Introduction to Psychology

Author

Huffman

ISBN 9781119178781

Printed in the United States of America 10 9 8 7 6 5 4 3 2 1

List of Titles

Real World Psychology

by Karen Huffman and Catherine A. Sanderson
Copyright © 2014, ISBN: 978-1-118-79777-8

Table of Contents

chapterone

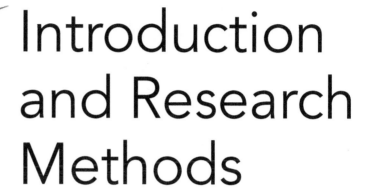

Great work

Introduction and Research Methods

CHAPTER OUTLINE

realworldpsychology

THINGS YOU'LL LEARN IN CHAPTER 1

Q1 How does your culture influence what you look for in a romantic partner?

Q2 Can diet, preschool education, and parental behavior increase a child's intelligence?

Q3 Are older people happier than younger people?

Q4 Why do heavy drinkers misreport their alcohol use?

Q5 How do spreading your study sessions and practice testing improve test scores?

THROUGHOUT THE CHAPTER, MARGIN ICONS FOR Q1–Q5 INDICATE WHERE THE TEXT ADDRESSES THESE QUESTIONS.

chapteroverview

Welcome to **Real World Psychology**! As our title suggests, we believe psychology's unique contributions to the scientific world are best shown through every day, real-life examples. Our innermost thoughts, our relationships, our politics, our "gut" feelings, and our deliberate decisions are all shaped by a complex psychological system that affects us at every level, from the cellular to the cultural. Psychology encompasses not only humankind but our nonhuman compatriots as well—from rats and pigeons to cats and chimps.

We invite you to let us know how your study of psychology (and this text) affects you and your life. You can reach us at khuffman@palomar.edu and casanderson@ amherst.edu. We look forward to hearing from you.

Warmest regards,

courtesy of Karen Huffman

courtesy of Catherine Sanderson

INTRODUCING PSYCHOLOGY

LEARNING OBJECTIVES

RETRIEVAL PRACTICE While reading the upcoming sections, respond to each Learning Objective in your own words. Then compare your responses to those found at www.wiley.com/college/huffman.

1 **DEFINE** psychology.

2 **IDENTIFY** modern psychology's seven major perspectives.

3 **SUMMARIZE** psychology's major career options.

Psychology The scientific study of behavior and mental processes.

The term **psychology** derives from the roots *psyche*, meaning "mind," and *logos*, meaning "word." Modern psychology is most commonly defined as the *scientific study of behavior and mental processes. Scientific* is a key feature of the definition because psychologists follow strict scientific procedures to collect and analyze their data. *Behavior* (such as crying, hitting, and sleeping) can be directly observed. *Mental processes* are private, internal experiences that cannot be directly observed (like feelings, thoughts, and memories).

For many psychologists, the most important part of the definition of psychology is the word *scientific*. Psychology places high value on *empirical evidence* that can be objectively tested and evaluated. Psychologists also emphasize **critical thinking**, *the process of objectively evaluating, comparing, analyzing, and synthesizing information* (Forshaw, 2013).

Critical thinking The process of objectively evaluating, comparing, analyzing, and synthesizing information.

Be careful not to confuse psychology with *pseudopsychologies*, which are based on common beliefs, folk wisdom, or superstitions. (*Pseudo* means "false.") These sometimes give the appearance of science, but they do not follow the basics of the scientific method. Examples include purported psychic powers, horoscopes, mediums, and self-help and "pop psych" statements such as "I'm mostly right-brained" or "We use only 10% of our brain." Given the popularity of these misleading beliefs, be sure to test your own possible myths in the *Psychology and You* section.

TEST YOURSELF: PSYCHOLOGY VERSUS PSEUDOPSYCHOLOGY

psychology and you

TRUE OR FALSE?

____1. The best way to learn and remember information is to "cram," or study it intensively during one concentrated period.

____2. Advertisers and politicians often use subliminal persuasion to influence our behavior.

____3. Most brain activity stops when we're asleep.

____4. Punishment is the most effective way to permanently change behavior.

____5. Eyewitness testimony is often unreliable.

____6. Polygraph ("lie detector") tests can accurately and reliably reveal whether a person is lying.

____7. Behaviors that are unusual or that violate social norms may indicate a psychological disorder.

____8. People with schizophrenia have two or more distinct personalities.

____9. Similarity is one of the best predictors of long-term relationships.

____10. In an emergency, as the number of bystanders increases, your chance of getting help decreases.

Henry Groskinsky/Time Life Pictures/Getty Images

The magician James Randi has dedicated his life to educating the public about fraudulent pseudopsychologists. Along with the prestigious MacArthur Foundation, Randi has offered $1 million to "anyone who proves a genuine psychic power under proper observing conditions" (Randi, 1997; The Amazing Meeting, 2011). Even after many years, the money has never been collected.

Answers: 1. False (Chapter 1), 2. False (Chapter 4), 3. False (Chapter 5), 4. False (Chapter 6), 5. True (Chapter 7), 6. False (Chapter 10), 7. True (Chapter 12), 8. False (Chapter 12), 9. True (Chapter 14), 10. True (Chapter 14)

Before we go on, we'd like to introduce you to a special feature in this text. In addition to the *Real World* research and practical applications you'll encounter throughout the text, we invited psychology professors from around the country to contribute their best stories and anecdotes, called "Voices from the Classroom."

Voices from the Classroom

The Joys of Teaching Intro Psych One of the things I like most is teaching a freshman class of Introduction to Psychology. Why? Because I can still remember how powerful my first psychology class was to me. My childhood consisted mainly of going to school and to church, two places that basically told me what to think. When I started college, I really didn't know how to think for myself. My first psych professor began class one day with a simple question. "If there was a pill that could make you happy all the time, would you take it?" He had no interest in a "correct" answer; he just wanted us to *think*. Why? Because psychology is the science of thought and behavior. That day in class, I realized that psychology could help me answer questions I had about *my own thoughts* and about *my own behaviors*. I was hooked. So, with that in mind, let me see if I can hook you with a question. In 1637, French philosopher Renee Descartes stated, (in Latin), "*Cogito ergo sum*," or in English, "I think, therefore I am." Here's my question: If you were brain dead, and no longer capable of action or thought, have you ceased to exist? Cool question, huh? Welcome to psychology!

Professor Keith W. Swain

Red Rocks Community College

Lakewood, Colorado

FIGURE 1.1 **WILLIAM JAMES (1842–1910)**

William James broadened psychology to include animal behavior and biological processes. In the late 1870s, James established the first psychology laboratory in the United States, at Harvard University.

Bettmann/Corbis Images

Psychoanalytic perspective An approach to understanding behavior and mental processes developed by Freud, which focuses on unconscious processes and unresolved conflicts.

Psychodynamic perspective An approach to understanding behavior and mental processes that emphasizes unconscious dynamics, internal motives, conflicts, and past experiences; actions are viewed as stemming from inherited instincts, biological drives, and attempts to resolve conflicts between personal needs and social requirements.

Behavioral perspective An approach to understanding behavior and mental processes that emphasizes objective, observable environmental influences on overt behavior.

Psychology's Past

Although people have long been interested in human nature, it was not until the first psychological laboratory was founded in 1879 that psychology as a science officially began. As interest in the new field grew, psychologists adopted various perspectives on the "appropriate" topics for psychological research and the "proper" research methods. These diverse viewpoints and subsequent debates molded and shaped modern psychological science.

Psychology's history as a science began in 1879, when Wilhelm Wundt [VILL-helm Voont], generally acknowledged as the "father of psychology," established the first psychological laboratory in Leipzig, Germany. Wundt and his followers were primarily interested in how we form sensations, images, and feelings. Their chief methodology was termed "introspection," and it relied on self-monitoring and reporting on conscious experiences (Freedheim & Weiner, 2013; Goodwin, 2012).

A student of Wundt's, Edward Titchener, brought his ideas to the United States. Titchener's approach, now known as *structuralism*, sought to identify the basic building blocks, or structures, of mental life through introspection and then to determine how these elements combine to form the whole of experience. Because introspection could not be used to study animals, children, or more complex mental disorders, however, structuralism failed as a working psychological approach. Although short-lived, it did establish a model for studying mental processes scientifically.

Structuralism's intellectual successor, *functionalism*, studied the way the mind functions to enable humans and other animals to adapt to their environment. William James was the leading force in the functionalist school (**Figure 1.1**). Although functionalism also eventually declined, it expanded the scope of psychology to include research on emotions and observable behaviors, initiated the psychological testing movement, and influenced modern education and industry.

During the late 1800s and early 1900s, while functionalism was prominent in the United States, the **psychoanalytic perspective** was forming in Europe. Its founder, Austrian physician Sigmund Freud, believed that a part of the human mind, the unconscious, contains thoughts, memories, and desires that lie outside personal awareness yet they still exert great influence. For example, according to Freud, a man who is cheating on his wife might slip up and say, "I wish you were her," when he consciously planned to say, "I wish you were here." Such seemingly meaningless, so-called Freudian slips supposedly reveal a person's true unconscious desires and motives.

Freud also believed many psychological problems are caused by unconscious sexual or aggressive motives and conflicts between "acceptable" and "unacceptable" behaviors (Chapter 11). His theory led to a system of therapy known as *psychoanalysis* (Chapter 13).

Modern Psychology

As summarized in **Table 1.1**, contemporary psychology reflects seven major perspectives: *psychodynamic, behavioral, humanistic, cognitive, biological, evolutionary,* and *sociocultural*. Although there are numerous differences between these seven perspectives, most psychologists recognize the value of each orientation and agree that no one view has all the answers.

Freud's nonscientific approach and emphasis on sexual and aggressive impulses have long been controversial, and today there are few strictly Freudian psychoanalysts left. However, the broad features of his theory remain in the modern **psychodynamic perspective**. The general goal of psychodynamic psychologists is to explore unconscious *dynamics*—internal motives, conflicts, and past experiences.

In the early 1900s, another major perspective appeared that dramatically shaped the course of modern psychology. Unlike earlier approaches, the **behavioral perspective** emphasizes objective, observable environmental influences on overt

TABLE 1.1 MODERN PSYCHOLOGY'S SEVEN MAJOR PERSPECTIVES

Perspectives	Major Emphases	Sample Research Questions	
Psychodynamic	Unconscious dynamics, motives, conflicts, and past experiences	How do adult personality traits or psychological problems reflect unconscious processes and early childhood experiences?	
Behavioral	Objective, observable, environmental influences on overt behavior; stimulus–response relationships and consequences for behavior	How do we learn both our good and bad habits? How can we increase desirable behaviors and decrease undesirable ones?	
Humanistic	Free will, self-actualization, and human nature as naturally positive and growth seeking	How can we promote a client's capacity for self-actualization and understanding of his or her own development? How can we promote international peace and reduce violence?	
Cognitive	Thinking, perceiving, problem solving, memory, language, and information processing	How do our thoughts and interpretations affect how we respond in certain situations? How can we improve how we process, store, and retrieve information?	
Biological	Genetic and biological processes in the brain and other parts of the nervous system	How might changes in neurotransmitters or damage to parts of the brain lead to psychological problems and changes in behavior and mental processes?	
Evolutionary	Natural selection, adaptation, and evolution of behavior and mental processes	How does natural selection help explain why we love and help certain people and hurt others? Do we have specific genes for aggression and altruism?	
Sociocultural	Social interaction and the cultural determinants of behavior and mental processes	How do the values and beliefs transmitted from our social and cultural environments affect our everyday psychological processes?	

FIGURE 1.2 B. F. SKINNER (1904–1990)

B. F. Skinner was one of the most influential psychologists of the twentieth century. Here he uses the so-called "Skinner box" to train a rat to press a lever for a reward.

Nina Leen/Time Life Pictures/Getty Images

behavior. Behaviorism's founder, John B. Watson (1913), rejected the practice of introspection and the influence of unconscious forces. Instead, Watson adopted Russian physiologist Ivan Pavlov's concept of *conditioning* (Chapter 6) to explain behavior as a result of observable stimuli (in the environment) and observable responses (behavioral actions).

Most early behaviorist research was focused on learning; nonhuman animals were ideal subjects for this research. One of the best-known behaviorists, B. F. Skinner, was convinced that behaviorist approaches could be used to "shape" human behavior (**Figure 1.2**).

As you'll discover in Chapters 6 and 13, therapeutic techniques rooted in the behavioristic perspective have been most successful in treating observable behavioral problems, such as those related to phobias and alcoholism (Kiefer & Dinter, 2013; May et al., 2013; Sarafino, 2012).

FIGURE 1.3 WHAT MAKES US HAPPY? | realworldpsychology

Research in positive psychology finds that our happiness increases when we give to others. When adults are given money and told to spend it on others, they experience higher levels of happiness than do those who are told to spend it on themselves (Dunn et al., 2008). Amazingly enough, even children as young as 2 years of age are happier when they give treats such as Goldfish crackers to other children than when they keep the treats for themselves (Aknin et al., 2012). Other research finds that those who experience more positive emotions also live longer than those with more negative emotions (Diener & Chan, 2011).

Humanistic perspective An approach to understanding behavior and mental processes that perceives human nature as naturally positive and growth seeking; it emphasizes free will and self-actualization.

Positive psychology The study of optimal human functioning; it emphasizes positive emotions, traits, and institutions.

Cognitive perspective An approach to understanding behavior and mental processes that focuses on thinking, perceiving, and information processing.

Biological perspective An approach to understanding behavior and mental processes that focuses on genetics and biological processes in the brain and other parts of the nervous system.

Evolutionary perspective An approach to understanding behavior and mental processes that stresses natural selection, adaptation, and evolution; it assumes that mental capabilities evolved over millions of years to serve particular adaptive purposes.

Although the psychoanalytic and behavioral perspectives dominated U.S. psychology for some time, in the 1950s a new approach emerged—the **humanistic perspective**, which stresses *free will* (voluntarily chosen behavior) and *self-actualization* (an inborn drive to develop all one's talents and capabilities). According to Carl Rogers and Abraham Maslow, two central humanist figures, all individuals naturally strive to develop and move toward self-actualization. Like psychoanalysis, humanist psychology developed an influential theory of personality and their own form of psychotherapy (Chapters 11 and 13). The humanistic approach also led the way to a contemporary research specialty known as **positive psychology**—the study of optimal human functioning (**Figure 1.3**) (Cummins, 2013; Diener, 2008; Seligman, 2003, 2011; Taylor & Sherman, 2008).

One of the most influential modern approaches, the **cognitive perspective**, recalls psychology's earliest days in that it emphasizes thoughts, perception, and information processing (Kellogg, 2011; Sternberg, 2012). Modern cognitive psychologists study the ways we gather, encode, and store information using a vast array of mental processes. These include perception, memory, imagery, concept formation, problem solving, reasoning, decision making, and language. Many cognitive psychologists also use an *information-processing approach*, likening the mind to a computer that sequentially takes in information, processes it, and then produces a response.

During the past few decades, scientists have explored the role of biological factors in almost every area of psychology. Using sophisticated tools and technologies, scientists who adopt this **biological perspective** examine behavior through the lens of genetics and biological processes in the brain and other parts of the nervous system. For example, research shows that genes influence many aspects of our behavior, including whether we finish high school and college, how kind we are to other people, and even whom we vote for in elections (Beaver et al., 2011; Hatemi & McDermott, 2012; Poulin et al., 2012).

The **evolutionary perspective** stresses natural selection, adaptation, and evolution of behavior and mental processes (Buss, 2011; Durrant & Ellis, 2013; Maner & Menzel, 2013). Its proponents argue that natural selection favors behaviors that enhance an organism's reproductive success. According to the evolutionary perspective, there's even an evolutionary explanation for the longevity of humans over other primates–it's grandmothers! Without them, a mother who has a two-year-old and then gives birth would have to devote her time and resources to the newborn at the expense of the older child. Grandmothers act as supplementary caregivers.

Finally, the **sociocultural perspective** emphasizes social interactions and cultural determinants of behavior and mental processes. Although we are often unaware of their influence, factors such as ethnicity, religion, occupation, and socioeconomic class have an enormous psychological impact on our mental processes and behavior (Berry et al., 2011; Boer & Fischer, 2013). For example, in countries with low levels of gender equality, women are more likely to be attracted by their partner's resources and men by physical attractiveness (Zentner & Mitura, 2012).

Sociocultural perspective An approach to understanding behavior and mental processes that emphasizes the social interaction and cultural determinants of behavior and mental processes.

Gender and Minority Influences

One of the first women to be recognized in the field of psychology was Mary Calkins. Her achievements are particularly noteworthy, considering the significant discrimination that she overcame. During the late 1800s and early 1900s, most colleges and universities provided little opportunity for women and ethnic minorities, either as students or as faculty members. In Mary Calkins' case, even after she completed all the requirements for a Ph.D. at Harvard University in 1895, and was described by William James as his brightest student, the university refused to grant the degree to a woman. Nevertheless, Calkins went on to perform valuable research on memory, and in 1905 served as the first female president of the American Psychological Association (APA). The first woman to receive her Ph.D. in psychology was Margaret Floy Washburn (Cornell, 1894), who wrote several influential books and served as the second female president of the APA.

Francis Cecil Sumner became the first African American to earn a Ph.D. in psychology. He earned it from Clark University in 1920 and later chaired one of the country's leading psychology departments, at Howard University. In 1971, one of Sumner's students, Kenneth B. Clark, became the first African American to be elected APA president. Clark's research with his wife, Mamie Clark, documented the harmful effects of prejudice and directly influenced the Supreme Court's landmark 1954 ruling against racial segregation in schools, Brown v. Board of Education **(Figure 1.4)**.

Sumner, Clark, Calkins, and Washburn, along with other important minorities and women, made significant and lasting contributions to psychology's development. In recent times, people of color and women have been actively encouraged to pursue graduate degrees in psychology. Today, women earning doctoral degrees in psychology greatly outnumber men, but minorities are still underrepresented (New Ph.D.s and Employment Outcomes, 2011; Willyard, 2011).

FIGURE 1.4 KENNETH CLARK (1914–2005) AND MAMIE PHIPPS CLARK (1917–1985)

Kenneth Clark and his wife, Mamie Phipps Clark, conducted experiments with black and white dolls to study children's attitudes about race. This research and their expert testimony contributed to the U.S. Supreme Court's ruling that racial segregation in public schools was unconstitutional.

Biopsychosocial Model

The seven major perspectives, as well as gender and minority influences, each make different contributions to modern psychology, which is why most contemporary psychologists do not adhere to one single intellectual perspective. Instead, a more integrative, unifying theme—the **biopsychosocial model**—has gained wide acceptance. This model views biological processes (genetics, neurotransmitters, evolution), psychological factors (learning, personality, motivation), and social forces (family, culture, ethnicity) as interrelated. It also sees all three factors as influences inseparable from the seven major perspectives **(Figure 1.5)**.

Why is the biopsychosocial model so important? As the old saying goes, "A fish doesn't know it's in water." Similarly, as individuals living alone inside our own heads, we're often unaware of the numerous, interacting factors that affect us—particularly cultural forces. For example, most North Americans and Western Europeans are raised to be very individualistic and are surprised to learn that over 70% of the world's population lives in collectivistic cultures. As you can see in **Table 1.2**, in *individualistic cultures*, the needs and goals of the individual are emphasized over the needs and goals of the group. When asked to complete the statement "I am . . . ,"

Biopsychosocial model An integrative, unifying theme of modern psychology that sees biological, psychological, and social processes as interacting influences.

FIGURE 1.5 **THE BIOPSYCHOSOCIAL MODEL** | realworldpsychology

When we consider people as individuals (**Figure a**), we don't always get a complete picture of their emotions and motivations.

Stepping back to see the same individuals in a broader context (**Figure b**) can provide new insights. With this "bigger picture" (the child's immediate surroundings and his or her group's behavior) in mind, can you better understand why each child might be feeling and acting as he or she is? The biopsychosocial model recognizes that there is usually no single cause for our behavior or our mental states (**Figure c**). For example, our moods and feelings are often influenced by genetics and neurotransmitters (biological), our learned responses and patterns of thinking (psychological), and our socioeconomic status and cultural views of emotion (sociocultural).

©Bonnie Jacobs/iStockphoto

©Jurgen Schulzki/Imagebroker/Age Fotostock America, Inc.

people from individualistic cultures tend to respond with personality traits ("I am shy"; "I am outgoing") or their occupation ("I am a teacher"; "I am a student").

In *collectivistic cultures*, however, the person is defined and understood primarily by looking at his or her place in the social unit (Berry et al., 2011; Dierdorff et al., 2011; Greenfield & Quiroz, 2013; McCrae, 2004, 2011). Relatedness, connectedness, and interdependence are valued, as opposed to separateness, independence, and individualism. When asked to complete the statement "I am . . . ," people from collectivistic cultures tend to mention their families or nationality ("I am a daughter"; "I am Chinese"). Keep in mind, however, that these sample countries and their sample values exist on a continuum, and that within each country there is a wide range of individual differences.

Looking back at the two photos from the two cultures in Figure 1.5, can you see how learning more about the biopsychosocial model offers increased understanding of ourselves, our friends, and our families, and how it may improve our understanding and sensitivity to other cultures? For example, North Americans generally define *sincerity* as behaving in accordance with our inner feelings, whereas people from collectivist cultures tend to see their equivalent word for sincerity as behavior that conforms to a person's role expectations and duties. (Yamada, 1997). This explains why collectivistic behaviors might appear insincere to a North American.

Careers in Psychology

Many people think of psychologists only as therapists, and it's true that the fields of clinical and counseling psychology do make up the largest specialty areas. However, many psychologists have no connection with therapy. Instead, they work as researchers, teachers, or consultants in academic, business, industry, and government

TABLE 1.2 — A COMPARISON BETWEEN INDIVIDUALISTIC AND COLLECTIVISTIC CULTURES	
Sample Individualistic Countries	**Sample Collectivistic Cultures**
United States	Hong Kong
Australia	China
Great Britain	India
Canada	Japan
The Netherlands	West Africa region
Germany	Thailand
New Zealand	Taiwan
Sample Individualistic Values	**Sample Collectivistic Values**
Independence	Interdependence
Individual rights	Obligations to others
Self-sufficiency	Reliance on group
Individual achievement	Group achievement
Independent living	Living with kin
Personal failure leads to shame and guilt	Failing the group leads to shame and guilt

settings, or in a combination of settings. As you can see in **Table 1.3**, there are several career paths and valuable life skills associated with a bachelor's degree in psychology. Of course, your options are even greater if you go beyond the bachelor's degree and earn your master's degree, Ph.D, or Psy.D—see **Table 1.4**. For more information about what psychologists do—and how to pursue a career in psychology—check out the websites of the American Psychological Association (APA) and the Association for Psychological Science (APS).

TABLE 1.3 — WHAT CAN I DO WITH A BACHELOR'S DEGREE IN PSYCHOLOGY? realworldpsychology
Top Careers with a Bachelor's Degree in Psychology
Management and administration
Sales
Social work
Labor-relations, personnel and training
Real estate, business services, insurance
Sample Skills Gained from a Psychology Major
Improved ability to predict and understand behavior
Better understanding of how to use and interpret data
Increased communication and interpersonal skills
Increased ability to manage difficult situations and high-stress environments
Enhanced insight into problem behavior
Note that the U.S. Department of Labor predicts only an average rate of growth for psychologists in the next decade. However, the good news is that a degree in our field, and this course in general psychology, will provide you with invaluable lifetime skills.

| TABLE 1.4 | SAMPLE CAREERS AND SPECIALTIES IN PSYCHOLOGY | real world psychology |

CAREER/SPECIALTY	DESCRIPTION
Biopsychologist/ neuroscientist	Investigates the relationship between biology, behavior, and mental processes, including how physical and chemical processes affect the structure and function of the brain and nervous system
Clinical psychologist	Specializes in the evaluation, diagnosis, and treatment of psychological disorders
Cognitive psychologist	Examines "higher" mental processes, including thought, memory, intelligence, creativity, and language
Comparative psychologist	Studies the behavior and mental processes of nonhuman animals; emphasizes evolution and cross-species comparisons
Counseling psychologist	Overlaps with clinical psychology, but generally works with less seriously disordered individuals and focuses more on social, educational, and career adjustment
Cross-cultural psychologist/ psychological anthropologist	Studies similarities and differences in and across various cultures and ethnic groups
Developmental psychologist	Studies the course of human growth and development from conception to death
Educational psychologist	Studies the processes of education and works to promote the academic, intellectual, social, and emotional development of children in the school environment
Environmental psychologist	Investigates how people affect and are affected by the physical environment
Experimental psychologist	Examines processes such as learning, conditioning, motivation, emotion, sensation, and perception in humans and other animals (Note that psychologists working in almost all other areas of specialization also conduct experiments.)
Forensic psychologist	Applies principles of psychology to the legal system, including jury selection, psychological profiling, assessment, and treatment of offenders
Gender and/or cultural psychologist	Investigates how men and women and different cultures vary from one another and how they are similar
Health psychologist	Studies how biological, psychological, and social factors affect health and illness
Industrial/ organizational psychologist	Applies principles of psychology to the workplace, including personnel selection and evaluation, leadership, job satisfaction, employee motivation, and group processes within the organization
Personality psychologist	Studies the unique and relatively stable patterns in a person's thoughts, feelings, and actions
Positive psychologist	Examines factors related to optimal human functioning
School psychologist	Collaborates with teachers, parents, and students within the educational system to help children with needs related to a disability and/or their academic and social progress; also provides evaluation and assessment of a student's functioning and eligibility for special services
Social psychologist	Investigates the role of social forces in interpersonal behavior, including aggression, prejudice, love, helping, conformity, and attitudes
Sports psychologist	Applies principles of psychology to enhance physical performance

Zigy Kaluzny/Getty Images, Inc.

Dolphin Inst./Photo Researchers

RETRIEVAL PRACTICE: INTRODUCING PSYCHOLOGY

Self-Test

Completing this self-test and comparing your answers with those in Appendix B provides immediate feedback and helpful practice for exams. Additional interactive, self-tests are available at www.wiley.com/college/huffman.

1. Psychology is defined as the _____.

    a. science of conscious and   b. empirical study of the mind
       unconscious forces   and behavior
    c. scientific study of the mind   d. scientific study of behavior
                                and mental processes

2. _____ rely on common beliefs, folk wisdom, or even superstitions and do not follow the basics of the scientific method.

    a. Pseudopsychologies   b. Sociologists
    c. Astronomers   d. Counselors

3. _____ is generally acknowledged to be the father of psychology.

    a. Sigmund Freud   b. B. F. Skinner
    c. Wilhelm Wundt   d. William James

4. Which of the following terms do not belong together?

    a. structuralism, unconscious   b. behaviorism, observable
       behavior   behavior
    c. psychoanalytic, unconscious d. humanism, free will
       conflict

Think Critically

1 Psychologists are among the least likely to believe in psychics, palmistry, astrology, and other paranormal phenomena. Why might that be?

2 Which of the seven modern perspectives of psychology do you most agree with? Why?

3 How might the biopsychosocial model explain difficulties or achievements in your own life?

realworldpsychology

How does your culture influence what you look for in a romantic partner?

HINT: LOOK IN THE MARGIN FOR ⓠ1

THE SCIENCE OF PSYCHOLOGY

RETRIEVAL PRACTICE While reading the upcoming sections, respond to each Learning Objective in your own words. Then compare your responses with those found at www.wiley.com/college/huffman.

1 COMPARE the fundamental goals of basic and applied research.
2 DESCRIBE the scientific method.
3 IDENTIFY psychology's four main goals.

LEARNING OBJECTIVES

In science, research strategies are generally categorized as either *basic* or *applied*. **Basic research** is most often conducted to advance core scientific knowledge, whereas **applied research** is designed to solve practical ("real world") problems (**Figure 1.6**). As you'll see in Chapter 6, classical and operant conditioning principles evolved from numerous *basic research* studies designed to advance the general understanding of how human and nonhuman animals learn. In Chapters 12 and 13, you'll also discover how *applied research* based on these principles has been used to successfully treat psychological disorders such as phobias. Similarly, in Chapter 7, you'll see how basic research on how we create, store, and retrieve our memories has led to practical applications in the legal field, such as a greater appreciation for the fallibility of eyewitness testimony.

Basic research Research that typically focuses on fundamental principles and theories; most often conducted in universities and research laboratories.

Applied research Research that is generally conducted outside the laboratory; its data are typically used for real world application.

FIGURE 1.6 APPLIED RESEARCH IN PSYCHOLOGY

Note how psychological research has helped design safe and more reliable appliances, machinery, and instrument controls (*Psychology Matters*, 2006).

Ⓐ Spatial correspondence
Controls for stovetops should be arranged in a pattern that corresponds to the placement of the burners.

Poorly designed   Well-designed

Ⓑ Visibility
Automobile gauges for fuel, temperature, and speed should be easily visible to the driver.

Ⓒ Arrangement of numbers
A top-down arrangement of numbers on a cell phone is more efficient than the bottom-up arrangement on a computer's key board.

Poorly designed   Well-designed

Poorly designed   Well-designed

Keep in mind that basic and applied research approaches are not polar opposites. Instead, they frequently share similar goals, and their outcomes interact, with one building on the other.

The Scientific Method

Like scientists in any other field, psychologists follow strict, standardized procedures so that others can understand, interpret, and repeat or test their findings. Most scientific investigations consist of six basic steps, collectively based on the **scientific method (Figure 1.7)**.

Have you wondered whether completing the Retrieval Practice exercises that follow the Learning Objectives, Self-Test, and Key Terms in each of the chapters of this text is worth your time? Have you thought, "Will I get a better grade on my exams if I do these exercises?" How would you use the scientific method to answer these general questions? Starting with Step 1, you could go to professional journals and read up on the research about retrieval practice that already exists on this topic. To complete Step 2, you would first form an educated guess based on your literature review in Step 1. You would then turn this guess into a statement, called a **hypothesis**, which provides predictions that can be tested in some way. You would then need to explicitly state how each of your variables in your hypothesis will be **operationally defined** (observed, manipulated, and measured). For example, a better grade on my exams might be operationally defined as earning one letter grade higher than the letter grade on my previous exam.

Using your initial question about the value of the Retrieval Practice exercises, your hypothesis and operational definitions might be: "Students who spend two hours studying Chapter 1 in this text and one hour completing the three Retrieval Practice exercises will earn higher scores on a standard academic exam than students who spend three hours using free-choice study techniques without completing the Retrieval Practice exercises."

Scientific method The cyclical and cumulative research process used for gathering and interpreting objective information in a way that minimizes error and yields dependable results.

Hypothesis A tentative and testable explanation about the relationship between two or more variables; a testable prediction or question.

Operational definition A precise description of how the variables in a study will be observed, manipulated, and measured.

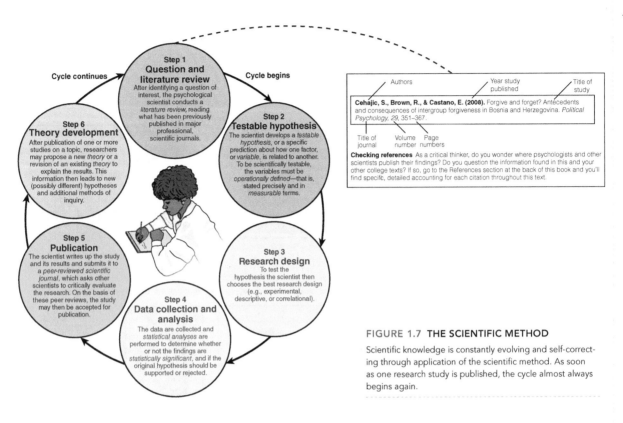

Cehajic, S., Brown, R., & Castano, E. (2008). Forgive and forget? Antecedents and consequences of intergroup forgiveness in Bosnia and Herzegovina. *Political Psychology, 29,* 351–367.

Checking references As a critical thinker, do you wonder where psychologists and other scientists publish their findings? Do you question the information found in this and your other college texts? If so, go to the References section at the back of this book and you'll find specific, detailed accounting for each citation throughout this text.

FIGURE 1.7 **THE SCIENTIFIC METHOD**

Scientific knowledge is constantly evolving and self-correcting through application of the scientific method. As soon as one research study is published, the cycle almost always begins again.

For Step 3, you would then most likely choose an experimental research design and solicit 100 volunteers from various classes, 50 of whom should be randomly assigned to Group 1 (Retrieval Practice) and the other 50 to Group 2 (no Retrieval Practice). After both groups study for three hours, you would present and score a 20-point quiz, followed by a statistical analysis (Step 4) to determine whether the difference in test scores between the two groups is **statistically significant**. To be statistically significant, the difference between the groups must be large enough that the result is probably not due to chance. In Step 5, you could publish your research, and then you go on to further investigate additional study techniques that might contribute to theory development on the most effective study methods, Step 6. [You'll be interested to know that research does exist on the superiority of retrieval practice on retention of material and improved exam scores (Agarwal et al., 2012; Karpicke & Smith, 2012), which is why they're emphasized in this text.]

Note also in Figure 1.7 that the scientific method is cyclical and cumulative. Scientific progress comes from repeatedly challenging and revising existing theories and building new ones. If numerous scientists, using different procedures or participants in varied settings, can repeat, or *replicate*, a study's findings, there is increased scientific confidence in the findings. If the findings cannot be replicated, researchers look for other explanations and conduct further studies. When different studies report contradictory findings, researchers may average or combine the results of all such studies and reach conclusions about the overall weight of the evidence, a popular statistical technique called **meta-analysis**. For example, one recent meta-analysis found that a healthy diet, high-quality preschool, and interactive reading with parents can all lead to increases in children's intelligence (Protzko et al., 2013).

After many related findings have been collected and confirmed, scientists may generate a **theory** to explain the data through a systematic, interrelated set of

Statistical significance A statistical statement of how likely it is that a study's result occurred merely by chance.

Meta-analysis A statistical technique for combining and analyzing data from many studies in order to determine overall trends.

Theory An organized, interrelated set of concepts that explain a phenomenon or body of data.

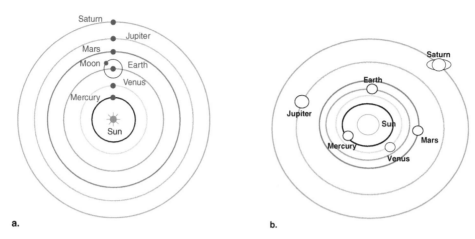

a. **b.**

FIGURE 1.8 **OPINIONS VERSUS FACTS—SCIENCE TO THE RESCUE!**

Early experiments, conducted primarily by *Nicolaus Copernicus* (1473–1543), led to a collection of facts and the ultimate theory that the Earth was not the center of the universe (as generally assumed at the time) **(Figure a)**. Instead, it rotated around the sun with the other planets in concentric circles. Later scientists (astronomers Johannes Kepler and Tycho Brahe) built on this Copernican (heliocentric) theory with additional experiments that led to a revised theory, in which the orbits were not mere circles but rather elliptical orbits. **(Figure b)**. Today, researchers have expanded the theory even further by demonstrating that our sun is not the center of the universe, but only a part of a galaxy that in turn is only one of many billions. Can you see how these incremental changes illustrate the value of scientific theories and their self-correcting nature?

concepts. In common usage, the term *theory* is often assumed to mean something is only a hunch or someone's personal opinion. In reality, scientific theories are evidence based, rigorously tested, and self-correcting (**Figure 1.8**).

Psychology's Four Main Goals

In contrast to *pseudopsychologies*, which we discussed earlier and which rely on unsubstantiated beliefs and opinions, psychology is based on rigorous scientific methods. When conducting their research, psychologists have four major goals—to *describe*, *explain*, *predict*, and *change* behavior and mental processes:

1. **Description** Description tells what occurred. In some studies, psychologists attempt to *describe*, or name and classify, particular behaviors by making careful scientific observations. Description is usually the first step in understanding behavior. For example, if someone says, "Boys are more aggressive than girls," what does that mean? The speaker's definition of aggression may differ from yours. Science requires specificity.

2. **Explanation** An explanation tells why a behavior or mental process occurred. *Explaining* a behavior or mental process requires us to discover and understand its causes. One of the most enduring debates in science is the **nature–nurture controversy** (Gruber, 2013; Tyson et al., 2011). Are we controlled by biological and genetic factors (the nature side) or by the environment and learning (the nurture side)? As you will see throughout the text, psychology (like all other sciences) generally avoids "either or" positions and focuses instead on *interactions*. Today, almost all scientists agree that most psychological, and even physical, traits reflect an interaction between nature and nurture. For example, research suggests numerous interacting causes or explanations for aggression, including culture, learning, genes, brain damage, and high levels of testosterone (Garfield et al.; 2011; Longino, 2013; Pournaghash-Tehrani, 2011).

3. **Prediction** Psychologists generally begin with description and explanation (answering the "whats" and "whys"). Then they move on to the higher-level goal

Nature–nurture controversy An ongoing dispute about the relative contributions of nature (heredity) and nurture (environment) in determining the development of behavior and mental processes.

of *prediction*, identifying "when" and under what conditions a future behavior or mental process is likely to occur. For instance, knowing that alcohol leads to increased aggression (Ferguson, 2010; Parker & McCaffree, 2013), we can predict that more fights will erupt in places where alcohol is consumed than in places where it isn't.

4. **Change** For some people, change as a goal of psychology brings to mind evil politicians or cult leaders brainwashing unknowing victims. However, to psychologists, *change* means applying psychological knowledge to prevent unwanted outcomes or bring about desired goals. In almost all cases, change as a goal of psychology is positive. Psychologists help people improve their work environment, stop addictive behaviors, become less depressed, improve their family relationships, and so on. Furthermore, as you may know from personal experience, it is very difficult (if not impossible) to change someone against her or his will. (*Here is an old joke*: Do you know how many psychologists it takes to change a light bulb? *Answer*: None. The light bulb has to want to change.)

RETRIEVAL PRACTICE: THE SCIENCE OF PSYCHOLOGY

Self-Test

Completing this self-test and comparing your answers with those in Appendix B provides immediate feedback and helpful practice for exams. Additional interactive, self-tests are available at www.wiley.com/college/huffman.

1. If you conducted a study on areas of the brain most affected by drinking alcohol, it would be _____ research.

    a. unethical   b. basic
    c. pseudopsychology   d. applied

2. A(n) _____ provides a precise definition of how the variables in a study will be observed and measured.

    a. meta-analysis   b. theory
    c. independent   d. operational definition
       observation

3. The goal of _____ is to tell what occurred, whereas the goal of _____ is to tell when.

    a. health psychologists;   b. description; prediction
      biological psychologists   d. pseudopsychologists;
    c. psychologists; psychiatrists   clinical psychologists

4. Label the six steps in the scientific method.

Think Critically

1 What is the difference between a scientific theory, an opinion, and a hunch?

2 Nonhuman animals are sometimes used in psychological research when it would be impractical or unethical to use human participants. What research questions might require the use of nonhuman animals?

3 Which side of the debate, nature or nurture, has had the most influence on your life?

realworldpsychology

Can diet, preschool education, and parental behavior increase a child's intelligence?

HINT: LOOK IN THE MARGIN FOR (Q2)

RESEARCH METHODS

RETRIEVAL PRACTICE While reading the upcoming sections, respond to each Learning Objective in your own words. Then compare your responses to those found at www.wiley.com/college/huffman.

1 DESCRIBE the four key types of descriptive research.
2 EXPLAIN how to interpret a correlation coefficient.
3 IDENTIFY the key components of experimental research.
4 DESCRIBE the ethical guidelines for psychological research.

Having studied the scientific method and psychology's four main goals, we can now examine how psychologists conduct their research. Psychologists generally draw on three major research methods—*descriptive, correlational,* and *experimental* (**Table 1.5**). Each of these approaches has advantages and disadvantages, and psychologists often use variations of all three methods to study a single problem. In fact, when multiple approaches lead to similar conclusions, scientists have an especially strong foundation for concluding that one variable does affect another in a particular way.

Descriptive Research

Descriptive research A research method in which the researcher observes and records behavior and mental processes without manipulating variables.

Almost everyone observes and describes others in an attempt to understand them, but in conducting **descriptive research**, psychologists do so systematically and scientifically. The key types of descriptive research are *naturalistic observation, survey/interview, case study,* and *archival research*.

Naturalistic Observation

Naturalistic observation The process of observing and recording a research participant's behavior and mental processes in his or her natural setting, without interfering.

When conducting **naturalistic observation**, researchers systematically observe and record participants' behavior in their natural setting, without interfering. Many settings lend themselves to naturalistic observation, from supermarkets to airports to outdoor settings. For example, Jane Goodall's classic naturalistic observations of wild chimpanzees provided invaluable insights into their everyday lives, such as their use of tools, acts of aggression, demonstrations of affection, and, sadly, even the killing of other chimps' babies (infantacide). In Chapter 5 you'll read about a study in which researchers used naturalistic observation to examine whether drivers

| TABLE 1.5 | PSYCHOLOGY'S THREE MAJOR RESEARCH METHODS |

Method	Purpose	Advantages	Disadvantages
Descriptive (naturalistic observation, survey/interview, case study, archival research)	Observe, collect, and record data (meets psychology's goal of description)	Minimizes artificiality, makes data collection easier, allows description of behavior and mental processes as they occur	Little or no control over variables, researcher or participant biases, cannot identify cause and effect
Correlational (statistical analyses of relationships between variables)	Identify relationships and assess how well one variable predicts another (meets psychology's goal of *prediction*)	Helps clarify relationships between variables that cannot be examined by other methods and allows prediction	Little or no control over variables, cannot identify cause and effect
Experimental (manipulation and control of variables)	Identify cause and effect (meets psychology's goal of *explanation*)	Allows researchers to have precise control over variables, helps identify cause and effect	Ethical concerns, practical limitations, artificiality of lab conditions, uncontrolled variables may confound results, researcher and participant biases

Note that the three methods are not mutually exclusive. Researchers may use one, two, or all three methods to explore the same topic.

talking on a cell phone were less likely to come to a complete stop at a stop sign (Strayer et al., 2011). Can you guess what they found?

The chief advantage of naturalistic observation is that researchers can obtain data about natural behavior rather than about behavior that is a reaction to an artificial experimental situation. But naturalistic observation can be difficult and time-consuming, and the lack of control by the researcher makes it difficult to conduct observations for behavior that occurs infrequently.

For a researcher who wants to observe behavior in a more controlled setting, *laboratory observation* has many of the advantages of naturalistic observation, but with greater control over the variables (**Figure 1.9**).

FIGURE 1.9 LABORATORY OBSERVATION

In this type of observation, the researcher brings participants into a specially prepared room in the laboratory, with one-way mirrors, or an inconspicuous camera, and microphones. While hidden from view, the researcher can observe school children at work, families interacting, or the like.

Survey/Interview

Psychologists use **surveys/interviews** to ask people to report their behaviors, opinions, and attitudes (Nestor & Schutt, 2012). In Chapter 6 you'll read about a study in which researchers interviewed 3- to 6-year-old girls about their preference for using game pieces depicting thinner or heavier women when playing Candy Land to measure preference for the thin ideal (Harriger et al., 2010). In Chapter 10, you'll read about the use of survey research to study how a person's first sexual experience may impact subsequent sexual relationships (Smith & Shaffer, 2013). One key advantage of this approach is that researchers can gather data from many more people than is generally possible with other research designs.

Unfortunately, most surveys/interviews rely on self-reported data, and not all participants are honest. As you might imagine, people are especially motivated to give less-than-truthful answers when asked about highly sensitive topics, such as infidelity, drug use, and pornography.

Survey/interview A research technique that questions a large sample of people to assess their behaviors and mental processes.

Case Studies

What if a researcher wants to investigate photophobia (fear of light)? In such a case, it would be difficult to find enough participants to conduct an experiment or to use surveys/interviews or naturalistic observation. For rare disorders or phenomena, researchers try to find someone who has the problem and study him or her intensively. This type of in-depth study of a single research participant, or a small group of individuals, is called a **case study** (Moore et al., 2012). In Chapter 9, we'll share a fascinating case study that examined the impact of severe neglect during childhood on language acquisition. This study obviously could not be conducted using another method, for ethical reasons, and because of the rarity of such severe deprivation.

Case study An in-depth study of a single research participant or a small group of individuals.

Archival research A descriptive research approach that studies existing data to find answers to research questions.

Archival Research

The fourth type of descriptive research is **archival research**, in which researchers study previously recorded data. For example, and as described in Chapter 14, using preexisting data from more than 50 years of Major League Baseball games, researchers revealed that more batters are deliberately hit by pitchers on hot days than on cooler days (Larrick et al., 2011). Interestingly, the new "digital democracy," based on spontaneous comments on Twitter or Facebook, may turn out to be an even better method of research than the traditional random sampling of adults. Researchers who used a massive archive of billions of stored data from Twitter found "tweet share" predicted the winner in 404 out of 435 competitive races in the U.S. House elections in 2010 (DiGrazia et al., 2013). Apparently, only the total amount of discussion—good or bad—is a very good predictor of votes.

"What I drink and what I tell the pollsters I drink are two different things."

Correlational research Research that measures the degree of relationship (if any) between two or more variables in order to determine how well one variable predicts another.

Correlation coefficient A number from –1.00 to +1.00 that indicates the direction and strength of the relationship between two variables.

Correlational Research

Data collected from descriptive research provides invaluable information on behavior and mental processes. However, when researchers are interested in examining more than one variable, they can take a further step and calculate the degree and type of relationship between the variables. As the name **correlational research** implies, when any two variables are co-related, a change in one is accompanied by a change in the other. For example, researchers in one study examined the link between happiness and age in a sample of more than 5,000 people across the United States (Sutin et al., 2013). This study revealed that, contrary to common stereotypes, happiness actually increases with age!

An important advantage of correlational studies is that they allow us to make predictions about one variable based on knowledge of another. For instance, suppose scientists notice a relationship between the use of cell phones and the number of traffic accidents, or between the hours of television viewing and performance on exams. First, they would carefully measure the two factors. Next, they would analyze their measurements using a statistical formula that gives a **correlation coefficient** (**Figure 1.10**).

FIGURE 1.10 INTERPRETING A CORRELATION COEFFICIENT

A correlation coefficient is a number from –1.00 to +1.00 that represents the direction and strength of a relationship between two variables. Understanding it is crucial to becoming an educated consumer of research.

- **Direction of the correlation** (left-hand column) The + or – sign in the correlation coefficient indicates the *direction* of the correlation, either positive or negative, which is often depicted in graphs called *scatterplots*. Each dot on these graphs represents one participant's score on both variables.
- **Strength of the correlation** (right-hand column) A correlation of +1.00 and a –1.00 magnitude both indicate the strongest possible relationship. As the number decreases and gets closer to 0.00, the relationship weakens. We interpret correlations close to zero as representing no relationship between the variables—like the "relationship" between broken mirrors and years of bad luck.

Direction of the correlation

Positive correlation

Zero correlation

Negative correlation

Strength of the Correlation

+1.00	Perfect positive relationship (100% of the variance)
+.80 to +.99	Very strong positive relationship (64–98% of the variance)
+.60 to +.79	Strong positive relationship (36–62% of the variance)
+.40 to +.59	Moderate positive relationship (16–35% of the variance)
+.20 to +.39	Weak positive relationship (4–15% of the variance)
0.00	No relationship (0% of the variance)
–.20 to –.39	Weak negative relationship (4–15% of the variance)
–.40 to –.59	Moderate negative relationship (16–35% of the variance)
–.60 to –.79	Strong negative relationship (36–62% of the variance)
–.80 to –.99	Very strong negative relationship (64–98% of the variance)
–1.00	Perfect negative relationship (100% of the variance)

Think Critically

Can you identify whether each of the following pairs most likely has a positive, negative, or zero correlation?

1. Health and exercise
2. Hours of TV viewing and student grades
3. Happiness and helpfulness
4. Hours of sleep and number of friends
5. Extraversion and loneliness

Answers: 1. positive, 2. negative, 3. positive, 4. zero, 5. negative

Chris Carroll/Corbis Images

Looking closely at the right-hand side of the chart in Figure 1.10, you'll note that while the numbers in the first column (+1.00 to –1.00) describe the *strength* of the relationship between two variables, what's often overlooked is the second column, which shows the actual percentage of *variance* (or how widely individuals in a group vary). We calculate this variance by multiplying the correlation number by itself (in this example .5 × .5 = 25%). It's important to understand this because people often over-interpret popular examples such as the .5 correlation between IQ (intelligence quotient) and GPA (grade point average) or the .4 correlation between IQ and income. Now that you understand more about correlations, you can see that your GPA has only a weak relationship with your IQ (25%) and that there is an even lower relationship (16%) between your IQ and your eventual income. The good news is that many factors other than IQ explain both GPA and income—mainly hard work, motivation, and perseverance.

In addition to providing more accurate prediction, correlational studies often point to *possible* causation. For example, smoking cigarettes and drinking alcohol while pregnant are highly correlated with birth defects (Agopian et al., 2013; Pruett et al., 2013). This strong correlation led to a large number of animal experiments and other research methods that added supportive evidence, which has helped convince pregnant mothers to avoid these drugs while pregnant—thus preventing many infant birth defects.

In other cases, it's important to emphasize that a correlation between two variables does not *necessarily* mean that one variable *causes* another (**Figure 1.11**). When people read media reports about correlations between stress and cancer or between a full moon and increased crime, they often mistakenly infer that stress causes cancer or that a full moon causes crime. In fact, a wide variety of possible third factors may cause someone to have greater susceptibility to both the correlated phenomena. This point is so important and critical to becoming an educated consumer of scientific research that we offer another example (**Figure 1.12**).

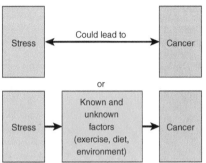

FIGURE 1.11 CORRELATION VERSUS CAUSATION

Research has found a strong correlation between stress and cancer (Chapter 3). However, this correlation does not tell us whether stress causes cancer, whether cancer causes stress, or whether other known and unknown factors, such as smoking, drinking, or pesticides could contribute to both stress and cancer. Can you think of a way to study the effects of stress on cancer that is not correlational?

FIGURE 1.12 REVISITING CORRELATION VERSUS CAUSATION

Ice cream consumption and drowning are highly correlated. Does this mean that eating ice cream causes people to drown? Of course not! A third factor, such as high temperatures, increases both ice cream consumption and participation in water-based activities.

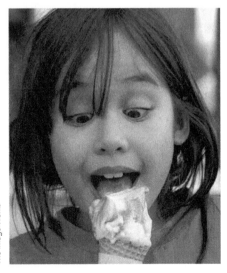

Norbert Schwerin/ The Image Works

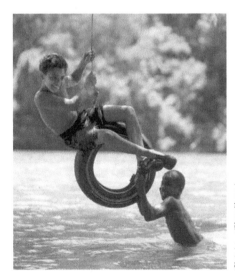

Chris Lowe/Photolibrary/ Getty Images

Experimental research A carefully controlled scientific procedure that involves the manipulation of variables to determine cause and effect.

Independent variable (IV) The variable that is manipulated to determine its causal effect on the dependent variable; also called the treatment variable.

Dependent variable (DV) The variable that is observed and measured for change; the factor that is affected by (or dependent on) the independent variable.

Experimental group The group that is manipulated (i.e., receives treatment) in an experiment.

Control group The group that is not manipulated (i.e., receives no treatment) during an experiment.

Sample bias A bias that may occur when research participants are unrepresentative of the larger population.

Random assignment A research technique that involves using chance to assign participants to experimental or control conditions, thus minimizing the possibility of biases or preexisting differences in the group.

Confounding variable A stimulus, other than the variable an experimenter inadvertently introduces into a research setting, that may affect the outcome of the study and lead to erroneous conclusions.

Experimental Research

As you've just seen, correlational studies are important because they reveal *associations* between variables. However, to determine *causation* (what causes what), we need **experimental research**. In Chapter 4, you'll discover how experiments were used to test the influence of pregnant women's food choices on taste preferences in their infants (Mennella et al., 2001). Similarly, in Chapter 13, you'll learn how experiments can help test the effectiveness of a particular psychotherapy approach at helping a spider-phobic person become comfortable enough to touch a tarantula (Hauner et al., 2012).

Experiments are considered the "gold standard" for scientific research because only through an experiment can researchers experimentally isolate and then examine a single factor's effect on a particular behavior (Goodwin, 2011). To accomplish this type of isolation and examination, an experiment has five critical components: a hypothesis (discussed earlier), an **independent variable (IV)**, a **dependent variable (DV)**, one or more **experimental group(s)**, and a **control group (Figure 1.13)**.

How can we prevent bias and errors when creating and setting up our experiments? Sample bias may occur when a particular group of participants does not accurately reflect the composition of the larger population from which they are drawn. For example, critics suggest that much psychological literature is biased because it primarily uses college students as subjects. A way to minimize sample bias is to randomly select participants who constitute a representative sample of the entire population of interest.

Even if we avoid **sample bias** with representative sampling, we can still introduce bias into the experiment when we assign participates to the experimental or control group. As you can see in Step 2 of Figure 1.13, assigning participants to either group using a chance or random system, such as a coin toss, guaranties that each participant is equally likely to be assigned to any particular group, a technique called random assignment. **Random assignment** also helps control for extraneous, **confounding variables** (such as time of day, lighting conditions, and room temperature), which must be held constant across experimental and control groups so that they do not affect the different groups' results (**Figure 1.14**).

©terex/iStockphoto

realworldpsychology **Do Aesthetics Affect Eating Behavior?**

To answer this question, a group of researchers modified the environment in one section of a fast food restaurant by dimming the lights and adding relaxing music, plants, candles, and tablecloths. They then randomly assigned customers to sit in either the original section of the restaurant or this new section (Wansink & Van Ittersum, 2012). All participants freely ordered whatever food they preferred, but those in the more relaxing part of the restaurant took longer to eat their meal and ate 18% fewer calories.

Can you see how the *random assignment* of the customers controlled for any potential *confounding variables*? All participants freely entered the same restaurant, and each individual was equally likely to be assigned to either section in the restaurant. Thanks to these controls, the researchers can legitimately conclude that the *independent variable* (IV) (relaxing versus standard restaurant condition) caused the change in the *dependent variables* (DVs) (time spent eating and number of calories consumed).

In addition to the controls mentioned above, a good scientific experiment has other invaluable techniques for protecting against potential sources of error from

FIGURE 1.13 **EXPERIMENTAL RESEARCH DESIGN**

When designing an experiment, researchers must follow certain steps to ensure that their results are scientifically meaningful. In this example, researchers want to test whether watching violent television shows increases aggression in children.

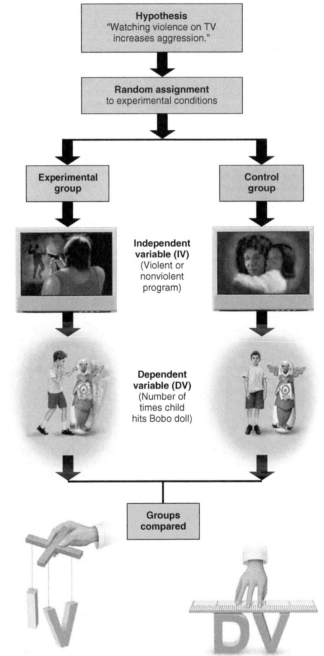

1 The experimenter begins by identifying the hypothesis.

2 In order to avoid sample bias, the experimenter randomly assigns subjects to two different groups.

3 Having at least two groups allows the performance of one group to be compared to that of another.

4 The experimental group watches violent programs while the control group watches nonviolent programs. The amount of violent TV watched is the independent variable (IV).

5 The experimenter then counts how many times the child hits, kicks, or punches a large plastic doll. The number of aggressive acts is the dependent variable (DV).

6 The experimenter relates differences in aggressive behavior (DV) to the amount of violent television watched (IV).

To help you remember the independent and dependent variables (IV and DV), carefully study these drawings and create a visual picture in your own mind of how:

The experimenter "manipulates" the IV to determine its causal effect on the DV.

The experimenter "measures" the DV, which "depends" on the IV.

FIGURE 1.14 CONTROLLING FOR CONFOUNDING VARIABLES

Recognizing that certain, outside variables may affect their experiment, researchers strive for balance between the experimental and control groups, making sure the variables are the same for both. Once balance is achieved, and the independent variable (IV) is added to the experimental group, the experimenters check to see if the scale's balance is significantly disrupted. If so, they can then say that the IV *caused* the change. However, if the IV is not "heavy" enough to make a significant difference, then the experiment "failed," and experimenters go back to further refine their approach—or start over.

both the researcher and the participants. For example, if experimenters' beliefs and expectations are not controlled for, they can affect participants' responses, producing flawed results. Imagine what might happen if an experimenter breathed a sigh of relief when a participant gave a response that supported the researcher's hypothesis. One way to prevent such **experimenter bias** from destroying the validity of participants' responses is to establish objective methods for collecting and recording data, such as using computers to present stimuli and record responses.

Experimenters also can skew their results if they assume that behaviors typical in their own culture are typical in all cultures—a bias known as **ethnocentrism**. One way to avoid this problem is to have researchers from two cultures each conduct the same study twice, once with their own culture and once with at least one other culture. This kind of *cross-cultural sampling* isolates group differences in behavior that stem from researchers' ethnocentrism.

Just as researchers can inadvertently introduce error (the experimenter bias), participants also can produce a similar error, called **participant bias**. For example, research measuring accuracy of reports of alcohol consumption demonstrates that heavy drinkers tend to under-report how much alcohol they are consuming (Northcote & Livingston, 2011). In this case, participants may try to present themselves in a good light—called the *social desirability response*—or deliberately attempt to mislead the researcher.

Experimenter bias Bias that occurs when a researcher influences research results in the expected direction.

Ethnocentrism The belief that one's culture is typical of all cultures; also, viewing one's own ethnic group (or culture) as central and "correct" and judging others according to this standard.

Participant bias Bias that can occur when experimental conditions influence the participant's behavior or mental processes.

Single-blind study An experiment where only the researcher, and not the participants, knows who is in either the experimental or control group.

Runzelkorn/Shutterstock

psychology and you **Understanding Social Desirability** Imagine you're in an experiment that asks you about sensitive and highly personal behaviors, such as whether you've ever abused drugs, cheated on a test, or shoplifted. Can you see why participants might give dishonest answers to such questions, either due to fear of the consequences or personal embarrassment?

Double-blind study An experimental technique in which both the researcher and the participants are unaware of (blind to) who is in the experimental or control groups.

Placebo An inactive substance or fake treatment used as a control technique, usually in drug research, or given by a medical practitioner to a patient.

Researchers attempt to control for this type of *participant bias* by offering anonymous participation and other guarantees of privacy and confidentiality. **Single-blind studies**, **double-blind studies**, and **placebos** offer additional safeguards (**Figure 1.15**).

Finally, one of the most effective (and controversial) ways of preventing participant bias is to temporarily deceive participants about the true nature of the research project. For example, in studies examining when and how people help others,

Participant

Experimenter

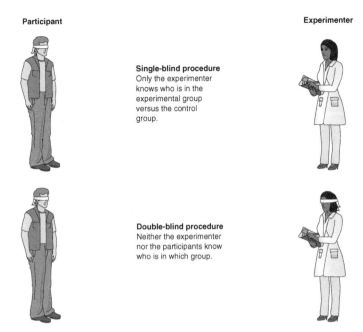

Single-blind procedure
Only the experimenter knows who is in the experimental group versus the control group.

Double-blind procedure
Neither the experimenter nor the participants know who is in which group.

FIGURE 1.15 A SINGLE- OR DOUBLE-BLIND EXPERIMENTAL DESIGN

To test a new drug, researchers administering the experimental drug and/or the participants taking the drug must be unaware of (or "blind" to) who is receiving a *placebo* (a fake pill or injection) and who is receiving the drug itself. Placebos are necessary because researchers know that the mere act of taking a pill or receiving an injection can change a participant's condition or responses, the so-called "placebo effect" (Barbui et al., 2011; Brown, 2013).

participants may not be told the true goal of the study because they might try to present themselves as more helpful than they actually would be in real life.

Recognizing that we've offered a large number of research problems and safeguards associated with the experimental method, we've gathered them all into **Figure 1.16**. Be sure to study it carefully. In addition, note that the problems and safeguards connected with descriptive and correlational research described earlier also apply to experimental research.

Before closing this section on research methods, we want to clarify that although experiments are considered the "gold standard" in research, descriptive and correlational methods also offer unique information that can help us live safer and more productive lives. For example, psychologists have repeatedly found high correlations between stress and disease (Chapter 3) and between cocaine use and heart attacks (Chapter 5). Can you see how we could never logistically or morally create human

FIGURE 1.16 POTENTIAL RESEARCH PROBLEMS AND SOLUTIONS

Researcher			
Potential problem	**Potential problem**	**Potential problem**	**Potential problem**
Experimenter bias	Ethnocentrism	Sample bias	Participant bias
Solution	**Solution**	**Solution**	**Solution**
Blind observers, single- and double-blind studies, placebos	Cross-cultural sampling	Random/representative sampling, random assignment	Anonymity, confidentiality, deception, single- and double-blind studies, placebos

PSYCHSCIENCE

POLITICS AND DATING RELATIONSHIPS

Are you more likely to date a person if his or her political preference (conservative, moderate, liberal, or none) matches your own? To scientifically test this question, participants were brought into a research lab and shown profiles of fictional people, which were made to look like those on popular online dating websites and manipulated in several ways, including religion, education, and political preference (Huber & Malhotra, 2012).

The researchers were somewhat surprised that compatibility in political views significantly affected how much participants stated they would like to date someone. But they were even more surprised to find that participants also rated the fictional person as more physically attractive when they believed they shared similar political beliefs!

To see whether this artificial laboratory study would accurately predict behavior in a real-life situation, the researchers then conducted a second study, using data from an existing dating website called *OkCupid*. Given that online messages sent from one person and replied to by another generally indicate a shared interest in dating, the researchers reported that shared political views increased interest by 9.5%.

Why is this research important? *Similarity* is one of the best predictors of long-term relationships (Chapter 14). But what happens if we restrict our dating (and friendship) partners to those

we already agree with? Aren't we more likely to fall victim to *groupthink* (Chapter 14) and *confirmation bias* (Chapter 8)?

RESEARCH CHALLENGE

1 Based on the information provided, did these two studies (Huber & Malhotra, 2012) use descriptive, correlational, and/or experimental research? (Tip: Be sure to look for two separate answers for the two different studies.)

2 If you chose:

- descriptive research, is this a naturalistic observation, survey/interview, case study, or archival research?
- correlational research, is this a positive, negative, or zero correlation?
- experimental research, label the IV, DV, experimental group(s), and control group.

>> CHECK YOUR ANSWERS IN APPENDIX B.

NOTE: The information provided in this study is admittedly limited, but the level of detail is similar to what is presented in most textbooks and public reports of research findings. Answering these questions, and then comparing your answers to those in the Appendix, will help you become a better critical thinker and consumer of scientific research.

experiments that would prove true cause and effect in these situations? Instead, we often have to rely on the accumulating weight of the evidence from nonexperimental studies and nonhuman animal experiments. If you'd like additional information about research methods and statistical analyses, see Appendix A at the back of this text. In addition, each chapter of this text offers an in-depth analysis of a hot topic in research (*Psych Science*), along with a self-grading *Research Challenge* (see the first example above).

Ethical Guidelines

So far, we've discussed how psychologists conduct research and analyze their data. Now we need to examine the general ethics that guide their research. The two largest professional organizations of psychologists, the American Psychological Association (APA) and the Association for Psychological Science (APS), both recognize the importance of maintaining high ethical standards in research, therapy, and all other areas of professional psychology. The preamble to the APA's publication *Ethical Principles of Psychologists and Code of Conduct* (2002, 2010) requires psychologists to maintain their competence, to retain objectivity in applying their skills, and to preserve the dignity and best interests of their clients, colleagues, students, research participants, and society.

Respecting the Rights of Human Participants

The APA and APS have developed rigorous guidelines regulating research with human participants, including:

- **Informed consent** Researchers must obtain an **informed consent** agreement from all participants *before* initiating an experiment. Participants are made aware of the nature of the study, what to expect, and significant factors that might influence their willingness to participate, including all physical risks, discomfort, and possibly unpleasant emotional experiences.

- **Voluntary participation** Participants must be told that they're free to decline to participate or to withdraw from the research at any time.

- **Restricted use of deception and debriefing** If participants knew the true purpose behind certain studies, they might not respond naturally. In one of the most famous studies in social psychology, researchers ordered participants to give electric shocks to another participant (who was really a confederate of the researcher and was not actually receiving any shocks). Although this study was testing participants' willingness to follow orders, they were told that the study was examining the use of shocks to assist with learning. Obviously in this case, participants' behavior could not be accurately measured if they were told the real focus of the study (Milgram, 1963). Therefore, researchers occasionally need to temporarily deceive participants about the actual reason for the experiment.

    However, when deception is necessary, important guidelines and restrictions still apply. One of the most important is **debriefing**, which is conducted once the data collection has been completed. The researchers provide a full explanation of the research, including its design and purpose, any deceptions used, and then clarify participants' misconceptions, questions, or concerns.

- **Confidentiality** All information acquired about people during a study must be kept private and not published in such a way that an individual's rights to privacy are compromised.

Informed consent A participant's agreement to take part in a study after being told what to expect.

Debriefing A discussion procedure conducted at the end of an experiment or study; participants are informed of the study's design and purpose, possible misconceptions are clarified, questions answered, and explanations are provided for any possible deception.

Respecting the Rights of Nonhuman Animals

Although they are used in only 7 to 8% of psychological research (APA, 2009; ILAR, 2009; MORI, 2005), nonhuman animals—mostly rats and mice—have made significant contributions to almost every area of psychology. Without nonhuman animals in *medical research*, how would we test new drugs, surgical procedures, and methods for relieving pain? *Psychological research* with nonhuman animals has led to significant advances in virtually every area of psychology—the brain and nervous system, health and stress, sensation and perception, sleep, learning, memory, motivation, and emotion.

Nonhuman animal research has also produced significant gains for some animal populations, such as the development of more natural environments for zoo animals and more successful breeding techniques for endangered species.

Despite the advantages, using nonhuman animals in psychological research remains controversial (Akins & Panicker, 2012; Baker & Serdikoff, 2013). While debate continues about ethical issues in such research, psychologists take great care in handling research animals. Researchers also actively search for new and better ways to protect the animals (Guidelines for Ethical Conduct, 2008; Pope & Vasquez, 2011).

Respecting the Rights of Psychotherapy Clients

Professional organizations such as the APA and APS, as well as academic institutions and state and local agencies, all may require that therapists, like researchers, maintain the highest ethical standards. Therapists must also uphold their clients' trust. All personal information and therapy records must be kept confidential, and records can be made available only to authorized persons and with the client's permission. However, therapists are legally required to break confidentiality if a client threatens violence to him- or herself or to others, if a client is suspected of abusing a child or an elderly person, and in other limited situations (Fisher, 2013; Kress et al., 2013; Tyson et al., 2011).

RETRIEVAL PRACTICE: RESEARCH METHODS

Self-Test

Completing this self-test and comparing your answers with those in Appendix B provides immediate feedback and helpful practice for exams. Additional interactive, self-tests are available at www.wiley.com/college/huffman.

1. In a case study, a researcher is most likely to _____.

a. interview many research subjects who have a single problem or disorder
b. conduct an in-depth study of a single research participant
c. choose and investigate a single topic
d. use any of these options, which describe different types of case studies

2. When a researcher observes or measures two or more variables to find relationships between them, without directly manipulating them or implying a causal relationship, he or she is conducting _____.

a. experimental research
b. a correlational study
c. non-causal metrics
d. a meta-analysis

3. If researchers gave participants varying amounts of a new memory drug and then gave them a story to read and measured their scores on a quiz, the _____ would be the IV, and the _____ would be the DV.

a. response to the drug; amount of the drug
b. experimental group; control group
c. amount of the drug; quiz scores
d. researcher variables; extraneous variables

4. A participant's agreement to take part in a study after being told what to expect is known as _____.

a. unethical pre-briefing
b. an experimental contract
c. a participant contract
d. informed consent

5. Debriefing is _____.

a. interviewing subjects after a study to find out what they were thinking during their participation
b. explaining the design and purpose of the study when it is over and revealing any deception used
c. disclosing potential physical and emotional risks and the nature of the study before it begins
d. interviewing subjects after a study to determine whether any deception used was effective in preventing them from learning the true purpose of the study

Think Critically

1 What is meant by the axiom "correlation is not causation"?

2 Cigarette companies have suggested that there is no scientific evidence that smoking causes lung cancer. How would you refute this claim?

realworldpsychology

Are older people happier than younger people?

Why do heavy drinkers misreport their alcohol use?

HINT: LOOK IN THE MARGIN FOR AND

STRATEGIES FOR STUDENT SUCCESS

RETRIEVAL PRACTICE While reading the upcoming sections, respond to each Learning Objective in your own words. Then compare your responses to those found at www.wiley.com/college/huffman.

1 **DESCRIBE** the steps you can take to improve your study habits.

2 **IDENTIFY** how you might improve your current time management habits.

In this section, you will find several well-researched study strategies and techniques guaranteed to make you a more successful college student. They are grouped together under *study habits* and *time management*.

Study Habits

Do you sometimes read a paragraph many times yet remember nothing from it? Here are four ways to successfully read (and remember) information in this and most other texts:

1. **Familiarization** The first step is to familiarize yourself with the general text so that you can take full advantage of its contents. In *Real World Psychology*, the Preface, Table of Contents, Glossary (both running through the text of each chapter and at the end of each chapter), References, Name Index, and Subject Index will help give you a bird's-eye view of the rest of the text. In addition, as you scan the book to familiarize yourself with its contents, you should also take note of the many tables, figures, photographs, and special feature boxes, all of which will enhance your understanding of the subject.

2. **Active Reading** The next step is to make a conscious decision to actively read and learn the material. Reading a text is *not* like reading a novel or fun articles on the Internet! You must tell your brain to slow down, focus on details, and save the material for future recall.

3. **Distributed practice** Spreading your study sessions out over time (distributed practice) is far more efficient than waiting until right before an exam and cramming in all the information at once (massed practice) (Chapter 7). If you were a basketball player, you wouldn't wait until the night before a big play-off game to practice. The same is true for exam preparation. Keep in mind that distributed practice is NOT simply rereading the chapter several times over a few days. As mentioned above, you need to actively focus and study what you're reading.

4. **Practice test taking** For most people, taking tests is NOT one of our favorite activities. However, it's important to note that research has clearly shown that practice test taking and distributed practice are two of the most efficient ways to study and learn (Carpenter, 2012; Dunlosky et al., 2013). Just as you need to repeatedly practice throwing baskets to become a good basketball player, you need to repeatedly practice your test taking skills. The easiest way to practice this skill (and to improve your grades) is by completing the Self-Tests and Think Critically Questions found in each chapter of this book. You also can easily access the free flashcards and other forms of self-testing on the student companion website for this text at www.wiley.com/college/huffman.

For more tips on improving your study habits, see *Psychology and You*.

psychology and you   **The Importance of Focus** Think about a time when you were trying to study for an important test, but you continued to find your mind wandering. Perhaps you started thinking about what you were going to eat for dinner, or what weekend plans you hoped to make. As you might imagine, this type of distracted studying isn't very effective! This book will give you strategies for active learning that will help you not only in your psychology class but in all your other classes!

©Zastavkin/iStockphoto

SQ4R method A study technique based on six steps: Survey, Question, Read, Recite, Review, and wRite.

One of the best ways to read actively is to use the **SQ4R method**, which was developed by Francis Robinson (1970). The initials stand for six steps in effective reading: **S**urvey, **Q**uestion, **R**ead, **R**ecite, **R**eview, and w**R**ite. As you might have guessed, *Real World Psychology* was designed to incorporate each of these steps (**Figure 1.17**).

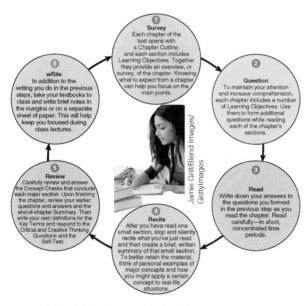

FIGURE 1.17 USING THE SQ4R METHOD

Follow these steps to improve your reading efficiency.

Time Management

If you find that you can't always strike a good balance between work, study, and social activities or that you aren't always good at budgeting your time, here are five basic time-management strategies:

- **Establish a baseline.** Before attempting any changes, simply record your day-to-day activities for one to two weeks. You may be surprised at how you spend your time.

- **Set up a realistic schedule.** Make a daily and weekly "to do" list, including all required activities, basic maintenance tasks (like laundry, cooking, child care, and eating), and a reasonable amount of down time. Then create a daily schedule of activities that includes time for each of these. To make permanent time-management changes, shape your behavior, starting with small changes and building on them.

- **Reward yourself.** Give yourself immediate, tangible rewards for sticking with your daily schedule.

- **Maximize your time.** To increase your efficiency, begin by paying close attention to the amount time you spend on true, focused studying versus the time you waste worrying, complaining, and/or fiddling around getting ready to study ("fretting and prepping"). Also be alert for hidden "time opportunities"—spare moments that normally go to waste that you might instead use productively.

---

psychology and you **Improving Your Grade** Here are five additional strategies for grade improvement and test taking that can further improve your success as a student:

- **Avoid highlighting and rereading** Marking with a yellow highlighter, or underlining potentially important portions of material, as well as rereading text material after initial reading, are common techniques students use while studying. Unfortunately, they are a waste of time! Research clearly shows that they are among the LEAST effective of all the major study techniques (Dunlosky et al., 2013). As previously discussed, you need to actively focus on your reading and these techniques encourage passive reading.

- **Take notes** While reading and listening to classroom lectures, ask yourself, "What is the main idea?" Write down key ideas and supporting details and examples. Effective note taking depends on active reading and active listening. Also, pay attention to the amount of pages and lecture time your text or instructors spend on various topics. It's generally a good indication of what is considered important for you to know.

- **Improve your general test-taking skills** Expect a bit of stress but don't panic. Pace yourself but don't rush. Focus on what you know. Skip over questions when you don't know the answers, and then go back if time allows. On multiple-choice exams, carefully read each question and all the alternative answers before responding. Answer all questions and make sure you have recorded your answers correctly.

- **Overlearn** Many people tend to study new material just to the point where they can recite the information, but they do not attempt to understand it more deeply. For best results, however, you should overlearn. In other words, be sure to fully understand how key terms and concepts are related to one another and also be able to generate examples other than the ones in the text. In addition, you should repeatedly review the material (by visualizing the phenomena that are described and explained in the text and by rehearsing what

you have learned) until the information is firmly locked in place. Overlearning is particularly important if you suffer from test anxiety.

- **Take study skills courses** Improve your reading speed and comprehension and your word-processing/typing skills by taking additional courses designed to develop these specific abilities. Also, don't overlook important human resources. Your instructors, roommates, classmates, friends, and family members often provide useful tips and encouragement.

Think Critically

1. What factors might prevent you from reading test questions carefully and responding accurately?
2. How could a friend or roommate help you improve your grades on tests?

RETRIEVAL PRACTICE: STRATEGIES FOR STUDENT SUCCESS

Self-Test

Completing this self-test and comparing your answers with those in Appendix B provides immediate feedback and helpful practice for exams. Additional interactive, self-tests are available at www.wiley.com/college/huffman.

1. List the six steps in the SQ4R method.

© Chris Schmidt/iStockphoto

2. One of the clearest findings in psychology is that _____ practice is a much more efficient way to study and learn than _____ practice.

a. spaced (distributed); massed
b. active; passive
c. applied; basic
d. none of these options

3. Research suggests that _____ might be two of the most important keys to improving grades.

a. highlighting and rereading
b. personal control and better time management
c. active studying and the SQ4R method
d. distributed practice and practice testing

4. _____ is particularly important if you suffer from test anxiety.

a. Overlearning
b. Hyper-soma control
c. Active studying
d. Passive listening

Think Critically

1 Identify how you might improve your current time management.

2 What do you think prevents you or the people you know from fully employing the strategies for student success presented in this chapter?

realworldpsychology

How do spreading your study sessions and practice testing improve test scores?

HINT: LOOK IN THE MARGIN FOR Q5

Summary

1 INTRODUCING PSYCHOLOGY 4

- **Psychology** is the scientific study of *behavior* and *mental processes*. The discipline places high value on *empirical evidence* and **critical thinking**. *Pseudopsychologies*, such as belief in psychic powers, are not based on scientific evidence.
- Wilhelm Wundt, considered the father of psychology, and his followers, including Edward Titchener, were interested in studying conscious experience. Their approach, *structuralism*, sought to identify the basic structures of mental life through introspection.
- The *functionalism* school, led by William James, studied the way the mind functions to enable humans and other animals to adapt to their environment.
- The **psychoanalytic perspective**, founded by Sigmund Freud, emphasized the influence of the unconscious mind, which lies outside personal awareness.
- Contemporary psychology reflects the ideas of seven major perspectives: **psychodynamic, behavioral, humanistic, cognitive, biological, evolutionary,** and **sociocultural**. Most contemporary psychologists embrace a unifying perspective known as the **biopsychosocial model**.
- Despite early societal limitations, women and minorities have made important contributions to psychology. Pioneers include Margaret Floy Washburn, Mary Calkins, Francis Cecil Sumner, and Kenneth and Mamie Clark.
- Psychologists work as therapists, researchers, teachers, and consultants, in a wide range of settings.

2 THE SCIENCE OF PSYCHOLOGY 13

- **Basic research** is aimed at advancing general scientific understanding, whereas **applied research** works to address real world problems.
- Most scientific investigations consist of six basic steps, collectively known as the **scientific method**. Scientific progress comes from repeatedly challenging and revising existing **theories** and building new ones.
- Psychology's four basic goals are to *describe, explain, predict,* and *change* behavior and mental processes through the use of

scientific methods. One of the most enduring debates in science is the **nature–nurture controversy**.

3 RESEARCH METHODS 18

- **Descriptive research** systematically observes and records behavior and mental processes without manipulating variables. The four major types of descriptive research are **naturalistic observation, survey/interview, case study,** and **archival research**.
- **Correlational research** measures the relationship between two variables. Researchers analyze their results using a **correlation coefficient**. Correlations can be positive or negative. A correlation between two variables does not necessarily mean that one causes the other.
- **Experimental research** manipulates and controls variables to determine cause and effect. An experiment has five critical components: **hypothesis, independent** and **dependent variables** and **experimental** and **control groups**. A good scientific experiment protects against potential sources of error from both the researcher and the participants through means such as **random assignment, placebos, single-blind studies** and **double-blind studies.**
- Psychologists must maintain high ethical standards. This includes respecting the rights of therapy clients and research participants (both human and nonhuman). **Informed consent** and **debriefing** are critical elements of any research that includes human participants. Researchers and clinicians are held professionally responsible for their actions by the APA and APS, their research institutions, and local and state agencies.

4 STRATEGIES FOR STUDENT SUCCESS 29

- Several well-documented techniques will help you understand and absorb written material most completely. They include familiarization, active reading through the **SQ4R method**, distributed practice, and practice testing.
- Additional techniques include effective time management (while studying and during an exam), avoiding highlighting and rereading, taking notes, improving general test-taking skills, overlearning, and study skills courses.

⊙applyingrealworldpsychology

We began this chapter with five intriguing Real World Psychology questions, and you were asked to revisit these questions at the end of each section. Questions like these have an important and lasting impact on all of our lives. See if you can answer these additional critical thinking questions related to real world examples.

Jonathan Selig/Getty Images

1 Nonhuman animals, like the mice in this photo, are sometimes used in psychological research when it would be impractical or unethical to use human participants. Do you believe nonhuman animal research is ethical? Why or why not?

2 What research questions might require the use of nonhuman animals? How would you ensure the proper treatment of these animals?

3 On p. 22, we discussed a potential experimental design to test whether watching violent TV might increase aggression in children. Assuming that we did find a significant increase, can you think of reasons the findings might not generalize to real world situations?

4 You may have heard that dog owners are healthier than cat owners, which leads some to believe that getting a dog would improve their health. Given this chapter's repeated warning that "correlation does not prove causation," can you think of an alternative explanation for why dog owners might be healthier?

5 People often confuse critical thinking with simply being critical and argumentative. How would you explain the true meaning and value of critical thinking?

6 How does psychology's emphasis on the scientific method contribute to critical thinking?

Key Terms

RETRIEVAL PRACTICE Write a definition for each term before turning back to the referenced page to check your answer.

- applied research 13
- archival research 19
- basic research 13
- behavioral perspective 6
- biological perspective 8
- biopsychosocial model 9
- case study 19
- cognitive perspective 8
- confounding variable 22
- control group 22
- correlational research 20
- correlation coefficient 20
- critical thinking 4
- debriefing 27
- dependent variable (DV) 22

- descriptive research 18
- double-blind study 24
- ethnocentrism 24
- evolutionary perspective 8
- experimental group 22
- experimental research 22
- experimenter bias 24
- humanistic perspective 8
- hypothesis 14
- independent variable (IV) 22
- informed consent 27
- meta-analysis 15
- naturalistic observation 18
- nature–nurture controversy 16
- operational definition 14

- participant bias 24
- placebo 24
- positive psychology 8
- psychoanalytic perspective 6
- psychodynamic perspective 6
- psychology 4
- random assignment 22
- sample bias 22
- scientific method 14
- single-blind study 24
- sociocultural perspective 9
- SQ4R method 30
- statistical significance 15
- survey/interview 19
- theory 15

chaptertwo

Neuroscience and Biological Foundations

CHAPTER OUTLINE

realworldpsychology

THROUGHOUT THE CHAPTER, MARGIN ICONS FOR Q1–Q5 INDICATE WHERE THE TEXT ADDRESSES THESE QUESTIONS.

chapteroverview

The brain is the last and grandest biological frontier, the most complex thing we have yet discovered in our universe. It contains hundreds of billions of cells interlinked through trillions of connections. The brain boggles the mind.

—James Watson
(Nobel Prize Winner)

Ancient cultures, including the Egyptian, Indian, and Chinese, believed the heart was the center of all thoughts and emotions. Today we know that the brain and the rest of the nervous system are the power behind our psychological life and much of our physical being. This chapter introduces you to the important and exciting field of *neuroscience* and *biopsychology*, the scientific study of the *biology* of behavior and mental processes, while also providing a foundation for understanding several fascinating discoveries and essential biological processes discussed throughout the text.

OUR GENETIC INHERITANCE

LEARNING OBJECTIVES

RETRIEVAL PRACTICE While reading the upcoming sections, respond to each Learning Objective in your own words. Then compare your responses with those found at www.wiley.com/college/huffman.

1 **DESCRIBE** how genetic material passes from one generation to the next.
2 **OUTLINE** the approaches scientists take to explore human genetic inheritance.
3 **EXPLAIN** the process of natural selection.

Behavioral genetics The study of the relative effects of heredity and the environment on behavior and mental processes.

Evolutionary psychology The branch of psychology that studies the application of the principles of evolution to explain behavior and mental processes.

Gene A segment of DNA (deoxyribonucleic acid) that occupies a specific place on a particular chromosome and carries the code for hereditary transmission.

Millions of years of evolution have contributed to what we are today. Our ancestors foraged for food, fought for survival, and passed on traits that were selected and transmitted down through the generations. How do these transmitted traits affect us today? For answers, psychologists often turn to **behavioral genetics**, the study of how heredity and environment affect us, and **evolutionary psychology**, the application of the principles of evolution to explain behavior and mental processes.

Behavioral Genetics

Genes are the most important and basic building blocks of our biological inheritance (Barnes, 2013) (**Figure 2.1**). Each of our human characteristics and behaviors is

FIGURE 2.1 **HEREDITARY CODE**

The genes we inherit from our biological parents help determine many of our physical traits (like height and hair color) and also are possible determinants of numerous behaviors (such as aggression, sensation-seeking, and sociability).

A Conception
At the moment of conception, a father's sperm and a mother's egg each contribute 23 chromosomes, for a total of 46.

B Cell nucleus
Each cell in the human body (except red blood cells) contains a nucleus.

C Chromosomes
Each cell nucleus contains 46 chromosomes, which are threadlike molecules of DNA (deoxyribonucleic acid).

D Genes
Each DNA molecule contains thousands of genes, which are the most basic units of heredity.

Nucleus

Thierry Berrod, Mona Lisa Production/Photo Researchers

FIGURE 2.2 **GENE–ENVIRONMENT INTERACTION**

Children who are malnourished may not reach their full potential genetic height or maximum intelligence. Can you see how environmental factors interact with genetic factors to influence many traits?

Per-Anders Pettersson/Getty Images

related to the presence or absence of particular genes that control the transmission of traits. In some traits, such as blood type, a single pair of genes (one from each parent) determines what characteristics we will possess. When two genes for a given trait conflict, the outcome depends on whether the gene is *dominant* or *recessive*. A dominant gene reveals its trait whenever the gene is present. In contrast, the gene for a recessive trait is normally expressed only if the other gene in the pair is also recessive.

It was once assumed that characteristics such as eye color, hair color, and height were the result of either one dominant gene or two paired recessive genes. But modern geneticists believe that these characteristics are *polygenic*, meaning they are controlled by multiple genes. Most polygenic traits like height and intelligence also are affected by environmental and social factors (**Figure 2.2**). Fortunately, most serious genetic disorders are not transmitted through a dominant gene. Can you guess why?

Why do scientists study human inheritance? As you'll see throughout this text, researchers are finding increasing evidence that our personality traits, cognitive abilities, behavioral habits, sexual orientation, and psychological disorders are all determined, at least in part, by genetic factors. For example, genetic or chromosomal abnormalities have been found to be important factors in Alzheimer's disease and schizophrenia, as well as in diabetes, heart disease, and cancer (**Figure 2.3**). Surprisingly, researchers have even discovered that our genes can influence which particular political party we identify with, as well as our political views, including beliefs about the death penalty, unemployment, and abortion (Hatemi & McDermott, 2012).

In addition to studying how genes affect us as individuals, behavioral geneticists also examine how and when they're transmitted from one generation to the next.

FIGURE 2.3 **SAVING HER OWN LIFE?**

realworldpsychology

In May 2013, actor Angelina Jolie announced that she had undergone a preventive double mastectomy (the removal of both of her breasts) to reduce her personal risk of developing breast cancer. She made this decision after learning that she carries a mutation in her BRAC1 gene, which leads to a 65% lifetime risk of developing breast cancer.

Daniel Zuchnik/Getty Images

FIGURE 2.4 IDENTICAL VERSUS FRATERNAL TWINS

Ⓐ Identical (*monozygotic*—one egg) twins share 100% of the same genes because they develop from a single egg fertilized by a single sperm. They also share the same placenta and have the same sex and same genetic makeup.

Ⓑ Fraternal (*dizygotic*—two eggs) twins share, on average, 50% of their genes because they are formed when two separate sperm fertilize two separate eggs. Although they share the same general environment within the womb, they are no more genetically similar than nontwin siblings. They're simply nine-month "womb mates."

Can you see why this makes the study of identical and fraternal twins a top priority? Identical twins share all their genes, whereas fraternal twins share only about half of their genes (**Figure 2.4**). Also, both sets of twins share the same parents and develop in relatively the same environment, thereby providing an invaluable "natural experiment." If heredity influences a trait or behavior to some degree, identical twins should be more alike than fraternal twins. For example, studies of intelligence show that identical twins have more similar intelligence test scores than fraternal twins (Plomin & Spinath, 2004; Trzaskowski et al., 2013), which suggests a genetic influence on intelligence.

In addition to twin studies, researchers also study families with biological and adopted children to determine whether adopted children are more like their adoptive parents (who controlled the home environment) or their biological parents (who controlled the genetic inheritance) (**Figure 2.5**). Research using these family studies has found that many traits and mental disorders, such as intelligence, sociability, and depression, are most strongly influenced by genetics (Davies et al., 2011; Kang et al., 2012; Stein et al., 2012).

Findings from research studies like these have allowed behavioral geneticists to estimate the **heritability** of various traits, which is the percentage of variation in a population attributable to heredity. If genetics contributed nothing to a trait, it would have a heritability estimate of 0%. If a trait is completely due to genetics, it would have a heritability estimate of 100%.

Before going on, it's very important to emphasize that *heritability estimates do not apply to individuals*. Height has one of the highest heritability estimates—around 90% (Plomin, 1990). But, it's impossible to predict with certainty an individual's height from a heritability estimate (**Figure 2.6**). Furthermore, *heritability does not trump environment*. For example, if you inherited a gene known to increase your chances of developing emphysema from smoking, you should not overreact. Smoking is an environmental factor, and if you never smoke you have little or no chance of developing emphysema.

Heritability A statistical formula that provides a percentage of variation in a population attributable to genetic factors rather than to differences in the environment.

FIGURE 2.5 ADOPTION STUDIES

If adopted children are more like their biological family in some trait, then genetic factors probably had the greater influence. Conversely, if adopted children resemble their adopted family, even though they do not share similar genes, then environmental factors may predominate.

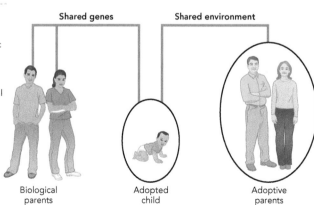

Shared genes   Shared environment

Biological parents   Adopted child   Adoptive parents

As we've seen, behavioral genetics studies help explain the role of heredity (nature) and the environment (nurture) in our individual behavior. To increase our understanding of genetic dispositions, we also need to look at universal behaviors transmitted from our evolutionary past.

Evolutionary Psychology

Evolutionary psychology suggests that many behavioral commonalities, from eating to fighting with our enemies, emerged and remain in human populations because they helped our ancestors (and ourselves) survive (Buss, 2011; Durrant & Ellis, 2013). This perspective stems from the writings of Charles Darwin (1859), who suggested that natural forces select traits that aid an organism's survival. This process of **natural selection** occurs when a particular genetic trait gives an organism a reproductive advantage over others. Because of natural selection, the fastest, strongest, smartest, or otherwise most fit organisms are most likely to live long enough to reproduce and thereby pass on their genes to the next generation.

Genetic mutations also help explain behavior. Everyone likely carries at least one gene that has mutated, or changed from the original. Very rarely, a mutated gene will be significant enough to change an individual's behavior. It might cause someone to be more or less social, risk taking, shy, or careful. If the gene then gives the person a reproductive advantage, he or she will be more likely to pass on the gene to future generations. However, this mutation doesn't guarantee long-term survival. Even a well-adapted population can perish if its environment changes too rapidly.

FIGURE 2.6 HEIGHT AND HERITABILITY

Imagine a small village, in which the average height of all adult women was 4 feet 5 inches. The heritability of height in this group could be quite high; women with short parents would be on average much shorter than women of tall parents. So how would you explain the difference in height between the parent and child in this photo?

Image Source/Getty Images

Natural selection The process by which heritable traits that increase an organism's chances of survival or reproduction are favored over less beneficial traits.

RETRIEVAL PRACTICE: OUR GENETIC INHERITANCE

Self-Test

Completing this self-test and comparing your answers with those in Appendix B provides immediate feedback and helpful practice for exams. Additional interactive, self-tests are available at www.wiley.com/college/huffman.

1. Behavioral genetics is the study of the relative effects of _____.

a. behavior and genetics on survival
b. heredity and environment on behavior and mental processes
c. genetics on natural selection
d. natural selection and adaptation

2. Evolutionary psychology studies the _____.

a. ways in which humans adapted their environment to survive and evolve
b. effects of genetics on humankind's behavior over the millennia
c. methods humans used to evolve and change behavior
d. application of evolutionary principles to explain behavior and mental processes.

3. _____ is a measure of the degree to which a characteristic is related to genetic versus environmental factors.

a. Heritability
b. Inheritance
c. Biological ratio
d. Genome biostatistics

4. The term _____ refers to a process by which heritable traits that increase an organism's chances of survival or reproduction are favored over less beneficial traits.

a. natural selection
b. devolution
c. survival of the fastest
d. reproductive success

Think Critically

1 Imagine that scientists were able to identify specific genes linked to serious criminal behavior. If it were possible to remove or redesign these genes, would you be in favor of this type of gene manipulation? Why or why not?

2 Using an evolutionary perspective, can you explain why people are more likely to help family members than to help strangers?

realworldpsychology

Can our genes influence whom we vote for in presidential elections?

HINT: LOOK IN THE MARGIN FOR

NEURAL BASES OF BEHAVIOR

LEARNING OBJECTIVES

Neuron The basic building block (nerve cell) of the nervous system, responsible for receiving, processing, and transmitting electrochemical information.

Glial cells The cells that provide structural, nutritional, and other support for neurons, as well as communication within the nervous system; also called glia or neuroglia.

Dendrites The branching fibers of neurons that receive neural impulses from other neurons and convey impulses toward the cell body.

Cell body The part of a neuron that contains the cell nucleus and other structures that help the neuron carry out its functions; also known as the soma.

Axon A long, tube-like structure that conveys impulses away from a neuron's cell body toward other neurons or to muscles or glands.

Action potential A neural impulse, or brief electrical charge, that carries information along the axon of a neuron; movement is generated when positively charged ions move in and out through channels in the axon's membrane.

RETRIEVAL PRACTICE While reading the upcoming sections, respond to each Learning Objective in your own words. Then compare your responses with those found at www.wiley.com/college/huffman.

1 **IDENTIFY** the key role and features of neurons.
2 **EXPLAIN** how neurons communicate throughout the body.
3 **DESCRIBE** the role of hormones and the endocrine system.

Our brain and the rest of our nervous system essentially consist of **neurons**. Each neuron is a tiny information-processing system with thousands of connections for receiving and sending electrochemical signals to other neurons. Each human body may have as many as 1 *trillion* neurons. (Note that a *neuron* is an individual cell, whereas a nerve is a group of neurons.)

Neurons are held in place and supported by **glial cells**, which make up about 90% of the brain's total cells. They also supply nutrients and oxygen, perform cleanup tasks, and insulate one neuron from another so that their neural messages are not scrambled. In addition, they play a direct role in nervous system communication (Burnstock, 2013; Thyssen et al., 2013; Weaver, 2012). However, the "star" of the communication show is still the neuron.

No two neurons are alike, but most share three basic features: **dendrites**, the **cell body**, and an **axon** (**Figure 2.7**). To remember how information travels through the neuron, think of these three in reverse alphabetical order: *Dendrite → Cell Body → Axon*.

How Do Neurons Communicate?

A neuron's basic function is to transmit information throughout the nervous system. Neurons "speak" in a type of electrical and chemical language. The process of neural communication begins within the neuron itself, when the dendrites and cell body receive electrical messages. These messages move along the axon in the form of a neural impulse, or **action potential** (**Figure 2.8**).

FIGURE 2.7 **KEY PARTS OF A NEURON**

Red arrows in the figure on the left indicate direction of information flow: dendrites → cell body → axon → terminal buttons of axon.

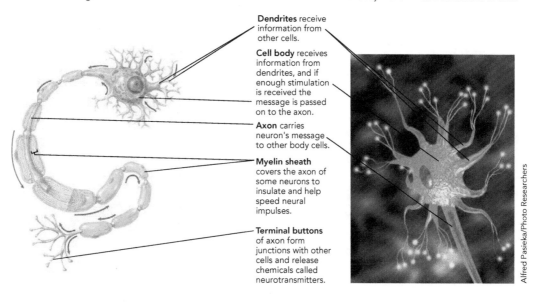

Dendrites receive information from other cells.

Cell body receives information from dendrites, and if enough stimulation is received the message is passed on to the axon.

Axon carries neuron's message to other body cells.

Myelin sheath covers the axon of some neurons to insulate and help speed neural impulses.

Terminal buttons of axon form junctions with other cells and release chemicals called neurotransmitters.

Alfred Pasieka/Photo Researchers

FIGURE 2.8 COMMUNICATION *WITHIN* THE NEURON

The process of neural communications begins within the neuron itself, when the dendrites and cell body receive information and conduct it toward the axon. From there, the information moves down the entire length of the axon via a brief traveling electrical charge called an *action potential*, which can be described in the following three steps:

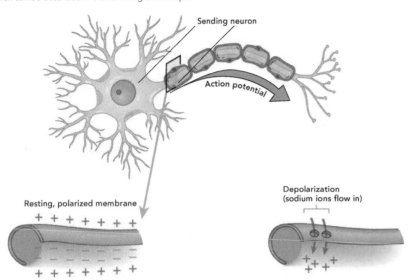

Sending neuron

Action potential

Resting, polarized membrane

Depolarization
(sodium ions flow in)

1 Resting potential

When an axon is not stimulated, it is in a polarized state, called the *resting potential*. "At rest," the fluid inside the axon has more negatively charged ions than the fluid outside. This results from the selective permeability of the axon membrane and a series of mechanisms, called *sodium-potassium pumps*, which pull potassium ions in and pump sodium ions out of the axon. The inside of the axon has a charge of about −70 millivolts relative to the outside.

2 Action potential initiation

When an "at rest" axon membrane is stimulated by a sufficiently strong signal, it produces an action potential (or depolarization). This action potential begins when the first part of the axon opens its "gates" and positively charged sodium ions rush through. The additional sodium ions change the previously negative charge inside the axon to a positive charge—thus depolarizing the axon.

Potassium ions
flow out

Depolarization

3 Spreading of action potential and repolarization

The initial depolarization (or action potential) of Step 2 produces a subsequent imbalance of ions in the adjacent axon membrane. This imbalance thus causes the action potential to spread to the next section. Meanwhile, "gates" in the axon membrane of the initially depolarized section open and potassium ions flow out, thus allowing the first section to repolarize and return to its resting potential.

Flow of depolarization

Action potential

Action potential

Action potential

© ImageSource/SuperStock

Overall summary

The sequential process of depolarization and repolarization moving the action potential from the cell body to the terminal buttons is similar to fans at an athletic event doing the "wave." One section of fans first stands up and waves their arms (action potential initiation), then sits down (resting potential), and then the "wave" spreads on. Note that this is an "all-or-none" event.

Myelin sheath The layer of fatty insulation wrapped around the axon of some neurons that increases the rate at which neural impulses travel along the axon.

Neural impulses move much more slowly than electricity moves through a wire. A neural impulse travels along a bare axon at only about 10 meters per second. (Electricity moves at 36 million meters per second.)

Some axons, however, are enveloped in fatty insulation, the **myelin sheath**. This sheath blankets the axon, with the exception of periodic *nodes*, points at which the myelin is very thin or absent. In a myelinated axon, the neural impulse moves about 10 times faster than in a bare axon because the action potential jumps from node to node rather than travel along the entire axon. Sadly, research shows that social isolation during the early weeks and months of life (as occurs for babies who are in orphanages) prevents cells from producing the right amount of myelin, which leads to long-term problems in cognitive functioning (Makinodan et al., 2012).

Communication *within* the neuron (Figure 2.8) is not the same as communication *between* neurons (**Figure 2.9**). Within the neuron, messages travel electrically,

---

FIGURE 2.9 COMMUNICATION *BETWEEN* NEURONS

Within the neuron (see Figure 2.8), messages travel electrically. Between neurons, messages are transmitted chemically. The three steps shown here summarize this chemical transmission.

1 Sending a chemical signal
When an action potential reaches the branching axon terminals, it triggers the terminal buttons at the axon's end to open and release thousands of neurotransmitters into the **synapse**, the tiny opening between the sending and receiving neuron. These chemicals then move across the synaptic gap and attach to the membranes of the receiving neuron. In this way, they carry the message from the sending neuron to the receiving neuron.

2 Receiving a chemical signal
After a chemical message flows across the synaptic gap, it attaches to the receiving neuron. It's important to know that each receiving neuron gets multiple neurotransmitter messages. As you can see in this close-up photo, the axon terminals from thousands of other nearby neurons almost completely cover the cell body of the receiving neuron. It's also important to understand that neurotransmitters deliver either excitatory or inhibitory messages, and that the receiving neuron will only produce an action potential and pass along the message if the number of excitatory messages outweigh the inhibitory messages.

Science Source/Photo Researchers, Inc.

3 Dealing with leftovers
Given that some neurons have thousands of receptors, which are only responsive to specific neurotransmitters, what happens to excess neurotransmitters or to those that do not "fit" into the adjacent receptor sites? The sending neuron normally reabsorbs the excess (called "reuptake"), or they are broken down by special enzymes.

FIGURE 2.10 **HOW POISONS AND DRUGS AFFECT OUR BRAINS** | *psychology and you*

Foreign chemicals, like poisons and drugs, can mimic or block ongoing actions of neurotransmitters, thus interfering with normal functions.

Normal neurotransmission

Postsynaptic receptor site

Neural impulse

Somewhat like a key fitting into a lock, receptor sites on receiving neurons' dendrites recognize neurotransmitters by their particular shape. When the shape of the neurotransmitter matches the shape of the receptor site a message is sent.

Neurotransmitters without the correct shape won't fit the receptors, so they cannot stimulate the dendrite, and that neurotransmitter's message is blocked.

Ⓐ Normal neurotransmitter activation Ⓑ Blocked neurotransmitter activation

How poisons and drugs affect neurotransmission

Some *agonist* drugs like the poison in the black widow spider or the nicotine in cigarettes, are similar enough in structure to a specific neurotransmitter (in this case, acetylcholine) that they mimic its effects on the receiving neuron, and a message is sent.

Some *antagonist* drugs block neurotransmitters like acetylcholine, which is vital in muscle action. Blocking it paralyzes muscles, including those involved in breathing, which can be fatal.

Ⓒ Agonist drug "mimics" neurotransmitter Ⓓ Antagonist drug fills receptor space and blocks neurotransmitter

altrendo images/Stockbyte/Getty Images, Inc.

Most snake venom and some poisons, like *botulinum* toxin (Botox®), seriously affect normal muscle contraction. Ironically, these same poisons are sometimes used to treat certain medical conditions involving abnormal muscle contraction—as well as for some cosmetic purposes.

whereas between neurons the messages are carried across the *synaptic gap* via chemicals called **neurotransmitters**.

Researchers have discovered hundreds of substances that function as neurotransmitters. For example, some **agonist drugs** enhance or "mimic" the action of particular neurotransmitters, whereas **antagonist drugs** block or inhibit the effects (**Figure 2.10**)

One benefit of studying the brain and its neurotransmitters is that it will help us understand some common medical problems. For example, we know that decreased levels of the neurotransmitter dopamine are associated with Parkinson's disease (PD), whereas excessively high levels of dopamine appear to contribute to some forms of schizophrenia. **Table 2.1** presents additional examples of the better-understood neurotransmitters.

Neurotransmitter A chemical messenger released by neurons that travels across the synapse and allows neurons to communicate with one another.

Agonist drug A substance that mimics and enhances a neurotransmitter's effect.

Antagonist drug A substance that blocks normal neurotransmitter functioning.

TABLE 2.1 HOW NEUROTRANSMITTERS AFFECT US

Which neurotransmitters best explain this professional tennis player's exceptional skills?

AP/Wide World Photos

Neurotransmitter	Known or Suspected Effects
Acetylcholine (ACh)	Muscle action, learning, memory, REM (rapid-eye-movement) sleep, emotion; decreased ACh plays a suspected role in Alzheimer's disease
Dopamine (DA)	Movement, attention, memory, learning, and emotion; excess DA associated with schizophrenia; too little DA linked with Parkinson's disease; also plays a role in addiction and the reward system
Endorphins	Mood, pain, memory, learning, blood pressure, appetite, and sexual activity
Epinephrine (or adrenaline)	Emotional arousal, memory storage, and metabolism of glucose necessary for energy release
GABA (gamma-aminobutyric acid)	Neural inhibition in the central nervous system; tranquilizing drugs, like Valium, increase GABA's inhibitory effects and thereby decrease anxiety
Norepinephrine (NE) [or noradrenaline (NA)]	Learning, memory, dreaming, emotion, waking from sleep, eating, alertness, wakefulness, reactions to stress; low levels of NE associated with depression; high levels of NE linked with agitated, manic states
Serotonin	Mood, sleep, appetite, sensory perception, arousal, temperature regulation, pain suppression, and impulsivity; low levels of serotonin associated with depression

Endorphin A chemical substance in the nervous system similar in structure and action to opiates; involved in pain control, pleasure, and memory.

Perhaps the best-known neurotransmitters are the endogenous opioid peptides, commonly known as **endorphins** (a contraction of *endogenous* [self-produced] and *morphine*). These chemicals mimic the effects of opium-based drugs such as morphine: They elevate mood and reduce pain. In fact, drinking alcohol causes endorphins to be released in parts of the brain that are responsible for feelings of reward and pleasure (Mitchell et al., 2012).

Endorphins also affect memory, learning, blood pressure, appetite, and sexual activity. For example, rats that are injected in the brain with an endorphin-like chemical eat considerably more M&Ms than they would under normal conditions, even consuming as much as 17 grams (more than 5% of their body weight; DiFeliceantonio et al., 2012). Although this may not seem like a lot of chocolate to you, it is the equivalent of a normal-sized adult eating 7.5 pounds of M&Ms in a single session!

Hormones and the Endocrine System

Endocrine system A network of glands located throughout the body that manufacture and secrete hormones into the bloodstream.

Hormone Chemical messengers manufactured and secreted by the endocrine glands, which circulate in the bloodstream to produce bodily changes or maintain normal bodily functions.

We've just seen how the nervous system uses neurotransmitters to transmit messages throughout the body. A second type of communication system also exists. This second system is made up of a network of glands, called the **endocrine system**, which uses **hormones** to carry its messages (**Figure 2.11**).

Why do we need two communication systems? Like e-mails we send to particular people, neurotransmitters deliver messages to specific receptors, which other neurons nearby probably don't "overhear." Hormones, in contrast, are like a global e-mail message that we send to everyone in our address book.

FIGURE 2.11 **THE ENDOCRINE SYSTEM**

This figure shows the major endocrine glands, along with some internal organs to help you locate the glands.

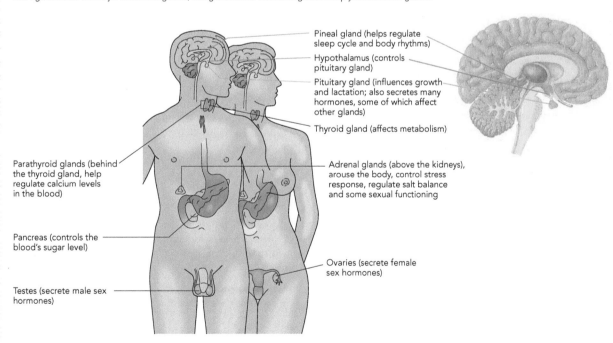

Pineal gland (helps regulate sleep cycle and body rhythms)

Hypothalamus (controls pituitary gland)

Pituitary gland (influences growth and lactation; also secretes many hormones, some of which affect other glands)

Thyroid gland (affects metabolism)

Parathyroid glands (behind the thyroid gland, help regulate calcium levels in the blood)

Adrenal glands (above the kidneys), arouse the body, control stress response, regulate salt balance and some sexual functioning

Pancreas (controls the blood's sugar level)

Ovaries (secrete female sex hormones)

Testes (secrete male sex hormones)

In addition, neurotransmitters are released from a neuron's terminal buttons into the **synapse**, a small open gap between neurons. In contrast, hormones are released from endocrine glands directly into our bloodstream. The messages are then carried by the blood throughout our bodies to any cell that will listen. Like our global e-mail recipients who may forward our message on to other people, messages from hormones are often forwarded on to other parts of the body. For example, a small part of the brain called the hypothalamus releases hormones that signal the pituitary (another small brain structure), which in turn stimulates or inhibits the release of other hormones.

Our hormone-releasing endocrine system has several important functions. It helps regulate long-term bodily processes, such as growth and sexual characteristics. It also maintains ongoing bodily processes, such as digestion and elimination. Finally, hormones control the body's response to emergencies. In times of crisis, the hypothalamus sends messages through two pathways—the neural system and the endocrine system (primarily the pituitary gland). The pituitary sends hormonal messages to the adrenal glands (located right above the kidneys). The adrenal glands then release *cortisol*, a stress hormone that boosts energy and blood sugar levels, *epinephrine* (commonly called adrenaline), and *norepinephrine* (or nonadrenaline). (Remember that these same chemicals also can serve as neurotransmitters.)

Synapse The gap between the axon tip of the sending neuron and the dendrite and/or cell body of the receiving neuron; during an action potential, neurotransmitters are released and flow across the synapse.

RETRIEVAL PRACTICE: NEURAL BASES OF BEHAVIOR

Self-Test

Completing this self-test and comparing your answers with those in Appendix B provides immediate feedback and helpful practice for exams. Additional interactive, self-tests are available at www.wiley.com/college/huffman.

1. An action potential is _____.

a. the likelihood that a neuron will take action when stimulated

b. the tendency for a neuron to be potentiated by neurotransmitters

c. a neural impulse that carries information along the axon of a neuron

d. the firing of a nerve, either toward or away from the brain

2. Too much of the neurotransmitter _____ may be related to schizophrenia, whereas too little may be related to Parkinson's disease.

a. acetylcholine

b. dopamine

c. norepinephrine

d. serotonin

3. Chemicals manufactured by endocrine glands and circulated in the bloodstream to change or maintain bodily functions are called _____.

a. vasopressors

b. gonadotropins

c. hormones

d. steroids

4. Chemical messengers that are released by axons and travel across the synapse are called _____.

a. chemical agonists

b. neurotransmitters

c. synaptic transmitters

d. neuroactivists

Think Critically

1 Why is it valuable for scientists to understand how neurotransmitters work at a molecular level?

2 What are some examples of how hormones affect your daily life?

realworldpsychology

Why can spending the first few months of life in an orphanage lead to long-term problems in cognitive functioning?

How can a chemical in the brain lead rats to binge-eat M&Ms?

HINT: LOOK IN THE MARGIN FOR Q2 AND Q3

NERVOUS SYSTEM ORGANIZATION

RETRIEVAL PRACTICE While reading the upcoming sections, respond to each Learning Objective in your own words. Then compare your responses with those found at www.wiley.com/college/huffman.

1 **IDENTIFY** the major elements of the nervous system.

2 **EXPLAIN** the role of the central nervous system (CNS).

3 **DESCRIBE** the components of the peripheral nervous system (PNS).

Have you heard the expression "Information is power"? Nowhere is this truer than in the human body. Without information, we could not survive. Neurons within our nervous system must take in sensory information from the outside world and then pass along this information to the entire human body. Just as the circulatory system handles blood, which conveys chemicals and oxygen, our nervous system uses chemicals and electrical processes to convey information.

The nervous system is divided and subdivided into several branches (**Figure 2.12**). The main branch includes the brain and a bundle of nerves that form the *spinal cord*. Because this system is located in the center of our body (within our skull and spine), it is called the **central nervous system (CNS)**. The CNS is primarily responsible for processing and organizing information.

The second major branch of our nervous system includes all the nerves outside the brain and spinal cord. This **peripheral nervous system (PNS)** carries messages (action potentials) to and from the central nervous system to the periphery of the body. Now, let's take a closer look at the CNS and the PNS.

Central nervous system (CNS) The part of the nervous system consisting of the brain and spinal cord.

Peripheral nervous system (PNS) The part of the nervous system composed of the nerves and neurons connecting the central nervous system (CNS) to the rest of the body.

FIGURE 2.12 **THE NERVOUS SYSTEM**

Central Nervous System (CNS)

The central nervous system (CNS) is the branch of the nervous system that makes us unique. Most other animals can smell, run, see, and hear far better than we can. But thanks to our CNS, we can process information and adapt to our environment in ways that no other animal can. Unfortunately, our CNS is also incredibly fragile. Unlike neurons in the PNS that can regenerate and require less protection, neurons in the CNS can suffer serious and permanent damage. However, the brain may not be as "hard wired" as we once thought.

Scientists long believed that after the first two or three years of life most animals, including humans, were unable to repair or replace damaged neurons in the brain or spinal cord. We now know that the brain is capable of lifelong **neuroplasticity** and **neurogenesis**.

Neuroplasticity

Rather than being a fixed, solid organ, the brain is capable of changing its structure and function as a result of usage and experience (Bowden et al., 2013; Marcotte et al., 2013). This "rewiring" is what makes our brains so wonderfully adaptive. For example, it makes it possible for us to learn a new sport or a foreign language.

Remarkably, this rewiring has even helped "remodel" the brain following strokes. For example, psychologist Edward Taub and his colleagues (2004, 2012) have had success working with stroke patients (**Figure 2.13**).

Neurogenesis

Our brains continually replace lost cells with new cells that originate deep within the brain and migrate to become part of its circuitry. The source of these newly created cells is neural **stem cells**—rare, immature cells that can grow and develop into any type of cell. Their fate depends on the chemical signals they receive. Experiments and clinical trials on both human and nonhuman animals have used stem cells for bone marrow transplants, and to repopulate or replace cells devastated by injury or disease. This research offers hope to patients suffering from strokes, Alzheimer's, Parkinson's, epilepsy, stress, and depression (e.g., Austin & Rini, 2013; Inden et al., 2013; Kim et al., 2013; Yin et al., 2012). In addition, stem cell injections into the eyes of patients with untreatable eye diseases and severe visual problems have led to dramatic improvements in vision (Schwartz et al., 2012).

Courtesy Taub Therapy Clinc/UAB Media Relations

FIGURE 2.13 A BREAKTHROUGH IN NEUROSCIENCE

By immobilizing the unaffected arm or leg and requiring rigorous and repetitive exercise of the affected limb, psychologist Edward Taub and colleagues "recruit" stroke patients' intact brain cells to take over for damaged cells. The therapy has restored function in some patients as long as 21 years after their strokes.

Neuroplasticity The brain's ability to reorganize and change its structure and function throughout the life span.

Neurogenesis The process by which new neurons are generated.

Stem cells Immature (uncommitted) cells that have the potential to develop into almost any type of cell, depending on the chemical signals they receive.

realworldpsychology **Stem Cell Therapy** Will stem cell transplants allow people paralyzed from spinal cord injuries to walk again? Scientists have had some success transplanting stem cells into spinal cord–injured nonhuman animals (Cusimano et al., 2012; Lee et al., 2011; Rossi, 2011; Sieber-Blum, 2010; Wang et al., 2013). When the damaged spinal cord was viewed several weeks later, the implanted cells had survived and spread throughout the injured area. More important, the transplant animals also showed some improvement in previously paralyzed parts of their bodies. Medical researchers have also recently begun testing the safety of embryonic stem cell therapy for human paralysis patients, and future trials may determine whether these cells will repair damaged spinal cords and/or improve sensation and movement in paralyzed areas (Conger, 2011; Curt et al., 2012; Robbins, 2013).

© 26ISO/iStockphoto

FIGURE 2.14 HOW THE SPINAL REFLEX OPERATES

In a simple reflex arc, a sensory receptor responds to stimulation and initiates a neural impulse that travels to the spinal cord. This signal then travels back to the appropriate muscle, which then contracts. The response is automatic and immediate in a reflex because the signal only travels as far as the spinal cord before action is initiated, not all the way to the brain. The brain is later "notified" of the action when the spinal cord sends along the message. What might be the evolutionary advantages of the reflex arc?

1 In a simple reflex circuit, skin receptors in the fingertips detect heat from the sauce pan, and then send neural messages to sensory neurons.

2 Sensory neurons send messages to interneurons, which in turn connect with motor neurons.

3 Motor neurons send messages to hand muscles, causing a withdrawal reflex. (This occurs before the brain perceives the actual sensation of pain.)

Spinal cord (cross section)

4 While the spinal reflex occurs, sensory neurons also send messages up the spinal cord to the brain.

5 A small structure in the brain, the thalamus, relays incoming sensory information to the higher, cortical areas of the brain.

6 An area of the brain, known as the somatosensory cortex, receives the message from the thalamus and interprets it as PAIN!

Now that we have discussed neuroplasticity and neurogenesis within the central nervous system (CNS), let's take a closer look at the spinal cord. Because of its central importance for psychology and behavior, we'll discuss the brain in detail in the next major section.

Spinal Cord

Beginning at the base of our brains and continuing down our backs, the spinal cord carries vital information from the rest of the body into and out of the brain. But the spinal cord doesn't simply relay messages. It can also initiate some automatic behaviors on its own. We call these involuntary, automatic behaviors **reflexes**, or *reflex arcs*, because the response to the incoming stimuli is automatically "reflected" back to the spinal cord, which allows an immediate action response without the delay of routing signals directly to the brain.

As you can see in the simple reflex arc depicted in **Figure 2.14**, a sensory receptor first responds to stimulation and initiates a neural impulse that travels to the spinal cord. This signal then travels back to the appropriate muscle, which contracts. The response is automatic and immediate in a reflex because the signal travels only as far as the spinal cord before action is initiated, not all the way to the brain. The brain is later "notified" of the action when the spinal cord sends along the message. What might be the evolutionary advantages of the reflex arc?

Reflex An innate, automatic response to a stimulus that has a biological relevance for an organism (for example, knee-jerk reflex).

We're all born with numerous reflexes, many of which fade over time (**Figure 2.15**). But even as adults, we still blink in response to a puff of air in our eyes, gag when something touches the back of the throat, and urinate and defecate in response to pressure in the bladder and rectum.

Kovalchynskyy Mykola/Shutterstock

psychology and you **Sexual Response Reflexes** Reflexes even influence our sexual responses. Certain stimuli, such as the stroking of the genitals, can lead to arousal and the reflexive muscle contractions of orgasm in both men and women. However, in order for us to have the passion, thoughts, and emotion we normally associate with sex, the sensory information from the stroking and orgasm must be carried by the spinal cord to the appropriate areas of the brain that receive and interpret these specific sensory messages.

Peripheral Nervous System (PNS)

The peripheral nervous system (PNS) is just what it sounds like—the part that involves nerves *peripheral* to (or outside) the brain and spinal cord. The chief function of the peripheral nervous system (PNS) is to carry information to and from the central nervous system (CNS). It links the brain and spinal cord to the body's sense receptors, muscles, and glands.

The PNS is subdivided into the somatic nervous system and the autonomic nervous system. The **somatic nervous system (SNS)** consists of all the nerves that connect to sensory receptors and skeletal muscles. The name comes from the term *soma*, which means "body," and the somatic nervous system plays a key role in communication throughout the entire body. In a kind of two-way street, the somatic nervous system (also called the skeletal nervous system) first carries sensory information to the brain and spinal cord (CNS) and then carries messages from the CNS to skeletal muscles.

> **Somatic nervous system (SNS)** A subdivision of the peripheral nervous system (PNS) that connects the central nervous system (CNS) to sensory receptors and controls skeletal muscles.

Think Critically

1 What might happen if infants lacked these reflexes?

2 Can you explain why most infant reflexes disappear within the first year?

FIGURE 2.15 TESTING FOR REFLEXES | *psychology and you*

If you have a newborn or young infant in your home, you can easily (and safely) test for these simple reflexes. (Most infant reflexes disappear within the first year of life. If they reappear in later life, it generally indicates damage to the central nervous system.)

Photos by Linnea Leaver Mavrides/ Courtesy Catherine Sanderson

Ⓐ Rooting reflex
Lightly stroke the cheek or side of the mouth, and watch how the infant automatically (reflexively) turns toward the stimulation and attempts to suck.

Ⓑ Grasping reflex
Place your finger or an object in the infant's palm and note the automatic grasp.

Ⓒ Babinski reflex
Lightly stroke the sole of the infant's foot, and the big toe will move toward the top of the foot, while the other toes fan out.

Autonomic nervous system (ANS) The subdivision of the peripheral nervous system (PNS) that controls the body's involuntary motor responses by connecting the sensory receptors to the central nervous system (CNS) and the CNS to the smooth muscle, cardiac muscle, and glands.

Sympathetic nervous system The subdivision of the autonomic nervous system (ANS) that is responsible for arousing the body and mobilizing its energy during times of stress; also called the "fight-or-flight" system.

Parasympathetic nervous system The subdivision of the autonomic nervous system (ANS) that is responsible for calming the body and conserving energy.

The other subdivision of the PNS is the **autonomic nervous system (ANS)**. The ANS is responsible for involuntary tasks, such as heart rate, digestion, pupil dilation, and breathing. Like an automatic pilot, the ANS can sometimes be consciously overridden. But as its name implies, the autonomic system normally operates on its own (autonomously).

The autonomic nervous system is further divided into two branches, the sympathetic and parasympathetic, which tend to work in opposition to each other to regulate the functioning of such target organs as the heart, the intestines, and the lungs. Like two children on a teeter-totter, one will be up while the other is down, but they essentially balance each other out. **Figure 2.16** illustrates a familiar example of the interaction between the sympathetic and parasympathetic nervous systems.

During stressful times, either mental or physical, the **sympathetic nervous system** mobilizes bodily resources to respond to the stressor. This emergency response is often called the "fight or flight" response. If you noticed a dangerous snake coiled and ready to strike, your sympathetic nervous system would increase your heart rate, respiration, and blood pressure; stop your digestive and eliminative processes; and release hormones, such as cortisol, into the bloodstream. The net result of sympathetic activation is to get more oxygenated blood and energy to the skeletal muscles, thus allowing you to cope with the stress—to either fight or flee.

In contrast to the sympathetic nervous system, the **parasympathetic nervous system** is responsible for calming our bodies and conserving energy. It returns our normal bodily functions by slowing our heart rate, lowering our blood pressure, and increasing our digestive and eliminative processes.

The sympathetic nervous system provides an adaptive, evolutionary advantage. At the beginning of human evolution, when we faced a dangerous bear or an aggressive human intruder, there were only two reasonable responses—fight or flight. The automatic mobilization of bodily resources can still be critical, even in modern times. However, less life-threatening events, such as traffic jams, also activate our sympathetic nervous system. As the next chapter discusses, ongoing sympathetic system response to such chronic, daily stress can become detrimental to our health. For a look at how the autonomic nervous system affects our sexual lives, see **Figure 2.17**.

FIGURE 2.16 ACTIONS OF THE AUTONOMIC NERVOUS SYSTEM (ANS)

The ANS is responsible for a variety of independent (autonomous) activities, such as salivation and digestion. It exercises this control through its two divisions—the sympathetic and parasympathetic branches.

Sympathetic dominance

Parasympathetic dominance

FIGURE 2.17 **AUTONOMIC NERVOUS SYSTEM AND SEXUAL AROUSAL** | *psychology and you*

The complexities of sexual interaction—and, in particular, the difficulties couples sometimes have in achieving sexual arousal or orgasm—illustrate the balancing act between the sympathetic and parasympathetic nervous systems.

Piotr Marcinski/Shutterstock

Ⓐ Parasympathetic dominance
Sexual arousal and excitement require that the body be relaxed enough to allow increased blood flow to the genitals—in other words, the nervous system must be in *parasympathetic dominance*. Parasympathetic nerves carry messages from the central nervous system directly to the sexual organs, allowing for a localized response (increased blood flow and genital arousal).

© 4774344sean/iStockphoto

Ⓑ Sympathetic dominance
During strong emotions, such as anger, anxiety, or fear, the body shifts to *sympathetic dominance*, which causes blood flow to the genitals and other organs to decrease because the body is preparing for "fight or flight." As a result, the person is unable (or less likely) to become sexually aroused. Any number of circumstances— performance anxiety, fear of unwanted pregnancy or disease, or tensions between partners—can trigger sympathetic dominance.

Ⓥoices from the Classroom

Burn Prevention—Thanks to the CNS and PNS To explain the importance of how well the CNS and PNS communicate with one another, I often ask my students to raise their hands if they have ever have been burned. Every student, every single time raises his or her hand. But, hands quickly drop when I ask, "How many have been burned more than 20 times?" Ultimately, I'm left only with people who work in environments with hot stimuli (i.e., bakers, cooks, welders, etc.). I explain that during the process of being burned, our PNS does an excellent job of sending info about hot stimuli sensed from the five senses to the CNS. The CNS then quickly learns to associate and detect hot stimuli picked up by the PNS: from the sounds of boiling water, the feel the heat from a red hot stove surface, the smell of something burning, to recognizing the flicking shadows of a flame. Once we've learned these associations between "hot stimuli" and being burned, getting burned again is a rare experience–thanks to the excellent relay system between the CNS and PNS!

Professor R. D. Landis
Weatherford Community College
Weatherford, Texas

RETRIEVAL PRACTICE: NERVOUS SYSTEM ORGANIZATION

Self-Test

Completing this self-test and comparing your answers with those in Appendix B provides immediate feedback and helpful practice for exams. Additional interactive, self-tests are available at www.wiley.com/college/huffman.

1. The _____ nervous system is responsible for fight or flight, whereas the _____ nervous system is responsible for maintaining calm.

a. central; peripheral
b. parasympathetic; sympathetic
c. sympathetic; parasympathetic
d. autonomic; somatic

2. The peripheral nervous system is _____.

a. composed of the spinal cord and peripheral nerves
b. less important than the central nervous system
c. contained within the skull and spinal column
d. a combination of all the nerves and neurons outside the brain and spinal cord

3. If you are startled by the sound of a loud explosion, the _____ nervous system will become dominant.

a. semiautomatic
b. afferent
c. parasympathetic
d. sympathetic

4. The central nervous system _____.

a. consists of the brain and spinal cord
b. is the most important nervous system
c. includes the automatic and other nervous systems
d. all these options

Think Critically

1 Some stem cell research comes from tissue taken from aborted fetuses, which has led to great controversy and severe restrictions in some states. Do you believe this specific form of research should be limited? If so, how and why?

2 What are some everyday examples of neuroplasticity—that is, of the way the brain is changed and shaped by experience?

realworldpsychology

How can stem cell injections lead to restored vision and improved recovery from strokes?

HINT: LOOK IN THE MARGIN FOR **Q4**

A TOUR THROUGH THE BRAIN

LEARNING OBJECTIVES

RETRIEVAL PRACTICE While reading the upcoming sections, respond to each Learning Objective in your own words. Then compare your responses with those found at www.wiley.com/college/huffman.

1 DESCRIBE how neuroscientists study the brain and nervous system.
2 IDENTIFY the major structures of the hindbrain, midbrain, and forebrain.
3 SUMMARIZE the major roles of the lobes of the cerebral cortex.
4 DESCRIBE how the brain is divided into two specialized hemispheres.

We begin our exploration of the brain with a discussion of the tools that neuroscientists use to study it. Then we offer a quick tour of the brain, beginning at its lower end, where the spinal cord joins the base of the brain, and then move upward, all the way to the top of the skull. As we move from bottom to top, "lower," basic processes, such as breathing, generally give way to more complex mental processes (**Figure 2.18**).

Biological Tools for Research

How do we know how the brain and nervous system work? The earliest explorers of the brain *dissected* the brains of deceased humans and conducted experiments on other animals using *lesioning* techniques (systematically destroying brain tissue to study the effects on behavior and mental processes). By the mid-1800s, this research had produced a basic map of the nervous system, including some areas of the brain. Early researchers also relied on clinical observations and case studies of living people who had experienced injuries, diseases, and disorders that affected brain functioning.

Modern researchers still use such methods, but they also employ other techniques to examine biological processes that underlie our behavior (**Table 2.2**). For example, recent advances in brain science have led to various types of brain-imaging scans, which can be used in both clinical and laboratory settings. Most of these methods are relatively *noninvasive*—that is, their use does not involve breaking the skin or entering the body.

Lower-Level Brain Structures

Having studied the tools scientists use for exploring the brain, we can now begin our tour. Let's talk first about brain size and complexity, which vary significantly from species to species. For example, fish and reptiles have smaller, less complex brains than do cats and dogs. The most complex brains belong to whales, dolphins, and higher primates, such as chimps, gorillas, and humans. The billions of neurons that make up the human brain control much of what we think, feel, and do. Certain brain structures are specialized to perform certain tasks, a process known as *localization of function*. However, most parts of the brain perform integrating, overlapping functions.

Science Pictures Limited/Photo Researchers

A photo of the human brain
This deceased human's brain is sliced down the center, split into right and left halves. Like the diagram below, only the right half of the brain is shown in this photo.

FIGURE 2.18 **THE HUMAN BRAIN**

Note on the left side of this figure how the forebrain, midbrain, and hindbrain radically change in their size and placement during prenatal development. The profile drawing in the middle highlights key structures and functions of the right half of the adult brain. As you read about each of these structures, keep this drawing in mind and refer to it as necessary. (The diagram shows the brain structures as if the brain were split vertically down the center and the left hemisphere were removed.)

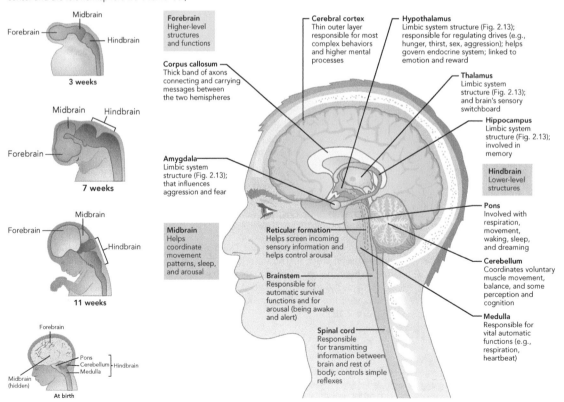

TABLE 2.2 SAMPLE TOOLS FOR BIOLOGICAL RESEARCH

Tool	Description	Purpose	
Electrical recordings Electrical activity throughout the brain sweeps in regular waves across its surface, and the electroencephalogram (EEG) is a read out of this activity.	Using electrodes attached to the skin or scalp, brain activity is detected and recorded on an EEG.	Reveals areas of the brain most active during particular tasks or mental states such as reading or sleeping; also traces abnormal brain waves caused by brain malfunctions, such as epilepsy or tumors.	 Larry Mulvehill/Photo Researchers, Inc.
CT (computed tomography) scan This CT scan used X-rays to locate a brain tumor, which is the deep purple mass at the top left.	Computer-created cross-sectional X-rays of the brain or other parts of the body produce 3-D images. Least expensive type of imaging and widely used in research.	Reveals the effects of strokes, injuries, tumors, and other brain disorders.	 Mehau Kulyk/Photo Researchers, Inc.
PET (positron emission tomography) scan The left PET scan shows brain activity when the eyes are open, whereas the one on the right is with the eyes closed. Note the increased activity, red and yellow, in the left photo when the eyes are open.	A radioactive form of glucose is injected into the bloodstream; a scanner records the amount of glucose used in particularly active areas of the brain and produces a computer-constructed picture of the brain.	Originally designed to detect abnormalities, now used to identify brain areas active during ordinary activities (such as reading or singing).	 N.I. H/Photo Researchers, Inc.
MRI (magnetic resonance imaging) Note the fissures and internal structures of the brain. The throat, nasal airways, and fluid surrounding the brain are dark.	Powerful electromagnets produce a high-frequency magnetic field that is passed through the brain.	Produces high-resolution 3-D pictures of the brain useful for identifying abnormalities and mapping brain structures and function.	 Scott Camazine/Photo Researchers, Inc.
fMRI (functional magnetic resonance imaging)	Newer, faster version of MRI that detects blood flow by picking up magnetic signals from blood, which has given up its oxygen to activate brain cells.	Measures blood flow, which indicates areas of the brain that are active and inactive during ordinary activities or responses (like reading or talking); also shows changes associated with various disorders.	 Science Photo Library/Photo Researchers, Inc.
Other methods: (a) Cell body or tract (myelin) staining, (b) Microinjections, and (c) Intrabrain electrical recordings	(a) Colors/stains selected neurons or nerve fibers. (b) Injects chemicals into specific areas of the brain. (c) Records activity of one or a group of neurons inside the brain.	Increases overall information of structure and function through direct observation and measurement. Intrabrain wire probes allow scientists to "see" individual neuron activity.	

Hindbrain

You're asleep and in the middle of a frightening nightmare. Your heart is racing, your breathing is rapid, and you're attempting to run away but find you can't move! Suddenly, your nightmare is shattered by a buzzing alarm clock. All your automatic behaviors and survival responses in this scenario are controlled or influenced by parts of the hindbrain. The **hindbrain** includes the medulla, pons, and cerebellum.

The **medulla** is essentially an extension of the spinal cord, with many neural fibers passing through it carrying information to and from the brain. It also controls many essential automatic bodily functions, such as respiration and heart rate.

The **pons** is involved in respiration, movement, sleeping, waking, and dreaming (among other things). It also contains axons that cross from one side of the brain to the other (*pons* is Latin for "bridge").

The cauliflower-shaped **cerebellum** (Latin for "little brain") is, evolutionarily, a very old structure. It coordinates fine muscle movement and balance (**Figure 2.19**). Researchers using functional magnetic resonance imaging (fMRI) have shown that parts of the cerebellum also are important for memory, sensation, perception, cognition, language, learning, and even "multitasking" (e.g., Bellebaum & Daum, 2011; Eichenbaum, 2013; Manganelli et al., 2013; Thompson, 2005; Wu et al., 2013).

Midbrain

The **midbrain** helps us orient our eye and body movements to visual and auditory stimuli, and it works with the pons to help control sleep and level of arousal. It also contains a small structure, the *substantia nigra*, that secretes the neurotransmitter dopamine. Parkinson's disease, an age-related degenerative condition, is related to the deterioration of neurons in the substantia nigra and the subsequent loss of dopamine.

Running through the core of the hindbrain, midbrain, and brainstem is the **reticular formation (RF)**. This diffuse, finger-shaped network of neurons helps screen incoming sensory information and alerts the higher brain centers to important events. Without our reticular formation, we would not be alert or perhaps even conscious.

Hindbrain The lower or hind region of the brain; collection of structures including the medulla, pons, and cerebellum.

Medulla The hindbrain structure responsible for vital, automatic functions, such as respiration and heartbeat.

Pons The hindbrain structure involved in respiration, movement, waking, sleep, and dreaming.

Cerebellum The hindbrain structure responsible for coordinating fine muscle movement, balance, and some perception and cognition.

Midbrain The collection of structures in the middle of the brain responsible for coordinating movement patterns, sleep, and arousal.

Reticular formation (RF) The diffuse set of neurons that helps screen incoming information and controls arousal.

FIGURE 2.19 **WALK THE LINE**

Asking drivers to perform tasks like walking the white line is a common test for possible intoxication. Why? The cerebellum, responsible for smooth and precise movements, is one of the first areas of the brain to be affected by alcohol.

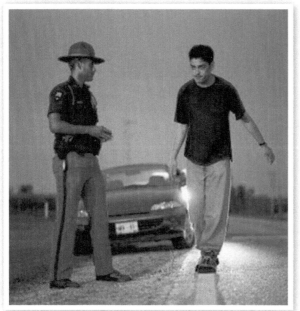

Bill Fritsch/Getty Images, Inc.

Forebrain The collection of upper-level brain structures including the thalamus, hypothalamus, limbic system, and cerebral cortex.

Thalamus The forebrain structure at the top of the brainstem that serves as the brain's switchboard, relaying sensory messages to the cerebral cortex.

Hypothalamus The small brain structure beneath the thalamus that helps govern drives (hunger, thirst, sex, and aggression) and hormones.

Forebrain

The **forebrain** is the largest and most prominent part of the human brain. It includes the cerebral cortex, hypothalamus, limbic system, and thalamus (**Figure 2.20**). The last three structures are located near the top of the brainstem. The cerebral cortex (discussed separately, in the next section) is wrapped above and around them. (*Cerebrum* is Latin for "brain," and *cortex* is Latin for "covering" or "bark.")

The **thalamus** integrates input from the senses, and it may also function in learning and memory (Barnes, 2013). It receives input from nearly all sensory systems, except smell, and then directs the information to the appropriate cortical areas. The thalamus also transmits some higher brain information to the cerebellum and medulla. Think of the thalamus as the switchboard in an air traffic control center that receives information from all aircraft and directs them to landing or takeoff areas.

Because the thalamus is the brain's major sensory relay center to the cerebral cortex, damage or abnormalities in the thalamus might cause the cortex to misinterpret or not receive vital sensory information. Interestingly, brain-imaging research links thalamus abnormalities to schizophrenia, a serious psychological disorder characterized by problems with sensory filtering and perception (Bor et al., 2011; Hazlett et al., 2012; Kubota et al., 2013).

Beneath the thalamus lies the kidney bean–sized **hypothalamus**. (*Hypo-* means "under.") This organ has been called the "master control center" for emotions and for many basic motives such as hunger, thirst, sex, and aggression (Feinstein, 2013; Hull, 2011; Moll et al., 2012). It regulates the body's internal environment, including temperature control, which it accomplishes by regulating the endocrine system.

FIGURE 2.20 **STRUCTURES OF THE FOREBRAIN**

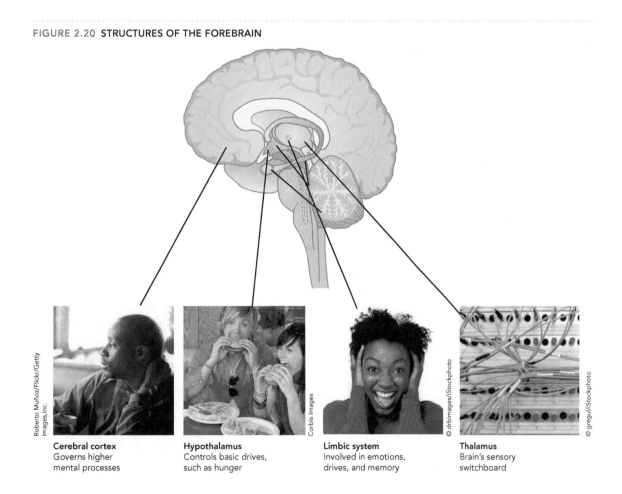

Cerebral cortex
Governs higher
mental processes

Hypothalamus
Controls basic drives,
such as hunger

Limbic system
Involved in emotions,
drives, and memory

Thalamus
Brain's sensory
switchboard

psychology and you   **Diet and the Hypothalamus** Have you ever gone on a diet to try to lose weight or lost weight but then struggled to maintain your new weight? One of the reasons long-term weight loss is so hard for many people is that eating a high-fat diet can lead to long-term changes in the hypothalamus (Thaler et al., 2012). These changes make it harder for the body to regulate its weight, meaning that you will continue to feel hungry even when you have just eaten plenty of food. Sadly, this process makes it hard to stick to a diet and thereby increases the risk of obesity.

© donmedia/iStockphoto

Hanging down from the hypothalamus, the *pituitary gland* is usually considered the master endocrine gland because it releases hormones that activate the other endocrine glands. The hypothalamus influences the pituitary through direct neural connections and through release of its own hormones into the blood supply of the pituitary. The hypothalamus also directly influences some important aspects of behavior, such as eating and drinking patterns.

An interconnected group of forebrain structures, known as the **limbic system**, is located roughly along the border between the cerebral cortex and the lower-level brain structures (**Figure 2.21**). The limbic system is generally responsible for emotions, drives, and memory. In Chapter 7, you'll discover how the **hippocampus**, a key part of the limbic system, is involved in forming and retrieving our memories. However, the limbic system's major focus of interest is the **amygdala**, which is linked to the production and regulation of emotions–especially aggression and fear (Armony, 2013; LeDoux, 1998, 2002, 2007; Pinho et al., 2013; Whalen et al., 2013).

Another well-known function of the limbic system is its role as part of the so-called "pleasure center," a set of brain structures whose stimulation leads to highly enjoyable feelings (Bjork et al., 2012; Kolb, 2013; Olds & Milner, 1954). Even though limbic system structures and neurotransmitters are instrumental in emotions, the frontal lobes of the cerebral cortex also play an important role.

The Cerebral Cortex

The gray, wrinkled **cerebral cortex**, the surface layer of the cerebral hemispheres, is responsible for most complex behaviors and higher mental processes. It plays such a vital role that many consider it the essence of life. In fact, physicians may declare a person legally dead when the cerebral cortex dies, even when the lower-level brain structures and the rest of the body are fully functioning.

Although the cerebral cortex is only about one-eighth of an inch thick, it's made up of approximately 30 billion neurons and nine times as many glial cells. Its numerous wrinkles, called *convolutions*, significantly increase its surface area. Damage to the cerebral cortex is linked to numerous problems, including suicide, substance abuse, and dementia (McKee et al., 2012). Evidence suggests that such trauma is particularly common in athletes who experience head injuries in sports like football, ice hockey, boxing, and soccer (**Figure 2.22**).

Limbic system The interconnected group of forebrain structures involved with emotions, drives, and memory, as well as major physiological functions.

Hippocampus The sea-horse shaped part of the limbic system involved in forming and retrieving memories.

Amygdala A part of the limbic system that controls emotions, like aggression and fear, and the formation of emotional memory.

Cerebral cortex The thin surface layer on the cerebral hemispheres that regulates most complex behavior, including sensations, motor control, and higher mental processes.

FIGURE 2.21 MAJOR BRAIN STRUCTURES COMMONLY ASSOCIATED WITH THE LIMBIC SYSTEM

Drew Hallowell/Philadelphia Eagles/Getty Images

FIGURE 2.22 DAMAGE TO THE BRAIN
realworldpsychology

On March 20, 2013, the owners of the National Football League voted to ban runners from leading with their helmets when they hit other players. This so-called "crown rule" is designed to help reduce concussions, as might have occurred on September 9, 2012, when Cleveland Browns running back Trent Richardson ran into Philadelphia Eagles safety Kurt Coleman, knocking his helmet into the air.

FIGURE 2.23
INFORMATION CROSSOVER

Our brain's right hemisphere controls the left side of our body, whereas the left hemisphere controls the right side.

Frontal lobes The two lobes at the front of the brain that govern motor control, speech production, and higher functions, such as thinking, personality, emotion, and memory.

The full cerebral cortex and the two cerebral hemispheres beneath it closely resemble an oversized walnut. The division, or *fissure*, down the center marks the separation between the left and right *hemispheres* of the brain, which make up about 80% of the brain's weight. The hemispheres are mostly filled with axon connections between the cortex and the other brain structures. Each hemisphere controls the opposite side of the body (**Figure 2.23**).

The cerebral hemispheres are each divided into four distinct areas, or lobes (**Figure 2.24**). Like the lower-level brain structures, each lobe specializes in somewhat different tasks, another example of localization of function. However, some functions overlap two or more lobes.

Frontal Lobes

Our two large **frontal lobes** coordinate messages received from all the other lobes. An area at the very back of these frontal lobes, known as the *motor cortex*, instigates all voluntary movement. In the lower-left frontal lobe lies *Broca's area*. In 1865, French physician Paul Broca discovered that damage to this area causes difficulty in speech, but not in language comprehension. This type of impaired language ability is known as *Broca's aphasia*.

Finally, the frontal lobes control most of our higher functions—the functions that distinguish humans from other animals, such as thinking, personality, emotion, and memory. Abnormalities in the frontal lobes are often observed in patients with schizophrenia (Chapter 13). For example, teenagers with schizophrenia often show loss of gray matter, as well as increases in cerebrospinal fluid in the frontal lobes (Arango et al., 2012). Research also shows that damage to the frontal lobes affects personality, motivation, drives, creativity, self-awareness, initiative, reasoning, and emotional behavior. But as you'll see in the *Psych Science* feature, updated information about the classic case of Phineas Gage indicates that our brains are remarkably flexible and

FIGURE 2.24 LOBES OF THE BRAIN

This is a view of the brain's left hemisphere showing its four lobes—*frontal, parietal, temporal,* and *occipital*. The right hemisphere has the same four lobes. Divisions between the lobes are marked by visibly prominent folds. Keep in mind that Broca's and Wernicke's areas occur only in the left hemisphere.

that damage to the frontal lobes (and other parts of the brain) may not be as permanent as we once thought—thanks to *neuroplasticity* and *neurogenesis*.

Temporal Lobes

The **temporal lobes** are responsible for hearing, language comprehension, memory, and some emotional control. The *auditory cortex*, which processes sound, is located at the top front of each temporal lobe. This area is responsible for receiving incoming sensory information and sending it on to the parietal lobes, where it is combined with other sensory information.

A part of the left temporal lobe called *Wernicke's area* aids in language comprehension. About a decade after Broca's discovery, German neurologist Carl Wernicke noted that patients with damage in this area could not understand what they read

Temporal lobes The two lobes on each side of the brain above the ears that are involved in audition (hearing), language comprehension, memory, and some emotional control.

PSYCHSCIENCE

PHINEAS GAGE—MYTHS VERSUS FACTS

In 1848, a 25-year-old railroad foreman named Phineas Gage had a metal rod (13½ pounds, 3 feet 7 inches long, and 1¼ inches in diameter) accidentally blown through the front of his face, destroying much of his brain's left frontal lobe. Amazingly, Gage was immediately able to sit up, speak, and move around, and he did not receive medical treatment until about 1½ hours later. After his wound healed, he tried to return to work, but was soon fired. The previously friendly, efficient, and capable foreman was now "fitful, impatient, and lacking in deference to his fellows" (Macmillan, 2000). In the words of his friends: "Gage was no longer Gage" (Harlow, 1868).

This so-called "American Crowbar Case" is often cited in current texts and academic papers as one of the earliest in-depth studies of an individual's survival after massive damage to the brain's frontal lobes. The evidence is clear that Gage did experience several dramatic changes in his behavior and personality after the accident, but the extent and permanence of these changes are in dispute. Most accounts of post-accident Gage report him as impulsive and unreliable until his death. However, more reliable evidence later showed that Gage spent many years driving stagecoaches—a job that required high motor, cognitive, and interpersonal skills (Macmillan, 2000, 2008; Macmillan & Lena, 2010).

So why bother reporting this controversy? As you'll note throughout this text, we discuss several popular misconceptions in psychology in order to clarify and correct them. Phineas Gage's story is particularly important because it highlights how a small set of reliable facts can be distorted and shaped to fit existing beliefs and scientific theories. For example, at the time of Gage's accident, little was known about how the brain functions, and damage to it was believed to be largely irreversible. Can you see how our current research techniques (e.g., Van Horn et al., 2012), along with our new understanding of *neurogenesis* and *neuroplasticity* might now explain the previously ignored evidence of Gage's significant recovery in later life?

RESEARCH CHALLENGE

1 Based on the information provided, did the researchers in this study of Phineas Gage use descriptive, correlational, and/or experimental research?

2 If you chose:

- descriptive research, is this a naturalistic observation, survey/interview, case study, or archival research?
- correlational research, is this a positive, negative, or zero correlation?
- experimental research, label the IV, DV, experimental group(s), and control group.

>>CHECK YOUR ANSWERS IN APPENDIX B.

NOTE: The information provided in this study is admittedly limited, but the level of detail is similar to what is presented in most textbooks and public reports of research findings. Answering these questions, and then comparing your answers to those in the Appendix, will help you become a better critical thinker and consumer of scientific research.

or heard, but they could speak quickly and easily. However, their speech was often unintelligible because it contained made-up words, sound substitutions, and word substitutions. This syndrome is now referred to as *Wernicke's aphasia*.

Occipital Lobes

The **occipital lobes** are responsible for, among other things, vision and visual perception. Damage to the occipital lobes can produce blindness, even if the eyes and their neural connection to the brain are perfectly healthy.

Parietal Lobes

The **parietal lobes** receive and interpret bodily sensations including pressure, pain, touch, temperature, and location of body parts. A band of tissue on the front of the parietal lobes, called the *somatosensory cortex*, receives information about touch in different body areas. Areas of the body with more somatosensory and motor cortex devoted to them (such as the hands and face) are most sensitive to touch and have the most precise motor control (**Figure 2.25**).

Association Areas

One of the most popular myths in psychology is that we use only 10% of our brain. This myth might have begun with early research which showed that approximately three-fourths of the cortex is "quiet" (with no precise, specific function responsive to electrical brain stimulation). These areas are not dormant, however. They are clearly engaged in interpreting, integrating, and acting on information processed by other parts of the brain. They are called **association areas** because they associate, or connect, various areas and functions of the brain. The association areas in the frontal lobes, for example, help in decision making and planning. Similarly, the association area right in front of the motor cortex aids in the planning of voluntary movement.

Occipital lobes The two lobes at the back of the brain that are primarily responsible for vision and visual perception.

Parietal lobes The two lobes located at the top of the brain, in which bodily sensations are received and interpreted.

Association areas The "quiet" areas in the cerebral cortex involved in interpreting, integrating, and acting on information processed by other parts of the brain.

FIGURE 2.25 BODY REPRESENTATION OF THE MOTOR CORTEX AND SOMATOSENSORY CORTEX

This drawing shows a vertical cross section taken from the left hemisphere's motor cortex and right hemisphere's somatosensory cortex. If body areas were truly proportional to the amount of tissue on the motor and somatosensory cortices that affect them, our bodies would look like the oddly shaped human figures draped around the outside edge of the cortex.

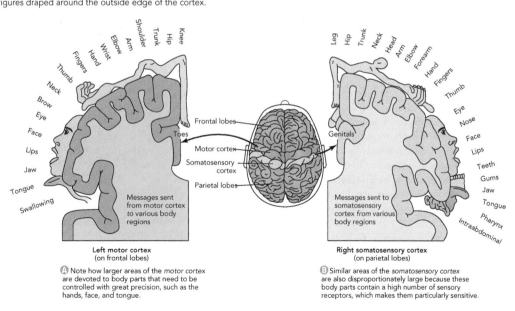

Left motor cortex
(on frontal lobes)

Ⓐ Note how larger areas of the *motor cortex* are devoted to body parts that need to be controlled with great precision, such as the hands, face, and tongue.

Right somatosensory cortex
(on parietal lobes)

Ⓑ Similar areas of the *somatosensory cortex* are also disproportionately large because these body parts contain a high number of sensory receptors, which makes them particularly sensitive.

FIGURE 2.26 VIEWS OF THE CORPUS CALLOSUM

In the photo on the left, a human brain was sliced vertically from the top to the bottom to expose the corpus callosum, which conveys information between the two hemispheres of the cerebral cortex. In the illustration on the right, a brain was cut horizontally, which shows how fibers, or *axons*, of the corpus callosum link to both the right and left hemispheres. Note: The deep, extensive cuts shown in these photos are to reveal the corpus callosum. In split-brain surgeries on live patients, only fibers within the corpus callosum itself are cut.

Two Brains in One?

We mentioned earlier that the brain's left and right cerebral hemispheres control opposite sides of the body. Each hemisphere also has separate areas of specialization. This is another example of localization of function, technically referred to as *lateralization*.

Early researchers believed the right hemisphere was subordinate or nondominant to the left, with few special functions or abilities. In the 1960s, landmark **split-brain surgeries** began to change this view.

The primary connection between the two cerebral hemispheres is a thick, ribbon-like band of neural fibers under the cortex called the **corpus callosum** (**Figure 2.26**). In some rare cases of severe epilepsy, when other forms of treatment have failed, surgeons cut the corpus callosum to stop the spread of epileptic seizures from one hemisphere to the other. Because this operation cuts the only direct communication link between the two hemispheres, it reveals what each half of the brain can do in isolation from the other. The resulting research has profoundly improved our understanding of how the two halves of the brain function.

For example, when someone has a brain stroke and loses his or her ability to speak, we know this generally points to damage on the left hemisphere, because this is where *Broca's area*, which controls speech production, is located (refer back to Figure 2.24). However, we now know that when specific regions of the brain are injured or destroyed their functions can sometimes be picked up by a neighboring region—even the opposite hemisphere.

Split-brain surgery The cutting of the corpus callosum to separate the brain's two hemispheres; used medically to treat severe epilepsy; also provides information on the functions of the two hemispheres.

Corpus callosum A bundle of neural fibers that connects the brain's two hemispheres.

---

realworldpsychology **The Myth of the "Neglected Right Brain"** Popular accounts of split-brain research have led to some exaggerated claims and unwarranted conclusions about differences between the left and right hemispheres. For example, courses and books directed at "right-brain thinking" and "drawing on the right side of the brain" often promise to increase our intuition, creativity, and artistic abilities by waking up our neglected and underused right brain. Contrary to this myth, research has clearly shown that the two hemispheres work together in a coordinated, integrated way, each making important contributions (Barnes, 2013).

If you are a member of a soccer or basketball team, you can easily understand this principle. Just as you and your teammates often specialize in different jobs, such as offense and defense, the hemispheres also somewhat divide their workload. However, like good team players, each of the two hemispheres is generally aware of what the other is doing.

© Debbi Smirnoff/iStockphoto

Although most split-brain surgery patients generally show very few outward changes in their behavior, other than fewer epileptic seizures, the surgery does create a few unusual responses. For example, one split-brain patient reported that when he dressed himself, he sometimes pulled his pants down with his left hand and up with his right (Gazzaniga, 2009). The subtle changes in split-brain patients normally appear only with specialized testing. See **Figure 2.27** for an illustration and description of this type of specialized test. Keep in mind that in actual split-brain surgery on live patients, only some fibers within the corpus callosum are cut (*not* the lower brain structures), and this surgery is performed only in rare cases of intractable epilepsy.

In our tour of the nervous system, the principles of localization of function, lateralization, and specialization recur: Dendrites receive information, the occipital lobes specialize in vision, and so on. Keep in mind, however, that, like a great soccer or basketball team, all parts of the brain and nervous system also play overlapping and synchronized roles.

FIGURE 2.27 SPLIT-BRAIN RESEARCH

Experiments on split-brain patients often present visual information to only the patient's left or right hemisphere, which leads to some intriguing results.

Ⓐ When a split-brain patient is asked to stare straight ahead while a photo of a screwdriver is flashed only to the right hemisphere, he will report that he "saw nothing."

Ⓑ However, when asked to pick up with his left hand what he saw, he can reach through and touch the items hidden behind the screen and easily pick up the screwdriver.

Ⓒ When the left hemisphere receives an image of a baseball, the split-brain patient can easily name it.

Assuming you have an intact, nonsevered corpus callosum, if the same photos were presented to you in the same way, you could easily name both the screwdriver and the baseball. Can you explain why? The answers lie in our somewhat confusing visual wiring system (as shown in drawings d and e below).

 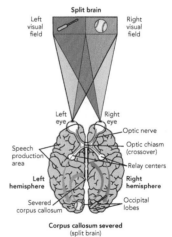

Ⓓ As you can see, our eyes normally connect to our brains in such a way that, when we look straight ahead, information from the left visual field travels to our right hemisphere (the blue line). In contrast, information from the right visual field travels to our left hemisphere (the red line). The messages received by either hemisphere are then quickly sent to the other across the corpus callosum (the red and blue arrows).

Ⓔ When the corpus callosum is severed (note the white line down the middle of the two hemispheres), a split-brain patient cannot verbalize what he sees. This is because in this particular task the visual information is presented only to the right hemisphere and the information cannot travel to the opposite (verbal) hemisphere.

RETRIEVAL PRACTICE: A TOUR THROUGH THE BRAIN

Self-Test

Completing this self-test and comparing your answers with those in Appendix B provides immediate feedback and helpful practice for exams. Additional interactive, self-tests are available at www.wiley.com/college/huffman.

1. Label the following structures/areas of the brain:

a. corpus callosum   b. amygdala
c. cerebellum   d. thalamus
e. hippocampus   f. cerebral cortex

2. Label the four lobes of the brain:

a. frontal   b. parietal
c. temporal   d. occipital

3. The _____ lobes are largely responsible for motor control, speech production, and higher functions, such as thinking, personality, and memory.

a. cortical   b. frontal
c. parietal   d. occipital

4. Although the left and right hemispheres sometimes perform different, specialized functions, they are normally in close communication and share functions, thanks to the _____.

a. thalamus   b. sympathetic nervous system
c. cerebellum   d. corpus callosum

Think Critically

1 Imagine that you are giving a speech. Name the cortical lobes involved in the following behaviors:

a. Seeing faces in the audience
b. Hearing questions from the audience
c. Remembering where your car is parked when you are ready to go home
d. Noticing that your new shoes are too tight and hurting your feet

2 What are some everyday examples of the different functions of the two hemispheres?

realworldpsychology

Why are former NFL athletes at increased risk of depression, dementia, and suicide?

HINT: LOOK IN THE MARGIN FOR **Q5**

Summary

1 OUR GENETIC INHERITANCE   36

- Neuroscience/biopsychology studies how biological processes relate to behavioral and mental processes.
- **Genes** (dominant or recessive) hold the code for inherited traits. **Behavioral geneticists** use studies of twins and families with biological and adopted children to help determine **heritability**, the relative influences of heredity and environment on various traits.
- **Evolutionary psychology** suggests that many behavioral commonalities emerged and remain in human populations through **natural selection** because they helped ensure our "genetic survival."

2 NEURAL BASES OF BEHAVIOR   40

- **Neurons**, supported by **glial cells**, receive and send electro-chemical signals to other neurons and to the rest of the body. Their major components are **dendrites**, a **cell body**, and an **axon**.

- Within a neuron, a neural impulse, or **action potential**, moves along the axon. Neurons communicate with each other using **neurotransmitters**, which are released at the **synapse** and attach to the receiving neuron. Neurons receive input from many synapses. Hundreds of different neurotransmitters regulate a wide variety of physiological processes. Many **agonist** and **antagonist drugs** and poisons act by mimicking or interfering with neurotransmitters.
- The **endocrine system** uses **hormones** to broadcast messages throughout the body. The system regulates long-term bodily processes, maintains ongoing bodily processes, and controls the body's response to emergencies.

3 NERVOUS SYSTEM ORGANIZATION   46

- The **central nervous system (CNS)** includes the brain and spinal cord. The CNS allows us to process information and adapt to our environment in ways that no other animal can. The spinal cord transmits information between the brain and the rest of the body, and it initiates involuntary **reflexes**. Although the CNS is very fragile, recent research shows that the brain is capable of lifelong **neuroplasticity** and **neurogenesis**. Neurogenesis is made possible by **stem cells**.

- The **peripheral nervous system (PNS)** includes all the nerves outside the brain and spinal cord. It links the brain and spinal cord to the body's sense receptors, muscles, and glands. The PNS is subdivided into the **somatic nervous system (SNS)**, which controls voluntrary movement, and the **autonomic nervous system (ANS)**, which is responsible for automatic behavior.
- The ANS includes the **sympathetic nervous system** and the **parasympathetic nervous system**. The sympathetic nervous system mobilizes the body's "fight or flight" response. The parasympathetic nervous system returns the body to its normal functioning.

4 A TOUR THROUGH THE BRAIN 52

- Neuroscientists have developed several tools to explore the human brain and nervous system. Early researchers used dissection and other methods like clinical observation and case studies of living people. Recent scientific advances include newer brain imaging scans, which have improved scientists' ability to examine these processes and to do so noninvasively.
- The brain is divided into the **hindbrain**, the **midbrain**, and the **forebrain**. The brainstem includes parts of each of these.

Certain brain structures are specialized to perform certain tasks thanks to *localization of function*.

- The hindbrain, including the **medulla**, **pons**, and **cerebellum**, controls automatic behaviors and survival responses.
- The midbrain helps us orient our eye and body movements, helps control sleep and arousal, and is involved with the neurotransmitter dopamine. The **reticular formation (RF)** runs through the core of the hindbrain, midbrain, and brainstem, and is responsible for screening information and managing our levels of alertness.
- Forebrain structures, including the **cerebral cortex**, **hypothalamus**, **limbic system**, and **thalamus**, integrate input from the senses, control basic motives, regulate the body's internal environment, and regulate emotions, learning, and memory.
- The **cerebral cortex**, part of the forebrain, governs most higher processing and complex behaviors. It is divided into two hemispheres, each controlling the opposite side of the body. The **corpus callosum** links the hemispheres. Each hemisphere is divided into **frontal**, **parietal**, **temporal**, and **occipital lobes**. Each lobe specializes in somewhat different tasks, but a large part of the cortex is devoted to integrating actions performed by different brain regions.
- **Split-brain** research shows that each hemisphere performs somewhat different functions, although they work in close communication.

◉ applyingrealworldpsychology

We began this chapter with five intriguing Real World Psychology questions, and you were asked to revisit these questions at the end of each section. Questions like these have an important and lasting impact on all of our lives. See if you can answer these additional critical thinking questions related to real world examples.

1 Most traits are polygenic, meaning they are controlled by more than one gene. Given that tongue curling is one of the few traits that depends on only one dominant gene, can you explain why both of the parents of the three boys in this photo are "noncurlers"?

2 Why might humans and other animals have evolved to possess complex traits such as tongue curling?

3 If neuroscientists were able to use brain scans to determine what a person is thinking, what might be the ethical considerations of this type of research?

4 Imagine that your friend "John" has suffered a major automobile accident, and now has right-sided paralysis. Given that he has lost his ability to speak, can you identify the specific section of the brain and which hemisphere was most likely damaged in the accident?

5 Some research suggests that women are better than men at multitasking. What part(s) of the brain would explain this possible difference?

Courtesy Karen Huffman

Key Terms

RETRIEVAL PRACTICE Write a definition for each term before turning back to the referenced page to check your answer.

- action potential 40
- agonist drug 43
- amygdala 57
- antagonist drug 43
- association areas 60
- autonomic nervous system (ANS) 50
- axon 40
- behavioral genetics 36
- cell body 40
- central nervous system (CNS) 46
- cerebellum 55
- cerebral cortex 57
- corpus callosum 61
- dendrites 40
- endocrine system 44
- endorphin 44
- evolutionary psychology 36

- forebrain 56
- frontal lobes 58
- gene 36
- glial cells 40
- heritability 38
- hindbrain 55
- hippocampus 57
- hormone 44
- hypothalamus 56
- limbic system 57
- medulla 55
- midbrain 55
- myelin sheath 42
- natural selection 39
- neurogenesis 47
- neuron 40
- neuroplasticity 47

- neurotransmitter 43
- occipital lobes 60
- parasympathetic nervous system 50
- parietal lobes 60
- peripheral nervous system (PNS) 46
- pons 55
- reflex 48
- reticular formation (RF) 55
- somatic nervous system (SNS) 49
- split-brain surgery 61
- stem cells 47
- sympathetic nervous system 50
- synapse 45
- temporal lobes 59
- thalamus 56

chapterfour

Sensation and Perception

CHAPTER OUTLINE

realworldpsychology

chapteroverview

Imagine that your visual field has been suddenly inverted and reversed. Things you normally expect to be on your right are now on your left, and those above your head are now below. How would you ride a bike, read a book, or even walk through your home? Do you think you could ever adapt to this upside-down world?

To answer that question, psychologist George Stratton (1896) invented, and for eight days wore, special prism goggles that flipped his view of the world from up to down and right to left. For the first few days, Stratton had a great deal of difficulty navigating in this environment and coping with everyday tasks. But by the third day, he noted:

Walking through the narrow spaces between pieces of furniture required much less care than hitherto. I could watch my hands as they wrote, without hesitating or becoming embarrassed thereby.

By the fifth day, Stratton had almost completely adjusted to his strange perceptual environment, and when he later removed the headgear, he quickly readapted.

What does this experiment have to do with everyday life? At this very moment, our bodies are being bombarded with stimuli from the outside world—light, sound, heat, pressure, texture, and so on—while our brains are floating in complete silence and utter darkness within our skulls. Stratton's experiment shows us that sensing the world is not enough. Our brains must receive, convert, and constantly adapt the information from our sense organs into useful mental representations of the world. How we get the outside world inside to our brains, and what our brains do with this information, are the key topics of this chapter.

UNDERSTANDING SENSATION

LEARNING OBJECTIVES

RETRIEVAL PRACTICE While reading the upcoming sections, respond to each Learning Objective in your own words. Then compare your responses with those found at www.wiley.com/college/huffman.

1 DESCRIBE how raw sensory stimuli are processed and converted to signals in the brain.

2 EXPLAIN how our experience of stimuli can be measured.

3 SUMMARIZE the factors involved in sensory adaptation.

Psychologists are keenly interested in our senses because they are our mind's window to the outside world. We're equally interested in how our mind perceives and interprets the information it receives from the senses.

Sensation begins with specialized receptor cells located in our sense organs (eyes, ears, nose, tongue, skin, and internal body tissues). When sense organs detect an appropriate stimulus (light, mechanical pressure, chemical molecules), they convert it into neural impulses (action potentials) that are transmitted to our brain. Through the process of **perception**, the brain then assigns meaning to this sensory information **(Table 4.1)**.

Processing

Our eyes, ears, skin, and other sense organs all contain special cells called receptors, which receive and process sensory information from the environment. For each sense, these specialized cells respond to a distinct stimulus, such as sound waves or odor molecules. Next, during the process of **transduction**, the receptors convert the energy from the specific sensory stimulus into neural impulses, which are sent to the brain. For example, in hearing, tiny receptor cells in the inner ear convert mechanical vibrations from sound waves into electrochemical signals. Neurons then carry these signals to the brain, where specific sensory receptors detect and interpret the information.

How does our brain differentiate between sensations, such as sounds and smells? Through a process known as **coding**, the brain interprets different physical

Sensation The process of detecting, converting, and transmitting raw sensory information from the external and internal environments to the brain.

Perception The processes of selecting, organizing, and interpreting sensory information into meaningful patterns; interpreting sensory images as having been produced by stimuli from the external, three-dimensional world.

Transduction The process whereby sensory receptors convert stimuli into neural impulses to be sent to the brain (for example, transforming light waves into neural impulses).

Coding The process in which neural impulses travel by different routes to different parts of the brain; it allows us to detect various physical stimuli as distinct sensations.

TABLE 4.1 SENSATION AND PERCEPTION

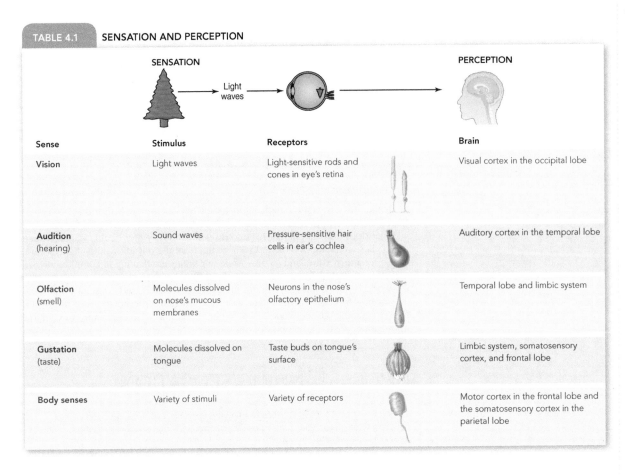

Sense	Stimulus	Receptors		Brain
Vision	Light waves	Light-sensitive rods and cones in eye's retina		Visual cortex in the occipital lobe
Audition (hearing)	Sound waves	Pressure-sensitive hair cells in ear's cochlea		Auditory cortex in the temporal lobe
Olfaction (smell)	Molecules dissolved on nose's mucous membranes	Neurons in the nose's olfactory epithelium		Temporal lobe and limbic system
Gustation (taste)	Molecules dissolved on tongue	Taste buds on tongue's surface		Limbic system, somatosensory cortex, and frontal lobe
Body senses	Variety of stimuli	Variety of receptors		Motor cortex in the frontal lobe and the somatosensory cortex in the parietal lobe

stimuli as distinct sensations because their neural impulses travel by different routes and arrive at different parts of the brain **(Figure 4.1)**.

We also have structures that purposefully reduce the amount of sensory information we receive. In this process of *sensory reduction*, we analyze and then filter incoming sensations before sending neural impulses on for further processing in other parts of our brain. Without this natural filtering of stimuli, we would constantly hear blood rushing through our veins and feel our clothes brushing against our skin. Some level of filtering is needed to prevent our brain from being overwhelmed with unnecessary information.

All species have evolved selective receptors that suppress or amplify information for survival. Humans, for example, cannot sense ultraviolet light, electric or magnetic fields, the ultrasonic sound of a dog whistle, or infrared heat patterns from warm-blooded animals, as some other animals can.

Psychophysics

How can scientists measure the exact amount of stimulus energy it takes to trigger a conscious experience? The answer come from the

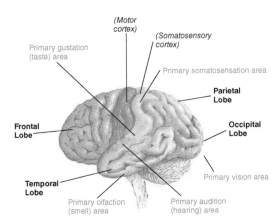

FIGURE 4.1 SENSORY PROCESSING WITHIN THE BRAIN

Neural messages from the various sense organs must travel to the brain in order for us to see, hear, smell, and so on. Shown here in the red-colored labels are the primary locations in the cerebral cortex for vision, hearing, taste, smell, and somatosensation (which includes touch, pain, and temperature sensitivity).

TABLE 4.2	EXAMPLES OF HUMAN ABSOLUTE THRESHOLDS
Sense	**Absolute Threshold**
Vision	A candle flame seen from 30 miles away on a clear, dark night
Audition (hearing)	The tick of an old-fashioned watch at 20 feet
Olfaction (smell)	One drop of perfume spread throughout a six-room apartment
Gustation (taste)	One teaspoon of sugar in 2 gallons of water
Body senses	A bee's wing falling on your cheek from a height of about half an inch

Psychophysics The study of the link between the physical characteristics of stimuli and the psychological experience of them.

Difference threshold The smallest physical difference between two stimuli that is consciously detectable 50% of the time; also called the *just noticeable difference* (*JND*).

Absolute threshold The minimum amount of stimulation necessary to consciously detect a stimulus 50% of the time.

field of **psychophysics**, which studies and measures the link between the physical characteristics of stimuli and the sensory experience of them.

One of the most interesting insights from psychophysics is that what is out there is not directly reproduced in here. At this moment, there are light waves, sound waves, odors, tastes, and microscopic particles touching us that we cannot see, hear, smell, taste, or feel. We are consciously aware of only a narrow range of stimuli in our environment. German scientist Ernst Weber (1795–1878) was one of the first to study the smallest difference between two weights that could be detected (Coren, 2013).

This **difference threshold**, which is also known as *Weber's Law of just noticeable differences* (*JND*), is the minimum difference that is consciously detectable 50% of the time. Another scientist, Gustav Fechner (1801–1887), expanded on Weber's law to determine what is called the **absolute threshold**, the minimum stimulation necessary to consciously detect a stimulus 50% of the time. See **Table 4.2** for a list of absolute thresholds for our various senses.

To measure your senses, an examiner presents a series of signals that vary in intensity and asks you to report which signals you can detect. In a hearing test, the softest level at which you can consistently hear a tone is your absolute threshold. The examiner then compares your threshold with those of people with normal hearing to determine whether you have hearing loss **(Figure 4.2)**.

Interestingly, many nonhuman animals have higher and lower thresholds than humans. For example, a dog's absolute and difference thresholds for smell are far more sensitive than those of a human. For this reason, specially trained dogs provide invaluable help in sniffing out dangerous plants, animals, drugs, and explosives; tracking criminals; and assisting in search-and-rescue operations **(Figure 4.3)**. Some researchers believe dogs can even detect chemical signs of certain illnesses, such as diabetes or cancer, and possibly even predict seizures in humans (Akers & Denbow, 2008; Buszewski et al., 2012; McCulloch et al., 2012).

Subliminal Stimuli

Have you heard some of the wild rumors about subliminal messages? During the 1970s, it was said that rock songs contained demonic messages, which could only be heard when the songs were played backwards! Similarly, in the 1990s many suggested that some Disney films contained obscene subliminal messages. For example, in the film *Aladdin*, the lead character supposedly whispers, "all good teenagers take off your clothes," and *The Lion King* reportedly showed close ups of the dust with a secret spelling out of the word "sex." In addition, at one time movie theaters were reportedly flashing messages like "Eat popcorn" and "Drink Cola-Cola" on the screen. Even though the messages were so brief that viewers weren't aware of seeing them, it was believed they increased consumption of these products (Blecha, 2004; Vokey & Read, 1985).

Can unconscious stimuli affect our behavior? As you've just discovered about *absolute thresholds*, it's clearly possible to perceive something without conscious awareness (Brooks et al., 2012; Irvine,

FIGURE 4.2 MEASURING THE ABSOLUTE AND DIFFERENCE THRESHOLDS FOR HEARING

© Carmen Martínez Banús/iStockphoto

2013; Smith, 2012). Experimental studies on **subliminal perception** commonly use an instrument, called a *tachistoscope,* to flash images too quickly for conscious recognition but slowly enough to be registered by the brain.

For example, in one study, experimenters subliminally presented photographs to two groups of participants who were receiving either a painful or a not-so-painful heat shock (Jensen et al., 2012). A photo of one man was presented every time the painful heat shock was delivered, whereas a different man's photo was presented every time the not-so-painful shock was delivered.

Next, the experimenters subliminally presented all participants with these same photos before they received a moderate shock. As predicted, participants from the group who saw the photo previously associated with the painful heat shock rated the moderate shock as more severe than those in the group who saw the photo associated with the not-so-painful shock.

FIGURE 4.3 PUTTING ANIMALS' HIGHER SENSORY RECEPTORS TO WORK

Subliminal perception The perception of stimuli presented below conscious awareness.

© ewg3D/iStockphoto

realworldpsychology **The Limits of Subliminal Perception**
Evidence that subliminal perception occurs doesn't necessarily mean that such processes lead to *subliminal persuasion.* Subliminal stimuli are basically weak stimuli. At best, they have a modest (if any) effect on consumer behavior, and they have absolutely no effect on the attitudes of youth listening to rock music or on citizens' voting behavior (Bermeritinger et al., 2009; Fennis & Stroebe, 2010; Salpeter & Swirsky, 2012). As for subliminal tapes promising to help you lose weight or relieve stress, save your money! Blank "placebo" tapes appear to be just as effective.

Sensory Adaptation

Imagine that friends have invited you to come visit their beautiful new baby. As they greet you at the door, you are overwhelmed by the odor of a wet diaper. Why don't your friends do something about that smell? The answer lies in the previously mentioned sensory reduction, as well as **sensory adaptation**. When a constant stimulus is presented for a length of time, sensation often fades or disappears. Receptors in our sensory system become less sensitive. They get "tired" and actually fire less frequently.

Sensory adaptation can be understood from an evolutionary perspective. We can't afford to waste attention and time on unchanging, normally unimportant stimuli. "Turning down the volume" on repetitive information helps the brain cope with an overwhelming amount of sensory stimuli and enables us to pay attention to change. Sometimes, however, adaptation can be dangerous, as when people stop paying attention to a small gas leak in the kitchen.

Although some senses, like smell and touch, adapt quickly, we never completely adapt to visual stimuli or to extremely intense stimuli, such as the odor of ammonia or the pain of a bad burn. From an evolutionary perspective, these limitations on sensory adaptation aid survival by reminding us, for example, to keep a watch out for dangerous predators, avoid strong odors and heat, and to take care of that burn.

If we don't adapt to pain, how do athletes keep playing despite painful injuries? In certain situations, including times of physical exertion, the body releases natural painkillers called *endorphins* (Chapter 2), which inhibit pain perception. This is the so-called "runner's high," which may help explain why athletes have been found to have a higher pain tolerance than nonathletes (Tesarz et al., 2012). (As a critical thinker, is it possible that individuals with a naturally high pain tolerance are just more attracted to athletics? Or does the experience of playing sports change your pain tolerance?)

In addition to endorphin release, one of the most widely accepted explanations of pain perception is the **gate-control theory of pain**, first proposed by Ronald

Sensory adaptation The process by which receptor cells become less sensitive due to constant stimulation.

Gate-control theory of pain The theory that pain sensations are processed and altered by certain cells in the spinal cord, which act as gates to interrupt and block some pain signals while sending others on to the brain.

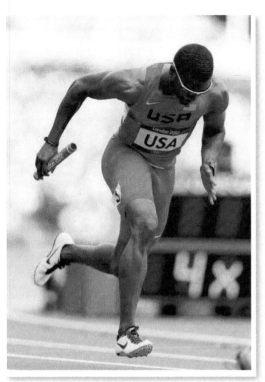

Ian MacNicol/Getty Images

FIGURE 4.4 OVERCOMING EXCRUCIATING PAIN!

realworldpsychology

Our body's ability to inhibit pain perception sometimes makes it possible for athletes to "play through" painful injuries. For example, Manteo Mitchell broke his left leg in the qualifying heats of the 4 × 400-meter relay race in the 2012 Olympics. Recalling the moment of the accident, Manteo said, "I felt it break . . . it hurt so bad . . . it felt like somebody literally just snapped my leg in half" (Moore, 2013). However, he continued running so that the American team could get into the finals. Many people admired his courage and determination, while others thought the potential for lasting damage was too high a price to pay for a medal or trophy. What do you think?

Melzack and Patrick Wall (1965). According to this theory, the experience of pain depends partly on whether or not the neural message gets past a "gatekeeper" in the spinal cord. Normally, the gate is kept shut, either by impulses coming down from the brain or by messages coming from large-diameter nerve fibers that conduct most sensory signals, such as touch and pressure. However, when body tissue is damaged, impulses from smaller pain fibers open the gate (Goldstein, 2014; Moayedi & Davis, 2013).

Can you see how this gate-control theory helps explain why massaging an injury or scratching an itch can temporarily relieve discomfort? It's because pressure on large-diameter neurons interferes with pain signals.

Messages from our brain also can control the pain gate, which explains how athletes and soldiers can carry on despite excruciating pain. When we're soothed by endorphins or distracted by competition or fear, our experience of pain can be greatly diminished **(Figure 4.4)**. Holding the hand of a loved one—or even just looking at a photograph of him or her—can also help reduce pain during a medical procedure (Master et al., 2009). Similarly, actively listening to music—meaning concentrating on specific musical cues in songs people know well, such as "Mary Had a Little Lamb"—can help reduce pain, especially among those who are very anxious (Bradshaw et al., 2012).

Research also suggests that the pain gate may be chemically controlled, that a neurotransmitter called *substance P* opens the pain gate, and that endorphins close it (Bianchi et al., 2008; Lin et al., 2012; Papathanassoglou et al., 2010). Other research finds that when normal sensory input is disrupted, the brain can generate pain and other sensations on its own (Melzack, 1999; Moayedi & Davis, 2013; Snijders et al., 2010).

For example, amputees sometimes continue to feel pain (and itching or tickling) long after a limb has been amputated. This *phantom limb pain* occurs because nerve cells send conflicting messages to the brain. The brain interprets this "static" as pain since the message arises in the area of the spinal cord responsible for pain signaling. When amputees are fitted with prosthetic limbs and begin using them, and sometimes when *mirror visual therapy* is used, phantom pain often disappears because the brain is somehow tricked into believing that there is no longer a missing limb (Foell & Flor, 2012; Giummarra & Moseley, 2011; Gracely et al., 2002; Plumbe et al., 2013).

(Mirror therapy involves a box with two mirrors—one facing each way. The amputee patient places his or her good limb into one side of the box and the amputated limb in the other. He or she then concentrates on looking into the mirror on the side that reflects the good limb, while making movements with both the good and amputated limbs. Thanks to the artificial feedback provided by the two mirrors, the patient sees only the reflected image of the good limb moving and interprets this as the phantom limb also moving.)

Now that we've studied how we perceive pain and how we might ignore or "play through" it, it's important to point out that other research finds that when we get anxious or dwell on our pain, we can intensify it (Lin et al., 2013; Ruscheweyh et al., 2013; Sullivan et al., 1998). Interestingly, social and cultural factors, such as well-meaning friends who ask chronic pain sufferers about their pain, may unintentionally reinforce and increase it (Flor, 2013; Jolliffe & Nicholas, 2004).

The following *Psychology and You* offers an assessment and strategies for managing your personal pain.

TEST YOURSELF: HOW WELL DO YOU MANAGE YOUR PAIN?

psychology and you

Score yourself on how often you use one or more of these strategies, using the following scale:
0 = never, 2 = seldom, 3 = occasionally, 4 = often, 5 = almost always, 6 = always.

_____ **1.** I do something I enjoy, such as watching TV or listening to music.

_____ **2.** I try to be around other people.

_____ **3.** I do something active, like household chores or projects.

_____ **4.** I try to feel distant from the pain, almost as if the pain were in somebody else's body.

_____ **5.** I try to think about something pleasant.

_____ **6.** I replay in my mind pleasant experiences from the past.

_____ **7.** I tell myself that I can overcome the pain.

_____ **8.** I don't think about the pain.

These questions are based on effective pain management techniques, such as distraction, ignoring pain, and reinterpreting it. Review those items that you checked as "never" or "seldom" and consider adding them to your pain management skills.

RETRIEVAL PRACTICE: UNDERSTANDING SENSATION

Self-Test

Completing this self-test and comparing your answers with those in Appendix B provides immediate feedback and helpful practice for exams. Additional interactive, self-tests are available at www.wiley.com/college/huffman.

1. Transduction is the process of converting _____.

   a. sensory stimuli into neural impulses that are sent along to the brain
   b. receptors into transmitters

   c. a particular sensory stimulus into a specific sensation
   d. receptors into neural impulses

2. Sensory reduction refers to the process of _____.

   a. reducing your dependence on a single sensory system
   b. decreasing the number of sensory receptors that are stimulated

   c. filtering and analyzing incoming sensations before sending a neural message on for further processing
   d. reducing environmental sensations by physically preventing your sensory organs from seeing, hearing, and so on

3. Experiments on subliminal perception have _____.

   a. supported its existence, but shown that it has little or no effect on persuasion
   b. shown that subliminal perception occurs only among children and some adolescents

   c. shown that subliminal messages affect only people who are highly suggestible
   d. failed to support the phenomenon

4. The _____ theory of pain helps explain why it sometimes helps to rub or massage an injured area.

   a. sensory adaptation
   b. gate-control
   c. just noticeable difference
   d. Lamaze

Think Critically

1 Sensation and perception are closely linked. What is the central distinction between the two?

2 If we sensed and attended equally to each stimulus in the world, the amount of information would be overwhelming. What sensory and perceptual processes help us lessen the din?

3 If we don't adapt to pain, why is it that people can sometimes "tune out" painful injuries?

realworldpsychology

Do athletes have a higher pain tolerance than non-athletes?

Can looking at a photograph of a loved one lead you to feel less pain?

HINT: LOOK IN THE MARGIN FOR (Q1) AND (Q2)

HOW WE SEE AND HEAR

LEARNING OBJECTIVES

RETRIEVAL PRACTICE While reading the upcoming sections, respond to each Learning Objective in your own words. Then compare your responses with those found at www.wiley.com/college/huffman.

1 **IDENTIFY** the three major characteristics of light and sound waves.

2 **EXPLAIN** how the eye captures and focuses light energy and how it converts it into neural signals.

3 **DESCRIBE** the path that sound waves take in the ear.

4 **SUMMARIZE** the two theories that explain how we distinguish among different pitches.

Many people mistakenly believe that what they see and hear is a copy of the outside world. In fact, vision and hearing are the result of what our brains create in response to light and sound waves. What we see and hear is based on wave phenomena, similar to ocean waves **(Figure 4.5)**.

In addition to wavelength/frequency shown in Figure 4.5, waves also vary in height (technically called *amplitude*). This wave height/amplitude determines the intensity of sights and sounds. Finally, waves also vary in range, or complexity, which mixes together waves of various wavelength/frequency and wave height/amplitude **(Figure 4.6)**.

Vision

Did you know that Major League batters can routinely hit a 90-miles-per-hour fastball four-tenths of a second after it leaves the pitcher's hand? How can the human eye receive and process information that fast? To understand the marvels of vision, we need to start with the basics—that light waves are a form of electromagnetic energy and only a small part of the full *electromagnetic spectrum* **(Figure 4.7)**.

To fully appreciate how our eyes turn these light waves into the experience we call *vision*, we need to first examine the various structures in our eyes that capture and focus the light waves. Then, we need to understand how these waves are transformed (transduced) into neural messages (action potentials) that our brain can process into images we consciously see. (Be sure to carefully study this step-by-step process in **Figure 4.8**.)

FIGURE 4.5 **WAVES OF LIGHT AND SOUND**

Ocean waves have a certain distance between them (the *wavelength*), and they pass by you at intervals. If you counted the number of passing waves in a set amount of time (for example, 5 waves in 60 seconds), you could calculate the *frequency* (the number of complete wavelengths that pass a point in a given time). Longer wavelength means lower frequency and vice versa.

© S. Greg Panosian/iStockphoto

FIGURE 4.6 **PROPERTIES OF LIGHT AND SOUND**

Wavelength	**Wave amplitude**	**Range of wavelengths**
The distance between successive peaks.	The height from peak to trough.	The mixture of waves.
Time →	Time →	Time →
Long wavelength/ low frequency = Reddish colors/ low-pitched sounds	*Low amplitude/ low intensity = Dull colors/ soft sounds*	*Small range/ low complexity = Less complex colors/ less complex sounds*
Time →	Time →	Time →
Short wavelength/ high frequency = Bluish colors/ high pitched sound	*High amplitude/ high intensity = Bright colors/ loud sounds*	*Large range/ high complexity = Complex colors/ complex sounds*

FIGURE 4.7 THE ELECTROMAGNETIC SPECTRUM FOR VISION

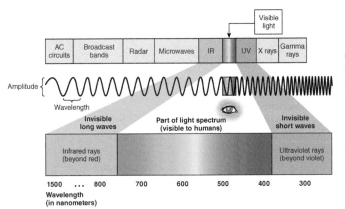

The full spectrum of electromagnetic waves contains very long wavelength AC circuits and radio waves at one end, and relatively short gamma ray waves at the other.

Only the light waves, in the middle of the electromagnetic spectrum can be seen by the human eye. Note how the longer visible wavelengths are the light waves that we see as red, and the shortest are those we perceive as blue. In between are the rest of the colors.

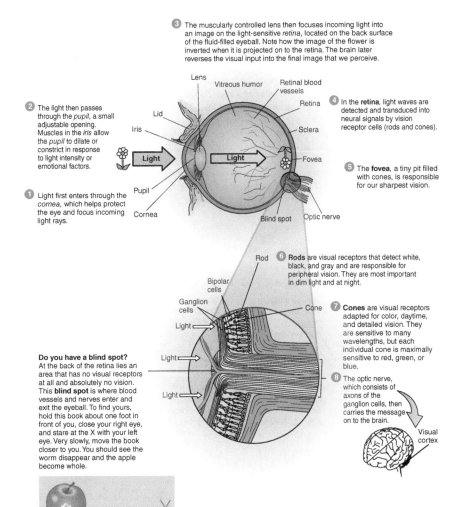

3 The muscularly controlled lens then focuses incoming light into an image on the light-sensitive *retina*, located on the back surface of the fluid-filled eyeball. Note how the image of the flower is inverted when it is projected on to the retina. The brain later reverses the visual input into the final image that we perceive.

2 The light then passes through the *pupil*, a small adjustable opening. Muscles in the *iris* allow the *pupil* to dilate or constrict in response to light intensity or emotional factors.

1 Light first enters through the *cornea*, which helps protect the eye and focus incoming light rays.

4 In the **retina**, light waves are detected and transduced into neural signals by vision receptor cells (rods and cones).

5 The **fovea**, a tiny pit filled with cones, is responsible for our sharpest vision.

6 **Rods** are visual receptors that detect white, black, and gray and are responsible for peripheral vision. They are most important in dim light and at night.

7 **Cones** are visual receptors adapted for color, daytime, and detailed vision. They are sensitive to many wavelengths, but each individual cone is maximally sensitive to red, green, or blue.

8 The optic nerve, which consists of axons of the ganglion cells, then carries the message on to the brain.

Do you have a blind spot?
At the back of the retina lies an area that has no visual receptors at all and absolutely no vision. This **blind spot** is where blood vessels and nerves enter and exit the eyeball. To find yours, hold this book about one foot in front of you, close your right eye, and stare at the X with your left eye. Very slowly, move the book closer to you. You should see the worm disappear and the apple become whole.

FIGURE 4.8 HOW OUR EYES SEE

Various structures of your eye work together to capture and focus the light waves from the outside world. Receptor cells in your retina (rods and cones) then convert these waves into messages that are sent along the optic nerve to be interpreted by your brain.

Retina The light-sensitive inner surface of the back of the eye, which contains the receptor cells for vision (rods and cones).

Blind spot The point at which the optic nerve leaves the eye, which contains no receptor cells for vision—thus creating a "blind spot."

Rods Photoreceptors concentrated in the periphery of the retina that are most active in dim illumination; rods do not produce sensation of color.

Cones Visual receptor cells that are concentrated near the center of the retina and are responsible for color vision and fine detail; they are most sensitive in brightly lit conditions.

Fovea A tiny pit in the center of the retina that is densely filled with cones; it is responsible for sharp vision.

Audition The sense or act of hearing.

Place theory for hearing The theory that pitch perception is linked to the particular spot on the cochlea's basilar membrane that is most stimulated; pitch is coded by the place at which activation occurs.

Frequency theory for hearing The theory that pitch perception occurs when a tone produces a rate of vibration in the basilar membrane equal to its frequency, with the result that pitch can be coded by the frequency of the neural response.

Vision Problems and Peculiarities

Thoroughly understanding the processes detailed in Figure 4.8 offers clues that help us understand several visual peculiarities. For example, small abnormalities in the eye sometimes cause images to be focused in front of the **retina** in the case of *nearsightedness (myopia)*, or behind it in the case of *farsightedness (hyperopia)*. In addition, during middle age, most people's lenses lose elasticity and the ability to accommodate for near vision, a condition known as *presbyopia*. Corrective lenses or laser surgery can often correct these visual acuity problems.

A visual peculiarity occurs where the optic nerve exits the eye. Because there are no receptor cells for visual stimuli in that area, we have a tiny hole, or **blind spot**, in our field of vision. (See Figure 4.8 for a demonstration.)

Two additional peculiarities happen when we go from a bright to dark setting and vice versa. Have you noticed that when you walk into a dark movie theater on a sunny afternoon, you're almost blind for a few seconds? The reason is that in bright light, the pigment inside the **rods** (refer to Figure 4.8) is bleached, making them temporarily nonfunctional. It takes a second or two for the rods to become functional enough again for you to see. This process of *dark adaptation* continues for 20 to 30 minutes.

In contrast, *light adaptation*, the adjustment that takes place when you go from darkness to a bright setting, takes about 7 to 10 minutes and is the work of the **cones**. Interestingly, a region in the center of the retina, called the **fovea**, has the greatest density of cones, which are most sensitive in brightly lit conditions. They're also responsible for color vision and fine detail.

Hearing

The sense or act of hearing, known as **audition**, has a number of important functions, ranging from alerting us to dangers to helping us communicate with others. In this section we talk first about sound waves, then about the ear's anatomy and function, and finally about problems with hearing.

Like the visual process, which transforms light waves into vision, the auditory system is designed to convert sound waves into hearing. Sound waves are produced by air molecules moving in a particular wave pattern. For example, vibrating objects like vocal cords or guitar strings create waves of compressed and expanded air resembling ripples on a lake that circle out from a tossed stone. Our ears detect and respond to these waves of small air pressure changes, our brain then interprets the neural messages resulting from these waves, and we hear!

To fully understand this process, pay close attention to the step-by-step diagram in **Figure 4.9**.

Pitch perception

How do we determine that certain sounds are from a child's voice and not from an adult's? We distinguish between high- and low-pitched sounds by the *frequency* of the sound waves. High-frequency sound waves, which produce high-pitched sounds, maximally stimulate the hair cells at different locations along the basilar membrane (refer to Figure 4.9). This is known as the **place theory for hearing**. Conversely, low-pitched sounds cause hair cells along the basilar membrane to bend and fire neural messages (action potentials) at the same rate as the frequency of that sound, the **frequency theory for hearing**.

In short, place theory best explains how we hear high-pitched sounds, whereas frequency theory is a better explanation for how we hear low-pitched sounds **(Table 4.3)**.

Interestingly, as we age, we tend to lose our ability to hear high-pitched sounds but are still able to hear low-pitched sounds. Given that young students can hear a cell phone ringtone that sounds at 17 kilohertz—too high for adult ears to detect—they can take advantage of this age-related hearing difference and call one another during

FIGURE 4.9 HOW OUR EARS HEAR

The **outer ear** captures and funnels sound waves into the eardrum. Next, three tiny bones in the **middle ear** pick up the ear-drum's vibrations, and transmit them to the **inner ear**. Finally, the snail-shaped **cochlea** in the inner ear transforms (transduces) the sound waves into neural messages (action potentials) that our brain processes into what we consciously hear.

1 The **outer ear** captures and funnels sound waves onto the tympanic membrane (ear drum).

2 Vibrations of the tympanic membrane strike the **middle ear's** ossicles (hammer, anvil, and stirrup). Then the stirrup hits the oval window.

3 Vibrations of the oval window create waves in the **inner ear's** cochlear fluid which deflects the basilar membrane. This movement bends the hair cells.

4 The hair cells communicate with the auditory nerve, which sends neural impulses to the brain.

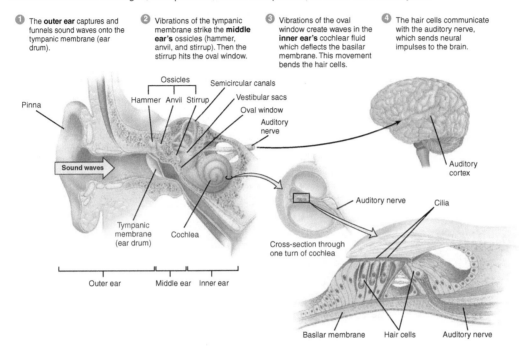

class **(Figure 4.10).** Ironically, the cell phone's ringtone that teachers can't hear is an offshoot of another device, called the Mosquito, which was originally designed to help shopkeepers annoy and drive away loitering teens!

Softness versus Loudness

How we detect a sound as being soft or loud depends on its amplitude (or wave height). Waves with high peaks and low valleys produce loud sounds; waves with relatively low peaks and shallow valleys produce soft sounds. The

Outer ear The pinna, auditory canal, and eardrum structures which funnel sound waves to the middle ear.

Middle ear The hammer, anvil, and stirrup structures of the ear, which concentrate eardrum vibrations onto the cochlea's oval window.

Inner ear The semicircular canals, vestibular sacs, and cochlea, which generate neural signals that are sent to the brain.

Cochlea [KOK-lee-uh] The fluid-filled, coiled tube in the inner ear that contains the receptors for hearing.

TABLE 4.3	HOW WE DISTINGUISH AMONG SOUNDS OF DIFFERENT PITCH		
Theory	**Frequency**	**Pitch**	**Example**
Place theory Hair cells are stimulated at different locations on basilar membrane.	High frequency	High-pitched sounds	A squeal or a child's voice
Frequency theory Hair cells fire at the same rate as the frequency for the sound.	Low frequency	Low-pitched sounds	A growl or an adult's voice

FIGURE 4.10 **STUDENTS EXPLOITING AGE-RELATED HEARING LOSS**

realworldpsychology

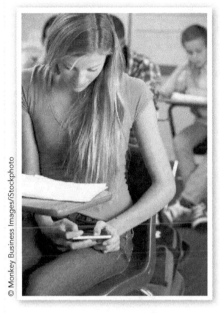

© Monkey Business Images/iStockphoto

Conduction hearing loss A type of hearing loss that results from damage to the mechanical system that conducts sound waves to the cochlea; also called conduction deafness.

Sensorineural hearing loss A type of hearing loss resulting from damage to cochlea's receptor (hair) hearing cells or to the auditory nerve; also called nerve deafness.

relative loudness or softness of sounds is measured on a scale of *decibels* (**Figure 4.11**).

Hearing Problems

What are the types, causes, and treatments of hearing loss? **Conduction hearing loss**, also called conduction deafness, results from problems with the mechanical system that conducts sound waves to the cochlea. Hearing aids that amplify the incoming sound waves, and some forms of surgery, can help with this type of hearing loss.

In contrast, **sensorineural hearing loss**, also known as nerve deafness, results from damage to the cochlea's receptor (hair) cells or to the auditory nerve. Disease and biological changes associated with aging can result in sensorineural hearing loss. But its most common (and preventable) cause is continuous exposure to loud noise, which can damage hair cells and lead to permanent hearing loss. Even brief exposure to really loud sounds, like a stereo or headphones at full blast, a jackhammer, or a jet airplane engine, can cause permanent nerve deafness (refer to Figure 4.11). In fact, a high volume on earphones can reach the same noise level as a jet engine! All forms of high volume noise can damage the coating on nerve cells, making it harder for the nerve cells to send information from the ears to the brain (Pilati et al., 2012). Q3

Although most hearing loss is temporary, damage to the auditory nerve or receptor cells is generally considered irreversible. The only treatment for auditory nerve damage is a small electronic device called a *cochlear implant*. If the auditory nerve is intact, the implant bypasses hair cells to stimulate the nerve. Currently, cochlear implants produce only a crude approximation of hearing, but the technology is improving.

FIGURE 4.11 **BEWARE OF LOUD SOUNDS**

The higher a sound's decibel reading, the more damaging it is to the ear.

psychology and you Strategies for Protecting Hearing

Given the limited benefits of medicine or technology to help improve hearing following damage, it's important to protect our sense of hearing. We can do this by avoiding exceptionally loud noises, wearing earplugs when we cannot avoid such stimuli, and paying attention to bodily warnings of possible hearing loss, including a change in our normal hearing threshold and *tinnitus*, a whistling or ringing sensation in the ears. These relatively small changes can have lifelong benefits!

Bernd Leitner Fotodesign/Shutterstock

RETRIEVAL PRACTICE: HOW WE SEE AND HEAR

Self-Test

Completing this self-test and comparing your answers with those in Appendix B provides immediate feedback and helpful practice for exams. Additional interactive, self-tests are available at www.wiley.com/college/huffman.

1. Identify the parts of the eye, placing the appropriate label on the figure to the right.

cornea	rod
iris	cone
pupil	fovea
lens	blind spot
retina	optic nerve

2. A visual acuity problem that occurs when the cornea and lens focus an image in front of the retina is called _____.

a. farsightedness   b. hyperopia
c. myopia   d. presbyopia

3. Identify the parts of the ear, placing the appropriate label on the figure to the right.

tympanic membrane	hammer
anvil	oval window
stirrup	cochlea

4. Chronic exposure to loud noise can cause permanent _____.

a. auditory illusions   b. auditory hallucinations
c. nerve deafness   d. conduction deafness

Think Critically

1 Which of your sensations, vision or hearing, would you most and least like to lose? Why?

2 Many people believe that blind people have supernatural hearing. How would you use terms like brain plasticity to explain that enhanced hearing might result from greater reliance on hearing or from just using auditory information more effectively?

3 Using what you've learned about pitch, how would you explain why an older person often has an easier time of hearing a man's voice than a woman's voice?

realworldpsychology

How can listening to loud music on headphones damage your hearing?

HINT: LOOK IN THE MARGIN FOR ⓠ3

OUR OTHER IMPORTANT SENSES

LEARNING OBJECTIVES

RETRIEVAL PRACTICE While reading the upcoming sections, respond to each Learning Objective in your own words. Then compare your responses with those found at www.wiley.com/college/huffman.

1 **DESCRIBE** how the information contained in odor molecules reaches the brain.

2 **EXPLAIN** how the information contained in food molecules reaches the brain.

3 **IDENTIFY** the body senses.

Vision and audition may be the most prominent of our senses, but the others—smell, taste, and the body senses—are also important for gathering information about our environment.

Smell and Taste

Smell and taste are sometimes referred as the *chemical senses* because they both rely on chemoreceptors that are sensitive to certain chemical molecules. Have you wondered why we have trouble we separating the two sensations? Smell and taste receptors are located near each other and closely interact **(Figure 4.12)**.

Our sense of smell, **olfaction**, is remarkably useful and sensitive. We possess more than 1,000 types of olfactory receptors, which allow us to detect more than 10,000 distinct smells. The nose is more sensitive to smoke than any electronic detector, and—through practice—blind people can quickly recognize others by their unique odors.

Some research on **pheromones**—chemicals found in natural body scents that affect various behaviors—supports the idea that certain chemical odors increase sexual behaviors—even in humans (Derntl et al., 2013; Kohl, 2012; Marazziti et al., 2010; Pause, 2012). However, others suggest that human sexuality is far more complex than that of other animals—and more so than perfume advertisements would have you believe.

Today, the sense of taste, **gustation**, may be the least critical of our senses. In the past, however, it probably contributed significantly to our survival. For example, humans and other animals have a preference for sweet foods, which are generally nonpoisonous and are good sources of energy. However, the major function of taste, aided by smell, is to help us avoid eating or drinking harmful substances. Because many plants that taste bitter contain toxic chemicals, an animal is more likely to survive if it avoids bitter-tasting plants (Cooper et al., 2002; Goldstein, 2014; Negri et al., 2012).

Learning and Culture

Many food and taste preferences also are learned from personal learning experiences (Liem et al., 2012; Yantis, 2013). For example, adults who are told a bottle of wine costs $90 rather than its real price of $10 report that it tastes better than the supposedly cheaper brand. Ironically, these false expectations actually trigger areas of the brain that respond to pleasant experiences (Plassmann et al., 2008). This means that in a neurochemical sense the wine we believe is better does in fact taste better!

The culture we live in also affects our taste preferences. Many Japanese children eat raw fish, and some Chinese children eat chicken feet as part of their normal diet. Although most U.S. children might consider these foods "yucky," they tend to love cheese, which children in many other cultures find repulsive. The upcoming *Psych Science* section describes how these tastes preferences are created very early in life.

Before going on, we need to update you on recent research findings on taste perception. It was long believed that we had only four distinct tastes: sweet, sour, salty, and bitter. However, we now know that we also have a fifth taste sense, *umami*, a word that means "delicious" or "savory" and refers to sensitivity to an amino acid called glutamate (Jinap & Hajeb, 2010; Lanfer et al., 2013). Glutamate is found in meats, meat broths, and monosodium glutamate (MSG).

Scientists also once believed that specific areas of the tongue were dedicated to detecting bitter, sweet, salty, and other tastes. Today, we know that taste receptors, like smell receptors, respond differentially to the varying shapes of food

Olfaction The sense or act of smelling.

Pheromones [FARE-oh-mones] Chemical signals released by organisms to communicate with other; they may affect behavior, including recognition of family members, aggression, territorial marking, and sexual mating.

Gustation The sense or act of taste.

FIGURE 4.12 **WHY WE ENJOY EATING PIZZA: OLFACTION PLUS GUSTATION**

realworldpsychology

What happens when we eat pizza? Taste receptor cells, as well as sensory cells that respond to touch and temperature, are activated on our tongues. Smell receptor cells in our nose are activated by odors from the pizza. This combined sensory information is then sent to the brain, where it is processed in various association regions of the cerebral cortex. These circuits, together with those that store memories related to our previous pizza experiences, work together to produce our perceptions of each pizza experience.

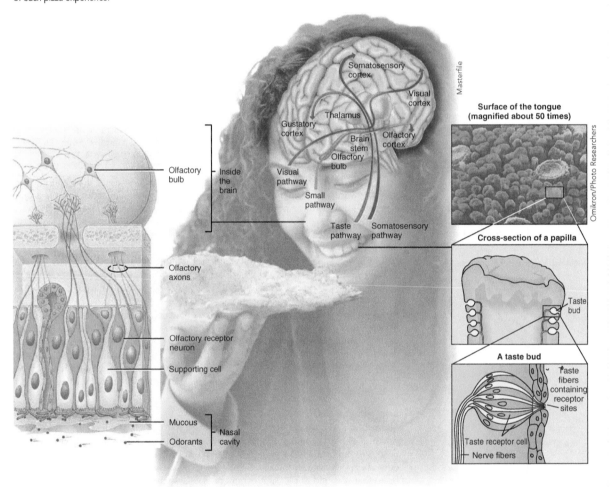

A **The smell pathway**

Olfactory receptor neurons (shown here in blue) transduce information from odorant molecules that enter the nose. The olfactory nerve carries this information into the olfactory bulb, where most information related to smell is processed before being sent on to other parts of the brain. (Note that olfaction is the only sensory system that is NOT routed through the thalamus.)

B **The taste pathway**

When we eat and drink, liquids and dissolved foods flow over papillae (the lavender circular areas) and into their pores to the taste buds, which contain the receptors for taste. These nerves carry information into the brain stem, thalamus, gustatory cortex, and somatosensory cortex.

PSYCHSCIENCE

CAN INFANTS LOVE CARROTS?

Would you believe that our taste preferences are shaped even before we are born? Researchers have conducted very clever studies to examine how the foods that pregnant women eat influence the types of tastes their babies prefer after birth. In one study, pregnant women who were planning to breast-feed were randomly assigned to one of three groups (Mennella et al., 2001):

- Women in one group drank carrot juice four times a week for three weeks during pregnancy.
- Women in another group drank carrot juice four times a week for three weeks after the baby was born.
- Women in the third group did not drink carrot juice.

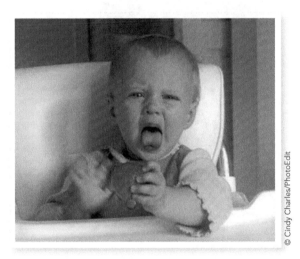

© Cindy Charles/PhotoEdit

The researchers then asked the mothers to rate their babies' facial reactions to different types of foods and to measure how much of a carrot-flavored cereal the babies ate. Babies who were exposed to the taste of carrots either during pregnancy or through breast milk ate more of the carrot-flavored cereal than babies who had no exposure to this taste. Thus showing that taste preferences may be established very early in life—in fact, even before birth.

RESEARCH CHALLENGE

1. Based on the information provided, did the study (Menella et al., 2001) use descriptive, correlational, and/or experimental research?

2. If you chose:
   - descriptive research, is this a naturalistic observation, survey/interview, case study, or archival research?
   - correlational research, is this a positive, negative, or zero correlation?
   - experimental research, label the IV, DV, experimental group(s), and control group.

>> CHECK YOUR ANSWERS IN APPENDIX B.
NOTE: The information provided in this study is admittedly limited, but the level of detail is similar to what is presented in most textbooks and public reports of research findings. Answering these questions, and then comparing your answers to those in the Appendix, will help you become a better critical thinker and consumer of scientific research.

and liquid molecules. The major taste receptors—taste buds—are distributed all over our tongues within little bumps called papillae (refer to Figure 4.12).

The Body Senses

In addition to smell and taste, we have three important body senses that help us navigate our world—skin, vestibular, and kinesthesis **(Figure 4.13)**.

Skin Senses

Our skin is uniquely designed for the detection of touch (or pressure), temperature, and pain **(Figure 4.13a)**. The concentration and depth of the receptors for each of these stimuli vary (Fitzpatrick & Mooney, 2012; Hsiao & Gomez-Ramirez, 2013). For example, touch receptors are most concentrated on the face and fingers and least concentrated in the back and legs. Getting a paper cut can feel so painful

FIGURE 4.13 OUR BODY SENSES—SKIN, VESTIBULAR, AND KINESTHESIS

Ⓐ Skin senses
The tactile senses rely on a variety of receptors located in different parts of the skin. Both humans and nonhuman animals are highly responsive to touch.

© Philip Dyer/iStockphoto

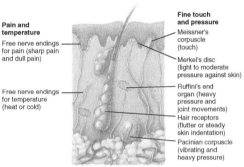

Pain and temperature

Free nerve endings for pain (sharp pain and dull pain)

Free nerve endings for temperature (heat or cold)

Fine touch and pressure

Meissner's corpuscle (touch)

Merkel's disc (light to moderate pressure against skin)

Ruffini's end organ (heavy pressure and joint movements)

Hair receptors (flutter or steady skin indentation)

Pacinian corpuscle (vibrating and heavy pressure)

Ⓑ Vestibular sense
Part of the "thrill" of amusement park rides comes from our vestibular sense becoming confused. The vestibular sense is used by the eye muscles to maintain visual fixation and sometimes by the body to change body orientation. We can become dizzy or nauseated if the vestibular sense becomes "confused" by boat, airplane, or automobile motion. Children between ages 2 and 12 years have the greatest susceptibility to motion sickness.

© RubberBall/Alamy Limited

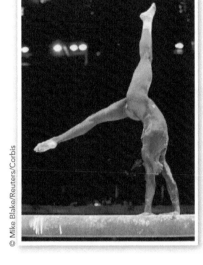

© Mike Blake/Reuters/Corbis

Ⓒ Kinesthesis
This athlete's finely-tuned behaviors are the result of information provided by receptors in her muscles, joints, and tendons that detect bodily position and movement.

because we have many receptors on our fingertips. Some receptors respond to more than one type of stimulation. For example, itching, tickling, and vibrating sensations seem to be produced by light stimulation of both pressure and pain receptors.

The benefits of touch are so significant for human growth and development that the American Academy of Pediatrics recommends that all mothers and babies have skin-to-skin contact in the first hours after birth. This type of contact, which is called *kangaroo care*, is especially beneficial for preterm and low-birth-weight infants, who then experience greater weight gain, fewer infections, and improved cognitive and motor development.

How does kangaroo care lead to these improvements in infant health? This type of skin-to-skin touch helps babies in several ways, including providing warmth (babies don't have to expend so much energy themselves to stay warm), reducing pain (babies have lower levels of stress and arousal, which improves immune functioning), and improving sleep quality (babies have more time and energy to devote to growth) (Johnston et al., 2011).

 Q4

Vestibular Sense

Our sense of balance, the **vestibular sense**, informs our brain of how our body, and particularly our head, are oriented with respect to gravity and three-dimensional space **(Figure 4.13b)**. When our head moves, liquid in the *semicircular canals*,

Vestibular sense The sense, located in the inner ear, that detects body movement and position with respect to gravity; also called the sense of balance.

located in our inner ear, moves and bends hair cell receptors. At the end of the semicircular canals are the *vestibular sacs*, which contain hair cells sensitive to our bodily movement relative to gravity (see again Figure 4.9). Information from the semicircular canals and the *vestibular sacs* is converted to neural impulses that are then carried to our brain.

Kinesthesis

Kinesthesis The sense, located in muscles, joints, and tendons, that detects bodily posture, orientation, and movement of body parts relative to each other.

The sense that provides the brain with information about bodily posture, orientation, and movement of individual body parts is called **kinesthesis (Figure 4.13c)**. Kinesthetic receptors are found throughout the muscles, joints, and tendons of our body. They tell our brain which muscles are being contracted or relaxed, how our body weight is distributed, where our arms and legs are in relation to the rest of our body, and so on.

RETRIEVAL PRACTICE: OUR OTHER IMPORTANT SENSES

Self-Test

Completing this self-test and comparing your answers with those in Appendix B provides immediate feedback and helpful practice for exams. Additional interactive, self-tests are available at www.wiley.com/college/huffman.

1. Most information related to smell is processed in the _____.

   a. nasal cavity   b. temporal lobe
   c. olfactory bulb   d. parietal lobe

2. Most of our taste receptors are found on the _____.

   a. olfactory bulb   b. gustatory cells
   c. taste buds   d. frenulum

3. The skin senses include _____.

   a. pressure   b. pain
   c. warmth and cold   d. all these

4. The weightlessness experienced by space travelers from zero gravity has its greatest effect on the _____ senses.

   a. visceral   b. reticular
   c. somasthetic   d. vestibular

Think Critically

1 From an evolutionary perspective, which is more important—smell or taste?

2 From a personal perspective, which sense is most important to you—your sense of smell, taste, skin senses, vestibular, or kinesthetic?

realworldpsychology

Why do premature babies grow faster when they receive skin-to-skin contact?

HINT: LOOK IN THE MARGIN FOR

UNDERSTANDING PERCEPTION

LEARNING OBJECTIVES

RETRIEVAL PRACTICE While reading the upcoming sections, respond to each Learning Objective in your own words. Then compare your responses with those found at www.wiley.com/college/huffman.

1 **DOCUMENT** the relationship between selective attention, feature detectors, and habituation.

2 **DESCRIBE** the four ways we organize sensory data.

3 **SUMMARIZE** the factors in perceptual interpretation.

We are ready to move from *sensation* and the major senses to *perception*, the process of selecting, organizing, and interpreting incoming sensations into useful mental representations of the world.

Normally, our perceptions agree with our sensations. When they do not, the result is called an **illusion**, a false or misleading impression produced by errors in the perceptual process or by actual physical distortions, as in desert mirages. Illusions provide psychologists with a tool for studying the normal process of perception **(Figure 4.14)**.

Note that illusions are NOT the same as hallucinations or delusions. *Hallucinations* are false sensory experiences that occur without external stimuli, such as hearing voices during a psychotic episode or seeing particular images after using some type of hallucinogenic drug, such as LSD or hallucinogenic mushrooms. *Delusions* refer to false beliefs, often of persecution or grandeur, that may accompany drug or psychotic experiences.

Illusion A false or misleading perception shared by others in the same perceptual environment.

Selection

In almost every situation, we confront more sensory information than we can reasonably pay attention to. Three major factors help us focus on some stimuli and ignore others: *selective attention, feature detectors,* and *habituation.*

Certain basic mechanisms for perceptual selection are built into the brain. For example, through the process of **selective attention (Figure 4.15)**, the brain picks out the information that is important to us and discards the rest (Haab et al., 2011; Kar, 2013; Lamy et al., 2013).

Selective attention The process of filtering out and attending only to important sensory messages.

FIGURE 4.14 **UNDERSTANDING PERCEPTUAL ILLUSIONS**
realworldpsychology

As you may have noticed, this text highlights numerous popular *myths* about psychology because it's important to understand and correct our misperceptions. For similar reasons, you need to know how illusions mislead out normal information processing and recognize that "seeing is believing, but seeing isn't always believe correctly" (Lilienfeld et al., 2010, p.7).

Ⓐ Müller-Lyer illusion
Which vertical line is longer? In fact, the two vertical lines are the same length, but psychologists have learned that people who live in urban environments normally see the one on the right as longer. This is because they have learned to make size and distance judgments from perspective cues created by right angles and horizontal and vertical lines of buildings and streets.

Ⓑ Ponzo illusion
Which of the two horizontal lines is longer? In fact, both lines are the exact same size, but the converging lines provide depth cues telling you that the top dark, horizontal, line is farther away than the bottom line and therefore much larger.

Think Critically

1 What do you think causes "errors" in the perceptual process, such as the optical illusions described here?

2 When you watch films of moving cars, the wheels appear to go backward. Can you explain this common visual illusion?

Ⓒ The horizontal-vertical illusion
Which is longer, the horizontal (flat) or the vertical (standing) line? People living in areas where they regularly see long straight lines, such as roads and train tracks, perceive the horizontal line as shorter because of their environmental experiences.

 Ⓓ Shepard's tables
Do these two table tops have the same dimensions? Get a ruler and check it for yourself.

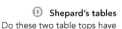

FIGURE 4.15 **SELECTIVE ATTENTION**

Have you noticed that when you're at a noisy party, you can still select and attend to the voices of people you find interesting, or that you can suddenly pick up on another group's conversation if someone in that group mentions your name? These are prime examples of *selective attention*, also called the "cocktail party phenomenon."

© Greg Hinsdale/Corbis

FIGURE 4.16 **LOCATION OF FEATURE DETECTORS IN THE BRAIN**

Feature detectors Specialized neurons that respond only to certain sensory information.

Habituation The brain's reduced responsiveness due to repeated stimulation of the same receptors.

In addition to selective attention, the brains of humans and other animals contain specialized cells, called **feature detectors**, which respond only to certain stimuli. For example, studies with humans have found feature detectors in the temporal and occipital lobes that respond maximally to faces **(Figure 4.16)**. Problems in these areas can produce a condition called *prosopagnosia* (*prosopon* means "face," and *agnosia* means "failure to know"). Interestingly, people with prosopagnosia can recognize that they are looking at a face. But they cannot say whose face is reflected in a mirror, even if it is their own or that of a friend or relative (Avidan et al., 2013; Stollhoff et al., 2011; Susilo & Duchaine, 2013).

Other examples of the brain's ability to filter experience are evidenced by **habituation**, a decrease in responding due to repeated stimulation of the same stimulus. Apparently, the brain is "prewired" to pay more attention to changes in the environment than to stimuli that remain constant. Developmental psychologists often use measurements of habituation to tell when a stimulus can be detected and discriminated by infants who are too young to speak. When presented with a new stimulus, infants pay attention, but with repetition their responses weaken.

Habituation also can help explain why attention and compliments from a stranger are generally more exciting than those from a long-term romantic partner. Unfortunately, some people (who haven't taken psychology courses or read this text) may misinterpret and overvalue this new attention. They may even leave good relationships, not realizing that they will also soon habituate to the new person!

©Yuri_Arcurs/iStockphoto

realworldpsychology **Using Selective Attention, Feature Detectors, and Habituation in Advertising** As advertisers and political operatives well know, people tend to automatically select stimuli that are intense, novel, moving, contrasting, and repetitious. For sheer volume of sales (or votes), if an ad gets your attention, that's all that matters. Whether you like the ad or not is irrelevant. This phenomenon also helps explain why sometimes you don't like a song when you first hear it on the radio or at a club, but after you've heard it hundreds of times, you actually might find it kind of catchy!

Organization

Raw sensory data are like the parts of a watch—the parts must be assembled in a meaningful way before they are useful. We organize sensory data in terms of form, constancy, depth, and color.

Form perception Gestalt psychologists were among the first to study how the brain organizes sensory impressions into a *gestalt*—a German word meaning "form" or "whole." They emphasized the importance of organization and patterning in enabling us to perceive the whole stimulus rather than perceive its discrete parts as separate entities. The Gestaltists proposed several laws of organization that specify how people perceive form **(Figure 4.17)**.

The most fundamental Gestalt principle of organization is our tendency to distinguish between the *figure* (our main focus of attention) and *ground* (the background or surroundings).

Your sense of figure and ground is at work in what you are doing right now—reading. Your brain is receiving sensations of black lines and white paper, but your brain is organizing these sensations into black letters and words on a white background. You perceive the letters as the figure and the white as the ground. If you make a great effort, you might be able to force yourself to see the page reversed, as though a black

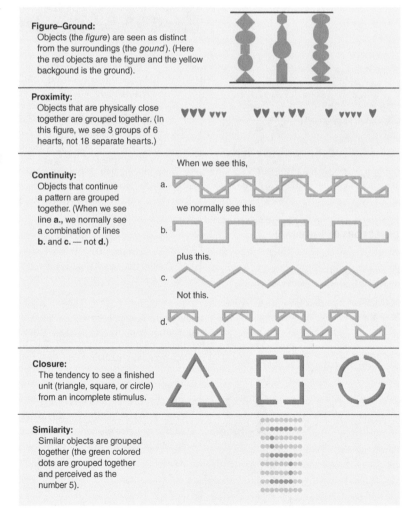

FIGURE 4.17 UNDERSTANDING GESTALT PRINCIPLES OF ORGANIZATION

Gestalt principles are based on the notion that we all share a natural tendency to force patterns onto whatever we see. Although the examples of the Gestalt principles in this figure are all visual, each principle applies to other modes of perception as well. For example, the Gestalt principle of *contiguity* cannot be shown because it involves nearness in time, not visual nearness. Similarly, the aural (hearing) effects of figure and ground aren't shown in this figure, but you've undoubtedly experienced them in a movie theater. Despite nearby conversations in the audience, you can still listen to the voices on the film because you make them your focus (the figure) versus the ground.

Figure–Ground:
Objects (the *figure*) are seen as distinct from the surroundings (the *gound*). (Here the red objects are the figure and the yellow backgound is the ground).

Proximity:
Objects that are physically close together are grouped together. (In this figure, we see 3 groups of 6 hearts, not 18 separate hearts.)

Continuity:
Objects that continue a pattern are grouped together. (When we see line **a.**, we normally see a combination of lines **b.** and **c.** — not **d.**)

When we see this,
a.

we normally see this
b.

plus this.
c.

Not this.
d.

Closure:
The tendency to see a finished unit (triangle, square, or circle) from an incomplete stimulus.

Similarity:
Similar objects are grouped together (the green colored dots are grouped together and perceived as the number 5).

FIGURE 4.18 UNDERSTANDING REVERSIBLE AND IMPOSSIBLE FIGURES

Ⓐ This so-called *reversible figure* demonstrates alternating figure–ground relations. It can be seen as a woman looking in a mirror or as a skull, depending on what you see as figure or ground.

Ⓑ When you first glance at this famous painting by the Dutch artist M.C. Escher, you detect specific features of the stimuli and judge them as sensible figures. But as you try to sort and organize the different elements into a stable, well-organized whole, you realize they don't add up—they're impossible. There is no one-to-one correspondence between your actual sensory input and your final perception.

M.C. Escher's "Concave and Convex" © 2012 The M.C. Escher Company-Holland. All rights reserved

background were showing through letter-shaped-holes in a white foreground. There are times, however, when it is very hard to distinguish the figure from the ground, as you can see in **Figure 4.18a**. This is known as a *reversible figure*. Your brain alternates between seeing the light areas as the figure and seeing them as the ground.

Like reversible figures, *impossible figures* help us understand perceptual principles—in this case, the principle of form organization **(Figure 4.18b)**.

Depth perception The ability to perceive three-dimensional space and to accurately judge distance.

Binocular cues Visual input from two eyes that allows perception of depth or distance.

Monocular cues Visual input from a single eye alone that contributes to perception of depth or distance.

Depth Perception

In our three-dimensional world, the ability to perceive the depth and distance of objects—as well as their height and width—is essential. **Depth perception** is learned primarily through experience. However, research using an apparatus called the *visual cliff* **(Figure 4.19)** suggests that some depth perception is inborn.

One mechanism by which we perceive depth is the interaction of both eyes to produce **binocular cues (Figure 4.20)**. The other relies on **monocular cues**, which work with each eye separately **(Figure 4.21)**.

Glass only

Shallow side

Floor as seen through the glass

FIGURE 4.19 VISUAL CLIFF

realworldpsychology

Crawling infants hesitate or refuse to move to the "deep end" of the visual cliff indicating that they perceive the difference in depth. The same is true for baby animals that walk almost immediately after birth. Even 2-month-old human infants show a change in heart rate when placed on the deep versus shallow side of the visual cliff (Adolph & Kretch, 2012; Banks & Salapatek, 1983; Gibson & Walk, 1960; Ueno et al., 2012).

FIGURE 4.20 BINOCULAR DEPTH CUES

How do we perceive a three-dimensional world with a two-dimensional receptor system? One mechanism is the interaction of both eyes to produce binocular cues.

Ⓑ Convergence

Hold your index finger at arm's length in front of you and watch it as you bring it closer until it is right in front of your nose. The amount of strain in your eye muscles created by the **convergence**, or turning inward of the eyes, is used as a cue by your brain to interpret distance.

Ⓐ Retinal disparity

Stare at your two index fingers a few inches in front of your eyes with their tips half an inch apart. Do you see the "floating finger"? Move it farther away and the "finger" will shrink. Move it closer and it will enlarge. Because our eyes are about 2½ inches apart, objects at different distances (such as the "floating finger") project their images on different parts of the retina, an effect called **retinal disparity**. Far objects project on the retinal area near the nose, whereas near objects project farther out, closer to the ears.

The binocular (two eyes) cues of **retinal disparity** and **convergence** are inadequate in judging distances longer than the length of a football field. Luckily, we have several monocular (one-eye) cues available separately to each eye. Imagine yourself as an artist and see whether you can identify each of the following cues in this beautiful photo of the Taj Mahal, a famous mausoleum in India (Figure 4.21):

- **Linear perspective** Parallel lines converge, or angle toward one another, as they recede into the distance.

- **Interposition** Objects that obscure or overlap other objects are perceived as closer.

- **Relative size** Close objects cast a larger retinal image than distant objects.

- **Texture gradient** Nearby objects have a coarser and more distinct texture than distant ones.

- **Aerial perspective** Distant objects appear hazy and blurred compared to close objects because of intervening atmospheric dust or haze.

- **Light and shadow** Brighter objects are perceived as being closer than darker objects.

- **Relative height** Objects positioned higher in our field of vision are perceived as farther away.

Two additional monocular cues for depth perception, **accommodation** of the lens of the eye and *motion parallax*, cannot be used by artists and are not shown in Figure 4.21. In *accommodation*, muscles that adjust the shape of the lens as it focuses on an object send neural messages to the brain, which interprets the signal to perceive distance. For near objects, the lens bulges; for

Retinal disparity The binocular cue of distance in which the separation of the eyes causes different images to fall on each retina.

Convergence A binocular depth cue in which the eyes turn inward (or converge) to fixate on an object.

Accommodation The process by which the eye's ciliary muscles change the shape (thickness) of the lens so that light is focused on the retina; adjustment of the eye's lens permitting focusing on near and distant objects.

FIGURE 4.21 MONOCULAR DEPTH CUES AND THE TAJ MAHAL

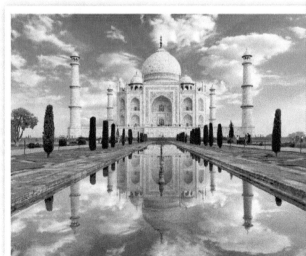

© Adam Kaz/iStockphoto

far objects, it flattens. *Motion parallax* (also known as *relative motion*) refers to the fact that when we are moving, close objects appear to whiz by, whereas farther objects seem to move more slowly or remain stationary. This effect can easily be seen when traveling by car or train.

Constancies Perception

To organize our sensations into meaningful patterns, we develop **perceptual constancies**, the learned tendency to perceive the environment as stable, despite changes in an object's *size, shape, color,* and *brightness*. Without perceptual constancy, things would seem to grow as we get closer to them, change shape as our viewing angle changes, and change color as light levels change (Durgin et al., 2012; Goldstein, 2014; Granrud, 2012).

Perceptual constancy The ability to retain an unchanging perception of an object despite changes in the sensory input.

Size constancy Regardless of the distance from us (or the size of the image it casts on our retina), *size constancy* allows us to interpret an object as always being the same size. For example, the image of the couple in the foreground of the photo **(Figure 4.22)** is much larger on our retina than the trees behind them. However, thanks to size constancy, we perceive them to be of normal size. Without this constancy, we would perceive people walking away from us as shrinking and as growing as they walked toward us. Although researchers have found evidence of size constancy in newborns, it also develops from learning and the environment. Case studies of people who have been blind since birth, and then have their sight restored, find that they initially have little or no size constancy (Sacks, 1995).

Color and brightness constancies Our perception of color and brightness remain the same even when the light conditions change. Look at the two dogs' fur in this photo **(Figure 4.23)**. We perceive the color and brightness as constant

FIGURE 4.22 **SIZE CONSTANCY**

courtesy Karen Huffman

FIGURE 4.23 **COLOR AND BRIGHTNESS CONSTANCIES**

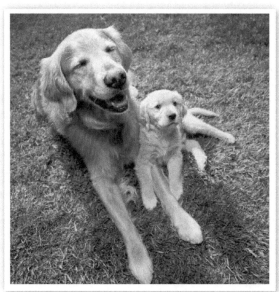

GK Hart/Vikki Hart/Getty Images, Inc.

FIGURE 4.24 **SHAPE CONSTANCY**

Note how as the coin is rotated, it changes shape, but we still perceive it as the same coin—thanks to shape constancy.

The so-called Ames room illusion (shown in this diagram) also illustrates size and shape constancy. To a viewer peering through the peephole, the Ames room appears to be a normal cubic-shaped room. But the true shape is trapezoidal. In addition, the walls are slanted and the floor and ceiling are at an incline. Because our brains mistakenly assume that the two people are the same distance away, we compensate for the apparent size difference by making the person on the left appear much smaller.

despite the fact that the wavelength of light reaching our retina may vary as the light changes.

Shape constancy One additional perceptual constancy is the tendency to perceive an object's shape as staying constant even when the angle of our view changes **(Figure 4.24)**.

Color perception

Our ability to perceive color is at least as remarkable and useful as depth perception. Humans may be able to discriminate among 7 million different hues, and research conducted in many cultures suggests that we all seem to see essentially the same colored world (Davies, 1998; Ozturk et al., 2013). Furthermore, studies of infants old enough to focus and move their eyes show that they are able to see color nearly as well as adults and have color preferences similar to those of adults (Franklin et al., 2010).

Although we know color is produced by different wavelengths of light, the actual way in which we perceive color is a matter of scientific debate. Traditionally, there have been two theories of color vision: the trichromatic (three-color) theory and the opponent-process theory. The **trichromatic theory of color** (from the Greek word *tri*, meaning "three," and *chroma*, meaning "color") suggests that we have three "color systems," each of which is maximally sensitive to red, green, or blue (Young, 1802). The proponents of this theory demonstrated that mixing lights of these three colors could yield the full spectrum of colors we perceive.

Trichromatic theory of color The theory that color perception results from three types of cones in the retina, each most sensitive to either red, green, or blue; other colors result from a mixture of these three.

chapter 4 SENSATION AND PERCEPTION

Opponent-process theory of color The theory that all color perception is based on three systems, each of which contains two color opposites (red versus green, blue versus yellow, and black versus white).

However, trichromatic theory doesn't fully explain color vision, and other researchers have proposed alternative theories. For example, the **opponent-process theory of color** agrees that we have three color systems, but it says that each system is sensitive to two opposing colors—blue and yellow, red and green, black and white—in an "on/off" fashion. In other words, each color receptor responds either to blue or yellow, or to red or green, with the black-or-white systems responding to differences in brightness levels. This theory makes a lot of sense because when different-colored lights are combined, people are unable to see reddish greens and bluish yellows. In fact, when red and green lights or blue and yellow lights are mixed in equal amounts, we see white. This opponent-process theory also explains *color afterimages*, a fun type of optical illusion in which an image briefly remains after the original image has faded (see *Test Yourself*).

TEST YOURSELF: UNDERSTANDING AND TESTING YOURSELF FOR COLOR AFTERIMAGES

psychology and you

Try staring at the dot in the middle of this color-distorted U.S. flag for 60 seconds. Then stare at a plain sheet of white paper. You should get interesting color aftereffects—red in place of green, blue in place of yellow, and white in place of black: a

"genuine" U.S. flag. (If you don't see the afterimage, blink once or twice and try again.)

What happened? As you stared at the green, black, and yellow colors, the neural systems that process those colors became fatigued. Then when you looked at the plain white paper, which reflects all wavelengths, a reverse opponent process occurred: Each fatigued receptor responded with its opposing red, white, and blue colors! This is a good example of color afterimages—and further support for the opponent-process theory.

Think Critically

1 In what kinds of situations do you think color afterimages are likely to occur?

2 Other than learning that our eyes can play tricks on our brain, why might illusions like this afterimage be important?

Today we know that both trichromatic and opponent-process theories are correct—they just operate at different levels in visual processing. Color vision is processed in a trichromatic fashion in the retina. In contrast, color vision during opponent processing involves the retina, optic nerve, and brain.

Color-Deficient Vision

Most people perceive three different colors—red, green, and blue—and are called *trichromats*. However, a small percentage of the population has a genetic deficiency in the red–green system, the blue–yellow system, or both. Those who perceive only two colors are called *dichromats*. People who are sensitive to only the black–white system are called *monochromats*, and they are totally color blind. If you'd like to test yourself for red–green color blindness, see *Test Yourself*.

TEST YOURSELF: UNDERSTANDING COLOR BLINDNESS

psychology and you

Are you color blind? People who suffer red–green deficiency have trouble perceiving the number in this design. Although we commonly use the term *color blindness*, most problems are color confusion rather than color blindness. Furthermore, most people who have some color blindness are not even aware of it.

Interpretation

After selectively sorting through incoming sensory information and organizing it, the brain uses this information to explain and make judgments about the external world. This final stage of perception—*interpretation*—is influenced by several factors, including sensory adaptation, perceptual set, frame of reference, and bottom-up or top-down processing.

Stratton's experiment with the inverting goggles, discussed in the chapter overview, illustrates the critical role that sensory adaptation plays in the way we interpret the information that our brains gather. Without his ability to adapt his perceptions to a skewed environment, Stratton would not have been able to function. His brain's ability to retrain itself to interpret his new surroundings allowed him to create coherence from what would otherwise have been chaos.

As you can see in the *Real World Psychology* example below, our previous experiences, assumptions, and expectations also affect how we interpret and perceive the world, by creating a **perceptual set**, or a readiness to perceive in a particular manner, based on expectations (Dunning & Balcetis, 2013). In other words, we largely see what we expect to see!

Perceptual set The readiness to perceive in a particular manner, based on expectations.

realworldpsychology

Crime and Perceptual Sets In some cases, our *perceptual sets*, or expectations, can have hazardous effects. For example, researchers asked both white and black participants to play a videogame in which they were told to shoot targets who were carrying a gun but not those who were unarmed (Correll et al., 2002).

Participants of both races made the decision to shoot an armed target more quickly if the target was black than white. They also chose NOT to shoot an unarmed target more quickly if the target was white than black.

This study points to the influence of our expectations on real-life situations in which police officers must decide almost instantly whether to shoot a potential suspect—and may partially explain why blacks are at greater risk than whites of being accidentally shot by police officers.

Foto Bouten/Shutterstock

chapter 4 SENSATION AND PERCEPTION

FIGURE 4.25 PERCEPTUAL SET?

When you look at this drawing, do you see a young woman looking back over her shoulder or an older woman with her chin buried in a fur collar? It may depend on your age. Younger students tend to first see a young woman, and older students first see an older woman. Although the basic sensory input stays the same, your brain's attempt to interpret ambiguous stimuli creates a type of perceptual dance, shifting from one interpretation to another (Gaetz et al., 1998).

Bottom-up processing Perceptual analysis that begins "at the bottom," with raw sensory data being sent "up" to the brain for higher-level analysis; it is data-driven processing that moves from the parts to the whole.

Top-down processing Perceptual analysis that starts "at the top," with higher-level cognitive processes (such as expectations and knowledge), and then works down; it is conceptually driven processing that moves from the whole to the parts.

In addition to possible problems with *perceptual set* (**Figure 4.25**), the way we perceive people, objects, or situations is also affected by the *frame of reference*, or context. An elephant is perceived as much larger when it is next to a mouse than when it stands next to a giraffe. This is the reason professional athletes who make huge amounts of money sometimes feel underpaid: They're comparing what they make to the pay of those around them, who also make huge sums, and not to the average person in the United States! The influence of frame of reference on perception also helps explain why people rate themselves as more athletic if they compare themselves to the Pope than to a professional basketball player (Mussweiler et al., 2004)!

Finally, recall that we began this chapter by discussing how we receive sensory information (sensation) and work our way upward to the top levels of perceptual processing (perception), **bottom-up processing**. In contrast, **top-down processing** begins with "higher," "top"-level processing of thoughts, previous experiences, expectations, language, and cultural background and works down to the sensory level (Antúnez et al., 2013; Chica et al., 2013; Freeman & Ambady, 2011; Zhaoping & Guyader, 2007) (see *Psychology and You*).

Jose Luis Pelaez/Iconica/Getty Images, Inc.

psychology and you **Reading and Processing** When first learning to read, you used bottom-up processing. You initially learned that certain arrangements of line and "squiggles" represented specific letters. You later realized that these letters make up words.

Now, yuor aiblity to raed uisng top-dwon prcessoing mkaes it psosible to unedrstnad thsi sntenece desipte its mnay mssipllengis.

Extrasensory perception (ESP) The perceptual, so-called "psychic," abilities that supposedly go beyond the known senses (for example, telepathy, clairvoyance, precognition, and psychokinesis).

Science and ESP

So far in this chapter, we have talked about sensations provided by our eyes, ears, nose, mouth, and skin. What about a so-called sixth sense? Can some people perceive things that cannot be perceived with the usual sensory channels, by using **extrasensory perception (ESP)**? Those who claim to have ESP profess to be able to read other people's minds (*telepathy*), perceive objects or events that are inaccessible to their normal senses (*clairvoyance*), predict the future (*precognition*), or move or affect objects without touching them (psychokinesis).

As we discussed in Chapter 1, each of these claims falls under the name *pseudopsychology,* including Daryl Bem's highly publicized research (Bem, 2011). Furthermore, virtually all reports and so-called studies of ESP have been successfully debunked (Alcock, 2011; Bones, 2012; Galak et al., 2012; Irwin, 2008; Shaffer & Jadwiszczok, 2010). Findings in ESP are notoriously "fragile" in that they do not hold up to intense scrutiny.

Perhaps the most serious weakness of ESP is its failure of replication by rivals in independent laboratories, which is a core requirement for scientific acceptance (Francis, 2012; Hyman, 1996; Rouder et al., 2013). (Recall also from Chapter 1 that magician James Randi and the MacArthur Foundation has offered $1 million to "anyone who proves a genuine psychic power under proper observing conditions." But even after many years, the money has never been collected!)

So why do so many people believe in ESP? One reason is that, as mentioned earlier in the chapter, our motivations and interests often influence our perceptions, driving us to selectively attend to things we want to see or hear. In addition, the subject of extrasensory perception often generates strong emotional responses. When individuals feel strongly about an issue, they sometimes fail to recognize the faulty reasoning underlying their beliefs.

Belief in ESP is particularly associated with illogical or noncritical thinking. For example, people often fall victim to the *fallacy of positive instances*, or the *confirmation bias*, noting and remembering events that confirm personal expectations and beliefs (the "hits") and ignoring nonsupportive evidence (the "misses"). Other times, people fail to recognize chance occurrences for what they are. Finally, human information processing often biases us to notice and remember the most vivid information. Rather than relying on scientific research based on analyzing numerous data points, we prefer colorful anecdotes and heartfelt personal testimonials.

Voices from the Classroom

ESP or Intuition? I had been dating my girlfriend for nearly three years when a job offer caused me to move to another state. Soon after moving, I realized that I needed to propose to her to show her how serious I was about our relationship. When she came in town to visit me, I proposed to her the day after we had been dating for four years. I told no one in advance of this proposal. I was very excited to share this news with my mother; my mom and I have always been close. Even though we lived far from each other, we talked at least once or twice a week. So, I called my mom to share the big news with her. I said, "Hi mom." The first thing my mother said was, "Are you engaged?" Was this ESP or just mother's intuition? What do you believe?

Professor David Baskind

Delta College

University Center, Michigan

RETRIEVAL PRACTICE: UNDERSTANDING PERCEPTION

Self-Test

Completing this self-test and comparing your answers with those in Appendix B provides immediate feedback and helpful practice for exams. Additional interactive, self-tests are available at www.wiley.com/college/huffman.

1. When our brain is sorting out and attending only to the most important messages from the senses, it is engaged in the process of _____.

a. sensory adaptation   b. sensory habituation

c. selective attention   d. selective sorting

2. In the _____ shown below, the discrepancy between figure and ground is too vague, and we may have difficulty perceiving which is figure and which is ground.

a. illusion   b. reversible figure

c. optical illusion   d. hallucination

3. The tendency for the environment to be perceived as remaining the same even with changes in sensory input is called _____.

a. perceptual constancy   b. the constancy of expectation

c. an illusory correlation   d. Gestalt's primary principle

4. The _____ of color vision says that color perception results from three types of cones in the retina.

a. tricolor theory   b. trichromatic theory

c. tripigment theory   d. opponent-process theory

5. A readiness to perceive in a particular manner is known as _____.

a. sensory adaptation   b. perceptual set

c. habituation   d. frame of reference

Think Critically

1 Can you explain how your own perceptual sets might create prejudice or discrimination?

2 How has reading this chapter's information about ESP influenced your beliefs about this topic?

3 Why do you think no one has ever received the $1 million dollar award that was offered for a provable case of ESP?

realworldpsychology

Why do people rate themselves as more athletic if they compare themselves to the Pope than to a professional basketball player?

HINT: LOOK IN THE MARGIN FOR

Summary

1 UNDERSTANDING SENSATION 92

- **Sensation** is the process by which we detect stimuli and convert them into neural signals (**transduction**). During **coding**, the neural impulses generated by different physical stimuli travel by separate routes and arrive at different parts of the brain. In sensory reduction, we filter and analyze incoming sensations.
- In **sensory adaptation**, sensory receptors fire less frequently with repeated stimulation so that sensation decreases over time.
- **Psychophysics** measures our experience of sensory stimuli. The **absolute threshold** is the minimum stimulation necessary to consciously detect a stimulus 50% of the time. The **difference threshold**, or just noticeable difference (JND), is the smallest difference between two stimuli that is consciously detectable 50% of the time.
- Subliminal stimuli, though perceivable, have a modest effect on behavior.
- According to the **gate-control theory**, our experience of pain depends partly on whether the neural message gets past a "gatekeeper" in the spinal cord, which researchers believe is chemically controlled.

2 HOW WE SEE AND HEAR 98

- Light and sound move in waves. Light waves are a form of electromagnetic energy, and sound waves are produced when air molecules move in a particular wave pattern. Both light waves and sound waves vary in wavelength/frequency, wave height/amplitude, and wave range/complexity.
- Light enters the eye at the front of the eyeball. The cornea protects the eye and helps focus light rays. The lens further focuses light, adjusting to allow focusing on objects at different distances. At the back of the eye, incoming light waves reach the **retina**, which contains light-sensitive **rods** and **cones**. A network of neurons in the retina transmits neural information to the brain.
- The **outer ear** gathers sound waves, the **middle ear** amplifies and concentrates the sounds, and the **inner ear** changes the mechanical energy of sounds into neural impulses. The frequency and intensity of sounds determine how we distinguish among sounds of different pitches and loudness, respectively.

3 OUR OTHER IMPORTANT SENSES 104

- Smell and taste, sometimes called the chemical senses, involve chemoreceptors that are sensitive to certain chemical molecules. In **olfaction**, odor molecules stimulate receptors in the olfactory epithelium, in the nose. The resulting neural impulse travels to the olfactory bulb, where the information is processed before being sent elsewhere in the brain. Our sense of taste (**gustation**) involves five tastes: sweet, sour, salty, bitter, and umami (umami means "savory" or "delicious"). The taste buds are clustered on our tongues within the papillae.
- The body senses— the skin senses, the **vestibular sense**, and **kinesthesis**—tell the brain what it's touching or being touched by, how the body is oriented, and where and how it is moving.

4 UNDERSTANDING PERCEPTION 108

- **Perception** is the process of selecting, organizing, and interpreting incoming sensations into useful mental representations of the world. **Selective attention** allows us to filter out unimportant sensory messages. **Feature detectors** are specialized cells that respond only to certain sensory information. **Habituation** is a decrease in responsiveness due to repeated stimulation of the same stimulus.
- To be useful, sensory data must be assembled in a meaningful way. We organize sensory data in terms of form, constancy, depth, and color. Size and shape constancy are demonstrated in the Ames room. Traditionally there have been two theories of color vision: the **trichromatic theory** and the **opponent-process theory**.
- **Perceptual adaptation**, **perceptual set**, frame of reference, and **bottom-up processing** versus **top-down processing** affect our interpretation of what we sense and perceive.

Lindsey Hebberd/Corbis

◉ applyingrealworldpsychology

We began this chapter with five intriguing Real World Psychology questions, and you were asked to revisit these questions at the end of each section. Questions like these have an important and lasting impact on all of our lives. See if you can answer these additional critical thinking questions related to real world examples.

1. The man in this photo willingly endures what would normally be excruciating pain. What information did you gain from this chapter that would help explain this man's behavior?
2. How has sensory adaptation been both advantageous and disadvantageous in your own life?
3. Why is it important to test all young children's vision and hearing capabilities?
4. If scientists could improve your sensory capabilities (for example, vision and hearing) far beyond the normal range, would you volunteer for this treatment? What might be the advantages and disadvantages?
5. Imagine yourself as a hiker who happens upon an unusual structure in the middle of the desert. How might information from this chapter help you capture this structure in a painting?

Key Terms

RETRIEVAL PRACTICE Write a definition for each term before turning back to the referenced page to check your answer.

- absolute threshold 94
- accommodation 113
- audition 100
- binocular cues 112
- blind spot 100
- bottom-up processing 118
- cochlea 101
- coding 92
- conduction hearing loss 102
- cones 100
- convergence 113
- depth perception 112
- difference threshold 94
- extrasensory perception (ESP) 118
- feature detectors 110

- fovea 100
- frequency theory for hearing 100
- gate-control theory of pain 95
- gustation 104
- habituation 110
- illusion 109
- inner ear 101
- kinesthesis 108
- middle ear 101
- monocular cues 112
- olfaction 104
- opponent-process theory of color 116
- outer ear 101
- perception 92
- perceptual constancy 114
- perceptual set 117

- pheromones 104
- place theory for hearing 100
- psychophysics 94
- retina 100
- retinal disparity 113
- rods 100
- selective attention 109
- sensation 92
- sensorineural hearing loss 102
- sensory adaptation 95
- subliminal perception 95
- top-down processing 118
- transduction 92
- trichromatic theory of color 115
- vestibular sense 107

chapterfive

States of Consciousness

realworldpsychology

THINGS YOU'LL LEARN IN CHAPTER 5

Q1 Can getting too little sleep increase your risk of getting a cold?

Q2 Can using a computer or iPad late at night make it harder to fall asleep?

Q3 Are you addicted to Facebook?

Q4 Can using marijuana decrease your IQ?

Q5 Can hypnosis decrease the pain of childbirth?

THROUGHOUT THE CHAPTER, MARGIN ICONS FOR Q1–Q5 INDICATE
WHERE THE TEXT ADDRESSES THESE QUESTIONS.

chapteroverview

Control of consciousness determines the quality of life.

—Mihaly Csikszentmihaly

With the arrival of humans, it has been said, the universe has suddenly become conscious of itself. This, truly, it the greatest mystery of all.

—V. S. Ramachandran

We all commonly use the term *consciousness*, but what exactly does it mean? Is it simple awareness? What would it be like to be unaware? How can we study and understand the contents of our own consciousness when the only tool of discovery is consciousness itself?

In this chapter, we begin with an exploration of how consciousness is affected by circadian rhythms. Next, we'll discuss two alternate states—sleep and dreaming—followed by psychoactive drugs. Finally, we explore additional routes to altered consciousness through meditation and hypnosis.

CONSCIOUSNESS, SLEEP, AND DREAMING

LEARNING OBJECTIVES

RETRIEVAL PRACTICE While reading the upcoming sections, respond to each Learning Objective in your own words. Then compare your responses with those found at www.wiley.com/college/huffman.

1 **DEFINE** consciousness and alternate states of consciousness (ASCs).

2 **EXPLAIN** how circadian rhythms affect our lives.

3 **REVIEW** the stages of sleep.

4 **COMPARE** and contrast the theories about why we sleep and dream.

5 **SUMMARIZE** the types of sleep disorders.

Consciousness An organism's awareness of internal events and of the external environment.

William James, the first U.S. psychologist, likened **consciousness** to a stream that's constantly changing yet always the same. It meanders and flows, sometimes where the person wills and sometimes not. However, the process of *selective attention* (Chapter 4) allows us to control this stream of consciousness through deliberate concentration and full attention. For example, at the present moment you are, we hope, fully awake and concentrating on the words on this page. At times, however, your control may weaken, and your attention may drift to thoughts of a laptop you want to buy, a job, or an attractive classmate.

In addition to meandering and flowing, your stream of consciousness also varies in range and depth. It is not an all-or-nothing phenomenon—you are not either conscious or unconscious. Instead, consciousness exists along a continuum.

Other than wakefulness, there are common altered states, such as sleep and dreaming, psychoactive drug states, meditation, and hypnosis. You may think of yourself as being unconscious while you sleep, or fully conscious while "high" on certain drugs, but that's not true. Rather, you are in an **alternate state of consciousness (ASC)**. In this chapter, you will learn about both everyday, wakeful consciousness and ASCs.

Before we begin, *Psych Science* describes how talking on a cell phone can lead to a dangerous drift down this meandering stream of consciousness.

Alternate state of consciousness (ASC) A mental state, other than ordinary waking consciousness, that occurs during sleep, dreaming, psychoactive drug use, and hypnosis.

PSYCHSCIENCE

WHY DRIVING AND CELL PHONE USE JUST DON'T MIX

Strayer et al (2011). Cognitivedistraction while multitasking in theautomobile. In B. Ross (Ed.), *The Psychology of Learning and Motivation, 54*, 29-58

Driving while using a cell phone
The photo on the left shows what a driver sees when not distracted by using a cell phone. In the photo on the right, note what the driver does NOT see while talking on a cell phone. Can you understand why cell phone use (including texting) leads to accidents?

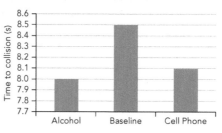

Does your state have laws about driving and talking—or texting—on a cell phone? These types of regulations are increasingly common, in part because of research conducted by psychologists that shows the extreme hazards of divided attention. Researchers in one study observed more than 1,700 drivers approaching an intersection and recorded whether the driver was talking on a cell phone as he or she approached the sign, and whether the car came to a complete stop (as the law requires) before going through the intersection. Their findings revealed that 75% of the drivers who were talking on a cell phone failed to come to a complete stop. In contrast, only 21% of those who were not talking on a cell phone failed to stop.

A follow-up laboratory study (also conducted by Strayer et al., 2011) recruited 40 volunteers and tested their skills on a driving simulator. Each volunteer was randomly assigned to one of three conditions:

- Driving while talking on a cell phone
- Driving while intoxicated (with a blood alcohol concentration of 0.08)
- Driving without talking on a cell phone or being intoxicated

The researchers examined a number of different measures of driving, including number of accidents, brake reaction time, and speed.

Can you predict what this research revealed? Both intoxicated drivers and drivers talking on a cell phone performed worse than those who were able to fully concentrate on driving (see the figure).

Keep in mind that all participants gave their informed consent for this research and that the "drunk drivers" were only tested in a driving simulator, not in an actual car.

RESEARCH CHALLENGE

1 Based on the information provided, did the study (Strayer et al., 2011) use descriptive, correlational, and/or experimental research?

2 If you chose:
- descriptive research, is this a naturalistic observation, survey/interview, case study, or archival research?
- correlational research, is this a positive, negative, or zero correlation?
- experimental research, label the IV, DV, experimental group(s), and control group.

>> CHECK YOUR ANSWERS IN APPENDIX B.
NOTE: The information provided in this study is admittedly limited, but the level of detail is similar to what is presented in most text books and public reports of research findings. Answering these questions, and then comparing your answers to those in the Appendix, will help you become a better critical thinker and consumer of scientific research.

Circadian Rhythms

Most animals have adapted to our planet's cycle of days and nights by developing a pattern of bodily functions that wax and wane over each 24-hour period. For humans, our alertness, core body temperature, moods, learning efficiency, blood pressure, metabolism, immune responses, and pulse rate all follow these **circadian rhythms** (Jones & Benca, 2013; Karatsoreos et al., 2011; Kyriacou & Hastings, 2010; Scheiermann et al., 2013). Usually, these activities reach their peak during the day and their low point at night **(Figure 5.1)**.

Circadian rhythm A consistent pattern of cyclical bodily activities, governed by an internal biological clock, that generally occurs on a 24- to 25-hour cycle. (*Circa* means "about," and *dies* means "day.")

© OSTILL/iStockphoto

realworldpsychology   **Circadian Challenges for Teenagers** Do you remember having trouble going to bed at a "reasonable hour" when you were a teenager and then having a really difficult time getting up each morning? This common pattern of staying up late at night and then sleeping longer in the morning appears to be a result of the natural shift in the timing of circadian rhythms that occurs during puberty (Carskadon et al., 1998). This shift is caused by a delay in the release of the hormone melatonin. In adults, this hormone is typically released around 10 p.m., signaling the body that it is time to go to sleep. But in teenagers, melatonin isn't released until around 1 a.m.–thus explaining why it's more difficult for teenagers to fall asleep as early as adults or younger children do.

Recognition of this unique biological shift in circadian rhythms among teenagers has led some school districts to delay the start of school in the morning. Research shows that even a 30-minute delay allows teenagers to be more alert and focused during class, as well as improvements in their moods and overall health (Owens et al., 2010). Even more importantly, delaying the start of school in one large county in Kentucky was associated with a 16.5% decrease in car crashes among teenage drivers over the next two years (Danner & Philips, 2008).

FIGURE 5.1 WHAT CONTROLS CIRCADIAN RHYTHMS?

Circadian rhythms are regulated by a part of the hypothalamus called the *suprachiasmatic nucleus* (SCN).

A The SCN receives information about light and darkness from the eyes and then sends control messages to the *pineal gland*, which releases the hormone *melatonin*. Like other feedback loops in the body, the level of melatonin in the blood is sensed by the SCN, which then can modify the output of the pineal to maintain the "desired" level.

B Melatonin is thought to influence sleep, alertness, and body temperature. Note how our degree of alertness and core body temperature rise and fall in similar ways.

Disruptions in circadian rhythms are not just a problem for teenagers. We all are at risk of serious health issues and personal concerns, including increased risk of cancer, heart disease, autoimmune disorders, obesity, sleep disorders, and accidents, as well as decreased concentration and productivity (Dawson et al., 2011; Eckel-Mahan & Sassone-Corsi, 2013; Halvig et al., 2013; Jackson et al., 2013; Karatsoreos et al., 2011; Kyriacou & Hastings, 2010; Narasimamurthy et al., 2012; Menegaux et al., 2013; Pilcher et al., 2013; Wyse, 2012; Zhu & Zee, 2012). The most serious disruptions and ill effects tend to be with physicians, nurses, police, and others—about 20% of employees in the United States—whose occupations require rotating "shift work" schedules. Typically divided into a first shift (8 a.m. to 4 p.m), second shift (4 p.m. to midnight) and a third shift (midnight to 8 a.m.), these work shifts often change from week to week, and clearly disrupt the workers' circadian rhythms. Some research suggests that shifting from days to evenings to nights may make it easier to adjust to rotating shift schedules—probably because it's easier to go to bed later than to get up earlier. Workers' health, productivity, and safety are also believed to increase when shifts are rotated every three weeks instead of every week and napping is allowed (Asaoka et al., 2013; Landy & Conte, 2013; Roth, 2012).

Image Source/Getty Images

Coping with disrupted circadian rhythms?

Although you might assume that only babies and small children need to nap, napping is actually very common among professional athletes. This extra sleep is important because they often play their games at night and in varying time zones, which disrupts their regular night-time sleep cycle (Abrams, 2011).

psychology and you **Understanding Jet Lag** Like shift work, flying across several time zones can also cause fatigue and irritability, decreased alertness and mental agility, as well as exacerbation of psychiatric disorders (Jones & Benca, 2013; Paul et al., 2011; Sack, 2010). Jet lag tends to be worse when we fly eastward because our bodies adjust more easily to going to bed later than to going to sleep earlier than normal.

© Pierivb/iStockphoto

Sleep Deprivation

One of the biggest problems with disrupted circadian rhythms is the corresponding disruptions in the amount and quality of our sleep, which poses its own set of hazards. Sleep deprivation is clearly associated with reduced cognitive and motor performance, irritability and other mood alterations, and increased cortisol levels, which are all signs of stress (Doane et al., 2010; Gupta & Gupta, 2013; Martella et al., 2011; Orzel-Gryglewska, 2010). Sleep deprivation also leads to impairment in the immune system, which is one reason adults who get fewer than seven hours of sleep a night are three times as likely to develop a cold as those who sleep at least eight hours a night (Ackerman et al., 2012; Cohen et al., 2009). In addition, sleep-deprived adults are more likely to become obese. This may be because getting inadequate amounts of sleep interferes with the production of hormones that control appetite (Knutson, 2012).

Perhaps the most frightening danger is that lapses in attention among sleep-deprived pilots, physicians, truck drivers, and other workers cause serious accidents and cost thousands of lives each year (Chiang et al., 2012; Hallvig et al., 2013; Jackson et al., 2013; Mansukhani et al., 2012; Williamson et al., 2011). Are you wondering if you're sleep-deprived? Take the two-part test in the following *Psychology and You* to find out.

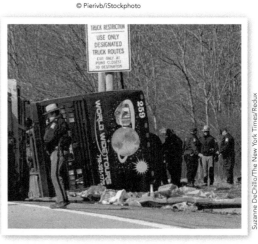
Suzanne DeChillo/The New York Times/Redux

Sleep deprivation can be fatal!

At 5:30 a.m. on March 12, 2011, a bus crashed on the outskirts of New York City, killing 15 people and injuring 14 others. In the three days prior to the crash, the bus driver had slept only during a few brief naps (McGeehan, 2012). The National Transportation Safety Board attributed the cause of this accident to driver fatigue.

TEST YOURSELF: SLEEP DEPRIVATION

psychology and you

Take the following test to determine whether you are sleep deprived.

Part 1 Set up a small mirror next to this text and trace the black star pictured here, using your nondominant hand, while watching your hand in the mirror. The task is difficult, and sleep-deprived people typically make many errors. If you are not sleep deprived, it still may be difficult to trace the star, but you'll probably do it accurately.

Part 2 Give yourself one point each time you answer yes to the following:

_____ **1.** I generally need an alarm clock or my cell phone alarm to wake up in the morning.

_____ **2.** I have a hard time getting out of bed in the morning.

_____ **3.** I try to only take late morning or early afternoon college classes because it's so hard to wake up early.

_____ **4.** People often tell me that I look tired and sleepy.

_____ **5.** I often struggle to stay awake during class, especially in warm rooms.

_____ **6.** I find it hard to concentrate and often nod off while I'm studying.

_____ **7.** I often feel sluggish and sleepy in the afternoon.

_____ **8.** I need several cups of coffee or other energy drinks to make it through the day.

_____ **9.** My friends often tell me I'm less moody and irritable when I've had enough sleep.

_____ **10.** I tend to get colds and infections, especially around final exams.

_____ **11.** When I get in bed at night, I generally fall asleep within four minutes.

_____ **12.** I try to catch up on my sleep debt by sleeping as long as possible on the weekends.

Pixtal/Age Fotostock America, Inc.

Effects of Sleep Deprivation
Insufficient sleep can seriously affect your college grades, as well as your physical health, motor skills, and overall mood.

The average student score is between 4 and 6. The higher your number, the greater your level of sleep deprivation.

Sources: Kaida et al., 2008; Mathis & Hess, 2009; National Sleep Foundation, 2012; Smith et al., 2012; Winerman, 2004.

Stages of Sleep

Having discussed our 24- to 25 hour circadian cycle, and the problems associated with its disruption, we now turn our attention to our cyclic patterns of sleep, which consist of five different stages. We begin with an exploration of how scientists study sleep. Surveys and interviews can provide general information, but for more detailed and precise data researchers in sleep laboratories use a number of sophisticated instruments **(Figure 5.2)**.

Imagine that you are a participant in a sleep experiment. When you arrive at the sleep lab, you are assigned one of several bedrooms. The researcher hooks you up to various physiological recording devices **(Figure 5.2a)**. You will probably need a night or two to adapt to the equipment before the researchers can begin to monitor your typical night's sleep. At first, you enter a relaxed, *presleep* state. As you continue relaxing, your brain's electrical activity slows even further. In the course of about an hour, you progress through several distinct stages of sleep, each progressively deeper **(Figure 5.2b)**. Then the sequence begins to reverse. Note that we don't necessarily go through all sleep stages in this exact sequence. But during the course of a night, people usually complete four to five cycles of light to deep sleep and back, each lasting about 90 minutes **(Figure 5.2c)**.

Figure 5.2b also shows an interesting phenomenon that occurs at the end of the first sleep cycle (and subsequent cycles). You reverse back through Stages 3, 2, and 1. At the end of Stage 1, you enter a very different phase noted by the characteristic rapid eye movements occurring under your closed eyelids. Researchers call this stage **rapid-eye-movement (REM) sleep**. During REM sleep, your scalp recordings display a pattern of small-amplitude, fast-wave activity, similar to an awake, vigilant person's brain waves. Your breathing and pulse rates become fast and irregular, and your genitals likely show signs of arousal. Yet your musculature is deeply relaxed and unresponsive. Because of these contradictory qualities, this REM stage is also sometimes referred to as *paradoxical sleep*.

Rapid-eye-movement (REM) sleep The fifth stage of sleep marked by rapid eye movements, high-frequency brain waves, paralysis of large muscles, and often dreaming.

FIGURE 5.2 **SCIENTIFIC STUDY OF SLEEP AND DREAMING**

Data collected in sleep labs has helped scientists understand the stages of sleep.

Ⓐ Participants in sleep research labs wear electrodes on their heads and bodies to measure brain and bodily responses during the sleep cycle. An electroencephalogram (EEG) detects and records brain-wave changes by means of small electrodes on the scalp. Other electrodes measure muscle activity and eye movements.

Ⓑ The stages of sleep, defined by telltale changes in brain waves, are indicated by the jagged lines. The compact brain waves of alertness gradually lengthen as we drift into Stages 1–4. Then we enter a fifth stage, called REM sleep, which has a different set of compact, faster brain waves.

Philippe Garo/Photo Researchers

Awake
Low-voltage, high-frequency beta waves

Drowsy
Alpha waves prominent

Stage 1 sleep
Theta waves prominent

Stage 2 sleep
Sleep spindles and mixed EEG activity

Slow-wave sleep (stage 3 and stage 4 sleep)
Progressively more delta waves (stage 4 shown)

REM sleep
Low-voltage, high-frequency waves

Ⓒ Your first sleep cycle generally lasts about 90 minutes from awake and alert, downward through Stages 1–4, and then back up through Stages 3, 2, and REM. If you sleep 8 hours, you'll typically go through approximately four or five sleep cycles (as shown by the vertical dotted lines). Note how the overall amount of REM sleep increases as the night progresses, while the amount of deep sleep (Stages 3 and 4) decreases.

Non-rapid-eye-movement (NREM) sleep Stages 1 through 4 of sleep during which a sleeper does not show rapid eye movements.

When awakened from REM sleep, people almost always report dreaming. Because REM sleep is so different from the other periods of sleep, Stages 1 through 4 are often collectively referred to as **non-rapid-eye-movement (NREM) sleep**. Dreams very similar to those from REM sleep also occur during NREM sleep, but less frequently (Chellappa et al., 2011; Wamsley et al., 2007).

Why Do We Sleep and Dream?

There are many myths and misconceptions about why we sleep and dream (see *Psychology and You*). Fortunately, scientists have carefully studied what sleep and dreaming do for us and why we spend approximately 25 years of our life in these alternate states of consciousness (ASCs).

TEST YOURSELF: HAVE YOU HEARD THESE COMMON MYTHS?

psychology and you

Before reading the facts about each myth, place a check by any statement that you currently believe to be true.

1. _____ *Everyone needs 8 hours of sleep a night to maintain sound mental and physical health.*

2. _____ *Dreams have special or symbolic meaning.*

3. _____ *Some people never dream.*

4. _____ *Dreams last only a few seconds and occur only in REM sleep.*

5. _____ *When genital arousal occurs during sleep, it means the sleeper is having a sexual dream.*

6. _____ *Most people dream only in black and white, and blind people don't dream.*

7. _____ *Dreaming of dying can be fatal.*

8. _____ *It's easy to learn new, complicated things, like a foreign language, while asleep.*

Facts:

1. *Fact:* Although the average is 7.6 hours of sleep a night, some people get by on an incredible 15 to 30 minutes. Others may need as much as 11 hours (Colrain, 2011; Daan, 2011; Doghramji, 2000; Maas et al., 1999).

2. *Fact:* Many people mistakenly believe that dreams can foretell the future, reflect unconscious desires, have secret meaning, reveal the truth, or contain special messages, but scientific research finds little or no support for these beliefs (Blum, 2011; Domhoff, 2010; Hobson et al., 2011; Lilienfeld et al., 2010; Montangero, 2012).

3. *Fact:* In rare cases, adults with certain brain injuries or disorders do not dream (Solms, 1997). But otherwise, virtually all adults regularly dream, but many don't remember doing so. Even people who firmly believe they never dream report dreams if they are repeatedly awakened during an overnight study in a sleep laboratory. Children also dream regularly. For example, between ages 3 and 8, they dream during approximately 25% of their sleep time (Foulkes, 1993, 1999).

4. *Fact:* Research shows that most dreams occur in real time. For example, a dream that seemed to last 20 minutes probably did last approximately 20 minutes (Dement & Wolpert, 1958). Dreams also occur in NREM sleep (Jones & Benca, 2013; Oudiette et al., 2012).

5. *Fact:* When sleepers are awakened during this time, they are no more likely to report sexual dreams than at other times.

6. *Fact:* People frequently report seeing color in their dreams. Those who are blind do dream, but they report visual images only if they lost their sight after approximately age 7 (Lilienfeld et al., 2010).

7. *Fact:* This is a good opportunity to exercise your critical thinking skills. Where did this myth come from? Although many people have personally experienced and recounted a fatal dream, how would we scientifically prove or disprove this belief?

8. *Fact:* Although some learning can occur doing the lighter stages (1 and 2) of sleep, processing and retention of this material is minimal (Lilienfeld et al., 2010; Ogilvie et al., 1989). Wakeful learning is much more effective and efficient.

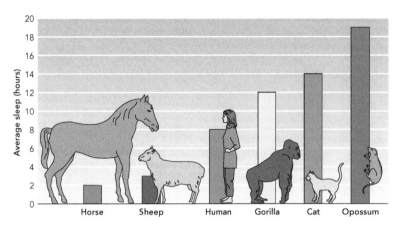

FIGURE 5.3 AVERAGE DAILY HOURS OF SLEEP FOR DIFFERENT MAMMALS

According to the adaptation/protection theory, differences in diet and number of predators affect different species' sleep habits. For example, opossums sleep many hours each day because they are relatively safe in their environment and are able to easily find food and shelter. In comparison, sheep and horses sleep very little because their diets require almost constant foraging for food in more dangerous open grasslands.

Four Sleep Theories

How do scientists explain our shared need for sleep? There are four key theories:

1. **Adaptation/protection theory** Sleep evolved because animals need to conserve energy and protect themselves from predators that are more active at night (Acerbi & Nunn, 2011; Drew, 2013; Siegel, 2008; Tsoukalas, 2012). As you can see in **Figure 5.3**, animals with the highest need to feed themselves and the lowest ability to hide tend to sleep the least.

2. **Repair/restoration theory** Sleep helps us recuperate from the depleting effects of daily waking activities. Essential chemicals and bodily tissues are repaired or replenished while we sleep. We recover not only from physical fatigue but also from emotional and intellectual demands (Colrain, 2011). When deprived of REM sleep, most people "catch up" later by spending more time than usual in this state (the so-called REM rebound), which further supports this theory.

3. **Growth/development theory** The percentage of deepest sleep (Stage 4) changes over the life span and coincides with changes in the structure and organization of the brain, as well as the release of growth hormones from the pituitary gland—particularly in children. As we age, our brains change less, and we release fewer of these hormones, grow less, and sleep less.

4. **Learning/memory theory** Sleep is important for learning and the consolidation, storage, and maintenance of memories (Fenn & Hambrick, 2012; Inostroza et al., 2013; Payne et al., 2012; Sara, 2010). This is particularly true for REM sleep, which increases after periods of stress or intense learning. For example, fetuses, infants, and young children, who generally are learning more than adults, spend far more of their sleep time in REM sleep **(Figure 5.4)**.

Adaptation/protection theory of sleep The theory that sleep evolved to conserve energy and provide protection from predators.

Repair/restoration theory of sleep The theory that sleep allows organisms to repair or recuperate from depleting daily waking activities.

Growth/development theory of sleep The theory that deep sleep (Stage 4) is correlated with physical development, including changes in the structure and organization of the brain; infants spend far more time in Stage 4 sleep than adults.

Learning/memory theory of sleep The theory that sleep is important for learning and for the consolidation, storage, and maintenance of memories.

FIGURE 5.4 AGING AND THE SLEEP CYCLE

Our biological need for sleep changes throughout our life span. The pie charts in this figure show the relative amounts of REM sleep, NREM sleep, and awake time the average person experiences as an infant, an adult, and an elderly person.

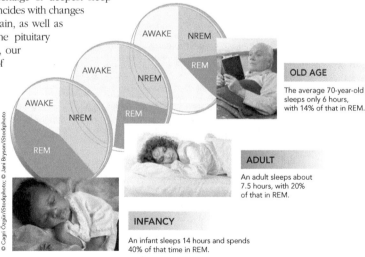

OLD AGE

The average 70-year-old sleeps only 6 hours, with 14% of that in REM.

ADULT

An adult sleeps about 7.5 hours, with 20% of that in REM.

INFANCY

An infant sleeps 14 hours and spends 40% of that time in REM.

From top to bottom: Glow Wellness/Getty Images, Inc.; © Cagri Özgür/iStockphoto; © Jani Bryson/iStockphoto

Wish-fulfillment view of dreams The Freudian belief that dreams provide an outlet for unacceptable desires.

Latent content of dreams According to Freud, a dream's unconscious, hidden meaning transformed into symbols within the dream's manifest content (story line).

Manifest content of dreams In Freudian dream analysis, the "surface," or remembered, story line, which contains symbols that mask the dream's latent content (the true meaning).

Activation–synthesis hypothesis of dreams The perspective that dreams are by-products of random stimulation of brain cells, which the brain attempts to combine (or synthesize) into coherent patterns, known as dreams.

Cognitive view of dreams The perspective that dreams are a type of information processing that help interpret daily experiences and organize them into memories.

Three Dream Theories

Now let's look at three theories of why we dream—and whether dreams carry special meaning or information.

One of the oldest and most scientifically controversial explanations for why we dream is Freud's **wish-fulfillment view**. Freud proposed that unacceptable desires, which are reportedly normally repressed, rise to the surface of consciousness during dreaming. We avoid anxiety, Freud believed, by disguising our forbidden unconscious needs (what Freud called the dream's **latent content**) as symbols (**manifest content**). For example, a journey supposedly symbolizes death; horseback riding and dancing could symbolize sexual intercourse; and a gun might represent a penis.

Most modern scientific research does not support Freud's view (Domhoff, 2004; Dufresne, 2007; Siegel, 2010). Critics also say that Freud's theory is highly subjective and that the symbols can be interpreted according to the particular analyst's view or training.

In contrast to Freud, a biological view called the **activation–synthesis hypothesis** suggests that dreams are a by-product of random stimulation of brain cells during REM sleep (Hobson, 1999, 2005; Wamsley & Stickgold, 2010). Alan Hobson and Robert McCarley (1977) proposed that specific neurons in the brain stem fire spontaneously during REM sleep and that the cortex struggles to "synthesize," or make sense of, this random stimulation by manufacturing dreams. This is *not* to say that dreams are totally meaningless. Hobson (1999, 2005) suggests that even if our dreams begin with essentially random brain activity, our individual personalities, motivations, memories, and life experiences guide how our brains construct the dream.

Finally, some researchers support the **cognitive view of dreams**, which suggests that dreams are simply another type of information processing. That is, our dreams help us organize and interpret our everyday, waking experiences and thoughts into memories. For example, some research reports strong similarities between dream content and waking thoughts, fears, and concerns (Domhoff, 2005, 2007, 2010; Erlacher & Schredl, 2004).

Gender Differences and Similarities

Men and women tend to share many of the common dream themes shown in **Table 5.1.** But women are more likely to report dreams of children, family members and other familiar people, household objects, and indoor events. In contrast, men tend to report dreams about strangers, violence, weapons, sexual activity, achievement, and outdoor events (Blume-Marcovici, 2010; Domhoff, 2003, 2007, 2010; Schredl, 2012). (As a critical thinker, can you see how attitudes toward "proper" male and female gender roles, like caring for children, sex, weapons, and violence, might have affected what the participants were willing to report?)

TABLE 5.1	TOP TEN COMMON DREAM THEMES

1. Being attacked or pursued
2. Falling
3. Sexual experiences
4. Being lost
5. Being paralyzed
6. Flying
7. Being naked in public
8. School, teachers, studying
9. Arriving too late
10. Death of close people or dead people as alive

Best View Stock /Getty Images, Inc.

Sources: Griffith, Miyagi, & Tago, 1958/2009; Nielsen et al., 2003; Schredl, 2010; Yu, 2012.

Culture and Dreams

Dreams about basic human needs and fears (like sex, aggression, and death) seem to be found in all cultures. Children around the world often dream about large, threatening monsters or wild animals. In addition, dreams around the world typically include more misfortune than good fortune, and the dreamer is more often the victim of aggression than the cause of it (Chang, 2012; Domhoff, 2003, 2007, 2010; Honig & Nealis, 2012; Yu, 2012).

Sleep–Wake Disorders

In any given year, an estimated 40 million Americans suffer from chronic sleep disorders, and another 30 million experience occasional sleep disorders serious enough to disrupt their daily activity (Purves & Piatt, 2012).

Judging by these statistics, and your own experiences, it's not surprising to learn that almost everyone has difficulty sleeping at some point in his or her lifetime. The most common or serious of these disorders are summarized in **Table 5.2**.

Although it's normal to have trouble sleeping before an exciting event, as many as 1 person in 10 may suffer from **insomnia**, and they experience persistent difficulty falling asleep or staying asleep or wakes up too early. Nearly everybody has insomnia at some time (Bastien, 2011; Colrain, 2011; Morin et al., 2013); a telltale sign is feeling poorly rested the next day. Most people with serious insomnia have other medical or psychological disorders as well (American Psychiatric Association, 2013; Boland & Alloy, 2013; Van Der Kloet, 2013).

Insomnia A sleep disorder characterized by persistent problems falling asleep, staying asleep, or awakening too early.

TABLE 5.2	SLEEP-WAKE DISORDERS
Label	**Characteristics**
Insomnia	Persistent difficulty falling asleep, maintaining sleep, or waking up too early
Narcolepsy	Sudden, irresistible onset of sleep during waking hours, characterized by sudden sleep attacks while standing, talking, or even driving
Breathing-Related Sleep Disorder (Sleep apnea)	Repeated interruption of breathing during sleep, causing loud snoring or poor-quality sleep and excessive daytime sleepiness
Nightmare	Bad dream that significantly disrupts REM sleep
NREM Sleep Arousal Disorder (Sleep terror)	Abrupt awakening with feelings of panic that significantly disrupts NREM sleep

realworldpsychology **The Hazards of Sleep Medication** To cope with insomnia, many people turn to nonprescription, over-the-counter sleeping pills, which generally don't work. In contrast, prescription tranquilizers and barbiturates do help people sleep, but they decrease Stage 4 and REM sleep, seriously affecting sleep quality. In the short term, limited use of drugs such as Ambien, Dalmane, Xanax, Halcion, and Lunesta may be helpful in treating sleep problems related to anxiety and acute, stressful situations. However, chronic users run the risk of psychological and physical drug dependence (Abadinsky, 2014; Farber & Banks, 2013). The hormone *melatonin* may provide a safer alternative. Some research suggests that taking even a relatively small dose (just .3 to .4 milligrams) can help people fall asleep and stay asleep (Brzezinski et al., 2005; Gooneratne et al., 2012).

Africa Studio/Shutterstock

Fortunately, there are many effective strategies for alleviating sleep problems without medication. For example, did you know that using a computer right before you try to fall asleep can make it harder to sleep (Wood et al., 2012)? Exposure to light from the electronic screens of a computer or an iPad reduces the level of melatonin in the body by about 22%, which makes it more difficult to fall asleep (especially for teenagers). See the following *Psychology and You* section for other recommendations about getting and staying asleep.

NATURAL SLEEP AIDS
psychology and you

Are you wondering what research recommends for sleep problems? Behavior therapy offers consistent benefits that you can apply in your own life (Constantino et al., 2007; Smith et al., 2005). For example, when you're having a hard time going to sleep, don't keep checking the clock and worrying about your loss of sleep. Instead, remove all TVs, stereos, and books and limit the use of your bedroom to sleep rather than to reading, watching movies, checking e-mail, and the like. If you need additional help, try some of the following suggestions.

During the Day

Exercise. Daily physical activity works away tension. But don't exercise vigorously late in the day, or you'll get fired up instead.

Keep regular hours. An erratic schedule can disrupt biological rhythms. Get up at the same time each day.

Avoid stimulants. Coffee, tea, soft drinks, chocolate, and some medications contain caffeine. Nicotine may be an even more potent sleep disrupter.

Avoid late meals and heavy drinking. Overindulgence can interfere with your normal sleep pattern.

Stop worrying. Focus on your problems at a set time earlier in the day.

Use presleep rituals. Follow the same routine every evening: listen to music, write in a diary, meditate.

Practice yoga. These gentle exercises help you relax.

In Bed

Use progressive muscle relaxation. Alternately tense and relax various muscle groups.

Use fantasies. Imagine yourself in a tranquil setting. Feel yourself relax.

Use deep breathing. Take deep breaths, telling yourself you're falling asleep.

Try a warm bath. This can induce drowsiness because it sends blood away from the brain to the skin surface.

Narcolepsy The sudden and irresistible compulsion to sleep during the daytime. (*Narco* means "numbness," and *lepsy* means "seizure.")

Sleep apnea A sleep disorder of the upper respiratory system that causes a repeated interruption of breathing during sleep; it also leads to loud snoring or poor-quality sleep and excessive daytime sleepiness.

Narcolepsy, a sleep disorder characterized by sudden and irresistible onsets of sleep during normal waking hours, afflicts about 1 person in 2,000 and generally runs in families (Kotagal & Kumar, 2013; Pedrazzoli et al., 2007; Raggi et al., 2011). During an attack, REM-like sleep suddenly intrudes into the waking state of consciousness. Victims may experience sudden, incapacitating attacks of muscle weakness or paralysis (known as cataplexy). They may even fall asleep while walking, talking, or driving a car. Although long naps each day and stimulant or antidepressant drugs can help reduce the frequency of attacks, both the causes and cure of narcolepsy are still unknown **(Figure 5.5)**.

Perhaps the most serious sleep disorder is **sleep apnea**. People with sleep apnea may fail to breathe for a minute or longer and then wake up gasping for breath. When they do breathe during their sleep, they often snore. Sleep apnea seems to result from blocked upper airway passages or from the brain's ceasing to send signals to the diaphragm, thus causing breathing to stop.

Unfortunately, people with sleep apnea are often unaware they have this disorder, and fail to understand how their repeated awakenings during the night leave them feeling tired and sleepy during the day. More importantly, they should know that sleep apnea can lead to high blood pressure, stroke, cancer, depression, and heart attack

FIGURE 5.5 **NARCOLEPSY**

Research on specially bred narcoleptic dogs has found degenerated neurons in certain areas of the brain (Siegel, 2000). Whether human narcolepsy results from similar degeneration is a question for future research. Note how this hungry puppy has lapsed suddenly from alert wakefulness to deep sleep even when offered his preferred food.

(Culebras, 2012; Emdin et al., 2013; Furukawa et al., 2010; Nieto et al., 2012; Nikolaou et al., 2011; Vitulano et al., 2013; Wheaton et al., 2012).

Treatment for sleep apnea depends partly on its severity. If the problem occurs only when you're sleeping on your back, sewing tennis balls to the back of your pajama top may help remind you to sleep on your side. Because obstruction of the breathing passages is related to obesity and heavy alcohol use (Roehrs & Roth, 2012; Sarkhosh et al., 2013), dieting and alcohol restriction are often recommended. For other sleepers, surgery, dental appliances that reposition the tongue, or machines that provide a stream of air to keep the airway open may provide help.

Recent findings suggest that even "simple" snoring (without the breathing stoppage characteristic of sleep apnea) can lead to heart disease and possible death (Jones & Benca, 2013; Li et al., 2012). Although occasional mild snoring is fairly normal, chronic snoring is a possible warning sign that should prompt people to seek help.

Two additional abnormal sleep disturbances are **nightmares** and **sleep terrors (Figure 5.6)**. *Sleepwalking*, which sometimes accompanies sleep terrors, usually occurs during NREM sleep. (Recall that large muscles are paralyzed during REM sleep, which explains why sleepwalking normally occurs during NREM sleep.) An estimated 4% of U.S. adults—meaning over 8 million people—have at least one episode of sleepwalking each year (Ohayon et al., 2012). *Sleeptalking* can occur during any stage of sleep, but it appears to arise most commonly during NREM sleep. It can consist of single indistinct words or long, articulate sentences. It is even possible to engage some sleep talkers in a limited conversation.

Nightmares, sleep terrors, sleepwalking, and sleeptalking are all more common among young children, but they can also occur in adults, usually during times of stress or major life events (Hiscock & Darvey, 2013; Hobson & Silvestri, 1999). Patience and soothing reassurance at the time of the sleep disruption are usually the only treatment recommended for both children and adults.

Nightmares Anxiety-arousing dreams that generally occur near the end of the sleep cycle, during REM sleep.

Sleep terrors Abrupt awakenings from NREM (non-rapid-eye-movement) sleep accompanied by intense physiological arousal and feelings of panic.

FIGURE 5.6 **NIGHTMARE OR SLEEP TERROR?**

Nightmares, or bad dreams, occur toward the end of the sleep cycle, during REM sleep. Less common but more frightening are sleep terrors, which occur early in the cycle, during Stage 3 or Stage 4 of NREM sleep. Like the child in this photo, the sleeper may sit bolt upright, screaming and sweating, walk around, and talk incoherently and may be almost impossible to awaken.

RETRIEVAL PRACTICE: CONSCIOUSNESS, SLEEP, AND DREAMING

Self-Test

Completing this self-test and comparing your answers with those in Appendix B provides immediate feedback and helpful practice for exams. Additional interactive, self-tests are available at www.wiley.com/college/huffman.

1. *Consciousness* is defined as _____.

   a. ordinary and extraordinary wakefulness

   b. an organism's awareness of internal events and of the external environment

   c. mental representations of the world in the here and now

   d. any mental state that requires thinking and processing of sensory stimuli

2. *Circadian rhythms* are _____.

   a. patterns that repeat themselves on a twice-daily schedule

   b. physical and mental changes associated with the cycle of the moon

   c. rhythmical processes in your brain

   d. biological changes that occur on a 24- to 25-hour cycle

3. The sleep stage marked by irregular breathing, eye movements, high-frequency brain waves, and dreaming is called _____ sleep.

   a. beta

   b. hypnologic

   c. REM

   d. transitional

4. The _____ theory says that sleep allows us to replenish what was depleted during daytime activities.

   a. repair/restoration

   b. evolutionary/circadian

   c. supply-demand

   d. conservation of energy

Think Critically

1 How are you affected by sleep deprivation and disruption of your circadian rhythms?

2 Which of the major theories of dreaming best explains your own dreams?

realworldpsychology

Can getting too little sleep increase your risk of getting a cold?

Can using a computer or an iPad late at night make it harder to fall asleep?

HINT: LOOK IN THE MARGIN FOR AND

PSYCHOACTIVE DRUGS

LEARNING OBJECTIVES

RETRIEVAL PRACTICE While reading the upcoming sections, respond to each Learning Objective in your own words. Then compare your responses with those found at www.wiley.com/college/huffman.

1 **EXPLAIN** how psychoactive drugs affect nervous system functioning.

2 **COMPARE** the four major categories of psychoactive drugs.

3 **DESCRIBE** the effects of club drugs on the nervous system.

Psychoactive drug A chemical that changes mental processes and conscious awareness, mood, and/or perception.

Agonist drug A drug that binds to a receptor and triggers a response in the cell, which mimics or enhances a neurotransmitter's effect.

Antagonist drug A drug that binds to a receptor and triggers a response in the cell, which blocks a neurotransmitter's effect.

Have you noticed how difficult it is to have a logical, nonemotional discussion about drugs? In our society, where the most popular **psychoactive drugs** are caffeine, tobacco, and ethyl alcohol, people often become defensive when these drugs are grouped with illicit drugs such as marijuana and cocaine. Similarly, marijuana users are disturbed that their drug of choice is grouped with "hard" drugs like heroin. Most scientists believe that there are good and bad uses of all drugs. The way drug use differs from drug abuse and how chemical alterations in consciousness affect a person, psychologically and physically, are important topics in psychology.

Alcohol, for example, has a diffuse effect on neural membranes throughout the nervous system. Most psychoactive drugs, however, act in a more specific way: by either enhancing a particular neurotransmitter's effect, as does an **agonist drug**, or inhibiting it, as does an **antagonist drug** (**Figure 5.7**).

Drugs

Agonist Drugs
(Enhance synaptic transmission)

Antagonist Drugs
(Inhibit synaptic transmission)

1 Synthesis, storage, and release

Neurotransmitter molecule

Sending neuron

Receiving neuron

Agonist drugs increase the neuron's ability to synthesize more transmitter molecules, store them more securely, or release them.

Leakage

Sending neuron

Receiving neuron

Antagonist drugs decrease the neuron's ability to synthesize, store, and release neurotransmitters.

2 Binding

Neurotransmitter molecule

Agonist drug molecule

Receiving neuron — Receptor binding site

Agonist drugs have shapes similar to that of some neurotransmitters, which allow them to bind with the receptor sites and mimic the neurotransmitter's message.

Neurotransmitter molecule

Antagonist drug molecule

Receiving neuron — Receptor binding site

Antagonist drugs bind with the receptor sites. However, the molecular shape of the drug is dissimilar enough to the neurotransmitter that its message is blocked.

3 Deactivation

Reuptake blocked by agonist drug molecule

Sending neuron

Receiving neuron

Agonist drugs block the deactivation of excess neurotransmitters by preventing reuptake or degradation. This blockage allows excess neurotransmitter molecules to remain in the synapse and thereby prolong activation of the receptor site.

?

No known deactivation effect with antagonist drugs

FIGURE 5.7 HOW DO AGONIST AND ANTAGONIST DRUGS PRODUCE THEIR PSYCHOACTIVE EFFECTS?

Most psychoactive drugs produce their mood, energy, and perception-altering effects by changing the body's supply of neurotransmitters. Note how they can alter the synthesis, storage, or release of neurotransmitters ❶. They also can change the neurotransmitters' effects on the receiving site of the receptor neuron ❷. After neurotransmitters carry their messages across the synapse, the sending neuron normally deactivates the excess, or leftover, neurotransmitter ❸. However, when agonist drugs block this process, excess neurotransmitters remain in the synapse, which prolongs the effect of the psychoactive drug.

Is drug abuse the same as drug addiction? The term **drug abuse** generally refers to drug taking that causes emotional or physical harm to oneself or others. Drug consumption among abusers is also typically compulsive, frequent, and intense. **Addiction** is a broad term that refers to a condition in which a person feels compelled to use a specific drug or almost any type of compulsive activity, from working to surfing the Internet (Potenza, 2013; Ross et al., 2010). In fact, the latest version of the *Diagnostic and Statistical Manual (DSM-5)*, which officially classifies mental disorders, now includes *gambling disorders* as part of their substance-related and addictive disorders category. But other disorders, like "sex addiction" or "exercise addiction" were not included due to insufficient evidence at this time (American Psychiatric Association, 2013).

Interestingly, some evidence shows that we can become addicted to Facebook and that risky trading in financial markets can create a high indistinguishable from that experienced in drug addiction (Andreassen et al., 2012; Zweig, 2007). Researchers in one study prompted people with a series of statements, such as "You feel an urge to use Facebook more and more," and "You become restless or troubled if you are prohibited from using Facebook" (Andreassen et al., 2012). The degree to which you agree with items like these may indicate that you are addicted, meaning that you feel unreasonably compelled to check and use Facebook throughout the day.

In addition to distinguishing between drug abuse and addiction, many researchers use the term **psychological dependence** to refer to the mental desire or craving to achieve a drug's effects, whereas **physical dependence** describes changes in bodily processes that make a drug necessary for minimum daily functioning. Physical dependence appears most clearly when the drug is withheld and the user undergoes **withdrawal** reactions, including physical pain and intense cravings.

Drug abuse Drug taking that causes emotional or physical harm to the drug user or others.

Addiction A broad term that describes a condition in which the body requires a drug (or specific activity) in order to function without physical and psychological reactions to its absence; it is often the outcome of tolerance and dependence.

Psychological dependence The psychological desire or craving to achieve a drug's effect.

Physical dependence The changes in bodily processes that make a drug necessary for minimal functioning.

Q3

Withdrawal The discomfort and distress, including physical pain and intense cravings, experienced after stopping the use of an addictive drug.

Keep in mind that psychological dependence is no less damaging than physical dependence. The craving in psychological dependence can be strong enough to keep the user in a constant drug-induced state—and to lure an addict back to a drug habit long after he or she has overcome physical dependence. After repeated use of a drug, many of the body's physiological processes adjust to higher and higher levels of the drug, producing a decreased sensitivity called **tolerance**.

Tolerance leads many users to escalate their drug use and experiment with other drugs in an attempt to re-create the original pleasurable altered state. Sometimes using one drug increases tolerance for another, a result known as *cross-tolerance*. Developing tolerance or cross-tolerance does not prevent drugs from seriously damaging the brain, heart, liver, and other organs.

Tolerance The bodily adjustment to continued use of a drug in which the drug user requires greater dosages to achieve the same effect.

Four Drug Categories

Psychologists divide psychoactive drugs into four broad categories: depressants, stimulants, opiates, and hallucinogens **(Table 5.3)**.

TABLE 5.3	EFFECTS OF THE MAJOR PSYCHOACTIVE DRUGS

	Category	Desired Effects	Undesirable Effects
RICHARD NOWITZ/NG Image Collection	**Depressants (sedatives)** Alcohol, barbiturates, anxiolytics, also known as antianxiety drugs or tranquilizers (Xanax), Rohypnol (roofies), Ketamine (Special K), Gamma-hydroxybutyrate (GHB)	Tension reduction, euphoria, disinhibition, drowsiness, muscle relaxation	Anxiety, nausea, disorientation, impaired reflexes and motor functioning, amnesia, loss of consciousness, shallow respiration, convulsions, coma, death
TAYLOR S. KENNEDY/NG Image Collection	**Stimulants** Cocaine, amphetamine, methamphetamine (crystal meth), MDMA (Ecstasy)	Exhilaration, euphoria, high physical and mental energy, reduced appetite, perceptions of power, sociability	Irritability, anxiety, sleeplessness, paranoia, hallucinations, psychosis, elevated blood pressure and body temperature, convulsions, death
	Caffeine	Increased alertness	Insomnia, restlessness, increased pulse rate, mild delirium, ringing in the ears, rapid heartbeat
SAM ABELL/NG Image Collection	Nicotine	Relaxation, increased alertness, sociability	Irritability, increased blood pressure, stomach pains, vomiting, dizziness, cancer, heart disease, emphysema
Uwe Schmid/OKAPIA/ Photo Researchers	**Opiates (Narcotics)** Morphine, heroin, codeine, oxycodone	Euphoria, "rush" of pleasure, pain relief, prevention of withdrawal discomfort, sleep	Nausea, vomiting, constipation, painful withdrawal, shallow respiration, convulsions, coma, death
JOEL SARTORE/NG Image Collection	**Hallucinogens (Psychedelics)** Lysergic acid diethylamide (LSD), mescaline (extract from the peyote cactus), psilocybin (extract from mushrooms)	Heightened aesthetic responses, euphoria, mild delusions, hallucinations, distorted perceptions and sensation	Panic, nausea, longer and more extreme delusions, hallucinations, perceptual distortions ("bad trips"), psychosis
	Marijuana	Relaxation, mild euphoria, nausea relief	Perceptual and sensory distortions, hallucinations, fatigue, increased appetite, lack of motivation, paranoia, possible psychosis

| TABLE 5.4 | ALCOHOL'S EFFECT ON THE BODY AND BEHAVIOR | |

Number of drinks[a] in two hours	Blood alcohol (content (%)[b]	Effect
(2)	0.05	Relaxed state; increased sociability
(3)	0.08	Everyday stress lessened
(4)	0.10	Movements and speech become clumsy
(7)	0.20	Very drunk; loud and difficult to understand; emotions unstable
(12)	0.40	Difficult to wake up; incapable of voluntary action
(15)	0.50	Coma and/or death

McPHOTO/Blickwinkel/Age Fotostock America, Inc.

[a]A drink refers to one 12-ounce beer, a 4-ounce glass of wine, or a 1.25-ounce shot of hard liquor.
[b]In America, the legal blood alcohol level for "drunk driving" varies from 0.05 to 0.12.

Depressants, sometimes called "downers," act on the central nervous system to suppress or slow bodily processes and to reduce overall responsiveness. Because tolerance and both physical and psychological dependence are rapidly acquired with these drugs, there is strong potential for abuse.

Although alcohol is primarily a depressant, at low doses it has stimulating effects, thus explaining its reputation as a "party drug." As consumption increases, symptoms of drunkenness appear. Alcohol's effects are determined primarily by the amount that reaches the brain **(Table 5.4)**. Because the liver breaks down alcohol at the rate of about 1 ounce per hour, the number of drinks and the speed of consumption are both very important. People can die after drinking large amounts of alcohol in a short period of time **(Figure 5.8)**. In addition, men's bodies are more efficient than women's at breaking down alcohol. Even after accounting for differences in size and muscle-to-fat ratio, women have a higher blood-alcohol level than men following equal doses of alcohol.

Alcohol should not be combined with any other drug; combining alcohol and barbiturates—both depressants—is particularly dangerous. Together, they can relax the diaphragm muscles to such a degree that the person suffocates.

Does this information surprise you? Take the quiz in *Psychology and You* to discover if some of your other ideas about alcohol are really misconceptions.

Depressant A drug that decreases bodily processes and overall responsiveness.

FIGURE 5.8 **ALCOHOL IS FAR TOO OFTEN FATAL**

On November 2, 2012, 19-year-old David Bogenberger, a finance major at Northern Illinois University, died of alcohol poisoning following hazing activities at his fraternity, Pi Kappa Alpha. His blood alcohol concentration was .35, which is five times the legal limit for driving in Illinois. Twenty-two members of his fraternity have been charged in his death.

Stimulant A drug that increases overall activity and general responsiveness.

Depressants suppress central nervous system activity, whereas **stimulants**, or "uppers," increase the overall activity and responsiveness of the central nervous system.

Cocaine is a powerful central nervous system stimulant extracted from the leaves of the coca plant. It produces feelings of alertness, euphoria, well-being, power, energy, and pleasure. But it also acts as an *agonist drug* to block the reuptake of our body's natural neurotransmitters that produce these same effects **(Figure 5.9)**.

Although cocaine was once considered a relatively harmless "recreational drug," even small initial doses can be fatal because cocaine interferes with the electrical system of the heart, causing irregular heartbeats and, in some cases, heart failure. It also can produce heart attacks, hypertension, and strokes by temporarily constricting blood vessels (Abadinsky, 2014; Kontak & Vongpatanasin, 2013; NIDA, 2010; Vidal et al., 2012), as well as cognitive declines and brain atrophy (Ersche et al., 2012). The most dangerous form of cocaine is the smokable, concentrated version known as "crack," or "rock." Its lower price makes it affordable and attractive to a large audience. And its greater potency makes it more highly addictive.

FIGURE 5.9 COCAINE: AN AGONIST DRUG IN ACTION

A The two figures depict how after releasing neurotransmitter into the synapse, the sending neuron normally reabsorbs (or reuptakes) excess neurotransmitter back into the terminal buttons.

Todd Gipstein//NG Image Collection

B This figure shows that when cocaine is present in the synapse, it will block the reuptake of dopamine, serotonin, and norepinephrine, and levels of these substances will increase. The result is overstimulation and a brief euphoric high. When the drug wears off, the depletion of neurotransmitters may cause the drug user to "crash."

Even legal stimulants can lead to serious problems. For example, the U.S. Public Health Service considers cigarette smoking the single most preventable cause of death and disease in the United States (Pearson et al., 2013). Researchers have found that nicotine activates the same brain areas as cocaine (Dandekar et al., 2011; David et al., 2013; Tronci & Balfour, 2011). Nicotine's effects—relaxation, increased alertness, and diminished pain and appetite—are so powerfully reinforcing that some people continue to smoke even after having a cancerous lung removed.

Opiates, or narcotics, which are derived from the opium poppy, are used medically to relieve pain (Connolly et al., 2013; Dalal & Bruera, 2013) because they mimic the brain's natural endorphins (Chapter 2), which numb pain and elevate mood. This creates a dangerous pathway to drug abuse, however. After repeated flooding with artificial opiates, the brain eventually reduces or stops the production of its own opiates. If the user later attempts to stop, the brain lacks both the artificial and normal level of painkilling chemicals, and withdrawal becomes excruciatingly painful **(Figure 5.10)**.

So far, we have discussed three of the four types of psychoactive drugs: depressants, stimulants, and opiates. One of the most intriguing alterations of consciousness comes from **hallucinogens**, drugs that produce sensory or perceptual distortions, including visual, auditory, and kinesthetic hallucinations. Some cultures have used hallucinogens for religious purposes, as a way to experience "other realities" or to communicate with the supernatural. In Western societies, most people use hallucinogens for their reported "mind-expanding" potential.

Hallucinogens are commonly referred to as *psychedelics* (from the Greek for "mind manifesting"). They include mescaline (derived from the peyote cactus), psilocybin (derived from mushrooms), phencyclidine (chemically derived), and LSD (lysergic acid diethylamide, derived from ergot, a rye mold).

LSD, or "acid," produces dramatic alterations in sensation and perception, including an altered sense of time, synesthesia (blending of the senses), and spiritual experiences. Perhaps because the LSD experience is so powerful, few people "drop acid" on a regular basis. Nevertheless, LSD can be an extremely dangerous drug. Bad LSD "trips" can be terrifying and may lead to accidents, deaths, or suicide. One 32-year-old man, with no known psychiatric disorder, intentionally removed his own testes after the first and single use of LSD combined with alcohol (Blacha et al., 2013)!

Marijuana, also called cannabis, is classified as a hallucinogen even though it has some properties of a depressant—it induces drowsiness and lethargy—and some of a narcotic—it acts as a weak painkiller. In low doses, marijuana produces mild euphoria; moderate doses lead to an intensification of sensory experiences and the illusion that time is passing slowly. High doses may produce hallucinations, delusions, and distortions of body image (Abadinsky, 2014; Gorelick et al., 2013; Hart & Ksir, 2013). The active ingredient in marijuana is THC, or tetrahydrocannabinol, which attaches to receptors that are abundant throughout the brain.

Kevin Winter/Getty Images

The High Cost of Drug Abuse

In July 2013, Cory Monteith, a 31-year-old actor who starred in the television show "Glee," died of an accidental overdose of heroin and alcohol. He struggled with addiction for years, and had recently undergone treatment for substance abuse addiction.

Opiate A drug derived from opium that numbs the senses and relieves pain.

Hallucinogen A drug that produces sensory or perceptual distortions.

FIGURE 5.10 HOW OPIATES CREATE PHYSICAL DEPENDENCE

Psychoactive drugs such as opiates affect the brain and body in a variety of ways.

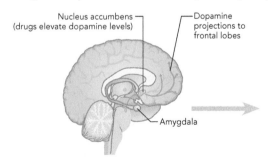

Nucleus accumbens (drugs elevate dopamine levels)

Dopamine projections to frontal lobes

Amygdala

Ⓐ Most researchers believe that increased dopamine activity in this so-called *reward pathway* of the brain accounts for the reinforcing effects of most addictive drugs.

Jim Varney/Science Photo Library/Photo Researchers, Inc.

Ⓑ Absence of the drug triggers withdrawal symptoms (e.g., intense pain and cravings).

Voices from the Classroom

Exercise, Marijuana, and Chocolate When discussing the benefits of exercise for stress relief, and the role of endorphins, I ask my students if they've heard the term "anandamide." Almost everyone say no. They're surprised to learn that it's a naturally produced neurotransmitter, like endorphins, which is released during exercise. And I tell them about a recent study that found male athletes who warmed up and cooled down and exercised for 45 minutes at 70% effort increased their anandamide release by 80%. They're even more surprised when I explain that anandamides bind to the same brain receptors as do the cannabinoid (THC/ marijuana) molecules. In that dark chocolate also has been found to promote anandamide release, I conclude the discussion by providing dark chocolate for the entire class.

Professor Jan Mendoza
Golden West College
Huntington Beach, California

Some research has found marijuana to be therapeutic in treating glaucoma (an eye disease), alleviating the nausea and vomiting associated with chemotherapy, and dealing with other health problems (Borgelt et al., 2013; Green & De-Vries, 2010; Hart & Ksir, 2013).

Chronic marijuana use, however, can lead to throat and respiratory disorders, impaired lung functioning and immune response, declines in testosterone levels, reduced sperm count, and disruption of the menstrual cycle and ovulation (Hall & Degenhardt, 2010; Karavolos et al., 2013; Rooke et al., 2013; Skinner et al., 2011).

Marijuana use can also lead to decreases in IQ. Researchers in one study examined IQ in a sample of more than 1,000 13-year-olds and then retested their IQs 25 years later (Meier et al., 2012). Findings revealed that teenagers who started smoking marijuana before age 18 and were addicted to this drug by age 38 showed decreases in IQ points, including drops of as much as 8 points for those who reported the heaviest use. Although some research supports the popular belief that marijuana serves as a "gateway" to other illegal drugs, other studies find little or no connection (Hart & Ksir, 2013; Kirisci et al., 2013; Panlilio et al., 2013).

Marijuana also can be habit forming, but few users experience the intense cravings associated with cocaine or opiates. Withdrawal symptoms are mild because the drug dissolves in the body's fat and leaves the body very slowly, which explains why a marijuana user can test positive for days or weeks after the last use.

Club Drugs

As you can see in **Figure 5.11**, and may know from television or newspapers, psychoactive drugs like Rohypnol (the "date rape drug," also called "roofies") and MDMA (3,4-methylenedioxymethylamphetamine, or "ecstasy") are among our nation's most popular drugs of abuse. Other "club" drugs, like GHB (gamma-hydroxybutyrate), Ketamine ("special K"), methamphetamine ("ice" or "crystal meth"), and LSD, are also gaining in popularity (DeMaria, 2012; Hopfer, 2011; Shimane et al., 2013; van Laar, 2012). However, these drugs can have very serious consequences. For example, recreational use of "ecstasy" is associated with a reduction in the neurotransmitter serotonin in the brain, which can lead to problems regulating mood, appetite, sleep, learning, memory, and even death (Di Iorio et al., 2012).

One of the most threatening recent trends in club drugs is the swallowing, injecting, or snorting of synthetic stimulants, called "bath salts," which are currently legally sold in small packets. Although marked "not for human ingestion," they are increasingly popular among those associated with the dance music scene. Widely available on the Internet and marketed with enticing names such as "White Lightning" or "Lovey Dovey," these bath salts produce cocaine or ecstasy-like effects. But they're far more toxic. Following reports of cases like Neil Brown, who slit his face and stomach repeatedly with a skinning knife, and numerous overdoses or deaths, several states now ban their sale (Baumann et al., 2013; Oz, 2011; Winder et al., 2013).

In addition, club drugs, like all illicit drugs, are particularly dangerous because there are no truth-in-packaging laws to protect buyers from unscrupulous practices. Sellers often substitute unknown cheaper, and possibly even more dangerous, substances for the ones they claim to be selling. Also, club drugs (like most psychoactive drugs) affect the motor coordination, perceptual skills, and reaction time necessary for safe driving.

Impaired decision making is a serious problem as well. Just as "drinking and driving don't mix," club drug use may lead to risky sexual behaviors and increased risk of sexually transmitted infections. Add in the fact that some drugs, like Rohypnol, are odorless, colorless, tasteless, and can easily be added to beverages by individuals who want to intoxicate or sedate others, and you can see that the dangers of club drug use go far beyond the drug itself.

FIGURE 5.11 **BEWARE OF CLUB DRUGS**

Although club drugs can produce initially desirable effects, such as MDMA's reported feelings of great empathy and connectedness with others, almost all psychoactive drugs can cause serious health problems—in some cases, even death (Chamberlin & Saper, 2009; Jaehne et al., 2011; National Institute on Drug Abuse, 2012).

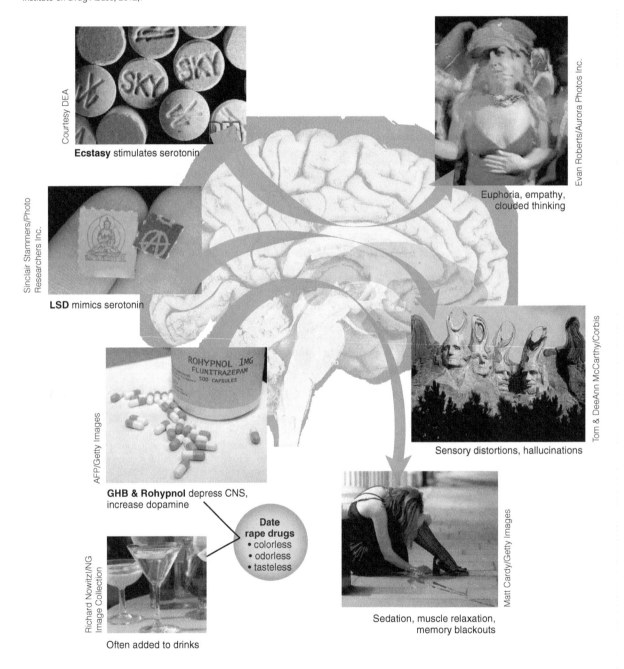

Courtesy DEA

Ecstasy stimulates serotonin

Evan Roberts/Aurora Photos Inc.

Euphoria, empathy, clouded thinking

Sinclair Stammers/Photo Researchers Inc.

LSD mimics serotonin

Tom & DeeAnn McCarthy/Corbis

Sensory distortions, hallucinations

AFP/Getty Images

GHB & Rohypnol depress CNS, increase dopamine

Date rape drugs
- colorless
- odorless
- tasteless

Richard Nowitz/ING Image Collection

Often added to drinks

Matt Cardy/Getty Images

Sedation, muscle relaxation, memory blackouts

RETRIEVAL PRACTICE: PSYCHOACTIVE DRUGS

Self-Test

Completing this self-test and comparing your answers with those in Appendix B provides immediate feedback and helpful practice for exams. Additional interactive, self-tests are available at www.wiley.com/college/huffman.

1. Psychoactive drugs _____.

   a. change conscious awareness, b. are addictive, mind altering, mood, or perception and dangerous to your health
   c. are illegal unless prescribed d. all these options by a medical doctor

2. Depressants include all the following *except* _____.

   a. antianxiety drugs   b. alcohol
   c. tobacco   d. Rohypnol

3. _____ drugs inhibit normal synaptic transmission, whereas _____ drugs enhance synaptic transmission.

   a. Antagonist; agonist   b. Agonist; antagonist
   c. Protagonist; agonist   d. Protagonist; co-agonist

4. Drug taking that causes emotional or physical harm to the drug user or others is known as _____.

   a. addiction   b. physical dependence
   c. psychological dependence d. drug abuse

Think Critically

1 Which is more important in creating addiction—physical dependence or psychological dependence?

2 Do you think marijuana use should be legal? Why or why not?

realworldpsychology

Are you addicted to Facebook?

Can using marijuana decrease your IQ?

HINT: LOOK IN THE MARGIN FOR AND

MEDITATION AND HYPNOSIS

LEARNING OBJECTIVES

RETRIEVAL PRACTICE While reading the upcoming sections, respond to each Learning Objective in your own words. Then compare your responses with those found at www.wiley.com/college/huffman.

1 **DESCRIBE** the effect of meditation on the nervous system.

2 **EXPLAIN** the features of the hypnotic state.

As we have seen, factors such as sleep, dreaming, and psychoactive drug use can create altered states of consciousness. Changes in consciousness also can be achieved by means of meditation and hypnosis.

Meditation

"Suddenly, with a roar like that of a waterfall, I felt a stream of liquid light entering my brain through the spinal cord . . . I experienced a rocking sensation and then felt myself slipping out of my body, entirely enveloped in a halo of light. I felt the point of consciousness that was myself growing wider, surrounded by waves of light" (Krishna, 1999, pp. 4–5).

This is how spiritual leader Gopi Krishna described his experience with **meditation**, a group of techniques designed to focus attention, block out distractions, and produce an altered state of awareness **(Figure 5.12)**. Although most people in the beginning stages of meditation report a simpler, mellow type of relaxation followed by a mild euphoria and a sense of timelessness. Some advanced meditators report experiences of profound rapture, joy, and/or strong hallucinations.

Meditation A group of techniques designed to alter consciousness; it's believed to enhance self-knowledge and well-being through reduced self-awareness.

FIGURE 5.12 BENEFITS OF MEDITATION | *psychology and you*

A Some meditation techniques, such as tai chi and hatha yoga, include body movements and postures, while in other techniques, the meditator remains motionless, chanting or focusing on a single point, like a candle flame.

B During meditation, the hypothalamus diminishes the sympathetic response and increases the parasympathetic response. Shutting down the so-called fight-or-flight response in this way allows for deep rest, slower respiration, and overall relaxation.

Dan Dalton/Getty Images

Cerebral cortex

Attention and focus are strengthened. The cortex thickens over time.

Cerebral white matter

Frontal lobe

Amygdala

Hypothalamus

Science Pictures Limited/Photo Researchers

Top view of head

Before meditation   During meditation

C Researchers have found that an increased area of the brain responds to sensory stimuli during meditation, suggesting that meditation enhances the coordination between the brain hemispheres (Kilpatrick et al., 2011; Lyubimov, 1992). Note how much the blue-colored areas enlarged and spread from the right to the left hemisphere during meditation.

How can we explain these effects? Brain imaging studies suggest that meditation's requirement to focus attention, block out distractions, and focus on a single object, emotion, or word, reduces the number of brain cells that must be devoted to the multiple, competing tasks normally going on within the brain's frontal lobes. This narrowed focus thus explains the feelings of timelessness and mild euphoria (Cvetkovic & Cosic, 2011; Wachholtz & Austin, 2013).

Research has also verified that meditation can produce dramatic changes in basic physiological processes, including heart rate, oxygen consumption, sweat gland responses, and brain activity. In addition, it's been somewhat successful in reducing pain, anxiety, and stress; lowering blood pressure; increasing creativity, and improving overall mental health (Colzato et al., 2012; Gans et al., 2013; Gordon et al., 2013; Grant et al., 2011). As you can see in **Figures 5.12b and c**, studies have also found that meditation can change the body's sympathetic and parasympathetic responses, and increase structural support for the sensory, decision-making, emotion regulation, and attention-processing centers of the brain (Libby et al., 2012; Lo & Chang, 2013; Malinowski, 2013; Tang & Posner, 2013; Urry et al., 2012).

Interestingly, one study provided participants with eight weeks of training in meditation and examined brain activation in response to upsetting images both before and after the training (Desbordes et al., 2012). Results indicated that after training participants showed lower levels of activation in the amygdala (a part of the brain that responds to emotion), even if they were not meditating at the time.

Hypnosis

Relax . . . your eyelids are so very heavy . . . your muscles are becoming more and more relaxed . . . your breathing is becoming deeper and deeper . . . relax . . . your eyes are closing . . . let go . . . relax.

Hypnosis An alternate state of consciousness characterized by deep relaxation and a trancelike state of heightened suggestibility and intense focus.

Hypnotists use suggestions like these to begin **hypnosis**, a trance-like state of heightened suggestibility, deep relaxation, and intense focus. Once hypnotized, some people can be convinced that they are standing at the edge of the ocean, listening to the sound of the waves and feeling the ocean mist on their faces. Invited to eat a "delicious apple" that is actually an onion, the hypnotized person may relish the flavor. Told they are watching a very funny or sad movie, hypnotized people may begin to laugh or cry at their self-created visions.

From the 1700s to modern times, entertainers and quacks have used (and abused) hypnosis **(Table 5.5)**, but physicians, dentists, and therapists also have long employed it as a respected clinical tool. Modern scientific research has removed much of the mystery surrounding hypnosis. A number of features characterize the hypnotic state (Jamieson & Hasegawa, 2007; Jensen et al., 2008; Robertson, 2013):

- Narrowed, highly focused attention (ability to "tune out" competing sensory stimuli)
- Increased use of imagination and hallucinations
- A passive and receptive attitude
- Decreased responsiveness to pain
- Heightened suggestibility, or a greater willingness to respond to proposed changes in perception ("This onion is an apple")

Today, even with available anesthetics, hypnosis is occasionally used in surgery and for the treatment of cancer, chronic pain and severe burns (Jensen et al., 2008, 2011; Montgomery et al., 2013; Nusbaum et al., 2011; Smith, 2011). It has found its best use in medical areas such as dentistry and childbirth, where patients have a high

TABLE 5.5	HYPNOSIS MYTHS AND FACTS
Myth	**Fact**
Faking Hypnosis participants are "faking it" and playing along with the hypnotist.	There are conflicting research positions about hypnosis. Although most participants are not consciously faking hypnosis, some researchers believe the effects result from a blend of conformity, relaxation, obedience, suggestion, and role playing. Other theorists believe that hypnotic effects result from a special altered state of consciousness. A group of "unified" theorists suggests that hypnosis is a combination of both relaxation/role playing and a unique alternate state or consciousness.
Forced hypnosis People can be hypnotized against their will or hypnotically "brainwashed."	Hypnosis requires a willing, conscious choice to relinquish control of one's consciousness to someone else. The best potential subjects are those who are able to focus attention, are open to new experiences, and are capable of imaginative involvement or fantasy.
Unethical behavior Hypnosis can make people behave immorally or take dangerous risks against their will.	Hypnotized people retain awareness and control of their behavior, and they can refuse to comply with the hypnotist's suggestions.
Superhuman strength Under hypnosis, people can perform acts of special superhuman strength.	When nonhypnotized people are simply asked to try their hardest on tests of physical strength, they generally can do anything a hypnotized person can do.
Exceptional memory Under hypnosis, people can recall things they otherwise could not.	Although the heightened relaxation and focus that hypnosis engenders improves recall for some information, it adds little if anything to regular memory, and hypnotized people also are more willing to guess. Because memory is normally filled with fabrication and distortion (Chapter 7), hypnosis generally increases the potential for error.

Sources: Hilgard, 1978, 1992; Lilienfeld et al., 2010; Lynn et al., 2010; Montgomery et al., 2013; Orne, 2006; Terhune et al., 2011; Wickramasekera, 2008.

degree of anxiety, fear, and misinformation. For example, some studies have found that women who use hypnosis in labor and childbirth experience lower levels of pain and a shorter duration of labor (Madden et al., 2012). Because tension and anxiety strongly affect pain, any technique that helps the patient relax is medically useful.

In psychotherapy, hypnosis can help patients relax, recall painful memories, and reduce anxiety. Despite the many myths about hypnosis, it has been used with modest success in the treatment of phobias and in helping people to lose weight, stop smoking, and improve study habits (Amundson & Nuttgens, 2008; Robertson, 2013; Smith, 2011).

One final note

Before going on to the next chapter, we'd like to take an unusual step for authors. We'd like to offer you, our reader, a piece of caring, personal and professional advice about alternate states of consciousness (ASCs). The core problem while you're in any ASC is that you're less aware of external reality, which places you at high risk. This applies to both men and women. Interestingly, we all recognize these dangers while sleeping and dreaming, and we've developed standard ways to protect ourselves. For example, when we're driving on a long trip and start to feel sleepy, we stop for coffee, walk around, and/or rent a hotel room before allowing ourselves to fall asleep.

Our simple advice to you is to follow this same "sleepy driver" logic and standards. If you decide to use drugs, meditate, undergo hypnosis, or engage in any other form of altered consciousness, research the effects and risks of your ASC and plan ahead for the best options for dealing with it—just like you set up a designated driver before drinking. Take care and best wishes,

Karen R. Huffman   *Catherine A. Sanderson*

RETRIEVAL PRACTICE: MEDITATION AND HYPNOSIS

Self-Test

Completing this self-test and comparing your answers with those in Appendix B provides immediate feedback and helpful practice for exams. Additional interactive, self-tests are available at www.wiley.com/college/huffman.

1. Alternate states of consciousness (ASCs) can be achieved in which of the following ways?

   a. during sleep and dreaming   b. via chemical channels
   c. through hypnosis and   d. all these options
      meditation

2. _____ is a group of techniques designed to focus attention, block out all distractions, and produce an alternate state of consciousness (ASC).

   a. Hypnosis   b. MDMA
   c. Parapsychology   d. Meditation

3. _____ is occasionally used in surgery and for the treatment of chronic pain and severe burns.

   a. Parasomnia   b. Meditation
   c. Hypnosis   d. Parapsychology

4. _____ is an alternate state of heightened suggestibility characterized by deep relaxation and a trancelike state.

   a. Meditation   b. Amphetamine psychosis
   c. Hypnosis   d. Daydreaming

Think Critically

1 Why is it almost impossible to hypnotize an unwilling participant?

2 Describe the possible health benefits of hypnosis and meditation.

realworldpsychology

Can hypnosis decrease the pain of childbirth?

HINT: LOOK IN THE MARGIN FOR

Summary

1 CONSCIOUSNESS, SLEEP, AND DREAMING 124

- **Consciousness**, an organism's awareness of internal events and the external environment, varies in its depth and exists along a continuum. We spend most of our time in waking consciousness, but also in various **alternate states of consciousness (ASCs)**, such as sleep and dreaming.

- Many physiological functions follow 24-hour **circadian rhythms**. Disruptions in these rhythms, as well as long-term sleep deprivation, lead to increased fatigue, cognitive and mood disruptions, and other health problems.

- During a normal night's sleep, we progress through four distinct stages of **non-rapid-eye-movement (NREM) sleep**, with periods of **rapid-eye-movement (REM) sleep** generally occurring at the end of each sleep cycle. Both REM and NREM sleep are important for our biological functioning.

- There are four major theories about why we sleep. **Adaptation/protection theory** proposes that sleep evolved to conserve energy and to provide protection from predators. The **repair/restoration theory** suggests that sleep helps us recuperate from the day's events. The **growth/development theory** argues that we use sleep for growth. The **learning/memory theory** says that we use sleep for consolidation, storage, and maintenance of memories.

- Three major theories about why we dream are Freud's **wish-fulfillment view**, the **activation–synthesis hypothesis**, and the **cognitive view**.

- Sleep–wake disorders include **insomnia, narcolepsy, sleep apnea, nightmares**, and **sleep terrors**. Natural sleep aids, based on behavior therapy, are helpful ways to treat sleep-wake disorders and avoid problems associated with medication.

2 PSYCHOACTIVE DRUGS 136

- **Psychoactive drugs** influence the nervous system in a variety of ways. Alcohol affects neural membranes throughout the entire nervous system. Most psychoactive drugs act in a more specific way, by either enhancing a particular neurotransmitter's effect—an **agonist drug**—or inhibiting it—an **antagonist drug**.

- The term **drug abuse** refers to drug-taking behavior that causes emotional or physical harm to oneself or others. **Addiction** refers to a condition in which a person feels compelled to use a specific drug. **Psychological dependence** refers to the mental desire or craving to achieve a drug's effects. **Physical dependence** refers to biological changes that make a drug necessary for minimum daily functioning, and **withdrawal** symptoms. Repeated use of a drug can produce decreased sensitivity, or **tolerance**. Sometimes, using one drug increases tolerance for another (**cross-tolerance**).

- Psychologists divide psychoactive drugs into four categories: **depressants** (such as alcohol, barbiturates, Rohypnol, and Ketamine), **stimulants** (such as caffeine, nicotine, cocaine, and amphetamines), **opiates** (such as morphine, heroin, and codeine), and **hallucinogens** (such as marijuana and LSD). Almost all psychoactive drugs may cause serious health problems and, in some cases, even death.

3 MEDITATION AND HYPNOSIS 144

- **Meditation** refers to techniques designed to focus attention, block out distractions, and produce an alternate state of consciousness. Researchers have verified that it can produce dramatic changes in basic physiological processes.

- Modern research has removed the mystery surrounding **hypnosis**, a trancelike state of heightened suggestibility, deep relaxation, and intense focus. It is used in psychotherapy and medicine, and it is especially useful for those with a high degree of anxiety, fear, and misinformation.

Dorling Kindersley/Getty Images, Inc.

Neo Vision/Getty Images, Inc.

 ◉ applyingrealworldpsychology

We began this chapter with five intriguing Real World Psychology questions, and you were asked to revisit these questions at the end of each section. Questions like these have an important and lasting impact on all of our lives. See if you can answer these additional critical thinking questions related to real world examples.

1 In which stage of sleep is the kitten in each photo, and how do you know?

2 Why might REM sleep serve an important adaptive function for cats?

3 Imagine that someone marketed a drug that allowed you to get complete rest and recuperation from only one hour of sleep, but it stopped you from dreaming. Would you take the drug? Why or why not?

4 Why do you think Freud's dream theory remains so popular, despite serious scientific questions and alternative modern theories?

5 Why do you think alcohol is more popular and culturally acceptable than the other drugs discussed in this chapter?

6 What are some possible ethical considerations of using hypnosis?

Key Terms

RETRIEVAL PRACTICE Write a definition for each term before turning back to the referenced page to check your answer.

- activation–synthesis hypothesis of dreams 132
- adaptation/protection theory of sleep 131
- addiction 137
- agonist drug 136
- alternate state of consciousness (ASC) 124
- antagonist drug 136
- circadian rhythm 126
- cognitive view of dreams 132
- consciousness 124
- depressant 139
- drug abuse 137
- growth/development theory of sleep 131
- hallucinogen 141
- hypnosis 146
- insomnia 133
- latent content of dreams 132
- learning/memory theory of sleep 131
- manifest content of dreams 132
- meditation 144
- narcolepsy 134
- nightmares 135
- non-rapid-eye-movement (NREM) sleep 130
- opiate 141
- physical dependence 137
- psychoactive drug 136
- psychological dependence 137
- rapid-eye-movement (REM) sleep 129
- repair/restoration theory of sleep 131
- sleep apnea 134
- sleep terrors 135
- stimulant 140
- tolerance 138
- wish-fulfillment view of dreams 132
- withdrawal 137

chaptersix

Learning

realworldpsychology

THINGS YOU'LL LEARN IN CHAPTER 6

Q1 Why can simply hearing the drill in a dentist's office—even if that drill is nowhere near you—make you feel anxious?

Q2 How can decreasing the cost of fruit and vegetables lead to healthier eating?

Q3 Why do gamblers have such trouble quitting, even when they continue to lose money?

Q4 Does watching sex on TV increase the risk of teen pregnancies?

Q5 Why can even young children recognize a picture of a snake much faster than a picture of a frog or caterpillar?

THROUGHOUT THE CHAPTER, MARGIN ICONS FOR Q1–Q5 INDICATE WHERE THE TEXT ADDRESSES THESE QUESTIONS.

chapteroverview

Imagine yourself in the following situations:

On your way to campus, you note a bad traffic jam up ahead and quickly decide to try a new shortcut someone mentioned several weeks ago.

Later, in your general psychology class, you watch a video on service dogs for the blind, and are amazed by these dogs opening and closing doors, helping their owners dress and undress, carrying items in a backpack, and even differentiating between classrooms, bathrooms, escalators, and elevators.

While leaving campus, you note that the pitcher on your college's baseball team ritualistically kicks the dirt twice with each foot, then spits in his glove, and finally taps the top of his ball cap three times before throwing each pitch.

Now ask yourself, how did you manage that new shortcut to campus? How did those guide dogs perform such amazing acts? Why did the baseball pitcher engage in such strange, superstitious rituals? All three of these sets of behavior are clearly not genetic or present at the moment of birth. Instead, they result from *learning*.

We usually think of learning as classroom activities, such as math and reading, or as motor skills, like riding a bike or playing the piano. But for psychologists, learning is an all-encompassing process allowing us to adapt to our ever-changing environment. We learn that certain objects or events, such as food or pain, are associated with our survival (classical conditioning). We also learn to avoid punishing situations, and to repeat acts that bring rewards (operant conditioning). Finally, we learn through personal insights and from watching others (cognitive-social learning). Without the ability to learn, we simply could not exist.

In this chapter, we will study these three forms of learning, followed by the biology of learning, which explains how our brain and nervous system change when we learn.

CLASSICAL CONDITIONING

RETRIEVAL PRACTICE While reading the upcoming sections, respond to each Learning Objective in your own words. Then compare your responses with those found at www.wiley.com/college/huffman.

1 DESCRIBE Pavlov and Watson's contributions to our understanding of learning.

2 EXPLAIN the three steps in classical conditioning.

3 SUMMARIZE the six principles of classical conditioning.

Learning A relatively permanent change in behavior or mental processes caused by experience.

Before we go on, we need to operationally define **learning** *as a relatively permanent change in behavior or mental processes caused by experience.* This relative permanence applies not only to bad habits, like texting while driving or procrastinating, but also to useful behaviors and emotions, such as training guide dogs for the blind or falling in love.

We begin this chapter with a study of one of the earliest forms of learning, *classical conditioning*, made famous by Pavlov's salivating dogs.

Beginnings of Classical Conditioning

Why does your mouth water when you stare at a large slice of delicious cake or a juicy steak? The answer to this question was accidentally discovered in the laboratory of Russian physiologist Ivan Pavlov (1849–1936). Pavlov's initial plan was to study the role of saliva in digestion by using a tube attached to dogs' salivary glands **(Figure 6.1)**.

Ironically, during these experiments, one of Pavlov's students noticed that even before receiving the actual food, many dogs began salivating at the mere sight of the food, the food dish, the smell of the food, or even just the sight of the person who customarily delivered the food! Pavlov's genius was in recognizing the importance of this

FIGURE 6.1 PAVLOV'S EXPERIMENTAL SETUP

Harness (to restrict movement by subject)

Tube for collecting saliva from subject's mouth

Amount of saliva recorded here

"unscheduled" salivation. He realized that the dogs were not only responding on the basis of hunger (a biological need), but also as a result of experience or learning.

Excited by this accidental discovery, Pavlov and his students conducted several experiments, including sounding a tone on a tuning fork just before food was placed in the dogs' mouths. After several pairings of the tone and food, dogs in the laboratory began to salivate on hearing the tone alone.

Pavlov and later researchers found that many things can become conditioned stimuli for salivation if they are paired with food—a bell, a buzzer, a light, and even the sight of a circle or triangle drawn on a card. This type of learning, in which a neutral stimulus (such as the tone on a tuning fork) comes to elicit a response after repeated pairings with a naturally occurring stimulus (like food), is now known as **classical conditioning**.

To fully understand classical conditioning, and how it applies to our everyday life, the first step is to recognize that **conditioning** is simply another word for learning. Next, we need to explain that classical conditioning is a three-step process—*before*, *during*, and *after conditioning*. A process that is explained in detail below and visually summarized in **Figure 6.2**.

Classical conditioning A type of learning that develops through involuntarily paired associations; a previously neutral stimulus (NS) is paired (associated) with an unconditioned stimulus (US) to elicit a conditioned response (CR).

Conditioning The process of learning associations between stimuli and behavioral responses.

FIGURE 6.2 THE BEGINNINGS AND A MODERN APPLICATION OF CLASSICAL CONDITIONING

Although Pavlov's initial experiment used a metronome, a ticking instrument designed to mark exact time, his best-known method (depicted here) involved a tone from a tuning fork. As you can see, the basic process of classical conditioning is simple. Just as you've been classically conditioned to respond to your cell phone's tones, or possibly to just the sight of a pizza box, Pavlov's dogs learned to respond to the tuning fork's tone. Unfortunately, many students get confused by these technical terms. So here's a tip that might help: The actual stimuli (tone and meat) remain the same—only their names change from neutral to conditioned or from unconditioned to conditioned. A similar name change happens for the response (salivation)—from unconditioned to conditioned.

Neutral stimulus (NS) A stimulus that, before conditioning, does not naturally bring about the response of interest.

Unconditioned stimulus (US) In classical conditioning, a stimulus that elicits an unconditioned response (UR) without previous conditioning.

Unconditioned response (UR) In classical conditioning, a learned reaction to an unconditioned stimulus (US) that occurs without previous conditioning.

Conditioned stimulus (CS) In classical conditioning, a previously neutral stimulus (NS) becomes conditioned through repeated pairings with an unconditioned stimulus (US), and it now elicits a conditioned response (CR).

Conditioned response (CR) In classical conditioning, a learned reaction to a conditioned stimulus (CS) that occurs because of previous repeated pairings with an unconditioned stimulus (US).

Conditioned emotional response (CER) Through classical conditioning, an emotion, such as fear, becomes a conditioned response to a previously neutral stimulus (NS).

STEP 1 Before conditioning, the sound of the tone does NOT lead to salivation, which makes the tone a **neutral stimulus (NS)**. Conversely, food naturally brings about salivation, which makes food an *unlearned*, **unconditioned stimulus (US)**. The initial, salivary reflex of salivation also is *unlearned*, so it is called an **unconditioned response (UR)**.

STEP 2 During conditioning, the tuning fork (NS) is repeatedly sounded right before the presentation of the meat (US).

STEP 3 After conditioning, the tone alone will bring about salivation. At this point, we can say that the dog is *classically conditioned*. The previously neutral stimulus (NS) (the tone) has now become a *learned*, **conditioned stimulus (CS)**, that produced a *learned*, **conditioned response (CR)** (the dog's salivation). (Note that the "R" in UR in Step 1 and the CR in this Step 3 refers to both "reflex" and "response.")

In sum, the overall goal of Pavlov's classical conditioning was for the dog to learn to associate the tone with the unconditioned stimulus (meat), and then to show the same response (salivation) to the tone as to the meat.

So what does a salivating dog have to do with your everyday life? Classical conditioning is a fundamental way that all animals, including humans, learn. The human feelings of excitement and/or compulsion to gamble, your love for your parents (or significant other), drooling at the sight of chocolate cake or pizza, and the almost universal fear of public speaking all largely result from classical conditioning.

How do we learn to be afraid of public speaking or of typically harmless things like mice and elevators? In a now-famous experiment, John Watson and Rosalie Rayner (1920) demonstrated how a fear of rats could be classically conditioned.

In this study, a healthy 11-month-old child, later known as "Little Albert," was first allowed to play with a white laboratory rat **(Figure 6.3)**. Like most other infants, Albert was curious and reached for the rat, showing no fear. Knowing that infants are naturally frightened by loud noises, Watson stood behind Albert and when he reached for the rat, Watson banged a steel bar with a hammer. The loud noise obviously frightened the child and made him cry. The rat was paired with the loud noise only seven times before Albert became classically conditioned and demonstrated fear of the rat even without the noise. The rat had become a CS that brought about the CR (fear).

Although this deliberate experimental creation of what's now called a **conditioned emotional response (CER)** remains a classic in psychology, it has been heavily criticized and would never be allowed under today's experimental guidelines

FIGURE 6.3 **LITTLE ALBERT'S FEARS**

Benjamin Harris

Ⓐ Watson and Rayner's famous "Little Albert" study demonstrated how some fears can originate through conditioning.

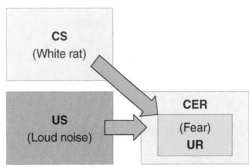

Ⓑ Using classical conditioning terms, we would say that the white rat (a neutral stimulus/NS) was paired with the loud noise (an unconditioned stimulus/US) to produce a conditioned emotional response (CER) in Albert, fear of the rat.

(Ethical Principles of Psychologists, 2010; Fridlund et al., 2012; Ollendick et al., 2012; Paul & Blumenthal, 1989). The research procedures used by Watson and Rayner violated several ethical guidelines for scientific research (Chapter 1). They not only deliberately created a serious fear in a child, but they also ended their experiment without *extinguishing* (removing) it. In addition, the researchers have been criticized because they did not measure Albert's fear objectively. Their subjective evaluation raises doubt about the degree of fear conditioned.

Despite such criticisms, this study of Little Albert showed us that many of our likes, dislikes, prejudices, and fears are examples of *conditioned emotional responses (CERs)*. For example, if your romantic partner always uses the same shampoo, simply the smell of that shampoo may soon elicit a positive response. In Chapter 13, you'll discover how Watson's research later led to powerful clinical tools for eliminating exaggerated and irrational fears of a specific object or situation, known as *phobias* (Cal et al., 2006; Field, 2006; Schachtman & Reilly, 2011; Schweckendiek et al., 2011). For more examples of how classical conditioning impacts everyday life, see **Figure 6.4**.

FIGURE 6.4 CLASSICAL CONDITIONING IN EVERYDAY LIFE

realworldpsychology

Have you ever wondered why people are prejudiced and discriminate against others? These behaviors, as well as advertising and medicine, are all heavily influenced by classical conditioning.

Ⓐ Prejudice

How do children, like the one holding the KKK sign in this photo, develop prejudice at such an early age? As shown in the diagram, children are naturally upset and become afraid (UR) when they see that their parents are upset and afraid (US). Over time, they may learn to associate their parents' reaction with all members of a disliked group (CS), thus becoming prejudiced like their parents.

Ⓑ Advertising

Magazine ads, TV commercials, and business promotions often use higher-order classical conditioning to pair their products or company logo, the neutral stimulus (NS), with previously conditioned pleasant images, like attractive models and celebrities, the conditioned stimulus (CS). These attractive models then trigger desired behaviors, the conditioned response (CR), such as purchasing their products (Krugman, 2013; Miller & Allen, 2012; Sweldens et al., 2010).

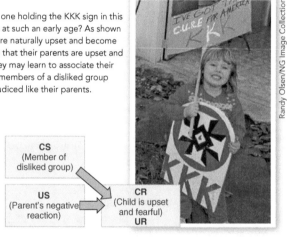

CS (Member of disliked group)

US (Parent's negative reaction)

CR (Child is upset and fearful) UR

Ⓒ Medicine

Classical conditioning also is used in the medical field. For example, a treatment designed for alcohol-addicted patients pairs alcohol with a nausea-producing drug. Afterward, just the smell or taste of alcohol makes the person sick. Some, but not all, patients have found this treatment helpful.

US (nausea drug) → UR (nausea)

CS + US (alcohol) (drug) → UR (nausea)

CS (alcohol) → CR (nausea)

Principles of Classical Conditioning

Fear and avoidance of dental work is very common. How did it develop? Imagine being seated in a dental chair, and, even though the drill is nowhere near you, its sound can make you feel anxious. Your anxiety is obviously not innate. Little babies don't cringe at the sound of a dental drill. Your fear of the drill, and maybe dentistry in general, involves one or more of the six principles shown in **Table 6.1**. As you'll discover in Chapters 12 and 13, the good news is that even people with serious dental phobias can learn to overcome them (Elsesser et al., 2013).

Acquisition, Stimulus Generalization, and Stimulus Discrimination

After Pavlov's original (accidental) discovery of classical conditioning, he conducted numerous experiments beyond the basic **acquisition** phase, a general term for the third step in classical conditioning in which the conditioned response (CR) is first elicited by the conditioned stimulus (CS).

One of his most interesting findings was that stimuli similar to the original conditioned stimulus (CS) also can elicit the conditioned response (CR). For example, after first conditioning dogs to salivate to the sound of low-pitched tones, Pavlov later demonstrated that the dogs would also salivate in response to higher-pitched tones. Similarly, after conditioning, the infant in Watson and Rayner's experiment ("Little Albert") feared not only rats but also a rabbit, a dog, and a bearded Santa Claus mask. This spreading or *generalizing* of the CR to similar stimuli, even though they have never been paired with the US, is called **stimulus generalization**.

In contrast, just as Pavlov's dogs learned to generalize and respond to similar stimuli, they also learned how to *discriminate* between similar stimuli. For example, when he gave the dogs food following a high-pitched tone, but not when he used a low-pitched tone, he found that they learned the difference between the two tones and only salivated to the high-pitched one. Likewise, Albert learned to recognize differences between rats and other stimuli, and presumably overcame his fear of Santa Claus. This ability to distinguish or discriminate between stimuli is known as **stimulus discrimination**.

© oneblink-cj/iStockphoto

Are you afraid of dentists?

Acquisition The final step in a classical conditioning experiment during which the conditioned stimulus (CS) elicits the conditioned response (CR).

Stimulus generalization The conditioned response (CR) is elicited not only by the conditioned stimulus (CS) but also by stimuli similar to the conditioned stimulus (CS).

Stimulus discrimination A conditioning process in which an organism learns to respond differently to stimuli that differ from the conditioned stimulus on some dimension.

TABLE 6.1	SIX PRINCIPLES AND APPLICATIONS OF CLASSICAL CONDITIONING	*psychology and you*
Process	**Description**	**Example**
Acquisition of basic classical conditioning	Process of learning a new response, in which the neutral stimulus (NS) and unconditioned stimulus (US) are first paired to produce the unconditioned response (UR); then the neutral stimulus (NS) becomes a conditioned stimulus (CS), eliciting a conditioned response (CR)	You learn to fear (CR) a dentist's drill (CS) because you associate it with the pain of your tooth extraction (US).
Stimulus generalization	Conditioned response (CR) is elicited not only by the conditioned stimulus (CS) but also by stimuli similar to the conditioned stimulus (CS)	You generalize your fear of the dentist's drill to your dentist's office and other dentists' offices.
Stimulus discrimination	Stimuli similar to the conditioned stimulus (CS) do not elicit the conditioned response (CR)	You are not afraid of your physician's office because you've learned to differentiate it from your dentist's office.
Extinction	Conditioned stimulus (CS) is presented alone, without the unconditioned stimulus (US); eventually the conditioned stimulus (CS) no longer elicits the conditioned response (CR)	You return several times to your dentist's office for routine checkups, with no dental drill; your fear (CR) gradually diminishes.
Spontaneous recovery	Sudden reappearance of a previously extinguished conditioned response (CR)	While watching a movie depicting dental drilling, your previous fear (CR) suddenly returns.
Higher-order conditioning	Neutral stimulus (NS) becomes a conditioned stimulus (CS) through repeated pairing with a previously conditioned stimulus (CS)	You fear just the sight of the sign outside your dentist's office, an originally neutral stimulus (NS). Why? It has become a conditioned stimulus (CS), associated with the previous conditioned stimulus (CS) of the dental drill.

oices from the Classroom

Stimulus Discrimination in Childhood Growing up, there was a park at the end of the street where I lived. After finishing my homework, I would join the neighborhood kids down at the park to play until dinner time. Our dads would all whistle to signal when it was time for us to come home for dinner. At first, I ran home when I heard any whistle (stimulus generalization). Then, I learned the sound of MY dad's whistle (stimulus discrimination). This enabled me to be able to play longer as my dinner time was often a half hour later than some of my friends.

Professor Amy Beeman
San Diego Mesa College
San Diego, California

Extinction, Spontaneous Recovery, and Higher-Order Conditioning

What do you think happened when Pavlov repeatedly sounded the tone without presenting food? The answer is that the dogs' salivation gradually declined, a process Pavlov called **extinction**—the gradual weakening of a conditioned response (CR).

Once extinguished, is a conditioned response (CR) gone for good? Extinction is not unlearning—it does not "erase" the learned connection between the stimulus and the response (Bouton et al., 2012; Storsve et al., 2012). Pavlov found that sometimes, after a conditioned response had apparently been extinguished, if he sounded the tone once again the dogs would salivate. This reemergence of a previously extinguished conditioned response (CR) after a period of rest is called **spontaneous recovery** (see *Psychology and You*).

Extinction The gradual disappearance of a conditioned response (CR); it occurs when an unconditioned stimulus (US) is withheld whenever the conditioned stimulus (CS) is presented.

Spontaneous recovery The sudden, reappearance of a previously extinguished conditioned response (CR) after a rest period.

psychology and you **Spontaneous Recovery** Have you ever felt renewed excitement at the sight of a former girlfriend or boyfriend, even though years have passed, you have a new partner, and extinction has occurred? This may be an example of spontaneous recovery. It also may help explain why people might misinterpret a sudden flare-up of feelings and be tempted to return to unhappy relationships. To make matters worse, when a conditioned stimulus is reintroduced after extinction, the conditioning occurs much faster the second time around—a phenomenon known as *reconditioning*.

The good news is that those who have taken general psychology (or read this book) are far less likely to make this mistake. Looking at **Figure 6.5**, you can see that even if you experience spontaneous recovery, your sudden peak of feelings for the old love partner will gradually return to their previously extinguished state. So don't overreact.

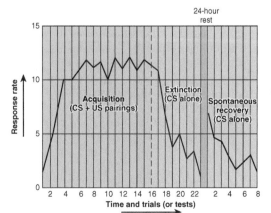

FIGURE 6.5 THREE KEY PRINCIPLES OF CLASSICAL CONDITIONING

During acquisition, the strength of the conditioned response (CR) rapidly increases and then levels off near its maximum. During extinction, the CR declines erratically until it is extinguished. After a "rest" period in which the organism is not exposed to the conditioned stimulus (CS), spontaneous recovery may occur, and the CS will once again elicit a (weakened) CR.

Higher-order conditioning A process in which a neutral stimulus (NS) becomes a conditioned stimulus (CS) through repeated pairings with a previously conditioned stimulus (CS).

Both spontaneous recovery and reconditioning help underscore why it can be so difficult for us to break bad habits (such as eating too much chocolate cake) or internalize new beliefs (such as egalitarian gender or racial beliefs). The phenomenon of **higher-order conditioning (Figure 6.6)** further expands our understanding of complex learned habits and associations.

FIGURE 6.6 THE POWER OF HIGHER-ORDER CONDITIONING | realworldpsychology

Children are not born salivating to the sight of McDonald's golden arches. So why do they beg adults to take them to "Mickey D's" after simply seeing an ad showing the golden arches? It's because of higher-order conditioning, which occurs when a neutral stimulus (NS) becomes a conditioned stimulus (CS) through repeated pairings with a previously conditioned stimulus (CS).

① First-order conditioning
If you wanted to demonstrate high-order conditioning in Pavlov's dogs, you would first condition the dogs to salivate in response to the sound of the tone. Similarly, children first learn to pair McDonald's restaurants with the food.

② Pairing NS with previously conditioned CS
Then, with Pavlov's dogs, you would pair a flash of light with the tone. Similarly, children later associate the two golden arches with the McDonald's restaurant.

③ Higher-order conditioning
Eventually, the dogs would salivate in response to the flash of light alone. Similarly, children salivate and beg to eat at Mickey D's when they see the golden arches.

Voices from the Classroom

Cats and Classical Conditioning To review the major principles of classical conditioning, I use several examples based on a cat's eating behavior. *Basic, initial classical conditioning* = cat meows to the sound of a spoon banging on the side of a food bowl. *Higher-order conditioning* = meowing occurs when the spoon drawer is opened. *Generalization* = meowing occurs when any kitchen drawer is opened. *Discrimination* = meowing occurs when just the spoon drawer is opened. *Extinction* = cat slowly stops meowing because canned cat food is banned due to cat's health issues. *Spontaneous recovery* = one day cat suddenly meows after hearing a spoon bang the side of the food bowl or when the spoon drawer is opened.

Professor Jeffrey Henriques
University of Wisconsin
Madison, Wisconsin

RETRIEVAL PRACTICE: CLASSICAL CONDITIONING

Self-Test

Completing this self-test and comparing your answers with those in Appendix B provides immediate feedback and helpful practice for exams. Additional interactive, self-tests are available at www.wiley.com/college/huffman.

1. _____ conditioning occurs when a neutral stimulus becomes associated with an unconditioned stimulus to elicit a conditioned response.

   a. Reflex   b. Instinctive
   c. Classical   d. Basic

2. The process of learning associations between environmental stimuli and behavioral responses is known as _____.

   a. maturation   b. contiguity learning
   c. conditioning   d. latent learning

3. In John Watson's demonstration of classical conditioning with Little Albert, the unconditioned stimulus was _____.

   a. symptoms of fear   b. a rat
   c. a bath towel   d. a loud noise

4. A baby is bitten by a small dog and then is afraid of all small animals. This is an example of _____.

   a. stimulus discrimination   b. extinction
   c. reinforcement   d. stimulus generalization

Think Critically

1 How might Watson and Rayner, who conducted the famous "Little Albert" study, have designed a more ethical study of conditioned emotional responses (CERs)?

2 Most classical conditioning is involuntary. Considering this, is it ethical for politicians and advertisers to use classical conditioning to influence our thoughts and behavior? Why or why not?

realworldpsychology

Why can simply hearing the drill in a dentist's office—even if that drill is nowhere near you—make you feel anxious?

HINT: LOOK IN THE MARGIN FOR (Q1)

OPERANT CONDITIONING

RETRIEVAL PRACTICE While reading the upcoming sections, respond to each Learning Objective in your own words. Then compare your responses with those found at www.wiley.com/college/huffman.

1 DESCRIBE Thorndike's and Skinner's contributions to operant conditioning research.
2 EXPLAIN how reinforcement and punishment influence behavior.
3 SUMMARIZE how shaping and schedules of reinforcement affect behavior.

As we've just seen, classical conditioning is based on what happens *before* we *involuntarily* respond: Something happens to us, and we learn a new response. In contrast, **operant conditioning** is based on what happens *after* we *voluntarily* perform a behavior: We do something and learn from the consequences **(Figure 6.7)**.

Note that *consequences* are the heart of operant conditioning. In classical conditioning, consequences are irrelevant—Pavlov's dogs still got to eat whether they salivated or not. But in operant conditioning, the organism voluntarily performs a behavior (an *operant*) that produces a consequence—either reinforcement or punishment. **Reinforcement** strengthens the response, making it more likely to recur. **Punishment** weakens the response, making it less likely to recur.

LEARNING OBJECTIVES

Operant conditioning Learning through voluntary behavior and its subsequent consequences; reinforcement increases behavioral tendencies, whereas punishment decreases them.

Reinforcement The adding or taking away of a stimulus following a response, which increases the likelihood of that response being repeated.

Punishment The adding or taking away of a stimulus following a response, which decreases the likelihood of that response being repeated.

FIGURE 6.7 CLASSICAL VERSUS OPERANT CONDITIONING

Classical conditioning is based on involuntary behavior, whereas operant conditioning is based on voluntary behavior.

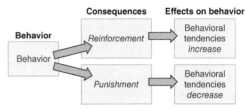

A Classical conditioning
The subject is passive and involuntarily pairs the originally neutral stimulus (NS) with an unconditioned stimulus (US), which produces a conditioned stimulus (CS) that leads to a learned, conditioned response (CR).

B Operant conditioning
The subject is active and voluntarily "operates" on the environment. The consequences (reinforcement or punishment) affect whether the behavior will increase or decrease.

 Thankfully, operant conditioning principles can be used to change our negative health-related behaviors by reinforcing healthy choices and punishing unhealthy ones. For example, only allowing yourself to watch TV while exercising will improve your general physical health. And, several studies have shown that decreasing the cost of fruits and vegetables, while increasing the price of soda, can lead people to make healthier food and drink choices (Eyles et al., 2012). Similarly, increasing the cost of smoking—often by increasing taxes on cigarettes—reduces smoking rates (Cavazos-Rehg et al., 2012; Wilson et al., 2012). The effect of increased taxes on cigarettes is particularly true for heavy smokers, who pay considerably more due to their higher consumption, and for teenagers, who tend to have less discretionary income.

Beginnings of Operant Conditioning

Law of effect Thorndike's rule that responses that produce a satisfying effect are more likely to occur again, whereas those that produce a discomforting effect become less likely to occur again.

Edward Thorndike (1874–1949), a pioneer of operant conditioning, determined that the frequency of a behavior is modified by its consequences (Thorndike, 1911). Thorndike's **law of effect** was an important first step in understanding how consequences can modify active, voluntary behaviors **(Figure 6.8)**.

FIGURE 6.8 THORNDIKE'S LAW OF EFFECT

In his most famous experiment, Thorndike put a cat inside a specially built puzzle box. When the cat stepped on a pedal inside the box (at first, through trial and error), the door opened, and the cat could get out and eat. With each additional success, the cat's actions became more purposeful, and it soon learned to open the door immediately (from Thorndike, 1898).

B. F. Skinner (1904–1990) extended Thorndike's law of effect to more complex behaviors. He also emphasized that reinforcement and punishment should always be presented *after* the behavior of interest has occurred. This was because Skinner believed that the only way to know how we have influenced someone's behavior is to check whether it increases or decreases. As he pointed out, we too often think we're reinforcing or punishing behavior when we're actually doing the opposite (see *Psychology and You*).

psychology and you   **The Challenge of Reinforcement** A professor may think she is encouraging shy students to talk by repeatedly praising them each time they speak up in class. But what if you are one of those shy students and are embarrassed by this extra attention? If so, you may actually decrease the number of times you talk in class. Can you see why it's important to always remember that what is reinforcing or punishing for one person may not be so for another?

Michele Cozzolino/Shutterstock

Reinforcement and Punishment

Reinforcers, which strengthen a response, can be a powerful tool in all parts of our lives. Psychologists group them into two types, primary and secondary. **Primary reinforcers** satisfy an intrinsic, unlearned biological need (like food, water, and sex). **Secondary reinforcers** are not intrinsic; the value of this reinforcer is learned (like money, praise, and attention). Each type of reinforcer can produce **positive reinforcement** or **negative reinforcement**, depending on whether certain stimuli are added or taken away **(Table 6.2)**.

Primary reinforcers Any stimuli that increase the probability of a response because of their innate, biological value, such as food and water.

Secondary reinforcers Any stimuli that increase the probability of a response because of their learned value, such as money and material possessions.

Positive reinforcement The adding (or presenting) of a stimulus, thereby strengthening a response and making it more likely to recur.

Negative reinforcement The taking away (or removing) of a stimulus, thereby strengthening a response and making it more likely to recur.

TABLE 6.2	HOW REINFORCEMENT INCREASES (OR STRENGTHENS) BEHAVIOR	*psychology and you*
	POSITIVE REINFORCEMENT Stimulus added (+) and behavior increases	**NEGATIVE REINFORCEMENT** Stimulus taken away (−) and behavior increases
PRIMARY REINFORCERS Satisfy biological needs	You hug your baby and he smiles at you. The "addition" of his smile increases the likelihood that you will hug him again. / You do a favor for a friend and she buys you lunch in return, which makes it more likely that you'll do more favors for your friend in the future.	You baby is crying, so you hug him and he stops crying. The "removal" of crying increases the likelihood that you will hug him again when he cries. / You take an aspirin for your headache, which takes away the pain, and makes it more likely that you'll take an aspirin again when you have future pains.
SECONDARY REINFORCERS Satisfy learned needs	You increase profits and receive $200 as a bonus. The "addition" of the bonus increases the likelihood that you'll work hard in the future to increase profits. / You study hard and receive a good grade on your psychology exam, which makes it more likely that you'll study hard in the future.	After high sales, your boss says you won't have to work on weekends. The "removal" of having to work on weekends makes it more likely that you'll work harder for high sales in the future. / You're allowed to skip the final exam because you did so well on your unit exams, which makes it more likely that you'll work hard to do well on unit exams in the future.

michaeljung/Shutterstock

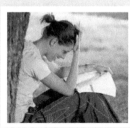

© diego_cervo/iStockphoto

Premack principle The use of a naturally occurring high-frequency response to reinforce and increase low-frequency responses.

Primary punishers Any stimuli that decrease the probability of a response because of their innate, biological value, such as hunger and thirst.

Secondary punishers Any stimuli that decrease the probability of a response because of their learned value, such as poor grades or a parking ticket.

Positive punishment The addition (or presenting) of a stimulus, thereby weakening a response and making it less likely to recur.

Negative punishment The taking away (or removing) of a stimulus, thereby weakening a response and making it less likely to recur.

Interestingly, when you make yourself do some necessary but tedious task—say, paying bills—before letting yourself go to the movies, you are not only using positive reinforcement, you're also using the **Premack principle**. This principle is named after psychologist David Premack, who found that any naturally occurring, high-frequency response can be used to reinforce and increase low-frequency responses (Goldfield, 2012; Poling, 2010). Recognizing that you love to go to movies, you intuitively tie your less desirable low-frequency activity (paying bills) to your high-frequency or highly desirable behavior (going to the movies).

It's very important to note that negative reinforcement is NOT punishment. The two concepts are actually completely opposite. Reinforcement (both positive and negative) *strengthens* a behavior, whereas punishment (both positive and negative) *weakens* a behavior. Knowing that this terminology is confusing, we encourage you to think of positive and negative in a *mathematical* sense. Instead of automatically assuming that positive means something "good" and negative means something "bad," recognize that in mathematics positive is adding something [+], and negative is taking something away [–].

As with reinforcement, there are two kinds of punishers—primary and secondary, and two kinds of punishment—positive and negative.

Primary punishers are unmet innate, biological needs (e.g., hunger, thirst, discomfort). **Secondary punishers** are unmet learned needs (e.g., poor grades, bad hair day, loss of an election). In turn, **positive punishment** is the addition (+) of a stimulus that decreases (or weakens) the likelihood of the response occurring again. **Negative punishment** is the taking away (–) of a reinforcing stimulus, which decreases (or weakens) the likelihood of the response occurring again **(Table 6.3)**. (To check your understanding of the principles of reinforcement and punishment, see **Figure 6.9**.)

Keep in mind that punishment is a difficult, and tricky, concept that's difficult to use appropriately and effectively. We often think we're punishing yet the behaviors continue. Similarly, we too often mistakenly think we're reinforcing when we're actually punishing. The key thing to remember is that punishment, by definition, is a process that adds or takes away something and causes a behavior to decrease. If

TABLE 6.3	HOW PUNISHMENT DECREASES (OR WEAKENS) BEHAVIOR	*psychology and you*

	POSITIVE PUNISHMENT Stimulus added (+) and behavior decreases (or weakens)	**NEGATIVE PUNISHMENT** Stimulus taken away (–) and behavior decreases (or weakens)	
PRIMARY PUNISHERS *Unlearned, biological needs are not met*	A rat receives an electric shock when it crosses an electric grid. The "addition" of the shock decreases the likelihood that the rat will cross the electric grid in the future. You must run four extra laps on a hot day because you were late to your gym class. Adding the four extra laps makes it less likely that you'll be late for gym class in the future.	A hungry child is denied dessert because she refused to eat her dinner. The "removal" of the dessert option decreases the likelihood of the child refusing to eat her dinner in the future. You lose sleep for several nights because you didn't study ahead of time in order to prepare for your final exams. The loss of sleep makes it less likely that you'll be unprepared for future final exams.	
SECONDARY PUNISHERS *Learned needs are not met*	A parent adds extra chores following a child's bad report card. The "addition" of the extra chores decreases the likelihood that the child will get a bad report card in the future. You study hard and still receive a low grade on your psychology exam. The "addition" of the low grade after studying hard decreases the likelihood that you will study hard the future.	A child's favorite toy is taken away because he/she disobeyed. The "removal" of the toy decreases the likelihood that the child will disobey in the future. Your bonus is taken away because of poor performance on your job. Removing the bonus makes it less likely that you'll turn in a poor performance in the future.	

© jtyler/iStockphoto

© ajikkafe/iStockphoto

FIGURE 6.9 USING THE "SKINNER BOX" FOR BOTH REINFORCEMENT AND PUNISHMENT

To test his behavioral theories, Skinner used an animal, usually a pigeon or a rat, and an apparatus that has come to be called a *Skinner Box.*

A In Skinner's basic experimental design, an animal (such as a rat) could press a lever and food pellets or shocks (administered through an electric grid on the cage floor) could be used to give the animal reinforcement or punishment.

B Are these examples of positive reinforcement, negative reinforcement, positive punishment, or negative punishment? Fill in the appropriate learning principle in the space provided.

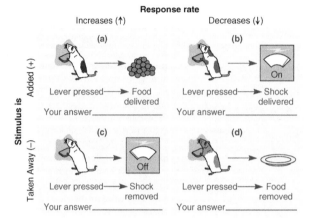

Answers: (a) positive reinforcement, (b) positive punishment, (c) negative reinforcement, (d) negative punishment

---

the behavior does not decrease it's NOT punishment! So it's always important to watch the actual behavior and not what you think should happen. Thus, if parents ignore all the A's on their child's report card ("taking away" encouraging comments) and ask repeated questions about the B's and C's, they may unintentionally be punishing the child's excellent grade achievement and weakening the likelihood of future A's. Similarly, dog owners who yell at or spank their dogs for finally coming to them ("adding" verbal or physical aggression) after being called several times are actually punishing the desired behavior—coming when called.

In addition to these problems with punishment, to be effective it should always be *clear, direct, immediate,* and *consistent.* However, in the real world, this is extremely hard to do. Police officers cannot stop every driver each and every time they speed. To make matters worse, when punishment is not immediate, during the delay, the behavior is likely to be reinforced on a partial schedule, which makes it highly resistant to extinction.

Think about gambling. It should be a punishing situation; gamblers usually lose far more than they win. However, the fact that they occasionally win keeps gamblers "hanging in there." Furthermore, some research demonstrates that pathological gamblers are less able to make an association between negative events (such as losing lots of money) and the stimuli that cause those events (such as gambling) (Brunborg et al., 2012).

Even if punishment immediately follows the misbehavior, the recipient may only learn what *not* to do, but not necessarily what he or she *should* do. It's much more efficient to teach someone by giving him or her clear examples of correct behavior than to simply punish the incorrect behavior.

(C) Voices from the Classroom

Operant Conditioning and Driving with Kids I have two children, who used to fight like cats and dogs, especially in the confined area of the car. Rather than punish them, I decided to ignore their bickering (as long as no arms or legs flew out the window). If we made it all the way to the shopping mall without an argument, I immediately praised them highly, showed excitement, and told them how great I felt. Another time when they made it to the mall without bickering, I stopped and we had ice cream on the way home. (Trips with bickering were ignored; no reinforcement.) Happily, within about five or six trips to the mall, there was virtually no bickering. It was awesome!

Professor Barbara Kennedy
Brevard Community College
Palm Bay, Florida

Is this positive or negative punishment?

Answer: It depends. If the child's behavior decreases, it would be punishment. Forcing him or her to sit in a chair away from other people and activities removes, or takes away (−), the opportunity to be near and interact with caregivers and/or playmates.

In sum, reinforcement and punishment can change behavior in laboratory settings, but evidence from real life suggests that these two approaches are not equal in their ease of application or effectiveness. Also, reinforcement is generally more ethical than punishment. However, punishment is sometimes necessary. If you decide to use it in cases of serious and potentially dangerous situations, keep in mind that punishment has at least seven important drawbacks:

1. **Passive aggressiveness** For the recipient, punishment often leads to frustration, anger, and possible aggression. But most of us have learned from experience that retaliatory aggression toward a punisher (especially one who is bigger and more powerful) is usually followed by more punishment. So instead, we may resort to subtle techniques, called *passive aggressiveness*, in which we deliberately show up late, "forget" to do an assigned chore, or complete the chore in a half-hearted way (Hopwood & Wright, 2012; Johnson, 2008).

2. **Avoidance behavior** No one likes to be punished, so we naturally try to avoid the punisher. If every time you come home a parent or spouse starts yelling at you, you will delay coming home—or will find another place to go.

3. **Inappropriate modeling** Have you ever seen a parent spank or hit his or her child for hitting another child? Ironically, the punishing parent may unintentionally serve as a "model" for the same behavior he or she is attempting to stop.

4. **Temporary suppression versus elimination** Punishment generally suppresses the behavior only temporarily, while the punisher is nearby.

5. **Learned helplessness** Research shows that nonhuman animals will fail to learn an escape response after experiencing inescapable aversive events (Jones et al., 2013; Maier, 1970; Seligman & Maier, 1967). Can you see how this phenomenon, known as *learned helplessness*, might explain, in part, why some people stay in abusive relationships (Miller et al., 2012)? Or why some students, who've experienced many failures in academic settings, might passively accept punishingly low grades, and/or engage in self-defeating behaviors, such as procrastination or minimal effort responses?

6. **Rewarded aggression** Because punishment often produces a decrease in undesired behavior, at least for the moment, the punisher is in effect rewarded for applying punishment.

7. **Perpetuated aggression** A vicious cycle may be established in which both the punisher and recipient are reinforced for inappropriate behavior— the punisher for punishing and the recipient for being fearful and submissive. This side effect partially explains the escalation of violence in family abuse and bullying (Anderson et al., 2008; Hamby & Grych, 2013; Miller et al., 2012).

Using this list of punishment's seven drawbacks, see if you can explain the following questions: Why do you think roommates, children, and spouses refuse to load the dishwasher despite repeated nagging? Why do drivers quickly slow down when they see a police car following behind and then quickly resume speeding once the police officer is out of sight? Given all the problems associated with punishment, why is it so often used?

The best answer to the dishwasher question may be item number 1—*passive aggressiveness*. The driver speeding up after the police officer leaves may be an example of number 4—*temporary suppression*. And the continued use of punishment, despite its drawbacks, may be best explained by the sixth and seventh points—*rewarded and perpetuated aggression*!

Shaping and Maintaining Behavior

It's easy to see how reinforcement is better than punishment for teaching and learning of most things, but how would you teach someone complex things like how to play the piano or to speak a foreign language? How do seals in zoos and amusement parks learn how to balance beach balls on their noses, or how to clap their flippers together on command from the trainers?

For new and complex behaviors such as these, which aren't likely to occur naturally, **shaping** is the key. Skinner believed that shaping, or *rewarding successive approximations*, explains a variety of abilities that each of us possesses, from eating with a fork to playing a musical instrument, to driving a car. Parents, athletic coaches, teachers, therapists, and animal trainers all use shaping techniques (Heinicke et al., 2013; Lefrancois, 2012; McDougall, 2013).

For example, Momoko, a female monkey, is famous in Japan for her water-skiing, deep-sea diving, and other amazing abilities **(Figure 6.10)**. Her animal trainers used the successive steps of shaping to teach her these skills. First, they reinforced Momoko (with a small food treat) for standing or sitting on the water ski. Then they reinforced her each time she accomplished a successive step in learning to water-ski.

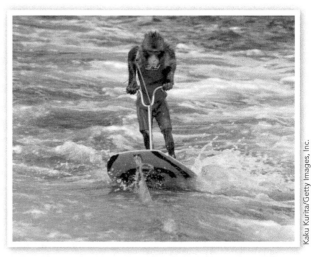

FIGURE 6.10 **CAN SHAPING TEACH A MONKEY TO WATERSKI?**

Now that we've discussed how we learn complex behaviors through shaping, you may want to know how to maintain it. When Skinner was training his animals, he found that learning was most rapid if the response was reinforced every time it occurred—a pattern called **continuous reinforcement**.

As you have probably noticed, however, real life seldom provides continuous reinforcement. Instead, most of our responses are reinforced only sometimes—a pattern called **partial (or intermittent) reinforcement**. Think of how parents or spouses keep nagging one another even when they're only occasionally reinforced, how telemarketers keep calling even when most people hang up on them, and how children keep whining even when parents only occasionally give in! The fact that these behaviors are only intermittently reinforced explains why they're so persistent—and so resistant to extinction! On a happier note, partial (intermittent) reinforcement also encourages productive, desirable behaviors like business owners who keep revising their product and students who keep plugging away at their college classes until they graduate. For better or worse, persistence pays off!

Keep in mind that a continuous schedule is best used in the initial stages of learning. However, once a task is well learned, you'll want to move on to a partial (intermittent) schedule—thanks to its strong resistance to extinction.

When using partial reinforcement, it's also important to note that some partial **schedules of reinforcement** are better suited for maintaining or changing behavior than others. As you can see in **Table 6.4**, there are four schedules—fixed ratio (FR), variable ratio (VR), fixed interval (FI), and **variable interval (VI)**.

Before going on, **Figure 6.11** offers even more examples of how operant conditioning applies to everyday life. In addition, if you're feeling a bit overwhelmed with all the terms and concepts for both classical and operant condtioning, carefully study the summary provided in **Table 6.5**. Also, note that while it's convenient to divide classical and operant conditioning into separate categories, almost all behaviors result from a combination of both forms of conditioning.

Shaping A training method where reinforcement is delivered for successive approximations of the desired response.

Continuous reinforcement A reinforcement pattern in which every correct response is reinforced.

Partial (intermittent) reinforcement A reinforcement pattern in which some, but not all, correct responses are reinforced.

Schedules of reinforcement Specific patterns of reinforcement (either fixed or variable) that determine when a behavior will be reinforced.

Fixed ratio (FR) schedule A schedule of reinforcement in which a reinforcer is delivered for the first response made after a fixed number of responses.

Variable ratio (VR) schedule A schedule of reinforcement in which a reinforcer is delivered for the first response made after a variable number of responses whose average is predetermined.

Fixed interval (FI) schedule A schedule of reinforcement in which a reinforcer is delivered for the first response made after a fixed period of time.

Variable interval (VI) schedule A schedule of reinforcement in which a reinforcer is delivered for the first response made after a variable period of time whose average is predetermined.

TABLE 6.4 FOUR SCHEDULES OF PARTIAL (INTERMITTENT) REINFORCEMENT | realworldpsychology

		Definitions	Response rates	Example
Ratio schedules (response based)	**Fixed ratio (FR)**	Reinforcement occurs after a predetermined number of responses	High rate of response, but a brief drop-off just after reinforcement	You receive a free flight from your frequent flyer program after accumulating a given number of flight miles.
	Variable ratio (VR)	Reinforcement occurs after a varying number of responses	High response rate, no pause after reinforcement, and very resistant to extinction	Slot machines are designed to pay out after an average number of responses (maybe every 10 times), but any one machine may pay out on the first responses, then seventh, then the twentieth.
Interval schedules (time based)	**Fixed Interval (FI)**	Rainforcement occurs after a fixed period of time	Responses tend to increase as the time for the next reinforcement is near, but drop off after reinforcement and during interval	You receive a monthly paycheck. Rat's behavior is reinforced with a food pellet when (or if) it presses a bar after 20 seconds have elapsed.
	Variable interval (VI)	Reinforcement occurs after varying periods of time	Relatively low, but steady, response rates because respondents cannot predict when reward will come	Your professor gives pop quizzes at random times throughout the course. Rat's behavior is reinforced with a food pellet after a response and a variable unpredictable interval of time.

FIGURE 6.11 OPERANT CONDITIONING IN EVERYDAY LIFE | realworldpsychology

Reinforcement and punishment shape behavior in many aspects of our lives.

Ⓐ Prejudice and discrimination
Although prejudice and discrimination show up early in life, children are not born believing others are inferior. What reinforcement might these boys receive for teasing this boy? Can you see how operant conditioning, beginning at an early age, can promote prejudice and discrimination?

Ⓑ Superstition
Like prejudice and discrimination, we are not born being superstitious, these attitudes are learned—partly through operant conditioning. Knocking on wood for good fortune, a bride wearing "something old" at her wedding, or this baseball player placing gum on his helmet are all superstitious behaviors that generally develop from accidental reinforcement. For example, the baseball player might have once placed his gum on his helmet and then hit a home run. He then associated the gum with winning and continued the practice for all later games.

Ⓒ Biofeedback
Biofeedback relies on operant conditioning to treat ailments such as anxiety and chronic pain. For example, chronic pain patients are sometimes connected to electrodes and watch a monitor screen with a series of flashing lights, or listen to different beeps, which display changes in their internal bodily functions. The patients then use the machine's "feedback," flashing lights or beeps, to gauge their progress as they try various relaxation strategies to receive corresponding relief from the pain of muscle tension.

TABLE 6.5	COMPARING CLASSICAL AND OPERANT CONDITIONING	
	Classical Conditioning	**Operant Conditioning**
Example	Cringing at the sound of a dentist's drill	A baby cries and you pick it up
Pioneers	Ivan Pavlov	Edward Thorndike
	John B. Watson	B. F. Skinner
Key Terms	Neutral stimulus (NS)	Reinforcers and punishers (primary/secondary)
	Unconditioned stimulus (US)	Reinforcement (positive/negative)
	Conditioned stimulus (CS)	Punishment (positive/negative)
	Unconditioned response (UR)	Superstition
	Conditioned response (CR)	Shaping
	Conditioned emotional response (CER)	Schedules of reinforcement (continuous/partial)
Major Similarities	Acquisition	Acquisition
	Generalization	Generalization
	Discrimination	Discrimination
	Extinction	Extinction
	Spontaneous recovery	Spontaneous recovery
	Higher-order conditioning	Higher-order conditioning
Major Differences	Subject is passive; learning based on involuntary responses and pairing of NS with US	Subject is active; learning based on voluntary responses and their consequences
	Order of effects (most effective when NS comes *before* US)	Order of effects (most effective when reinforcement or punishment come *after* behavior)

RETRIEVAL PRACTICE: OPERANT CONDITIONING

Self-Test

Completing this self-test and comparing your answers with those in Appendix B provides immediate feedback and helpful practice for exams. Additional interactive, self-tests are available at www.wiley.com/college/huffman.

1. Learning in which voluntary responses are controlled by their consequences is called _____.

a. self-efficacy   b. operant conditioning
c. classical conditioning   d. shaping

2. An employer who gives his or her employees a cash bonus after they've done a good job is an example of _____.

a. positive reinforcement   b. incremental conditioning
c. classical conditioning   d. bribery

3. _____ reinforcers normally satisfy an unlearned biological need.

a. Positive   b. Negative
c. Primary   d. none of these options

4. The most effective way to decrease the probability of your teenager engaging in undesired behaviors is to use _____.

a. punishment and negative reinforcement   b. modeling and extinction
c. extinction and negative reinforcement   d. all of these options

Think Critically

1 You observe a parent yelling "No!" to his or her child who is screaming for candy in a supermarket. Given what you've learned about operant conditioning, can you predict how both the parent and the child will respond in similar future situations?

2 Can you think of a better alternative to yelling "No!"?

realworldpsychology

How can decreasing the cost of fruit and vegetables lead to healthier eating?

Why do gamblers have such trouble quitting, even when they continue to lose money?

HINT: LOOK IN THE MARGIN FOR (Q2) AND (Q3)

COGNITIVE-SOCIAL LEARNING

LEARNING OBJECTIVES

RETRIEVAL PRACTICE While reading the upcoming sections, respond to each Learning Objective in your own words. Then compare your responses with those found at www.wiley.com/college/huffman.

1 SUMMARIZE the cognitive-social theory of learning.
2 DESCRIBE insight learning and latent learning.
3 EXPLAIN the principles of observational learning.

So far, we have examined learning processes that involve associations between a stimulus and an observable behavior. Although some behaviorists believe that almost all learning can be explained in such stimulus–response terms, other psychologists feel that all of learning can not be explained solely by operant and classical conditioning. **Cognitive-social learning theory** (also called cognitive-social learning or cognitive-behavioral theory) incorporates the general concepts of conditioning, but rather than relying on a simple S–R (stimulus and response) model, this theory emphasizes the interpretation or thinking that occurs within the organism: S–O–R (stimulus–organism–response).

> **Cognitive-social learning theory** A theory that emphasizes the roles of thinking and social learning.

According to this view, humans have attitudes, beliefs, expectations, motivations, and emotions that affect learning. Furthermore, humans and many nonhuman animals also are social creatures that are capable of learning new behaviors through the observation and imitation of others. For example, children who perceive that at least one of their parents is physically active are much more likely to be physically active themselves (Voss & Sandercock, 2013).

Insight and Latent Learning

Early behaviorists likened the mind to a "black box" whose workings could not be observed directly. German psychologist Wolfgang Köhler (1887-1967) wanted to look inside the box. He believed that there was more to learning—especially learning to solve a complex problem—than responding to stimuli in a trial-and-error fashion.

In one of a series of experiments, Köhler placed a banana just outside the reach of a caged chimpanzee. To reach the banana, the chimp had to use a stick placed near the cage to extend its reach. Köhler noticed that the chimp did not solve the problem in a random trial-and-error fashion. Instead, he seemed to sit and think about the situation for a while. Then, in a flash of **insight**, the chimp

> **Insight** A sudden understanding or realization of how a problem can be solved.

picked up the stick and maneuvered the banana to within its grasp (Köhler, 1925). Köhler called this *insight learning* because some internal mental event, which he could only describe as "insight," went on between the presentation of the banana and the use of the stick to retrieve it. (See **Figure 6.12** for another example of how Köhler's chimps solved a different version of the same problem.)

Like Köhler, Edward C. Tolman (1898–1956) believed that previous researchers underestimated human and nonhuman animals' cognitive processes and cognitive learning. He noted that, when allowed to roam aimlessly in an experimental maze with no food reward at the end, rats seemed to develop a **cognitive map**, or mental representation of the maze.

To further test the idea of cognitive learning, Tolman allowed one group of rats to aimlessly explore a maze, with no reinforcement. A second group was reinforced with food whenever they reached the end of the maze. The third group was not rewarded during the first 10 days of the trial, but starting on day 11, they found food at the end of the maze.

As expected from simple operant conditioning, the first and third groups were slow to learn the maze, whereas the second group, which had reinforcement, showed fast, steady improvement. However, when the third group started receiving reinforcement (on the 11th day), their learning quickly caught up to the group that had been reinforced every time (Tolman & Honzik, 1930). This showed that the nonreinforced rats had been thinking and building cognitive maps of the area during their aimless wandering and that their **latent learning** only showed up when there was a reason to display it (the food reward).

Cognitive maps and latent learning are not limited to rats. For example, a chipmunk will pay little attention to a new log in its territory (after initially checking it for food). When a predator comes along, however, the chipmunk heads directly for and hides beneath the log. Recent experiments provide additional clear evidence of latent learning and the existence of internal, cognitive maps in both human and nonhuman animals (Lew, 2011; Nadel, 2013; Redish & Ekstrom, 2013) **(Figure 6.13)**.

Observational Learning

In addition to classical and operant conditioning and cognitive processes (such as insight and latent learning), we also learn many things through **observational learning**. From birth to death, observational learning is very important to our

FIGURE 6.12 COGNITIVE-SOCIAL LEARNING

In a second Köhler experiment, chimpanzees were placed in a room with several scattered boxes, none of which was high enough to enable them to reach the banana. They initially ran around and unproductively jumped for the banana. Then, all of a sudden, they saw the solution—they stacked the boxes and then used them to climb up and grab the banana! (Also, note how the chimp in the background is engaged in observational learning, our next topic.)

Cognitive map A mental image of a three-dimensional space that an organism has navigated.

Latent learning Hidden learning that exists without behavioral signs.

Observational learning The learning of new behaviors or information by watching and imitating others (also known as social learning or modeling).

Ty Milford/Masterfile

FIGURE 6.13 COGNITIVE MAPS IN HUMANS

This young woman rides through her neighborhood for fun, without a specific destination. However, she is developing her own internal cognitive maps, and she could probably easily return to the local park even though she might not be able to give specific directions. Can you think of examples of similar cognitive maps from your own life?

Albert Bandura

Albert Bandura

FIGURE 6.14 **BANDURA'S BOBO DOLL STUDY**

biological, psychological, and social survival (the *biopsychosocial model*). Watching others helps us avoid dangerous stimuli in our environment, teaches us how to think and feel, and shows us how to act and interact socially (Hora & Klassen, 2012; Kalat, 2013).

Unfortunately, watching others also may lead to negative outcomes. For example, one correlational study found that teenagers who watched high levels of televised sexual content were twice as likely to become pregnant or get a partner pregnant within the next three years compared to teens who watched low levels (Chandra et al., 2008). Further research suggests that these unintended pregnancies may reflect the fact that mainstream media focuses on glamorized, casual sex, while ignoring the risks and consequences (Strasburger, 2010).

Much of our knowledge about the power of observational learning initially came from the work of Albert Bandura and his colleagues (Bandura, 2007; Bandura, Ross, & Ross, 1961; Bandura & Walters, 1963). Wanting to know whether children learn to be aggressive by watching others be aggressive, Bandura and his colleagues set up several experiments. They allowed children to watch a live or televised adult model punch, throw, and hit a large inflated Bobo doll **(Figure 6.14 top)**. Later, the children were allowed to play in the same room with the same toys. As Bandura hypothesized, children who had seen the live or televised aggressive model were much more aggressive with the Bobo doll than children who had not seen the modeled aggression **(Figure 6.14 bottom)**. In other words, "Monkey see, monkey do."

Thanks to the Bobo doll studies and his other experiments, Bandura established that observational learning requires at least four separate processes: *attention*, *retention*, *reproduction*, and *motivation* **(Figure 6.15)**.

FIGURE 6.15 **BANDURA'S FOUR KEY FACTORS IN OBSERVATIONAL LEARNING**

A child wanting to become a premier ballerina would need to incorporate these four factors to maximize learning.

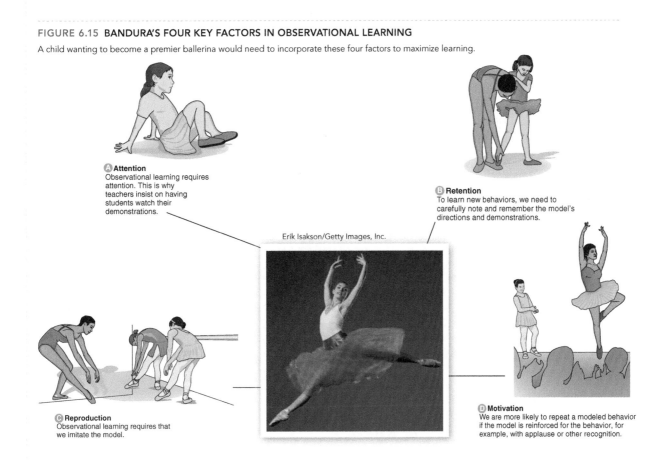

Erik Isakson/Getty Images, Inc.

A Attention
Observational learning requires attention. This is why teachers insist on having students watch their demonstrations.

B Retention
To learn new behaviors, we need to carefully note and remember the model's directions and demonstrations.

C Reproduction
Observational learning requires that we imitate the model.

D Motivation
We are more likely to repeat a modeled behavior if the model is reinforced for the behavior, for example, with applause or other recognition.

PSYCHSCIENCE

THE (SCARY) POWER OF OBSERVATIONAL LEARNING

Karl Prouse/Catwalking/Getty Images

© aldomurillo/iStockphoto

© chrisgramly/iStockphoto

What do we learn from images like these? Researchers in one study wanted to know whether the preference for the thin ideal is seen even in very young children, who should have little exposure to this type of media image of women (Harriger et al., 2010). To examine this question, these researchers asked preschool girls (ages 3 to 5) to play a game of either Candy Land or Chutes and Ladders with them. The girls were told they could select which of three game piece characters they wanted to be. Unlike the women in the photos above, these game piece characters were exactly the same, except in terms of their body size (one character was thin, one was average, one was fat).

If the girls had no preference for a particular body type, then about 33% of the girls should have randomly chosen one of the three figures. However, the researchers found that the girls showed an overwhelming preference for the character with the thin figure:

- 69% chose the thin figure.
- 20% chose the average figure.
- Only 11% chose the fat figure.

When asked to explain why they chose a particular figure, many of the girls expressed negative attitudes about the fat figure. For example, one girl said, "I hate her because she has a fat stomach." Another girl said, "I don't want to be her; she's fat and ugly." This research sadly suggests that this preference for the thinness norm emerges very early in life.

RESEARCH CHALLENGE

1. Based on the information provided, did this study (Harriger et al., 2010) use descriptive, correlational, and/or experimental research?

2. If you chose:
   - descriptive research, is this a naturalistic observation, survey/interview, case study, or archival research?
   - correlational research, is this a positive, negative, or zero correlation?
   - experimental research, label the IV, DV, experimental group(s), and control group.

>> CHECK YOUR ANSWERS IN APPENDIX B.

NOTE: The information provided in this study is admittedly limited, but the level of detail is similar to what is presented in most textbooks and public reports of research findings. Answering these questions, and then comparing your answers to those in the Appendix, will help you become a better critical thinker and consumer of scientific research.

RETRIEVAL PRACTICE: COGNITIVE-SOCIAL LEARNING

Self-Test

Completing this self-test and comparing your answers with those in Appendix B provides immediate feedback and helpful practice for exams. Additional interactive, self-tests are available at www.wiley.com/college/huffman.

1. Insight is _____.

    a. based on unconscious classical conditioning

    b. an innate human reflex

    c. a sudden flash of understanding

    d. an artifact of operant conditioning

2. When walking to your psychology class, you note that the path you normally take is blocked for construction, so you quickly choose an alternate route. This demonstrates that you've developed _____ of your campus.

    a. a hidden, latent mastery

    b. insight into the layout

    c. a cognitive map

    d. none of these options

3. Latent learning occurs without being rewarded and _____.

    a. remains hidden until a future time when it is needed

    b. is easily extinguished

    c. serves as a discriminative stimuli

    d. has been found only in nonhuman species

4. Bandura's observational learning studies focused on how _____.

    a. rats learn cognitive maps through exploration

    b. children learn aggressive behaviors by observing aggressive models

    c. cats learn problem solving through trial and error

    d. chimpanzees learn problem solving through reasoning

Think Critically

1 What are some examples of how insight learning has benefited you in your life?

2 Are there instances in which observational learning has worked to your advantage?

realworldpsychology

Does watching sex on TV increase the risk of teen pregnancies?

HINT: LOOK IN THE MARGIN FOR

BIOLOGY OF LEARNING

LEARNING OBJECTIVES

RETRIEVAL PRACTICE While reading the upcoming sections, respond to each Learning Objective in your own words. Then compare your responses with those found at www.wiley.com/college/huffman.

1 **EXPLAIN** how learning changes the brain.
2 **DESCRIBE** the biological foundation for empathy.
3 **SUMMARIZE** the role of evolution in learning.

So far in this chapter, we have considered how external forces—from reinforcing events to our observations of others—affect learning. But we also know that for changes in behavior to persist over time, lasting biological changes must occur within the organism. In this section, we will examine neurological and evolutionary influences on learning.

Neuroscience and Learning

Each time we learn something, either consciously or unconsciously, that experience creates new synaptic connections and alterations in a wide network of our brain

FIGURE 6.16 **ENVIRONMENTAL ENRICHMENT AND THE BRAIN** | realworldpsychology

For humans and nonhuman animals alike, environmental conditions play an important role in enabling learning. How might a classroom rich with stimulating toys, games, and books foster intellectual development in young children?

structures, including the cortex, cerebellum, hippocampus, hypothalamus, thalamus, and amygdala.

Evidence that learning changes brain structure first emerged in the 1960s, from studies of animals raised in enriched versus deprived environments. Compared with rats raised in a stimulus-poor environment, those raised in a colorful, stimulating "rat Disneyland" had a thicker cortex, increased nerve growth factor (NGF), more fully developed synapses, more dendritic branching, and improved performance on many tests of learning and memory (Hamilton et al., 2012; Harati et al., 2011; Lorez-Arnaiz et al., 2007; Speisman et al., 2013).

Admittedly, it is a big leap from rats to humans, but research suggests that the human brain also responds to environmental conditions **(Figure 6.16)**. For example, older adults who are exposed to stimulating environments generally perform better on intellectual and perceptual tasks than those who are in restricted environments (Daffner, 2010; Petrosini et al., 2013; Schaie, 1994, 2008).

Similarly, babies who spend their early weeks and months of life in an orphanage, and receive little or no one-on-one care or attention, show deficits in the cortex of the brain, indicating that early environmental conditions may have a lasting impact on cognitive development (Almas et al., 2012; Sheridan et al., 2012). The good news, however, is that children who are initially placed in an orphanage but later move on to foster care—where they receive more individual attention—show some improvements in brain development.

Mirror Neurons and Imitation

Recent research has identified another neurological influence on learning processes, particularly imitation. When an adult models a facial expression, even very young infants will respond with a similar expression **(Figure 6.17)**. At 9 months, infants will imitate facial actions a full day after first seeing them (Heimann & Meltzoff, 1996).

How can newborn infants so easily imitate the facial expressions of others? Using fMRIs and other brain-imaging techniques,

FIGURE 6.17 **INFANT IMITATION—EVIDENCE OF MIRROR NEURONS?**

In a series of well-known studies, Andrew Meltzoff and M. Keith Moore (1977, 1985, 1994) found that newborns could imitate such facial movements as tongue protrusion, mouth opening, and lip pursing.

From: A.N. Meltzoff & M.K. Moore, "Imitation of facial and manual gestures by human neonates." Science, 1977, 198, 75–78.

Mirror neuron A type of neuron that fires (or activates) when an action is performed, as well as when observing the actions or emotions of another; believed to be responsible for empathy, imitation, language, and the deficits of some mental disorders.

researchers have identified specific **mirror neurons** believed to be responsible for human empathy and imitation (Ahlsén, 2008; Baird et al., 2011; Caggiano et al., 2011; Haker et al., 2013). These neurons are found in several key areas of the brain, and are believed to be responsible for how we identify with what others are feeling and imitate their actions. When we see another person in pain, one reason we empathize and "share their pain" may be that our mirror neurons are firing. Similarly, if we watch others who are smiling, our mirror neurons make it harder for us to frown.

Mirror neurons were first discovered by neuroscientists who implanted wires in the brains of monkeys to monitor areas involved in planning and carrying out movement (Ferrari et al., 2005; Rizzolatti et al., 2002, 2006). When these monkeys moved and grasped an object, specific neurons fired, but they also fired when the monkeys simply observed another monkey performing the same or similar tasks.

Carlos E. Santa Maria/Shutterstock

realworldpsychology   **Mirror Neurons** Have you noticed how spectators at an athletic event sometimes slightly move their arms or legs in synchrony with the athletes? Mirror neurons may be the underlying biological mechanism for this imitation. Deficiencies in these neurons also might help explain the emotional deficits of children and adults with autism or schizophrenia, who often misunderstand the verbal and nonverbal cues of others (Enticott et al., 2012; Kana et al., 2011; Rizzolatti, 2012).

Although scientists are excited about the promising links between mirror neurons and human emotions, imitation, language, learning, and learning disabilities, we do not yet know how they develop. In addition, other researchers have suggested that more research is needed to justify the claims for the role of mirror neurons (Baird et al., 2011; Thomas, 2012). Stay tuned.

Evolution and Learning

Humans and other animals are born with various innate reflexes and instincts. Although these biological tendencies help ensure evolutionary survival, they are inherently inflexible. Learning allows us to more flexibly respond to complex environmental cues, such as spoken words and written symbols, which in turn enables us to survive and prosper in a constantly changing world.

Because animals can be classically conditioned to salivate to tones and operantly conditioned to perform a variety of novel behaviors, such as a seal balancing a ball on its nose, learning theorists initially believed that the fundamental laws of conditioning would apply to almost all species and all behaviors. However, researchers have discovered that some associations are much more readily learned than others.

For example, when a food or drink is associated with nausea or vomiting, that particular food or drink more readily becomes a conditioned stimulus (CS) that triggers a conditioned **taste aversion**. Like other classically conditioned responses, taste aversions develop involuntarily.

Taste-aversion A classically conditioned dislike for, and avoidance of, a specific food whose ingestion is followed by illness.

© robtek/iStockphoto

psychology and you   **Taste Aversion** Years ago, a young woman named Rebecca unsuspectingly bit into a Butterfinger candy bar filled with small, wiggling maggots. Horrified, she ran gagging and screaming to the bathroom. Many years later, Rebecca still feels nauseated when she sees a Butterfinger candy bar. Can you see how stimulus discrimination explains why she doesn't feel similarly nauseated by the sight of her boyfriend, who bought her the candy?

Rebecca's graphic (and true!) story illustrates an important evolutionary process. Being biologically prepared to quickly associate nausea with food or drink is obviously adaptive because it helps us avoid that or similar food or drink in the future (Domjan, 2005; Garcia, 2003; Lotem & Halpern, 2012; Swami, 2011).

Further evidence comes from John Garcia and his colleague Robert Koelling (1966) who produced a taste aversion in lab rats by pairing sweetened water (NS) and a shock (US), which produced nausea (UR). After being conditioned and then recovering from the illness, the rats refused to drink the sweetened water (CS) because of the conditioned taste aversion. Remarkably, however, Garcia also discovered that only certain neutral stimuli could produce the nausea. Pairings of a noise (NS) with the shock (US) produced no taste aversion.

Similarly, perhaps because of the more "primitive" evolutionary threat posed by snakes, darkness, spiders, and heights, people tend to more easily develop phobias of these stimuli and situations far more easily than of guns, knives, and electrical outlets. Research also shows that both adults and very young children have an innate ability to very quickly identify the presence of a snake, whereas they are less able to quickly identify other (non-life-threatening) objects, including a caterpillar, flower, or toad (LoBue & DeLoache, 2008; Young et al., 2012). We apparently inherit a built-in (innate) readiness to form associations between certain stimuli and responses—but not others. This is known as **biological preparedness**.

Just as Garcia couldn't produce classically conditioned noise–nausea associations, other researchers have found that an animal's natural behavior pattern can interfere with operant conditioning. For example, early researchers tried to teach a chicken to play baseball (Breland & Breland, 1961). Through shaping and reinforcement, the chicken first learned to pull a loop that activated a swinging bat and then learned to actually hit the ball. But instead of running to first base, it would chase the ball as if it were food. Regardless of the lack of reinforcement for chasing the ball, the chicken's natural behavior took precedence. This type of biological behavior, is known as **instinctive drift**, along with taste aversions and the variability in phobic responses, are all examples of biological preparedness.

In this chapter, we've discussed three general types of learning, classical, operant, and cognitive-social. We've also examined the biological effect on learning. As humans, we also have the capacity to learn and change thanks to our ability to remember, think, and to use language, as well as our individual forms of intelligence. Each of these exciting topics are discussed in the next two chapters.

Biological preparedness The built-in (innate) readiness to form associations between certain stimuli and responses.

Instinctive drift The tendency for conditioned responses to revert (drift back) to innate response patterns.

RETRIEVAL PRACTICE: BIOLOGY OF LEARNING

Self-Test

Completing this self-test and comparing your answers with those in Appendix B provides immediate feedback and helpful practice for exams. Additional interactive, self-tests are available at www.wiley.com/college/huffman.

1. _____ neurons may be responsible for human empathy and imitation.

   a. Motor   b. Sensitivity
   c. Empathy   d. Mirror

2. Rebecca's story of becoming nauseated and vomiting after eating a spoiled candy bar is a good example of _____.

   a. a biological imperative   b. a taste aversion
   c. learned empathy   d. negative reinforcement

3. Being innately predisposed to form associations between certain stimuli and responses is called _____.

   a. prejudice   b. vicarious learning
   c. superstitious priming   d. biological preparedness

4. A biological constraint where an animal's conditioned responses tend to shift toward innate response patterns is called _____.

   a. biological preparedness   b. reflexes
   c. instinctive drift   d. taste aversion

Think Critically

1 If mirror neurons explain human empathy, could they also explain why first responders (like police and firefighters) are more vulnerable to job burnout? Why or why not?

2 Do you have any taste aversions? If so, how would you use information in this chapter to remove them?

realworldpsychology

Why can even young children recognize a picture of a snake much faster than a picture of a frog or caterpillar?

HINT: LOOK IN THE MARGIN FOR Q5

Summary

1 CLASSICAL CONDITIONING 152

- **Learning** is a relatively permanent change in behavior or mental processes caused by experience. Pavlov discovered a fundamental form of **conditioning** (learning) called **classical conditioning**, a type of learning that develops through involuntarily paired associations. A previously **neutral stimulus (NS)** becomes associated with an **unconditioned stimulus (US)** to elicit a **conditioned response (CR)**.
- In the "Little Albert" study, Watson and Rayner demonstrated how many of our likes, dislikes, prejudices, and fears are examples of a **conditioned emotional response (CER)**, which develops in response to a previously neutral stimulus (NS).
- **Acquisition**, the first of six key principles of classical conditioning, occurs when the **conditioned stimulus (CS)** leads to a CR. **Stimulus generalization** occurs when an event similar to the originally conditioned stimulus triggers the same conditioned response. With experience, animals learn to distinguish between an original conditioned stimulus and similar stimuli—**stimulus discrimination**. **Extinction** is a gradual weakening or suppression of a previously conditioned response. However, if a conditioned stimulus is reintroduced after extinction, an extinguished response may **spontaneously recover**. **Higher-order conditioning** occurs when the NS becomes a CS through repeated pairings with a previous CS.

2 OPERANT CONDITIONING 159

- In **operant conditioning**, an organism learns as a result of voluntary behavior and its subsequent consequences. **Reinforcement** strengthens the response, while **punishment** weakens the response.
- Thorndike developed the **law of effect**, in which responses that produce a satisfying effect are more likely to recur, whereas those that produce a discomforting effect become less likely to recur. Skinner extended Thorndike's law of effect to more complex behaviors.
- **Primary reinforcers** and **primary punishers** are innate, whereas **secondary reinforcers** and **secondary punishers** are learned. Each type of reinforcer can produce **positive reinforcement** or **negative reinforcement,** and both of these

forms of reinforcement strengthen the response they follow. Negative reinforcement is NOT punishment. Both **positive punishment** and **negative punishment** weaken a response.
- Punishment can have serious side effects: passive aggressiveness, avoidance behavior, inappropriate modeling, temporary suppression, learned helplessness, rewarded aggression, and perpetuated aggression.
- Organisms learn complex behaviors through **shaping**, in which reinforcement is delivered for successive approximations of the desired response.
- **Schedules of reinforcement** refers to the rate or interval at which responses are reinforced. Most behavior is rewarded and maintained through one of four partial schedules of reinforcement: **fixed ratio (FR)**, **variable ratio (VR)**, **fixed interval (FI)**, or **variable interval (VI)**.

3 COGNITIVE-SOCIAL LEARNING 168

- **Cognitive-social learning theory** emphasizes cognitive and social aspects of learning. Köhler discovered that animals sometimes learn through sudden **insight**, rather than through trial and error. Tolman provided evidence of hidden, **latent learning** and internal **cognitive maps**.
- Bandura's research found that children who watched an adult behave aggressively toward an inflated Bobo doll were later more aggressive than those who had not seen the aggression. According to Bandura, **observational learning** requires attention, retention, reproduction, and motivation.

4 BIOLOGY OF LEARNING 172

- Learning creates structural changes in the brain. Early evidence for such changes came from research on animals raised in enriched environments versus deprived environments.
- **Mirror neurons** fire when an action is performed, as well as when observing the actions or emotions of another.
- Learning is an evolutionary adaptation that enables organisms to survive and prosper in a constantly changing world. Researchers have identified biological constraints that limit the generality of conditioning principles: **biological preparedness** and **instinctive drift**.

Chris Fitzgerald/CandidatePhotos/NewsCom

⊙ applyingrealworldpsychology

We began this chapter with five intriguing Real World Psychology questions, and you were asked to revisit these questions at the end of each section. Questions like these have an important and lasting impact on all of our lives. See if you can answer these additional critical thinking questions related to real world examples.

1 What principles of learning best explain why politicians kiss babies?

2 What other stimuli or symbols do politicians use in their campaigns that are based on learning principles?

3 Have you ever used learning principles to get others to do what you want? Was it ethical?

4 How could the media be used to promote desirable traits and behaviors in the viewing public?

5 Imagine if someone developed a secret pill that could make alcohol, tobacco, and fatty foods an immediate taste aversion for everyone. Would that be a good or bad thing? Assuming that it was safe, would you take the pill? Why or why not?

Key Terms

RETRIEVAL PRACTICE   Write a definition for each term before turning back to the referenced page to check your answer.

- acquisition 156
- biological preparedness 175
- classical conditioning 153
- cognitive map 169
- cognitive-social learning theory 168
- conditioned emotional response (CER) 154
- conditioned response (CR) 154
- conditioned stimulus (CS) 154
- conditioning 153
- continuous reinforcement 165
- extinction 157
- fixed interval (FI) schedule 165
- fixed ratio (FR) schedule 165
- higher-order conditioning 158

- insight 168
- instinctive drift 175
- latent learning 169
- law of effect 160
- learning 152
- mirror neurons 174
- negative punishment 162
- negative reinforcement 161
- neutral stimulus (NS) 154
- observational learning 169
- operant conditioning 159
- partial (intermittent) of reinforcement 165
- positive punishment 162
- positive reinforcement 161
- Premack principle 162

- primary punishers 162
- primary reinforcers 161
- punishment 159
- reinforcement 159
- schedules of reinforcement 165
- secondary punishers 162
- secondary reinforcers 161
- shaping 165
- spontaneous recovery 157
- stimulus discrimination 156
- stimulus generalization 156
- taste aversion 174
- unconditioned response (UR) 154
- unconditioned stimulus (US) 154
- variable interval (VI) schedule 165
- variable ratio (VR) schedule 165

chapterseven

Memory

realworldpsychology

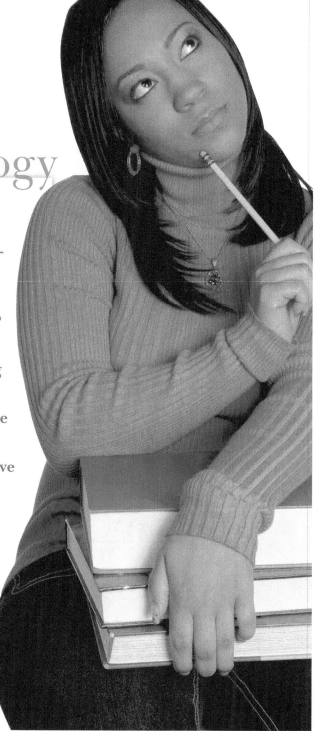

THINGS YOU'LL LEARN IN CHAPTER 7

Q1 Do daydreamers actually have better working-memory skills than people who don't daydream?

Q2 How can taking a nap improve your memory?

Q3 Can merely imagining engaging in a behavior create a false memory of actually performing that behavior?

Q4 Why might exposure to pornography interfere with memory?

Q5 Does accuracy increase when eyewitnesses have only a few seconds to make an identification?

THROUGHOUT THE CHAPTER, MARGIN ICONS FOR Q1–Q5 INDICATE WHERE THE TEXT ADDRESSES THESE QUESTIONS.

Sleep mask: © evemilla/iStockphoto; Man with thought bubble: © holicow/iStockphoto; Male athlete running: © 4x6/iStockphoto; Blocks spelling x-rated: © morrbyte/iStockphoto; Woman swearing on a bible: © qingwa/iStockphoto; Girl deep in thought: © John Cooke/iStockphoto

chapteroverview

When H.M. was 27, he underwent brain surgery to correct his severe epileptic seizures. Although the surgery improved his medical problem, now something was clearly wrong with H.M.'s long-term memory. When his uncle died, he grieved in a normal way. But soon after, he began to ask why his uncle never visited him. H.M. had to be repeatedly reminded of his uncle's death, and each reminder would begin a new mourning process.

H.M. lived another 55 years not recognizing the people who cared for him daily. Each time he met his caregivers, read a book, or ate a meal, it was as if for the first time (Barbeau, Puel, & Pariente, 2010; Carey, 2008; Corkin, 2002). Sadly, H.M. died in 2008—never having regained his long-term memory.

What should we make of this true, real-life example? What would it be like to be H.M.—existing only in the present moment, unable to learn and form new memories? How can we remember our second-grade teacher's name, but forget the name of someone we just met? In this chapter, you'll discover answers to these and other fascinating questions about memory.

THE NATURE OF MEMORY

LEARNING OBJECTIVES

RETRIEVAL PRACTICE While reading the upcoming sections, respond to each Learning Objective in your own words. Then compare your responses with those found at www.wiley.com/college/huffman.

1 **REVIEW** the core principles of the major memory models.

2 **DESCRIBE** the purpose of sensory memory.

3 **EXPLAIN** the function of short-term memory (STM) and how it operates as our working memory.

4 **DESCRIBE** the functions and various types of long-term memory (LTM).

5 **EXPLAIN** how organization, elaborative rehearsal, and retrieval cues improve long-term memory.

Memory The internal record or representation of some prior event or experience; the mental capacity to encode, store, and retrieve information.

Constructive process The process of organizing and shaping information during processing, storage, and retrieval of memories.

Memory allows us to learn from our experiences and to adapt to ever-changing environments. Without it, we would have no past or future. Yet our memories are also highly fallible. Although some people think of **memory** as a gigantic library or an automatic video recorder, our memories are not exact recordings of events. Instead, memory is a **constructive process** through which we actively organize and shape information as it is being processed, stored, and retrieved. As expected, this construction often leads to serious errors and biases, which we'll discuss throughout the chapter.

Memory Models

To understand memory (and its constructive nature), you need a model of how it operates. Over the years, psychologists have developed numerous models for memory, and we'll focus on the two most important ones.

Encoding, Storage, and Retrieval (ESR) Model

Encoding, storage, and retrieval (ESR) model A memory model which suggests that memory is formed through three processes: *encoding* (getting information in), *storage* (retaining information for future use), and *retrieval* (recovering information).

Encoding The process by which a mental representation is formed in memory.

Storage The retention of encoded information over time.

According to the **encoding, storage, and retrieval (ESR) model**, the barrage of information that we encounter every day goes through three basic operations: *encoding, storage,* and *retrieval.* Each of these processes represents a different function that is closely analogous to the parts and functions of a computer **(Figure 7.1)**.

To input data into a computer, you begin by typing letters and numbers on the keyboard. The computer then translates these keystrokes into its own electronic language. In a roughly similar fashion, your brain **encodes** sensory information (sound, visual images, and other senses) into a neural code (language) it can understand and use.

Once information is *encoded*, it must be **stored**. Computer information is normally stored on a flash drive or hard drive, whereas human information is stored in the brain.

FIGURE 7.1 ENCODING, STORAGE, AND RETRIEVAL

The encoding, storage, and retrieval model of memory can be compared to a computer's information processing system.

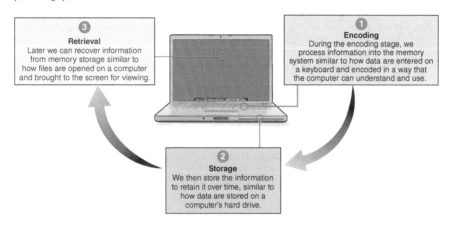

③ Retrieval
Later we can recover information from memory storage similar to how files are opened on a computer and brought to the screen for viewing.

① Encoding
During the encoding stage, we process information into the memory system similar to how data are entered on a keyboard and encoded in a way that the computer can understand and use.

② Storage
We then store the information to retain it over time, similar to how data are stored on a computer's hard drive.

Finally, information must be **retrieved**, or taken out of storage. We retrieve stored information by going to files on our computer or to "files" in our brain. Keep this model in mind. To do well in college, or almost any other pursuit, you must successfully encode, store and retrieve a large amount of facts and concepts. Throughout this chapter, we'll discuss ways to improve your memory during each of these processes.

Retrieval The recovery of information from memory storage.

Three-Stage Memory Model

Since the late 1960s, the most highly researched and widely used memory model has been the **three-stage memory model** (Atkinson & Shiffrin, 1968; Eichenbaum, 2013; Nairne & Neath, 2013). It remains the leading paradigm in memory research because it offers a convenient way to organize the major findings. According to this model, three different storage "boxes," or memory stages, hold and process information. Each stage has a different purpose, duration, and capacity **(Figure 7.2)**. Let's discuss each stage in more detail.

Three-stage memory model A memory model which suggests that memory storage requires passage of information through three stages (sensory, short-term, and long-term memory).

FIGURE 7.2 THE TRADITIONAL THREE-STAGE MEMORY MODEL

Each "box" represents a separate memory system that differs in purpose, duration, and capacity. When information is not transferred from sensory memory or short-term memory, it is assumed to be lost. Information stored in long-term memory can be retrieved and sent back to short-term memory for use.

Sensory memory The initial memory stage, which holds sensory information; it has relatively large capacity but the duration is only a few seconds.

FIGURE 7.3 SPERLING'S TEST FOR ICONIC MEMORY

Short-term memory (STM) The second memory stage, which temporarily stores sensory information and decides whether to send it on to long-term memory (LTM); its capacity is limited to five to nine items and it has a duration of about 30 seconds.

Chunking The process of grouping separate pieces of information into a single unit (or chunk) on the basis of similarity or some other organizing principle.

Sensory Memory

Everything we see, hear, touch, taste, and smell must first enter our **sensory memory**. Once it's entered, the information remains in sensory memory just long enough for our brain to locate relevant bits of data and transfer it on to the next stage of memory. For visual information, known as *iconic memory*, the visual image (icon) stays in sensory memory only about one-half a second before it rapidly fades away.

In an early study of iconic sensory memory, George Sperling (1960) flashed an arrangement of 12 letters like the ones in **Figure 7.3** for 1/20 of a second. Most people, he found, could recall only 4 or 5 of the letters. But when instructed to report just the top, middle, or bottom row, depending on whether they heard a high, medium, or low tone, they reported almost all the letters correctly. Apparently, all 12 letters are held in sensory memory right after they are viewed, but only those that are immediately attended to are noted and processed.

Like the fleeting visual images in iconic memory, auditory stimuli (what we hear) is also temporary but a weaker "echo," or *echoic memory*, of this auditory input lingers for up to four seconds (Inui et al., 2010; Neisser, 1967; Radvansky, 2011). Why are iconic and auditory memories so fleeting? We cannot process all incoming stimuli, so lower brain centers need only a few seconds to "decide" if the information is important enough to promote to conscious awareness **(Figure 7.4).**

Early researchers believed that sensory memory had an unlimited capacity. However, later research suggests that sensory memory does have limits and that stored images are fuzzier than once thought (Franconeri et al., 2013; Goldstein, 2010; Moulin, 2011).

Short-Term Memory (STM)

The second stage of memory processing, **short-term memory (STM)**, temporarily stores and processes sensory stimuli. If the information is important, STM organizes and sends this information along to long-term (LTM)—otherwise, information decays and is lost. STM also retrieves stored memories from LTM. Otherwise, information decays and is lost.

The capacity and duration of STM are limited (Bankó & Vidnyánsky, 2010; Nairne & Neath, 2013). To extend the *capacity* of STM, you can use a technique called **chunking** (Glicksohn & Cohen, 2011; Miller, 1956; Oberauer et al., 2013; Thornton & Conway, 2013). Have you noticed that your credit card, Social Security, and telephone numbers are almost always grouped into three or four units separated

FIGURE 7.4 DEMONSTRATING ICONIC AND ECHOIC MEMORIES *psychology and you*

Ⓐ Visual Images—Iconic Memory
To demonstrate the duration of visual memory, or *iconic memory*, swing a flashlight in a dark room. Because the image, or icon, lingers for a fraction of a second after the flashlight is moved, you see the light as a continuous stream, as in this photo, rather than as a succession of individual points.

Ⓑ Auditory Stimuli—Echoic Memory
Think back to a time when someone asked you a question while you were deeply absorbed in a task. Did you ask "What?" and then immediately find you could answer them without hearing their repeated response? Now you know why. A weaker "echo" (echoic memory) of auditory information is available for up to four seconds.

by hyphens? The reason is that it's easier to remember numbers in chunks rather than as a string of single digits.

Chunking also helps in football. What do you see when you observe this arrangement of players from a page of a football playbook **(Figure 7.5)**? To the inexpert eye, it looks like a random assembly of lines and arrows, and a naive person generally would have little or no understanding or appreciation of the skills required in football. But experienced players and seasoned fans generally recognize many or all of the standard plays. To them, the scattered lines form meaningful patterns—classic arrangements that recur often. Just as you group the letters of this sentence into meaningful words and remember them long enough to understand the meaning of the sentence, expert football players group the different football plays into easily recalled patterns (or chunks).

You can also extend the *duration* of your STM almost indefinitely by consciously "juggling" the information—a process called **maintenance rehearsal**. You are using maintenance rehearsal when you look up a phone number and repeat it over and over until you key in the number.

People who are good at remembering names also know to take advantage of maintenance rehearsal. They repeat the name of each person they meet, aloud or silently, to keep it active in STM. They also make sure that other thoughts (such as their plans for what to say next) don't intrude.

As you can see in **Figure 7.6**, short-term memory is more than just a passive, temporary "holding area." Given that active processing of information also occurs in STM, many researchers prefer the term **working memory** (Baddeley, 1992, 2007; Barrouillet & Camos, 2012; Brady & Tenenbaum, 2013; Thornton & Conway, 2013). All our conscious thinking occurs in this "working memory," and the manipulation of information that occurs here helps explain some of the memory errors and false constructions described in this chapter.

Interestingly, people who daydream while completing simple tasks may show even higher working-memory capabilities (Levinson et al., 2012). Researchers in one study first tested participants on their level of working memory, meaning how much information they could hold in their minds at one time. The participants then completed relatively mindless tasks, such as pressing a button each time a certain letter appeared on a computer screen. Participants were asked periodically whether their minds were focused on the assigned task or were wandering to other thoughts. People with higher working-memory scores reported more mind wandering during the mindless task, presumably because they needed to spend less attention on the simple task. These findings suggest that having better working-memory skills may allow for more daydreaming!

FIGURE 7.5 CHUNKING IN FOOTBALL

Maintenance rehearsal The memory-improvement technique of repeating information over and over to maintain it in short-term memory (STM).

Working memory An alternate term for short-term memory (STM), which emphasizes the active processing of information.

Q1

Three-stage memory model

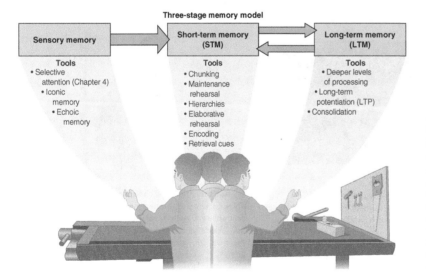

Sensory memory	Short-term memory (STM)	Long-term memory (LTM)
Tools	**Tools**	**Tools**
• Selective attention (Chapter 4)	• Chunking	• Deeper levels of processing
• Iconic memory	• Maintenance rehearsal	• Long-term potentiation (LTP)
• Echoic memory	• Hierarchies	• Consolidation
	• Elaborative rehearsal	
	• Encoding	
	• Retrieval cues	

FIGURE 7.6 HOW WORKING MEMORY MIGHT WORK

Given that short-term memory (STM) is active, or *working*, It helps to visually picture STM as a "workbench," with a "worker" at the bench who selectively attends to certain sensory information and also sends and retrieves it from long-term memory (LTM). The worker also manipulates the incoming, transferred, and retrieved information. Note the "tools" the "worker" uses during the three stages of processing.

Long-term memory (LTM) The third stage of memory, which stores information for long periods of time; the capacity is virtually limitless, and the duration is relatively permanent.

Explicit/declarative memory A subsystem within long-term memory (LTM) that consciously stores facts, information, and personal life experiences.

Semantic memory A subsystem of long-term memory (LTM) that stores general knowledge; a mental encyclopedia or dictionary.

Episodic memory A subsystem of long-term memory (LTM) that stores autobiographical events and the contexts in which they occurred; a mental diary of a person's life.

Implicit/nondeclarative memory A subsystem within long-term memory (LTM) that unconsciously stores procedural skills and simple classically conditioned responses.

Long-Term Memory (LTM)

Once information has been transferred from STM, it is organized and integrated with other information in **long-term memory (LTM)**. LTM serves as a storehouse for information that must be kept for long periods. When we need the information, it is sent back to STM for our conscious use. Compared with sensory memory and short-term memory, long-term memory has relatively unlimited *capacity* and *duration* (Eichenbaum, 2013). But, just as with any other possession, the better we label and arrange our memories, the more readily we'll be able to retrieve them.

How do we store the vast amount of information we collect over a lifetime? Several types of LTM exist **(Figure 7.7)**.

Explicit/declarative memory refers to intentional learning or conscious knowledge. If asked to remember your phone number or your mother's name, you can easily state (*declare*) the answers directly (*explicitly*).

Explicit/declarative memory can be further subdivided into two parts. **Semantic memory** is memory for general knowledge, rules, events, facts, and specific information. It is our mental encyclopedia. In contrast, **episodic memory** is like a mental diary. It records the major events (*episodes*) in our lives. Some of our episodic memories are short-lived, whereas others can last a lifetime.

Have you ever wondered why most adults can recall almost nothing of the years before they reached age 3? Research suggests that a concept of self, sufficient language development, and growth of the frontal lobes of the cortex (along with other structures) may be necessary for us to encode and retrieve early events many years later (Bauer & Lukowski, 2010; Pathman & Bauer, 2013; Rose et al., 2011).

Implicit/nondeclarative memory refers to unintentional learning or unconscious knowledge. Try telling someone else how you tie your shoelaces without demonstrating the actual behavior. Because your memory of this skill is unconscious and hard to describe (*declare*) in words, this type of memory is sometimes referred to as *nondeclarative*.

Implicit/nondeclarative memory consists of *procedural* motor skills, like tying your shoes or riding a bike, as well as *classically conditioned memory* responses, such as fears or taste aversions.

FIGURE 7.7 TYPES OF LONG-TERM MEMORY (LTM)

LTM is divided and subdivided into various types.

Implicit/nondeclarative memory also includes **priming**, in which prior exposure to a stimulus (*prime*) facilitates or inhibits the processing of new information (McKoon & Ratcliff, 2012; Northup & Mulligan, 2013; Schmitz & Wentura, 2012). Priming often occurs even when we do not consciously remember being exposed to the prime.

Priming A process in which a prior exposure to a stimulus (or prime) facilitates or inhibits the processing of new information, even when one has no conscious memory of the initial learning and storage.

© CBW/Alamy Inc.

> **psychology and you** **How Our Moods Are Primed** Have you ever felt nervous being home alone while reading a Stephen King novel, experienced sadness after hearing about a tragic event in the news, or developed amorous feelings while watching a romantic movie? These are all examples of how the situation we are in may influence our mood, in conscious or unconscious ways. Given this new insight into how priming can "set you up" for certain emotions, can you see how others who haven't studied psychology might be more likely to mislabel or overreact to their emotions?

Improving Long-Term Memory

There are several ways we can improve long-term memory. These include *organization, rehearsal* (or *repetition*), and *retrieval*.

One additional trick for giving your memory a boost is to use **mnemonic** devices to encode items in a special way (see *Improving Your Memory Using Mnemonic Devices* on the next page). However, these devices take practice and time, and some students find that they get better results using the other well-researched principles discussed throughout this chapter.

Mnemonic A strategy or device that uses familiar information during the encoding of new information to enhance subsequent access to the information in memory.

Organization

To successfully encode information for LTM, we need to *organize* material into hierarchies. This means arranging a number of related items into broad categories that we further divide and subdivide. (This organizational strategy for LTM is similar to the strategy of chunking material in STM.) For instance, by grouping small subsets of ideas together (as subheadings under larger, main headings and within diagrams, tables, and so on), we hope to make the material in this book more understandable and *memorable*.

Admittedly, organization takes time and work. But you'll be happy to know that some memory organization and filing is done automatically while you sleep (Groch et al., 2013; Payne et al., 2012; Stickgold & Walker, 2013; Verleger et al., 2011). In fact, research shows that people who rest and close their eyes for as little as 10 minutes show greater memory for details of a story they've just heard (Dewar et al., 2012). Unfortunately, despite claims to the contrary, research shows that we can't recruit our sleeping hours to memorize new material, such as a foreign language.

Rehearsal

Like organization, *rehearsal* also improves encoding for both STM and LTM. If you need to hold information in STM for longer than 30 seconds, you can simply keep repeating it (maintenance rehearsal). But storage in LTM requires *deeper levels of processing*, called **elaborative rehearsal**.

The immediate goal of elaborative rehearsal is to *understand*—not to memorize. Fortunately, this attempt to understand is one of the best ways to encode new information into long-term memory.

Elaborative rehearsal A technique for improving memory by linking new information to previously stored material; also known as deeper levels of processing.

IMPROVING YOUR MEMORY USING MNEMONIC DEVICES

psychology and you

These three mnemonics improve memory by tagging information to physical locations (*method of loci*), organizing information into main and subsidiary topics (an *outline*), and using familiar information to remember the unfamiliar (*acronyms*).

Ⓐ Method of loci

Greek and Roman orators developed the *method of loci* to keep track of the many parts of their long speeches. Orators would imagine the parts of their speeches attached to places in a courtyard. For example, if an opening point in a speech was the concept of *justice*, they might visualize a courthouse placed in the first corner of their garden. Continuing this imaginary garden walk, the second point the orator might make would be about the prison system, and the third would be the need for balance in government.

Ⓑ Outline organization

When listening to lectures and/or reading the text, draw a vertical line approximately 3 inches from the left margin of your notebook paper. Write main headings from the chapter outline to the left of the line and add specific details and examples from the lecture or text on the right, as in this example:

Outline	Details and Examples from Lecture and Text
1. Nature of Memory	_____
a. Memory Models	_____
b. Sensory Memory	_____
c. Short-Term Memory (STM)	_____

Ⓒ Acronyms

To use the *acronym method*, create a new code word from the first letters of the items you want to remember. For example, to recall the names of the Great Lakes, think of *HOMES* on a *great lake* (Huron, Ontario, Michigan, Erie, Superior). Visualizing homes on each lake also helps you remember your code word *homes*.

Think Critically

1 How could you use the method of loci to remember several items on your grocery shopping list?

2 How would you use the acronym method to remember the names of the last seven presidents of the United States?

Retrieval

Finally, effective *retrieval* is critical to improving long-term memory. There are two types of **retrieval cues (Figure 7.8)**. *Specific* cues require you only to *recognize* the correct response. *General* cues require you to *recall* previously learned material by searching through all possible matches in LTM—a much more difficult task.

Retrieval cue A prompt or stimulus that aids recall or retrieval of a stored piece of information from long-term memory (LTM).

> psychology and you   **The Power of Retrieval Cues** Whether cues require recall or only recognition is not all that matters. Imagine that while house hunting, you walk into a stranger's kitchen and are greeted with the unmistakable smell of freshly baked bread. Instantly, the aroma transports you to your grandmother's kitchen, where you spent many childhood afternoons doing your homework. You find yourself suddenly thinking of the mental shortcuts your grandmother taught you to help you learn your multiplication tables. You hadn't thought about these little tricks for years, but somehow a whiff of baking bread brought them back to you. Why?

© M Studio/iStockphoto

In this imagined baking bread episode, you have stumbled upon the **encoding-specificity principle** (Tulving & Thompson, 1973). In most cases, we're able to remember better when we attempt to recall information in the *same* context in which we learned it (Lin et al., 2013; Unsworth et al., 2012). Have you noticed that you tend to do better on exams when you take them in the same seat and classroom in which you originally studied the material? This happens because the matching location acts as a retrieval cue for the information.

People also remember information better if their moods during learning and retrieval match (Forgas & Eich, 2013; Howe & Malone, 2011). This phenomenon, called *mood congruence*, occurs because a given mood tends to evoke memories that are consistent with that mood. When you're sad (or happy or angry), you're

Encoding-specificity principle The principle that retrieval of information is improved if cues received at the time of recall are consistent with those present at the time of encoding.

FIGURE 7.8 RECALL VERSUS RECOGNITION

Can you *recall*, in order, the names of the planets in our solar system? If not, it's probably because recall, like questions on an essay exam, requires retrieval using only general, nonspecific cues—like naming the planets. In contrast, a recognition task only requires you to identify the correct response, like a multiple-choice exam. Note how much easier it is to *recognize* the names of the planets when you're provided a specific retrieval cue, in this case the first three letters of each planet: Mer-, Ven-, Ear-, Mar-, Jup-, Sat-, Ura-, Nep-, Plu-. (Note that in 2006, Pluto was officially declassified as a planet and is now considered a "dwarf planet.")

Antonio M. Rosario/Photographer's Choice/Getty Images

more likely to remember events and circumstances from other times when you were sad (or happy or angry).

Finally, memory retrieval is most effective when we are in the same state of consciousness as we were in when the memory was formed. For example, people who are intoxicated will better remember events that happened in a previous drunken state, compared to when they are sober (Nasehi et al., 2010; Sanday et al., 2013). This is called *state-dependent retrieval.*

RETRIEVAL PRACTICE: THE NATURE OF MEMORY

Self-Test

Completing this self-test and comparing your answers with those in Appendix B provides immediate feedback and helpful practice for exams. Additional interactive, self-tests are available at www.wiley.com/college/huffman.

1. Information in _____ lasts only a few seconds or less and has a relatively large (but not unlimited) storage capacity.

   a. perceptual processes   b. working memory
   c. short-term storage   d. sensory memory

2. _____ is the process of grouping separate pieces of information into a single unit.

   a. Chunking   b. Collecting
   c. Conflation   d. Dual-coding

3. In answering this question, the correct multiple-choice option may serve as a _____ for recalling accurate information from your long-term memory.

   a. specificity code   b. retrieval cue
   c. priming pump   d. flashbulb stimulus

4. The encoding-specificity principle says that information retrieval is improved when _____.

   a. both maintenance and elaborative rehearsal are used
   b. reverberating circuits consolidate information
   c. conditions of recovery are similar to encoding conditions
   d. long-term potentiation is accessed

Think Critically

1 What are some of the possible advantages and disadvantages of the fact that memory is a constructive process?

2 If you were forced to lose one type of memory—sensory, short-term, or long-term—which would you select? Why?

realworldpsychology

Do daydreamers actually have better working-memory skills than people who don't daydream?

How can taking a nap improve your memory?

HINT: LOOK IN THE MARGIN FOR AND

FORGETTING

LEARNING OBJECTIVES

RETRIEVAL PRACTICE While reading the upcoming sections, respond to each Learning Objective in your own words. Then compare your responses with those found at www.wiley.com/college/huffman.

1 DESCRIBE Ebbinghaus's research on learning and forgetting.
2 REVIEW the five key theories about why we forget.
3 EXPLAIN the six most important factors that contribute to forgetting.

Psychologists have long been interested in how and why we forget. Hermann Ebbinghaus first introduced the experimental study of learning and forgetting in 1885 (**Figure 7.9**).

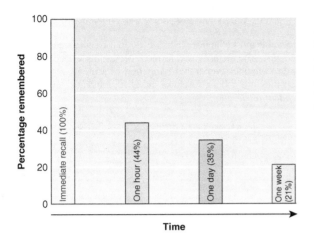

FIGURE 7.9 **HOW QUICKLY WE FORGET**

Using himself as a subject, Ebbinghaus calculated how long it took to learn a list of three-letter *nonsense syllables*, such as *SIB* and *RAL*. He found that one hour after he knew a list perfectly, he remembered only 44% of the syllables. A day later he recalled 35%, and a week later only 21%.

Although Ebbinghaus's research showed a dramatic drop in his previously learned material, keep in mind that meaningful material is much more memorable than nonsense syllables. Furthermore, after some time had passed and Ebbinghaus thought he had completely forgotten the list, he discovered that *relearning* it took less time than the initial learning took. Similarly, if your college requires you to repeat some of the math or foreign language courses you took in high school, you'll be happily surprised by how much you recall and how much easier it is to relearn the information the second time around.

More recent research based on Ebbinghaus's discoveries has identified an ideal time to practice something you have just learned. Practicing too soon is a waste of time, but if you practice too late, you will already have forgotten what you learned. The ideal time to practice is when you are about to forget.

Polish psychologist Piotr Wozniak used Ebbinghaus's insight regarding the ideal practice time to create a software program called SuperMemo. The program can be used to predict the future state of an individual's memory and help the person schedule reviews of learned information at the optimal time. So far the program has been applied mainly to language learning, helping users retain huge amounts of vocabulary. But Wozniak hopes that someday programs like SuperMemo will tell people when to wake and when to exercise, help them remember what they have read and whom they have met, and remind them of their goals (Wolf, 2008).

Theories of Forgetting

Although we all sometimes wish we had complete recall of everything we've learned, if we truly couldn't forget, our minds would be filled with meaningless data, such as what we ate for breakfast every morning and every conversation we've ever had. Similarly, think of the pain we'd continuously endure if we couldn't distance ourselves from tragedy through forgetting. The ability to forget is essential to the proper functioning of memory, and psychologists have developed several theories to explain why forgetting occurs **(Figure 7.10)**: *decay, interference, motivated forgetting, encoding failure,* and *retrieval failure.* Each theory focuses on a different stage of the memory process or a particular type of problem in processing information.

In *decay theory,* memory is processed and stored in a physical form—for example, in a network of neurons. Connections between neurons probably deteriorate over time, leading to forgetting. This theory explains why skills and memory degrade if they go unused ("use it or lose it").

In *interference theory,* forgetting is caused by two competing memories, particularly memories with similar qualities. At least two types of interference exist: *retroactive* and *proactive* **(Figure 7.11).** When new information leads to forgetting old material, it is called **retroactive interference** (acting backward in time). Learning your new phone number may cause you to forget your old phone number (old,

Retroactive interference A memory error in which new information interferes with remembering old information; it is backward-acting interference.

FIGURE 7.10 WHY WE FORGET: FIVE KEY THEORIES

Which of the five theories of forgetting best applies to this cartoon?

Proactive interference A memory error in which old information interferes with remembering new information; it is forward-acting interference.

"retro," information is forgotten). Conversely, when old information leads to forgetting of new information, it is called **proactive interference** (acting forward in time). Old information (like the Spanish you learned in high school) may interfere with your ability to learn and remember your new college course in French.

Motivated forgetting theory is based on the idea that we forget some information for a reason. According to Freudian theory, people forget unpleasant or anxiety-producing information, either consciously or unconsciously.

In *encoding failure theory*, our sensory memory receives the information and passes it to STM. But during STM, we may overlook precise details, and may not fully encode it, which would result in a failure to pass along a complete memory for proper storage in LTM.

FIGURE 7.11 RETROACTIVE INTERFERENCE AND PROACTIVE INTERFERENCE

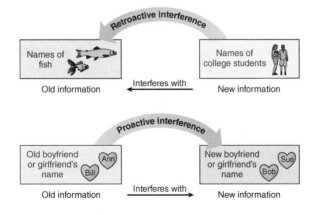

Ⓐ Retroactive (backward-acting) **interference** occurs when new information interferes with old information. This example comes from a story about an absent-minded ichthyology professor (fish specialist) who refused to learn the name of his college students. Asked why, he said, "Every time I learn a student's name, I forget the name of a fish!"

Ⓑ Proactive (forward-acting) **interference** occurs when old information interferes with new information. Have you ever been in trouble because you used an old partner's name to refer to your new partner? You now have a guilt-free explanation—proactive interference.

TEST YOURSELF: WHICH IS THE REAL PENNY?

psychology and you

If you want a simple (but fascinating) example of *encoding failure*, try to identify the correct penny among this sample of 10. Despite having seen a real penny thousands of times in our lives, most of us have difficulty recognizing the details. The U.S. penny has eight easily distinguishing characteristics (Lincoln's head, the date it was minted, which way Lincoln is facing, and so on). However, the average person can only remember three characteristics (Nickerson & Adams, 1979). Because we can easily recognize pennies by their size and color, we don't encode the fine details and pass them on for storage in LTM. Can you see how this applies to reading a textbook? You can't read a text the way you read a novel. You need to pay close attention to details in order to "recognize" the correct answers on exams!

(a) (b) (c) (d) (e)

(f) (g) (h) (i) (j)

According to *retrieval failure theory*, memories stored in LTM aren't forgotten. They're just momentarily inaccessible. For example, the **tip-of-the-tongue (TOT) phenomenon**—the feeling that a word or an event you are trying to remember will pop out at any second—is known to result from interference, faulty cues, and high emotional arousal.

Tip-of-the-tongue (TOT) phenomenon Feeling that specific information is stored in your long-term memory but being temporarily unable to retrieve it.

Factors Involved in Forgetting

Since Ebbinghaus's original research, scientists have discovered numerous factors that contribute to forgetting. Six of the most important are the *misinformation effect*, the *serial- position effect*, *source amnesia*, the *sleeper effect*, *spacing of practice*, and *culture*.

Many people (who haven't studied this chapter or taken a psychology course) believe that when they're recalling an event, they're remembering it as if it were a kind of instant replay. However, as you know, our memories are highly fallible and filled with personal constructions that we create during encoding and storage. Research on the **misinformation effect** shows that information that occurs *after an event* may further alter and revise those constructions.

For example, in one study, participants completed an interview in one room and then answered questions about it in another room (Morgan et al., 2012). Participants who received neutral questions like "Was there a telephone in the room?" answered accurately for the most part, making errors on only 10% of the questions. However, other participants were asked questions such as "What color was the telephone?" which falsely implied that there had been a telephone in the room. Of these respondents, 98% "remembered" a telephone. Other

Misinformation effect A memory distortion that results from misleading post-event information.

Voices from the Classroom

"False Daughter" Memories One of the co-authors of this book, Karen Huffman, is a dear friend of mine and we've co-taught intro psych for many years. During our times together in the classroom, we've often told stories about our own children to provide real-life examples of various psychological principles. Ironically, in the chapter on memory, we suddenly realized that some of the stories we were currently telling our students about our respective daughters were becoming blended in our own minds. We couldn't remember whether certain events happened to one of my three daughters or to Karen's only daughter! For us, this became a perfect, personal example of both the *constructive* nature of memory, as well as *source amnesia*!

Professor Katie Townsend-Merino
Palomar College
San Marcos, CA

experiments have created false memories, by showing subjects doctored photos of themselves taking a completely fictitious hot-air balloon ride or by asking subjects to simply imagine an event, such as having a nurse remove a skin sample from their finger. In these and similar cases, a large number of subjects later believed that the misleading information was correct and that the fictitious or imagined events actually occurred (Fazio et al., 2013; Hess et al., 2012; Wright et al., 2013).

Some research even suggests that watching someone else engage in a behavior, or merely *imagining* ourselves doing that behavior, can lead us to (falsely) believe that we've actually done that activity ourselves. For example, one study asked students to read a series of statements, such as "shake the bottle," and were then told to either imagine performing that action or to watch a video of someone else performing it. When the students were asked two weeks later to recall which actions they had performed, they "remembered" performing 23% of the actions they had seen someone else doing in the video and "remembered" performing 33% of the actions they had imagined doing themselves (Lindner et al., 2010)!

In addition to having problems with the misinformation effect, study participants who are asked to memorize lists of words remember some words better than others, depending on where they occurred in the list, a result known as the **serial-position effect**. They remember the words at the beginning (*primacy effect*) and the end (*recency effect*) better than those in the middle of the list, which are quite often forgotten (Bonk & Healy, 2010; Overstreet & Healy, 2011).

The reasons for the serial-position effect are complex, but they have interesting real-life implications. For example, a potential employer's memory of you might be enhanced if you are either the first or the last candidate interviewed.

Each day we read, hear, and process an enormous amount of information, and it's easy to get confused about who said what to whom and in what context. Forgetting the true source of a memory is known as **source amnesia** (Kleider et al., 2008; Leichtman, 2006; Paterson et al., 2011).

When we first hear something from an unreliable source, we tend to disregard that information in favor of a more reliable source. However, as the source of the information is forgotten (source amnesia), the unreliable information is no longer discounted. This is called the **sleeper effect** (see *Real World Psychology*) (Appel & Richter, 2007; Ecker et al., 2011; Nabi & Moyer-Gusé, 2013).

Serial-position effect A characteristic of memory retrieval in which information at the beginning and end of a series is remembered better than material in the middle.

Source amnesia A memory error caused by forgetting the true source of a memory (also called source confusion or source misattribution).

Sleeper effect A memory error in which information from an unreliable source that was initially discounted later gains credibility because the source is forgotten.

© Tampa Bay Times/ZUMAPRESS/Alamy Inc.

realworldpsychology   **The Power of Negative Political Campaigns**

Think back to a recent heated political election. What type of television advertisements most readily come to mind? People are most likely to recall ads that rely on creating negative feelings about one of the candidates. These negative advertisement work because they stick with us, even if we initially have negative feelings about them (Lariscy & Tinkham, 1999). Over time, the "facts" stay in our memory, and we forget the source, illustrating both source amnesia and the sleeper effect!

Distributed practice A study technique in which practice (or study) sessions are interspersed with rest periods.

Massed practice A study technique in which time spent learning is grouped (or massed) into long, unbroken intervals; also known as cramming.

If we try to memorize too much information at once (as when students "cram" before an exam), we're not likely to learn and remember as much as we would with more distributed study (Dunn et al., 2013; Fulton et al., 2013; Karpicke & Bauernschmidt, 2011). **Distributed practice** refers to spacing your learning periods, with rest periods between sessions. Cramming is called **massed practice** because the time spent learning is massed into long, unbroken intervals. For example, researchers in one study asked musicians to practice a note sequence in three practice sessions that were separated by either 5 minutes, 6 hours, or 24 hours (Simmons, 2012). Those whose practice sessions were separated by 24 hours showed significantly greater memory of the notes than those with shorter times between practice sessions.

Finally, as illustrated in **Figure 7.12**, cultural factors can play a role in how well people remember what they have learned.

(c) Ferdinando Scianna/MagnumPhotos, Inc.

FIGURE 7.12 CULTURE AND MEMORY

In many societies, tribal leaders pass down vital information through orally related stories. As a result, children living in these cultures have better memories for information that is related through stories than do other children. Can you think of other ways in which culture might influence memory?

RETRIEVAL PRACTICE: FORGETTING

Self-Test

Completing this self-test and comparing your answers with those in Appendix B provides immediate feedback and helpful practice for exams. Additional interactive, self-tests are available at www.wiley.com/college/huffman.

1. According to the _____ theory of forgetting, memory is processed and stored in a physical form, and connections between neurons deteriorate over time.

a. decay
b. interference
c. motivated forgetting
d. retrieval failure

2. The _____ theory suggests that forgetting is caused by two competing memories, particularly memories with similar qualities.

a. decay
b. interference
c. motivated forgetting
d. encoding failure

3. Which of the following is *not* one of the six factors that contribute to forgetting outlined in the text?

a. misinformation effect
b. serial-position effect
c. race and/or ethnicity
d. source amnesia

4. Distributed practice is a learning technique in which _____.

a. students are distributed (spaced) equally throughout the room
b. learning periods alternate with nonlearning rest periods
c. learning decays faster than it can be distributed
d. several students study together, distributing various subjects according to their individual strengths

Think Critically

1 Briefly describe an example from your own life of source amnesia and the sleeper effect.

2 Why might advertisers of shoddy services or products benefit from channel surfing if the television viewer is skipping from news programs to cable talk shows to infomercials?

realworldpsychology

Can merely imagining engaging in a behavior create a false memory of actually performing that behavior?

HINT: LOOK IN THE MARGIN FOR Q3

BIOLOGICAL BASES OF MEMORY

LEARNING OBJECTIVES

RETRIEVAL PRACTICE While reading the upcoming sections, respond to each Learning Objective in your own words. Then compare your responses with those found at www.wiley.com/college/huffman.

1 **DESCRIBE** two kinds of biological changes that occur when we learn something new.

2 **EXPLAIN** the effect of hormones on memory.

3 **IDENTIFY** some brain areas involved in memory.

4 **EXPLAIN** how injury and disease can affect memory.

A number of biological changes occur when we learn something new. Among them are neuronal and synaptic changes and hormonal changes. We discuss these changes in this section, along with the questions of where memories are located and what causes memory loss.

Neuronal and Synaptic Changes

We know that learning modifies the brain's neural networks (Chapters 2 and 6). As you learn to play tennis, for example, repeated practice builds specific neural pathways that make it easier and easier for you to get the ball over the net. This **long-term potentiation (LTP)** happens in at least two ways.

First, as early research with rats raised in enriched environments showed (Rosenzweig et al., 1972), repeated stimulation of a synapse can strengthen the synapse by causing the dendrites to grow more spines (Chapter 6). This results in more synapses, more receptor sites, and more sensitivity.

Second, when learning and memory occur, there is a measurable change in the amount of neurotransmitter released, which thereby increases the neuron's efficiency in message transmission. Research with *Aplysia* (sea slugs) clearly demonstrates this effect **(Figure 7.13)**.

Long-term potentiation (LTP) A long-lasting increase in neural excitability, which may be a biological mechanism for learning and memory.

FIGURE 7.13 **HOW DOES A SEA SLUG LEARN AND REMEMBER?**

After repeated squirting with water, followed by a mild shock, the sea slug, *Aplysia*, releases more neurotransmitters at certain synapses. These synapses then become more efficient at transmitting signals that allow the slug to withdraw its gills when squirted. As a critical thinker, can you explain why this ability might provide an evolutionary advantage?

© Wolfgang Pölzer/Alamy Inc.

Further evidence comes from research with genetically engineered "smart mice," which have extra receptors for a neurotransmitter named NMDA (N-methyl-d-aspartate). These mice performed significantly better on memory tasks than did normal mice (Brim et al., 2013; Mohamad et al., 2013; Tang et al., 2001; Tsien, 2000).

Although it is difficult to generalize from sea slugs and mice, research on long-term potentiation (LTP) in humans also supports the idea that LTP is one of the major biological mechanisms underlying learning and memory (Berger et al., 2008; Kullmann & Lamsa, 2011; Shin et al., 2010).

Hormonal Changes and Emotional Arousal

When stressed or excited, we naturally produce hormones that arouse the body, such as *epinephrine* and *cortisol* (Chapter 3). These hormones in turn affect the amygdala (a brain structure involved in emotion), which then stimulates the hippocampus and cerebral cortex (parts of the brain that are important for memory storage). Research has shown that epinephrine or cortisol, or electrical stimulation of the amygdala, increase the encoding and storage of new information (Hupbach & Fieman, 2012; Jurado-Berbel et al., 2010; McIntyre et al., 2012). However, prolonged or excessive stress and emotional arousal can increase, as well as interfere with, memory (Baucom et al., 2012; Guenzel et al., 2013; Morgan et al., 2012; Schilling et al., 2013).

Interestingly, some research suggests that exposure to pornography can disrupt memory. Researchers in one study (Laier et al., 2013) asked men to view a series of both pornographic and nonpornographic images and judge whether they had previously seen each image. Men who saw the nonsexual images gave 80% correct answers, whereas men who saw the pornographic images gave only 67% correct answers. Can you see how sexual arousal interferes with working memory and how it may help explain these findings?

The powerful effect of hormones on memory also can be seen in what are known as **flashbulb memories (FBMs)**—vivid, detailed, and near-permanent images associated with surprising or strongly emotional events (Brown & Kulik, 1977). In such situations, we secrete a flood of hormones when we initially experience or learn of the event, and then we replay the event in our minds again and again, actions that both make for stronger memories. In addition to widely shared public events, such as the Boston Marathon bombings on April 15, 2013, your personal flashbulb memories might include your first kiss, the birth of your first child, or the loss of a loved one.

Despite their intensity, flashbulb memories may not be as accurate as you might think (Kvavilashvili et al., 2010; Lanciano et al., 2010; Schmidt, 2012). For example, when asked how he heard the news of the September 11, 2001, attacks, President George W. Bush's answers contained several errors (Greenberg, 2004). Our flashbulb memories for specific details (particularly the time and place the emotional event occurred) are fairly accurate (Rimmele et al., 2012). But, overall, flashbulb memories, like all other memories, are not perfect recordings of events. What separates them from ordinary, everyday memories is their vividness and our subjective confidence in their accuracy. Keep in mind that confidence is not the same as accuracy—an important point we'll return to in the last part of this chapter.

Where Are Memories Located?

Early memory researchers believed that memory was *localized*, or stored in a particular brain area. Later research suggests that, in fact, memory tends to be localized not in a single area but in many separate areas throughout the brain **(Figure 7.14)**.

Flashbulb memory (FBM) A recall of vivid, detailed, and near-permanent images associated with surprising or strongly emotional events; it may or may not be accurate.

FIGURE 7.14 THE BRAIN AND MEMORY

Damage to any one of these areas can affect encoding, storage, and retrieval of memories.

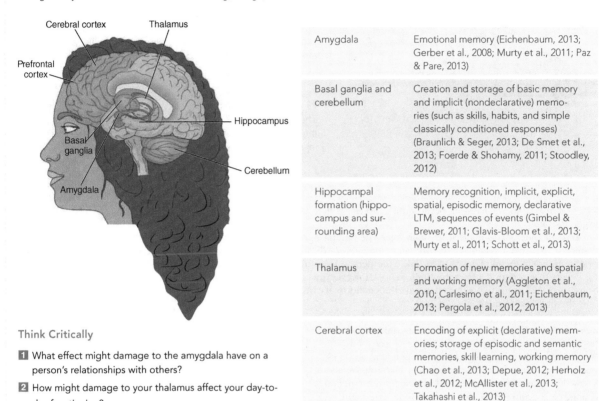

Amygdala	Emotional memory (Eichenbaum, 2013; Gerber et al., 2008; Murty et al., 2011; Paz & Pare, 2013)
Basal ganglia and cerebellum	Creation and storage of basic memory and implicit (nondeclarative) memories (such as skills, habits, and simple classically conditioned responses) (Braunlich & Seger, 2013; De Smet et al., 2013; Foerde & Shohamy, 2011; Stoodley, 2012)
Hippocampal formation (hippocampus and surrounding area)	Memory recognition, implicit, explicit, spatial, episodic memory, declarative LTM, sequences of events (Gimbel & Brewer, 2011; Glavis-Bloom et al., 2013; Murty et al., 2011; Schott et al., 2013)
Thalamus	Formation of new memories and spatial and working memory (Aggleton et al., 2010; Carlesimo et al., 2011; Eichenbaum, 2013; Pergola et al., 2012, 2013)
Cerebral cortex	Encoding of explicit (declarative) memories; storage of episodic and semantic memories, skill learning, working memory (Chao et al., 2013; Depue, 2012; Herholz et al., 2012; McAllister et al., 2013; Takahashi et al., 2013)

Think Critically

1 What effect might damage to the amygdala have on a person's relationships with others?

2 How might damage to your thalamus affect your day-to-day functioning?

Today, research techniques are so advanced that we can experimentally induce and measure memory-related brain changes as they occur—on-the-spot reporting! For example, James Brewer and his colleagues (1998) used functional magnetic resonance imaging (fMRI) to locate areas of the brain responsible for encoding memories of pictures. They showed 96 pictures of indoor and outdoor scenes to participants while scanning their brains, and then they later tested participants' ability to recall the pictures. Brewer and his colleagues identified the *right prefrontal cortex* and the *parahippocampal cortex* as being the most active during the encoding of the pictures. These are only two of several brain regions involved in memory storage.

Biological Causes of Memory Loss

The leading cause of neurological disorders—including memory loss—among young U.S. men and women between the ages of 15 and 25 is *traumatic brain injury*. These injuries most commonly result from car accidents, falls, blows, and gunshot wounds.

Traumatic brain injury happens when the skull suddenly collides with another object. Compression, twisting, and distortion of the brain inside the skull all cause serious and sometimes permanent damage to the brain. The frontal and temporal

FIGURE 7.15 TWO TYPES OF AMNESIA

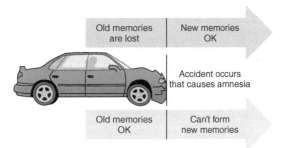

Old memories are lost | New memories OK

Accident occurs that causes amnesia

Old memories OK | Can't form new memories

🅐 Retrograde amnesia
The person loses memories of events that occurred *before* the accident, yet has no trouble remembering things that happened afterward (old, "retro" memories are lost).

🅑 Anterograde amnesia
The person cannot form new memories for events that occur *after* the accident. Anterograde amnesia also may result from a surgical injury or from diseases such as chronic alcoholism.

lobes often take the heaviest hit because they directly collide with the bony ridges inside the skull.

Loss of memory as a result of brain injury or trauma is called *amnesia*, and there are two major types—*retrograde* and *anterograde* (**Figure 7.15**). In **retrograde amnesia** (acting backward in time), the person loses memory (is amnesic) for events that occurred *before* the brain injury. However, the same person has no trouble remembering things that happened after the injury. As the name implies, only the old, "retro," memories are lost.

What causes retrograde amnesia? In cases where the individual is only amnesic for the events right before the brain injury, the cause may be a failure of consolidation. We learned earlier that during long-term potentiation (LTP), our neurons change to accommodate new learning. We also know that it takes a certain amount of time for these neural changes to become fixed and stable in long-term memory, a process known as **consolidation**. Like heavy rain on wet cement, the brain injury "wipes away" unstable memories because the cement has not had time to harden (*retrograde amnesia*).

In contrast to retrograde amnesia, in which people lose memories for events *before* a brain injury, some people lose memory for events that occur *after* a brain injury, which is called **anterograde amnesia** (acting forward in time). This type of amnesia generally results from a surgical injury or from diseases such as chronic alcoholism. Continuing our analogy with wet cement, anterograde amnesia would be like having permanently hardened cement. You can't lay down new long-term memories because the cement is hardened.

Keep in mind that retrograde amnesia is normally temporary. Unfortunately, anterograde amnesia is most often permanent, but patients show surprising abilities to learn and remember implicit/nondeclarative tasks (such as procedural motor skills like mowing a lawn).

Another way to understand these two forms of amnesia is to compare them to the functions of a computer. Experiencing retrograde amnesia would be like having your latest stored data (memories) erased from your hard drive. In contrast, having anterograde amnesia would be similar to disconnecting your hard drive from the computer—no new data (memories) could be stored.

Retrograde amnesia The loss of memory for events before a brain injury; backward-acting amnesia.

Consolidation The process by which neural changes associated with recent learning become durable and stable.

Anterograde amnesia The inability to form new memories after a brain injury; forward-acting amnesia.

Amnesia at work
Fifty-five-year-old Kay Delaney slipped and hit her head at work, which led to severe memory loss. Sadly, she now believes she's only 34 and has no memory of the past 21 years, including raising her three children. Is this an example of retrograde or anterograde amnesia?

Casey Gutteridge/SWNS

FIGURE 7.16 THE EFFECT OF ALZHEIMER'S DISEASE ON THE BRAIN

Ⓐ Normal brain
Note the high amount of red and yellow color (signs of brain activity) in the positron emission tomography scans of the normal brain.

Ⓑ Brain of an Alzheimer's disease patient
The reduced activity in the brain of the Alzheimer's disease patient is evident. The loss is most significant in the temporal and parietal lobes, which indicates that these areas are particularly important for storing memories.

Science Source/Photo Researchers

Science Source/Photo Researchers

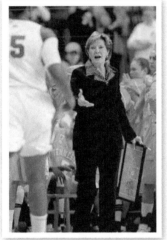

© Duncan Williams/Icon SMI/Corbis

Pat Summit, coach of the Tennessee Lady Vols basketball team from 1974 until 2012 and the winningest college basketball coach of all time, announced in 2011 that she had early-stage Alzheimer's disease.

Alzheimer's disease (AD) A chronic organic brain syndrome characterized by gradual loss of memory, decline in intellectual ability, and deterioration of personality.

Like traumatic brain injuries, disease can alter the physiology of the brain and nervous system, affecting memory processes. For example, **Alzheimer's disease (AD)** is a progressive mental deterioration that occurs most commonly in old age **(Figure 7.16)**. The most noticeable early symptoms are disturbances in memory, which become progressively worse until, in the final stages, the person fails to recognize loved ones, needs total nursing care, and ultimately dies.

Alzheimer's does not attack all types of memory equally. A hallmark of the disease is an extreme decrease in *explicit/declarative memory* (Irish et al., 2011; Libon et al., 2007; Satler et al., 2007). Alzheimer's patients fail to recall facts, information, and personal life experiences, yet they still retain some *implicit/nondeclarative* memories, such as simple classically conditioned responses and procedural tasks like brushing their teeth.

Brain autopsies of people with Alzheimer's show unusual *tangles* (structures formed from degenerating cell bodies) and *plaques* (structures formed from degenerating axons and dendrites). Hereditary Alzheimer's generally strikes its victims between the ages of 45 and 55. Some experts believe the cause of Alzheimer's is primarily genetic, but others think instead that genetic makeup may make some people more susceptible to environmental triggers (Bettens et al., 2013; Sillén et al., 2011; Yu et al., 2013).

© Alexsi/iStockphoto

realworldpsychology   **A New Treatment for Alzheimer's Disease?**
Researchers have recently experimented with electrical brain stimulation for patients with severe epilepsy (Suthana et al., 2012). Those who received stimulation to a particular part of the cortex, which is one of the first parts of the brain to be damaged in patients with Alzheimer's disease, showed improvement in memory. This technique also may be useful in treating patients with Alzheimer's and other forms of severe memory loss.

RETRIEVAL PRACTICE: BIOLOGICAL BASES OF MEMORY

Self-Test

Completing this self-test and comparing your answers with those in Appendix B provides immediate feedback and helpful practice for exams. Additional interactive, self-tests are available at www.wiley.com/college/huffman.

1. The long-lasting increase in neural excitability believed to be a biological mechanism for learning and memory is called _____.

    a. maintenance rehearsal   b. adrenaline activation
    c. long-term potentiation   d. the reverberating response

2. Your vivid memory of what you were doing when you were first informed about your parents' impending divorce is an example of _____.

    a. encoding specificity   b. long-term potentiation
    c. latent learning   d. a flashbulb memory

3. Ralph can't remember anything that happened to him before he fell through the floor of his tree house. His lack of memory of events before his fall is called _____ amnesia.

    a. retroactive   b. proactive
    c. anterograde   d. retrograde

4. A progressive mental deterioration characterized by severe memory loss that occurs most commonly in elderly people is called

    _____.

    a. retrieval loss syndrome   b. prefrontal cortex
       deterioration
    c. Alzheimer's disease   d. age-related amnesia

Think Critically

1 What might be the evolutionary benefit of flashbulb memories?

2 How might Alzheimer's disease affect a person's relationships with others?

realworldpsychology

Why might exposure to pornography interfere with memory?

HINT: LOOK IN THE MARGIN FOR Q4

MEMORY DISTORTIONS

RETRIEVAL PRACTICE While reading the upcoming sections, respond to each Learning Objective in your own words. Then compare your responses with those found at www.wiley.com/college/huffman.

1 **EXPLAIN** why our memories sometimes become distorted.
2 **DESCRIBE** problems with using eyewitnesses in the criminal justice system.
3 **DISTINGUISH** between false and repressed memories.

LEARNING OBJECTIVES

At this point in your life, you've undoubtedly experienced a painful breakup of a serious love relationship and/or witnessed similar breakups among your close friends. During these breakups, did you wonder how the reported experiences of two people in the same partnership could be so different? Why would each partner reconstruct his or her own personal memory of the relationship?

There are several reasons we shape, rearrange, and distort our memories. One of the most common is our need for *logic* and *consistency*. When we're initially forming new memories or sorting through old ones, we fill in missing pieces, make "corrections," and rearrange information to make it logical and consistent with our previous experiences or personal desires. For example, if you left a relationship because you found a new partner, you might rearrange your memories to suit your belief that you are just a weak-willed person who can't stay faithful or that you were mismatched from the beginning. However, if you were the one left behind, you might reconstruct your memories and now believe that you're doomed to lose people you love or that your partner was a manipulative "player" from the beginning. Of course, not all memory reconstructions are so dramatic. However, it's important that we recognize and remember the fallibility of our memory processes during initial encoding, current storage, and future retrieval. To experience first-hand the constructive nature of memory, try the memory test below.

We also shape and construct our memories for the sake of *efficiency*. We summarize, augment, and tie new information in with related memories in LTM. Similarly, when we need to retrieve the stored information, we leave out seemingly unimportant elements or misremember the details.

Despite all their problems and biases, our memories are normally fairly accurate and serve us well in most situations. They have evolved to encode, store, and retrieve general and/or vital information, such as the location of various buildings on our college campus or looking both ways when we cross the street. However, when faced with tasks that require encoding, storing, and retrieving precise details like those in a scholarly text, remembering names and faces of

---

TEST YOURSELF: A PERSONAL MEMORY TEST

psychology and you

Carefully read through all the words in the following list.

Sour	Chocolate	Pie	Bitter	Soda
Nice	Heart	Honey	Good	Honey
Honey	Cake	Candy	Taste	
Artichoke	Tart	Sugar	Tooth	

Now cover the list and write down all the words you remember.

Number of correctly recalled words:

15 to 18 words = excellent memory

10 to 14 words = average

5 to 9 words = below average

4 or fewer words = you might need a nap

How did you do? Do you have a good or excellent memory? Did you recall seeing the words *sleep* and *doctor*? Did you recall seeing the words "sour" and "honey"? Most students do, and it's a good example of the *serial-position effect*—the first and last words in the list (p. 00). Did you remember the word "artichoke" and "honey"? If you recalled "artichoke," it illustrates the power of *distinctiveness*, whereas if you remembered seeing "honey" it's because it was repeated three times.

Both of these examples demonstrate how distinctive and/ or repeated material are more easily encoded, stored, and recalled. Finally, did you see the word "*sweet*"? Look back over the list. That word is not there, yet most students commonly report seeing it. Why? As mentioned in the introduction to this chapter, memory is not a faithful duplicate of an event; it is a *constructive process*. We actively shape and build on information as it is encoded and retrieved.

Think Critically

1 Other than this example of seeing the word "sweet," can you think of another example in which you created a false memory?

2 How might constructive memories create misunderstandings at work and in our everyday relationships?

potential clients, or recalling where we left our house keys, our brains are not as well-equipped.

Memory and the Criminal Justice System

When our memory errors come into play in the criminal justice system, they may lead to wrongful judgments of guilt or innocence with possible life or death consequences!

In the past, one of the best forms of trial evidence a lawyer could have was an *eyewitness*—"I was there; I saw it with my own eyes." Unfortunately, research has identified several problems with eyewitness testimony (Cutler & Kovera, 2013; Herve et al., 2013; Loftus, 2000, 2001, 2007, 2011). One of the most serious is that it's relatively easy to create false memories (Fazio et al., 2013; Frenda et al., 2011; Loftus & Cahill, 2007; Strange et al., 2011; Wright et al., 2013).

Even more troubling are the findings that once false memories have been formed, they can multiply over time and last for years. Researchers in one study showed participants pictures of an event, such as a girl's wallet being stolen (Zhu et al., 2012). Participants then read a series of statements about the event, which included both accurate information (for instance, the person who took the girl's wallet was a man) and false information (the person who took the girl's wallet put it in his pants pocket, when in reality the picture showed him hiding the wallet in his jacket). Initially, after reading these statements, participants identified only 31% of the false events as having occurred. However, when participants were asked 1½ years later which events had occurred, they identified 39% of the false statements as true, indicating that false memories not only last but can even multiply over time. What might be the implications of this research for eyewitness testimony in court?

Recall our earlier discussion of the misinformation effect and how experimenters created a false memory of seeing a telephone in a room (page 191). Participants who were asked neutral questions, such as "Was there a telephone in the room?" made errors on only 10% of the queries (Morgan et al., 2013). In contrast, when participants were asked "What color was the telephone?" falsely implying that a telephone had been in the room, 98% "remembered" it being there. The *Psych Science* box further describes how our biases can influence our "memory" of an event.

Problems with eyewitness recollections are so well established and important that judges now allow expert testimony on the unreliability of eyewitness testimony and routinely instruct jurors on its limits (Cutler & Kovea, 2013; Pezdek, 2012). If you serve as a member of a jury or listen to accounts of crimes in the news, remind yourself of these problems. Also, keep in mind that research participants in eyewitness studies generally report their inaccurate memories with great self-assurance and strong conviction (Douglass & Pavletic, 2012; Goodwin et al., 2013; Jaeger et al., 2012). Eyewitnesses to an actual crime may similarly identify an innocent person as the perpetrator with equally high confidence **(Figure 7.17)**. In one experiment, participants watched people committing a staged crime. Only an hour later, 20% of the eyewitnesses identified innocent

FIGURE 7.17 THE DANGERS OF EYEWITNESS TESTIMONY

realworldpsychology

Damon Thibodeaux served 15 years in prison for killing his step-cousin before being released on September 28, 2012, after he was officially cleared via DNA testing. He was convicted at age 22 based in part on testimony by two eyewitnesses.

© Michael DeMocker/TheTimes Picayune/Landov

PSYCHSCIENCE

DO WE "REMEMBER" WHAT WE WANT TO REMEMBER?

Photo left and right: Reprinted from Journal of Experimental Social Psychology Volume 49, Issue 2, Steven J. Frenda et al. False memories of fabricated political events. Copyright 2013, with permission from Elsevier

To study how false memories are formed, researchers in one recent study asked more than 5,000 participants about their memories of several political events (Frenda et al., 2013). Some of these political events had actually occurred, such as George W. Bush's winning the 2000 presidential election. However, other political events had been deliberately created by the experimenters to appear as if they had occurred when in fact they had not. Each fabricated story included a photograph supposedly showing the event. Participants were then asked whether they remembered the event occurring and how they felt about it at the time.

Can you predict what these researchers found? In line with prior research on the ease with which false memories are created, approximately half the participants "remembered" that the false event happened, and about 27% "remembered" seeing it reported on the news. Interestingly, participants' political orientation influenced the formation of false memories.

For example, participants who were politically liberal were significantly more likely to create a false memory of President George W. Bush supposedly socializing with a famous baseball star during the Hurricane Katrina disaster (see the fabricated photo on the left). In contrast, participants who were politically conservative were more likely to falsely remember seeing

President Barack Obama supposedly shaking hands with the President of Iran (note the fabricated photo on the right). These findings indicate that we are particularly likely to form false memories of events that fit with, and reinforce, our preexisting attitudes.

RESEARCH CHALLENGE

1 Based on the information provided, did this study (Frenda et al., 2013) use descriptive, correlational, and/or experimental research?

2 If you chose:

- descriptive research, is this a naturalistic observation, survey/interview, case study, or archival research?
- correlational research, is this a positive, negative, or zero correlation?
- experimental research, label the IV, DV, experimental group(s), and control group.

>> CHECK YOUR ANSWERS IN APPENDIX B.

NOTE: The information provided in this study is admittedly limited, but the level of detail is similar to what is presented in most textbooks and public reports of research findings. Answering these questions, and then comparing your answers to those in the Appendix, will help you become a better critical thinker and consumer of scientific research.

people from mug shots, and a week later, 8% identified innocent people in a lineup (Brown et al., 1977).

 Ironically, research now suggests that the accuracy of eyewitness testimony can be improved if people are asked to make very fast judgments (Brewer et al., 2012). In fact, giving people only a few seconds to identify the culprit in a lineup increases the accuracy of such identifications by 20 to 30%, compared to allowing people to take as long as they want to make a decision. **Figure 7.18** offers further tips for improving eyewitness testimony.

"Thank you, gentlemen—you may all leave except for No. 3."

© The New Yorker Collection 2006 Tom Cheney from Cartoonbank.com

FIGURE 7.18 EYEWITNESSES AND POLICE LINEUPS

As humorously depicted in this cartoon, officials now recommend that suspects should never "stand out" from the others in a lineup. Witnesses also are cautioned to not assume that the real criminal is in the lineup, and they should never "guess" when asked to make an identification.

False Versus Repressed Memories

Like eyewitness testimony, false memories can have serious legal, personal, and social implications. Consider this true story of psychologist Elizabeth Loftus, one of modern psychology's most famous memory scientists.

When Elizabeth was 14, her mother drowned in the family's pool. Decades later, a relative told Elizabeth that she, Elizabeth, had been the one to find her mother's body. Despite her initial shock, Elizabeth's memories slowly started coming back. Her recovery of these gruesome childhood memories, although painful, initially brought great relief. It also seemed to explain why she had always been fascinated by the topic of memory.

Then her brother called to say there had been a mistake! The relative who told Elizabeth that she had been the one to discover her mother's body later remembered— and other relatives confirmed—that it had actually been Aunt Pearl, not Elizabeth. Loftus, an expert on memory distortions, had unknowingly created her own *false memory*.

Creating false memories may be somewhat common, but can we recover true memories that are buried in childhood? *Repression* is the supposed unconscious coping mechanism by which we prevent anxiety-provoking thoughts from reaching consciousness. According to some research, repressed memories are *actively* and *consciously* "forgotten" in an effort to avoid the pain of their retrieval (Anderson et al., 2004; Boag, 2012). Others suggest that some memories are so painful that they exist only in an *unconscious* corner of the brain, making them inaccessible to the individual (Haaken, 2010; Mancia & Baggott, 2008). In these cases, therapy supposedly would be necessary to unlock the hidden memories.

Repression is a complex and controversial topic in psychology. No one doubts that some memories are forgotten and later recovered. What some question is the idea that *repressed memories* of painful experiences (especially childhood sexual abuse) are stored in the unconscious mind (Klein, 2012; Lambert et al., 2010; Loftus & Cahill, 2007).

Critics suggest that most people who have witnessed or experienced a violent crime or are adult survivors of childhood sexual abuse have intense, persistent memories. They have trouble *forgetting*, not remembering. Some critics also wonder whether therapists sometimes inadvertently create false memories in their clients during therapy. Some worry that if a clinician even suggests the possibility of abuse, the client's own *constructive processes* may lead him or her to create a false memory. The client might start to incorporate portrayals of abuse from movies and books into his or her own memory, forgetting their original sources and eventually coming to see them as reliable.

This is not to say that all psychotherapy clients who recover memories of sexual abuse (or other painful incidents) have invented those memories. For example, some research suggests that children may remember experiencing sexual abuse but not understand or recognize those behaviors as abuse until adulthood (McNally, 2012).

Unfortunately, the repressed memory debate has grown increasingly bitter, and research on both sides is hotly contested. The stakes are high because lawsuits and criminal prosecutions of sexual abuse are sometimes based on recovered memories of childhood sexual abuse. As researchers continue exploring the mechanisms underlying delayed remembering, we must be careful not to ridicule or condemn people who recover true memories of abuse. In the same spirit, we must protect innocent people from wrongful accusations that come from false memories. Hopefully, with continued research (and perhaps new technology) we may someday better protect the interests of both the victim and the accused.

RETRIEVAL PRACTICE: MEMORY DISTORTIONS

Self-Test

Completing this self-test and comparing your answers with those in Appendix B provides immediate feedback and helpful practice for exams. Additional interactive, self-tests are available at www.wiley.com/college/huffman.

1. Problems with eyewitness recollections are so well established and important that judges now _____.

   a. allow expert testimony on the unreliability of eyewitness testimony
   b. routinely instruct jurors on the limits and unreliability of eyewitness recollections
   c. both the above
   d. none of the above

2. Researchers have demonstrated that it is _____ to create false memories.

   a. relatively easy
   b. rarely possible
   c. moderately difficult
   d. never possible

3. Dave was told the same childhood story of his father saving his neighbor from a fire so many times that he is now sure it is true, but all the evidence proves it never happened. This is an example of _____.

   a. a repressed memory
   b. deluded childhood fantasies
   c. a false memory
   d. early-onset juvenile dementia

4. _____ memories are related to anxiety-provoking thoughts or events that are supposedly prevented from reaching consciousness.

   a. Suppressed
   b. Flashbulb
   c. Flashback
   d. Repressed

Think Critically

1 As an eyewitness to a crime, how could you use information in this chapter to improve your memory for specific details?

2 If you were a juror, what would you say to the other jurors about the reliability of eyewitness testimony?

realworldpsychology

Does accuracy increase when eyewitnesses have only a few seconds to make an identification?

HINT: LOOK IN THE MARGIN FOR

Summary

1 THE NATURE OF MEMORY   180

- **Memory** is an internal representation of some prior event or experience. It's also a **constructive process** that organizes and shapes information. Major perspectives on memory include the **encoding, storage, and retrieval (ESR) model** and the **three-stage memory model**.
- Information enters memory in three stages: **encoding, storage,** and **retrieval**. In contrast, the **three-stage memory model** proposes that information is stored and processed in **sensory memory, short-term memory (STM),** and **long-term memory (LTM)**; these differ in purpose, duration, and capacity.
- **Chunking** and **maintenance rehearsal** improve STM's duration and capacity. Researchers think of STM as our **working memory**.
- **LTM** is an almost unlimited storehouse for information that must be kept for long periods. The two major types of LTM are

explicit/declarative memory and **implicit/nondeclarative memory**. Organization and **elaborative rehearsal** improve encoding. **Retrieval cues** help stimulate retrieval of information from LTM. According to the **encoding-specificity principle**, retrieval is improved when conditions of recovery are similar to encoding conditions.

2 FORGETTING   188

- Researchers have proposed that we forget information through decay, **retroactive** and **proactive interference**, motivated forgetting, encoding failure, and retrieval failure.
- Early research by Ebbinghaus showed that we tend to forget newly learned information quickly, but we relearn the information more readily the second time.

- Six factors that contribute to forgetting are the **misinformation effect**, the **serial-position effect** (primacy and recency effects), **source amnesia**, the **sleeper effect**, spacing of practice as in **distributed** versus **massed practice**, and culture.

3 BIOLOGICAL BASES OF MEMORY 194

- Learning modifies the brain's neural networks through **long-term potentiation (LTP)**, strengthening particular synapses and affecting the ability of neurons to release their neurotransmitters.
- Stress hormones affect the amygdala, which stimulates brain areas that are important for memory storage. Heightened arousal from these hormones also can increase the encoding and storage of new information and the formation of **flashbulb memories (FBMs)**.
- Research using advanced techniques, such as fMRI, has indicated that several brain regions are involved in memory storage.

- Two major types of amnesia are **retrograde** and **anterograde amnesia**. Traumatic brain injuries and disease, such as **Alzheimer's disease (AD)**, can cause memory loss.

4 MEMORY DISTORTIONS 199

- People shape, rearrange, and distort memories in order to create logic, consistency, and efficiency. Despite all their problems and biases, our memories are normally fairly accurate and usually serve us well.
- When memory errors occur in the context of the criminal justice system, they can have serious legal and social consequences. Problems with eyewitness recollections are well established. Judges often allow expert testimony on the unreliability of eyewitnesses.
- False memories are well-established phenomenon, which are relatively common and easy to create. However, memory *repression* (especially of childhood sexual abuse) is a complex and controversial topic.

⊚ applyingrealworldpsychology

We began this chapter with five intriguing Real World Psychology questions, and you were asked to revisit these questions at the end of each section. Questions like these have an important and lasting impact on all of our lives. See if you can answer these additional critical thinking questions related to real world examples.

1 Many people think they can perfectly recall elaborate memories about how they felt or what they said when they first learned about devastating events, like the Boston Marathon bombings. What do you recall about this particular event? Do your memories fit with what flashbulb memory (FBM) research suggests?

2 Despite documented errors with FBMs, most people are very confident in their personal accuracy. What problems might result from this overconfidence?

3 Human memory is often compared to the workings of a computer. Based on your own experience, what are the advantages and limits of this comparison?

4 Amnesia is a common theme for Hollywood movies and television. How might these portrayals, which are often inaccurate, negatively influence the public's perception?

5 What memory improvement techniques described in this chapter have you found to be helpful in your everyday life? What new strategies do you plan to try?

Boston Globe/Getty Images

Key Terms

RETRIEVAL PRACTICE Write a definition for each term before turning back to the referenced page to check your answer.

chaptereight

Thinking, Language, and Intelligence

CHAPTER OUTLINE

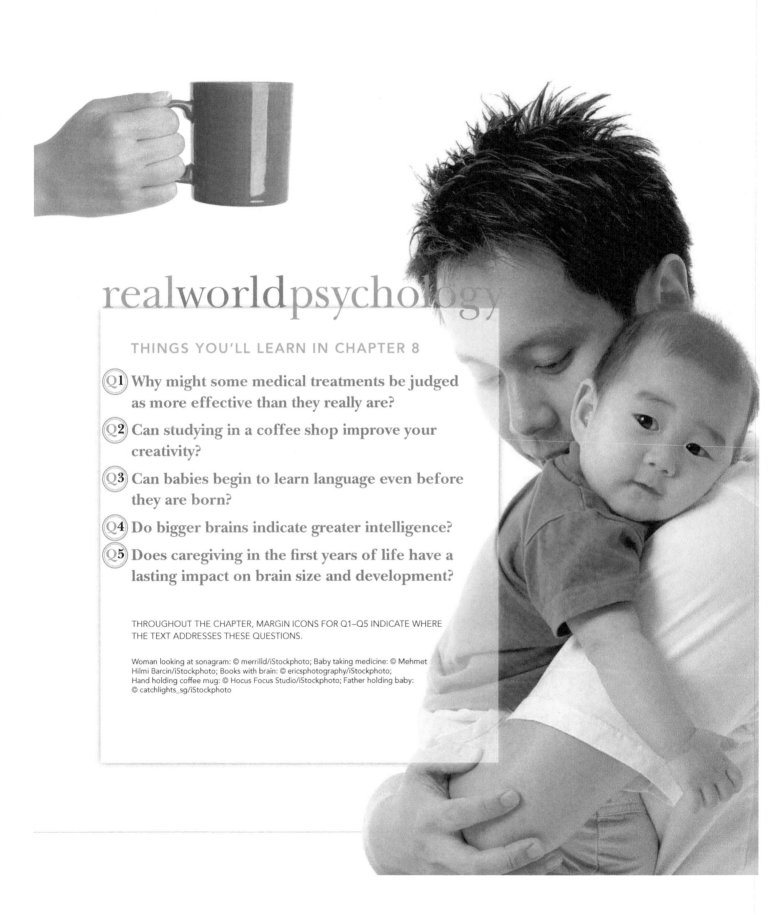

realworldpsychology

THINGS YOU'LL LEARN IN CHAPTER 8

Q1 Why might some medical treatments be judged as more effective than they really are?

Q2 Can studying in a coffee shop improve your creativity?

Q3 Can babies begin to learn language even before they are born?

Q4 Do bigger brains indicate greater intelligence?

Q5 Does caregiving in the first years of life have a lasting impact on brain size and development?

THROUGHOUT THE CHAPTER, MARGIN ICONS FOR Q1–Q5 INDICATE WHERE THE TEXT ADDRESSES THESE QUESTIONS.

chapteroverview

Intellectual growth should commence at birth and cease only at death.

—Albert Einstein

You've undoubtedly heard of Albert Einstein, the German-born physicist who developed the theory of relativity and the well-known equation $E = mc^2$, which foreshadowed the development of nuclear power. But did you know that as a young child Einstein spoke so rarely and slowly that his parents feared that something was seriously wrong with him? Their concerns were obviously unfounded. Einstein is considered to be a true genius—one of the smartest people of all time--and we now know that many brilliant people were "late talkers" in childhood.

In this chapter, we focus on thinking, language, and intelligence--each of which was central to Einstein's achievements. These topics are also key to understanding how we think about, describe, and successfully navigate the world around us. We begin with the first topic—*thinking*.

THINKING

LEARNING OBJECTIVES

RETRIEVAL PRACTICE While reading the upcoming sections, respond to each Learning Objective in your own words. Then compare your responses with those found at www.wiley.com/college/huffman.

1 **DESCRIBE** the roles of mental images and concepts in thinking.
2 **DESCRIBE** the three stages of problem solving.
3 **IDENTIFY** the barriers to problem solving.
4 **EXPLAIN** the characteristics associated with creativity.

Cognition The mental activities involved in acquiring, storing, retrieving, and using knowledge.

If you go on to major in psychology, you'll discover that researchers often group thinking, language, and intelligence under the larger umbrella of **cognition**, the mental activities of acquiring, storing, retrieving, and using knowledge. And, technically, we discuss cognition throughout this text (for example, chapters on sensation and perception, consciousness, learning, and memory). However, in this section we limit our discussion to *thinking*—what it is and where it's located.

Every time we take in information and mentally act on it, we're thinking. These thought processes are both localized and distributed throughout our brains in networks of neurons. For example, during problem solving or decision making, our brains are most active in the *prefrontal cortex*. This region associates complex ideas; makes plans; forms, initiates, and allocates attention; and supports multitasking. In addition to the localization of thinking processes, the prefrontal cortex also links to other areas of the brain, such as the limbic system (Chapter 2), to synthesize information from several senses (Anderson et al., 2011; Collins & Adams, 2013). Now that we know where thinking occurs, we need to discuss its basic components.

Cognitive Building Blocks

Imagine yourself lying, relaxed, in the warm, gritty sand on an ocean beach. Do you see palms swaying in the wind? Can you smell the salty sea and taste the dried salt on your lips? Can you hear children playing in the surf? What you've just created is a **mental image**, a mental representation of a previously stored sensory experience, which includes visual, auditory, olfactory, tactile, motor, and gustatory imagery (McKellar, 1972). We all have a mental space where we visualize and manipulate our sensory images (Borst et al., 2011; Ganis & Schendan, 2013; Weisberg & Reeves, 2013; Zvyagintsev et al., 2013).

In addition to mental images, our thinking also includes forming **concepts**, or mental representations of a group or category (Goldstone et al., 2013; Jern & Kemp, 2013). Concepts can be concrete (like car and concert) or abstract (like intelligence and beauty). They are essential to thinking and communication because they simplify and organize information. Normally, when you see a new object or encounter a new situation, you relate it to your existing conceptual structure and categorize it according to where it fits. For example, if you see a metal box with four wheels driving on

Mental image The mental representation of a previously stored sensory experience, including visual, auditory, olfactory, tactile, motor, or gustatory imagery (for example, visualizing a train and hearing its horn).

Concept The mental representation of a group or category.

FIGURE 8.1 CONCEPTS

When forming concepts, we most often use prototypes, artificial concepts, and hierarchies to simplify and categorize information. For example, when we encounter a bird, we fit it into our existing concept of a bird.

Stephen St. John/NG Image Collection

A **Prototypes**

When initially learning about the world, a young child develops a general, natural concept based on a typical representative, or **prototype**, of *bird* after a parent points out a number of examples. Once the child develops the prototype of a *bird*, he or she is then able to quickly classify all flying animals, such as this robin, correctly.

Gordon Wiltsie/NG Image Collection

B **Artificial concepts**

We create **artificial concepts** from logical rules or definitions. When an example doesn't quite fit the prototype, like this penguin, we must review our artificial concept of a bird: warm-blooded animals that fly, have wings and beaks, and lay eggs. Although this penguin doesn't fly, it has wings, a beak, and lays eggs. So it must be a bird.

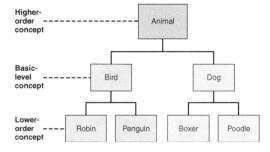

C **Hierarchies**

Creating **hierarchies**, or subcategories within broader concepts, makes mastering new material faster and easier. Note, however, that we tend to begin with basic-level concepts (the middle row on the diagram) when we first learn something (Rosch, 1978). For example, a child develops the basic-level concept for bird before learning the higher-order concept *animal* or the lower-order concept *robin*.

---

the highway, you know it is a car, even if you've never seen that particular model before. How do we learn concepts? They develop through the environmental interactions of three major building blocks (Prasada et al., 2012; Weisberg & Reeves, 2013):

- **Prototypes** When initially learning about the world, a young child develops a general, natural concept based on a typical representative, or **prototype**, of *bird* after a parent points out a number of examples. Once the child develops the prototype of a *bird*, he or she then is able to quickly classify all flying animals, such as this robin, correctly.

- **Artificial concepts** We create artificial *(or formal)* concepts from logical rules or definitions. When an example doesn't quite fit the prototype, like a penguin, we must review our artificial concept of a bird: warm-blooded animals that fly, have wings and beaks, and lay eggs. Although this penguin doesn't fly, it has wings, a beak, and lays eggs. So it must be a bird.

- **Hierarchies** Creating *hierarchies*, or subcategories within broader concepts, helps us master new material more quickly and easily **(Figure 8.1)**. Note, however, that we tend to begin with basic-level concepts (the middle row on the diagram) when we first learn something (Rosch, 1978). For example, a child develops the basic-level concept for *bird* before learning the higher-order concept *animal* or the lower-order concept *robin*.

Prototype The example that embodies the "best" or most typical features of a concept or category.

Artificial concept A clearly defined concept based on a set of logical rules; also known as a formal concept.

Solving Problems

Several years ago in Los Angeles, a 12-foot-high tractor-trailer got stuck under a bridge that was 6 inches too low. After hours of towing, tugging, and pushing, the police and transportation workers were stumped. Then a young boy happened by and asked, "Why don't you let some air out of the tires?" It was a simple, creative suggestion—and it worked.

Our lives are filled with problems—some simple, some difficult. In all cases, problem solving requires moving from a given state (the problem) to a goal state (the solution), a process that usually has three steps: *preparation, production,* and *evaluation* (Bourne et al., 1979). Note in **Figure 8.2** that during the preparation stage, we identify and separate relevant from irrelevant facts, and define the ultimate goal. Then, during the production stage, we generate possible solutions, called

FIGURE 8.2 THREE STEPS TO THE GOAL

There are three stages of problem solving that help you attain a goal, such as moving to a new home.

1 Preparation

Begin by clarifying the problem using these three steps in preparation.

- Define the ultimate goal. Move to a new home close to work.

- Outline your limits and/or desires.
  - ✓ Must allow pets.
  - ✓ Must be close enough to walk.
  - ✓ I prefer a house to an apartment building.
  - ✓ Fireplaces are nice.

- Separate the negotiable from the nonnegotiable.
  - ✓ Must allow pets.
  - ✓ Must be close enough to walk.
  - * I prefer a house to an apartment building.
  - * Fireplaces are nice.

2 Production

Next, test your possible paths and solutions with one or both of these methods.

- Use an **algorithm**, a logical step-by-step procedure that, if followed correctly, will eventually solve the problem. But algorithms may take a long time—especially for complex problems. Look at every ad in the paper and call all of those that allow pets.

- Use a **heuristic**, a simple rule for problem solving that does not guarantee a solution, but offers a likely shortcut to it. Work backwards from the solution—start by drawing a 1-mile radius around work to narrow the search.

3 Evaluation

Did your possible solutions solve the problem?

- If no, then you must return to the production and/or preparation stages.

- If yes, then take action to achieve your goal.

Algorithm A logical, step-by-step procedure that, if followed correctly, will always eventually solve the problem.

Heuristic A cognitive strategy, or "rule of thumb," often used as a shortcut for problem solving; does not guarantee a solution to a problem but does narrow the alternatives.

hypotheses, by using *algorithms* and *heuristics*. **Algorithms**, as problem-solving strategies, are guaranteed to lead to an eventual solution. But they are not practical in many situations. **Heuristics**, or simplified rules based on experience, are much faster but do not guarantee a solution. Finally, during the evaluation stage we judge the hypotheses generated during the production stage against the criteria established in the preparation stage.

In addition to using these three steps, we also sometimes solve problems with a sudden flash of *insight*, like Köhler's chimps who stacked boxes to reach the bananas (Chapter 6). On other occasions, we may mentally set our problem aside for a while, in an *incubation period*, and then find that the solution comes to mind without further conscious thought.

Barriers to Problem Solving

Why are some problems so difficult to solve? The reason may be that we often stick to problem-solving strategies that have worked in the past, called **mental sets**, rather than try new, possibly more effective ones **(Figure 8.3)**.

Besides relying on mental sets, we sometimes fail to solve problems because we think of objects as functioning only in their prescribed, customary way—a phenomenon called **functional fixedness**. When a child uses soft cushions to build a fort, or you use a table knife instead of a screwdriver to tighten a screw, you both have successfully avoided functional fixedness. Similarly, the individual who discovered a way to retrofit diesel engines to allow them to use discarded restaurant oil as fuel has overcome functional fixedness—and may become very wealthy! For a test of your own functional fixedness, carefully examine **Figure 8.4**.

Other barriers to effective problem solving stem from our tendency to ignore important information. Have you ever caught yourself agreeing with friends who support your political opinions and discounting conflicting opinions? This inclination to seek confirmation for our preexisting beliefs and to overlook contradictory evidence is known as **confirmation bias** (Christandl et al., 2011; Hernandez & Preston, 2013; Moreno & Johnston, 2013; Nickerson, 1998).

In some cases, this bias can have serious consequences. For example, researchers in one study examined the reported treatment outcomes in medical research studies (Hrobjartsson et al., 2013). In some of these studies, the person who evaluated the effectiveness of the treatment did not know whether the patient received a particular treatment (these researchers were blind to condition). In other cases, however, the researcher who evaluated the treatment was aware of which treatment each patient received. Can you guess their findings? Studies in which the researcher was aware of which treatment the patient received found the treatment to be more effective than those in which the researcher did not have this information. The problem isn't just that the participants in this research setting, who had previous knowledge, fell victim to the confirmation bias, but how it undoubtedly occurs in everyday life. Medical doctors, therapists, and others who treat our ailments all have preexisting beliefs based on their professional training and clinical experience. But once they develop a preferred treatment, they may only seek confirmatory evidence of preexisting beliefs. Thus, certain treatments may be judged as being more effective than they actually are, and possibly more effective ones are ignored.

Mental set A problem-solving strategy that has worked in the past, which we continue to use rather than try new strategies.

Functional fixedness The inability to think of an object functioning other than in its usual or customary way; adversely affects problem solving and creativity.

Confirmation bias The bias of preferring information that confirms preexisting positions or beliefs, while ignoring or discounting contradictory evidence.

FIGURE 8.3 THE NINE-DOT PROBLEM

Without lifting your pencil, can you draw no more than four lines to connect all nine dots? If not, the reason may be that you're trying to use *mental sets*—problem-solving strategies that have worked well for you in the past. Try "thinking outside the box" and then compare your answer to the solution presented at the end of the chapter.

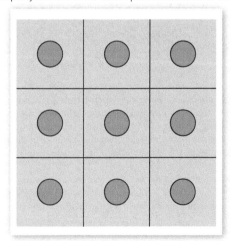

FIGURE 8.4 OVERCOMING FUNCTIONAL FIXEDNESS

Can you use these supplies to mount the candle on a wall so that it can be lit in the normal way and without toppling over? The solution is at the end of the chapter.

© Willard/iStockphoto

realworldpsychology Sports Fans and Superstitious Beliefs

Have you heard of the *Sports Illustrated* magazine's "cover jinx"? The belief is that once a team or person appears on the cover of this magazine, something bad will soon befall them. For example, on November 20, 2012, the previously winning Notre Dame football team was on the cover and then lost 42–14 to Alabama in the National Championship Game on January 7, 2013. Can you see how people who believe in the "jinx" might tend to look for examples to support it but fail to see examples that don't? For example, the New York Yankees and Michael Jordan have had the most covers by a team and individual, respectively; and their exceptional winning histories were anything but "jinxed."

On a similar note, researchers in one study asked participants to compare two handwriting samples for a supposed note written by a bank robber and handed to a bank teller. Participants were told that one handwriting sample was from the supposed bank robber, whereas the other sample was supposedly from a suspect who had been arrested for committing the crime (Kukucka & Kassin, 2012). Participants who were also informed that the suspect had already confessed to the crime judged his handwriting sample as more similar than participants who were not given this additional information.

Just as some people used their superstitious beliefs in the *Sports Illustrated* "cover jinx," these research participants used the suspect's supposed confession to search for confirming evidence. However, while sports fans' misplaced beliefs are relatively unimportant, this research suggests the confirmation bias may have serious repercussions in actual legal judgments.

Another barrier to problem solving sometimes results from our improper use of heuristics (see again Figure 8.2). For example, when we use the **availability heuristic**, we take a mental shortcut and judge something based on the information that is readily available in our memories. In other words, we give greater credence to information and examples that readily spring to mind (Fortune & Goodie, 2012; Kahneman & Tversky, 1973; Miller et al., 2012; Tversky & Kahneman, 1974, 1993).

Availability heuristic A cognitive strategy (or shortcut) that involves making judgments based on information that is readily available in memory.

psychology and you The Pros and Cons of Heuristics

Thankfully, the availability heuristic as a mental shortcut is often appropriate and helpful. If you note that your professor consistently lowers points on assignments that are turned in late, you'll be more likely to turn in your paper on time. However, when a rare event makes a vivid impression on us, we sometimes erroneously overestimate its likelihood. For example, horrific images of plane crashes easily come to mind, and we tend to think such crashes are more common than they actually are. Similarly, if you easily recall images of your grandfather smoking cigarettes his entire life and living to be 100, you may fail to recognize the uniqueness of this one personal example. More importantly, you may ignore or distort the larger and factually based serious dangers of smoking. In addition, sensationalistic media coverage of rare instances of children being kidnapped while walking to school, or occasional bullying on a school bus, may create an erroneous availability heuristic, and parents may needlessly drive their children to and from school.

© dlHunter/iStockphoto

Representativeness heuristic A cognitive strategy (or shortcut) that involves making judgments based on how well an object or event matches (represents) an existing prototype in our minds.

Like the availability heuristic, the **representativeness heuristic** both helps and hinders good decision making. Using this heuristic, we estimate the probability of an event based on how well an individual or event matches (or *represents*) an existing prototype in our minds (Fisk et al., 2006; Pachur et al., 2013; Read & Grushka-Cockayne, 2011). When we see a dark, cloudy sky, we decide to carry an umbrella because these circumstances match our mind's prototype of "signs of impending rain." In this case, the umbrella decision is likely correct.

Problems occur when we misjudge and overestimate how much someone shares the characteristics of a group they belong to. For example, a principal who believes that women are naturally better with children might hire a woman for an elementary school teaching position over a better-qualified man simply because of her membership in the group of women.

The important take-home message here is to be aware of the potential biases that sometimes limit our good judgment and ability to solve problems. At the same time, we need to remember that cognitive strategies, such as the availability and representativeness heuristics, provide mental shortcuts that are generally far more likely to help than to hurt us (Pohl et al., 2013). They allow immediate "inferences that are fast, frugal, and accurate" (Todd & Gigerenzer, 2000, p. 736).

Creativity

Everyone exhibits a certain amount of creativity in some aspects of life. Even when doing ordinary tasks, like planning an afternoon of errands, you are being somewhat creative. Similarly, if you've ever tightened a screw with a penny or used a thick book on a chair as a booster seat for a child, you've found creative solutions to problems.

How would psychologists operationally define creativity? Conceptions of creativity are obviously personal and depend on our culture, but most agree that a creative solution or performance generally produces original, appropriate, and valued outcomes in a novel way. Three characteristics are also associated with **creativity**: *originality*, *fluency*, and *flexibility*. Thomas Edison's development of the first "practical" light bulb offers a prime example of each of these characteristics **(Table 8.1)**.

Creativity The ability to produce original, appropriate, and valued outcomes in a novel way; consists of three characteristics—originality, fluency, and flexibility.

Do we need special conditions to increase creativity? Interestingly, researchers in one study examined how the sounds in our environment influence creativity (Mehta et al., 2012). Participants were asked to engage in various exercises testing creativity, such as coming up with unusual ways to use common objects. Some participants performed this task in a relatively quiet environment (50 decibels), whereas others did so in an environment with a moderate level of ambient noise (70 dB), and still others worked in a loud environment (85 dB). Can you predict the findings? Participants in the environment with a moderate level of background noise were the most creative, suggesting that having some type of noise distraction encourages people to think more creatively than a very quiet setting, which may explain why some people find they're more creative while studying in a coffee shop!

TABLE 8.1	THREE ELEMENTS OF CREATIVE THINKING		
	Explanations	**Thomas Edison Examples**	
Originality	Seeing unique or different solutions to a problem	After noting that electricity passing through a conductor produces a glowing red or white light, Edison, like others before him, imagined using this light for practical applications.	
Fluency	Generating a large number of possible solutions	Edison and his team of scientists, termed "Edison's Pioneers," tried literally hundreds of different materials to find one that would heat to the point of glowing white without burning up.	
Flexibility	Shifting with ease from one type of problem-solving strategy to another	When they couldn't find the perfect long-lasting filament material, Edison and his team used the best they had and tried heating it in a vacuum. Finally success—they had created the first practical light bulb. (It burned nearly 14 hours, quite an accomplishment for the time).	

Courtesy U. S. Department of the Interior, National Parks Service, Edison National Historic Site

Think Critically

1 Can you identify which of the three characteristics of creativity (originality, fluency, or flexibility) best explains your personal experiences with being creative?

2 Creativity is usually associated with art, poetry, and the like. What are other areas in which creativity is highly valued?

Divergent thinking An aspect of creativity characterized by an ability to produce unusual but appropriate alternatives from a single starting point.

How do we measure creativity? Most tests focus on **divergent thinking**, a type of thinking in which we develop many possibilities from a single starting point (Baer, 1994, 2013). In contrast to *convergent thinking*, in which we work to solve a specific problem, divergent thinking is open-ended and focused on generating unusual, novel solutions. For example, when assigned a research paper, many students have trouble coming up with something on their own. They're thinking "inside the box" when they focus on the specific problem of completing the assignment in a way that will please the professor. This is convergent thinking. Instead, most professors want to develop creative, divergent thinking and encourage (force?) their students to dig deeper to come up with their own unique ideas.

Psychologists have developed several methods to test for divergent thinking. For example, the Unusual Uses Test requires you to think of as many uses as possible for an object, such as a brick. In the Anagrams Test, you're asked to reorder the letters in a word to make as many new words as possible. To test your overall creativity, try the activities in *Are You Creative?*

TEST YOURSELF: ARE YOU CREATIVE?

psychology and you

- Find 10 coins and arrange them in the configuration shown here. By moving only 2 coins, form two rows that each contain 6 coins. The solution is at the end of the chapter.

- In five minutes, see how many words you can make using the letters in the word *hippopotamus*.

- In five minutes, list all the things you can do with a paper clip.

How did you do? If you'd like help increasing your score, research suggests that creativity requires the coming together of six interrelated resources, as shown in **Table 8.2**. You can study this list and then strengthen yourself in the areas in which you need improvement.

TABLE 8.2	RESOURCES OF CREATIVE PEOPLE
Intellectual ability	Enough intelligence to see problems in a new light
Knowledge	Sufficient basic knowledge of the problem to effectively evaluate possible solutions
Thinking style	Novel ideas and ability to distinguish between the worthy and worthless
Personality	Willingness to grow and change, take risks, and work to overcome obstacles
Motivation	Sufficient motivation to accomplish the task and more internal than external motivation
Environment	An environment that supports creativity

Kevin Mazur/TAS/Getty Images

Which resources best explain Taylor Swift's phenomenal success?

Sources: Mieg, 2011; Sternberg, 2010; Sternberg & Lubart, 1996.

RETRIEVAL PRACTICE: THINKING

Self-Test

Completing this self-test and comparing your answers with those in Appendix B provides immediate feedback and helpful practice for exams. Additional interactive, self-tests are available at www.wiley.com/college/huffman.

1. The mental activities involved in acquiring, storing, retrieving, and using knowledge are collectively known as _____.

a. perception   b. consciousness
c. cognition   d. awareness

2. Rosa is shopping in a new supermarket and wants to find a standard type of mustard. Which problem-solving strategy would be most efficient?

a. algorithm   b. heuristic
c. instinct   d. mental set

3. _____ is a logical step-by-step procedure that, if followed, will always produce the solution.

a. An algorithm   b. A problem-solving set
c. A heuristic   d. Brainstorming

4. _____ is the ability to produce valued outcomes in a novel way.

a. Problem solving   b. Functional flexibility
c. Incubation   d. Creativity

Think Critically

1 During problem solving, do you use primarily algorithms or heuristics? What are the advantages of each?

2 Would you prefer to be highly creative or highly intelligent? Why?

realworldpsychology

Why might some medical treatments be judged as more effective than they really are?

Can studying in a coffee shop improve your creativity?

HINT: LOOK IN THE MARGIN FOR (Q1) AND (Q2)

LANGUAGE

RETRIEVAL PRACTICE While reading the upcoming sections, respond to each Learning Objective in your own words. Then compare your responses with those www.wiley.com/college/huffman.

1 IDENTIFY the building blocks of language.
2 DESCRIBE the prominent theories of how language and thought interact.
3 DESCRIBE the major stages of language development.
4 REVIEW the evidence that nonhuman animals are able to learn and use language.

Using **language** enables us to mentally manipulate symbols, thereby expanding our thinking. Whether it's spoken, written, or signed, language also allows us to communicate our thoughts, ideas, and feelings.

To produce language, we first build words using **phonemes** [FO-neems] and **morphemes** [MOR-feems]. Then we string words into sentences using rules of **grammar**, such as *syntax* and *semantics* (**Figure 8.5**).

What happens in our brains when we produce and comprehend language? Recall from Chapter 2 that for most of us, our language centers are located in the left frontal

LEARNING OBJECTIVES

Language A form of communication using sounds and symbols combined according to specified rules.

Phoneme The smallest basic unit of speech or sound in any given language that makes a meaningful difference in speech production and reception.

Morpheme The smallest meaningful unit of language; formed from a combination of phonemes.

Grammar The system of rules (syntax and semantics) used to create language and communication.

FIGURE 8.5 **BUILDING BLOCKS OF LANGUAGE**

Grammar

System of rules (syntax and semantics) used to generate acceptable language, thus enabling us to communicate with and understand others.

They were in my psychology class.
versus
They was in my psychology class.

Syntax	*Semantics*
Grammatical rules for putting words in correct order	A system of rules for using words to create meaning
I am happy. versus *Happy I am.*	*I went out on a limb for you.* versus *Humans have several limbs.*

Morphemes

Smallest meaningful units of language; created by combining phonemes. (*Function morphemes* are prefixes and suffixes. *Content morphemes* are root words.)

unthinkable = un·think·able
(prefix = *un*, root word = *think*, suffix = *able*)

Phonemes

Smallest distinctive sound unit that makes up every language

p in pansy; *ng* in sting

"GOT IDEA. TALK BETTER. COMBINE WORDS. MAKE SENTENCES."

Sidney Harris/ScienceCartoonPlus.com

lobe, with *Broca's area* linked to speech production and *Wernicke's area* being important for language comprehension. Language, just like our thought processes, is both localized and distributed throughout our brain **(Figure 8.6)**. For example, the amygdala is active when we engage in a special type of language—cursing or swearing. Why? Recall from Chapter 2 that the amygdala is linked to emotions, especially fear and rage. So it's logical that the brain regions activated by swearing or hearing swear words would be the same as those for fear and aggression. Keep in mind, however, that in our everyday conversations, both areas are active at the same time, along with other parts of the brain. Note also in Figure 8.6 *Broca's area* (which is responsible for speech generation) and *Wernicke's area* (which controls language comprehension). Other parts of the brain also are activated during different types of language generation and listening.

FIGURE 8.6 **LANGUAGE AND THE BRAIN**

Left hemisphere

Frontal lobe

Broca's area

Wernicke's area

Hippocampus

Temporal lobe

Amygdala

Masterfile

FIGURE 8.7 USING PET SCANS TO STUDY LANGUAGE AND THE BRAIN

WDCN/Univ. College London/Photo Researchers

Ⓐ Language generated in the frontal lobe (center left) has its cognition checked in the temporal lobe (lower right).

WDCN/Univ. College London/Photo Researchers

Ⓑ Working out the meaning of heard words makes areas of the temporal lobe light up.

WDCN/Univ. College London/Photo Researchers

Ⓒ Repeating words increases activity in Broca's area and Wernicke's area, as well as a motor region responsible for pronouncing words (reddish area at the top).

How do we know which parts of the brain are involved with language? Scientists can track brain activity through a colored *positron emission tomography (PET) scan*. Injection of the radioactive isotope oxygen-15 into the bloodstream of the subject makes areas of the brain with high metabolic activity "light up" in red and orange on the scan **(Figure 8.7)**.

Language and Thought

Does the fact that you speak English instead of German—or Chinese instead of Swahili—determine how you reason, think, and perceive the world? Linguist Benjamin Whorf (1956) believed so. As evidence for his *linguistic relativity hypothesis*, Whorf offered a now classic example: Because Inuits (previously known as Eskimos) supposedly have many words for snow (*apikak* for "first snow falling," *pukak* for "snow for drinking water," and so on), they can reportedly perceive and think about snow differently from English speakers, who have only one word—*snow*.

Though intriguing, Whorf's hypothesis has not fared well. He apparently exaggerated the number of Inuit words for snow (Pullum, 1991) and ignored the fact that English speakers have a number of terms to describe various forms of snow, such as *slush*, *sleet*, *hard pack*, and *powder*. Other research has directly contradicted Whorf's theory. For example, Eleanor Rosch (1973) found that although people of the Dani tribe in New Guinea possess only two color names—one indicating cool, dark colors, and the other describing warm, bright colors—they discriminate among multiple hues as well as English speakers do.

Whorf apparently was mistaken in his belief that language *determines* thought. But there is no doubt that language *influences* thought (Deutscher, 2010; Jarvis, 2011; Ottenheimer, 2013; Warren, 2013). People who speak both Chinese and English report that the language they're currently using affects their sense of self (Berry et al., 2011; Matsumoto, 2010). When using Chinese, they tend to conform to Chinese cultural norms; when speaking English, they tend to adopt Western norms.

realworldpsychology **Language, Business, and the Military** Our words influence the thinking of those who hear them. That's why companies avoid *firing* employees. Instead, employees are *outplaced* or *nonrenewed*. Similarly, the military uses terms like *preemptive strike* to cover the fact that they attacked first and *tactical redeployment* to refer to a retreat. Furthermore, research has shown that consumers who receive a *rebate* are less likely to spend the money than those who receive a *bonus* (Epley, 2008).

© DoxaDigital/iStockphoto

218

FIGURE 8.8 **CAN YOU IDENTIFY THIS EMOTION?**

Infants as young as 2.5 months can nonverbally express emotions, such as joy, surprise, or anger.

Myrleen Ferguson Cafe/PhotoEdit

Cooing The vowel-like sounds infants produce beginning around 2 to 3 months of age.

Babbling The vowel/consonant combinations that infants begin to produce at about 4 to 6 months of age.

Overextension The overly broad use of a word to include objects that do not fit the word's meaning (or example, calling all men "Daddy").

Telegraphic speech The two- or three-word sentences of young children that contain only the most necessary words.

Overgeneralization The grammatical error of applying the basic rules of grammar even to cases that are exceptions to the rule (for example, saying "mans" instead of "men"); also known as overregularization.

Language Development

From birth, a child communicates through facial expressions, eye contact, and body gestures **(Figure 8.8)**. Babies only hours old begin to "teach" their caregivers when and how they want to be held, fed, and played with. Babies even start to learn language before they are born. For example, researchers in one study played sounds from two different languages—English and Swedish—for babies at hospitals in both the United States and Sweden shortly after birth (Moon et al., 2012). These babies were given special pacifiers that were hooked up to a computer, and the more times they sucked on the pacifier, the more times they heard the vowels. Half the babies heard sounds from the language they'd been exposed to in utero, whereas the others heard vowels from a different language. In both countries, the babies who heard the foreign vowels sucked more frequently than those who heard sounds from their native language, suggesting that babies have already become familiar—through listening to their mother's voice—with the sounds in their native language and are now more interested in hearing novel sounds!

Eventually, children also communicate verbally, progressing through several distinct stages of language acquisition. These stages are summarized in **Table 8.3**. By age 5, most children have mastered basic grammar and typically use about 2,000 words (a level of mastery considered adequate for getting by in any given culture). Past

TABLE 8.3 **LANGUAGE ACQUISITION**

Birth to 12 months

FEATURES	EXAMPLES
Crying (reflexive in newborns) becomes more purposeful	hunger cry, anger cry, and pain cry
Cooing (vowel-like sounds) at 2–3 months	"ooooh," "aaaah"
Babbling (consonants added) at 4–6 months	"bahbahbah," "dahdahdah"

12 months to 2 years

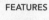

FEATURES	EXAMPLES
Babbling resembles language of the environment, and child understands sounds relate to meaning	"Mama," "juice," "up"
Speech consists of one-word utterances	
Expressive ability more than doubles once words are joined into short phrases	"Daddy milk," "no night-night!"
Overextension (using words to include objects that do not fit the word's meaning)	all men = "Daddy" all furry animals = "doggy"

2 years to 5 years

FEATURES	EXAMPLES
Telegraphic speech (like telegrams, omits nonessential connecting words)	"Me want cookie" "Grandma go bye-bye?"
Vocabulary increases at a phenomenal rate	
Child acquires a wide variety of grammar rules	adding –ed for past tense, adding s to form plurals
Overgeneralization (applying basic rules of grammar even to cases that are exceptions to the rule)	"I goed to the zoo" "Two mans"

this point, vocabulary and grammar gradually improve throughout life (Esquivel & Acevedo, 2013; Oller et al., 2014; Rowe & Levine, 2011).

Some theorists believe that language capability is innate, primarily a matter of maturation. Noam Chomsky (1968, 1980) suggests that children are "prewired" with a neurological ability known as a **language acquisition device (LAD)** that enables them to analyze language and to extract the basic rules of grammar. This mechanism needs only minimal exposure to adult speech to unlock its potential. As evidence for this *nativist position*, Chomsky observes that children everywhere progress through the same stages of language development at about the same ages. He also notes that babbling is the same in all languages and that deaf babies babble just like hearing babies.

Nurturists argue that the nativist position doesn't fully explain individual differences in language development. They hold that children learn language through a complex system of rewards, punishments, and imitation. For example, parents smile and encourage any vocalizations from a very young infant. Later, they respond even more enthusiastically when the infant babbles "mama" or "dada." In this way, parents unknowingly use *shaping* (Chapter 6) to help babies learn language.

Language acquisition device (LAD) According to Chomsky, an innate mechanism that enables a child to analyze language and extract the basic rules of grammar.

Can Human Animals Talk with Nonhuman Animals?

Without question, nonhuman animals communicate. They regularly send warnings, signal sexual interest, share locations of food sources, and so on. But can nonhuman animals master the complexity of human language? Since the 1930s, many language studies have attempted to answer this question by probing the language abilities of chimpanzees, gorillas, and other animals (Berwick et al., 2011; Call, 2011; Lyn et al., 2011; Ottenheimer, 2013; Stegmann, 2013).

One of the most successful early studies was conducted by Beatrice and Allen Gardner (1969), who recognized chimpanzees' manual dexterity and ability to imitate gestures. The Gardners used American Sign Language (ASL) with a chimp named Washoe. By the time Washoe was 4 years old, she had learned 132 signs and was able to combine them into simple sentences such as "Hurry, gimme toothbrush" and "Please tickle more." The famous gorilla Koko also uses ASL to communicate; she reportedly uses more than 1,000 words **(Figure 8.9)**.

FIGURE 8.9 SIGNING

According to her teacher, Penny Patterson, Koko has used ASL to converse with others, talk to herself, joke, express preferences, and even lie (Linden, 1993; Patterson, 2002).

FIGURE 8.10 **COMPUTER-AIDED COMMUNICATION**

Apes lack the necessary anatomical structures to vocalize the way humans do. For this reason, language research with chimps and gorillas has focused on teaching the animals to use sign language or to "speak" by pointing to symbols on a keyboard. Do you think this amounts to using language the same way humans do?

Michael Nichols/NG image Collection

"ALTHOUGH HUMANS MAKE SOUNDS WITH THEIR MOUTHS AND OCCASIONALLY LOOK AT EACH OTHER, THERE IS NO SOLID EVIDENCE THAT THEY ACTUALLY COMMUNICATE WITH EACH OTHER."

Sidney Harris/ScienceCartoonPlus.com

In another well-known study, a chimp named Lana learned to use symbols on a computer to get things she wanted, such as food, a drink, and a tickle from her trainers and to have her curtains opened (Rumbaugh et al., 1974) **(Figure 8.10)**.

Dolphins also are often the subject of interesting language research (May-Collado, 2010). Communication with dolphins is done by means of hand signals or audible commands transmitted through an underwater speaker system. In one typical study, trainers gave dolphins commands made up of two- to five-word sentences, such as "Big ball—square—return," which meant that they should go get the big ball, put it in the floating square, and return to the trainer (Herman et al., 1984). By varying the syntax (for example, the order of the words) and specific content of the commands, the researchers showed that dolphins are sensitive to these aspects of language.

Psychologists disagree about how to interpret the findings on apes and dolphins. Most believe that nonhuman animals communicate but that their ideas are severely limited. For example, some critics claim that apes and dolphins are unable to convey subtle meanings, use language creatively, or communicate at an abstract level (Jackendoff, 2003; Siegala & Varley, 2008).

Others propose that these animals do not truly understand language but are simply operantly conditioned (Chapter 6) to imitate symbols to receive rewards (Savage-Rumbaugh, 1990; Terrace, 1979). Finally, still others suggest that data regarding animal language has not always been well documented (Font & Carazo, 2010; Willingham, 2001; Wynne, 2007).

Proponents of animal language respond that apes can use language creatively and have even coined some words of their own. For example, Koko signed "finger bracelet" to describe a ring and "eye hat" to describe a mask (Patterson & Linden, 1981). Proponents also argue that, as demonstrated by the dolphin studies, animals can be taught to understand basic rules of sentence structure.

Still, the gap between human and nonhuman animals' language is considerable. Current evidence suggests that, at best, nonhuman animal language is less complex and less creative and has fewer rules than any language used by humans.

RETRIEVAL PRACTICE: LANGUAGE

Self-Test

Completing this self-test and comparing your answers with those in Appendix B provides immediate feedback and helpful practice for exams. Additional interactive, self-tests are available at www.wiley.com/college/huffman.

1. _____ is the set of rules that (syntax and semantics) used to create language and communication.

a. Syntax   b. Semantics
c. Pragmatics   d. Grammar

2. What are the three building blocks of language?

a. grammar, phonemes, and morphemes
b. semantics, structure, and phonemes
c. pragmatics, phonemes, and morphemes
d. grammar, prefix, and suffix

3. According to Chomsky, the innate mechanism that enables a child to analyze language is known as a(n) _____.

a. telegraphic understanding device (TUD)
b. language acquisition device (LAD)
c. language and grammar translator (LGT)
d. overgeneralized neural net (ONN)

4. Human language differs from the communication of nonhuman animals in that it _____.

a. is used more creatively
b. is more complex
c. has more rules
d. all of these options

Think Critically

1 Describe a personal example of language influencing your thinking.

2 Review the evidence that nonhuman animals are able to learn and use language. Do you think apes and dolphins have true language? Why or why not?

realworldpsychology

Can babies begin to learn language even before they are born?

HINT: LOOK IN THE MARGIN FOR

INTELLIGENCE

RETRIEVAL PRACTICE While reading the upcoming sections, respond to each Learning Objective in your own words. Then compare your responses with those www.wiley.com/college/huffman.

1 **IDENTIFY** the key theories and types of intelligence.

2 **DESCRIBE** how intelligence is measured.

3 **DISCUSS** the relative contributions of nature and nurture to IQ.

4 **EXPLAIN** the importance of between versus group differences in intelligence.

LEARNING OBJECTIVES

Many people equate intelligence with "book smarts." For others, the definition of intelligence depends on the characteristics and skills that are valued in a particular social group or culture (Hunt, 2011; Sternberg, 2013). For example, the Mandarin word that corresponds most closely to the word *intelligence* is a character meaning "good brain and talented" (Matsumoto, 2000). The word is also associated with traits like imitation, effort, and social responsibility (Keats, 1982).

Even among Western psychologists there is debate over the definition of intelligence. In this discussion, we rely on a formal definition of **intelligence**—*the global capacity to think rationally, act purposefully, profit from experience, and deal effectively with the environment* (Wechsler, 1944, 1977).

Intelligence The global capacity to think rationally, act purposefully, profit from experience, and deal effectively with the environment.

The Nature of Intelligence

In the 1920s, British psychologist Charles Spearman first observed that high scores on separate tests of mental abilities tend to correlate with each other. Spearman

General intelligence (g) Spearman's term for overall, general intellectual ability.

Fluid intelligence (gf) Aspects of innate intelligence, including reasoning abilities, memory, and speed of information processing; relatively independent of education and tends to decline as people age.

Crystallized intelligence (gc) Knowledge and skills gained through experience and education and the ability to access that knowledge; intelligence that tends to increase over the life span.

Emotional intelligence (EI) The ability to perceive, appraise, express, and regulate emotions accurately and appropriately.

(1923) thus proposed that intelligence is a single factor, which he termed **general intelligence (g)**. He believed that *g* underlies all intellectual behavior, including reasoning, solving problems, and performing well in all areas of cognition. Spearman's work laid the foundations for today's standardized intelligence tests (Matlin, 2013; Wright, 2011).

About a decade later, L. L. Thurstone (1938) proposed 7 primary mental abilities: verbal comprehension, word fluency, numerical fluency, spatial visualization, associative memory, perceptual speed, and reasoning. J. P. Guilford (1967) later expanded this number, proposing that as many as 120 factors are involved in the structure of intelligence.

Around the same time, Raymond Cattell (1963, 1971) reanalyzed Thurstone's data and argued against the idea of multiple intelligences. He believed that two subtypes of g exist:

- **Fluid intelligence (gf)** refers to innate, inherited reasoning abilities, memory, and speed of information processing. Fluid intelligence is relatively independent of education and experience, and like other biological capacities, it declines with age (Jost et al., 2011; Murray et al., 2011; Rozencwajg et al., 2005).

- **Crystallized intelligence (gc)** refers to the store of knowledge and skills gained through experience and education (Hunt, 2011; Sternberg, 2013). Crystallized intelligence tends to increase over the life span.

Today there is considerable support for the concept of g as a measure of academic smarts. However, many contemporary cognitive theorists believe that intelligence is not a single general factor but a collection of many separate specific abilities.

One of these cognitive theorists, Howard Gardner, believes that people have many kinds of intelligences. The fact that brain-damaged patients often lose some intellectual abilities while retaining others suggests to Gardner that different intelligences are located in discrete areas throughout the brain. According to *Gardner's theory of multiple intelligences* (1983, 1999, 2008, 2011), people have different profiles of intelligence because they are stronger in some areas than others **(Table 8.4)**. They also use their intelligences differently to learn new material, perform tasks, and solve problems.

Robert Sternberg's *triarchic theory of successful intelligence* also assumes multiple abilities. As shown in **Table 8.5**, Sternberg theorized that three separate, learned aspects of intelligence exist: (1) *analytic*, (2) *creative*, and (3) *practical* (Sternberg, 1985, 2007, 2012).

Sternberg (1985, 1999, 2013) emphasizes the process underlying thinking rather than just the product. He also stresses the importance of applying mental abilities to real-world situations rather than testing mental abilities in isolation. In short, Sternberg avoids the traditional idea of intelligence as an innate form of "book smarts" and instead emphasizes successful intelligence as the learned ability to adapt to, shape, and select environments in order to accomplish personal and societal goals.

Finally, in addition to the multiple intelligences proposed by Gardner and Sternberg, Daniel Goleman's research (1995, 2000, 2008) and best-selling books have popularized the concept of **emotional intelligence (EI)**, based on original work by Peter Salovey and John Mayer (1990).

Voices from the Classroom

Multiple Intelligences and Being "Word Smart" When discussing Gardner's multiple intelligences to identify our strengths and weaknesses, I remind students of the 2012 Olympics winner Gabby Douglas's physical genius as she flies through the air or Louis Sullivan's spatial wizardry in his architectural skyscrapers in Chicago. Then I share my personal example. I am "word" smart, which served me well in earning a doctoral degree. But I never got the basketball in the hoop, never hit the softball with the bat, and even today, quickly move when I see a Ping Pong ball headed my way. Yes, I'm kinesthetically challenged. Gardner's theory is a beneficial tool for recognizing our strengths and weaknesses.

Professor Carmon Weaver Hicks

Ivy Tech Community College

Madison, Indiana

TABLE 8.4	GARDNER'S MULTIPLE INTELLIGENCES

Type of Intelligence	Possible Careers	
Linguistic Language, such as speaking, reading a book, writing a story	Novelist, journalist, teacher	
Spatial Mental maps, such as figuring out how to pack multiple presents in a box or how to draw a floor plan	Engineer, architect, pilot	
Bodily/kinesthetic Body movement, such as dancing, soccer, and football	Athlete, dancer, ski instructor	
Intrapersonal Understanding oneself, such as setting achievable goals or recognizing self-defeating emotions	Increased success in almost all careers	
Logical/mathematical Problem solving or scientific analysis, such as following a logical proof or solving a mathematical problem	Mathematician, scientist, engineer	
Musical Musical skills, such as singing or playing a musical instrument	Singer, musician, composer	
Interpersonal Social skills, such as managing diverse groups of people	Salesperson, manager, therapist, teacher	
Naturalistic Being attuned to nature, such as noticing seasonal patterns or using environmentally safe products	Biologist, naturalist	
Spiritual/existential Attunement to meaning of life and death and other conditions of life	Philosopher, theologian	

Source: Adapted from Gardner, 1983, 1999, 2008, 2011.

TABLE 8.5	STERNBERG'S TRIARCHIC THEORY OF SUCCESSFUL INTELLIGENCE

	Analytical Intelligence	Creative Intelligence	Practical Intelligence
Sample skills	Good at analysis, evaluation, judgment, and comparison skills	Good at invention, coping with novelty, and imagination skills	Good at application, implementation, execution, and utilization skills
Methods of assessment	Intelligence tests assess the meaning of words based on context, and how to solve number-series problems	Open-ended tasks, writing a short story, drawing a piece of art, solving a scientific problem requiring insight	Tasks requiring solutions to practical, personal problems

Emotional intelligence (EI) is generally defined as *the ability to perceive, appraise, express, and regulate emotions accurately and appropriately.* In other words, an emotionally intelligent person successfully combines the three components of emotions (cognitive, physiological, and behavioral). Proponents of EI have suggested ways in which the close collaboration between emotion and reason may promote personal well-being and growth (Salovey et al., 2000) **(Figure 8.11)**.

FIGURE 8.11 HOW DO WE DEVELOP EMOTIONAL INTELLIGENCE?
The mother in this photo appears to be empathizing with her young daughter and helping her to recognize and manage her own emotions. According to Goleman, this type of modeling and instruction is vital to the development of emotional intelligence.

realworldpsychology

Should We Teach EI in Schools? Popular accounts such as Goleman's have suggested that traditional measures of human intelligence ignore a crucial range of abilities that characterize people who excel in real life: self-awareness, impulse control, persistence, zeal and self-motivation, empathy, and social deftness. Goleman also proposes that many societal problems, such as domestic abuse and youth violence, can be attributed to low EI. Therefore, he argues, EI should be fostered and taught to everyone. In line with this, researchers in one study found that elementary schools in which emotional intelligence is taught show higher levels of warmth between students and teachers, more leadership among students, and teachers with a greater focus on students' interests and motivations (Rivers et al., 2012).

Critics fear that a handy term like EI invites misuse, but their strongest reaction is to Goleman's proposals for teaching EI. For example, Paul McHugh, director of psychiatry at Johns Hopkins University, suggests that Goleman is "presuming that someone has the key to the right emotions to be taught to children. We don't even know the right emotions to be taught to adults" (cited in Gibbs, 1995, p. 68).

Measuring Intelligence

Different IQ tests approach the measurement of intelligence from different perspectives. However, most are designed to predict grades in school. Let's look at the most commonly used IQ tests.

The *Stanford-Binet Intelligence Scale* is loosely based on the first IQ tests developed in France around the turn of the twentieth century by Alfred Binet. In the United States, Lewis Terman (1916) developed the Stanford-Binet (at Stanford University) to test the intellectual ability of U.S.-born children ages 3 to 16. The test is revised periodically—most recently in 2003. The test is administered individually and consists of such tasks as copying geometric designs, identifying similarities, and repeating number sequences.

In the original version of the Stanford-Binet, results were expressed in terms of a mental age. For example, if a 7-year-old's score equaled that of an average 8-year-old, the child was considered to have a mental age of 8. To determine the child's

FIGURE 8.12 ITEMS SIMILAR TO THOSE ON THE WECHSLER ADULT INTELLIGENCE SCALE (WAIS)

These are sample, simulated items resembling those found in the Wechsler Adult Intelligence Scale, Fourth Edition (WAIS-IV). Previous editions of the WAIS included sections, such as Picture Arrangement, Block Design, and Object Assembly, which were dropped to increase reliability, and user friendliness. WAIS-IV also takes less time to administer and the results show smaller differences based on level of education or racial/ethnic group membership. *Source:* Based on simulated items from the Wechsler Adult Intelligence Scale, Fourth Edition (WAIS-IV).

Ⓐ **Visual Puzzles**
The test administrator asks: "Which three pieces go together to make this puzzle?"

Ⓑ **Figure Weights**
The test administrator asks: "Which one of these works to balance the scale?"

intelligence quotient (IQ), mental age was divided by the child's chronological age (actual age in years) and multiplied by 100.

The most widely used intelligence test today, the *Wechsler Adult Intelligence Scale (WAIS),* was developed by David Wechsler in the early 1900s. He later created a similar test for school-aged children. Like the Stanford-Binet, Wechsler's tests yield an overall intelligence score, but there are separate scores for verbal intelligence (such as vocabulary comprehension, and knowledge of general information) and performance (such as arranging blocks to match a given pattern) **(Figure 8.12)**. The advantages of Wechsler's test are that different abilities can be evaluated either separately or together, and the test can be used with non-English speakers (in which case the verbal portion is omitted).

Today, most intelligence test scores are expressed as a comparison of a single person's score to a national sample of similar-aged people **(Figure 8.13)**. Even though the actual IQ is no longer calculated using the original formula comparing mental and chronological ages, the term *IQ* remains as a shorthand expression for intelligence test scores.

What makes a good test? How are the tests developed by Binet and Wechsler any better than those published in popular magazines and presented on television programs? To be scientifically acceptable, all psychological tests must fulfill three basic requirements:

- **Standardization** Intelligence tests (as well as personality, aptitude, and most other tests) must be **standardized** in two senses (Gregory, 2011; Kolen & Hendrickson, 2013; Plucker & Esping, 2013). First, every test must have *norms,*

Intelligence quotient (IQ) An index of intelligence initially derived from standardized tests and by dividing mental age by chronological age and then multiplying by 100; now derived by comparing individual scores with the scores of others of the same age.

Standardization A set of uniform procedures for treating each participant in a test, interview, or experiment or for recording data.

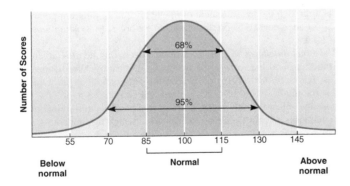

FIGURE 8.13 THE DISTRIBUTION OF SCORES ON THE STANFORD-BINET INTELLIGENCE TEST

Sixty-eight percent of children score within one standard deviation (16 points) above or below the national average, which is 100 points. About 16% score above 116, and about 16% score below 84.

Reliability The degree to which a test produces similar scores each time it is used; stability or consistency of the scores produced by an instrument.

Validity The degree to which a test measures what it is intended to measure.

or average scores, developed by giving the test to a representative sample of people (a diverse group of people who resemble those for whom the test is intended). Second, testing procedures must be standardized. All test takers must be given the same instructions, questions, and time limits, and all test administrators must follow the same objective score standards.

- **Reliability** is usually determined by retesting subjects to see whether their test scores change significantly (Geisinger, 2013; Gregory, 2011). Retesting can be done via the *test–retest method*, in which participants' scores on two separate administrations of the same test are compared, or via the *split-half method*, which splits a test into two equivalent parts (such as odd and even questions) and determines the degree of similarity between the two halves.

- **Validity** is the ability of a test to measure what it is designed to measure. The most important type of validity is *criterion-related validity*, or the accuracy with which test scores can be used to predict another variable of interest (known as the criterion). Criterion-related validity is expressed as the *correlation* (Chapter 1) between the test score and the criterion. If two variables are highly correlated, then one can be used to predict the other. Thus, if a test is valid, its scores will be useful in predicting an individual's behavior in some other specified situation. One example is using intelligence test scores to predict grades in college.

Voices from the Classroom

The Value of IQ Testing Intelligence tests, given under the appropriate circumstances, can be very valuable. If a student is struggling in school and the reasons are not obvious, an intelligence test can offer insight into that student's struggle. If the test results indicate a learning disability, such as dyslexia, then that student has a right to accommodations in school, which can ultimately help that student succeed.

Another example of the usefulness of intelligence tests is a personal one. My youngest son has significant facial paralysis and speech articulation difficulties due to a rare genetic condition. His school thought it best to place him in a special education classroom. I vehemently disagreed and had a psychologist test his intellectual level. When the results came back that his intelligence was completely normal, the school had no choice but to place him in a general education classroom, right where I knew he belonged all along!

Professor Paulina Multhaupt
Macomb Community College
Clinton Township, Michigan

Can you see why a test that is standardized and reliable but not valid is worthless? For example, a test for skin sensitivity may be easy to standardize (the instructions specify exactly how to apply the test agent), and it may be reliable (similar results are obtained on each retest). But it certainly would not be valid for predicting college grades.

Extremes in Intelligence

One of the best methods for judging the validity of a test is to compare people who score at the extremes. Despite the uncertainties discussed in the previous section, intelligence tests provide one of the major criteria for assessing mental ability at the extremes—specifically, for diagnosing *intellectual disability* and *mental giftedness*.

The clinical label *intellectually disabled* (previously referred to as *mentally retarded*) is applied when someone has significant deficits in general mental abilities, such as reasoning, problem solving, and academic learning. And these deficits result in impairments of adaptive functioning including communication, social participation, and personal independence (American Psychiatric Association, 2013).

Fewer than 3% of people are classified as having an intellectual disability **(Table 8.6)**. Of this group, 85% have only mild intellectual disability, and many become self-supporting, integrated members of society. Furthermore, people can score low on some measures of intelligence and still be average or even gifted in others (Armstrong et al., 2013; Meyer, 2011; Olson, 2010; Kreger Silverman, 2013). The most dramatic examples are people with **savant syndrome**. People with savant syndrome generally score very low on IQ tests (usually between 40 and 70), yet they demonstrate exceptional skills or brilliance in specific areas, such as rapid calculation, art, memory, or musical ability **(Figure 8.14)**.

Some forms of intellectual disability stem from genetic abnormalities, such as Down syndrome, fragile-X syndrome, and phenylketonuria (PKU). Other causes are environmental, including prenatal exposure to alcohol and other drugs, extreme

Savant syndrome A condition in which a person with generally limited mental abilities exhibits exceptional skill or brilliance in some limited field.

TABLE 8.6	DEGREES OF INTELLECTUAL DISABILITY			
	Level of Disability	IQ Scores	Characteristics	
	Mild (85%)	50–70	Usually able to become self-sufficient; may marry, have families, and secure full-time jobs in unskilled occupations	
	Moderate (10%)	35–49	Generally able to perform simple unskilled tasks; may contribute to a certain extent to their livelihood	
	Severe (3–4%)	20–34	Generally able to follow daily routines, but with continual supervision; with training, may learn basic communication skills	
	Profound (1–2%)	below 20	Generally able to perform only the most rudimentary behaviors, such as walking, feeding themselves, and saying a few phrases	

Pie chart: General population; Intellectually disabled 1–3%; 85% Mild, 1–2% Profound, 3–4% Severe, 10% Moderate

deprivation or neglect in early life, and brain damage from physical trauma, such as auto accidents or sports injuries. However, in many cases, there is no known cause of the intellectual disability. At the other end of the intelligence spectrum are people with especially high IQs (typically defined as being in the top 1 or 2%).

In 1921, Lewis Terman identified 1,500 gifted children—affectionately nicknamed the "Termites"—with IQs of 140 or higher and tracked their progress through adulthood. The number who became highly successful professionals was many times the number a random group would have provided (Kreger Silverman, 2013; Leslie, 2000; Terman, 1954). Those who were most successful tended to have extraordinary motivation, and they also had someone at home or school who was especially encouraging (Goleman, 1980). Unfortunately, some "Termites" also became alcoholics, got divorced, and committed suicide at close to the national rate (Campbell & Feng, 2011; Leslie, 2000; Terman, 1954). In sum, a high IQ is no guarantee of success in every endeavor; it only offers more intellectual opportunities.

Nature, Nurture, and IQ

Psychologists have long debated several important questions related to intelligence: How is brain functioning related to intelligence? What factors—environmental or hereditary—influence an individual's intelligence? Are IQ tests culturally biased? These questions, and the controversies surrounding them, are discussed in this section.

The Brain's Influence on Intelligence

A basic tenet of neuroscience is that all mental activity (including intelligence) results from neural activity in the brain. Most recent research on the biology of intelligence has focused on brain functioning. For example, neuroscientists have found that people who score highest on intelligence tests also respond more quickly on tasks requiring perceptual judgments (Bowling & Mackenzie, 1996; Posthuma et al., 2001; Sternberg, 2013).

In addition to a faster response time, research using positron emission tomography (PET) scans to measure brain activity (Chapter 2) suggests that intelligent brains work smarter, or more efficiently, than less-intelligent brains (Jung & Haier, 2007; Neubauer et al., 2004; Posthuma et al., 2001) **(Figure 8.15)**.

© Justin Sutcliffe/Redux Pictures

FIGURE 8.14 SAVANT SYNDROME—AN UNUSUAL FORM OF INTELLIGENCE

Derek Paravicini, a musical savant, pictured here, was born premature, blind, and with a severe learning disability. In spite of all these challenges, he plays the concert piano entirely by ear and has a repertoire of thousands of memorized pieces.

FIGURE 8.15 **DO INTELLIGENT BRAINS WORK MORE EFFICIENTLY?**

In PET scan images red and yellow indicate more activity in relevant brain areas. Note how during problem-solving tasks, low-IQ brains (left) show more activity than high-IQ brains (right). This research suggests that lower-IQ brains actually work harder, although less efficiently, than higher-IQ brains.

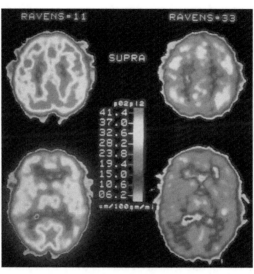

Courtesy Richard J. Haier, University of California-Irvine

Does size matter? It makes logical sense that bigger brains would be smarter; after all, humans have larger brains than less intelligent species, such as dogs. (Some animals, such as whales and dolphins, have larger brains than humans, but our brains are larger relative to our body size.) In fact, brain-imaging studies have found a significant correlation between brain size (adjusted for body size) and intelligence (Christensen et al., 2008; Colom et al., 2013; Deary et al., 2007). On the other hand, Albert Einstein's brain was no larger than normal (Witelson et al., 1999). In fact, some of Einstein's brain areas were actually smaller than average, but the area responsible for processing mathematical and spatial information was 15% larger than average.

Genetic and Environmental Influences on Intelligence

Similarities in intelligence between family members are due to a combination of hereditary (shared genetic material) and environmental factors (similar living arrangements and experiences). Researchers who are interested in the role of heredity in intelligence often focus on identical (monozygotic) twins because they share 100% of their genetic material, as shown in **Figure 8.16**.

Why are some people intellectually gifted, whereas others struggle? As identical twin studies demonstrate, genetics play an important role. In Figure 8.15, note the

FIGURE 8.16 **GENETIC AND ENVIRONMENTAL INFLUENCES ON IQ**

Note the higher correlations between identical twins' IQ test scores compared to correlations between all other pairs. Genes no doubt play a significant role in intelligence, but these effects are difficult to separate from environmental influences. (Based on Bouchard & McGue, 1981; Bouchard et al., 1998; Molenaar et al., 2013).

PhotoDisc, Inc./Getty Images

3 Year Old Children

Normal   Extreme Neglect

FIGURE 8.17 NEGLECT AND IQ

These images illustrate the negative impact of neglect on the developing brain. The CT scans on the left are from healthy three-year-old children with an average head size (50th percentile). The image on the right is from a series of three, three-year-old children following severe sensory-deprivation neglect in early childhood.

Each child's brain is significantly smaller than average and each has abnormal development of cortex (cortical atrophy) and other abnormalities suggesting abnormal development of the brain.

With kind permission from Springer Science+Business Media: Perry, B.D. Childhood experience and the expression of genetic potential: what childhood neglect tells us about nature and nurture Brain and Mind 3: 79-100, 2002.

higher correlations between identical twins' IQ scores compared to the correlations between all other pairs (Bouchard & McGue, 1981; Bouchard et al., 1998; McGue et al., 1993; Trzaskowski et al., 2013). Although heredity equips each of us with innate intellectual capabilities, the environment significantly influences whether a person will reach his or her full intellectual potential (Dickens & Flynn, 2001; Sangwan, 2001). For example, early malnutrition can retard a child's brain development, which in turn affects the child's curiosity, responsiveness to the environment, and motivation for learning—all of which can lower the child's IQ. The reverse is also true: An enriching early environment can set the stage for intellectual growth.

The long-running Minnesota Study of Twins, an investigation of identical twins raised in different homes and reunited only as adults (Bouchard, 1994, 1999; Bouchard et al., 1998; Johnson et al., 2007), found that genetic factors appear to play a surprisingly large role in the IQ scores of identical twins.

However, such results are not conclusive. Adoption agencies tend to look for similar criteria in their choice of adoptive parents. Therefore, the homes of these "reared apart" twins were actually quite similar. In addition, these twins shared the same nine-month prenatal environment, which also might have influenced their brain development and intelligence (White et al., 2002). Further evidence of the way the environment may affect intelligence comes from brain scans of children who are seriously neglected **(Figure 8.17)**.

realworldpsychology   **Multiple Sad Effects of Neglect and Abuse** In addition to permanent brain changes, children who lack reliable care and stable attachment or who experience deliberate abuse in the first few years of life show not only lower intelligence but also less empathy for others and a greater vulnerability to later substance abuse and addiction (Luby et al., 2012). In contrast, children who are enrolled in high-quality preschool programs and are regularly read to by their parents show increases in IQ. These studies provide further evidence that the environment, for better or worse, has a major impact (Protzko et al., 2013).

Twin Design/Shutterstock

Between Versus Within Group Differences

One of the most controversial issues in psychology is historic group differences in average IQ scores between black and white people in the United States. As we've just seen, intelligence in general does show a high degree of heritability. However, it's VERY important to recognize that heritability cannot explain *between*-group differences! Note the overall difference between the average height of plants on the left and

FIGURE 8.18 GENETICS VERSUS ENVIRONMENT

Note that even when you begin with the same package of seeds (genetic inheritance), the average height of corn plants in the fertile soil will be greater than the average height of corn plants in the poor soil (environmental influences). Therefore, no valid or logical conclusions can be drawn about the overall genetic differences between the two groups of plants because the two environments (soil) are so different. Similar logic must be applied to intelligence scores between ethnic groups.

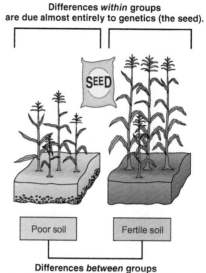

Differences *within* groups are due almost entirely to genetics (the seed).

SEED

Poor soil   Fertile soil

Differences *between* groups are due almost *entirely* to environment (the soil).

those on the right in **Figure 8.18**. Just as we cannot say that the difference *between* these two groups of plants is due to heredity, we similarly cannot say that differences in IQ *between* any two ethnic groups are due to heredity.

Note also the considerable variation in height *within* the group of plants on the left and those *within* the group on the right. Just as some plants are taller than others, there are blacks who score high on IQ tests and whites who score low, while the reverse is equally true. Always remember that the greatest differences in IQ scores occur when we compare individuals *within* groups—not *between* groups.

Why are we calling such attention to this *between*- and *within*-group distinction? In 1969, Arthur Jensen sparked a heated debate when he argued that genetic factors are "strongly implicated" as the cause of ethnic differences in intelligence. A book by Richard J. Herrnstein and Charles Murray titled *The Bell Curve: Intelligence and Class Structure in American Life* reignited this debate in 1994, when the authors claimed that African Americans score below average in IQ because of their "genetic heritage."

Although there is no clear resolution to this ongoing debate, some of the strongest proponents of the "heritability of intelligence" argument seem to ignore the "fertile soil" background of the groups who score highest on IQ tests. As an open-minded, critical thinker, carefully consider these important research findings:

- Environmental and cultural factors may override genetic potential and later affect IQ test scores. Like plants that come from similar seeds, but are placed in poor versus enriched soil, minority children are more likely to grow up in lower socioeconomic conditions, which may hamper their true intellectual potential. Also, in some ethnic groups and economic classes, a child who excels in school may be ridiculed for trying to be different from his or her classmates. Moreover, if children's own language and dialect do not match their education system or the IQ tests they take, they are obviously at a disadvantage (Cathers-Schiffman & Thompson, 2007; García & Náñez, 2011; Johnson et al., 2010; Sidhu et al., 2010; Sternberg & Grigorenko, 2008). Furthermore, environmental stress can also lead to short-term decreases in test scores (see *Psych Science*).

- Traditional IQ tests may be culturally biased. If standardized IQ tests contain items that reflect white, middle-class culture, they will discriminate against minority-group members whose language, knowledge and values differ from those of the white majority (Abedi, 2013; Suzuki et al., 2013). Researchers have attempted to create a *culture-fair* or *culture-free* IQ test, but they have found it

PSYCHSCIENCE

THE IMPACT OF EXPOSURE TO HOMICIDE ON INTELLIGENCE

Researchers in one study were interested in examining whether exposure to violence, and in particular to homicides, in their local community could have an impact on children's test scores (Sharkey, 2010). To test this question, researchers reviewed scores on both vocabulary and reading tests for African American children (ages 5 to 17) in a local public school. They then compared the test scores of children who were tested in the week after a homicide in their neighborhood to those of other children in the same neighborhood who were tested at different times. Sadly, their findings reveal that exposure to a nearby homicide in the week before the testing led to lower scores on both vocabulary and reading scores than scores achieved by peers in the same neighborhood who were tested at different times. Can you understand how and why children who are exposed to violence in their environment may therefore suffer short-term decreases in their cognitive abilities? How might this exposure to violence also affect their social and emotional well being?

RESEARCH CHALLENGE

1 Based on the information provided, did this study (Sharkey, 2010) use descriptive, correlational, and/or experimental research?

2 If you chose:

- descriptive research, is this a naturalistic observation, survey/interview, case study, or archival research?
- correlational research, is this a positive, negative, or zero correlation?
- experimental research, label the IV, DV, experimental group(s), and control group.

>> CHECK YOUR ANSWERS IN APPENDIX B.
NOTE: The information provided in this study is admittedly limited, but the level of detail is similar to what is presented in most textbooks and public reports of research findings. Answering these questions, and then comparing your answers to those in the Appendix, will help you become a better critical thinker and consumer of scientific research.

virtually impossible to do. Past experiences, motivation, test-taking abilities, and previous experiences with tests are powerful influences on IQ scores.

- Intelligence (as measured by IQ tests) is not a fixed trait. Around the world, IQ scores have increased over the past half century. This well-established phenomenon, known as the *Flynn effect*, may be due to improved nutrition, better public education, more proficient test-taking skills, and rising levels of education for a greater percentage of the world's population (Flynn, 1987, 2007, 2010; Huang & Hauser, 1998; Pietschnig et al., 2011; Watkins & Smith, 2013).

- Selectively highlighting IQ scores from one group (African American) is deceptive because race and ethnicity, like intelligence itself, are almost impossible to define. Depending on the definition we use, there are between 3 and 300 races, and no race is pure in a biological sense (Fujimura et al., 2010; Kite, 2013; Sternberg & Grigorenko, 2008). Furthermore, like President Barack Obama, Tiger Woods, and Mariah Carey, many people today self-identify as multiracial.

- Negative stereotypes about minority groups can cause some group members to doubt their abilities. This phenomenon, called **stereotype threat** may, in turn, reduce their intelligence test scores (Owens & Massey, 2011; Ryan & Sackett, 2013; Tomasetto & Appoloni, 2013).

Stereotype threat Awareness of a negative stereotype that affects oneself and may lead to impairment in performance.

In the first study of stereotype threat, Claude Steele and Joshua Aronson (1995) recruited Black and White University students (with similar ability levels) to complete a difficult verbal exam. In the group of students who were told that the exam was diagnostic of their intellectual abilities, Blacks underperformed in relation to Whites. However, in the non-diagnostic group taking the same exam, there were no differences between the two group scores.

This and other research suggests that stereotype threat occurs because members of stereotyped groups are anxious that they will fulfill their group's negative stereotype. This anxiety in turn hinders their performance on tests. Some people cope with stereotype threat by *disidentifying*, telling themselves they don't care about the

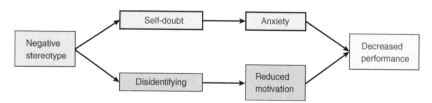

FIGURE 8.19 HOW STEREOTYPE THREAT LEADS TO DECREASED PERFORMANCE

test scores (Major et al., 1998). Unfortunately, this attitude reduces motivation and also leads to decreased performance **(Figure 8.19)**.

Stereotype threat affects many social groups, including African Americans, women, Native Americans, Latinos, low-income people, elderly people, and white male athletes (Joanisse et al., 2013; Keller & Bless, 2008; Owens & Massey, 2011). This research helps explain some group differences in intelligence and achievement tests. As such, it underscores why relying solely on such tests to make critical decisions affecting individual lives—for example, in hiring, college admissions, or clinical application—is unwarranted and possibly even unethical.

What's the good news? First, some early research suggested that having Barack Obama as a positive role model improved academic performance by African Americans—thus offsetting the stereotype threat (Marx et al., 2009) **(Figure 8.20)**. Second, people who have the opportunity to self-affirm, or validate, their identities in some type of meaningful way do not show the negative effects of stereotype threat. For example, African American first-year college students who receive information about how to feel more connected to their college or university show higher

FIGURE 8.20 "OBAMA EFFECT" VERSUS STEREOTYPE THREAT | realworldpsychology

Preliminary research found a so-called "Obama effect," which promised to offset problems related to the stereotype threat (Dillon, 2009). However, later studies found either no relationship between test performance and positive thoughts about Obama or mixed results (Aronson et al., 2009; Smith, 2012).

Reuters/Larry Downing/Landov

GPAs as well as better health three years later (Walten & Cohen, 2011). Similarly, African American adults with hypertension, or high blood pressure, who self-affirm by focusing on positive moments in their lives show higher levels of adherence to their blood pressure medication (Ogedegbe et al., 2011).

So what's the most important take-away message? In this chapter, we've explored three cognitive processes (*thinking, language,* and *intelligence*), each of which is greatly affected by numerous interacting factors. To solve problems, be creative, communicate with others, and adapt to our environment requires various mental abilities, most of which are not genetic and can be easily learned (see *Psychology and You*).

psychology and you   **Optimizing Your Well-Being** In Chapter 1, we introduced you to the field of *positive psychology*—the scientific study of optimal human functioning. One of the key researchers in this area, Martin Seligman, believes optimal well-being results from five core factors: *Positive emotion, Engagement, Relationships, Meaning,* and *Accomplishment* (PERMA). To learn more about positive psychology and these five factors, while also gaining invaluable personal insights, visit Dr. Seligman's home page. While there, be sure to complete one or more of the free, scientifically validated surveys: www.authentichappiness.sas .upenn.edu.

© Yuri/iStockphoto

RETRIEVAL PRACTICE: INTELLIGENCE

Self-Test

Completing this self-test and comparing your answers with those in Appendix B provides immediate feedback and helpful practice for exams. Additional interactive, self-tests are available at www.wiley.com/college/huffman.

1. The definition of intelligence in this book stresses the global capacity to _____.

  a. successfully perform within relationships, in school, and on the job
  b. read, write, and do computations at home and at work
  c. perform verbally and physically within the environment
  d. think rationally, act purposefully, profit from experience, and deal effectively with the environment

2. Which is the most widely used intelligence test?

  a. Wechsler Intelligence Scale for Children
  b. Wechsler Adult Intelligence Scale
  c. Stanford-Binet Intelligence Scale
  d. Binet-Terman Intelligence Scale

3. The development of uniform procedures for administering and scoring a test is called _____.

  a. norming
  b. procedural protocol
  c. standardization
  d. normalization

4. _____ suggested that people differ in their "profiles of intelligence" and that each person shows a unique pattern of strengths and weaknesses.

  a. Spearman
  b. Binet
  c. Wechsler
  d. Gardner

Think Critically

1 How would someone with exceptionally low or high emotional intelligence behave?

2 Do you believe IQ test are culturally biased? Why or why not?

realworldpsychology

Do bigger brains indicate greater intelligence?

Does caregiving in the first years of life have a lasting impact on brain size and development?

HINT: LOOK IN THE MARGIN FOR Q4 AND Q5

Summary

1 THINKING 208

- Thinking is a central aspect of **cognition**. Thought processes are distributed throughout the brain in neural networks. **Mental images** and **concepts** aid our thought processes. There are three major building blocks for concepts—**prototypes, artificial concepts**, and hierarchies.
- **Problem solving** usually has three steps: *preparation, production*, and *evaluation*. **Algorithms** and **heuristics** help us produce solutions.
- Barriers to problem solving include **mental sets, functional fixedness, confirmation bias, availability heuristic**, and the **representativeness heuristic.**
- **Creativity** is the ability to produce valued outcomes in a novel way. Tests of creativity usually focus on **divergent thinking**.

2 LANGUAGE 215

- **Language** supports thinking and enables us to communicate. To produce language, we use **phonemes, morphemes**, and **grammar** (syntax and semantics). Several different parts of our brain are involved in producing and listening to language.
- According to Whorf's **linguistic relativity hypothesis**, language determines thought. Generally, Whorf's hypothesis is not supported. However, language does strongly influence thought.
- Children communicate nonverbally from birth. Their verbal communication proceeds in stages: *prelinguistic*, which includes crying, **cooing**, and **babbling**, and *linguistic*, which includes single utterances, **telegraphic speech**, and acquisition of rules of grammar.
- According to Chomsky, humans are "prewired" with a **language acquisition device (LAD)** that enables language development. Nurturists hold that children learn language through rewards, punishments, and imitation. Most psychologists hold an intermediate view.
- Research with chimpanzees, gorillas, and dolphins suggests that these animals can learn and use basic rules of language.

However, critics suggest nonhuman animal language is less complex, less creative, and not as rule-laden as human language.

3 INTELLIGENCE 221

- There is considerable debate over the meaning of **intelligence**. Here it is defined as the global capacity to think rationally, act purposefully, and deal effectively with the environment.
- Spearman proposed that intelligence is a single factor, which he termed **general intelligence (g)**. Thurstone and Guilford argued that intelligence included numerous distinct abilities. Cattell proposed two subtypes of *g*: **fluid intelligence (gf)** and **crystallized intelligence (gc)**. Many contemporary cognitive theorists, including Gardner and Sternberg, believe that intelligence is a collection of many separate specific abilities. Goleman believes that **emotional intelligence (EI)**, the ability to empathize and manage our emotions and relationships, is just as important as any other kind of intelligence.
- Early intelligence tests computed a person's mental age to arrive at an **intelligence quotient (IQ)**. Today, two of the most widely used intelligence tests are the *Stanford-Binet Intelligence Scale* and the *Wechsler Adult Intelligence Scale (WAIS)*. Intelligence tests commonly compare the performance of an individual with other individuals of the same age. To be scientifically acceptable, all psychological tests must fulfill three basic requirements: **standardization, reliability**, and **validity**.
- Intelligence tests provide one of the major criteria for assessing **intellectual disability** and **mental giftedness**, both of which exist on a continuum. Studies of people who are intellectually gifted found that they had more intellectual opportunities and tended to excel professionally. However, a high IQ does not guarantee success in every endeavor.
- Most recent research on the biology of intelligence has focused on brain functioning, not size. Research indicates that intelligent people's brains respond especially quickly and efficiently.
- In answer to the question of how race affects IQ, heredity and intelligence are interacting, inseparable factors.

◉ applyingrealworldpsychology

We began this chapter with five intriguing Real World Psychology questions, and you were asked to revisit these questions at the end of each section. Questions like these have an important and lasting impact on all of our lives. See if you can answer these additional critical thinking questions related to real world examples.

T K Wanstal/The Image Works

1 Jerry Levy and Mark Newman, the two men shown in this photo, are identical twins who were separated at birth and first met as adults at a firefighter's convention. Research shows that IQ tends to be highly correlated for identical twins, but do you believe identical twins share a special connectedness? Why or why not?

2 Does the brothers' choosing the same uncommon profession seem like a case of special "twin-telepathy"? If so, how might *confirmation bias* contribute to the perception of twin-telepathy?

3 What is the role of emotional intelligence (EI) in business? Should it be a factor in hiring and promotions? What might be the advantages and drawbacks if it did?

4 Should preschools and elementary schools be required to teach children multiple languages? Why or why not?

5 Which of the barriers to problem solving described in this chapter are the biggest problems for you? How will you work to overcome them?

Key Terms

RETRIEVAL PRACTICE   Write a definition for each term before turning back to the referenced page to check your answer.

- algorithm 210
- artificial concept 209
- availability heuristic 212
- babbling 218
- cognition 208
- concept 208
- confirmation bias 211
- cooing 218
- creativity 213
- crystallized intelligence (*gc*) 222
- divergent thinking 214
- emotional intelligence (EI) 222

- fluid intelligence (*gf*) 222
- functional fixedness 211
- general intelligence (*g*) 222
- grammar 215
- heuristic 210
- intelligence 221
- intelligence quotient (IQ) 225
- language 215
- language acquisition device (LAD) 219
- mental image 208
- mental set 211
- morpheme 215

- overextension 218
- overgeneralization 218
- phoneme 215
- prototype 209
- reliability 226
- representativeness heuristic 212
- savant syndrome 226
- standardization 225
- stereotype threat 231
- telegraphic speech 218
- validity 226

Solutions

Nine-dot problem solution (page 211)

People find this puzzle difficult because they see the arrangement of dots as a square—a mental set that limits possible solutions.

Candle problem solution (page 211)

Use the tacks to mount the matchbox tray to the wall. Light the candle and use some melted wax to mount the candle to the matchbox.

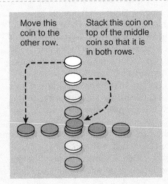

Move this coin to the other row.

Stack this coin on top of the middle coin so that it is in both rows.

Coin problem solution (page 214)

Wechsler Adult Intelligence Scale solution (page 225)

Ⓑ "Which one of these works to balance the scale?"

From the middle image, we deduce an empty scale would be out of balance, since we need two stars added to the right just to be in balance.

From the first image, since we know that the scale is two stars heavy on the left, if adding one star to the already heavier left side balances with one ball, a ball must equal three stars!

The final image shows three stars and one ball on the left. To balance on the right, we match what is shown on the left AND ADD two stars since we know the scale, by itself, is two stars heavy on the left.

Therefore we need one ball and five stars to balance. But that is NOT one of the answers! But we know one ball equals three stars. Looking at the possible answers, we see that two stars and two balls (1+1+3+3=8 stars) is the same as one ball and five stars (3+1+1+1+1=8 stars)—and that is the answer!

Ⓐ "Which three pieces go together to make this puzzle?"

Rotate 180 degrees ...

Rotate 90 degrees to the right ...

Rotate 180 degrees ...

chapternine

Life Span Development

realworldpsychology

THINGS YOU'LL LEARN IN CHAPTER 9

Q1 Are our childhood friends' predictions of our adult personality better than our own self-ratings?

Q2 Does prenatal exposure to smoke increase the risk of obesity later in life?

Q3 Why do teenagers seem to sleep so much?

Q4 Do babies learn faster when they're sitting up than when they're lying down?

Q5 Do today's college students want women to propose marriage?

THROUGHOUT THE CHAPTER, MARGIN ICONS FOR Q1–Q5 INDICATE WHERE THE TEXT ADDRESSES THESE QUESTIONS.

pillows: © karammiri/iStockphoto; baby: © jfairone/iStockphoto; cigarette: © milosluz/iStockphoto; smoke: © Nocturnus/iStockphoto; three students: londoneye/Getty Images; woman proposing: © Pojoslaw/Shutterstock

chapteroverview

Are you one of the lucky ones who grew up with loving parents who documented every stage of your development with photos, videos, and/or journals—starting with your birth, first smile, first day of school, and all the way to your high school graduation? If so, you have a head start on the material in this chapter. As you might expect, studying development across the entire life span is a monumental task, so we've organized this chapter into three major sections—*physical, cognitive,* and *social-emotional development.* Before we begin, we need to briefly examine the research issues and methods psychologists use to study development.

STUDYING DEVELOPMENT

LEARNING OBJECTIVES

RETRIEVAL PRACTICE While reading the upcoming sections, respond to each Learning Objective in your own words. Then compare your responses with those found at www.wiley.com/college/huffman.

1 **SUMMARIZE** the three most important debates or questions in developmental psychology.

2 **CONTRAST** the cross-sectional research design with the longitudinal research design.

Developmental psychology The study of age-related changes in behavior, mental processes, and stages of growth, from conception to death.

Maturation The continuing influence of heredity throughout development; age-related physical and behavioral changes characteristic of a species.

Critical period A time of special sensitivity to specific types of learning, which shapes the capacity for future development.

Imprinting An inherited, primitive form of rapid learning (within a critical period) in which some infant animals physically follow and form an attachment to the first moving object they see and/or hear.

Just as some parents carefully document their child's progress throughout his or her life span, the field of **developmental psychology** studies growth and change throughout the eight major stages of life—from conception to death, or "womb to tomb" **(Table 9.1)**. Their studies have led to three key theoretical issues.

Theoretical Issues

Almost every area of research in human development frames questions around three major issues:

1. **Nature or nurture?** How do both genetics (nature) and life experiences (nurture) influence development? According to the *nature position,* development is largely governed by automatic, genetically predetermined signals in a process known as **maturation**. Just as a flower unfolds in accord with its genetic blueprint, humans crawl before we walk and walk before we run.

   In addition, naturists believe there are **critical periods**, or windows of opportunity, that occur early in life when exposure to certain stimuli or experiences is necessary for proper development. For example, many newborn animals form rigid attachments to particular stimuli shortly after birth, a process called **imprinting (Figure 9.1)**.

TABLE 9.1	LIFE SPAN DEVELOPMENT

Stage	Approximate Age
Prenatal	Conception to birth
Infancy	Birth to 18 months
Early childhood	18 months to 6 years
Middle childhood	6 to 12 years
Adolescence	12 to 20 years
Young adulthood	20 to 45 years
Middle adulthood	45 to 60 years
Later adulthood	60 years to death

THE FOUR AGES OF MAN

INFANCY   CHILDHOOD   YOUTH   MATURITY

© The New Yorker Collection 1991 Michael Crawford from cartoon bank.com. All Rights Reserved.

Human children also may have critical periods for normal development. Research has shown that appropriate social interaction in the first few weeks of life is essential for creating normal cognitive and social development (Ekas et al., 2013; Feldman, 2014). Sadly, a study of both Israeli and Palestinian children also found that exposure to serious military/political violence at age 8 is associated with more aggressive behavior later on, whereas witnessing such violence at later ages doesn't lead to such aggression (Boxer et al., 2013). These and other similar studies provide further evidence for critical periods—at least in the early years (see *Psych Science*).

2. **Stages or continuity?** Some developmental psychologists suggest that development generally occurs in *stages* that are discrete and qualitatively different from one to another, whereas others believe it follows a *continuous pattern*, with gradual but steady and quantitative (measurable) changes **(Figure 9.2)**.

Nina Leen/Time Life Pictures/Getty Images

FIGURE 9.1 **CRITICAL PERIODS AND IMPRINTING**
Konrad Lorenz's (1937) early studies of *imprinting* found that baby geese will attach to (or imprint on) the first suitable moving stimulus they see within a certain *critical period*—normally the first 36 hours of their lives. While baby geese normally imprint on their mother, Lorenz discovered that if he was the first moving creature the geese observed, they would imprint and follow him everywhere.

PSYCHSCIENCE

DEPRIVATION AND DEVELOPMENT

What happens if a child is deprived of appropriate stimulation during a critical period of development? Consider the story of Genie, the so-called "wild child." From the time she was 20 months old until authorities rescued her at age 13, Genie was locked alone in a tiny, windowless room. By day, she sat naked and tied to a child's toilet with nothing to do and no one to talk to. At night, she was immobilized in a kind of straitjacket and "caged" in a covered crib. Genie's abusive father forbade anyone to speak to her for those 13 years. If Genie made noise, her father beat her while he barked and growled like a dog.

AP/Wide World Photos

Genie's tale is a heartbreaking account of the lasting scars from a disastrous childhood. In the years after her rescue, Genie spent thousands of hours receiving special training, and by age 19 she could use public transportation and was adapting well to special classes at school. Genie was far from normal, however. Her intelligence scores were still close to the cutoff for intellectual disability. And although linguists and psychologists worked with her for many years, she was never able to master grammatical structure, and was limited to sentences like "Genie go." This suggests that because of her extreme childhood isolation and abuse, Genie, like other seriously neglected or environmentally isolated children, missed a necessary critical period for language development

(Baird, 2010; Curtiss, 1977; LaPointe, 2005; Raaska et al., 2013; Rymer, 1993; Saxton, 2010; Sylvestre & Mérette, 2010). To make matters worse, she was also subjected to a series of foster home placements, some of which were emotionally and physically abusive. According to the latest information, Genie now lives in a privately run facility for mentally underdeveloped adults (James, 2008).

RESEARCH CHALLENGE

1 Based on the information provided, did this study (Rymer, 1993) use descriptive, correlational, and/or experimental research?

2 If you chose:
- descriptive research, is this a naturalistic observation, survey/interview, case study, or archival research?
- correlational research, is this a positive, negative, or zero correlation?
- experimental research, label the IV, DV, experimental group(s), and control group.

>> CHECK YOUR ANSWERS IN APPENDIX B.
NOTE: The information provided in this study is admittedly limited, but the level of detail is similar to what is presented in most textbooks and public reports of research findings. Answering these questions, and then comparing your answers to those in the Appendix, will help you become a better critical thinker and consumer of scientific research.

FIGURE 9.2 **STAGES VERSUS CONTINUITY IN DEVELOPMENT**

There is an ongoing debate about whether development is better characterized by discrete stages or by gradual, continuous development.

Ⓐ Stage theorists think development results from discrete, qualitative changes.

Ⓑ Continuity theorists believe development results from gradual, quantitative (incremental) changes.

3. Stability or change? Which of our traits are stable and present throughout our life span, and what aspects will change? Psychologists who emphasize *stability* hold that measurements of personality taken during childhood are important predictors of adult personality; those who emphasize *change* disagree.

Research Approaches

To answer these three controversies and other questions, developmental psychologists typically use all the research methods discussed in Chapter 1. To study the entire human life span, they also need two additional techniques—*cross sectional* and *longitudinal* (**Figure 9.3**).

The **cross-sectional design** examines people of various ages (such as 20, 40, 60, and 80) all at the same time to see how each age differs at that one specific time of measurement. For example, one cross-sectional study examined women in

Cross-sectional design A research technique that measures individuals of various ages at one point in time and provides information about age differences.

FIGURE 9.3 **CROSS-SECTIONAL VERSUS LONGITUDINAL RESEARCH**

To study development, psychologists may use either a cross-sectional or longitudinal design for their research.

CROSS-SECTIONAL RESEARCH

			Advantages	Disadvantages
Different participants of various ages are compared at one point in time to determine age-related *differences*	**Group One** 20-year-old participants	Research done in 2013	• Provides information about age differences • Quick and less expensive • Typically larger sample	• Cohort effects difficult to separate • Restricted generalizability (measures behaviors and mental processes at only one point in time)
	Group Two 40-year-old participants			
	Group Three 60-year-old participants			

LONGITUDINAL RESEARCH

The **same** participants are studied at various ages to determine age-related *changes*	**Study One** Participants are 20 years old	Research done in 2013	• Provides information about age changes • Increased confidence in results • More in-depth information per participant	• More expensive and time consuming • Restricted generalizability (typically smaller sample due to participant dropouts over time)
	Study Two Same participants are now 40 years old	Research done in 2033		
	Study Three Same participants are now 60 years old	Research done in 2053		

three different age groups (ages 22–34, 35–49, and 50–65) to examine whether body weight dissatisfaction changes with age (Siegel, 2010). Unfortunately, female body dissatisfaction appears to be quite stable—and relatively high—across the life span.

In contrast, a **longitudinal design** takes repeated measures of one person or a group of same-aged people over a long period of time to see how the individual or the group changes over time. For example, a group of developmental researchers wondered if peer ratings of personality taken during childhood might be better predictors of later adult personality than self-ratings (Martin-Storey et al., 2012)? They first asked grade school children in 1976-1978 to rate themselves and their peers on several personality factors, such as likeability, aggression, and social withdrawal. In 1999-2003, the researchers returned and asked the same participants, now in mid-adulthood, to complete a second series of personality tests. As hypothesized, the peer ratings were better than self-ratings in predicting adult personality. Does this finding surprise you? If so, try contacting some of your childhood peers and then compare notes on how you remember one another's personality as children and now as adults.

Now that you have a better idea of these two types of research, if you were a developmental psychologist interested in studying intelligence in adults, which design would you choose—cross-sectional or longitudinal? Before you decide, note the different research results shown in **Figure 9.4**.

Why do the two methods show such different results? Cross-sectional studies sometimes confuse genuine age differences with *cohort effects*—differences that result from specific histories of the age group studied. As shown in the top line in Figure 9.4, the 81-year-olds measured by the cross-sectional design have dramatically lower scores than the 25-year-olds. But is this due to aging, or perhaps to broad environmental differences, such as less formal education or poor nutrition? Because the different age groups, called *cohorts*, grew up in different historical periods, the results may not apply to people growing up at other times. With the cross-sectional design, age effects and cohort effects are sometimes inextricably tangled.

Longitudinal studies also have limits. They are expensive in terms of time and money, and it is difficult for us to generalize their results. Because participants often drop out or move away during the extended test period, the experimenter may end up with a self-selected sample that differs from the general population in important ways. Each method of research has strengths and weaknesses (as you recall from the right-hand side of Figure 9.3). Keep these differences in mind when you read the findings of developmental research.

Before we go on, it's important to point out that modern researchers sometimes combine both cross-sectional and longitudinal designs into one study. For example, in Chapter 1, we discussed a study that examined whether well-being decreases with age (Sutin et al., 2013). When these researchers examined their combined cross-sectional and longitudinal data from two independent samples taken over 30 years, they initially found that well-being *declined* with age. However, when they then controlled for the fact that older cohorts started out with lower levels of well-being, they found that all the cohorts *increased* rather than decreased in well-being with age. The reversal in findings was explained by the fact that the older group of people had experienced instances of major turmoil in their younger years, including the Great Depression. This means that this group started out with lower levels of well-being than those who grew up during more prosperous times.

Can you see why this combination of two research designs is important? It offers a more accurate and positive view of well-being in old age than what was indicated in either the cross-sectional design or the longitudinal design. It also suggests some troubling possibilities for today's young adults who are entering a stagnant workforce and high unemployment. As the study's authors say, this "economic turmoil may impede [their] psychological, as well as financial, growth even decades after times get better" (Sutin et al., 2013, p. 384).

Longitudinal design A research design that measures a single individual or group of individuals over an extended period and gives information about age changes.

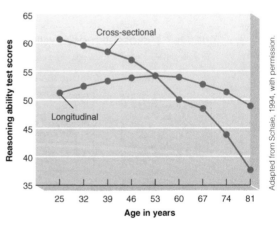

FIGURE 9.4 **WHICH RESULTS ARE "TRUE"?**

Cross-sectional studies have shown that reasoning and intelligence reach their peak in early adulthood and then gradually decline. In contrast, longitudinal studies have found that a marked decline does not begin until about age 60.

RETRIEVAL PRACTICE: STUDYING DEVELOPMENT

Self-Test

Completing this self-test and comparing your answers with those in Appendix B provides immediate feedback and helpful practice for exams. Additional interactive, self-tests are available at www.wiley.com/college/huffman.

1. _____ studies age-related changes in behavior and mental processes from conception to death.

   a. Thanatology   b. Teratogenology
   c. Human development   d. Developmental psychology

2. _____ is governed by automatic, genetically predetermined signals.

   a. The cohort effect   b. Secondary aging
   c. Thanatology   d. Maturation

3. What three major questions are studied in developmental psychology?

   a. nature versus nurture,   b. nature versus nurture,
      stages versus continuity,   "chunking" versus continuity,
      and stability versus change   and instability versus change
   c. nature versus nurture,   d. none of these
      stages versus continuity, and
      stagnation versus instability

4. _____ studies are the most time-efficient method, whereas _____ studies provide the most in-depth information per participant.

   a. Latitudinal; longitudinal   b. Neo-gerontology; longitudinal
   c. Cross-sectional; longitudinal d. Class-racial; longitudinal

Think Critically

1️⃣ Which of the three important debates or questions in developmental psychology do you find most valuable? Why?

2️⃣ Based on what you have learned about critical periods, can you think of a circumstance in your own development, or that of your friends, when a critical period might have been disrupted or lost?

realworldpsychology

Are our childhood friends' predictions of our adult personality better than our own self-ratings?

HINT: LOOK IN THE MARGIN FOR (Q1)

PHYSICAL DEVELOPMENT

LEARNING OBJECTIVES

RETRIEVAL PRACTICE While reading the upcoming sections, respond to each Learning Objective in your own words. Then compare your responses with those found at www.wiley.com/college/huffman.

1️⃣ **IDENTIFY** the three phases of prenatal physical development.
2️⃣ **SUMMARIZE** physical development during early childhood.
3️⃣ **DESCRIBE** the physical changes that occur during adolescence and adulthood.

After studying the photos of your two authors as they've aged over the life span **(Figure 9.5)** (or after reviewing your own similar photos), you may be amused and surprised by all the dramatic changes in physical appearance. But have you stopped to appreciate the incredible underlying process that transforms all of us from birth to death? In this section, we will explore the fascinating processes of physical development from conception through childhood, adolescence, and adulthood.

Prenatal Development

Your prenatal development began at conception, when your mother's egg, or ovum, united with your father's sperm cell **(Figure 9.6)**. At that time, you were

Photos courtesy of Catherine Sanderson

Photos courtesy of Karen Huffman

FIGURE 9.5 CHANGES IN PHYSICAL DEVELOPMENT OVER THE LIFE SPAN

As this series of photos of your two textbook authors show, physical changes occur throughout our lives. Our cognitive, social, and emotional processes, as well as our personalities also are continually changing, but the changes aren't as visible. (The top row is Catherine Sanderson at ages 1, 5, 10, 30, and the bottom row is Karen Huffman at ages 1, 4, 10, 30 and 60.)

FIGURE 9.6 CONCEPTION

Millions of sperm are released when a man ejaculates into a woman's vagina.

Francis Leroy, Biocosmos/Photo Researchers

David M. Phillips/Photo Researchers

Ⓐ Only a few hundred sperm survive the arduous trip up to the egg.

Ⓑ Although a joint effort is required to break through the outer coating, only one sperm will actually fertilize the egg.

Germinal period The first stage of prenatal development, beginning with ovulation and followed by conception and implantation in the uterus; the first two weeks of pregnancy.

Embryonic period The second stage of pre-natal development, which begins after uterine implantation and lasts through the eighth week.

Fetal period The third, and final, stage of pre-natal development (eight weeks to birth); char-acterized by rapid weight gain in the fetus and the fine detailing of bodily organs and systems.

a single cell barely 1/175 of an inch in diameter—smaller than the period at the end of this sentence. This new cell, called a *zygote*, then began a process of rapid cell division that resulted in a multimillion-celled infant (you) some nine months later.

The vast changes that occur during the nine months of a full-term pregnancy are usually divided into three stages: the **germinal period**, the **embryonic period**, and the **fetal period** (**Figure 9.7**).

During pregnancy, the *placenta* connects the fetus to the mother's uterus and serves as the link for delivery of food and excretion of wastes. It also screens out some, but not all, harmful substances. Environmental hazards such as X-rays and toxic waste, drugs, and diseases can still cross the placental barrier (**Table 9.2**).

FIGURE 9.7 PRENATAL DEVELOPMENT

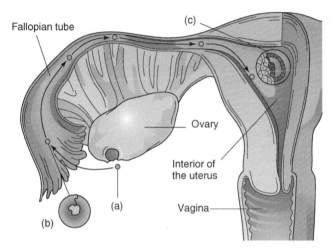

Fallopian tube
(c)
Ovary
Interior of the uterus
Vagina
(a)
(b)

1 **Germinal period: From conception to implantation**
After discharge from either the left or right ovary (a), the ovum travels to the opening of the fallopian tube.

If fertilization occurs (b), it normally takes place in the first third of the fallopian tube. The fertilized ovum is referred to as a zygote.

When the zygote reaches the uterus, it implants itself in the wall of the uterus (c) and begins to grow tendril-like structures that intertwine with the rich supply of blood vessels located there. After implantation, the organism is known as an embryo.

3 **Fetal period: From the end of the second month to birth**
At four months, all the actual body parts and organs are established. The fetal stage is primarily a time for increased growth and "fine detailing."

Petit Format/Nestle/Photo Researchers

2 **Embryonic period: From implantation to eight weeks**
At eight weeks, the major organ systems have become well differ-entiated. Note that at this stage, the head grows at a faster rate than other parts of the body.

Biophoto Associates/Photo Researchers

TABLE 9.2	SAMPLE PRENATAL ENVIRONMENTAL CONDITIONS THAT ENDANGER A CHILD
Maternal Factors	**Possible Effects on Embryo, Fetus, Newborn, or Young Child**
Malnutrition	Low birth weight, malformations, less developed brain, greater vulnerability to disease
Stress exposure	Low birth weight, hyperactivity, irritability, feeding difficulties
Exposure to X-rays	Malformations, cancer
Legal and illegal drugs: Alcohol, nicotine, cocaine, methamphetamine	Inhibition of bone growth, hearing loss, low birth weight, fetal alcohol syndrome (FAS), intellectual disability, attention deficits in childhood, death
Diseases: German measles (rubella), herpes, HIV/AIDS, toxoplasmosis	Blindness, deafness, intellectual disability, heart and other malformations, brain infection, spontaneous abortion, premature birth, low birth weight, death

Sources: Abadinsky, 2014; Levinthal, 2011; Maisto et al., 2014; Whitbourne, 2011.

These influences generally have the most devastating effects during the first three months of pregnancy, making this a *critical period* in development.

What about the father's role? Environmentally, a father's smoking may pollute the air the mother breathes, and genetically, he may transmit heritable diseases. In addition, research suggests that alcohol, opiates, cocaine, various gases, lead, pesticides, and industrial chemicals can damage his sperm (Baker & Nieuwenhuijsen, 2008; Ji et al., 2013; Levy et al., 2011; Miranda-Contreras et al., 2013).

Perhaps the most important—and generally avoidable—danger to a fetus comes from drugs, both legal and illegal. Nicotine and alcohol are major **teratogens**, environmental agents that cause damage during prenatal development. Mothers who smoke tobacco or drink alcohol during pregnancy have significantly higher rates of premature births, low-birth-weight infants, and fetal deaths. Their children also show increased behavior and cognitive problems **(Figure 9.8)** (Brady et al., 2013; Espy et al., 2011; Larkby et al., 2011; Pruett et al., 2013). Research also has shown that children whose mothers smoked during pregnancy are more likely to be obese as adolescents, perhaps because in-utero exposure to nicotine changes a part of the brain that increases a preference for fatty foods (Haghighi et al., 2013).

Teratogen An environmental agent that causes damage during prenatal development; comes from the Greek word *teras*, meaning "malformation."

Andy Levin/Science Source

FIGURE 9.8 FETAL ALCOHOL SYNDROME

Prenatal exposure to alcohol can result in a neurotoxic syndrome called **fetal alcohol syndrome (FAS)**, including facial abnormalities and stunted growth. But the most disabling features of FAS are brain damage and neurobehavioral problems, ranging from hyperactivity and learning disabilities to intellectual disability, depression, and psychoses (National Organization on Fetal Alcohol Syndrome, 2012; Pruett et al., 2013; Shaffer & Kipp, 2013; Sowell et al., 2008; Warren & Murray, 2013).

Fetal alcohol syndrome (FAS) A combination of birth defects, including organ deformities and mental, motor, and/or growth retardation, that result from maternal alcohol abuse.

Early Childhood Development

Like the prenatal period, early childhood is also a time of rapid physical development. Let's explore three key areas of change in early childhood: *brain, motor,* and *sensory/perceptual development.*

Brain Development

Our brain and other parts of the nervous system grow faster than any other part of the body during both prenatal development and the first two years of life, as illustrated in **Figure 9.9**. This brain development and learning occur primarily because neurons grow in size and because the number of axons and dendrites, as well as the extent of their connections, increases (DiPietro, 2000; Gilles & Nelson, 2012).

Motor Development

Compared to the hidden, internal changes in brain development, the orderly emergence of active movement skills, known as *motor development,* is easily observed and measured. A newborn's first motor abilities are limited to *reflexes,* or involuntary responses to stimulation. For example, the rooting reflex occurs when something touches a baby's cheek: The infant will automatically turn its head, open its mouth, and root for a nipple.

In addition to simple reflexes, the infant soon begins to show voluntary control over the movement of various body parts **(Figure 9.10)**. Thus, a helpless newborn, who cannot even lift her head, is soon transformed into an active toddler capable of crawling, walking, and climbing. In fact, babies are highly motivated to begin walking because they can move faster than when crawling, and they get better with practice (Adolph et al., 2012). Keep in mind that motor development is largely due to natural maturation, but, like brain development, it can also be affected by environmental influences such as disease and neglect.

Sensory and Perceptual Development

At birth, and during the final trimester of pregnancy, the developing child's senses are quite advanced (Colombo et al., 2013; Shaffer & Kipp, 2013). For example, research shows that a newborn infant prefers his or her mother's voice, providing evidence that the developing fetus can hear sounds outside the mother's body (Von Hofsten, 2013). In addition, a newborn can smell most odors and distinguish between sweet, salty, and bitter tastes. Breast-fed newborns also recognize the odor of their mother's milk compared to other mother's milk, formula, and other substances (Allam et al., 2010; Aoyama et al., 2010; Nishitani et al., 2009). Similarly, the newborn's sense of touch and pain is highly developed, as evidenced by reactions to circumcision and to heel pricks for blood testing, and by the fact that their pain reactions are lessened by the smell of their own mother's milk (Nishitani et al., 2009; Rodkey & Riddell, 2013; Williamson, 1997).

The newborn's sense of vision, however, is poorly developed. At birth, an infant is estimated to have vision between 20/200 and 20/600 (Haith & Benson, 1998). Imagine what the infant's visual life is like: The level of detail you see at 200 or 600 feet (if you have 20/20 vision) is what an infant sees at 20 feet. Within the first few months, vision quickly improves, and by 6 months it is 20/100 or better. At 2 years, visual acuity is nearly at the adult level of 20/20 (Courage & Adams, 1990).

One of the most interesting findings in infant sensory and perceptual research concerns hearing. Not only can the newborn hear quite well at birth, but also, during the last few months in the womb, the fetus can hear sounds outside the mother's body. This raises the interesting possibility of fetal learning, and some have advocated special stimulation for the fetus as a way of increasing intelligence, creativity, and general alertness (Muenssinger et al, 2013, Partanen et al., 2013; Van de Carr & Lehrer, 1997).

FIGURE 9.9 BRAIN DEVELOPMENT

The brain undergoes dramatic changes from conception through the first few years of life. Keep in mind, however, that our brains continue to change and develop throughout our life span.

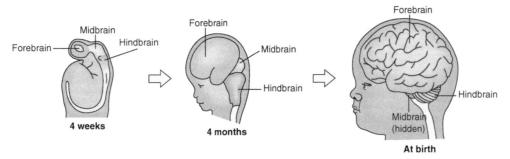

4 weeks **4 months** **At birth**

Ⓐ Prenatal brain development

Recall from Chapter 2 that the human brain is divided into three major sections—the hindbrain, midbrain, and forebrain. Note how at three weeks after conception these three brain sections are one long neural tube, which later becomes the brain and spinal cord.

At birth **3 months** **15 months** **6 years** **14 years**

Ⓑ Brain growth in the first two years

As infants learn and develop, synaptic connections between active neurons strengthen, and dendritic connections become more elaborate. Synaptic pruning (reduction of unused synapses) helps support this process. Myelination, the accumulation of fatty tissue coating the axons of nerve cells, continues until early adulthood.

Newborn **2 years** **5 years** **15 years** **Adult**

Ⓒ Brain and body changes over our life span

There are dramatic changes in our brain and body proportions as we grow older. At birth, our heads were one-fourth our total body's size, whereas in adulthood, our head is one-eighth.

Chin up — 2.2 mo.
Rolls over — 2.8 mo.
Sits with support — 2.9 mo.
Sits alone — 5.5 mo.
Stands holding furniture — 5.8 mo.
Walks holding on — 9.2 mo.
Stands alone — 11.5 mo.
Walks alone — 12.1 mo.
Walks up steps — 17.1 mo.

FIGURE 9.11 **READY FOR RESPONSIBILITY?** realworldpsychology

Adolescence is not a universal concept. Unlike the United States and other Western nations, some non-industrialized countries have no need for a slow transition from childhood to adulthood; children simply assume adult responsibilities as soon as possible.

The clearest and most dramatic physical sign of puberty is the *growth spurt*, which is characterized by rapid increases in height, weight, and skeletal growth **(Figure 9.12)** and by significant changes in reproductive structures and sexual characteristics. Maturation and hormone secretion cause rapid development of the ovaries, uterus, and vagina and the onset of menstruation (*menarche*) in the adolescent female. In the adolescent male, the testes, scrotum, and penis develop, and he experiences his first ejaculation (*spermarche*). The testes and ovaries in turn produce hormones that lead to the development of secondary sex characteristics, such as the growth of pubic hair, deepening of the voice and growth of facial hair in men, and growth of breasts in women **(Figure 9.13)**.

Have you ever wondered why teenagers seem to sleep so much? Researchers have found that puberty is triggered by changes in the brain, including the release of certain hormones, which occur only during periods of *deep sleep* (Shaw et al., 2012). This finding suggests that getting adequate, deep (slow-wave) sleep (see Chapter 5) during adolescence is an essential part of activating the reproductive system. Can you see why the increasing number of sleep problems in adolescents is a cause for concern, and why parents should actually be encouraging "oversleeping" in their teenagers?

Adulthood

Age-related physical changes that occur after the obvious pubertal changes are less dramatic. Other than some modest increases in height and muscular development during the late teens and early twenties, most individuals experience only minor physical changes until middle age.

For women, *menopause*, the cessation of the menstrual cycle, which occurs somewhere between the ages of 45 and 55, is the second most important life milestone in physical development. The decreased production of estrogen (the dominant female hormone) produces certain physical changes, including decreases in some types of cognitive and memory skills (Weber et al., 2013). However, the popular belief that menopause (or "the change of life") causes serious psychological mood swings, loss of sexual interest, and depression is not supported by current research (Matlin, 2012; Moilanen et al., 2010). In fact, most studies find that postmenopausal women report relief, increased libido, and other positive reactions to the end of their menstrual cycles (Chrisler, 2008; Strauss, 2010).

Sergey Novikov/Shutterstock

FIGURE 9.12 ADOLESCENT GROWTH SPURT

Note the gender differences in height gain during puberty. Most girls are about two years ahead of boys in their growth spurt and are therefore taller than most boys between the ages of 10 and 14.

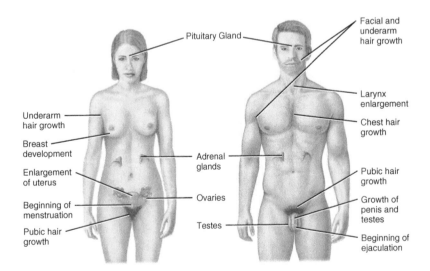

FIGURE 9.13 SECONDARY SEX CHARACTERISTICS

Complex physical changes in puberty primarily result from hormones secreted from the ovaries and testes, the pituitary gland in the brain, and the adrenal glands near the kidneys.

In contrast to women, men experience a more gradual decline in hormone levels, and most men can father children until their seventies or eighties. Physical changes such as unexpected weight gain, decline in sexual responsiveness, loss of muscle strength, and graying or loss of hair may lead some men (and women as well) to feel depressed and to question their life progress. They often see these alterations as a biological signal of aging and mortality. Such physical and psychological changes in some men are generally referred to as the *male climacteric* (or *andropause*). However, the popular belief that almost all men (and some women) go through a deeply disruptive midlife crisis, experiencing serious dissatisfaction with their work and personal relationships, is largely a myth.

After middle age, most physical changes in development are gradual and occur in the heart and arteries and in the sensory receptors. For example, cardiac output (the volume of blood pumped by the heart each minute) decreases, whereas blood pressure increases due to the thickening and stiffening of arterial walls. Visual acuity and depth perception decline, hearing acuity lessens (especially for high-frequency sounds), smell sensitivity decreases, and there is some decline in cognitive and memory skills (Baldwin & Ash, 2011; Edelstein et al., 2013; Fletcher & Rapp, 2013; Heinrich & Schneider, 2011; Siegler et al., 2013).

Sadly, television, magazines, movies, and advertisements too often present aging as a time for endless attempts at hiding gray hair, preventing or hiding wrinkles, avoiding or restoring thin or balding hair, and recovering lost sexual potency. Such negative portrayals contribute to our society's widespread **ageism**—prejudice or discrimination based on physical age. However, a recent survey of more than 1,000 older adults revealed an increase in well-being with age, contrary to what negative stereotypes about aging might predict (Jeste et al., 2012). Furthermore, as advertising companies consider the huge number of aging baby boomers, there has been a recent shift toward more positive and accurate portrayals of aging as a time of vigor, interest, and productivity.

Ageism Prejudice or discrimination based on physical age; similar to racism and sexism in its negative stereotypes.

Mark Wilson/Getty Images

realworldpsychology **Achievement in Later Years** Our cognitive abilities generally grow and improve throughout our life span, as demonstrated by the achievements of people like Ruth Bader Ginsburg. Justice Ginsburg worked tirelessly as a staunch courtroom advocate for many years, and now in her eighties continues to serve as a Supreme Court Justice for the United States—only the second of four woman to be appointed to this high honor.

RETRIEVAL PRACTICE: PHYSICAL DEVELOPMENT

Self-Test

Completing this self-test and comparing your answers with those in Appendix B provides immediate feedback and helpful practice for exams. Additional interactive, self-tests are available at www.wiley.com/college/huffman.

1. Teratogens are _____

a. maternal defects that cause damage during neo-natal development.

b. environmental agents that cause damage during prenatal development.

c. popular children's toys that studies have shown cause damage during early childhood development.

d. environmental diseases that cause damage during early childhood development.

2. The _____ is the first stage of prenatal development, which begins with ovulation and ends with implantation in the uterus (the first two weeks).

a. embryonic period

b. zygote stage

c. critical period

d. germinal period

3. Which of the following is *not* true regarding infant sensory and perceptual development?

a. A newborn's vision is almost 20/20 at birth.

b. A newborn's sense of pain is highly developed at birth.

c. An infant can recognize, and prefers, its own mother's breast milk by smell.

d. An infant can recognize, and prefers, its own mother's breast milk by taste.

4. The clearest and most physical sign of puberty is the _____, characterized by rapid increases in height, weight, and skeletal growth.

a. menses
b. spermarche
c. growth spurt
d. age of fertility

5. Some employers are reluctant to hire older workers (50 years of age and older) because of a generalized belief that they are sickly and will take too much time off. This is an example of _____.

a. discrimination
b. prejudice
c. ageism
d. all the above

Think Critically

1 If a mother knowingly ingests a quantity of alcohol, which causes her child to develop fetal alcohol syndrome (FAS), is she guilty of child abuse? Why or why not?

2 Based on what you have learned about development during late adulthood, do you think this period is inevitably a time of physical and mental decline? Why or why not?

realworldpsychology

Does prenatal exposure to smoke increase the risk of obesity later in life?

Why do teenagers seem to sleep so much?

HINT: LOOK IN THE MARGIN FOR ⓠ2 AND ⓠ3

COGNITIVE DEVELOPMENT

RETRIEVAL PRACTICE While reading the upcoming sections, respond to each Learning Objective in your own words. Then compare your responses with those found at www.wiley.com/college/huffman.

1 **EXPLAIN** the role of schemas, assimilation, and accommodation in cognitive development.

2 **DESCRIBE** the major characteristics of Piaget's four stages of cognitive development.

3 **COMPARE** Piaget's theory of cognitive development to Vygotsky's.

LEARNING OBJECTIVES

•

Just as a child's body and physical abilities change, his or her way of knowing and perceiving the world also grows and changes. Jean Piaget [pee-ah-ZHAY] provided some of the first great demonstrations of how children develop thinking and reasoning abilities. He showed that an infant begins at a cognitively "primitive" level and that intellectual growth progresses in distinct stages, motivated by an innate need to know.

To appreciate Piaget's contributions, we need to consider three major concepts: schemas, assimilation, and accommodation. **Schemas** are the most basic units of intellect. They act as patterns that organize our interactions with the environment, like an architect's drawings or a builder's blueprints (see *Test Yourself*).

Schema The cognitive structures, framework, or "blueprints" of knowledge, regarding objects, people, and situations, which grow and differentiate with experience.

TEST YOURSELF: DO YOU HAVE AN ARTISTIC SCHEMA?

psychology and you

Study the "impossible figure" to the right, and then try drawing this figure without tracing it. Students with artistic training generally find it relatively easy to reproduce, whereas the rest of us find it very hard or "impossible." This is because we lack the necessary artistic schema and cannot assimilate what we see. With practice and training, we could accommodate the new information and easily draw the figure.

© amana images inc./Alamy

FIGURE 9.14 ACCOMMODATION

An infant uses accommodation to make the transition from milk to solid foods.

Assimilation In Piaget's theory, applying existing mental patterns (schemas) to new information; new information is incorporated (assimilated) into existing schemas; works in tandem with accommodation.

Accommodation According to Piaget, the process of adjusting (accommodating) existing mental patterns (schemas) or developing new ones to better fit with new information; works in tandem with assimilation.

Sensorimotor stage Piaget's first stage of cognitive development (birth to approximately age 2), in which schemas are developed through sensory and motor activities.

Object permanence The Piagetian term for an infant's recognition that objects (or people) continue to exist even when they cannot be seen, heard, or touched directly.

In the first few weeks of life, for example, the infant apparently has several *schemas* based on the innate reflexes of sucking, grasping, and so on. These schemas are primarily motor and may be little more than stimulus-and-response mechanisms (for example, the nipple is presented, and the baby sucks). Soon, other schemas emerge. The infant develops a more detailed schema for eating solid food, a different schema for the concepts of "mother" and "father," and so on.

Assimilation and *accommodation* are the two major processes by which schemas grow and change over time. **Assimilation** is the process of absorbing new information into existing schemas. For instance, infants use their sucking schema not only in sucking nipples but also in sucking blankets and fingers. In **accommodation**, existing ideas are modified to fit new information. Accommodation generally occurs when new information or stimuli cannot be assimilated. New schemas are developed or old schemas are changed to better fit with the new information. An infant's first attempt to eat solid food with a spoon is a good example of accommodation **(Figure 9.14)**.

Interestingly, researchers in one study found that babies who sat upright in infant seats while they explored different objects were much better at distinguishing between those objects than babies who were lying down while they explored (Woods & Wilcox, 2013). Although the researchers weren't exactly sure why sitting up helped babies learn more about different objects, it may be that a sitting position allows babies to better reach for, hold, and manipulate objects.

Stages of Cognitive Development

According to Piaget, all children go through approximately the same four stages of cognitive development, regardless of the culture in which they live **(Table 9.3)**. Piaget also believed that these stages cannot be skipped because skills acquired at earlier stages are essential to mastery at later stages.

Sensorimotor Stage

The **sensorimotor stage** lasts from birth until "significant" language acquisition (about age 2). During this time, children explore the world and develop their schemas primarily through their senses and motor activities—hence the term *sensorimotor*. One important concept that infants lack at the beginning of the sensorimotor stage is **object permanence**—an understanding that objects continue to exist even when they cannot be seen, heard, or touched **(Figure 9.15)**. The attainment of object permanence generally signals a transition from the sensorimotor to the preoperational stage.

FIGURE 9.15 OBJECT PERMANENCE

Prior to about 8 months of age, infants tend to lack object permanence, as shown by the child in the first two photos, who apparently believes the toy no longer exists once it is blocked from sight. In contrast, the older child in the third photo knows that the object still exists even if it is hidden—as shown by her attempt to seek out the toy that is hidden under the sofa. Thus demonstrating that she has formed a mental representation (a schema) of the object and has acquired a recognition of object permanence.

Doug Goodman/Photo Researchers/Getty Images

Doug Goodman/Photo Researchers/Getty Images

Heleen Sitter/The Image Bank/Getty Images

| TABLE 9.3 | PIAGET'S FOUR STAGES OF COGNITIVE DEVELOPMENT |

Sensorimotor stage (birth to age 2)

Limits

- Beginning of stage lacks object permanence (understanding that things continue to exist even when not seen, heard, or felt)

Abilities

- Uses senses and motor skills to explore and develop cognitively

Example

- Children at this stage like to play with their food.

Jeff R Clow/Flickr/Getty Images

Preoperational stage (ages 2 to 7)

Limits

- Cannot perform "operations" (lacks reversibility)
- Intuitive thinking versus logical reasoning
- Egocentric thinking (inability to consider another's point of view)
- Animistic thinking (believing all things are living)

Abilities

- Has significant language and thinks symbolically

Example

- Children at this stage often believe the moon follows them.

© Igor Demchenkov/iStockphoto

Concrete operational stage (ages 7 to 11)

Limits

- Cannot think abstractly and hypothetically
- Thinking tied to concrete, tangible objects and events

Abilities

- Can perform "operations" on concrete objects
- Understands conservation (realizing that changes in shape or appearance can be reversed)
- Less egocentric
- Can think logically about concrete objects and events

Example

- Children at this stage begin to question the existence of Santa.

Hill Street Studios/Blend Images/Getty Images, Inc.

Formal operational stage (age 11 and over)

Limits

- Adolescent egocentrism at the beginning of this stage, with related problems of the personal fable and imaginary audience

Abilities

- Can think abstractly and hypothetically

Example

- Children at this stage show great concern for physical appearance.

© Adrian Burke/Corbis Images

Preoperational stage Piaget's second stage of cognitive development (roughly age 2 to 7), characterized by the ability to employ significant language and to think symbolically, but the child lacks operations (reversible mental processes), and thinking is egocentric and animistic.

Egocentrism In cognitive development, the inability to take the perspective of another person; a hallmark of Piaget's preoperational stage.

Preoperational Stage

During the **preoperational stage** (roughly ages 2 to 7), language advances significantly, and the child begins to think symbolically—using symbols, such as words, to represent concepts. Three other qualities characterize this stage: *lack of operations, egocentrism,* and *animism.*

Piaget labeled this period "preoperational" because the child *lacks operations,* or reversible mental processes. For instance, if a preoperational boy who has a brother is asked, "Do you have a brother?" he will easily respond, "Yes." However, when asked, "Does your brother have a brother?" he will answer, "No!" To understand that his brother has a brother, he must be able to reverse the concept of "having a brother."

Children at this stage have difficulty understanding that there are points of view other than their own, which is known as **egocentrism**. The preschooler who moves in front of you to get a better view of the TV or repeatedly asks questions while you are talking to someone else on the telephone is demonstrating egocentrism. Children of this age assume that others see, hear, feel, and think exactly as they do.

Voices from the Classroom

Egocentrism and a Dump Truck! It was getting close to my brother's birthday, and I called him up. After we chatted, he put his 4-year-old son Josh on the phone. I asked Josh, "What do you think we should get your dad for his birthday?" It took him very little time to blurt out, "A dump truck!" Being aware of Josh's personal love of bulldozers and dump trucks, which obviously wouldn't be my brother's choice for a birthday present, I realized that my nephew was in Piaget's preoperational stage and demonstrating egocentrism.

Professor David Baskind
Delta College
University Center, Michigan

Children in the preoperational stage also believe that objects such as the sun, trees, clouds, and bars of soap have motives, feelings, and intentions (for example, "dark clouds are angry" and "soap sinks because it is tired"). *Animism* refers to the belief that all things are living (or animated).

Concrete operational stage Piaget's third stage of cognitive development (roughly age 7 to 11), in which the child can perform mental operations on concrete objects and understand reversibility and conservation, but thinking is tied to concrete, tangible objects and events.

Conservation According to Piaget, the understanding that certain physical characteristics (such as volume) remain unchanged, even though appearances may change.

Concrete Operational Stage

At approximately age 7, children enter the **concrete operational stage**. During this time, many important thinking skills emerge. However, as the name implies, thinking tends to be limited to *concrete,* tangible objects and events. Unlike preoperational children, children in this stage are less egocentric in their thinking and become capable of true logical thought. As most parents know, children now stop believing in Santa Claus because they logically conclude that one man can't deliver presents to everyone in one night.

Because they understand the concept of *reversibility,* concrete operational children also can now successfully perform "operations." They recognize that certain physical attributes (such as volume) remain unchanged, although the outward appearance is altered, in a process known as **conservation**. Tests for conservation can identify whether a child is in the preoperational or the concrete operational stage (see *Putting Piaget to the Test*).

PUTTING PIAGET TO THE TEST
psychology and you

If you have access to children in the preoperational or concrete operational stages, try some of the following experiments, which researchers use to test Piaget's various forms of conservation. The equipment is easily obtained, and you will find their responses fascinating. Keep in mind that this should be done as a game. The child should not feel that he or she is failing a test or making a mistake.

Type of conservation task (average age at which concept is fully grasped)	Your task as experimenter . . .	Child is asked . . .
Length (ages 6–7)	**Step 1** Center two sticks of equal length. Child agrees that they are of equal length. **Step 2** Move one stick.	**Step 3** "Which stick is longer?" Preoperational child will say that one of the sticks is longer. Child in concrete stage will say that they are both the same length.
Substance amount (ages 6–7)	**Step 1** Center two identical clay balls. Child acknowledges that the two have equal amounts of clay. **Step 2** Flatten one of the balls.	**Step 3** "Do the two pieces have the same amount of clay?" Preoperational child will say that the flat piece has more clay. Child in concrete stage will say that the two pieces have the same amount of clay.
Liquid volume (ages 7–8)	**Step 1** Present two identical glasses with liquid at the same level. Child agrees that liquid is at the same height in both glasses. **Step 2** Pour the liquid from one of the short, wide glasses into the tall, thin one.	**Step 3** "Do the two glasses have the same amount of liquid?" Preoperational child will say that the tall, thin glass has more liquid. Child in concrete stage will say that the two glasses have the same amount of liquid.
Area (ages 8–10)	**Step 1** Center two identical pieces of cardboard with wooden blocks placed on them in identical positions. Child acknowledges that the same amount of space is left open on each piece of cardboard. **Step 2** Scatter the blocks on one piece of the cardboard.	**Step 3** "Do the two pieces of cardboard have the same amount of open space?" Preoperational child will say that the cardboard with scattered blocks has less open space. Child in concrete stage will say that both pieces have the same amount of open space.

Think Critically

1. Based on their responses, are the children you tested in the preoperational or concrete stage?

2. If you repeat the same tests with each child, do their answers change? Why or why not?

Formal Operational Stage

The final period in Piaget's theory, the **formal operational stage**, typically begins around age 11. In this stage, children begin to apply their operations to abstract concepts in addition to concrete objects. They also become capable of hypothetical thinking ("What if?"), which allows systematic formulation and testing of concepts.

Formal operational stage Piaget's fourth stage of cognitive development (around age 11 and beyond), characterized by abstract and hypothetical thinking.

For example, before filling out applications for part-time jobs, adolescents may think about possible conflicts with school and friends, the number of hours they want to work, and the kind of work for which they are qualified. Formal operational thinking also allows the adolescent to construct a well-reasoned argument based on hypothetical concepts and logical processes. Consider the following argument:

1. If you hit a glass with a feather, the glass will break.

2. You hit the glass with a feather.

What is the logical conclusion? The correct answer, "The glass will break," is contrary to fact and direct experience. Therefore, the child in the concrete operational stage would have difficulty with this task, whereas the formal operational thinker understands that this problem is about abstractions that need not correspond to the real world.

Along with the benefits of this cognitive style come several problems. Adolescents in the early stages of the formal operational period demonstrate a type of egocentrism different from that of the preoperational child. Adolescents certainly recognize that others have unique thoughts and perspectives. However, they may fail to differentiate between what they are thinking and what others are thinking. For example, if they get a new haircut or fail to make the sports team, they may be overly concerned about how others will react. Instead of considering that everyone is equally wrapped up in his or her own appearance, concerns, and plans, they tend to believe that they are the center of others' thoughts and attentions. David Elkind (1967, 2000, 2007) referred to this as the *imaginary audience*.

In sharp, ironic contrast to believing that others are always watching and evaluating them (the imaginary audience), Piaget believed that adolescents also often feel that they are special and unique. They alone are having insights or difficulties that no one else understands or experiences. Elkind described this as the *personal fable*.

In sum, the imaginary audience apparently results from an inability to differentiate the self from others, whereas the personal fable may be a product of differentiating too much. Thankfully, these two forms of adolescent egocentrism tend to decrease during later stages of the formal operational period.

© fstop123/iStockphoto

psychology and you **Understanding Your Own Adolescent Egocentrism** Do these descriptions of the imaginary audience and personal fable ring true for you? If so, do you now understand how these beliefs might help explain some of the problems and challenges you faced in adolescence? For example, many teens have difficulty accepting comfort and support from parents due to their belief that no one has ever felt or experienced what they have. One young woman remembered being very upset in middle school when her mother tried to comfort her over the loss of an important relationship. "I felt like she couldn't possibly know how it felt—no one could. I couldn't believe that anyone had ever suffered like this or that things would ever get better."

The most important danger of adolescent egocentrism is undoubtedly the fact that several forms of risk taking, such as engaging in sexual intercourse without protection, driving dangerously, and experimenting with drugs, seem to arise from the personal fable (Alberts et al., 2007; Flavell et al., 2002; Hill & Lapsley, 2011; Moshman, 2011). Adolescents have a sense of uniqueness, invulnerability, and immortality. They do recognize the dangers of risky activities, but given their adolescent egocentrism and personal fable, they believe the rules and statistical dangers just don't apply to them.

As a critical thinker, can you see how these Piagetian concepts of the imaginary audience and personal fable meet psychology's goal of *description* (Chapter 1)? If so, you'll also note how **Figure 9.16** and the following *Real World Psychology* offer biological insights toward the goal of *explanation*.

FIGURE 9.16 **BIOLOGY AND TEEN RISK TAKING**

Ⓐ Can you see how this type of risk-taking behavior may reflect the personal fable—adolescents' tendency to believe they are unique and special and that dangers don't apply to them?

Growth

Pruning

Ⓑ During early childhood (ages 3–6), the frontal lobes experience a significant increase in the connections between neurons, which helps explain a child's rapid cognitive growth.

Ⓒ This rapid synaptic growth shifts to the temporal and parietal lobes during the ages of 7 to 15, which corresponds to their significant increases in language and motor skills.

Ⓓ During the teen years (ages 16–20), synaptic pruning is widespread in the frontal lobes.

realworldpsychology **Brain and Behavior in Adolescence**
Adolescents are often criticized for their exaggerated, self-conscious concern for what others think, as well as for their extreme mood swings, poor decisions, and risky behaviors **(Figure 9.16)**. Rather than simply describing and labeling these as the imaginary audience and personal fable, psychologists now believe these effects may be largely due to their less-developed frontal lobes (Bunge & Toga, 2013; Christakou et al., 2011; Moshman, 2011; Pokhrel et al., 2013). In contrast to the rapid synaptic growth experienced in the earlier years **(Figures 9.16b and c)**, the adolescent's brain actively destroys (prunes) unneeded connections **(Figure 9.16d)**. Although it may seem counterintuitive, this pruning actually improves brain functioning by making the remaining neurons more efficient. Full maturity of the frontal lobes occurs around the mid-twenties. Recall from Chapter 2 that our frontal lobes are largely responsible for higher-level cognitive functioning, such as emotional regulation, planning ahead, and avoiding reckless behavior.

Vygotsky Versus Piaget

As influential as Piaget's account of cognitive development has been, there are other important theories, and criticisms of Piaget, to consider. For example, Russian psychologist Lev Vygotsky emphasized the sociocultural influences on a child's cognitive development, rather than Piaget's internal schemas. According to Vygotsky, children construct knowledge through their culture, language, and collaborative social interactions with more experienced thinkers (Mahn & John-Steiner, 2013; Trawick-Smith & Dziurgot, 2011). Unlike Piaget, Vygotsky believed that adults play an important

FIGURE 9.17 VYGOTSKY'S ZONE OF PROXIMAL DEVELOPMENT (ZPD)

Have you heard of "instructional scaffolding"? This term refers to providing support during the learning process that is tailored to the needs of the student. Vygotsky was one of the first to apply the general idea of scaffolding to early cognitive development. He proposed that the most effective teaching focuses on tasks between those a learner can do without help (the lower limit) and those he or she cannot do even with help (the upper limit). In this *zone of proximal development (ZPD)*, tasks and skills can be "stretched" to higher levels with the guidance and encouragement of a more knowledgeable person.

Upper limit (tasks beyond reach at present)

Zone of proximal development (ZPD) (tasks achievable with guidance)

Lower limit (tasks achieved without help)

© omgimages/iStockphoto

Zone of proximal development (ZPD) In Vygotsky's theory of cognitive development, the area between what children can accomplish on their own and what they can accomplish with the help of others who are more competent.

instructor role in development and that this instruction is particularly helpful when it falls within a child's **zone of proximal development (ZPD) (Figure 9.17)**.

Having briefly discussed Vygotsky's alternative theory, let's consider two major criticisms of Piaget—*underestimated abilities* and *underestimated genetic and cultural influences*. Research shows that Piaget may have underestimated young children's cognitive development. As you've just seen, Piaget believed that infancy and early childhood were a time of extreme egocentrism, in which children have little or no understanding of the perspective of others. However, later research finds that empathy develops at a relatively young age **(Figure 9.18)**. Furthermore, even newborn babies tend to cry in response to the cry of another baby (Diego & Jones, 2007; Geangu et al., 2010). Also, preschoolers will adapt their speech by using shorter, simpler expressions when talking to 2-year-olds as compared to talking with adults.

Piaget's model, like other stage theories, has also been criticized for not sufficiently taking into account genetic and cultural differences (Cole & Gajdamaschko, 2007; Shweder, 2011; Zelazo et al., 2010). Despite criticisms, however, Piaget's contributions to psychology are enormous. As one scholar put it, "assessing the impact of Piaget on developmental psychology is like assessing the impact of Shakespeare on English literature or Aristotle on philosophy—impossible" (Beilin, 1992, p. 191).

Ermolaev Alexander/Shutterstock

FIGURE 9.18 ARE PREOPERATIONAL CHILDREN ALWAYS EGOCENTRIC?

Some toddlers and preschoolers clearly demonstrate empathy for other people. How does this ability to take another's perspective contradict Piaget's beliefs about egocentrism in very young children?

RETRIEVAL PRACTICE: COGNITIVE DEVELOPMENT

Self-Test

Completing this self-test and comparing your answers with those in Appendix B provides immediate feedback and helpful practice for exams. Additional interactive, self-tests are available at www.wiley.com/college/huffman.

1. _____ was one of the first scientists to demonstrate that a child's intellect is fundamentally different from an adult's.

    a. Baumrind   b. Beck
    c. Piaget   d. Elkind

2. _____ occurs when existing schemas are used to absorb new information, whereas _____ makes changes and modifications to the schemas.

    a. Adaptation;   b. Adaptation; reversibility
       accommodation
    c. Egocentrism;   d. Assimilation; accommodation
       postschematization

3. A child's belief that the moon follows him as he travels in a car is an example of _____.

    a. sensorimotor delusions   b. formal operational thinking
    c. wet concrete thinking   d. animism

4. The ability to think abstractly and hypothetically occurs in Piaget's _____ stage.

    a. egocentric   b. postoperational
    c. formal operational   d. concrete operational

Think Critically

1 Piaget's theory states that all children progress through all the discrete stages of cognitive development in order and without skipping any. Do you agree with this theory? Do you know any children who seem to contradict this theory?

2 Based on what you've learned about schemas, what are some new schemas you've developed as part of your transition from high school to college?

realworldpsychology

Do babies learn faster when they're sitting up than when they're lying down

HINT: LOOK IN THE MARGIN FOR Q4

SOCIAL-EMOTIONAL DEVELOPMENT

RETRIEVAL PRACTICE While reading the upcoming sections, respond to each Learning Objective in your own words. Then compare your responses with those found at www.wiley.com/college/huffman.

LEARNING OBJECTIVES

1 **DESCRIBE** how attachment and parenting styles influence social-emotional development.

2 **SUMMARIZE** the central characteristics of Kohlberg's theory of moral development.

3 **REVIEW** Erikson's eight stages of psychosocial development.

4 **DESCRIBE** how sex and gender affect development.

In addition to physical and cognitive development, developmental psychologists study the way social and emotional factors affect development over the life span. In this section, we focus on *attachment*, *parenting styles*, *moral reasoning*, *personality*, *sex*, and *gender*.

Attachment

An infant arrives in the world with a multitude of behaviors that encourage a strong bond of **attachment** with primary caregivers. Returning to our earlier discussion of the nature–nurture controversy, researchers who advocate the nativist, or innate, position suggest that newborn infants are biologically equipped with verbal and

Attachment A strong emotional bond with special others that endures over time.

nonverbal behaviors (such as crying, clinging, and smiling) and imprinting ("following") behaviors (such as crawling and walking after the caregiver) that elicit instinctive nurturing responses from the caregiver (Bowlby, 1969, 1989, 2000).

Touch

Harry Harlow and his colleagues (1950, 1966, 1971) also investigated the variables that might affect attachment. They created two types of wire-framed surrogate (substitute) "mother" monkeys: one covered by soft terry cloth and one left uncovered **(Figure 9.19)**. The infant monkeys were fed by either the cloth or the wire mother, but they otherwise had access to both mothers. The researchers found that monkeys "reared" by a cloth mother clung frequently to the soft material of their surrogate mother and developed greater emotional security and curiosity than did monkeys assigned to the wire mother.

Thanks in part to Harlow's research, psychologists discovered that *contact comfort*, the pleasurable tactile sensations provided by a soft and cuddly "parent," is a powerful contributor to attachment **(Figure 9.20)**. Further support comes from a study described in Chapter 4 which shows that touch is an essential part of normal human infant development. This is why hospitals now encourage premature babies to receive "kangaroo care," in which babies have skin-to-skin contact with a parent (Schneider et al., 2012).

Although physical contact between caregiver and child appears to be an innate, biological part of attachment, Mary Ainsworth and her colleagues (1967, 1978) discovered several interesting differences in the type and levels of human attachment **(Figure 9.21)**. Note, however, that while Ainsworth studied

---

FIGURE 9.19 **HARLOW'S STUDY AND CONTACT COMFORT**

Although Harlow's studies of attachment in infant monkeys would be considered unethical today, it did clearly demonstrate that *touch*, and not *feeding*, is crucial to an infant's attachment.

Nina Leen/Time Life Pictures/Getty Images

FIGURE 9.20 **THE POWER OF TOUCH**

Parents around the world tend to kiss, nuzzle, comfort, and respond to their children with lots of physical contact, which points out its vital role in infant development. It also provides support for the biological, nature argument for attachment.

Marili Forastieri/Digital Vision/ Getty Images

FIGURE 9.21 RESEARCH ON INFANT ATTACHMENT

For most children, parents are the earliest and most important factor in social development, and the attachment between parent and child is of particular interest to developmental psychologists. In fact, research shows that strong levels of social connectedness, meaning social attachments to friends and parents, have a stronger impact on well-being in adulthood than does academic achievement in adolescence (Olsson et al., 2012).

1. The baby plays while the mother is nearby.

2. A stranger enters the room, speaks to the mother, and approaches the child.

3. The mother leaves and the stranger stays in the room with an unhappy baby.

4. The mother returns and the stranger leaves.

5. The baby is reunited with the mother.

Ⓐ Strange situation procedure
Mary Ainsworth and her colleagues (1967, 1978, 2010) found significant differences in the typical levels of attachment between infants and their mothers using a technique called the strange situation procedure, in which they observed how infants responded to the presence or absence of their mother and a stranger.

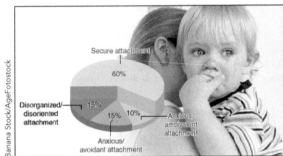

Secure
Seeks closeness with mother when stranger enters. Uses her as a safe base from which to explore, shows moderate distress on separation from her, and is happy when she returns.
Anxious/ambivalent
Infant becomes very upset when mother leaves the room and shows mixed emotions when she returns.
Anxious/avoidant
Infant does not seek closeness or contact with the mother and shows little emotion when the mother departs or returns.
Disorganized/disoriented
Infant exhibits avoidant or ambivalent attachment, often seeming either confused or apprehensive in the presence of the mother.

Banana Stock/AgeFotostock

Ⓑ Degrees of attachment
Using the strange situation procedure, Ainsworth found that children could be divided into three groups: *Secure, anxious/avoidant, and anxious/ambivalent*. A later psychologist, Mary Main, added a fourth category, *disorganized/disoriented* (Main & Solomon, 1986, 1990).

attachment between mothers and infants, later research demonstrated that *both* mothers and fathers have a lasting impact on development (Khaleque & Rohner, 2011).

In addition to finding varying levels of infant attachment to parents, researchers also have observed that these early patterns of attachment tend to be related to our later adult styles of romantic love (Fraley et al., 2013; Graham, 2011; Hatfield & Rapson, 2010; Kilmann et al., 2013; Sprecher & Fehr, 2011; Tatkin, 2011). If we developed a secure, anxious/ambivalent, anxious/avoidant, or disorganized/disoriented style as infants, we tend to follow these same patterns in our adult approach to intimacy and affection. For example, young adults who experienced either unresponsive or overintrusive parenting during childhood are more likely to avoid committed romantic relationships as adults (Dekel & Farber, 2012). You can check your own romantic attachment style in *Test Yourself*. However, keep in mind that it's always risky to infer causation from correlation (see Chapter 1). Even if early attachment experiences are correlated with our later relationships, they do not determine them. Throughout life, we can learn new social skills and different approaches to all our relationships.

TEST YOURSELF: WHAT'S YOUR ROMANTIC ATTACHMENT STYLE?

psychology and you

Thinking of your current and past romantic relationships, place a check next to the statement that best describes your feelings about relationships.

_____**1.** *I find it relatively easy to get close to others and am comfortable depending on them and having them depend on me. I don't often worry about being abandoned or about someone getting too close.*

_____**2.** *I am somewhat uncomfortable being close. I find it difficult to trust partners completely or to allow myself to depend on them. I am nervous when anyone gets close, and love partners often want me to be more intimate than is comfortable for me.*

_____**3.** *I find that others are reluctant to get as close as I would like. I often worry that my partner doesn't really love me or won't stay with me. I want to merge completely with another person, and this desire sometimes scares people away.*

According to research, 55% of adults agree with item 1 (secure attachment), 25% choose number 2 (anxious/avoidant attachment), and 20% choose item 3 (anxious/ambivalent attachment) (adapted from Fraley & Shaver, 1997; Hazan & Shaver, 1987). Note that the percentages for these adult attachment styles do not perfectly match those in Figure 9.21, partly because the disorganized/disoriented attachment pattern was not included in this measurement of adult romantic attachments.

Think Critically

1 Do your responses as an adult match your childhood attachment experiences?

2 Does your romantic attachment style negatively affect your present relationship? If so, how might you use this new information to make positive changes?

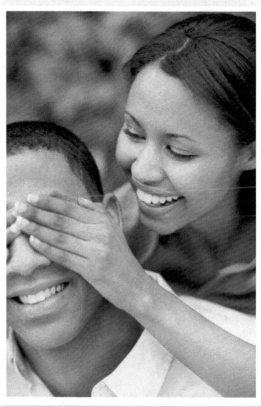

© GlobalStock / iStockphoto

Parenting Styles

How much of our personality comes from the way our parents treat us as we're growing up? Researchers since the 1920s have studied the effects of different methods of childrearing on children's behavior, development, and mental health. For example, when researchers did follow-up studies of children with the various levels of attachment we just discussed, they found that infants with a secure attachment style had caregivers who were sensitive and responsive to their signals of distress, happiness, and fatigue (Ainsworth, 1967; Ainsworth et al., 1978; Gini et al., 2007; Higley, 2008; Völker, 2007). Anxious/avoidant infants had caregivers who were aloof and distant, and anxious/ambivalent infants had inconsistent caregivers who alternated between strong affection and indifference. Follow-up studies found that, over time, securely attached children were the most sociable, emotionally aware, enthusiastic, cooperative, persistent, curious, and competent (Flaherty & Sadler, 2011; Friedman et al., 2013; Johnson et al., 2007).

Other studies by Diana Baumrind (1980, 1995, 2013) found that parenting styles could be reliably divided into four broad patterns—*permissive-neglectful,*

| TABLE 9.4 | PARENTING STYLES | realworldpsychology |

Parenting style	Description	Example	Effect on children
Permissive-neglectful (permissive-indifferent) (low C, low W)	Parents make few demands, with little structure or monitoring, and show little interest or emotional support; may be actively rejecting.	"I don't care about you—or what you do."	Children tend to have poor social skills and little self-control (being overly demanding and disobedient).
Permissive-indulgent (low C, high W)	Parents set few limits or demands, but are highly involved and emotionally connected.	"I care about you—and you're free to do what you like!"	Children often fail to learn respect for others and tend to be impulsive, immature, and out of control.
Authoritarian (high C, low W)	Parents are rigid and punitive, while also being low on warmth and responsiveness.	"I don't care what you want. Just do it my way, or else!"	Children tend to be easily upset, moody, aggressive, and often fail to learn good communication skills.
Authoritative (high C, high W)	Parents generally set and enforce firm limits, while also being highly involved, tender, and emotionally supportive.	"I really care about you, but there are rules and you need to be responsible."	Children become self-reliant, self-controlled, high achieving, and emotionally welladjusted; also seem more content, goal oriented. friendly, and socially competent.

Sources: Baumrind, 1991, 1995, 2013; Celada, 2011; Driscoll et al., 2008; Martin & Fabes, 2009; McKinney et al., 2008; Topham et al., 2011.

permissive-indulgent, authoritarian, and *authoritative*—which can be differentiated by their degree of *control/demandingness* (*C*) and *warmth/responsiveness* (*W*) **(Table 9.4)**.

Moral Development

Developing a sense of right and wrong, or morality, is a part of psychological development. Consider what you would do in the following situation:

> In Europe, a cancer-ridden woman was near death, but an expensive drug existed that might save her. The woman's husband, Heinz, begged the druggist to sell the drug cheaper or to let him pay later. But he refused. Heinz became desperate and broke into his store and stole it. (Adapted from Kohlberg, 1964, pp. 18–19)

Was Heinz right to steal the drug? What do you consider moral behavior? Is morality "in the eye of the beholder," or are there universal moral truths and principles? Whatever your answer, your ability to think, reason, and respond to Heinz's dilemma may demonstrate your current level of moral development.

One of the most influential researchers in moral development was Lawrence Kohlberg (1927–1987). He presented what he called "moral stories" like the Heinz dilemma to people of all ages, not to see whether they judged Heinz right or wrong but to examine the reasons they gave for their decisions. On the basis of his findings, Kohlberg (1964, 1984) developed a model of moral development with three broad levels in the evolution of moral reasoning, and each of the three levels composed of two distinct stages **(Figure 9.22)**. Individuals at each stage and level may or may not support Heinz's stealing of the drug, but their reasoning changes from level to level.

FIGURE 9.22 KOHLBERG'S STAGES OF MORAL DEVELOPMENT

Lawrence Kohlberg believed that individuals progress through three levels and six stages of moral development.

POSTCONVENTIONAL LEVEL

CONVENTIONAL LEVEL

PRECONVENTIONAL LEVEL

(Stages 1 and 2—birth to adolescence) Moral judgment is *self-centered*. What is right is what one can get away with, or what is personally satisfying. Moral understanding is based on rewards, punishments, and the exchange of favors.

1 Punishment-obedience orientation

Focus is on self-interest—obedience to authority and avoidance of punishment. Because children at this stage have difficulty considering another's point of view, they also ignore people's intentions.

2 Instrumental-exchange orientation

Children become aware of others' perspectives, but their morality is based on reciprocity—an equal exchange of favors.

(Stages 3 and 4—adolescence and young adulthood) Moral reasoning is *other-centered*. Conventional societal rules are accepted because they help ensure the social order.

3 Good-child orientation

Primary moral concern is being nice and gaining approval, and judges others by their intentions—"His heart was in the right place."

4 Law-and-order orientation

Morality based on a larger perspective—societal laws. Understanding that if everyone violated laws, even with good intentions, there would be chaos.

(Stages 5 and 6—adulthood) Moral judgments based on *personal standards for right and wrong*. Morality also defined in terms of abstract principles and values that apply to all situations and societies.

5 Social contact orientation

Appreciation for the underlying purposes served by laws. Societal laws are obeyed because of the "social contract," but they can be morally disobeyed if they fail to express the will of the majority or fail to maximize social welfare.

6 Universal-ethics orientation

"Right" is determined by universal ethical principles (e.g., nonviolence, human dignity, freedom) that moral authorities might view as compelling or fair. These principles apply whether or not they conform to existing laws.

Sources: Based on Kohlberg, L. "Stage and Sequence: The Cognitive Developmental Approach to Socialization," in D. A. Goslin, *The handbook of socialization theory and research.* Chicago: Rand McNally, 1969, p. 376 (Table 6.2).

Preconventional level The first level of Kohlberg's theory of moral development, where morality is based on rewards, punishment, and exchange of favors.

Conventional level The second level of Kohlberg's theory of moral development, where moral judgments are based on compliance with the rules and values of society.

Postconventional level The highest level of Kohlberg's theory of moral development, where individuals develop personal standards for right and wrong and define morality in terms of abstract principles and values that apply to all situations and societies.

Assessing Kohlberg's Theory

Kohlberg's ideas have led to considerable research on how we think about moral issues (Carlo et al., 2013; Krettenauer et al., 2013; Malti, 2013; Mitchell & Ziegler, 2013; Paciello et al., 2013). But his theories have also been the focus of three major areas of criticism:

1. *Moral reasoning versus behavior* Are people who achieve higher stages on Kohlberg's scale really more moral than others? Or do they just "talk a good game"?

   Some researchers have shown that a person's sense of moral identity, meaning the use of moral principles to define oneself, is often a good predictor of his or her behavior in real-world situations (Johnston et al., 2013; Stets & Carter, 2012). But others have found that situational factors are better predictors of moral behavior (Bandura, 1986, 1991, 2008; Minnameier & Schmidt, 2013; van

Ijizendoorn et al., 2013). For example, research participants are more likely to steal when they are told the money comes from a large company rather than from individuals (Greenberg, 2002). And both men and women will tell more sexual lies during casual relationships than during close relationships (Williams, 2001).

2. *Cultural differences* Cross-cultural studies confirm that children from a variety of cultures generally follow Kohlberg's model and progress sequentially from his first level, the *preconventional*, to his second, the *conventional* (Rest et al., 1999; Snarey, 1995). However, other studies find differences among cultures (Jensen, 2011; LePage et al., 2011; Rai & Fiske, 2011). For example, cross-cultural comparisons of responses to Heinz's moral dilemma show that Europeans and Americans tend to consider whether they like or identify with the victim in questions of morality. In contrast, Hindu Indians consider social responsibility and personal concerns two separate issues (Miller & Bersoff, 1998). Researchers suggest that the difference reflects the Indians' broader sense of social responsibility.

Furthermore, in India, Papua New Guinea, and China, as well as in Israeli kibbutzim, people don't choose between the rights of the individual and the rights of society (as the top levels of Kohlberg's model require). Instead, most people seek a compromise solution that accommodates both interests (Killen & Hart, 1999; Miller & Bersoff, 1998). Thus, Kohlberg's standard for judging the highest level of morality (the postconventional) may be more applicable to cultures that value individualism over community and interpersonal relationships.

3. *Possible gender bias* Researcher Carol Gilligan criticized Kohlberg's model because on his scale women often tend to be classified at a lower level of moral reasoning than men. She suggested that this difference occurred because Kohlberg's theory emphasizes values more often held by men, such as rationality and independence, while de-emphasizing common female values, such as concern for others and belonging (Gilligan, 1977, 1990, 1993; Kracher & Marble, 2008). However, most follow-up studies of Gilligan's specific theory, have found few, if any, gender differences (Bateman & Valentine, 2010; Fumagalli et al., 2010; Mercadillo et al., 2011; Smith, 2007).

Ragnar Singsaas /Getty Images, Inc.

realworldpsychology **Morality—Personal Trait or the Situation?** Which do you believe is the better predictor of moral behavior— the person or the situation? You've undoubtedly seen this dilemma when students are faced with a choice to cheat on an exam or shoplift. How about the case of Lance Armstrong, who chose to use performance-enhancing drugs in sports competition? Was it the situation or his personal morality that most influenced his behavior?

Personality Development

Like Piaget and Kohlberg, Erik Erikson (1902–1994) developed a stage theory of development. He identified eight **psychosocial stages** of social development **(Figure 9.23)**, each marked by a psychosocial crisis or conflict related to a specific developmental task. Erikson believed that the more successfully we overcome each psychosocial crisis, the better chance we have to develop in a healthy manner (Erikson, 1950).

Also like Piaget and Kohlberg, Erikson's insights and theory have stimulated considerable research (Conzen, 2010; Fukase & Okamoto, 2010; Marcia & Josselson, 2013; Zhang & He, 2011). However, Erikson also has critics (Beyers & Seiffge-Krenke, 2010; Spano et al., 2010). First, Erikson's psychosocial stages are difficult to test scientifically.

Psychosocial stages Erikson's theory that individuals pass through eight developmental stages, each involving a specific crisis that must be successfully resolved; each stage incorporates both the sexual and social aspects of an individual's development.

FIGURE 9.23 ERIKSON'S EIGHT STAGES OF PSYCHOSOCIAL DEVELOPMENT

Erikson identified eight stages of development, each of which is associated with its own unique psychosocial crisis.

1 Trust versus mistrust (birth–age 1)

Infants learn to *trust* or *mistrust* their caregivers and the world based on whether or not their needs—such as food, affection, safety—are met.

2 Autonomy versus shame and doubt (ages 1–3)

Toddlers start to assert their sense of independence (*autonomy*). If caregivers encourage this self-sufficiency, the toddler will learn to be independent versus feelings of *shame* and *doubt*.

3 Initiative versus guilt (ages 3–6)

Preschoolers learn to *initiate* activities and develop self-confidence and a sense of social responsibility. If not, they feel irresponsible, anxious, and *guilty*.

4 Industry versus inferiority (ages 6–12)

Elementary school-aged children who succeed in learning new, productive life skills, develop a sense of pride and competence (*industry*). Those who fail to develop these skills feel inadequate and unproductive (*inferior*).

5 Identity versus role confusion (ages 12–20)

Adolescents develop a coherent and stable self-definition (identity) by exploring many roles and deciding who or what they want to be in terms of career, attitudes, and so on. Failure to resolve this *identity crisis* may lead to apathy, withdrawal, and/or *role confusion*.

6 Intimacy versus isolation (early adulthood)

Young adults form lasting, meaningful relationships, which help them develop a sense of connectedness and *intimacy* with others. If not, they become psychologically *isolated*.

7 Generativity versus stagnation (middle adulthood)

The challenge for middle-aged adults is to be nurturant of the younger generation. Failing to meet this challenge leads to self-indulgence and a sense of *stagnation*.

8 Ego integrity versus despair (late adulthood)

During this stage, older adults reflect on their past. If this reflection reveals a life well-spent, the person experiences self-acceptance and satisfaction (*ego integrity*). If not, he or she experiences regret and deep dissatisfaction

Second, the labels he used to describe the eight stages may not be entirely appropriate cross-culturally. For example, in individualistic cultures, *autonomy* is highly preferable to *shame and doubt*. But in collectivist cultures, the preferred resolution might be *dependence* or *merging relations* (Berry et al., 2011). Despite their limits, Erikson's stages have greatly contributed to the study of development throughout the life span. And, like Piaget and Kohlberg, Erikson remains a major figure in developmental psychology.

Sex and Gender Influences on Development

Imagine for a moment what your life would be like if you were a member of the other sex. Would you think differently? Would you be more or less sociable and outgoing? Would your career plans or friendship patterns change? In this section, we will explore how our development is affected by *sex* (a biological characteristic determined at the moment of conception), **gender** (psychological and sociocultural meanings added to biological maleness or femaleness), **gender roles** (societal expectations for "appropriate" male and female attitudes and behaviors), and *cultural differences*.

Sex and Gender Differences

Physical anatomy is the most obvious biological sex difference between men and women. In addition to biological sex differences, scientists have also noted numerous gender differences that affect our cognitive and personality development **(Table 9.5)**. Keep in mind that these variations are statistically small, however, and represent few meaningful differences.

Gender-Role Development

By age 2, children are well aware of gender roles. They recognize that boys "should" be strong, independent, aggressive, dominant, and achieving, whereas girls "should" be soft, dependent, passive, emotional, and "naturally" interested in children (Collins, 2011; Endendijk et al., 2013; King, 2012; Leaper, 2013; Matlin, 2012; Wood, 2013). For example, one large-scale study of more than 10,000 U.S. adults found that compared to men, women have higher levels of sensitivity and warmth, whereas men score higher on dominance and vigilance (Del Giudice et al., 2012). The existence of similar gender roles in many cultures suggests that evolution and biology may play a role in their formation. However, most research emphasizes two major theories of gender-role development: *social learning* and *cognitive developmental* **(Figure 9.24)**.

Social-learning theorists emphasize the power of the immediate situation and observable behaviors on gender-role development. Girls learn how to be "feminine," and boys learn how to be "masculine" in two major ways: (1) They receive rewards or punishments for specific gender-role behaviors, and (2) they watch and imitate the behavior of others, particularly the same-sex parent (Bandura, 1989, 2008; Collins, 2011; Fulcher, 2011; Risman & Davis, 2013). A boy who puts on his father's tie or baseball cap wins big, indulgent smiles from his parents. But what would happen if he put on his mother's nightgown or lipstick? Parents, teachers, and friends generally reward or punish behaviors according to traditional gender-role expectations. Thus, a child "socially learns" what it means to be male or female.

According to the *cognitive-developmental theory*, social learning is part of gender-role development, but it's much more than a passive process of receiving rewards or punishments and modeling others. Instead, cognitive developmentalists argue that children actively observe, interpret, and judge the world around them

Gender A psychological and sociocultural phenomenon referring to learned sex-related behaviors and attitudes of males and females.

Gender roles The societal expectations for "appropriate" male and female attitudes and behavior and expressed publicly by the individual.

TABLE 9.5	RESEARCH-SUPPORTED SEX AND GENDER DIFFERENCES	
Behavior	**More Often Shown by Men**	**More Often Shown by Women**
Sexual	• Begin masturbating sooner in life cycle and higher overall occurrence rates • Start sexual life earlier and have first orgasm through masturbation • More likely to recognize their own sexual arousal • More orgasm consistency with sexual partner	• Begin masturbating later in life cycle and lower overall occurrence rates • Start sexual life later and have first orgasm from partner stimulation • Less likely to recognize their own sexual arousal • Less orgasm consistency with sexual partner
Touching	• Touched, kissed, and cuddled less by parents • Less physical contact with other men and respond more negatively to being touched • More likely to initiate both casual and intimate touch with sexual partner	• Touched, kissed, and cuddled more by parents • More physical contact with other women and respond more positively to being touched • Less likely to initiate either casual or intimate touch with sexual partner
Friendship	• Larger number of friends and express friendship by shared activities	• Smaller number of friends and express friendship by shared communication about self
Personality	• More aggressive from a very early age • More self-confident of future success • Attribute success to internal factors and failures to external factors • Achievement more task oriented; motives are mastery and competition • More self-validating • Higher self-esteem	• Less aggressive from a very early age • Less self-confident of future success • Attribute success to external factors and failures to internal factors • Achievement more socially directed, with emphasis on self-improvement; higher work motives • More dependent on others for validation • Lower self-esteem
Cognitive abilities	• Slightly superior in math and visuospatial skills	• Slightly superior in verbal skills

Sources: Blair & Lee, 2013; Bull et al., 2013; Casey, 2013; Crooks & Baur, 2013; King, 2012; Leaper, 2013; Masters & Johnson, 1961, 1966, 1970; Shibley Hyde & DeLamater, 2014; Wood, 2013.

(Bem, 1981, 1993; Hollander et al., 2011; Leaper, 2013). As children process information about the world, they also create internal rules governing correct behaviors for boys and for girls. On the basis of these rules, they form *gender schemas* (mental images) of how they should act.

Maartje van Caspel/Getty Images

realworldpsychology **Gender Roles and Teenagers** How do gender roles affect older children? Researchers in one study asked teenagers (ages 13 to 16) to describe two positive and two negative stories about themselves (Fivush et al., 2012). When the researchers examined the stories, they found striking differences. The stories told by girls were generally longer, more coherent, more detailed, and more descriptive of their own feelings and emotions. The boys' stories, in contrast, were more matter-of-fact and less self-reflective. What causes such differences? One factor may be that parents talk to boys and girls about emotions in different ways.

Androgyny

One way to overcome rigid or destructive gender-role stereotypes is to express both the "masculine" and "feminine" traits found in each individual—for example, being assertive and aggressive when necessary but also gentle and nurturing. Combining characteristics in this way is known as **androgyny [an-DRAH-juh-nee]**. Researchers

Androgyny [an-DRAH-juh-nee] Exhibiting both masculine and feminine traits; from the Greek *andro* for "male" and *gyn* for "female."

FIGURE 9.24 GENDER-ROLE DEVELOPMENT

Social-learning theory focuses on a child's passive process of learning about gender through observation, rewards, and punishments, whereas cognitive-developmental theory emphasizes a child's active role in building a gender schema.

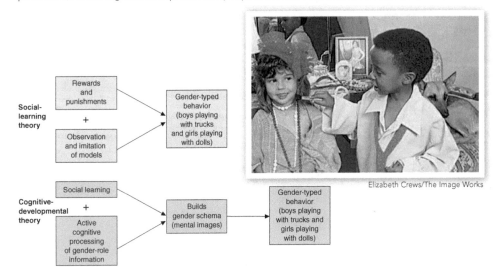

Elizabeth Crews/The Image Works

have found that this blending of traits leads to higher self-esteem and more success and adjustment in today's complex society because it allows us to display whatever behaviors and traits are most appropriate in a given situation (Bem, 1981, 1993; Huang et al., 2012; Kark et al., 2012; Stoltzfus et al., 2011; Wood, 2013).

Recent studies also show that gender roles are becoming less rigidly defined (Cotter et al., 2011; Hollander et al., 2011; Signorielli, 2013). Asian American and Mexican American groups show some of the largest changes toward androgyny, and African Americans remain among the most androgynous of all ethnic groups (Denmark et al., 2005; Duval, 2006; Renzetti et al., 2006).

Ironically, a recent survey of college students at a comparatively liberal university in California found that more than two-thirds of both women and men strongly prefer traditional gender roles when it comes to marriage proposals. In fact, the title of the published research article is: "Girls don't propose! Ew." (Robnett & Leaper, 2013). Furthermore, over 60% of the women surveyed were either "very willing" or "somewhat willing" to take their husband's surname.

Rachael Robnett, the lead author on this research, suggested that this type of "benevolent sexism" looks positive on the surface, but it contributes to power differentials between men and women and does a disservice to women (Lasnier, 2013). What do you think? Would relationships be better if both men and women were free to propose, and if they both kept their own names when they married?

RETRIEVAL PRACTICE: SOCIAL-EMOTIONAL DEVELOPMENT

Self-Test

Completing this self-test and comparing your answers with those in Appendix B provides immediate feedback and helpful practice for exams. Additional interactive, self-tests are available at www.wiley.com/college/huffman.

1. According to Harlow's research with cloth and wire surrogate mother monkeys, _____ is the most important variable for attachment.

a. contact comfort

b. "comfort food"

c. neonatal breast feeding

d. age group peer contact ("free play" periods)

2. According to Kohlberg, moral judgment is self-centered and based on obtaining rewards and avoiding punishment during the _____ level of moral development.

a. trust versus mistrust

b. industry versus inferiority

c. conventional

d. preconventional

3. Calvin would like to wear baggy, torn jeans and a nose ring, but he is concerned that others will disapprove. Calvin is at Kohlberg's _____ level of morality.

a. conformity
b. approval seeking
c. conventional
d. preconventional

4. According to Erikson, industry is the result of the successful completion of the _____ stage of development.

a. infancy and toddlerhood
b. ages 6 through 12
c. young adulthood
d. middle adulthood

Think Critically

1 Describe how attachment has influenced your social development. Which of Ainsworth's attachment styles best describes you?

2 What stage of moral development do you think you would qualify for, according to Kohlberg? Do you agree or disagree with this categorization?

3 How have your sex and gender affected your social development?

realworldpsychology

Do today's college students want women to propose marriage?

HINT: LOOK IN THE MARGIN FOR (Q5)

Summary

1 STUDYING DEVELOPMENT 238

- **Developmental psychology** is the study of age-related changes in behavior and mental processes from conception to death. Development is an ongoing, lifelong process.
- The three most important debates or questions in human development are about *nature versus nurture* (including studies of **maturation** and **critical periods**), *stages versus continuity*, and *stability versus change*.
- Developmental psychologists use two special techniques in their research: **cross-sectional design** and **longitudinal design**. Although both have valuable attributes, each also has disadvantages. Cross-sectional studies can confuse genuine age differences with *cohort effects*. On the other hand, longitudinal studies are expensive and time-consuming, and their results are restricted in generalizability.

2 PHYSICAL DEVELOPMENT 242

- Prenatal development begins at conception and is divided into three stages: the **germinal period**, the **embryonic period**, and the **fetal period**. During pregnancy, the *placenta* serves as the link for food and the excretion of wastes, and it screens out some harmful substances—but not **teratogens**, such as alcohol and nicotine.
- Early childhood is a time of rapid physical development, including brain, motor, and sensory/perceptual development. During *adolescence*, both boys and girls undergo dramatic changes in appearance and physical capacity. **Puberty** is the period of adolescence when a person becomes capable of reproduction. During adulthood, most individuals experience only minor physical changes until middle age. Around age 45–55, women experience *menopause*, the cessation of the menstrual cycle. At the same time, men experience a gradual decline in the production of sperm and testosterone, as well as other physical changes, known as the *male climacteric*.
- After middle age, most physical changes in development are gradual and occur in the heart and arteries and in the sensory receptors. One of the greatest problems for the elderly is

the various negative stereotypes that contribute to our society's widespread **ageism**.

3 COGNITIVE DEVELOPMENT 251

- Three major concepts are central to Piaget's theory: **schemas**, **assimilation**, and **accommodation**. According to Piaget, all children progress through four stages of cognitive development: the **sensorimotor stage**, the **preoperational stage**, the **concrete operational stage**, and the **formal operational stage**. As they move through these stages, children acquire progressively more sophisticated ways of thinking.
- Piaget's account of cognitive development has been enormously influential, but it has also received significant criticisms. For example, Vygotsky emphasized the sociocultural influences on a child's cognitive development, rather than Piaget's internal schemas. He also believed that adults play an important instructor role in development and that this instruction is particularly helpful when it falls within a child's **zone of proximal development (ZPD)**. Piaget has also been criticized for underestimating children's abilities, as well as the genetic and cultural influences on cognitive development.

4 SOCIAL-EMOTIONAL DEVELOPMENT 259

- Harlow's and his colleagues' research with monkeys raised by cloth or wire "mothers" found that *contact comfort* might be the most important factor in **attachment**.
- Using the strange situation procedure, Ainsworth found that children could be divided into three groups: Secure, anxious/avoidant, and anxious/ambivalent. Mary Main, later added a fourth category, disorganized/disoriented.
- In addition to attachment patterns, Baumrind's four parenting styles—*permissive-neglectful*, *permissive-indulgent*, *authoritarian*, and *authoritative*—also affect a child's social development.
- Kohlberg proposed three levels in the evolution of moral reasoning: the **preconventional level** (Stages 1 and 2), the **conventional level** (Stages 3 and 4), and the **postconventional level** (Stages 5 and 6).

- Erikson identified eight **psychosocial stages** of development, each marked by a crisis (such as the adolescent *identity crisis*) related to a specific developmental task.
- In addition to biological *sex* differences, scientists have found numerous **gender** differences relevant to social-emotional development. Most research emphasizes two major theories of **gender-role** development: social learning and cognitive developmental. **Androgyny**, combining both "masculine" and "feminine" traits, helps offset rigid gender-role stereotypes.

◉ applyingrealworldpsychology

We began this chapter with five intriguing Real World Psychology questions, and you were asked to revisit these questions at the end of each section. Questions like these have an important and lasting impact on all of our lives. See if you can answer these additional critical thinking questions related to real world examples.

1. People are often surprised, amused, and sometimes even critical of infants, like the one in this photo, who messily play with their food. Using Piaget's stage of sensorimotor development, explain why this type of "messiness" is a healthy, normal example of cognitive development.

2. What schemas might the child build by "exploring" her food in this way?

3. How might the various attachment styles correlate with Baumrind's parenting styles? Which parenting style do you believe is the best? Why?

4. Do you believe that men and women reason differently about morality? If so, what might be the pros and cons of these differences?

5. Which Eriksonian stage do you think best explains your current personality and life choices?

6. Upon completion of your study of this chapter, which side of the nature–nurture debate do you most support? Why?

KidStock/Blend Images /Getty Images, Inc.

Key Terms

RETRIEVAL PRACTICE Write a definition for each term before turning back to the referenced page to check your answer.

- accommodation 252
- ageism 250
- androgyny [an-drah-juh-nee] 268
- assimilation 252
- attachment 259
- concrete operational stage 254
- conservation 254
- conventional level 264
- critical period 238
- cross-sectional design 240
- developmental psychology 238

- egocentrism 254
- embryonic period 244
- fetal alcohol syndrome (FAS) 245
- fetal period 244
- formal operational stage 255
- gender 267
- gender roles 267
- germinal period 244
- imprinting 238
- longitudinal design 241
- maturation 238

- object permanence 252
- postconventional level 264
- preconventional level 264
- preoperational stage 254
- psychosocial stages 265
- puberty 248
- schema 251
- sensorimotor stage 252
- teratogen 245
- zone of proximal development (ZPD) 258

chapterten

Motivation and Emotion

CHAPTER OUTLINE

realworldpsychology

THINGS YOU'LL LEARN IN CHAPTER 10

Q1 Why might paying students to get good grades be a good idea?

Q2 How can just looking at pictures of high-fat foods make you feel hungry?

Q3 Is motivation a better predictor of math success in children than IQ?

Q4 How can a simple smile reduce stress?

Q5 Why do emotional expressions of Olympic athletes appear the same across all cultures?

THROUGHOUT THE CHAPTER, MARGIN ICONS FOR Q1–Q5 INDICATE WHERE THE TEXT ADDRESSES THESE QUESTIONS.

chapteroverview

What motivates you? Why are you in college and struggling to achieve your lifetime dreams? How do you feel about some of the chronic anxieties and frustrations that generally come with being in college?

Research in *motivation* and *emotion* attempts to answer such "what," "why," and "how" questions. *Motivation* refers to a set of factors that activate, direct, and maintain behavior, usually toward some goal. *Emotion*, on the other hand, refers to a subjective feeling that includes arousal (heart pounding), cognitions (thoughts, values, and expectations), and expressive behaviors (smiles, frowns, and running). In other words, motivation energizes and directs behavior, whereas emotion is the "feeling" response. (Both *motivation* and *emotion* come from the Latin *movere*, meaning "to move.")

In this chapter, we begin with the major theories and concepts of motivation, followed by several important sources of motivation—hunger, eating, achievement, and sexuality. Then we turn to the basic components and theories related to emotion. We conclude with a look at how culture and evolution affect emotion.

THEORIES OF MOTIVATION

LEARNING OBJECTIVES

RETRIEVAL PRACTICE While reading the upcoming sections, respond to each Learning Objective in your own words. Then compare your responses with those found at www.wiley.com/college/huffman.

1 **SUMMARIZE** the three biologically based theories of motivation.

2 **EXPLAIN** how incentives and cognitions affect motivation.

3 **DESCRIBE** how biopsychosocial theories apply to motivation.

Years of research on motivation has created six major theories, which fall into three general categories—*biological*, *psychological*, and *biopsychosocial* **(Table 10.1)**. While studying these theories, try to identify which theory best explains your personal behaviors, such as going to college or choosing a lifetime partner. This type of personal focus will not only improve your exam performance but also may lead to increased self-knowledge and personal motivation!

TABLE 10.1	SIX MAJOR THEORIES OF MOTIVATION	
	Theory	**Description**
Which of the six theories of motivation best explains this behavior?	**Biological**	
	1. Instinct	Motivation results from innate, biological instincts, which are unlearned responses found in almost all members of a species.
	2. Drive reduction	Motivation begins with a biological need (a lack or deficiency) that elicits a *drive* toward behavior that will satisfy the original need and restore homeostasis.
	3. Optimal arousal	Organisms are motivated to achieve and maintain an optimal level of arousal.
	Psychological	
	4. Incentive	Motivation results from external stimuli that "pull" the organism in certain directions.
	5. Cognitive	Motivation is affected by expectations and attributions, or how we interpret or think about our own or others' actions.
	Biopsychosocial	
	6. Maslow's hierarchy of needs	Lower needs like hunger and safety must be satisfied before advancing to higher needs (such as belonging and self-actualization).

Mattias Klum/NG Image Collection

Name That Theory
Curiosity is an important aspect of both human and nonhuman experience. Which of the six theories of motivation best explains this behavior?

© imaginary_nl/iStockphoto

FIGURE 10.1 **INSTINCTS**

Ⓐ Instinctual behaviors are obvious in many animals. Birds build nests, bears hibernate, and salmon swim upstream to spawn.

Ⓑ Sociobiologists such as Edward O. Wilson (1975, 1978) believe that humans also have instincts, like competition or aggression, that are genetically transmitted from one generation to another.

© asiseeit /iStockphoto

Biological Theories

Many theories of **motivation** focus on inborn biological processes that control behavior. Among these biologically oriented theories are *instinct*, *drive-reduction*, and *arousal* theories.

One of the earliest researchers, William McDougall (1908), proposed that humans had numerous instincts, such as repulsion, curiosity, and self-assertiveness. Other researchers later added their favorite instincts, and by the 1920s, the list of recognized instincts had become impossibly long. One researcher found listings for more than 10,000 human instincts (Bernard, 1924).

In addition, the label *instinct* led to unscientific, circular explanations—"men are aggressive because they are instinctively aggressive" or "women are maternal because they have a natural maternal instinct." However, in recent years, a branch of biology called sociobiology has revived the case for **instincts** when strictly defined as a *fixed, unlearned response patterns found in almost all members of a species* **(Figure 10.1)**.

In the 1930s, the concepts of drive and drive reduction began to replace the theory of instincts. According to **drive-reduction theory** (Hull, 1952), when biological needs such as for food, water, and oxygen are unmet, a state of tension known as a *drive* is created. The organism is then motivated to reduce that drive. Drive-reduction theory is based largely on the biological concept of **homeostasis**, a term that literally means "standing still" and describes the body's natural tendency to maintain a state of internal balance **(Figure 10.2)**.

Motivation A set of factors that activate, direct, and maintain behavior, usually toward some goal.

Instinct Fixed, unlearned response patterns found in almost all members of a species.

Drive-reduction theory The theory that motivation begins with a physiological need (a lack or deficiency) that elicits a drive toward behavior that will satisfy the original need; once the need is met, a state of balance (homeostasis) is restored, and motivation decreases.

Homeostasis The body's tendency to maintain a relatively balanced and stable internal state, such as a constant internal temperature.

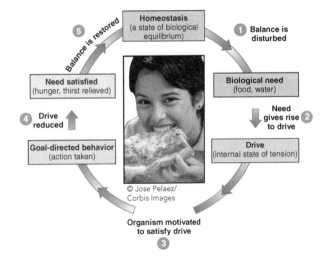

5 Balance is restored
Homeostasis (a state of biological equilibrium)
1 **Balance is disturbed**
Need satisfied (hunger, thirst relieved)
Biological need (food, water)
Need gives rise to drive 2
4 **Drive reduced**
Drive (internal state of tension)
Goal-directed behavior (action taken)
© Jose Pelaez/ Corbis Images
Organism motivated to satisfy drive
3

FIGURE 10.2 **DRIVE-REDUCTION THEORY**
realworldpsychology

When we are hungry or thirsty, the disruption of our normal state of equilibrium creates a drive that motivates us to search for food or water. Once action is taken and the need is satisfied, homeostasis is restored, and our motivation decreases.

Optimal-arousal theory The theory that organisms are motivated to achieve and maintain an optimal level of arousal.

In addition to having obvious biological needs, humans and other animals are innately curious and require a certain amount of novelty and complexity from the environment.

According to **optimal-arousal theory**, organisms are motivated to achieve and maintain an optimal level of arousal that maximizes their performance. Both too much and too little arousal diminish performance **(Figure 10.3)**. The desired amount of arousal also may vary from person to person (see *Test Yourself*).

FIGURE 10.3 **OPTIMAL LEVEL OF AROUSAL**

realworldpsychology

Our need for stimulation (the arousal motive) suggests that behavior efficiency increases as we move from deep sleep to increased alertness. However, once we pass the maximum level of arousal, our performance declines.

TEST YOURSELF: SENSATION SEEKING

psychology and you

What motivates people to bungee jump over deep canyons or white-water raft down dangerous rivers? According to research, these "high-sensation seekers" may be biologically "prewired" to need a higher-than-usual level of stimulation (Zuckerman, 1979, 1994, 2013).

To sample the kinds of questions asked on tests of levels of sensation seeking, circle the choice (a or b) that best describes you:

1. a. I would like a job that requires a lot of traveling.

    b. I would prefer a job in one location.

2. a. I get bored seeing the same old faces.

    b. I like the comfortable familiarity of everyday friends.

3. a. The most important goal of life is to live it to the fullest and experience as much as possible.

    b. The most important goal of life is to find peace and happiness.

4. a. I would like to try parachute jumping.

    b. I would never want to try jumping out of a plane, with or without a parachute.

5. a. I prefer people who are emotionally expressive even if they are a bit unstable.

    b. I prefer people who are calm and even-tempered.

Source: Zuckerman, M. (1978, February). The search for high sensation, *Psychology Today*, pp. 38–46.

Imagemore/Getty Images

Think Critically

1 If your answers to the brief quiz above indicate that you are a high-sensation seeker, what do you do to satisfy that urge, and what can you do to make sure it doesn't get out of control?

2 If you are low in sensation seeking, has this trait interfered with some aspect of your life? If so, what could you do to improve your functioning in this area?

How did you score on the sensation-seeking scale? Research suggests that four distinct factors characterize sensation seeking (Legrand et al., 2007; Manna et al., 2013; Peer & Rosenbloom, 2013; Zuckerman, 2004, 2008, 2013).

1. Thrill and adventure seeking (skydiving, driving fast, or trying to beat a train)

2. Experience seeking (travel, unusual friends, drug experimentation)

3. Disinhibition ("letting loose")

4. Susceptibility to boredom (lower tolerance for repetition and sameness)

Can you see how being very high or very low in sensation seeking might cause problems in relationships with two individuals who score toward opposite extremes? This is true not just between partners or spouses but also between parent and child and therapist and patient. There also might be job difficulties for high-sensation seekers in routine clerical or assembly-line jobs and for low-sensation seekers in highly challenging and variable occupations.

Psychological Theories

Instinct and drive-reduction theories explain some motivations, but why do we continue to eat after our biological need has been completely satisfied? Why do some of us work overtime when our salary is sufficient to meet all basic biological needs? These questions are best answered by psychosocial theories that emphasize incentives and cognition.

Unlike drive-reduction theory, which states that internal factors *push* people in certain directions, **incentive theory** maintains that external stimuli *pull* people toward desirable goals or away from undesirable ones. Most of us initially eat because our hunger "pushes" us (drive-reduction theory). But the sight of apple pie or ice cream too often "pulls" us toward continued eating (incentive theory).

Researchers interested in increasing good grades, adherence to school rules, and regular school attendance found that paying middle-school students $2.00 daily for each goal met was enough incentive to produce higher reading test scores, especially for boys, and those with disciplinary problems in the past (Fryer, 2010). But as you'll discover later in this chapter, this type of *extrinsic reward* (paying students for achieved goals) may create problems of its own.

According to *cognitive theories*, motivation is directly affected by *attributions*, or the ways in which we interpret or think about our own and others' actions (see *Psychology and You*).

Incentive theory The theory that motivation results from external stimuli that "pull" an organism in certain directions.

---

psychology and you   Using Attributions to Explain Grades
Imagine that you receive a high grade on a test in your psychology course. You can interpret that grade in several ways: You earned it because you really studied, you "lucked out" because the test was easy, or the textbook was exceptionally interesting and helpful (our preference!). People who attribute their successes to personal ability and effort tend to work harder toward their goals than people who attribute their successes to luck (Beacham et al., 2011; Martinko et al., 2011; Weiner, 1972, 1982; Zhou & Urhahne, 2013).

© Maridav/iStockphoto

Expectancies, or what we believe or assume will happen, are also important to motivation (Reinhard & Dickhäuser, 2011; Schmidt et al., 2013; Senko & Hulleman, 2013) **(Figure 10.4)**. If you anticipate that you will receive a promotion at work, you're more likely to work overtime for no pay than if you do not expect a promotion.

Don Smetzer/PhotoEdit

FIGURE 10.4 EXPECTANCIES AS PSYCHOLOGICAL MOTIVATORS

What expectations might these students have that would motivate them to master a new language?

Hierarchy of needs Maslow's view that basic human motives form a hierarchy; the lower motives (such as physiological and safety needs) must be met before advancing to higher needs (such as belonging and self-actualization).

Self-actualization The humanistic term for the inborn drive to develop all one's talents and capabilities.

Biopsychosocial Theories

Research in psychology generally emphasizes either biological or psychosocial factors (nature or nurture). But biopsychosocial factors almost always provide the best explanation, and theories of motivation are no exception. One researcher who recognized this was Abraham Maslow (1954, 1970, 1999). Maslow believed we all have numerous needs that compete for fulfillment but that some needs are more important than others. For example, your need for food and shelter is generally more important than your need for good grades.

Maslow's **hierarchy of needs** prioritizes human needs, starting with survival needs (which must be met before others) at the bottom and social, spiritual needs at the top **(Figure 10.5)**.

Maslow's hierarchy of needs seems intuitively correct: A starving person would first look for food, then love and friendship, and then self-esteem. This prioritizing and the concept of **self-actualization**, the inborn drive to develop all our talents and capabilities, are important factors in motivation, and Maslow's work has had a major impact on psychology, economics, and other related fields (Brink & van Bronswijk, 2013; Serlin, 2011; Stoll & Ha-Brookshire, 2012). For example, standard marketing texts often use Maslow's hierarchy of needs to imply that brand consumption is a natural, driving force in shopping behaviors. Ironically, Maslow's work and humanistic ideals would emphasize less, not more, consumption (Hackley, 2007).

Maslow's critics argue that parts of Maslow's theory are poorly researched and biased toward Western preferences for individualism. Furthermore, his theory presupposes that the lower needs must be satisfied before someone can achieve self-actualization, but people sometimes seek to satisfy higher-level needs even when their lower-level needs have not been met (Cullen & Gotell, 2002; Kress et al., 2011; Neher, 1991). For example, protestors all over the world have used starvation as a way to protest unfair laws and political situations.

FIGURE 10.5 **MASLOW'S HIERARCHY OF NEEDS**

Maslow's theory of motivation suggests that we all share a compelling need to "move up"—to grow, improve ourselves, and ultimately become "self-actualized."

Self-actualization needs: to find self-fulfillment and realize one's potential

Esteem needs: to achieve, be competent, gain approval, and excel

Belonging and love needs: to affiliate with others, be accepted, and give and receive affection

Safety needs: to feel secure and safe, to seek pleasure and avoid pain

Physiological needs: hunger, thirst, and maintenance of internal state of the body

Nam Y Huh/©AP/Wide World Photos

Which of Maslow's five levels of need are on display in this photo? Can you see how the needs of the rescuer clearly differ from those of the person who is being rescued?

RETRIEVAL PRACTICE: THEORIES OF MOTIVATION

Self-Test

Completing this self-test and comparing your answers with those in Appendix B provides immediate feedback and helpful practice for exams. Additional interactive, self-tests are available at www.wiley.com/college/huffman.

1. Motivation is best defined as _____.

a. a set of factors that activate, direct, and maintain behavior, usually toward a goal

b. the physiological and psychological arousal that occurs when a person really wants to achieve a goal

c. what makes you do what you do

d. goal-directed unconscious thoughts

2. This diagram illustrates the _____ theory, in which motivation decreases once homeostasis occurs.

a. cognitive

b. hierarchy of needs

c. incentive

d. drive-reduction theory

3. _____ says people are "pulled" by external stimuli to act a certain way.

a. Cognitive theory

b. Incentive theory

c. Maslow's hierarchy of needs

d. Drive reduction theory

4. According to Maslow's _____, some motives have to be satisfied before a person can advance to fulfilling higher motives.

a. psychosexual stages of development

b. moral stages of development

c. psychosocial stages of development

d. hierarchy of needs

Think Critically

1 Why are modern sociobiological theories of instincts more scientifically useful than older instinct theories?

2 At what level would you rank yourself on Maslow's hierarchy of needs? What can you do to advance to a higher level?

realworldpsychology

Why might paying students to get good grades be a good idea?

HINT: LOOK IN THE MARGIN FOR (Q1)

MOTIVATION AND BEHAVIOR

RETRIEVAL PRACTICE While reading the upcoming sections, respond to each Learning Objective in your own words. Then compare your responses with those found at www.wiley.com/college/huffman.

1 DESCRIBE how internal (biological) and external (psychosocial) factors direct hunger and eating as well as how they are involved in serious eating disorders.

2 IDENTIFY the traits of high achievers and explain why they are more motivated than others.

3 SUMMARIZE the major factors in human sexuality.

4 COMPARE intrinsic and extrinsic motivation.

LEARNING OBJECTIVES

Why do people put themselves in dangerous situations? Why do salmon swim upstream to spawn? Behavior results from many motives. For example, we discuss the need for sleep in Chapter 5, and we look at aggression, altruism, and interpersonal attraction in Chapter 14. Here, we focus on three basic motives: hunger, achievement, and sexuality. Then we turn to a discussion of how different kinds of motivation affect our intrinsic interests and performance.

Hunger and Eating

What motivates hunger? Is it your growling stomach? Or is it the sight of a juicy hamburger or the smell of a freshly baked cinnamon roll?

The Stomach

Early hunger researchers believed that the stomach controlled hunger, contracting to send hunger signals when it was empty. Today, we know it's more complicated. As dieters who drink lots of water to keep their stomachs feeling full have been disappointed to discover, sensory input from an empty stomach is not essential for feeling hungry. In fact, humans and nonhuman animals without stomachs continue to experience hunger.

However, there is a connection between the stomach and feeling hungry. Receptors in the stomach and intestines detect levels of nutrients, and specialized pressure receptors in the stomach walls signal feelings of either emptiness or *satiety* (fullness). The stomach and other parts of the gastrointestinal tract also release chemical signals that play a role in hunger (Hellström, 2013; Moran & Daily, 2011; Nicolaidis, 2011).

Biochemistry

Like the stomach, the brain and other parts of the body produce numerous neurotransmitters, hormones, enzymes, and other chemicals that affect hunger and satiety (Arumugam et al., 2008; Cooper et al., 2011; Hellström, 2013; Stadlbauer et al., 2013). Research in this area is complex because of the large number of known (and unknown) bodily chemicals and the interactions among them. It's unlikely that any one chemical controls our hunger and eating. Other internal factors, such as *thermogenesis*—the heat generated in response to food ingestion—also play a role (Acheson et al., 2011; Drapeau & Gallant, 2013; Ping-Delfos & Soares, 2011).

The Brain

In addition to its chemical signals, particular brain structures also influence hunger and eating. Let's look at the *hypothalamus*, which helps regulate eating, drinking, and body temperature.

Early research suggested that one area of the hypothalamus, the lateral hypothalamus (LH), stimulates eating, while another area, the ventromedial hypothalamus (VMH), creates feelings of satiation, signaling the animal to stop eating. When the VMH area was destroyed in rats, researchers found that the rats overate to the point of extreme obesity **(Figure 10.6)**. In contrast, when the LH area was destroyed, the animals starved to death if they were not force-fed.

FIGURE 10.6 HOW THE BRAIN AFFECTS EATING

Several areas of the brain are active in the regulation of hunger.

Ⓐ This diagram shows a section of the human brain, including the ventromedial hypothalamus (VMH) and the lateral hypothalamus (LH), which are involved in the regulation of hunger.

Hypothalamus
Pituitary gland

Lateral hypothalamic area

Ventromedial hypothalamic region

Ⓑ After the ventromedial area of the hypothalamus of the rat on the left was destroyed, its body weight tripled. A rat of normal weight is shown on the right for comparison.

Olivier Voisin/Photo Researchers

Later research, however, showed that the LH and VMH areas are not simple on–off switches for eating. For example, lesions (damage) to the VMH make animals picky eaters that reject a wide variety of foods. The lesions also increase insulin secretion, which may cause overeating (Challem et al., 2000; Figlewicz & Sipols, 2010). Today, researchers know that the hypothalamus plays an important role in hunger and eating, but it is not the brain's "eating center." In fact, hunger and eating, like virtually all other behaviors, are influenced by numerous neural circuits that run throughout the brain (Berman et al., 2013; Nolan-Poupart et al., 2013; van der Laan et al., 2011).

Psychosocial Factors

The internal motivations for hunger we've discussed (the stomach, biochemistry, and the brain) are powerful. But *psychosocial factors*—for example, spying a luscious dessert or a McDonald's billboard, or even simply noticing that it's almost lunchtime—can be equally important stimulus cues for hunger and eating. In fact, researchers in one study found that simply looking at pictures of high-fat foods, such as hamburgers, cookies, and cake, can stimulate parts of the brain in charge of appetite, thereby increasing feelings of hunger and cravings for sweet and salty foods (Luo et al., 2013).

Another important psychosocial influence on when, what, where, and why we eat is cultural conditioning. North Americans, for example, tend to eat dinner at around 6 p.m., whereas people in Spain and South America tend to eat around 10 p.m. When it comes to *what* we eat, have you ever eaten rat, dog, or horse meat? If you are a typical North American, this might sound repulsive to you, yet most Hindus in India would feel a similar revulsion at the thought of eating meat from cows.

In sum, numerous biological and psychosocial factors operate in the regulation of hunger and eating **(Figure 10.7)**, and researchers are still struggling to discover and explain how all these processes work together.

FIGURE 10.7 **KEY MECHANISMS IN HUNGER REGULATION**

Different parts of your body communicate with your brain to trigger feelings of hunger.

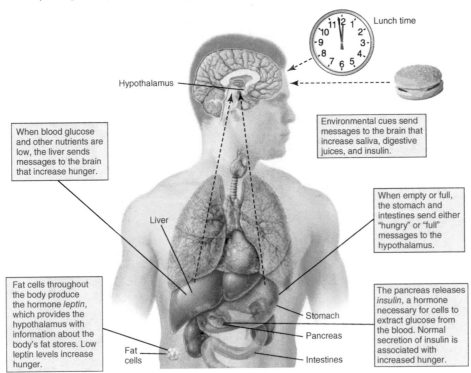

Eating Disorders

The same biopsychosocial forces that explain hunger and eating also play a role in four serious eating disorders: *obesity, anorexia nervosa, bulimia nervosa*, and *binge-eating disorder*.

Obesity

Imagine yourself being born and living your life on another planet, but you could receive all the Earth's normal television channels. Given that almost all the television stars, newscasters, and commercial spokespeople you've ever seen are very thin, would you wonder why there are so many ads promoting weight loss? How would you explain the recent news that obesity has reached epidemic proportions in the United States and other developed nations?

Obviously, there is large gap between the select few appearing on television and the real world. In fact, according to the latest 2013 data, more than one-third of adults in the United States are considered to be overweight, and another third are considered to be medically obese (American Heart Association, 2013; Corsica & Perri, 2013; Gallup Well-Being, 2013). In 2013, obesity was officially classified as a disease in the DSM-5 (American Psychiatric Association, 2013). (See Chapter 12 for a discussion of the DSM-5.)

Obesity Having a body mass index of 30 or above, based on height and weight.

What is **obesity**? The most widely used measure of weight status is *body mass index (BMI)*, which is a single numerical value that calculates height in relation to weight (see *Psychology and You*). Sadly, obesity is one of our greatest health threats because of its significant contribution to serious illnesses like heart disease, diabetes, stroke and certain cancers (American Heart Association, 2013; Corsica & Perri, 2013). In addition, each year, billions of dollars are spent treating serious and life-threatening medical problems related to obesity, with consumers spending billions more on largely ineffective weight-loss products and services.

Controlling weight is a particularly difficult task for people in the United States. We are among the most sedentary people of all, and we've become accustomed to "supersized" cheeseburgers, "Big Gulp" drinks, and huge servings of dessert (Duffey & Popkin, 2013; Fisher et al., 2013; Herman & Polivy, 2008). We've also learned that we should eat three meals a day, whether we're hungry or not; that "tasty" food requires lots of salt, sugar, and fat; and that food is an essential part of the workplace and all social gatherings **(Figure 10.8)**.

FIGURE 10.8 A FATTENING ENVIRONMENT | realworldpsychology

One of the most popular television programs, *The Biggest Loser*, shows how difficult it is for contestants to lose weight. Even more difficult, and seldom shown, is how hard it is to maintain weight loss. To make it permanent, we need to make permanent lifestyle changes regarding exercise and the amount and types of foods we eat and when we eat them.
Can you see how our everyday environments, such as in the workplace shown here, might prevent a person from making healthy lifestyle changes?

Dave Kotinsky/Getty Images

Christian Thomas/Getty Images

psychology and you **Calculating Your Own BMI** To determine your BMI, use the *Adult BMI Calculator* at the Centers for Disease Control and Prevention site: http://www.cdc.gov/healthyweight/assessing/bmi/adult_bmi/

Or follow these three steps:

1. Multiply your weight in pounds by 703.
2. Multiply your height in inches by itself (e.g., If you are 63 inches in height, you would multiply 63 x 63).
3. Divide step 1 by step 2.

If your BMI is:	You are:
18.5 and below	Underweight
18.5 to 24.9	Normal weight
25.0 to 29.9	Overweight
30.0 and above	Obese

Note: If your BMI is due to muscle or bone, rather than fat, it's possible to have a high BMI and still be healthy.

Source: Centers for Disease Control and Prevention, 2011.

However, we all know some people who can seemingly eat anything they want and still not add pounds. This may be a result of their ability to burn calories more effectively in the process of thermogenesis, a higher metabolic rate, or other factors. Adoption and twin studies indicate that genetics also plays a role (Andersson & Walley, 2011; Bernhard et al., 2013; Xia & Grant, 2013). Unfortunately, identifying the genes for obesity is difficult. Researchers have isolated a large number of genes that contribute to normal and abnormal weight (Camarena et al., 2004; Warrington et al., 2013; Xia & Grant, 2013).

The good news is that one of these identified genes may provide a potential genetic explanation for why some people overeat and run a greater risk for obesity. Recent research finds that people who carry variants of the FTO gene don't feel full after eating and overeat because they have higher blood levels of ghrelin—a known hunger-producing hormone (Karra et al., 2013). But the researchers cautioned that more research is needed, and that human appetite and obesity are undoubtedly more complex than a single hormone. In addition, this focus on genes should not encourage people to feel helpless against obesity. Ghrelin also can be reduced by exercise and a high-protein diet (Thompson, 2013; Williams, 2013).

Other Eating Disorders

Like obesity, the other major eating disorders—*anorexia nervosa, bulimia nervosa,* and *binge-eating disorder*—are widespread. They're also found in all cultures, ethnicities, and socioeconomic classes, but are more common in women (American Psychiatric Association, 2013; Insel, 2012; Mond & Arrighi, 2011; Smink et al., 2012). **Anorexia nervosa** is characterized by an overwhelming fear of becoming obese, a need for control, the use of dangerous weight-loss measures, and a body image that is so distorted that even a skeletal, emaciated body is perceived as fat. The resulting extreme malnutrition often leads to emaciation, osteoporosis, bone fractures, interruption of menstruation, and loss of brain tissue. A significant percentage of individuals with anorexia nervosa ultimately die of the disorder (Akey et al., 2013; Kaye et al., 2013; Reel, 2013).

Occasionally, a person suffering from anorexia nervosa succumbs to the desire to eat and gorges on food, then vomits or takes laxatives. However, this type of bingeing and purging is more characteristic of **bulimia nervosa**. Individuals with bulimia go on recurrent eating binges and then purge by self-induced vomiting or the use of laxatives. They often show impulsivity in other areas, sometimes engaging in excessive shopping, alcohol abuse, or petty shoplifting (Claes et al., 2011;

Anorexia nervosa An eating disorder characterized by severe loss of weight resulting from self-imposed starvation and an obsessive fear of obesity.

Bulimia nervosa An eating disorder characterized by recurrent episodes of consuming large quantities of food (bingeing), followed by self-induced vomiting (purging), extreme exercise, laxative use, and other medications.

Binge-eating disorder An eating disorder characterized by recurrent episodes of consuming large amounts of food in a discrete period of time, while feeling a lack of control, but not followed by purge behaviors.

Fischer et al., 2013; Vaz-Leal et al., 2011). The vomiting associated with bulimia nervosa causes severe damage to the teeth, throat, and stomach. It also leads to cardiac arrhythmia, metabolic deficiencies, and serious digestive disorders.

Note that bulimia is similar to but not the same as **binge-eating disorder**. This disorder involves recurrent episodes of consuming large amounts of food in a discrete period of time, while feeling a lack of control over eating. However, the individual does not try to purge (American Psychiatric Association, 2013). Individuals with binge-eating disorder generally eat more rapidly than normal, eat until they are uncomfortably full and eat when not feeling physically hungry. They also tend to eat alone because of embarrassment at the large quantities they are consuming, and they feel disgusted, depressed, or very guilty after bingeing.

There are many suspected causes of anorexia nervosa, bulimia nervosa, and binge-eating disorder. Some theories focus on physical causes, such as hypothalamic disorders, low levels of various neurotransmitters, and genetic or hormonal disorders. Other theories emphasize psychosocial factors, such as a need for perfection, a perceived loss of control, teasing about body weight, destructive thought patterns, depression, dysfunctional families, distorted body image, and emotional or sexual abuse (e.g., American Psychiatric Association, 2013; Caqueo-Urizar et al., 2011; Friederich et al., 2013; Heaner & Walsh, 2013; Jenkins et al., 2013; Kaye et al., 2013; Kreipe et al., 2012; Steiger et al., 2013).

Culture and ethnicity also play important roles in eating disorders (George & Franko, 2010; Pilecki et al., 2012; Swanson et al., 2012). For instance, African Americans report fewer eating and dieting disorders and greater body satisfaction than do Caucasian and European Americans (Taylor et al., 2013; Watson et al., 2013; Whaley et al., 2011). Interestingly, binge-eating disorder appears to be equally represented across racial/ethnic minority groups in the United States (Franko et al., 2013; Taylor et al., 2013). This research suggests that both culture and biology help explain eating disorders. Regardless of the causes, it is important to recognize the symptoms of anorexia, bulimia, and binge-eating disorder **(Table 10.2)** and to seek therapy if the symptoms apply to you.

TABLE 10.2	DSM-5 SYMPTOMS OF ANOREXIA NERVOSA, BULIMIA NERVOSA, AND BINGE-EATING DISORDER

Anorexia Nervosa	Bulimia Nervosa	Binge-Eating Disorder	
• Body mass index equal to or below 17	• Recurrent episodes of binge eating	• Recurrent episodes of binge eating	
• Intense fear of becoming fat or gaining weight, or persistent behavior that interferes with weight gain, even though underweight	• During the episode of binge eating, consuming, in a discrete period of time, an amount of food that is much larger than most people would consume	• During the episode of binge eating, consuming, in a discrete period of time, an amount of food that is much larger than most people would consume	
• Disturbance in one's body image or perceived weight	• Feeling a lack of control over eating during the episode of binge eating	• Feeling a lack of control over eating during the episode of binge eating	Chris Wolf/Getty Images
• Denial of seriousness of abnormally low body weight	• Purging behavior (self-induced vomiting; misuse of laxatives, diuretics, or other medications)	• No compensatory purging behavior (self-induced vomiting; misuse of laxatives, diuretics, or other medications)	Many celebrities, like Lady Gaga, have publicly shared their battles with eating disorders. But does this type of publicity increase or decrease the chance that their fans will suffer similar problems?
• Self-evaluation unduly influenced by body shape or weight	• Fasting and/or excessive exercise to prevent weight gain	• During the episode of binge eating, eating more rapidly than normal, eating until uncomfortably full and when not feeling physically hungry, eating alone because of embarrassment, feeling disgusted, depressed, or very guilty after bingeing	
	• Self-evaluation unduly influenced by body shape or weight		

Source: American Psychiatric Association, 2013.

The key point to remember is that all eating disorders are serious and chronic conditions that require treatment. In fact, some studies find that they have the highest mortality rates of all mental illnesses (Akey et al., 2013; Friederich et al., 2013; Insel, 2012; Reel, 2013)!

Achievement

Do you wonder what motivates Olympic athletes to work so hard for a gold medal? What about someone like Oprah Winfrey, famous television star, thriving businesswoman, and generous philanthropist? Or Mark Zuckerberg, cofounder of Facebook? What drives some people to high achievement?

The key to understanding what motivates high-achieving individuals lies in what psychologist Henry Murray (1938) identified as a high need for achievement (nAch), or **achievement motivation**. Several traits distinguish people who have this high nAch (Deaner, 2013; McClelland, 1958, 1987, 1993; Mokrova et al., 2013; Schunk & Zimmerman, 2013; Senko et al., 2008; Sheard, 2013):

Achievement motivation The desire to excel, especially in competition with others.

- **Preference for moderately difficult tasks** People high in nAch (need for achievement) avoid tasks that are too easy because they offer little challenge or satisfaction. They also avoid extremely difficult tasks because the probability of success is too low.

- **Competitiveness** High-achievement-oriented people are more attracted to careers and tasks that involve competition and an opportunity to excel.

- **Preference for clear goals with competent feedback** High-achievement-oriented people tend to prefer tasks with clear outcomes and situations in which they can receive feedback on their performance. They also prefer criticism from a harsh but competent evaluator to criticism from one who is friendlier but less competent.

- **Self-regulation and personal responsibility** High-achievement-oriented people purposefully control their thoughts and behaviors to attain their goals. In addition, they prefer being personally responsible for a project so that they can feel satisfied when the task is well done.

- **Mental toughness and persistence** High-achievement-oriented people have a mindset that allows them to persevere through difficult circumstances. It includes attributes like sacrifice and self-denial, which overcome obstacles while also maintaining concentration and motivation when things are going well. In one study, 47% of high nAch individuals persisted on an "unsolvable task" until time was called, compared with only 2% of people with low nAch.

- **More accomplished** People who have high nAch scores do better than others on exams, earn better grades in school, and excel in their chosen professions.

Achievement orientation appears to be largely learned in early childhood, primarily through interactions with parents **(Figure 10.9)**. Highly motivated children tend to have parents who encourage independence and frequently reward successes (Aunola et al., 2013; Katz et al., 2011; Pomerantz & Kempner, 2013). In fact, children's motivation for academic success—along with their study skills—are better predictors of long-term math achievement than IQ (Murayama et al., 2012). Our cultural values also affect achievement needs (Chi, 2013; Greenfield & Quiroz, 2013; Xu & Barnes, 2011).

Q3

FIGURE 10.9 FUTURE ACHIEVER

A study by Richard de Charms and Gerald Moeller (1962) found a significant correlation between the achievement themes in children's literature and the industrial accomplishments of various countries.

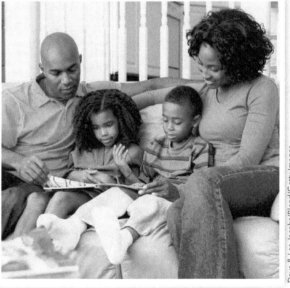

Dave & Les Jacobs/Blend/Getty Images

Sexuality

Obviously, there is strong motivation to engage in sexual behavior: It's essential for the survival of our species, and it's also pleasurable. But *sexuality* includes much more than reproduction. For most humans (and some other animals), a sexual relationship fulfills many needs, including the need for connection, intimacy, pleasure, and the release of sexual tension. Given the large role sex plays throughout our lives, can you predict how the quality of the first sexual experience might affect later relationships? See the *Psych Science* box.

PSYCHSCIENCE

DO INITIAL SEXUAL EXPERIENCES HAVE A LASTING IMPACT?

To study this question, researchers asked 331 young men and women to anonymously complete a questionnaire measuring degree of anxiety, regret, and contentment surrounding their first sexual act, as well as rating their current sex life (Smith & Shaffer, 2013).

As you might expect, those who reported more positive first-time experiences also reported higher levels of physical and emotional satisfaction in their subsequent and current relationships. Specifically, those who felt loved and respected by their partner during their first sexual experience found later encounters more emotionally satisfying. Sadly, people who described feelings of anxiety and negativity during their first sexual experience reported lower sexual satisfaction with their current sex lives.

Why is this research important? Some people may believe that the first sexual experience is "no big deal" or something you just have to get out of the way. However, this research reveals that it may have a lasting impact.

RESEARCH CHALLENGE

1. Based on the information provided, did this study (Smith & Shaffer, 2013) use descriptive, correlational, and/or experimental research?

2. If you chose:
   - descriptive research, is this a naturalistic observation, survey/interview, case study, or archival research?
   - correlational research, is this a positive, negative, or zero correlation?
   - experimental research, label the IV, DV, experimental group(s), and control group.

>> CHECK YOUR ANSWERS IN APPENDIX B.

Note: The information provided in this study is admittedly limited, but the level of detail is similar to what is presented in most textbooks and public reports of research findings. Answering these questions, and then comparing your answers to those in the Appendix, will help you become a better critical thinker and consumer of scientific research.

William Masters and Virginia Johnson (1966) were the first to conduct laboratory studies on what happens to the human body during sexual activity. They attached recording devices to male and female volunteers and monitored or filmed their physical responses as they moved from nonarousal to orgasm and back to nonarousal. They labeled the bodily changes during this series of events a **sexual response cycle (Figure 10.10)**. Researchers have further characterized differences between sexual response patterns in men and women **(Figure 10.11)**.

Sexual response cycle Masters and Johnson's description of the four-stage bodily response to sexual arousal, which consists of excitement, plateau, orgasm, and resolution.

Sexual Orientation

Of course, an important part of people's sexuality is the question of to whom they are sexually attracted. What leads some people to be sexually interested in members of their own sex, the opposite sex, or both sexes? The roots of human **sexual orientation** are poorly understood. However, most studies suggest that genetics and biology play the dominant role (Ashley, 2013; Bao & Swaab, 2011; Hines, 2013; LeVay, 2011; Segal, 2013). For example, studies on identical twins found that if one identical twin was gay, the second twin was also gay 48 to 65% of the time, whereas

Sexual orientation A primary erotic attraction toward members of the same sex (homosexual, gay, lesbian), both sexes (bisexual), or the other sex (heterosexual).

FIGURE 10.10 **MASTERS AND JOHNSON'S VIEW OF THE SEXUAL RESPONSE CYCLE**

Masters and Johnson identified a typical four-stage pattern of sexual response. Note that this simplified description does not account for individual variation and should not be used to judge what's "normal."

2 During the **plateau phase**, physiological and sexual arousal continue at heightened levels. In men, the penis becomes more engorged and erect while in the woman, the vagina expands. As arousal reaches its peak, both sexes may experience a feeling that orgasm is imminent and inevitable.

3 The **orgasm phase** involves a highly intense and pleasurable release of tension. In women, muscles around the vagina squeeze the vaginal walls in and out and the uterus pulsates. Muscles at the base of the penis contract in the man, causing ejaculation, the discharge of seminal fluid.

1 The **excitement phase** can last for minutes or hours. Arousal is initiated through touching, fantasy, or erotic stimuli. Heart rate and respiration increase and increased blood flow to the genital region causes penile or clitoral erection, and vaginal lubrication in women.

4 Physiological responses gradually return to normal during the **resolution phase**. After one orgasm, most men enter a **refractory phase**, during which further excitement to orgasm is considered impossible. Many women (and some men), however, are capable of multiple orgasms in fairly rapid succession.

the rate for fraternal twins was 26 to 30% (Ando et al., 2013; Hyde, 2005; Långstrom et al., 2010; Moutinho et al., 2011).

Research with rats and sheep hints that prenatal hormone levels may also affect fetal brain development and sexual orientation (Bagermihl, 1999; Hines, 2013; Roselli et al., 2011). However, the effects of hormones on human sexual orientation are unknown. Furthermore, no well-controlled study has ever found a difference in adult hormone levels between heterosexuals and gays and lesbians (Hall & Schaeff, 2008; Hines, 2013; LeVay, 2003, 2011).

FIGURE 10.11 **DIFFERENCES BETWEEN MALE AND FEMALE SEXUAL RESPONSE PATTERNS**

Although the overall pattern of sexual response is similar in the two sexes, there is more variation in specific patterns among women.

A Immediately after orgasm, men generally enter a refractory period, which lasts from several minutes to up to a day.

B Female sexual responses generally follow one or more of three basic patterns.

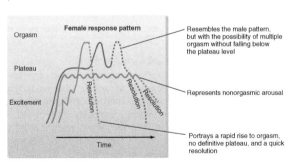

chapter 10 MOTIVATION AND EMOTION

TABLE 10.3 SEXUAL ORIENTATION MYTHS

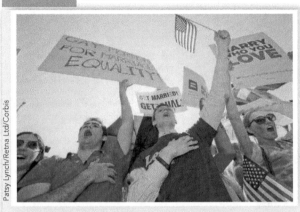

Patsy Lynch/Retna Ltd/Corbis

Myth #1: *Seduction theory:* Gays and lesbians were seduced as children by adults of their own sex.

Myth #2: *"By default" theory:* Gays and lesbians were unable to attract partners of the other sex or have experienced unhappy heterosexual experiences.

Myth #3: *Poor parenting theory:* Sons become gay because of domineering mothers and weak fathers. Daughters become lesbians because their mothers were weak or absent or their fathers were their primary role model.

Myth #4: *Modeling theory:* Children raised by gay and lesbian parents usually end up adopting their parents' sexual orientation.

On June 26, 2013, the U.S. Supreme Court ruled the federal Defense of Marriage Act (DOMA), which defined marriage as a union between one man and one woman, unconstitutional. This decision, along with other judicial and legislative action and changing societal views surrounding gay marriage, has brought attitudes about sexual orientation into full public debate.

Scientific research has disproved several widespread myths and misconceptions about homosexuality (Asley, 2013; Bergstrom-Lynch, 2008; Drucker, 2010; LeVay, 2003, 2011) **(Table 10.3)**. Although mental health authorities long ago discontinued labeling homosexuality as a mental illness, homosexuality continues to be a divisive societal issue. Gays, lesbians, bisexuals, and transgendered people often confront **sexual prejudice**, and many endure verbal and physical attacks, disrupted family and peer relationships, and high rates of anxiety, depression, and suicide (Johns et al., 2013; Nadal, 2013; Plöderl et al., 2013; Rivers, 2011). Sexual prejudice is a socially reinforced phenomenon, not an individual pathology (as the older term *homophobia* implies).

Sexual prejudice A negative attitude toward an individual because of her or his sexual orientation.

Extrinsic Versus Intrinsic Motivation

Should parents reward children for getting good grades? There is an ongoing controversy within psychological research over whether giving external, or extrinsic, rewards increases or decreases motivation (e.g., Anderman & Dawson, 2011; Anik et al., 2011; Babula, 2013; Deci & Moller, 2005; Deci & Ryan, 2012; Gunderman & Kamer, 2011; Kerr et al., 2013). Some researchers are concerned that providing such **extrinsic motivation** will seriously affect the individual's internal, **intrinsic motivation**. When we perform a task for no ulterior purpose, we are intrinsically motivated ("because I like it" or "because it's fun"). In contrast, when we perform a task for a reward, we are extrinsically motivated.

Extrinsic motivation Motivation based on external rewards or threats of punishment.

Intrinsic motivation Motivation resulting from internal, personal satisfaction from a task or activity.

© perkmeup /iStockphoto

realworldpsychology **Problems with Extrinsic Rewards** Some research has shown that people who are given extrinsic rewards like money or praise for an intrinsically satisfying activity, such as watching TV, playing cards, or even engaging in sex, often lose enjoyment and interest and may decrease the time they spend on the activity (Hennessey & Amabile, 1998; Kohn, 2000; Moneta & Siu, 2002). For example, one study of visitors to a national park found that those who were intrinsically motivated had measurably higher positive feelings and higher life-satisfaction levels than those who were extrinsically motivated (Cini et al., 2013). Similarly, 2-year-olds who receive rewards for helping someone else—which, like going to a national park, should be an intrinsically rewarding activity—are later less likely to offer help than are those who receive no reward (Warneken & Tomasello, 2008).

FIGURE 10.12 WHEN EXTRINSIC REWARDS ARE MOTIVATING

Extrinsic rewards used to control or gain approval inhibit intrinsic motivation (**a**). But when they inform or provide valuable feedback, they tend to increase motivation and enjoyment (**b**).

Ⓐ If extrinsic rewards are used to control or gain approval—for example, when schools pay all students for simple attendance or when parents give children approval or privileges for achieving good grades—they often decrease motivation (Eisenberger & Armeli, 1997; Eisenberger & Rhoades, 2002; Houlfort, 2006).

Ⓑ Extrinsic rewards can be motivating if they are used to produce intrinsic motivation. For example, when superior performance is recognized with an award or a special "no strings attached" treat (Deci, 1995), it may increase enjoyment.

As it turns out, not all extrinsic motivation is bad. As you can see in **Figure 10.12a**, it depends on how extrinsic rewards are used. When they are used to control or gain approval, as when schools pay all students for simple attendance or parents give children approval or privileges for good grades, they often decrease motivation (Eisenberger & Armeli, 1997; Eisenberger & Rhoades, 2002; Houlfort, 2006). On the other hand, extrinsic rewards can be motivating if they are used to inform a person of improved or superior performance or as a special "no strings attached" treat (Deci, 1995; Emmett & McGee, 2013; Panagopoulos, 2013). (See **Figure 10.12b**.) In fact, they may intensify the desire to do well again.

oices from the Classroom

When Extrinsic Motivation Becomes Intrinsic When I discuss the topic of motivation, I always tell my students a piece of my life story. I am a first-generation college student. Neither of my parents had a high school diploma. Their goal was to have their children graduate from high school. After graduation, I was working in a local grocery store and realized that that I didn't want to do that for my entire life. Wanting more in life, I began attending the local community college when I was 23 years old, where I soon met with academic success. Boy, did it feel good! I enjoyed succeeding in my classes. Maybe I could do this college thing! I put together a plan to finish community college, get a B.S. degree in psychology, and eventually a Ph.D. What began as *extrinsic motivation* turned into *intrinsic motivation*. These are not just esoteric concepts; they apply to real life!

Professor Vicki Ritts
St. Louis Community College, Meramec Campus
St. Louis, Missouri

RETRIEVAL PRACTICE: MOTIVATION AND BEHAVIOR

Self-Test

Completing this self-test and comparing your answers with those in Appendix B provides immediate feedback and helpful practice for exams. Additional interactive, self-tests are available at www.wiley.com/college/huffman.

1. Maria appears to be starving herself and has obviously lost a lot of weight in just a few months. You suspect she might be suffering from _____.

   a. anorexia nervosa   b. bulimia nervosa
   c. obesity phobia   d. none of these options

2. The desire to excel, especially in competition with others, is known as _____.

   a. drive-reduction theory   b. intrinsic motivation
   c. achievement motivation   d. all these options

3. _____ is a term for negative attitudes toward someone based on his or her sexual orientation.

   a. Heterophobia   b. Heterosexism
   c. Sexual prejudice   d. Sexual phobia

4. A high school began paying students $5 for each day they attended school. Overall rates of attendance increased in the first few weeks and then fell below the original starting point. The most likely reason is that _____.

   a. the students felt going to school wasn't worth $5   b. money is a secondary reinforcer, not a primary one
   c. extrinsic rewards decreased the intrinsic value of attending school   d. the students' expectancies changed to fit the situation

Think Critically

1 Most adults (and many children) find it difficult to control their weight. Using information from this chapter, can you identify the factors or motives that best explain your experience?

2 How can you restructure elements of your personal, work, or school life to increase intrinsic motivation over extrinsic?

realworldpsychology

How can just looking at pictures of high-fat foods make you feel hungry?

Is motivation a better predictor of math success in children than IQ?

HINT: LOOK IN THE MARGIN FOR AND

COMPONENTS AND THEORIES OF EMOTION

LEARNING OBJECTIVES

RETRIEVAL PRACTICE While reading the upcoming sections, respond to each Learning Objective in your own words. Then compare your responses with those found at www.wiley.com/college/huffman.

1 DESCRIBE the biological, cognitive, and behavioral components of emotion.
2 COMPARE the three major theories of emotion.
3 EXPLAIN cultural similarities and differences in emotion.
4 REVIEW the problems with relying on polygraph testing as a lie detector.

Emotion A complex pattern of feelings that includes arousal (heart pounding), cognitions (thoughts, values, and expectations), and expressive behaviors (smiles, frowns, and gestures).

Emotions play an important role in our lives. They color our dreams, memories, and perceptions. When they are disordered, they contribute significantly to psychological problems (Christenfeld & Mandler, 2013; Whalen et al., 2013). But what do we really mean by the term **emotion**? In everyday usage, we use it to describe feeling states; we feel "thrilled" when our political candidate wins an election, "dejected" when our candidate loses, and "miserable" when our loved ones reject us. Obviously, what you and I mean by these terms, or what we individually experience with different emotions, can vary greatly among individuals.

Three Components of Emotion

Psychologists define and study emotion according to three basic components—*biological*, *cognitive*, and *behavioral*.

Biological (Arousal) Component

Internal physical changes occur in our bodies whenever we experience an emotion. Imagine walking alone on a dark street and having someone jump from behind a stack of boxes and start running toward you. How would you respond? Like most other people, you would probably interpret the situation as threatening and would run. Your predominant emotion, fear, would inspire several physiological reactions, such as increased heart rate and blood pressure, perspiration, and goose bumps (piloerection). Such biological reactions are controlled by certain brain structures and by the autonomic branch of the nervous system (ANS).

Our emotional experiences appear to result from important interactions between several areas of the brain, particularly the *cerebral cortex* and *limbic system* (Feinstein, 2013; Langenecker et al., 2005; Panksepp, 2005; Whalen et al., 2013). As we discuss in Chapter 2, the cerebral cortex, the outermost layer of the brain, serves as our body's ultimate control and information-processing center, including our ability to recognize and regulate our emotions.

Studies of the limbic system, located in the innermost part of the brain, have shown that one area, the **amygdala**, plays a key role in emotion—especially fear **(Figure 10.13)**. It sends signals to the other areas of the brain, causing increased heart rate and all the other physiological reactions related to fear.

Emotional arousal sometimes occurs without our conscious awareness. According to psychologist Joseph LeDoux (1996, 2002, 2007), when the *thalamus* (our brain's sensory switchboard) receives sensory inputs, it sends separate messages up to the cortex, which "thinks" about the stimulus, and to the amygdala, which immediately activates the body's alarm system. Although this dual pathway occasionally leads to "false alarms," such as when we mistake a stick for a snake, LeDoux believes it is a highly adaptive warning system essential to our survival. He states that "the time saved by the amygdala in acting on the thalamic interpretation, rather than waiting for the cortical input, may be the difference between life and death" (LeDoux, 1996, p. 166).

As important as the brain is to emotion, it is the *autonomic nervous system* (Chapter 2) that produces the obvious signs of arousal. These largely automatic responses result from interconnections between the ANS and various glands and muscles **(Figure 10.14)**.

Cognitive (Thinking) Component

Emotional reactions are very individual: What you experience as intensely pleasurable may be boring or aversive to another. To study the cognitive (thought) component of emotions, psychologists typically use self-report techniques, such as paper-and-pencil tests, surveys, and interviews. However, people are sometimes unable or unwilling to accurately remember or describe their emotional states. For these reasons, our cognitions about our own and others' emotions are difficult to measure scientifically. This is why many researchers supplement participants' reports on their emotional experiences with methods that assess emotional experience indirectly (e.g., measuring physiological responses such as heart rate, pupil dilation, blood flow).

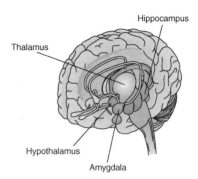

FIGURE 10.13 THE LIMBIC SYSTEM'S ROLE IN EMOTION

In addition to being involved in drive regulation, memory, and other functions, the limbic system is very important in emotions. It consists of several subcortical structures that form a border (or limbus) around the brain stem.

Amygdala A part of the limbic system structure linked to the production and regulation of emotions.

Sympathetic		Parasympathetic
Pupils dilated	**Eyes**	Pupils constricted
Decreased saliva	**Mouth**	Increased saliva
Vessels constricted (skin cold and clammy)	**Skin**	Vessels dilated (normal blood flow)
Respiration increased	**Lungs**	Respiration normal
Increased heart rate	**Heart**	Decreased heart rate
Increased epinephrine and norepinephrine	**Adrenal glands**	Decreased epinephrine and norepinephrine
Decreased motility	**Digestion**	Increased motility

FIGURE 10.14 EMOTION AND THE AUTONOMIC NERVOUS SYSTEM

During emotional arousal, the sympathetic branch of the autonomic nervous system prepares the body for fight or flight. (The hormones epinephrine and norepinephrine keep the system under sympathetic control until the emergency is over.) The parasympathetic branch returns the body to a more relaxed state (homeostasis).

FIGURE 10.15 DUCHENNE SMILE

People who show a Duchenne, or real, smile
(**a**) and laughter elicit more positive responses
from strangers and enjoy better interpersonal
relationships and personal adjustment
than those who use a social smile (**b**) (Keltner
et al., 1999; Platt et al., 2013; Prkachin &
Silverman, 2002).

Courtesy Richard Hosey

Behavioral (Expressive) Component

Emotional expression is a powerful form of communication, and facial expressions may be our most important form of emotional communication. Researchers have developed sensitive techniques to measure subtleties of feeling and to differentiate honest expressions from fake ones. Perhaps most interesting is the difference between the *social smile* and the *Duchenne smile* (named after French anatomist Duchenne de Boulogne, who first described it in 1862) **(Figure 10.15)**. In a false, social smile, our voluntary cheek muscles are pulled back, but our eyes are unsmiling. Smiles of real pleasure, on the other hand, use the muscles not only around the cheeks but also around the eyes.

The Duchenne smile illustrates the importance of nonverbal means of communicating emotion. We all know that people communicate in ways other than speaking or writing. However, few people recognize the full importance of nonverbal signals.

© Ocean/Corbis

psychology and you **The Power of Nonverbal Cues** Imagine yourself as a job interviewer. Your first applicant greets you with a big smile, full eye contact, a firm handshake, and an erect, open posture. The second applicant doesn't smile, looks down, offers a weak handshake, and slouches. Whom do you think you will hire?

Psychologist Albert Mehrabian would say that you're much less likely to hire the second applicant due to his or her "mixed messages." Mehrabian's research suggests that when we're communicating feelings or attitudes and our verbal and nonverbal dimensions don't match, the receiver trusts the predominant form of communication, which is about 93% nonverbal and consists of the way the words are said and the facial expression rather than the literal meaning of the words (Mehrabian, 1968, 1971, 2007).

Unfortunately, Mehrabian's research is often overgeneralized, and many people misquote him as saying that "over 90% of communication is nonverbal." Clearly, if a police officer says, "Put your hands up," his or her verbal words might carry 100% of the meaning. However, when we're confronted with a mismatch between verbal and nonverbal communication, it is safe to say that we pay far more attention to the nonverbal because we believe it more often tells us what someone is really thinking or feeling. The importance of nonverbal communication, particularly facial expressions, is further illustrated by the popularity of smileys and other emoticons in our everyday e-mail and text messages.

Three Major Theories of Emotion

Researchers generally agree that emotion has biological, cognitive, and behavioral components, but there is less agreement about *how* we become emotional (Christenfeld & Mandler, 2013). The major competing theories are the *James-Lange, Cannon-Bard,* and *Schachter and Singer's two-factor theories* **(Figure 10.16)**.

FIGURE 10.16 **COMPARING THREE MAJOR THEORIES OF EMOTION**

Gordon Wiltsie/National Geographic/Getty Images

Imagine that you're walking in the desert and suddenly see a coiled snake on the path next to you. What emotion would you experience? Most people would say they would be very afraid. But why? Common sense tells us that our hearts pound and we tremble when we're afraid or that we cry when we're sad. But according to the **James-Lange theory**, felt emotions begin with physiological arousal of the ANS (Chapter 2). This arousal (a pounding heart, breathlessness, trembling all over) then causes us to experience the emotion we call "fear." Contrary to popular opinion, James wrote: "We feel sorry because we cry, angry because we strike, afraid because we tremble" (James, 1890).

In contrast, the **Cannon-Bard theory** proposes that arousal and emotion occur separately but simultaneously. Following perception of an emotion-provoking stimulus, the thalamus (a subcortical brain structure) sends two simultaneous messages: one to the ANS, which causes physiological arousal, and one to the brain's cortex, which causes awareness of the felt emotion.

Finally, Schachter and Singer's **two-factor theory** suggests that our emotions start with physiological arousal followed by a conscious, cognitive appraisal. We then look to external cues from the environment and to others around us to find a label and explanation for the arousal. Therefore, if we cry at a wedding, we label our emotion as joy or happiness. If we cry at a funeral, we label the emotion as sadness.

In their classic study demonstrating this effect, Schachter and Singer (1962) gave research participants injections of epinephrine (adrenaline), a hormone/neurotransmitter that produces feelings of arousal, or saline shots (a placebo) and then exposed the participants to either a happy or angry confederate **(Figure 10.17)**. The way participants responded suggested that arousal could be labeled happiness or anger, depending on the context. Thus, Schachter and Singer's research demonstrated that emotion is determined by two factors: physiological arousal and cognitive appraisal (labeling).

Schachter and Singer's two-factor theory may have important practical implications. Depending on the cues present in our environment, we apparently can interpret exactly the same feelings of arousal in very different ways. For example, if

James-Lange theory A theory of emotion which suggests that the subjective experience of emotion results from physiological changes rather than being their cause ("I feel sad because I'm crying"); in this view, each emotion is physiologically distinct.

Cannon-Bard theory A theory which states that emotions and physiological changes occur simultaneously ("I'm crying and feeling sad at the same time"); in this view, all emotions are physiologically similar.

Two-factor theory Schachter and Singer's theory that emotion depends upon two factors—physiological arousal and cognitive labeling of that arousal.

FIGURE 10.17 **SCHACHTER AND SINGER'S CLASSIC STUDY**

Experimenter	**Informed group**	**Ignorant group**	**Misinformed group**	**Placebo group**
	Got epinephrine; told about effects	Got epinephrine; told nothing about effects	Got epinephrine; deceived about effects	Got saline instead of epinephrine; told nothing about effects

Ⓐ Participants in this study were first told that this was a study of how certain vitamins affect visual skills, and then they were asked for permission to be injected with a small shot of the vitamin "Suproxin." (This injection actually was a shot of the hormone/neurotransmitter epinephrine [or adrenaline], which triggers feelings of arousal such as racing heart, flushed skin, and trembling hands.) Those participants who gave permission were then divided into four groups and given injections. Those in the three groups who received the shot of epinephrine were correctly informed about the drug's effects, ignorant of the effects, or misinformed about the effects. Those in the fourth placebo group received a neutral, saline solution.

Happy confederate

I feel strange, it must be the injection

I feel strange, sort of "happy" like that fella

I feel strange. I guess I feel very happy like that guy over there

I feel strange, sort of happy like that fella

Ⓑ Each participant was then placed in a room with either a "happy" or an "angry" trained confederate (who was actually an accomplice of the experimenter). Both the participants and confederate were told that before they could take the supposed vision test, they needed to complete a questionnaire and allow time for the drug to take effect. The confederate was instructed in each condition to behave in line with his supposed emotion: He acted joyously in the happy condition—flying paper airplanes, bouncing a ball, etc.—and acted irate in the angry condition—complaining about the experiment, refusing to answer some items on the questionnaire, etc. As predicted, when participants were placed in a room with the happy confederate, they rated themselves as happy. They also behaved in a more joyous way, engaging in more "happy" acts, just like the confederate had modeled. When placed with the angry, irritated confederate, they reported feeling angry and behaved more irately. Although the subjects were feeling similar effects of the epinephrine, they labeled those effects differently (happy or angry), depending on the external cues in their environment, and acted accordingly.

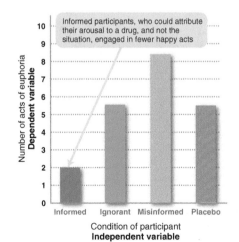

Informed participants, who could attribute their arousal to a drug, and not the situation, engaged in fewer happy acts

Number of acts of euphoria
Dependent variable

Condition of participant
Independent variable

Ⓒ This effect on emotions was most apparent in the groups that were misinformed about the true effects of the injections. Why? Those in the informed group correctly attributed their arousal to the drug rather than to the environment.

you're shy or afraid of public speaking, try interpreting your feelings of nervousness as the result of too much coffee or the heating in the room. Some research on this type of *misattribution of arousal* has had positive outcomes (Chafin et al., 2008; Inzlicht & Al-Khindi, 2012; Thornton & Tizard, 2010).

Later research on emotion has supported or discounted parts of all three of these major theories and added some new ideas. For example, as we saw earlier in discussing the behavioral component of emotion, facial expressions like the Duchenne smile help us express our emotions. And, according to the **facial-feedback hypothesis**, movements of our facial muscles produce and/or intensify our subjective experience of emotion (see *Psychology and You*). More specifically, sensory input (such as seeing a snake) is first routed to subcortical areas of the brain that activate facial movements. These facial changes then initiate and intensify emotions (Adelmann & Zajonc, 1989; Ceschi & Scherer, 2001; Dimberg & Söderkvist, 2011; Neal & Chartrand, 2011; Sander, 2013; Vrticka et al., 2013). Researchers in one study asked participants to maintain a smile while they were engaging in a stress-inducing task, such as keeping their hand in a bucket of very cold ice water (Kraft & Pressman, 2012). Compared to participants who held their face in a neutral position, those who smiled had lower heart rates, showing that smiling can help reduce the experience of stress—thus supporting the facial-feedback hypothesis.

Voices from the Classroom

Two-Factor Theory and "No Fear" Skiing This is an example I give for Schachter and Singer's two-factor theory of emotion, involving physiological arousal and a "label" based on a cognitive appraisal of the environment/situation. Once while snow skiing, I allowed myself to ski faster and faster, trying to keep up with my friend, Pete, who had suddenly zoomed passed me from behind. Because Pete was skiing that fast, I must be able to also, so I was "exhilarated" instead of "afraid" to be skiing that fast.

Then I fell. When I looked up, Pete kept skiing without waiting for me. That was odd. Then I turned to look behind and I saw Pete! The fast skier was in fact a different skier wearing the same style ski jacket as Pete's. Had I known he was not Pete, I would never have skied that fast without labeling my experience as "fear" instead of "exhilaration."

Professor Charles Dufour
University of Maine
Orono, Maine

Facial-feedback hypothesis The hypothesis that movements of the facial muscles produce and/or intensify our subjective experience of emotion.

psychology and you
Testing the Facial-Feedback Hypothesis Hold a pen or pencil between your teeth with your mouth open. Spend about 30 seconds in this position. How do you feel? According to research, pleasant feelings are more likely when teeth are showing than when they are not.

Source: Adapted from Strack et al., 1988.

Mark Owens/John Wiley & Sons, Inc.

Other research emphasizes specific pathways between the *thalamus, amygdala,* and *cerebral cortex* to help explain different emotional responses, such as the almost instantaneous emotional response to some stimuli versus our slower-developing responses (Armony, 2013; Lazarus, 1991, 1998; LeDoux, 1996, 2003, 2007; Paz & Pare, 2013; Somerville et al., 2013; Zajonc, 1984).

Applying this specific pathway idea to our earlier example of hiking in the woods and noticing a large snake near your foot, your first response would most likely be to freeze in fear or jump away to safety. Only later would you be able to logically evaluate the danger this particular snake posed. This type of two-phase fear response is a result of two different pathways for sensory data in the brain **(Figure 10.18)**.

Evolution, Culture, and Emotion

Early research indicated that people in all cultures express, recognize, and experience several basic emotions, such as happiness, surprise, anger, sadness, fear, and disgust, in essentially the same way (Darwin, 1872; Ekman & Friesen, 1971; Izard, 1971; Plutchik, 1980; Tomkins, 1962). In other words, across cultures, a frown is recognized as a sign of displeasure and a smile as a sign of pleasure.

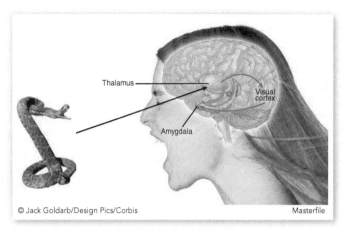

© Jack Goldarb/Design Pics/Corbis   Masterfile

FIGURE 10.18 **FAST AND SLOW PATHWAYS FOR FEAR**

When sensory input arrives at the thalamus, the thalamus sends it along a fast route directly to the amygdala (the red arrow), as well as along a slower, more indirect route to the visual cortex (the blue arrow). This speedy, direct route allows us to quickly respond to a feared stimulus (like the snake) even before we're consciously aware of our emotions or behaviors. In contrast, the indirect route, engaging the visual cortex, provides more detailed information that allows us to consciously evaluate the danger of this particular snake and our most appropriate response.

© Ocean/Corbis

© Kevork Djansezian/AP Photo

FIGURE 10.19 **CAN YOU IDENTIFY THESE EMOTIONS?**

Most people easily recognize the emotional expression of happiness, such as the man in the photo on the top. However, on occasion, our facial expressions don't seem to match our presumed emotions, as is the case in the photo on the bottom. In this case, Halle Berry was the first black actress to win the highly-coveted Best Actress award, yet she looks sad rather than happy.

Interestingly, researchers in one study asked participants from both the United States and South Korea to select from a list of options the emotions portrayed by Olympic athletes who had just won a medal (Matsumoto & Hwang, 2012). Across both countries, participants rated faces that showed grimaces or yelling, clenched fists, and arms raised above the shoulders as indicating "triumph." Similarly, participants in both cultures rated faces with a small smile and heads tilted back, and arms sticking out away from the body with hands open as showing "pride."

From an evolutionary perspective, the idea of universal facial expressions makes adaptive sense because such expressions signal others about our current emotional state (Ekman & Keltner, 1997). Charles Darwin first advanced the evolutionary theory of emotion in 1872. He proposed that expression of emotions evolved in different species as a part of survival and natural selection. For example, fear helps animals avoid danger, whereas expressions of anger and aggression are useful when fighting for mates or resources. Modern evolutionary theory suggests that basic emotions originate in the *limbic system*. Given that higher brain areas like the cortex developed later than the subcortical limbic system, evolutionary theory proposes that basic emotions evolved before thought.

Studies with infants provide further support for an evolutionary basis for emotions. For example, infants only a few hours old show distinct expressions of emotion that closely match adult facial expressions, and by the age of 7 months they can reliably interpret and recognize emotional information across both face and voice (Field et al., 1982; Grossman, 2013; Meltzoff & Moore, 1977, 1985, 1994). And all infants, even those who are born deaf and blind, show similar facial expressions in similar situations (Field et al., 1982; Gelder et al., 2006). In addition, a recent study showed that families may have characteristic facial expressions, shared even by family members who have been blind from birth (Peleg et al., 2006). This collective evidence points to a strong biological, evolutionary basis for emotional expression and decoding.

In contrast to the evolutionary approach, other researchers suggest that emotions are much more complex than originally thought (Fernández-Dols, 2013; Mead, 1928; Miyamoto & Ryaff, 2011; Nelson & Russell, 2013; Ortony & Turner, 1990). For example, although we may all share similar facial expressions for some emotions, each culture has its own *display rules* governing how, when, and where to express them (De Leersnyder et al., 2013; Ekman, 1993, 2004; Fok et al., 2008; Glikson & Erez, 2013; Koopmann-Holm & Matsumoto, 2011; Matsumoto & Hwang, 2011). In addition to culture, gender, family background, norms, and individual differences also affect our emotions and their expression (**Figure 10.19**).

realworldpsychology **Understanding Display Rules for Emotions**

How do we learn our culture's display rules? Parents and other adults pass along their culture's specific display rules to children by responding negatively or ignoring some emotions and being supportive and sympathetic to others. Public physical contact is also governed by display rules. North Americans and Asians are less likely than people in other cultures to touch each other; only the closest family members and friends might hug in greeting or farewell. In contrast, Latin Americans and Middle Easterners often kiss, embrace, and hold hands as a sign of casual friendship (Axtell, 2007). Some Middle Eastern men commonly greet one another with a kiss. Can you imagine this same behavior among men in North America, who generally shake hands or pat one another's shoulders?

Behrouz Mehri/AFP/Getty Images

The Polygraph as a Lie Detector

We've discussed the three major theories of emotion, and the way emotions are affected by culture and evolution. Now we turn our attention to one of the hottest, and most controversial, topics in emotion research—the **polygraph**.

Traditional polygraph tests are based on the theory that when people lie, they feel guilty and anxious. Special sensors supposedly detect these testable emotions by measuring sympathetic and parasympathetic nervous system responses (Grubin, 2010; Tomash & Reed, 2013) **(Figure 10.20)**.

The problem is that lying is only loosely related to anxiety and guilt. Some people become nervous even when telling the truth, whereas others remain calm when deliberately lying. A polygraph cannot tell which emotion is being felt (nervousness, excitement, sexual arousal, and so on) or whether a response is due to emotional arousal or something else. One study found that people could affect the level of arousal shown on the polygraph by about 50% simply by pressing their toes against the floor or biting their tongues (Honts & Kircher, 1994). In fact, although proponents claim that polygraph tests are 90% accurate or better, actual tests show error rates ranging between 25 and 75% (DeClue, 2003; Handler et al., 2009; Iacono, 2008). Countless millions of dollars have been spent on new and improved lie-detection

Polygraph An instrument that measures sympathetic arousal (heart rate, respiration rate, blood pressure, and skin conductivity) to detect emotional arousal, which in turn supposedly reflects lying versus truthfulness.

FIGURE 10.20 POLYGRAPH TESTING | realworldpsychology

Polygraph testing is based on the assumption that when we lie, we feel guilty, fearful, or anxious.

Ⓐ During a standard polygraph test, a band around the person's chest measures breathing rate, a cuff monitors blood pressure, and finger electrodes measure sweating, or galvanic skin response (GSR).

Ⓑ Note how the GSR rises sharply in response to the question "Have you ever taken money from this bank?"

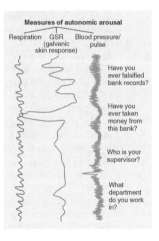

techniques (Kluger & Masters, 2006). Perhaps the most promising is the use of brain scans like the *functional magnetic resonance imaging (fMRI)*. Unfortunately, each of these new lie-detection techniques has potential problems and researchers have questioned their reliability and validity, while civil libertarians and judicial scholars question their ethics and legality (Ganis et al., 2011; Gómez-Restrepo, 2007; Roskies et al., 2013; Schweitzer & Saks, 2011).

For these reasons, legal and scientific research suggests caution in using the polygraph as a lie detector (DeClue, 2003; Handler et al., 2013; Tomash & Reed, 2013; Van Iddekinge et al., 2012).

RETRIEVAL PRACTICE: COMPONENTS AND THEORIES OF EMOTION

Self-Test

Completing this self-test and comparing your answers with those in Appendix B provides immediate feedback and helpful practice for exams. Additional interactive, self-tests are available at www.wiley.com/college/huffman.

1. The three components of emotion are _____.

a. cognitive, biological, and behavioral
b. perceiving, thinking, and acting
c. positive, negative, and neutral
d. active/passive, positive/negative, and direct/indirect

2. According to the _____, emotions and physiological changes occur simultaneously

a. Cannon-Bard theory
b. James-Lange theory
c. facial-feedback hypothesis
d. two-factor theory

3. The _____ suggests that we look to external rather than internal cues to understand emotions.

a. Cannon-Bard theory
b. James-Lange theory
c. facial feedback hypothesis
d. two-factor theory

4. The polygraph, or lie detector, measures primarily the _____ component of emotions.

a. physiological
b. articulatory
c. cognitive
d. subjective

Think Critically

1 If you were going on a date with someone or applying for an important job, how might you use the three key theories of emotion to increase the chances that things will go well?

2 Why do you think people around the world experience and express the same basic emotions, and what evolutionary advantages might help explain these similarities?

3 After reading the section on polygraph tests, would you be willing to take a "lie detector" test if you were accused of a crime? Why or why not?

realworldpsychology

How can a simple smile reduce stress?

Why do emotional expressions of Olympic athletes appear the same across all cultures?

HINT: LOOK IN THE MARGIN FOR (Q4) AND (Q5)

Summary

1 THEORIES OF MOTIVATION   274

- The three major biological theories of **motivation** provide roles for **instincts**, drives (produced by the body's need for **homeostasis**), and arousal (the need for novelty, complexity, and stimulation).
- Psychological theories emphasize the role of incentives, attributions, and expectancies in cognition.
- Maslow's **hierarchy of needs** theory takes a biopsychosocial approach. It prioritizes needs, with survival needs at the bottom and social and spiritual needs at the top. Although the theory has made important contributions, some critics argue that it is poorly researched and biased toward Western individualism.

2 MOTIVATION AND BEHAVIOR   279

- Hunger is one of the strongest motivational drives, and both biological factors (the stomach, biochemistry, the brain) and psychosocial factors (stimulus cues and cultural conditioning) affect hunger and eating. These factors play a similar role in **obesity, anorexia nervosa, bulimia nervosa**, and **binge-eating disorder**.
- A high need for achievement (nAch), or **achievement motivation**, is generally learned in early childhood primarily through interactions with parents.
- The human motivation for sex is extremely strong. Masters and Johnson first studied and described the **sexual response cycle**,

the series of physiological and sexual responses that occurs during sexual activity. Other sex research has focused on the roots of **sexual orientation**, and most studies suggest that genetics and biology play the dominant role. Sexual orientation remains a divisive issue, and gays, lesbians, bisexuals, and transgendered people often confront **sexual prejudice**.

• Providing **extrinsic motivation** like money or praise for an intrinsically satisfying activity can undermine people's enjoyment and interest—their **intrinsic motivation**—for the activity.

3 COMPONENTS AND THEORIES OF EMOTION 290

• **Emotion** has biological components (brain and autonomic nervous system), cognitive components (thoughts), and behavioral components (expressive).

• The major theories about how the components of emotion interact are the **James-Lange theory**, **Cannon-Bard theory**, and Schachter and Singer's **two-factor theory**. Each emphasizes different sequences or aspects of the three elements. Other research emphasizes how different pathways in the brain trigger faster and slower emotional responses.

• Some researchers believe there are basic, universal emotions shared by people of all cultures, who also express and recognize the basic emotions in essentially the same way. These findings and studies with infants support this evolutionary theory of emotion. However, other researchers question the existence of basic emotions. *Display rules* for emotional expressions vary across cultures.

• **Polygraph** tests attempt to detect lying by measuring physiological signs of guilt and anxiety. However, because lying is only loosely related to these emotions, most judges and scientists have serious reservations about using polygraphs as accurate lie detectors.

⊙ applyingrealworldpsychology

We began this chapter with five intriguing Real World Psychology questions, and you were asked to revisit these questions at the end of each section. Questions like these have an important and lasting impact on all of our lives. See if you can answer these additional critical thinking questions related to real world examples.

Tetra Images/SuperStock, Inc.

1 Nonhuman animals, like the kitten in this photo, sometimes display what we humans would label "curiosity." How might this trait be important for the survival and achievement of both human and nonhuman animals?

2 How do you think nonhuman animal motivation, like this kitten's, might differ from that of humans?

3 Think about your favorite hobbies or recreational activities (for example, riding your bike, watching TV, playing videogames). How would you explain these activities using the six theories of motivation (see Table 10.1, p. 274)?

4 Imagine yourself in a career as a health psychologist (Chapter 3). What type of public health efforts would you recommend to treat the rising epidemic and dangers associate with eating disorders?

5 Think back to a time when you felt very angry and upset over a misunderstanding with a special friend. Which of the three key components of emotion (biological, cognitive, or behavioral) best accounted for the intensity of your feelings? Which of the three major theories (the James-Lange, Cannon-Bard, or two-factor theory) best explains your overall emotional experience?

6 Do you believe people can (and should) control their emotions? Why or why not?

Key Terms

RETRIEVAL PRACTICE Write a definition for each term before turning back to the referenced page to check your answer.

chaptereleven

Personality

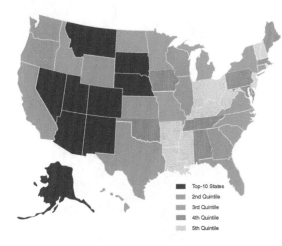

Top-10 States
2nd Quintile
3rd Quintile
4th Quintile
5th Quintile

realworldpsychology

Q1 Are some people with highly negative attitudes toward gay people repressing their own sexual desires?

Q2 Can personality traits predict the type of music we like?

Q3 What parenting skills are also associated with increased marital satisfaction?

Q4 Does helping parents prepare a meal increase a child's preference for healthy foods?

Q5 Can our genes predict how much we will give to charity?

Q6 Why do people from different states vary in their entrepreneurial spirit?

THROUGHOUT THE CHAPTER, MARGIN ICONS FOR Q1–Q6 INDICATE WHERE THE TEXT ADDRESSES THESE QUESTIONS.

chapteroverview

You have a strong need for other people to like and admire you. You tend to be critical of yourself. Although you have some personality weaknesses, you are generally able to compensate for them. At times, you have serious doubts about whether you have made the right decision or done the right thing.

—Adapted from Ulrich et al., 1963

Does this sound like you? A high percentage of research participants who read a similar personality description reported that the description was "very accurate"— even after they were informed that it was a *phony* horoscope (Hyman, 1981). Other research shows that about three-quarters of adults read newspaper horoscopes and that many of them believe astrological horoscopes were written especially for them (Sugarman et al., 2011; Wyman & Vyse, 2008).

Why are such spurious personality assessments so popular? One reason is that they seem to tap into our unique selves. Supporters of these horoscopes, however, ignore the fact that the traits they supposedly reveal are characteristics that almost everyone shares. Do you know anyone who doesn't "have a strong need for other people to like and admire" them? The traits in horoscopes are also generally flattering, or at least neutral.

Unlike the pseudopsychologies such as these newspaper horoscopes and Chinese fortune cookies, the descriptions presented by personality researchers are based on empirical studies. In this chapter, we examine the most prominent theories and up-to-date findings in personality research. We also explore professional techniques that psychologists use to assess personality.

Voices from the Classroom

Personality in the Dating World I once went on a date with someone who had the personality of an annoyed Chihuahua. What's weird about that statement is you know *exactly* what I mean. That's right, she was the woman with the high-pitched voice, angrily barking at the waiter, and shivering because she didn't wear enough clothes, right? And then there's me, the golden retriever sitting across the table from her, smiling away at the waiter, reassuring him that he's doing a great job, nervously drinking from everyone's water glasses, and despite not liking her very much, deeply hoping she still liked me. Of course, the key word here is *personality*. One's personality is that impression we give ourselves, (and others), of who we are: a unique pattern created from a combination of our typical thoughts, feelings, and behaviors. But I don't want to leave you with the wrong impression. While I may think that it would feel good to have strangers scratch my head in public, I tend to not do that.

Professor Keith W. Swain

Red Rocks Community College

Arvada, Colorado

PSYCHOANALYTIC/PSYCHODYNAMIC THEORIES

LEARNING OBJECTIVES

RETRIEVAL PRACTICE While reading the upcoming sections, respond to each Learning Objective in your own words. Then compare your responses with those found at www.wiley.com/college/huffman.

1 **DISCUSS** the major concepts of psychoanalytic/psychodynamic theories of personality.

2 **EXPLAIN** how Adler's, Jung's, and Horney's theories differ from Freud's thinking.

3 **EXPLORE** the major contributions and criticisms of Freud's psychoanalytic theories.

Before discussing the following psychoanalytic/psychodynamic theories, we need to provide a basic definition of **personality** as *a unique and relatively stable pattern of thoughts, feelings, and actions*. In other words, it describes how we are different from other people and what patterns of behavior are typical of us. We might qualify as an "extrovert," for example, if we're talkative and outgoing most of the time. Or we may be described as "conscientious" if we're responsible and self-disciplined most of the time. (Keep in mind that *personality* is not the same as *character*, which refers to our ethics, morals, values, and integrity.)

Freud's Psychoanalytic Theory

One of the earliest theories of personality was Sigmund Freud's psychoanalytic perspective, which emphasized unconscious processes and unresolved past conflicts. Working from about 1890 until he died in 1939, Freud developed a theory of personality that has been one of the most influential—and controversial—theories in all of science (Barenbaum & Winter, 2013; Bornstein et al., 2013; Cautin, 2011; Cordón, 2012). Let's examine some of Freud's most basic and debatable concepts.

Freud called the mind the "psyche" and asserted that it contains three *levels of consciousness*, or awareness: the **conscious**, the **preconscious**, and the **unconscious (Figure 11.1)**. For Freud, the unconscious is all-important because it reportedly stores our most primitive, instinctual motives, plus anxiety-laden thoughts and memories, which are normally blocked from our personal awareness. However, it supposedly still has an enormous impact on our behavior—like the hidden part of the iceberg that sunk the ocean liner *Titanic*.

Interestingly, because many of our unconscious thoughts and motives are unacceptable and threatening, Freud believed that they are normally *repressed* (held out of awareness)—unless they are unintentionally revealed by dreams or slips of the tongue, later called *Freudian slips* **(Figure 11.2)**.

Freud believed that most psychological disorders originate from repressed memories or sexual and aggressive instincts hidden in the unconscious. To treat these disorders, he developed a form of therapy called *psychoanalysis* (Chapter 13).

Personality A unique and relatively stable pattern of thoughts, feelings, and actions.

Conscious In Freudian terms, thoughts or motives that a person is currently aware of or is remembering.

Preconscious Freud's term for thoughts, motives, or memories that exist just beneath the surface of awareness and can be called to consciousness when necessary.

Unconscious Freud's term for a part of the psyche that stores repressed urges and primitive impulses.

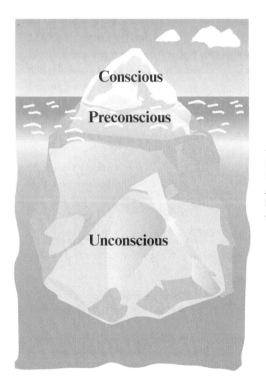

FIGURE 11.1 FREUD'S THREE LEVELS OF CONSCIOUSNESS

Although Freud never used the analogy himself, his levels of awareness are often compared to an iceberg:

- The tip of the iceberg would be analogous to the *conscious* mind, which is above the water and open to easy inspection.
- The *preconscious* mind (the area only shallowly submerged) contains information that can be viewed with a little extra effort.
- The large base of the iceberg is somewhat like the *unconscious*, completely hidden from personal inspection.

FIGURE 11.2 FREUDIAN SLIPS

Freud believed that a small slip of the tongue (now known as a *Freudian slip*) can reflect unconscious feelings that we normally keep hidden.

"Good morning, beheaded—uh, I mean beloved."

Id According to Freud, the primitive, unconscious component of personality that operates irrationally and acts on the pleasure principle.

Pleasure principle In Freud's theory, the principle on which the id operates—seeking immediate gratification.

Ego In Freud's theory, the rational, decision-making component of personality that operates according to the reality principle; from the Latin term *ego*, meaning "I."

Reality principle According to Freud, the principle on which the conscious ego operates as it seeks to delay gratification of the id's impulses until appropriate outlets and situations can be found.

Superego In Freud's theory, the aspect of personality that operates on the morality principle; the "conscience" that internalizes society's values, standards, and morals.

Morality principle In Freudian terms, the principle on which the superego operates; feelings of guilt result if its rules are violated.

Defense mechanisms In Freudian theory, the ego's protective method of reducing anxiety by self-deception and distorting reality.

In addition to proposing that the mind functions at three levels of consciousness, Freud also believed personality was composed of three mental structures: *id*, *ego*, and *superego* **(Figure 11.3)**.

According to Freud, the **id** is made up of innate biological instincts and urges. It is immature, impulsive, and irrational. The id is also totally unconscious and serves as the reservoir of mental energy. When its primitive drives build up, the id seeks immediate gratification to relieve the tension—a concept known as the **pleasure principle**. In other words, the id is like a newborn baby. It wants what it wants when it wants it!

Freud further believed that the second part of the psyche, the **ego**, is responsible for planning, problem solving, reasoning, and controlling the potentially destructive energy of the id. In Freud's system, the ego corresponds to the *self*—our conscious identity of ourselves as persons.

One of the ego's tasks is to channel and release the id's energy in ways that are compatible with the external world. Thus, the ego is responsible for delaying gratification when necessary. Contrary to the id's pleasure principle, the ego operates on the **reality principle** because it can understand and deal with objects and events in the real world.

The final part of the psyche to develop is the **superego**, a set of ethical rules for behavior. The superego develops from internalized parental and societal standards. It constantly strives for perfection and is therefore as unrealistic as the id. Some Freudian followers have suggested that the superego operates on the **morality principle** because violating its rules results in feelings of guilt. When the ego fails to satisfy both the id and the superego, anxiety slips into our conscious awareness. Because anxiety is uncomfortable, we avoid it through **defense mechanisms (Figure 11.4)**.

FIGURE 11.3 FREUD'S PERSONALITY STRUCTURE

According to Freud, personality is composed of three structures—the id, ego, and superego. Note how the ego is primarily conscious and preconscious, whereas the id is entirely unconscious.

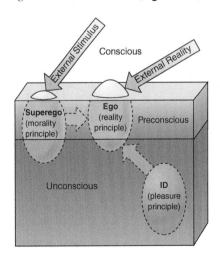

FIGURE 11.4 WHY DO WE USE DEFENSE MECHANISMS? realworldpsychology

(A) Freud believed defense mechanisms help us deal with unconscious conflicts, explaining why these physicians may *intellectualize* and distance themselves from the gruesome aspects of their work to avoid personal anxieties. Defense mechanisms can be healthy and helpful if we use them in moderation or on a temporary basis.

(B) Unfortunately, defense mechanisms almost always distort reality, and they create some of our most dangerous habits through a vicious self-reinforcing cycle. For example, an alcoholic who uses his paycheck to buy drinks may feel very guilty, but he can easily reduce this conflict by *rationalizing* that he deserves to relax and unwind with alcohol because he works so hard.

In addition to intellectualization and rationalization (shown in Figure 11.4), Freud identified several other defense mechanisms **(Table 11.1)**.

Although defense mechanisms are now an accepted part of modern psychology, other Freudian ideas are more controversial. For example, according to Freud, strong biological urges residing within the id push all children through five universal **psychosexual stages (Figure 11.5)**. The term *psychosexual* reflects Freud's belief that children experience sexual feelings from birth (in different forms from those experienced by adolescents or adults).

Psychosexual stages In Freudian theory, five developmental periods (oral, anal, phallic, latency, and genital) during which particular kinds of pleasures must be gratified if personality development is to proceed normally.

TABLE 11.1	SAMPLE PSYCHOLOGICAL DEFENSE MECHANISMS	
Defense Mechanism	**Description**	**Example**
Repression	Preventing painful or unacceptable thoughts from entering consciousness	Forgetting the details of a tragic accident
Sublimation	Redirecting socially unacceptable impulses into acceptable activities	Redirecting aggressive impulses by becoming a professional fighter
Denial	Refusing to accept an unpleasant reality	Alcoholics refusing to admit their addiction
Rationalization	Creating a socially acceptable excuse to justify unacceptable behavior	Justifying cheating on an exam by saying "everyone else does it"
Intellectualization	Ignoring the emotional aspects of a painful experience by focusing on abstract thoughts, words, or ideas	Discussing your divorce without emotion while ignoring underlying pain
Projection	Transferring unacceptable thoughts, motives, or impulses to others	Becoming unreasonably jealous of your mate while denying your own attraction to others
Reaction formation	Not acknowledging unacceptable impulses and overemphasizing their opposite	Promoting a petition against adult bookstores even though you are secretly fascinated by pornography
Regression	Reverting to immature ways of responding	Throwing a temper tantrum when a friend doesn't want to do what you'd like
Displacement	Redirecting impulses from the original source toward a less threatening person or object	Yelling at a coworker after being criticized by your boss

FIGURE 11.5 FREUD'S FIVE PSYCHOSEXUAL STAGES OF DEVELOPMENT

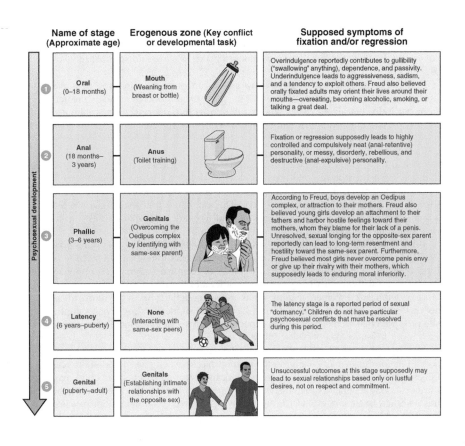

Name of stage (Approximate age)	Erogenous zone (Key conflict or developmental task)		Supposed symptoms of fixation and/or regression
1 Oral (0–18 months)	Mouth (Weaning from breast or bottle)		Overindulgence reportedly contributes to gullibility ("swallowing" anything), dependence, and passivity. Underindulgence leads to aggressiveness, sadism, and a tendency to exploit others. Freud also believed orally fixated adults may orient their lives around their mouths—overeating, becoming alcoholic, smoking, or talking a great deal.
2 Anal (18 months–3 years)	Anus (Toilet training)		Fixation or regression supposedly leads to highly controlled and compulsively neat (anal-retentive) personality, or messy, disorderly, rebellious, and destructive (anal-expulsive) personality.
3 Phallic (3–6 years)	Genitals (Overcoming the Oedipus complex by identifying with same-sex parent)		According to Freud, boys develop an Oedipus complex, or attraction to their mothers. Freud also believed young girls develop an attachment to their fathers and harbor hostile feelings toward their mothers, whom they blame for their lack of a penis. Unresolved, sexual longing for the opposite-sex parent reportedly can lead to long-term resentment and hostility toward the same-sex parent. Furthermore, Freud believed most girls never overcome penis envy or give up their rivalry with their mothers, which supposedly leads to enduring moral inferiority.
4 Latency (6 years–puberty)	None (Interacting with same-sex peers)		The latency stage is a reported period of sexual "dormancy." Children do not have particular psychosexual conflicts that must be resolved during this period.
5 Genital (puberty–adult)	Genitals (Establishing intimate relationships with the opposite sex)		Unsuccessful outcomes at this stage supposedly may lead to sexual relationships based only on lustful desires, not on respect and commitment.

Inferiority complex Adler's idea that feelings of inferiority develop from early childhood experiences of helplessness and incompetence.

Freud held that if a child's needs are not met or are overindulged at one particular psychosexual stage, the child may become *fixated*, and a part of his or her personality will remain stuck at that stage. Furthermore, under stress, individuals supposedly may return, or *regress*, to a stage at which earlier needs were frustrated or overly gratified. Obviously, Freud's theory does not imply that children should engage in sexual activity with each other, or with adults; such activity is clearly abuse and can have lasting consequences.

Psychodynamic/Neo-Freudian Theories

Some initial followers of Freud later rebelled and proposed theories of their own; they became known as *neo-Freudians*.

Alfred Adler (1870–1937) was the first to leave Freud's inner circle. Instead of seeing behavior as motivated by unconscious forces, Adler believed it is purposeful and goal directed. According to his *individual psychology*, we are motivated by our goals in life—especially our goals of obtaining security and overcoming feelings of inferiority (Carlson & Englar-Carlson, 2013).

Adler believed that almost everyone suffers from an **inferiority complex**, or deep feelings of inadequacy and incompetence that arise from our feelings of helplessness as infants. According to Adler, these early feelings result in a "will-to-power" that can take one of two paths. It can lead children to strive to develop superiority over others through dominance, aggression, or expressions of envy. Or, on a more positive note, it can encourage them to develop their full potential and creativity and to gain mastery and control in their lives (Adler, 1964, 1998) **(Figure 11.6)**.

FIGURE 11.6 **AN UPSIDE TO FEELINGS OF INFERIORITY?**

Adler suggested that the will-to-power could be positively expressed through social interest—by identifying with others and cooperating with them for the social good. Can you explain how these volunteers might be fulfilling their will-to-power interest?

© Hero Images/Corbis

Another early Freud follower turned dissenter, Carl Jung [Yoong], developed *analytical psychology*. Like Freud, Jung (1875–1961) emphasized unconscious processes, but he believed that the unconscious contains positive and spiritual motives as well as sexual and aggressive forces.

Jung also thought that we have two forms of unconscious mind: the personal unconscious and the collective unconscious. The *personal unconscious* is created from our individual experiences, whereas the **collective unconscious** is identical in each person and is inherited (Jung, 1946, 1959, 1969). The collective unconscious consists of primitive images and patterns of thought, feeling, and behavior that Jung called **archetypes (Figure 11.7)**.

Because of archetypal patterns in the collective unconscious, we perceive and react in certain predictable ways. One set of archetypes refers to gender roles (Chapter 9). Jung claimed that both males and females have patterns for feminine aspects of personality—*anima*—and masculine aspects of personality—*animus*—which allow us to express both masculine and feminine personality traits and to understand the opposite sex.

Like Adler and Jung, psychoanalyst Karen Horney [HORN-eye] was an influential follower of Freud who later came to reject major aspects of Freudian theory. She is credited with having developed a creative blend of Freudian, Adlerian, and Jungian theory, along with the first feminist critique of Freud's theory (Horney, 1939, 1945). Horney emphasized women's positive traits and suggested that most of Freud's ideas about female personality reflected male bias and misunderstanding. For example, she proposed that women's everyday experience with social inferiority led to power envy, not to Freud's idea of biological *penis envy*.

Horney also emphasized that personality development depends largely on social relationships—particularly on the relationship between parent and child. She believed that when a child's needs are not met by nurturing parents, the child may develop lasting feelings of helplessness and insecurity. The way people respond to this so-called **basic anxiety**, in Horney's view, sets the stage for later adult psychological health. She believed that everyone copes with this basic anxiety in one of

Collective unconscious Jung's concept of the part of an individual's unconscious that is inherited, evolutionarily developed, and common to all members of the species.

Archetypes According to Jung, the universal, inherited, primitive, and symbolic representations of a particular experience or object, which reside in the collective unconscious.

Basic anxiety According to Horney, feelings of helplessness and insecurity that adults experience because as children they felt alone and isolated in a hostile environment.

Roger Wood/Corbis

FIGURE 11.7 **ARCHETYPES IN THE COLLECTIVE UNCONSCIOUS?**

According to Jung, the collective unconscious is the ancestral memory of the human race and explains similarities in religion, art, symbolism, and dream imagery across cultures, such as the repeated symbol of the snake in ancient Egyptian tomb painting. Can you think of other explanations, such as the fact that snakes pose an evolutionary danger across time and cultures?

FIGURE 11.8 ORAL FIXATION OR SIMPLE SELF-SOOTHING?

Is this an example of Freud's earliest stage of psycho-sexual development, or just a part of all infants' normal sucking behaviors?

© PonyWang/iStockphoto

three ways—we move toward, away from, or against other people—and that psychological health requires a balance among these three styles.

In sum, Horney proposed that our adult personalities are shaped by our childhood relationship with our parents—not by fixation or regression at some stage of psychosexual development, as Freud argued.

Evaluating Psychoanalytic Theories

Before going on, let's consider the major criticisms of Freud's psychoanalytic theories:

- **Inadequate empirical support** Many psychoanalytic concepts—such as the psychosexual stages—cannot be empirically tested.
- **Overemphasis on sexuality, biology, and unconscious forces** Modern psychologists believe Freud underestimated the role of learning and culture in shaping personality **(Figure 11.8)**.
- **Sexism** Many psychologists, beginning with Karen Horney, reject Freud's theories as derogatory toward women.

In contrast to the claim of inadequate empirical support, numerous modern studies have supported certain Freudian concepts like the defense mechanisms and the belief that a lot of our information processing occurs outside our conscious awareness (*automatic processing*, Chapter 5, and *implicit memories*, Chapter 7). In addition, a recent study found that people who identify as having a heterosexual orientation but show a strong sexual attraction to same-sex people in psychological tests tend to have more homophobic attitudes and higher levels of hostility toward gay people (Weinstein et al., 2012). Can you see how Freud's theory might suggest that these negative attitudes and beliefs spring from unconscious repression of same-sex desires? Moreover, many contemporary clinicians still value Freud's insights about childhood experiences and unconscious influences on personality development (Bornstein et al., 2013; Celes, 2010; De Sousa, 2011; Kring et al., 2012; Siegel, 2010).

Today there are few Freudian purists. Instead, modern psychodynamic theorists and psychoanalysts tend to place less emphasis on sexual instincts and more on sociocultural influences on personality development.

Q1

RETRIEVAL PRACTICE: PSYCHOANALYTIC/PSYCHODYNAMIC THEORIES

Self-Test

Completing this self-test and comparing your answers with those in Appendix B provides immediate feedback and helpful practice for exams. Additional interactive, self-tests are available at www.wiley.com/college/huffman.

1. _____ is defined as a unique and relatively stable pattern of thoughts, feelings, and actions.

  a. Character   b. Trait
  c. Temperament   d. Personality

2. In Freudian terms, the _____ operates on the pleasure principle, seeking immediate gratification. The _____ operates on the reality principle, and the _____ contains the conscience and operates on the morality principle.

  a. psyche; ego; id   b. id; ego; superego
  c. conscious; preconscious; unconscious   d. oral stage; anal stage; phallic stage

3. According to Freud, when anxiety slips into our conscious awareness, we tend to avoid it through the use of _____.

  a. latency overcompensation   b. the Oedipus complex
  c. regression to the oral stage   d. defense mechanisms

4. Used excessively, defense mechanisms can be dangerous because they _____.

a. block intellectualization   b. become ineffective

c. distort reality   d. become fixated

5. Three of the most influential neo-Freudians were _____.

a. Plato, Aristotle, and Descartes

b. Dr. Laura, Dr. Phil, and Dr. Ruth

c. Adler, Jung, and Horney

d. None of these options

Think Critically

1 If scientists have so many problems with Freud, why do you think his theories are still popular with the public? Should psychologists continue to discuss his theories (and include them in textbooks)?

2 What is a possible example of sexism in Freud's psychoanalytic theory?

realworldpsychology

Are some people with highly negative attitudes toward gay people repressing their own sexual desires?

HINT: LOOK IN THE MARGIN FOR Q1

TRAIT THEORIES

RETRIEVAL PRACTICE While reading the upcoming sections, respond to each Learning Objective in your own words. Then compare your responses with those found at www.wiley.com/college/huffman.

1 **EXPLAIN** how early trait theorists approached the study of personality.

2 **IDENTIFY** the Big Five personality traits.

3 **SUMMARIZE** the major contributions and criticisms of trait theory.

LEARNING OBJECTIVES

Think for a moment about the key personality characteristics of your best friend. For example, you might say: *He's a great guy who's a lot of fun to be with. But I sometimes get tired of his constant jokes and pranks. On the other hand, he does listen well and will be serious when I need him to be.*

When describing another's personality, we generally use terms that refer to that person's most frequent and typical characteristics ("fun," "constant jokes and pranks," "listens well"). These unique and defining characteristics are the foundation for the *trait approach*, which seeks to discover what characteristics form the core of human personality.

Early Trait Theorists

An early study of dictionary terms found almost 4,500 words that described personality **traits** (Allport & Odbert, 1936). Faced with this enormous list, Gordon Allport (1937) believed that the best way to understand personality was to arrange a person's unique personality traits into a hierarchy, with the most pervasive or important traits at the top.

Later psychologists reduced the list of possible personality traits using a statistical technique called *factor analysis*, in which large arrays of data are grouped into more basic units (factors). Raymond Cattell (1950, 1965, 1990) condensed the list of traits to 16 source traits. Hans Eysenck (1967, 1982, 1990) reduced the list even further. He described personality as a relationship among three basic types of traits: *extroversion–introversion*, *neuroticism* (the tendency

Trait A relatively stable personality characteristic that can be used to describe someone.

toward insecurity, anxiety, guilt, and moodiness), and *psychoticism* (being out of touch with reality).

Modern Trait Theory

Factor analysis was also used to develop the most promising modern trait theory, the **five-factor model (FFM)** (Costa & McCrae, 2011; McCrae & Costa, 2013; Soto et al., 2011). A handy way to remember this model is to note that the first letters of the five words spell *ocean* **(Figure 11.9)**.

Combining previous research findings and the long list of possible personality traits, researchers discovered that these five traits came up repeatedly, even when different tests were used:

O Openness People who rate high in this factor are original, imaginative, curious, open to new ideas, artistic, and interested in cultural pursuits. Low scorers tend to be conventional, down-to-earth, narrower in their interests, and not artistic. Interestingly, critical thinkers tend to score higher than others on this factor (Clifford et al., 2004).

C Conscientiousness This factor ranges from responsible, self-disciplined, organized, and achieving at the high end to irresponsible, careless, impulsive, lazy, and undependable at the other.

E Extroversion This factor contrasts people who are sociable, outgoing, talkative, fun loving, and affectionate at the high end with introverted individuals who tend to be withdrawn, quiet, passive, and reserved at the low end.

A Agreeableness Individuals who score high in this factor are good-natured, warm, gentle, cooperative, trusting, and helpful, whereas low scorers are irritable, argumentative, ruthless, suspicious, uncooperative, and vindictive.

N Neuroticism (*or emotional stability*) People who score high in neuroticism are emotionally unstable and prone to insecurity, anxiety, guilt, worry, and moodiness. People at the other end are emotionally stable, calm, even-tempered, easygoing, and relaxed.

This five-factor model (FFM) has led to numerous research follow-ups and intriguing insights about personality. For example, researchers who examined personality traits in 243 people age 95 and older discovered that these older adults were more likely to show particular traits, such as optimism, extraversion, and conscientiousness. They also were less likely to show other traits, such as negative affect (Kato et al., 2012). Can you see how these findings indicate that personality traits may help predict how long we live?

What about nonhuman animals? Do you think they have distinct personalities? If so, do they also have specific personality traits that might be associated with a longer life span? (See *Psych Science.*)

Evaluating Trait Theories

The five-factor model (FFM) is the first model to achieve the major goal of trait theory—to describe and organize personality characteristics using the smallest number of traits. There also is strong cross-cultural research support for the FFM. Psychologist David Buss and his colleagues (1989, 1990, 2003) surveyed more than 10,000 men and women from 37

Five-factor model (FFM) A comprehensive descriptive personality system that includes openness, conscientiousness, extroversion, agreeableness, and neuroticism; informally called the Big Five.

FIGURE 11.9 THE FIVE-FACTOR MODEL (FFM)

Different adjectives may describe your personality, depending on whether you score high or low in each of the "Big Five" traits. Note that the lines on the right, below each of the five factors, indicate that scores on each factor exist on a continuum from low scorers to high scorers.

Big Five traits	Low scorers	High scorers
1 **O**penness	Down-to-earth Uncreative Conventional Not curious	Imaginative Creative Original Curious
2 **C**onscientiousness	Negligent Lazy Disorganized Late	Conscientious Hard-working Well-organized Punctual
3 **E**xtroversion	Loner Quiet Passive Reserved	Joiner Talkative Active Affectionate
4 **A**greeableness	Suspicious Critical Ruthless Irritable	Trusting Lenient Soft-hearted Good-natured
5 **N**euroticism	Calm Even-tempered Comfortable Unemotional	Worried Temperamental Self-conscious Emotional

PSYCHSCIENCE

DO ANIMALS HAVE UNIQUE PERSONALITIES?

Martin Harvey/Digital Vision/Getty Images

Pet owners have long believed that their dogs and cats have unique personalities, and a growing body of research tends to agree with them (Brodin et al., 2013; Gosling & John, 1999; Zuckerman, 2013). Moreover, the use of personality ratings has become a common tool for managing farm and zoo animals (Grand et al., 2012).

Dog lovers might be interested in knowing that when 78 dogs of all shapes and sizes were rated by both owners and strangers, a strong correlation was found on traits such as affection versus aggression, anxiety versus calmness, and intelligence versus stupidity. Researchers also found that personalities vary widely within a breed, which means that not all pit bulls are aggressive and not all Labrador retrievers are affectionate (Gosling et al., 2004).

To discover whether particular personality traits were associated with a longer life expectancy in nonhuman animals, researchers studied 298 gorillas in zoos and sanctuaries across North America. Using standardized measures similar to the FFM, they asked zoo keepers, volunteers, researchers, and caretakers who knew the gorillas well to score each gorilla's personality. With these scorings, they reliably identified four distinct personality traits: *dominance, extroversion, neuroticism,* and *agreeableness* (Weiss et al., 2013).

Next, the researchers examined the association between levels of each of these personality traits and life expectancy. They found that gorillas scoring high on extroversion, which included behaviors such as sociability, activity, play, and curiosity, lived longer lives. This link was found in both male and female gorillas and across all the different types of environments in which this research was conducted.

What might explain this link? One possibility is that extroverted ape—just like extroverted people—develop stronger social networks, which helps increase survival and reduce stress. Can you think of other possible explanations?

RESEARCH CHALLENGE

1. Based on the information provided, did this study (Weiss et al., 2013) use descriptive, correlational, and/or experimental research?

2. If you chose:
   - descriptive research, is this a naturalistic observation, survey/interview, case study, or archival research?
   - correlational research, is this a positive, negative, or zero correlation?
   - experimental research, label the IV, DV, experimental group(s), and control group.

>>CHECK YOUR ANSWERS IN APPENDIX B.
NOTE: The information provided in this study is admittedly limited, but the level of detail is similar to what is presented in most textbooks and public reports of research findings. Answering these questions, and then comparing your answers to those in the Appendix, will help you become a better critical thinker and consumer of scientific research.

countries and found a surprising level of agreement in the characteristics that men and women value in a mate **(Table 11.2)**. Note that both sexes tend to prefer mates with traits that closely match the FFM—dependability (conscientiousness), emotional stability (low neuroticism), pleasing disposition (agreeableness), and sociability (extroversion) to the alternatives.

Why is there such a high degree of shared preferences for certain personality traits? Scientists suggest that these traits may provide an evolutionary advantage to people who are more conscientious, extroverted, and agreeable—and less neurotic. The evolutionary advantage also is confirmed by other cross-cultural studies (Brumbaugh & Wood, 2013; Figueredo et al., 2011; McCrae, 2011; Rushton & Irwing, 2011) and comparative studies with dogs, chimpanzees, and other species (Adams, 2011; Gosling, 2008; Mehta & Gosling, 2006; Weiss et al., 2013).

| TABLE 11.2 | MATE PREFERENCES AND THE FIVE-FACTOR MODEL (FFM) | realworldpsychology |

What Men Want in a Mate

1. Mutual attraction—love
2. Dependable character
3. Emotional stability and maturity
4. Pleasing disposition
5. Good health
6. Education and intelligence
7. Sociability
8. Desire for home and children
9. Refinement, neatness
10. Good looks

What Women Want in a Mate

1. Mutual attraction—love
2. Dependable character
3. Emotional stability and maturity
4. Pleasing disposition
5. Education and intelligence
6. Sociability
7. Good health
8. Desire for home and children
9. Ambition and industriousness
10. Refinement, neatness

Source: Based on Buss et al., 1990.

© Michelle Marsan/Shutterstock

 Q2

In addition to having strong cross-cultural support, trait theories, like the FFM, allow us to predict real-life preferences and behaviors. For example, using the FFM, people who are extraverted have been found to prefer upbeat, energetic, and rhythmic types of music, such as rap and hip-hop. People who are open to experience prefer complex, intense, and rebellious music, such as classical and rock (Langemeyer et al., 2012). As you might expect, personality may also affect your career choice and job satisfaction (see *Test Yourself*).

TEST YOURSELF: MATCHING YOUR PERSONALITY WITH YOUR CAREER

psychology and you

Are some people better suited for certain jobs than others? According to psychologist John Holland's *personality-job-fit theory*, a match (or "good fit") between our individual personality and our career choice is a major factor in determining job satisfaction (Holland, 1985, 1994). Research shows that a good fit between personality and occupation helps increase subjective well-being, job success, and job satisfaction. In other words, people tend to be happier and like their work when they're well matched to their jobs (Joeng et al., 2013; Perkmen & Sahin, 2013; Williamson & Lounsbury, 2013). Check this table to see what job would be a good match for your personality.

Personality Characteristics	Holland Personality Type	Matching/Congruent Occupations
Shy, genuine, persistent, stable, conforming, practical	1. *Realistic:* Prefers physical activities that require skill, strength, and coordination	Mechanic, drill press operator, assembly-line worker, farmer
Analytical, original, curious, independent	2. *Investigative:* Prefers activities that involve thinking, organizing, and understanding	Biologist, economist, mathematician, news reporter
Sociable, friendly, cooperative, understanding	3. *Social:* Prefers activities that involve helping and developing others	Social worker, counselor, teacher, clinical psychologist
Conforming, efficient, practical, unimaginative, inflexible	4. *Conventional:* Prefers rule-regulated, orderly, and unambiguous activities	Accountant, bank teller, file clerk, manager
Imaginative, disorderly, idealistic, emotional, impractical	5. *Artistic:* Prefers ambiguous and unsystematic activities that allow creative expression	Painter, musician, writer, interior decorator
Self-confident, ambitious, energetic, domineering	6. *Enterprising:* Prefers verbal activities with opportunities to influence others and attain power	Lawyer, real estate agent, public relations specialist, small business manager

Source: Adapted and reproduced with special permission of the publisher, Psychological Assessment Resources, Inc., 16204 North Florida Avenue, Lutz, Florida 33549, from the *Dictionary of Holland Occupational Codes*, 3rd edition, by Gary D. Gottfredson, Ph.D., and John L. Holland, Ph.D., Copyright 1982, 1989, 1996. Further reproduction is prohibited without permission from PAR, Inc.

Trait theories, particularly the FFM, have proven to be successful at *describing* personality and predicting certain behaviors and preferences. However, critics argue that they fail to consider situational determinants of personality or to offer sufficient *explanations* for why people develop specific traits (Chamorro-Premuzic, 2011; Cheung et al., 2011; Furguson et al., 2011). And although trait theories have documented fairly high levels of personality stability over the life span, they have failed to identify which characteristics last a lifetime and which are most likely to change (Allemand et al., 2013; Boyce et al., 2013; Kandler et al., 2012; McCrae, 2011).

realworldpsychology   **Can Personality Change?** Prior to serving jail time for dog fighting, NFL quarterback Michael Vick relied almost exclusively on his natural athletic ability. Out of jail, he became a great teammate—the first to the field and the last to leave, and in 2010, he was named NFL's "Comeback Player of the Year" (Wilner, 2011). Do you think this change is permanent? Why or why not?

Jonathan Ernst/Getty Images, Inc.

RETRIEVAL PRACTICE: TRAIT THEORIES

Self-Test

Completing this self-test and comparing your answers with those in Appendix B provides immediate feedback and helpful practice for exams. Additional interactive, self-tests are available at www.wiley.com/college/huffman.

1. _____ is a statistical technique that groups large arrays of data into more basic units.

   a. MMPI   b. FFM
   c. Factor analysis   d. Regression analysis

2. What are the "Big Five" personality traits in the five-factor model?

   a. conscientiousness, openness, extroversion, agreeableness, and neuroticism
   b. openness, conscientiousness, introversion, agreeableness, and neuroticism
   c. shyness, conscientiousness, extroversion, agreeableness, and neuroticism
   d. shyness, conscientiousness, introversion, agreeableness, and neuroticism

3. People who score high in _____ are emotionally unstable and prone to insecurity, anxiety, guilt, worry, and moodiness.

   a. openness   b. conscientiousness
   c. extroversion   d. neuroticism

4. Trait theories of personality have been criticized for _____.

   a. failing to explain why people develop specific traits
   b. not including a large number of central traits
   c. failing to identify which traits last and which are transient
   d. not considering situational determinants of personality
   e. all but one of these options

Think Critically

1 After reading the descriptions for each of the Big Five personality dimensions, how well do you think they describe your key traits? Thinking of someone you know very well, can you predict how he or she might score on each of these traits?

2 What limitations do you believe trait theory has when we are looking at human development over the life span?

realworldpsychology

Can personality traits predict the type of music we like?

HINT: LOOK IN THE MARGIN FOR (Q2)

HUMANISTIC THEORIES

RETRIEVAL PRACTICE While reading the upcoming sections, respond to each Learning Objective in your own words. Then compare your responses with those found at www.wiley.com/college/Huffman.

1 EXPLAIN the importance of the self in Rogers's theory of personality.

2 DESCRIBE how Maslow's hierarchy of needs affects personality.

3 IDENTIFY the pros and cons of humanistic theories.

Self-actualization The humanistic term for the inborn drive to realize one's full potential and to develop all one's inherent talents and capabilities.

Humanistic theories of personality emphasize each person's internal feelings, thoughts, and sense of basic worth. In contrast to Freud's generally negative view of human nature, humanists believe that people are naturally good (or, at worst, neutral) and that they possess a natural tendency toward **self-actualization**, the inborn drive to develop all their talents and capabilities.

According to this view, our personality and behavior depend on how we perceive and interpret the world, not on traits, unconscious impulses, or rewards and punishments. Humanistic psychology was developed largely by Carl Rogers and Abraham Maslow.

Rogers's Theory

Self-concept A person's relatively stable self-perception, or mental model, based on life experiences, particularly the feedback and perception of others.

To psychologist Carl Rogers (1902–1987), the most important component of personality is our **self-concept**, the way we see and feel about ourselves. Rogers emphasized that mental health and adjustment reflect the degree of overlap (congruence) between our perceived real and ideal selves (see *Test Yourself*). This self-perception is relatively stable over time and develops from our life experiences, particularly the feedback and perception of others.

TEST YOURSELF: MEASURING YOUR PERSONAL SELF-CONCEPT

psychology and you

Stop for a moment and briefly describe yourself as you'd *ideally* like to be and as how you *actually* are. Now draw two circles, labeled "real self" and "ideal self," depicting how much your two perceived selves overlap. According to Carl Rogers, if your *real* self and *ideal* self are nearly the same, with considerable overlap in the two circles, you have congruence between your two "selves" and a positive self-concept. Unfortunately, many people have experienced negative life events and feedback from others that have led to negative self-concepts. In Rogers's view, poor mental health and personality maladjustment develop from a mismatch, or *incongruence*, between our ideal and real selves.

Congruence

Real Self | Ideal Self

Well-adjusted individual
Considerable overlap between the ideal and real selves

Incongruence

Real Self | Ideal Self

Poorly adjusted individual
Little overlap between the ideal and real selves

Why do some people develop negative self-concepts and poor mental health? Rogers believed that such outcomes generally result from early childhood experiences with parents and other adults who make their love and acceptance *conditional* and contingent on behaving in certain ways and expressing only certain feelings. Imagine being a child who is repeatedly told that your naturally occurring negative feelings and behaviors (which we all have) are totally unacceptable and unlovable. Can you see how your self-concept may become distorted? And why as an adult you might develop a shy, avoidant personality, always doubting the love and approval of others because they don't know "the real person hiding inside"?

To help children develop their fullest personality and life potential, Rogers cautioned that adults need to create an atmosphere of **unconditional positive regard**—a warm and caring environment in which a child is never disapproved of as a person. Interestingly, parents who engage in responsive caregiving, a form of unconditional positive regard, also tend to show this same pattern of behavior toward their spouses, which in turn leads to higher levels of relationship satisfaction (Millings et al., 2013). This suggests that unconditional positive regard is important in all types of relationships.

This is *not* to say that adults must approve of everything a child does. Rogers emphasizes that we must separate the value of the person from his or her behaviors—encouraging the person's innate positive nature, while discouraging destructive or hostile behaviors. Humanistic psychologists in general suggest that both children and adults must control their behavior so they can develop a healthy self-concept and satisfying relationships with others **(Figure 11.10)**.

Unconditional positive regard Rogers's term for love and acceptance with no contingencies attached.

Maslow's Theory

Like Rogers, Abraham Maslow believed there is a basic goodness to human nature and a natural tendency toward *self-actualization*. Maslow saw personality development as a natural progression from lower to higher levels—a basic *hierarchy of needs*. As newborns, we focus on physiological needs like hunger and thirst, and then as we grow

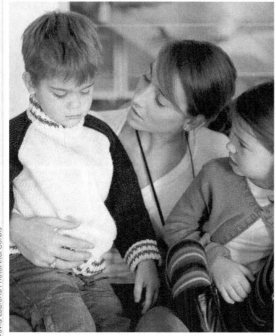

FIGURE 11.10 **UNCONDITIONAL POSITIVE REGARD**

In response to a child who is angry and hits his younger sister, the parent acknowledges that it is the behavior that is unacceptable, and not the child: "I know you're angry with your sister, but we don't hit. And you won't be able to play with her for a while unless you control your anger."

FIGURE 11.11 MASLOW'S HIERARCHY OF NEEDS

Although our natural movement is upward from physical needs toward the highest level, *self-actualization*, Maslow also believed we sometimes "regress" toward a lower level—especially under stressful conditions. For example, during national disasters, people first rush to stockpile food and water (physiological needs) and then often clamor for a strong leader to take over, enforce the rules, and make things right (safety needs).

and develop, we move on through four higher levels **(Figure 11.11)**. Cross-cultural support for Maslow's theory comes from recent surveys of people from 123 countries, which found that people from around the world do share a focus on the same basic needs, and when those needs are met, they report higher levels of happiness.

According to Maslow, self-actualization is the inborn drive to develop all our talents and capacities. It requires understanding our own potential, accepting ourselves and others as unique individuals, and taking a problem-centered approach to life (Maslow, 1970). Self-actualization is an ongoing process of growth rather than an end product or accomplishment.

Maslow believed that only a few, rare individuals, such as Albert Einstein, Mohandas Gandhi, and Eleanor Roosevelt, become fully self-actualized. However, he saw self-actualization as part of every person's basic hierarchy of needs. (See Chapter 10 for more information about Maslow's theory.)

Evaluating Humanistic Theories

Humanistic psychology was extremely popular during the 1960s and 1970s. It was seen as a refreshing new perspective on personality after the negative determinism of the psychoanalytic approach and the mechanical nature of learning theories (Chapter 6). Although this early popularity has declined, humanistic theories have provided valuable insights that are useful for personal growth and self-understanding. They also play a major role in contemporary counseling and psychotherapy, as well as in modern childrearing, education, and managerial practices (DeRobertis, 2013; Greenberg et al., 2013; Tennen et al., 2013).

However, humanistic theories have also been criticized (Cervone & Pervin, 2010; Chamorro-Premuzic, 2011; Funder, 2000; Schmid, 2013) for the following:

1. **Naïve assumptions** Some critics suggest that humanistic theories are unduly optimistic and overlook the negative aspects of human nature. For example, how would humanists explain immoral politicians, the spread of terrorism, and humankind's ongoing history of war and murder?

2. **Poor testability and inadequate evidence** Like many psychoanalytic terms and concepts, humanistic concepts such as unconditional positive regard and self-actualization are difficult to define operationally and to test scientifically.

3. **Narrowness** Like trait theories, humanistic theories have been criticized for merely describing personality rather than explaining it. For example, where does the motivation for self-actualization come from? To say that it is an "inborn drive" doesn't satisfy those who favor using experimental research and hard data to learn about personality.

RETRIEVAL PRACTICE: HUMANISTIC THEORIES

Self-Test

Completing this self-test and comparing your answers with those in Appendix B provides immediate feedback and helpful practice for exams. Additional interactive, self-tests are available at www.wiley.com/college/huffman.

1. The _____ approach emphasizes internal experiences, like feelings, thoughts, and the basic worth of the individual.

a. humanistic   b. psychodynamic
c. personalistic   d. motivational

2. Rogers suggested that _____ is necessary for a child to develop his or her fullest personality and life potential.

a. authoritative parenting   b. a challenging environment
c. unconditional positive regard   d. a friendly neighborhood

3. _____ believed in the basic goodness of individuals and their natural tendency toward self-actualization.

a. Karen Horney   b. Alfred Adler
c. Abraham Maslow   d. Carl Jung

4. A major criticism of humanistic psychology is that most of its concepts and assumptions _____.

a. are invalid   b. are unreliable
c. cannot be tested scientifically   d. lack a theoretical foundation

Think Critically

1 Do you agree with Rogers that unconditional positive regard from parents is key to healthy personality development? Why or why not?

2 Thinking of the traits of a fully self-actualized person, can you identify someone who exhibits all or most of these qualities? What criticism of humanistic theories is also a weakness of trait theories?

realworldpsychology

What parenting skills are also associated with increased marital satisfaction?

HINT: LOOK IN THE MARGIN FOR (Q3)

SOCIAL-COGNITIVE THEORIES

RETRIEVAL PRACTICE While reading the upcoming sections, respond to each Learning Objective in your own words. Then compare your responses with those found at www.wiley.com/college/Huffman.

1 **EXPLAIN** Bandura's concept of self-efficacy and Rotter's concept of locus of control.
2 **SUMMARIZE** the attractions and criticisms of the social-cognitive perspective on personality.

LEARNING OBJECTIVES

As you've just seen, psychoanalytic/psychodynamic, trait, and humanistic theories all tend to focus on internal, personal factors in personality development. In contrast, today's *social-cognitive* theories emphasize the influence of our *social* interpersonal interactions with the environment, along with our *cognitions*—our thoughts, feelings, expectations, and values.

Bandura's and Rotter's Approaches

Albert Bandura (also discussed in Chapter 6) has played a major role in reintroducing thought processes into personality theory. Cognition, or thought, is central to his concept of **self-efficacy**, which is very similar to our everyday notion of self-confidence (Bandura, 1997, 2011, 2012).

Self-efficacy Bandura's term for a person's learned expectation of success in a given situation; also, another term for self-confidence.

According to Bandura, if you have a strong sense of self-efficacy, you believe you can generally succeed and reach your goals, regardless of past failures and current obstacles. Your self-efficacy will in turn affect which challenges you choose to accept and the effort you expend in reaching goals. For example, one study found that children who assisted their parents with meal preparation reported higher self-efficacy for selecting and eating healthy foods (Chu et al., 2013).

psychology and you **Self-efficacy in Daily Life** The classic children's story *The Little Engine That Could* illustrates how we learn self-efficacy through our personal experiences with success. The little engine starts up a steep hill, saying, "I think I can, I think I can." After lots of hard work and perseverance, he ends up at the top of the hill and says, "I know I can, I know I can."

Bandura emphasized that self-efficacy is a *learned* expectation of success, but only in a given situation. It doesn't necessarily transfer to other circumstances. Bandura would suggest that the little engine's new-found self-efficacy will help him climb future hills. However, it wouldn't necessarily improve his overall speed or his ability to turn sharp corners. Similarly, self-defense training significantly affects a woman's belief that she can improve her odds of escaping from or disabling a potential assailant or rapist. But it does not lead her to feel more capable in all areas of her life (Weitlauf et al., 2001).

How then can we transfer self-efficacy to other parts of our everyday life? If you've experienced success as an athlete, a parent, or even a videogame player, consider how the skills you've demonstrated in these areas can be transferred to your academic life. Instead of saying, "I just can't find time to study" or "I never do well on tests," remind yourself of how your ongoing success in athletics, parenting, or videogames has resulted from good time management, hours of practice, patience, hard work, and perseverance. Applying skills that are the same as or similar to skills you've successfully used before will help move you from "I can't" to "I think I can." And then when you get your first high grade in a difficult course, you can move on to "I know I can, I know I can!"

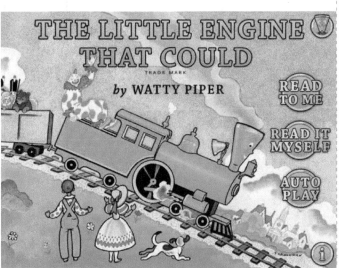

Reciprocal determinism Bandura's belief that a complex reciprocal interaction exists among the individual, his or her behavior, and environmental stimuli.

How does self-efficacy affect personality? Bandura sees personality as being shaped by **reciprocal determinism**, how the *person* (his or her personality, thoughts, expectations, etc.), *environment*, and *behavior* interact and influence one another **(Figure 11.12)**. Using Bandura's concept of self-efficacy, can you see how your own beliefs will affect how others respond to you and thereby influence your chance for success? Your belief ("I can succeed") will affect behaviors ("I'll work hard and ask for a promotion"), which in turn will affect the environment ("My employer recognized my efforts and promoted me").

Julian Rotter's theory is similar to Bandura's in that it suggests that learning experiences create *cognitive expectancies* that guide behavior and influence the environment (Rotter, 1954, 1990). According to Rotter, your behavior or personality is determined by (1) what you expect to happen following a specific action and (2) the reinforcement value attached to specific outcomes.

To understand your personality and behavior, Rotter would use personality tests that measure your internal versus external *locus of control* (Chapter 3). Rotter's tests ask subjects to respond to statements such as, "People get ahead in this world primarily by luck and connections rather than by hard work and perseverance" and "When someone doesn't like you, there is little you can do about it." As you may suspect, people with an external locus of control think the environment and external

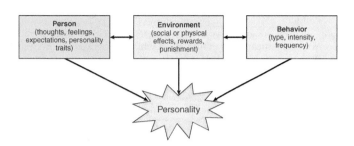

| Person (thoughts, feelings, expectations, personality traits) | Environment (social or physical effects, rewards, punishment) | Behavior (type, intensity, frequency) |

Personality

FIGURE 11.12 BANDURA'S THEORY OF RECIPROCAL DETERMINISM

According to Albert Bandura, personality is determined by a three-way, reciprocal interaction of the internal characteristics of the person, the external environment, and the person's behavior.

forces have primary control over their lives, whereas people with an *internal locus of control* think they can personally control events in their lives through their own efforts **(Figure 11.13)**.

Evaluating Social-Cognitive Theories

The social-cognitive perspective holds several attractions. First, it offers testable, objective hypotheses and operationally defined terms, and it relies on empirical data. Second, social-cognitive theories emphasize how the environment affects, and is affected by, individuals. Walter Mischel, a social-cognitive theorist, ignited the classic *person–situation debate* when he suggested that our personalities change according to a given situation (Mischel, 1968, 1984, 2004; Mischel & Shoda, 2008). Most of us behave differently in different situations—a shy person who never speaks up in large crowds may be very talkative at home or with friends.

Recognizing this flexibility, Mischel initially argued that personality traits are relatively poor predictors of actual behavior. He later softened his position, and said that behavior emerges from the interplay between personality characteristics and situational forces.

While this person versus situation debate continues, critics argue that social-cognitive theories focus too much on situational influences. They also suggest that this approach fails to adequately acknowledge the stability of personality, as well as unconscious, emotional, and biological influences (Ahmetoglu & Chamorro-Premuzic, 2013; Cook, 2013; Westen, 1998, 2007).

"We're encouraging people to become involved in their own rescue."

FIGURE 11.13 LOCUS OF CONTROL AND ACHIEVEMENT

Despite this cartoon's humorous message, research does link a perception of control with higher achievement, greater life satisfaction, and better overall mental health (Fitzgerald & Clark, 2013; Greene & Murdock, 2013; Herbert et al., 2013; You et al., 2011; Zampieri & Pedrosa de Souza, 2011).

RETRIEVAL PRACTICE: SOCIAL-COGNITIVE THEORIES

Self-Test

Completing this self-test and comparing your answers with those in Appendix B provides immediate feedback and helpful practice for exams. Additional interactive, self-tests are available at www.wiley.com/college/huffman.

1. According to Bandura, _____ relies on a person's belief about whether he or she can successfully engage in behaviors related to personal goals.

a. self-actualization   b. self-esteem
c. self-efficacy   d. self-congruence

2. Bandura's theory of _____ suggests that the person, behavior, and environment all interact to produce personality.

a. self-actualization   b. self-esteem maximization
c. self-efficacy   d. reciprocal determinism

3. According to Rotter, people with a(n) _____ believe the environment and external forces control events, whereas those with a(n) _____ believe in personal control.

a. self-actualized personality;   b. external locus of control;
    efficacy personality   internal locus of control
c. fatalistic view;   d. global locus of control;
    humanistic opinion   selfish locus of control

4. Walter Mischel, a social-cognitive theorist, ignited the classic person–situation debate when he suggested that _____.

a. our personalities change   b. our personalities change
    according to a given   according to prenatal
    situation   nutrition
c. our personalities seldom   d. our personalities change
    change over our lifetimes   according to our horoscope

Think Critically

1 How would Bandura's social-cognitive concept of self-efficacy explain why bright students sometimes don't do well in college?

2 Do you have an internal or external locus of control? How might this affect your academic and lifetime achievement?

realworldpsychology

Does helping parents prepare a meal increase a child's preference for healthy foods?

HINT: LOOK IN THE MARGIN FOR Q4

BIOLOGICAL THEORIES

LEARNING OBJECTIVES

RETRIEVAL PRACTICE While reading the upcoming sections, respond to each Learning Objective in your own words. Then compare your responses with found at www.wiley.com/college/Huffman.

1 **SUMMARIZE** the roles that brain structures, neurochemistry, and genetics play in personality.
2 **EXPLAIN** the contributions and limitations of biological theories.
3 **DESCRIBE** how the biopsychosocial model integrates different theories of personality.

In this section, we explore how biological factors influence our personalities. We conclude with a discussion of how all theories of personality ultimately interact in the *biopsychosocial model*.

Three Major Contributors to Personality

Hans Eysenck, the trait theorist mentioned earlier in the chapter, was one of the first to propose that personality traits are biologically based—at least in part. And modern research agrees that certain brain structures, neurochemistry, and genetics all may contribute to some personality characteristics. For example, how do we decide in the real world which risks are worth taking and which are not? Modern research using functional magnetic resonance imaging (fMRI) and other brain mapping techniques documents specific areas of the brain that correlate with trait impulsiveness and areas that differ between people with risk-averse and those with risk-seeking personalities (Cox et al., 2010; Schilling et al., 2013).

Earlier research also found that increased electroencephalographic (EEG) activity in the left frontal lobes of the brain is associated with sociability (or extroversion), whereas greater EEG activity in the right frontal lobes is associated with shyness or introversion versus extroversion (Fishman & Ng, 2013; Tellegen, 1985).

A major limitation of research on brain structures and personality is the difficulty of identifying which structures are uniquely connected with particular personality traits. Neurochemistry seems to offer more precise data on how biology influences personality. For example, sensation seeking (Chapter 11) has consistently been linked with levels of monoamine oxidase (MAO), an enzyme that regulates levels of neurotransmitters such as dopamine (Lee, 2011; Zuckerman, 1994, 2004). Dopamine also seems to be correlated with addictive personality traits, novelty seeking, and extroversion (Blum et al., 2013; Camperio et al., 2013; Marusich et al., 2011; Nemoda et al., 2011; Thomson et al., 2013).

realworldpsychology   **Biology's Impact on Personality** How can neurochemistry have such effects? Studies suggest that high-sensation seekers and extroverts tend to experience less physical arousal than introverts from the same stimulus (Figueredo et al., 2011; Fishman & Ng, 2013; Munoz & Anastassiou-Hadjicharalambous, 2011). Extroverts' low arousal apparently motivates them to seek out situations that will elevate their arousal. Moreover, it is believed that a higher arousal threshold is genetically transmitted. In other words, personality traits like sensation seeking and extroversion may be inherited.

© FurmanAnna/iStockphoto

This recognition that genetic factors have an important influence on personality has contributed to the relatively new field called *behavioral genetics* (Lessov-Schlaggar et al., 2013; Maxson, 2013), which attempts to determine the extent to which behavioral differences among people are due to genetics as opposed to the environment (Chapter 2). One interesting study found that when participants' saliva was genetically tested, those who had a "niceness gene" were more likely to report engaging in various types of prosocial behaviors, such as giving blood and engaging in volunteer work and making charitable contributions (Poulin et al., 2012). This finding suggests that even how nice we are may be at least partially based on our biology!

One way to measure genetic influences is to compare similarities in personality between identical twins and fraternal twins. For example, studies of the five-factor model (FFM) personality traits suggest that genetic factors contribute about 40 to 50% of personality (Bouchard, 1997, 2004; Eysenck, 1967, 1990; Kan et al., 2013; McCrae et al., 2004; Plomin, 1990; Slutske et al., 2013; Veselka et al., 2011).

In addition to conducting twin studies, researchers compare the personalities of parents with those of their biological children and their adopted children. Studies of extroversion and neuroticism have found that parents' traits correlate moderately with those of their biological children and hardly at all with those of their adopted children (Bouchard, 1997; McCrae et al., 2000).

Evaluating Biological Theories

Modern research in biological theories has provided exciting insights, and it has established clear links between some personality traits and various brain areas, neurotransmitters, and/or genetics. However, it's important to keep in mind that personality traits are never the result of a single biological process. For example, studies do show a strong inherited basis for personality, but researchers are careful not to overemphasize genetics (Ahmetoglu & Chamorro-Premuzic, 2013; Beauchamp et al., 2011; Chadwick, 2011; Cook, 2013). Some believe the importance of the unshared environment—aspects of the environment that differ from one individual to another, even within a family—has been overlooked. Others fear that research on "genetic determinism" could be misused to "prove" that an ethnic or a racial group is inferior, that male dominance is natural, or that social progress is impossible.

In sum, there is no doubt that biological studies have produced valuable results. However, as is true for all the theories discussed in this chapter, no single personality theory explains everything we need to know about personality. Each theory offers different insights into how a person develops the distinctive set of characteristics we call "personality." That's why instead of adhering to any one theory, many psychologists believe in the *biopsychosocial approach*, or the idea that several factors—biological, psychological, and social—overlap in their contributions to personality **(Figure 11.14)**.

FIGURE 11.14 MULTIPLE INFLUENCES ON PERSONALITY

Research indicates that three major factors influence personality: genetic (inherited) factors, nonshared environmental factors (the way each individual's genetic factors react and adjust to his or her environment), and shared environmental factors (parental and family experiences).

Rosanne Olson/Stone/Getty Images

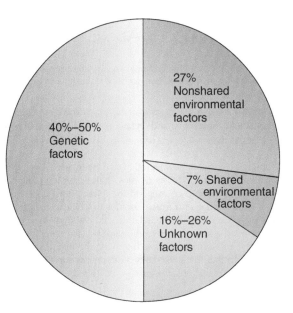

Source: Bouchard, 1997, 2004; Eysenck, 1967, 1990; Jang et al., 2006; McCrae et al., 2004; Plomin, 1990; Weiss et al., 2008

RETRIEVAL PRACTICE: BIOLOGICAL THEORIES

Self-Test

Completing this self-test and comparing your answers with those in Appendix B provides immediate feedback and helpful practice for exams. Additional interactive, self-tests are available at www.wiley.com/college/huffman.

1. _____ was one of the earliest theorists to suggest that personality traits are biologically based—at least in part.

   a. Albert Bandura   b. Hans Eysenck
   c. Abraham Maslow   d. Karen Horney

2. Dopamine is reportedly involved in the personality trait(s) _____.

   a. conscientiousness, extroversion, and altruism
   b. extroversion and neuroticism
   c. impulsivity, aggression and altruism
   d. novelty seeking, extroversion, and sensation seeking

3. _____ theories emphasize the importance of genetics in the development of personality.

   a. Behavioral genetics   b. Behavioral metrics
   c. Social/personal genetics   d. Biometrical engineering

4. The _____ approach represents a blending of several theories of personality.

   a. inherited basis   b. biopsychosocial
   c. social/overlap   d. none of these options

Think Critically

1 If biological factors explain certain personality traits, what advice would you give to someone who is painfully shy and wants to become more outgoing?

2 Given that many of the same brain structures most closely associated with personality are also linked with emotions, what does this suggest about the role of emotions in our personalities?

realworldpsychology

Can our genes predict how much we will give to charity?

HINT: LOOK IN THE MARGIN FOR Q5

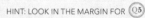

PERSONALITY ASSESSMENT

RETRIEVAL PRACTICE While reading the upcoming sections, respond to each Learning Objective in your own words. Then compare your responses with those found at www.wiley.com/college/Huffman.

1 SUMMARIZE the four major methods psychologists use to measure personality.
2 DESCRIBE the benefits and limitations of each method of personality assessment.
3 DISCUSS the three logical fallacies associated with pseudo-personality tests.

Numerous unscientific methods have been used over the decades to assess personality (**Figure 11.15**). As we saw in the opening paragraphs of this chapter, even today, some people consult fortune-tellers, horoscope columns in the newspaper, tarot cards, and even fortune cookies in Chinese restaurants. But scientific research has provided much more reliable and valid methods for measuring personality. Clinical and counseling psychologists, psychiatrists, and other helping professionals use these modern methods to help with the diagnosis of patients and to assess their progress in therapy. Personality assessments can be grouped into a few broad categories: *interviews*, *observations*, *objective tests*, and *projective tests*.

Interviews and Observation

We all use informal "interviews" to get to know other people. When first meeting someone, we usually ask about his or her job, academic interests, family, or hobbies. Psychologists also use interviews. In an unstructured format, interviewers get

LEARNING OBJECTIVES

FIGURE 11.15 **PERSONALITY AND BUMPS ON THE HEAD?**

In the 1800s, if you wanted to have your personality assessed, you would go to a phrenologist, who would determine your personality by measuring the bumps on your skull and comparing the measurements with a chart that associated different areas of the skull with particular traits, such as *sublimity* (ability to squelch natural impulses, especially sexual) and *ideality* (ability to live by high ideals). What traits might be measured if we still believed in phrenology today?

© Bettmann/CORBIS

impressions and pursue hunches or let the interviewee expand on information that promises to disclose personality characteristics. In structured interviews, the interviewer asks specific questions in order to evaluate the interviewee's responses more objectively and compare them with others' responses.

In addition to conducting interviews, psychologists also assess personality by directly and methodically observing behavior. They look for examples of specific behaviors and follow a careful set of evaluation guidelines. For instance, a psychologist might arrange to observe a troubled client's interactions with his or her family. Does the client become agitated by the presence of certain family members and not others? Does he or she become passive and withdrawn when asked a direct question? Through careful observation, the psychologist gains valuable insights into the client's personality as well as family dynamics **(Figure 11.16)**.

Objective Tests

Objective personality tests, or inventories, are the most widely used method of assessing personality, for two reasons: They can be administered to a large number of people relatively quickly, and they can be evaluated in a standardized fashion. Some objective tests measure one specific personality trait, such as sensation seeking (Chapter 10) or locus of control. However, psychologists in clinical, counseling, and industrial settings often wish to assess a range of personality traits. To do so, they generally use multitrait, or *multiphasic*, inventories.

The most widely studied and clinically used multitrait test is the **Minnesota Multiphasic Personality Inventory (MMPI)**—or its revision, the MMPI-2 (Butcher, 2000, 2011; Butcher & Perry, 2008; Silverstein, 2013; Tennen et al., 2013). This test consists of more than 500 statements to which participants respond with *True, False*, or *Cannot Say*. The following are examples of the kinds of statements found on the MMPI:

My stomach frequently bothers me.

I have enemies who really wish to harm me.

I sometimes hear things that other people can't hear.

I would like to be a mechanic.

I have never indulged in any unusual sex practices.

Minnesota Multiphasic Personality Inventory (MMPI) The most widely researched and clinically used self-report personality test. (MMPI-2 is the revised version.)

FIGURE 11.16 **BEHAVIORAL OBSERVATION**

How might careful observation help a psychologist better understand a troubled client's personality and family dynamics?

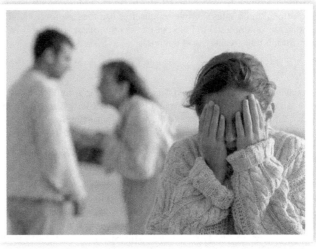

David De Lossy/Getty Images

TABLE 11.3	SUBSCALES OF THE MMPI-2
Clinical Scales	**Typical Interpretations of High Scores**
1. Hypochondriasis	Numerous physical complaints
2. Depression	Seriously depressed and pessimistic
3. Hysteria	Suggestible, immature, self-centered, demanding
4. Psychopathic deviate	Rebellious, nonconformist
5. Masculinity–femininity	Interests like those of the other sex
6. Paranoia	Suspicious and resentful of others
7. Psychasthenia	Fearful, agitated, brooding
8. Schizophrenia	Withdrawn, reclusive, bizarre thinking
9. Hypomania	Distractible, impulsive, dramatic
10. Social introversion	Shy, introverted, self-effacing
Validity Scales	**Typical Interpretations of High Scores**
1. L (lie)	Denies common problems, projects a "saintly" or false picture
2. F (confusion)	Answers are contradictory
3. K (defensiveness)	Minimizes social and emotional complaints Many items left unanswered
4. ? (cannot say)	

Did you notice that some of these questions are about very unusual, abnormal behavior? Although there are many "normal" questions on the full MMPI, the test is designed primarily to help clinical and counseling psychologists diagnose psychological disorders. MMPI test items are grouped into 10 clinical scales, each measuring a different disorder **(Table 11.3)**. There are also a number of validity scales designed to reflect the extent to which respondents (1) distort their answers in an attempt to fake psychological disturbances or to appear more psychologically healthy than they really are, (2) do not understand the items, (3) are being uncooperative, and/or (4) genuinely cannot answer the questions.

Other objective personality measures are less focused on psychological disorders. A good example is the NEO Personality Inventory–Revised, which assesses the dimensions of the five-factor model.

Note that personality tests like the MMPI are often confused with *career inventories*, or vocational interest tests. Career counselors use these latter tests (along with aptitude and achievement tests) to help people identify occupations and careers that match their unique traits, values, and interests.

Projective Tests

Unlike objective tests, **projective tests** use unstructured stimuli that subjects can perceive in many ways. When you listen to a piece of music or look at a picture, you might say that the music is sad or that the people in the picture look happy—but not everyone would have the same interpretation. Some psychologists believe that these different interpretations reveal important things about each individual's personality.

As the name implies, projective tests are meant to allow each person to project his or her own unconscious conflicts, psychological defenses, motives, and personality traits onto the test materials. Because respondents may be unable or unwilling to express their true feelings if asked directly, the ambiguous stimuli reportedly provide an indirect "psychological X-ray" of important unconscious processes (Hogan, 2006). Two of the most widely used projective tests are the **Rorschach Inkblot Test** and the **Thematic Apperception Test (TAT)** (Choca, 2013; Silverstein, 2013) **(Figure 11.17)**.

Projective test A method of personality assessment in which an individual is presented with a standardized set of ambiguous stimuli, such as inkblots or abstract drawings, which allow the test taker to project his or her unconscious onto the test material; the individual's responses are assumed to reveal inner feelings, motives, and conflicts.

Rorschach Inkblot Test A projective test based on 10 cards with symmetrical abstract patterns, known as inkblots, which asks respondents to describe what they "see" in the image; the subject's response is thought to be a projection of unconscious processes.

Thematic Apperception Test (TAT) A projective test in which pictures of ambiguous scenes are presented to an individual, who is encouraged to generate stories about them; the responses supposedly reflect a projection of the respondent's unconscious processes.

FIGURE 11.17 SAMPLE PROJECTIVE TESTS

The verbal or written responses participants make to projective tests reportedly reflect unconscious, hidden parts of their personalities that they unintentionally "project" onto the stimuli.

Ⓐ The *Rorschach Inkblot Test* was introduced in 1921 by Swiss psychiatrist Hermann Rorschach. With this technique, individuals are shown 10 inkblots like the one shown here, one at a time, and are asked to report what figures or objects they see in each of them.

Ⓑ Created by personality researcher Henry Murray in 1938, the *Thematic Apperception Test (TAT)* consists of a series of ambiguous black-and-white pictures that are shown to the test taker, who is asked to create a story related to each one.

Photolibrary/Getty Images

Are Personality Measurements Accurate?

Let's evaluate the strengths and the challenges of each of the four methods of personality assessment: *interviews, observation, objective tests,* and *projective tests.*

Interviews and Observations

Both interviews and observations can provide valuable insights into personality, but they are time-consuming and expensive. Furthermore, raters of personality tests frequently disagree in their evaluations of the same individuals. Interviews and observations also take place in unnatural settings, and, in fact, the very presence of an observer can alter a subject's behavior.

Objective Tests

Tests like the MMPI-2 provide specific, objective information about a broad range of personality traits in a relatively short period. However, they are also subject to at least three major criticisms:

1. **Deliberate deception and social desirability bias** Some items on personality inventories are easy to see through, so respondents may intentionally, or unintentionally, fake particular personality traits. In addition, some respondents want to look good and will answer questions in ways that they perceive are socially desirable. To avoid these problems, the MMPI-2 has built-in validity scales described earlier. In addition, personality researchers and some businesses avoid self-reports. Instead, they rely on other people, such as friends or coworkers, to rate an individual's personality, as well as how their personality influences their work performance (Connelly & Hülsheger, 2012). Given that most personality tests are based on self-report measures, and that three meta-analyses involving over 44,000 participants found that ratings from others were better predictors of actual behavior, academic achievement, and job performance (Connelly & Ones, 2010), can you see why other-ratings are so important?

2. **Diagnostic difficulties** In addition to the problems with all self-report inventories, when they are used for diagnosis, overlapping items sometimes make it difficult to pinpoint a disorder (Ben-Porath, 2013; Graham, 1991). Clients with severe disorders also sometimes score within the normal range, and normal clients sometimes score within the elevated range (Borghans et al., 2011; Morey, 2013).

3. **Cultural bias and inappropriate use** Some critics think the standards for "normalcy" on objective tests fail to recognize the impact of culture (Hill et al., 2012). For example, Latinos generally score higher on the masculine end of the masculinity–femininity scale of the MMPI-2 than respondents from North American and Western European cultures (Dana, 2005; Ketterer, 2011; Mundia, 2011). However, this tendency probably reflects traditional gender roles and cultural training more than any individual personality traits. Similarly, some recent research examining personality traits in members of the Tsimané culture, a community of foragers and farmers in Bolivia with relatively little contact with the outside world, reveals two distinct dimensions of personality—prosociality and industriousness—instead of the more widely accepted five personality traits (Gurven et al., 2012).

Differences in personality may also be seen in different parts of a single country. For example, one study of over half a million people in the United States revealed regional differences in personality traits linked with entrepreneurial activity, defined as business-creation and self-employment rates (Obschonka et al., 2013). As you can see in **Figure 11.18**, certain regions are much more entrepreneurial than others. Why? The authors of the study suggested that the higher scores in the West, for example, might be a reflection of America's historical migration patterns of people moving from the East into the West (or from outside of America). They cite other research (e.g., Rentfrow et al., 2008) that suggests this selective migration may have had a lasting effect on personality due to the heritability of personality traits and the passing on of norms and values within the regions.

What do you think? How would you explain the differences? Can you see the overall value of expanding our study of personality from just looking at differences between individuals to examining regional differences, and how this expansion might increase our understanding of how personality is formed and its potential applications?

Projective Tests

Although projective tests are extremely time-consuming to administer and interpret, their proponents suggest that because the method is unstructured, respondents may be more willing to talk honestly about sensitive topics. Critics point out, however, that the *reliability* and *validity* (Chapter 8) of projective tests is among the lowest of all tests of personality (Gacono et al., 2008; Krug, 2013; Wood et al., 2011). (Recall from Chapter 8 that reliability—the consistency of test results—and reliability—whether the test actually measures what it was designed to measure—are the two most important measures of a good test.)

As you can see, each of these methods has limits, which is why psychologists typically combine the results from various scientific methods to create a fuller picture of any individual's personality. However, you're unlikely to have access to this type of professional analysis, so what's the most important take-home message? Beware of pop-psych books and pop-culture personality quizzes in magazines and websites! They may be entertaining, but they're rarely based on standardized testing or scientific research of any kind, and you should never base important decisions on their input.

Finally, throughout this text, we have emphasized the value of critical thinking, which also is useful in evaluating personality tests (see *What's Wrong With Pseudo-Personality Quizzes?*).

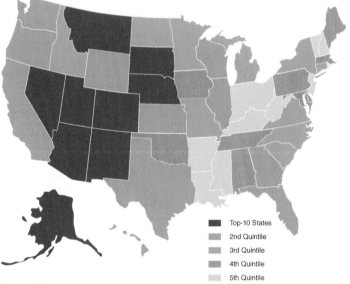

FIGURE 11.18 **ENTREPRENEURSHIP IN THE UNITED STATES**

- Top-10 States
- 2nd Quintile
- 3rd Quintile
- 4th Quintile
- 5th Quintile

WHAT'S WRONG WITH PSEUDO-PERSONALITY QUIZZES?

psychology and you

The personality horoscope presented in the chapter opener (p. 302) contains several logical fallacies. Using your critical thinking skills, can you see how the following three factors help explain why so many people believe in phony personality descriptions and predictions?

BARNUM EFFECT

We often accept pseudo-personality descriptions and horoscope predictions because we think they are accurate. We tend to believe these tests have somehow tapped into our unique selves. In fact, they are ambiguous, broad statements that fit just about anyone (e.g., "You have a strong need for other people to like and admire you"). The existence of such generalities led to the term the *Barnum effect*, named for the legendary circus promoter P.T. Barnum, who said, "Always have a little something for everyone" (Wyman & Vyse, 2008).

FALLACY OF POSITIVE INSTANCES

Look again at the introductory personality profile and count the number of times you agree with the statements. According to the *confirmation bias* (Chapter 8), we tend to notice and remember events that confirm our expectations and ignore those that are nonconfirming. If we see ourselves as independent thinkers, for example, we ignore the "needing to be liked by others" part and vice versa.

SELF-SERVING BIAS

Now check the overall tone of the bogus personality profile. Can you see how the traits are generally positive and flattering—or at least neutral? According to the *self-serving bias*, we tend to prefer information that maintains our positive self-image (Krusemark et al., 2008; Shepperd et al., 2008). In fact, research shows that the more favorable a personality description is, the more people believe it, and the more likely they are to believe it is personally unique (Guastello et al., 1989).

Taken together, these three logical fallacies help explain the common support for pop-psych personality tests and newspaper horoscopes. They offer something for everyone (*Barnum effect*). We pay attention only to what confirms our expectations (*confirmation bias*). And we like flattering descriptions (*self-serving bias*). You can test your understanding of these three biases in the following:

TESTING YOUR CRITICAL THINKING

Using the information in this *Psychology and You* section, can you identify the two major fallacies in this cartoon?

Answer: The self-serving bias and the Barnum effect.

RETRIEVAL PRACTICE: PERSONALITY ASSESSMENT

Self-Test

Completing this self-test and comparing your answers with those in Appendix B provides immediate feedback and helpful practice for exams. Additional interactive, self-tests are available at www.wiley.com/college/huffman.

1. In the 1800s, if you wanted to have your personality assessed, you would go to a phrenologist, who would determine your personality by studying/measuring _____.

   a. projective tests   b. ambiguous stimuli results
   c. inkblot stain responses   d. bumps on your head

2. The most widely researched and clinically used self-report personality test is the _____.

   a. MMPI   b. Rorschach Inkblot Test
   c. TAT   d. SVII

3. The Rorschach Inkblot Test is an example of a(n) _____ test.

   a. projective   b. ambiguous stimuli
   c. inkblot   d. all these options

4. Two important criteria for evaluating the usefulness of tests used to assess personality are _____.

   a. concurrence and prediction   b. reliability and validity
   c. consistency and correlation   d. diagnosis and prognosis

Think Critically

1 Which method of personality assessment (interviews, behavioral observation, objective testing, or projective testing) do you think is likely to be most informative? Can you think of circumstances in which one kind of assessment might be more effective than the others?

2 Why do you think objective personality tests like the MMPI are so popular and so widely used?

realworldpsychology

Why do people from different states vary in their entrepreneurial spirit?

HINT: LOOK IN THE MARGIN FOR (Q6)

Summary

1 PSYCHOANALYTIC/PSYCHODYNAMIC THEORIES   302

- Freud, the founder of psychodynamic theory, believed that the mind contained three *levels of consciousness*: **conscious**, **preconscious**, and **unconscious**. He believed that most psychological disorders originated from unconscious memories and instincts. Freud also asserted that personality was composed of the **id**, the **ego**, and the **superego**. When the ego fails to satisfy both the id and the superego, anxiety slips into conscious awareness, which triggers **defense mechanisms**. In addition, Freud believed that all children go through five **psychosexual stages**, which affect personality development.
- *Neo-Freudians* such as Adler, Jung, and Horney were influential followers of Freud who later rejected major aspects of Freudian theory.

2 TRAIT THEORIES   309

- Allport believed that the best way to understand personality was to arrange a person's unique personality **traits** into a hierarchy. Cattell and Eysenck later reduced the list of possible personality traits using *factor analysis*.
- The **five-factor model (FFM)** identifies major dimensions of personality, or the *Big Five*.

3 HUMANISTIC THEORIES   314

- According to Rogers, mental health and self-esteem are related to the degree of congruence between our **self-concept** and life experiences. Rogers argued that poor mental health results when young children do not receive **unconditional positive regard** from caregivers.

- Maslow saw personality as the quest to fulfill basic physiological needs and to move toward the highest level of **self-actualization**.

4 SOCIAL-COGNITIVE THEORIES 317

- Cognition is central to Bandura's concept of **self-efficacy**. According to Bandura, self-efficacy affects which challenges we choose to accept and the effort we expend in reaching goals. His concept of **reciprocal determinism** states that self-efficacy beliefs will also affect others' responses to us.
- Rotter's theory says that learning experiences create *cognitive expectancies* that guide behavior and influence the environment. Rotter believed that having an internal versus external *locus of control* affects personality and achievement.

5 BIOLOGICAL THEORIES 320

- Certain brain areas may contribute to personality. However, neurochemistry seems to offer more precise data on how biology influences personality. Research in *behavioral genetics* indicates that genetic factors also strongly influence personality.

- Instead of adhering to any one theory of personality, many psychologists believe in the biopsychosocial approach—the idea that several factors overlap in their contributions to personality.

6 PERSONALITY ASSESSMENT 323

- In an unstructured interview format, interviewers get impressions and pursue hunches or let the interviewee expand on information that promises to disclose personality characteristics. In structured interviews, interviewers ask specific predetermined questions so they can evaluate and compare multiple interviewee's responses more objectively. Psychologists also assess personality by directly observing behavior.
- **Objective personality tests** are widely used because we can administer them broadly and relatively quickly and evaluate them in a standardized fashion. To assess a range of personality traits, psychologists use multitrait inventories, such as the **MMPI**.
- **Projective tests** use unstructured stimuli that can be perceived in many ways. Projective tests, such as the **Rorschach Inkblot Test**, supposedly allow each person to project his or her own unconscious conflicts, psychological defenses, motives, and personality traits onto the test materials.

Cameron/Corbis Images

◎ applyingrealworldpsychology

We began this chapter with six intriguing Real World Psychology questions, and you were asked to revisit these questions at the end of each section. Questions like these have an important and lasting impact on all of our lives. See if you can answer these additional critical thinking questions related to real world examples.

1 As first discussed in Chapter 9 and throughout this chapter, early childhood relationships, particularly between parent and child, are very important to our personality development and overall psychological health. According to the five psychosexual stages of development, how might Freud interpret this woman and her son's obvious attachment to one another? Can you think of an alternative, more logical, explanation for their attachment?

2 How would Rogers's emphasis on unconditional positive regard and Bandura's social-cognitive concept of self-efficacy relate to this mother's display of pleasure at her son's attempt to dry her hair?

3 Can you identify one or more defense mechanisms that you use in your life? If you find them to be unhealthy, what can you do to change them?

4 If you agree that self-actualization is a worthy goal, what are you doing to move in that direction?

5 Which theory of personality discussed in this chapter do you find most useful in understanding yourself and others? Why?

Key Terms

RETRIEVAL PRACTICE Write a definition for each term before turning back to the referenced page to check your answer.

- archetypes 307
- basic anxiety 307
- collective unconscious 307
- conscious 303
- defense mechanisms 304
- ego 304
- five-factor model (FFM) 310
- id 304
- inferiority complex 306

- Minnesota Multiphasic Personality Inventory (MMPI) 324
- morality principle 304
- personality 303
- pleasure principle 304
- preconscious 303
- projective test 325
- psychosexual stages 305
- reality principle 304
- reciprocal determinism 318

- Rorschach Inkblot Test 325
- self-actualization 314
- self-concept 314
- self-efficacy 317
- superego 304
- Thematic Apperception Test (TAT) 325
- trait 309
- unconditional positive regard 315
- unconscious 303

chaptertwelve

Psychological Disorders

realworldpsychology

THINGS YOU'LL LEARN IN CHAPTER 12

Q1 How can media coverage of mass shootings create negative misperceptions about people with mental illness?

Q2 Do people with a phobia see the object that frightens them as larger than it really is?

Q3 Can eating fast food lead to depression later on?

Q4 Why might children who experience trauma be at increased risk of developing schizophrenia later in life?

Q5 How do changes in the brain help explain severe antisocial personality disorder?

Q6 Are symptoms of depression in women more distressing, deserving of sympathy, and difficult to treat than the same signs in men?

THROUGHOUT THE CHAPTER, MARGIN ICONS FOR Q1–Q6 INDICATE WHERE THE TEXT ADDRESSES THESE QUESTIONS.

chapteroverview

Are you excited? Throughout history, psychological disorders have been the subject of intense fascination. Now, you finally get to read and study the part of psychology you've probably been waiting for from the very beginning! Hopefully, while reading this chapter, you'll recognize how the earlier chapters have prepared you for a better understanding and appreciation of the complex issues surrounding abnormal behavior. We begin with a discussion of how psychological disorders are identified, explained, and classified. Then we explore six major categories of psychological disorders: anxiety disorders, depressive and bipolar disorders, schizophrenia, obsessive-compulsive disorder (OCD), and personality disorders. We close with a look at gender and cultural factors related to mental disorders.

STUDYING PSYCHOLOGICAL DISORDERS

LEARNING OBJECTIVES

RETRIEVAL PRACTICE While reading the upcoming sections, respond to each Learning Objective in your own words. Then compare your responses with those found at www.wiley.com/college/huffman.

1 DESCRIBE abnormal behavior and the four criteria for identifying psychological disorders.

2 EXPLAIN how perspectives on the causes of psychological disorders have changed throughout history.

3 DISCUSS the purposes and criticisms of the *Diagnostic and Statistical Manual of Mental Disorders* (DSM).

Most people agree that neither the artist who stays awake for 72 hours finishing a painting nor the shooter who kills 20 young school children is behaving normally. But what exactly is "normal"? How do we distinguish between eccentricity in the first case and abnormal behavior in the second?

Identifying and Explaining Psychological Disorders

Abnormal behavior Patterns of behaviors, thoughts, or emotions considered pathological (diseased or disordered) for one or more of these four reasons: deviance, dysfunction, distress, or danger.

Mental health professionals generally agree on four criteria for identifying **abnormal behavior** (or psychopathology). Often called the four D's, these signs are *deviance, dysfunction, distress,* and *danger* **(Figure 12.1)**. Keep in mind that abnormal behavior, like intelligence or creativity, exists on a continuum.

As you consider these criteria, remember that no single criterion is adequate for identifying all forms of abnormal behavior. Furthermore, when considering the two criteria *deviance* and *danger*, note that judgments of what is deviant vary historically and cross-culturally and that the public generally overestimates the danger posed by the mentally ill. (See **Table 12.1** for more about this and other myths of mental illness.)

What causes abnormal behavior? Historically, evil spirits and witchcraft have been blamed (Amin & Noggle, 2013; Goodwin, 2012; Millon, 2004; Petry, 2011; Riva et al., 2011). Stone Age people, for example, believed that abnormal behavior stemmed from demonic possession; the "therapy" was to bore a hole in the skull so the evil spirit could escape, a process we call *trephining*. During the European Middle Ages, a troubled person was sometimes treated with *exorcism*, an effort to drive the Devil out by praying, fasting, making noise, and beating the sufferer and administering terrible-tasting brews. During the fifteenth century, as the Renaissance got under way, many believed that some individuals chose to consort with the Devil. These supposed witches were often tortured, imprisoned for life, or executed.

As the Middle Ages ended, special mental hospitals called *asylums* began to appear in Europe. Initially designed to provide quiet retreats from the world and to protect society (Barlow & Durand, 2012; Coleborne & Mackinnon, 2011; Hamlett & Hoskins, 2013; Millon, 2004), the asylums unfortunately became overcrowded, inhumane prisons.

FIGURE 12.1 FOUR CRITERIA FOR IDENTIFYING ABNORMAL BEHAVIOR

Behavior may be considered abnormal if it meets one or more of these four criteria.

Ⓐ Deviance

Behaviors, thoughts, or emotions may be considered abnormal when they deviate from a society or culture's norms or values. For example, it's normal to be a bit concerned if friends are whispering, but abnormal if you're equally concerned when total strangers are whispering.

Ian West/Alamy

Ⓑ Dysfunction

When someone's dysfunction interferes with his or her daily functioning, such as drinking to the point that you cannot hold a job, stay in school, or maintain relationships, it would be considered abnormal behavior.

Ⓒ Distress

Behaviors, thoughts, or emotions that cause significant personal distress may qualify as abnormal. Self-abuse relationship problems, and suicidal thoughts all indicate serious personal\distress and unhappiness.

Ⓓ Danger

If someone's thoughts, emotions, or behaviors present a danger to self or others, such as engaging in road rage to the point of physical confrontation, it would be considered abnormal.

Digital Vision/Getty Images

| TABLE 12.1 | COMMON MYTHS ABOUT MENTAL ILLNESS | realworldpsychology |

- *Myth: Mentally ill people are often dangerous and unpredictable.*

   Fact: Only a few disorders, such as some psychotic and antisocial personality disorders, are associated with violence. The stereotype that connects mental illness and violence persists because of prejudice, selective media attention, and negative portrayals in movies and on television.

- *Myth: People with psychological disorders act in bizarre ways and are very different from normal people.*

   Fact: This is true for only a small minority of individuals and during a relatively brief portion of their lives. In fact, sometimes even mental health professionals find it difficult to distinguish normal from abnormal behaviors without formal screening.

- *Myth: Mental disorders are a sign of personal weakness.*

   Fact: Psychological disorders are a function of many factors, such as exposure to stress, genetic predispositions, and a host of personal and sociocultural experiences., and family background. Mentally disturbed individuals can't be blamed for their illness any more than we blame people who develop cancer or other illnesses.

- *Myth: A mentally ill person is only suited for low-level jobs and never fully recovers.*

   Fact: Like all other illnesses, mental disorders are complex, and their symptoms, severity, and prognoses differ for each individual. With therapy, the vast majority of those who are diagnosed as mentally ill eventually improve and lead normal, productive lives. Moreover, the extreme symptoms of some mental disorders are generally only temporary. For example, U.S. President Abraham Lincoln, British Prime Minister Winston Churchill, scientist Isaac Newton, and other high achieving people all suffered from serious mental disorders at various times throughout their careers.

Is this behavior abnormal? Eccentric? Yes. Mentally disordered? Probably not.

Sources: Barnow & Balkin, 2013; Famous people with mental illness, 2011; Famous people with schizophrenia, 2011; Hooley et al., 2013; Lilienfeld et al., 2010.

FIGURE 12.2 SEVEN PSYCHOLOGICAL PERSPECTIVES

As you can see in this diagram, the seven major perspectives differ in their various explanations for the general causes of psychological disorders, but there is still considerable overlap.

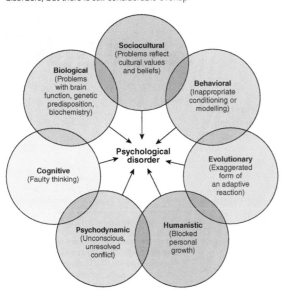

Medical model The diagnostic perspective which assumes that diseases (including mental illness) have physical causes that can be diagnosed, treated, and possibly cured.

Psychiatry The branch of medicine that deals with the diagnosis, treatment, and prevention of mental disorders.

Improvement came in 1792, when Philippe Pinel, a French physician, was placed in charge of a Parisian asylum. Believing that inmates' behavior was caused by underlying physical illness, he insisted that they be unshackled and removed from their unlighted, unheated cells. Many inmates improved so dramatically that they could be released. Pinel's **medical model** eventually gave rise to the modern specialty of **psychiatry**.

Unfortunately, when we label people "mentally ill," we may create new problems. One of the most outspoken critics of the medical model, psychiatrist Thomas Szasz (1960, 2004, 2012), believed it encourages people to believe they have no responsibility for their actions. Furthermore, he contended that mental illness is a myth used to label individuals who are peculiar or offensive to others and that these labels can become self-perpetuating. In other words, a person may begin to behave according to his or her diagnosed disorder.

In addition to potential problems for the identified person, the public also may develop negative attitudes about those labeled as mentally ill and about mental illness in general. This is particularly common following intensive media coverage of mass shootings committed by someone with such a disorder, despite the fact that most people with mental illness are not violent (McGinty et al., 2013).

Despite these potential dangers, the medical model—and the concept of mental illness—remains a founding principle of psychiatry. Psychology, in contrast, offers a multifaceted approach to explaining abnormal behavior, as shown in **Figure 12.2**.

Voices from the Classroom

Dangerous and Painful Labels Our society seems to have a fascination with labeling people, especially people who struggle with psychiatric disorders. I wonder why that is. Should we really be calling someone a schizophrenic? An anorexic? An autistic? We don't refer to people by their illness in other fields, so why do we in psychology? I have a close friend, who happens to be a brilliant physician and an amazing mother of four, who has struggled with a handful of severe episodes of major depressive disorder. Thankfully, she has always recovered from these episodes. That said, they seem to creep up on her and have the power to really throw her life off kilter. Knowing that her depression easily spirals into terrifying suicidal thoughts and urges, she admits herself to the hospital for treatment. While she is under care from the hospital staff, she doesn't want to be called the depressive or the mental patient. It is dehumanizing and offensive. Undergoing treatment for any psychiatric disorder is challenging enough. Our society doesn't need to make it any harder by labeling people and chipping away at their self-esteem. If we really want to label people, perhaps we should use their legal label . . . their actual name.

Professor Paulina Multhaupt
Macomb Community College
Clinton Township, Michigan

Classifying Psychological Disorders

Without a clear, reliable system for classifying the wide range of psychological disorders, scientific research on them would be almost impossible, and communication among mental health professionals would be seriously impaired. Fortunately,

FIGURE 12.3 THE INSANITY PLEA—GUILTY OF A CRIME OR MENTALLY ILL?

On March 27, 2012, JetBlue Airways captain Clayton Osbon dangerously disrupted a cross-country flight by running through the cabin, screaming about terrorists and religion. He was later charged with interference with a flight crew and was found not guilty by reason of insanity after a neuropsychologist testified that he had a "brief psychotic disorder" brought on by lack of sleep. Osbon was allowed to go free but with several restrictions, including not being allowed to fly or board any commercial or private planes. The insanity plea is used in fewer than 1% of all cases that reach trial and is successful in only a fraction of those (Claydon, 2012; Dirks-Linhorst, 2013; Goldstein et al., 2013).

© STRINGER/Reuter/ Corbis

mental health specialists share a uniform classification system, the ***Diagnostic and Statistical Manual of Mental Disorders (DSM)*** (American Psychiatric Association, 2013). This manual has been updated and revised several times, and the latest, fifth edition, was published in 2013.

Each revision of the *DSM* has expanded the list of disorders and changed the descriptions and categories to reflect both the latest in scientific research and any changes in the way abnormal behaviors are viewed within our social context (Hauser & Johnston, 2013; Widiger, 2013). For example, take the terms **neurosis** and **psychosis**. In previous editions of the *DSM*, the term *neurosis* reflected Freud's belief that all neurotic conditions arise from unconscious conflicts (Chapter 11). Now, conditions that were previously grouped under the heading *neurosis* have been formally studied and redistributed as separate categories. Unlike neurosis, the term *psychosis* is still listed in the current edition of the *DSM* because it remains useful for distinguishing the most severe mental disorders, such as schizophrenia.

What about the term *insanity*? Where does it fit in? **Insanity** is a legal term indicating that a person cannot be held responsible for his or her actions or is incompetent to manage his or her own affairs because of mental illness. In the law, the definition of mental illness rests primarily on a person's inability to tell right from wrong **(Figure 12.3)**.

Understanding and Evaluating the *DSM*

To understand a disorder, we must first name and describe it. The *DSM* identifies and describes the symptoms of approximately 400 disorders, which are grouped into 22 categories **(Table 12.2)**. Note that we focus on only the first 7 in this chapter (categories 8–11 are discussed in other chapters; 12–21 are beyond the scope of this book). Also, keep in mind that people may be diagnosed with more than one disorder at a time, a condition referred to as **comorbidity**.

Classification and diagnosis of mental disorders are essential to scientific study. Without a system such as the *DSM*, we could not effectively identify and diagnose the wide variety of disorders, predict their future courses, or suggest appropriate treatment. The *DSM* also facilitates communication among professionals and patients, and it serves as a valuable educational tool.

Unfortunately, the *DSM* does have limitations and potential problems. For example, critics suggest that it may be casting too wide a net and *overdiagnosing*. Given that insurance companies compensate physicians and psychologists only if each client is assigned a specific *DSM* code number, can you see how compilers of the *DSM* may be encouraged to add more diagnoses?

In addition, the *DSM* has been criticized for a potential *cultural bias*. It does provide a culture-specific section and a glossary of culture-bound syndromes, such as *amok* (Indonesia), *genital retraction syndrome* (Asia), and *windigo psychosis* (First Nations' cultures), which we discuss later in this chapter. However, the overall classification still reflects a Western European and U.S. perspective (Gellerman & Lu, 2011; Malhi, 2013; Sachdev, 2013).

Perhaps the most troubling criticism of the *DSM* is its possible overreliance on the medical model and the way it may unfairly label people. Consider the classic study conducted by David Rosenhan (1973) in which he and his seven colleagues presented themselves at several hospital admissions offices complaining of hearing voices (a classic symptom of schizophrenia). Aside from making this single false complaint

Diagnostic and Statistical Manual of Mental Disorders (DSM) A classification system developed by the American Psychiatric Association that is used to describe abnormal behaviors.

Neurosis An outmoded term and category dropped from *DSM*-111, in which a person does not have signs of brain abnormalities and does not display grossly irrational thinking or violate basic norms but does experience subjective distress.

Psychosis A serious mental disorder characterized by extreme mental disruption and defective or lost contact with reality.

Insanity The legal (not clinical) designation for the state of an individual judged to be legally irresponsible or incompetent to manage his or her own affairs because of mental illness.

Comorbidity The co-occurrence of two or more disorders in the same person at the same time, as when a person suffers from both depression and alcoholism.

TABLE 12.2 SUBCATEGORIES OF MENTAL DISORDERS IN THE *DSM*

1. *Anxiety disorders* Problems associated with excessive fear and anxiety and related behavioral disturbances.

2. *Depressive disorders* Problems characterized by the presence of sad, empty, or irritable mood.

3. *Bipolar and related disorders* Problems associated with alternating episodes of depression and mania.

4. *Schizophrenia spectrum and other psychotic disorders* Group of disorders characterized by delusions, hallucinations, disorganized thinking or motor behavior, and negative symptoms, such as diminished emotional expression.

5. *Obsessive-compulsive and related disorders* Group of disorders characterized by the presence of obsessions, compulsions, preoccupations, and/or repetitive behaviors or mental acts.

6. *Dissociative disorders* Group of disorders characterized by the disruption and/or discontinuity in the normal integration of consciousness, memory, identity, emotion, perception, body representation, motor control, and behavior.

7. *Personality disorders* Problems related to an enduring pattern of experience and behavior that deviates markedly from the expectations of an individual's culture, and leads to distress or impairment.

8. *Trauma- and stressor-related disorders* Problems associated with exposure to a traumatic or stressful event (see Chapter 3).

9. *Sleep–wake disorders* Dissatisfaction regarding the quality, timing, and amount of sleep (see Chapter 5).

10. *Substance-related and addictive disorders* A cluster of cognitive, behavioral, and physiological symptoms related to alcohol, tobacco, other drugs, and gambling (see Chapter 5).

11. *Feeding and eating disorders* Problems related to persistent disturbance of eating or eating-related behavior (see Chapter 10).

12. *Paraphilic disorders* Problems involving an intense and persistent sexual interest causing distress or impairment to the person or whose satisfaction has entailed personal harm, or risk of harm, to others (see optional Chapter 15).

13. *Sexual dysfunctions* A significant disturbance in a person's ability to respond sexually or to experience sexual pleasure (see optional Chapter 15).

14. *Gender dysphoria* Distress that may accompany the incongruence between a person's experienced or expressed gender and one's assigned gender (see optional Chapter 15).

15. *Neurodevelopmental disorders* Developmental deficits that typically manifest early in development, often before the child enters grade school, and produce impairments of personal, social, academic, or occupational functioning.

16. *Somatic symptom and related disorders* Problems related to unusual preoccupation with physical health or physical symptoms producing significant distress and impairment.

17. *Elimination disorders* Problems related to the inappropriate elimination of urine or feces, usually first diagnosed in childhood or adolescence.

18. *Disruptive, impulse-control, and conduct disorders* Problems related to kleptomania (impulsive stealing), pyromania (setting of fires), and other disorders characterized by inability to resist impulses, drives, or temptations to perform certain acts harmful to self or others.

19. *Neurocognitive disorders* A group of disorders involving cognitive function, including Alzheimer's disease, Huntington's disease, and physical trauma to the brain.

20. *Other mental disorders* Residual category of mental disorders causing significant distress or impairment but do not meet the full criteria for any other disorder in DSM-5.

21. *Medication-induced movement disorders and other adverse effects of medication* These are not mental disorders but are included because of their importance in the management by medication and differential diagnosis of mental disorders.

22. *Other conditions that may be a focus of clinical attention* These are not mental disorders but are included to draw attention to and document issues that may be encountered in routine clinical practice.

Sources: American Psychiatric Association, 2013; American Psychiatric Association, NICHY, 2012.

and providing false names and occupations, the researchers answered all questions truthfully. Not surprisingly, given their reported symptom, they were all diagnosed with mental disorders and admitted to the hospital. Once there, the "patients" stopped reporting any symptoms and behaved as they normally would, yet none were ever recognized by hospital staff as phony. Note that all of them were eventually released, after an average stay of 19 days, but only with a label on their permanent record of "schizophrenia in remission." Can you see the inherent dangers and "stickiness" of all forms of labels? Once the label "nerd," "jock," "criminal," or "mental patient" is applied, they may become self-fulfilling, and in the case of "criminal" or "mentally ill" they involve serious legal and employment issues.

Having noted the real and potential dangers of the label of mental illness, we need to explore a very common *Psych Science* question before going on: Are creative people at increased risk of suffering from mental illness?

PSYCHSCIENCE

CREATIVITY AND MENTAL DISORDERS

© Fox Searchlight Pictures/Photofest

What do you picture when you think of a creative genius? Thanks to movies, television, and novels, many people share the stereotypical image of an eccentric inventor or deranged artist, like the lead ballerina in the film *Black Swan*.

Is there an actual link between creativity and mental disorders? Researchers interested in this question collected data from more than 1 million people, including their specific professions, whether they had ever been diagnosed and treated for a mental disorder, and if so what type (Kyaga et al., 2012). Kyaga and his colleagues found that individuals in generally creative professions (scientific or artistic) were no more likely to suffer from investigated psychiatric disorders than control subjects. However, bipolar disorder was significantly more common in artists and scientists, and particularly in authors.

What do you think? How would you explain this intriguing association between certain creative professions and bipolar disorder? Does the manic phase of bipolar disorder increase the energy levels of artists, scientists, and authors, giving them greater access to creative ideas than they would otherwise have? Or does it interfere with their overall output? Can you see how variables like choice of occupation might confound these results (Patra & Balhara, 2012)? As you'll discover later in this chapter, there is a strong genetic component in bipolar disorders. And, just as you are much more likely to enter a profession similar to that of your parents because of familiarity, access, and modeling, children of artists, scientists, and authors are more likely to choose similar professions—thus possibly explaining the link between creativity and mental illness.

If you find these questions fascinating and the lack of answers frustrating, you may be the perfect candidate for a career as a research psychologist. Recall from Chapter 1 that the scientific method is circular and never-ending—but guaranteed to excite!

RESEARCH CHALLENGE

1 Based on the information provided, did this study (Kyaga et al., 2012) use descriptive, correlational, and/or experimental research?

2 If you chose:

- descriptive research, is this a naturalistic observation, survey/interview, case study, or archival research?
- correlational research, is this a positive, negative, or zero correlation?
- experimental research, label the IV, DV, experimental group(s), and control group.

>>CHECK YOUR ANSWERS IN APPENDIX B.

NOTE: The information provided in this study is admittedly limited, but the level of detail is similar to what is presented in most textbooks and public reports of research findings. Answering these questions, and then comparing your answers to those in the Appendix, will help you become a better critical thinker and consumer of scientific research.

RETRIEVAL PRACTICE: STUDYING PSYCHOLOGICAL DISORDERS

Self-Test

Completing this self-test and comparing your answers with those in Appendix B provides immediate feedback and helpful practice for exams. Additional interactive, self-tests are available at www.wiley.com/college/huffman.

1. *Abnormal behavior* is defined as _____.

   a. statistically infrequent patterns of pathological emotion, thought, or action

   b. patterns of emotion, thought, and action that are considered disordered

   c. patterns of behaviors, thoughts, or emotions considered pathological for one or more of four reasons: deviance, dysfunction, distress, or danger

   d. all these options

2. _____ is the branch of medicine that deals with the diagnosis, treatment, and prevention of mental disorders.

   a. Psychology

   b. Psychiatry

   c. Psychobiology

   d. Psychodiagnostics

3. In the early treatment of psychological disorders, _____ was used to allow evil spirits to escape, whereas _____ was designed to drive the Devil out through prayer, fasting, and so on.

   a. trephining; exorcism

   b. demonology; hydrotherapy

   c. the medical model; the dunking test

   d. none of these options

4. Label the seven psychological perspectives on psychological disorders.

a. _____ (Problems reflect cultural values and beliefs)

g. _____ (Problems with brain function, genetic predisposition, biochemistry)

b. _____ (Inappropriate conditioning or modelling)

Psychological disorder

f. _____ (Faulty thinking)

c. _____ (Exaggerated form of an adaptive reaction)

e. _____ (Unconscious, unresolved conflict)

d. _____ (Blocked personal growth)

Think Critically

1 Can you think of cases in which someone might have a psychological disorder not described by the four criteria deviance, dysfunction, distress, and/or danger?

2 Do you think the insanity plea, as it is currently structured, should be abolished? Why or why not?

realworldpsychology

How can media coverage of mass shootings create negative misperceptions about people with mental illness?

HINT: LOOK IN THE MARGIN FOR Q1

ANXIETY DISORDERS

LEARNING OBJECTIVES

RETRIEVAL PRACTICE While reading the upcoming sections, respond to each Learning Objective in your own words. Then compare your responses with those found at www.wiley.com/college/huffman.

1 **DESCRIBE** anxiety disorders and the symptoms of generalized anxiety disorder (GAD), panic disorder, and phobias.

2 **SUMMARIZE** how psychological, biological, and sociocultural factors contribute to anxiety disorders.

Anxiety disorder A mental disorder characterized by overwhelming tension and irrational fear accompanied by physiological arousal.

Have you ever faced a very important exam, job interview, or first date and broken out in a cold sweat, felt your heart pounding, and had trouble breathing? If so, you have some understanding of anxiety, but the experiences and symptoms of those who suffer from **anxiety disorders** are much more intense and life disrupting. Fortunately, anxiety disorders are also among the easiest to treat and offer some of the best chances for recovery (Chapter 13).

realworldpsychology **Coping with Anxiety Disorders** What would you do if you were a promising new professional basketball player expected to fly all over the country with your team but suffered from an intense fear of flying? This is just one of the many challenges facing NBA rookie player Royce White, who speaks openly about his illness and personal experiences, hoping to boost public awareness of mental illness. Although twice as many women as men are diagnosed with anxiety disorders, men like White also suffer from this widespread disease. In fact, anxiety disorders are the most frequently occurring mental disorders in the general population (Essau & Petermann, 2013; National Institute of Mental Health, 2011; Zerr et al., 2011).

Describing Anxiety Disorders

In this section, we discuss three anxiety disorders: *generalized anxiety disorder* (GAD), *panic disorder*, and *phobias* **(Figure 12.4)**. Although we cover these disorders separately, two or more often occur together (Corr, 2011; Johnston et al., 2013; Leyfer et al., 2013).

Generalized Anxiety Disorder

Sufferers of **generalized anxiety disorder (GAD)** experience fear and worries that are not focused on any one specific threat, which is why it's referred to as *generalized* (Hooley et al., 2013; Robichaud, 2013; Zink et al., 2013). Their anxiety also is chronic and uncontrollable and lasts at least six months. Because of persistent muscle tension and autonomic fear reactions, people with this disorder may develop headaches, heart palpitations, dizziness, and insomnia, making it even harder to cope with normal daily activities. The disorder affects twice as many women as men (Horwath & Gould, 2011).

Generalized anxiety disorder (GAD) An anxiety disorder characterized by persistent, uncontrollable, and free-floating, nonspecified anxiety.

Panic Disorder

Sudden but brief attacks of intense apprehension that cause trembling, dizziness, and difficulty breathing are symptoms of **panic disorder**. *Panic attacks* generally happen after frightening experiences or prolonged stress (and sometimes even after exercise). Panic disorder is diagnosed when several apparently spontaneous panic

Panic disorder An anxiety disorder in which sufferers experience sudden and inexplicable panic attacks; symptoms include difficulty breathing, heart palpitations, dizziness, trembling, terror, and feelings of impending doom.

FIGURE 12.4 **ANXIETY DISORDERS**

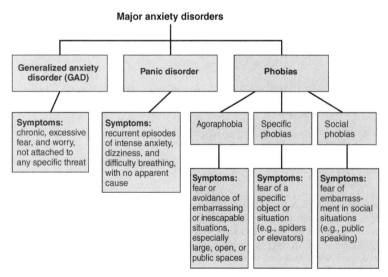

FIGURE 12.5 SPIDER PHOBIA

Can you imagine being so frightened by a spider that you would try to jump out of a speeding car to get away from it? This is how a person suffering from a phobia might feel.

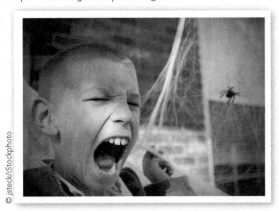

Phobia A persistent and intense, irrational fear and avoidance of a specific object or situation.

attacks lead to a persistent concern about future attacks. A common complication of panic disorder is agoraphobia, discussed in the next section (Horwath & Gould, 2011; Kircher et al., 2013).

Phobias

Phobias include a strong, irrational fear and avoidance of objects or situations that are usually considered harmless (elevators or the dentist, for example). Although the person recognizes that the fear is irrational, the experience is still one of overwhelming anxiety, and a full-blown panic attack may follow. The fifth edition of the *DSM* divides phobias into separate categories: agoraphobia, specific phobias, and social anxiety disorder (social phobia).

People with *agoraphobia* restrict their normal activities because they fear having a panic attack in crowded, enclosed, or wide-open places where they would be unable to receive help in an emergency. In severe cases, people with agoraphobia may refuse to leave the safety of their homes.

A *specific phobia* is a fear of a specific object or situation, such as needles, rats, spiders, or heights. Claustrophobia (fear of closed spaces) and acrophobia (fear of heights) are the specific phobias most often treated by therapists. People with specific phobias generally recognize that their fears are excessive and unreasonable, but they are unable to control their anxiety and will go to great lengths to avoid the feared stimulus **(Figure 12.5)**.

One factor that helps explain why people with phobias have such extreme reactions is that they perceive the feared objects as larger than they actually are. Researchers in one study asked people with spider phobias to stand beside a glass tank and observe five different tarantulas (Vasey et al., 2012). They were then asked to estimate the size of each tarantula by drawing a line on an index card to illustrate its length. Those who reported experiencing the highest levels of fear while standing beside the tank drew the longest lines.

People with *social anxiety disorder* (or *social phobia*) are irrationally fearful of embarrassing themselves in social situations. Fear of public speaking and of eating in public are the two most common social phobias. The fear of public scrutiny and potential humiliation may become so pervasive that normal life is impossible (Kariuki & Stein, 2013; Moitra et al., 2011; Stopa et al., 2013).

Explaining Anxiety Disorders

Why do people develop anxiety disorders? Research has focused on the roles of psychological, biological, and sociocultural processes (the *biopsychosocial model*) **(Figure 12.6)**.

FIGURE 12.6 ANXIETY DISORDERS AND THE BIOPSYCHOSOCIAL MODEL

The biopsychosocial model takes into account the wide variety of factors than can contribute to anxiety disorders.

Psychological Factors

Researchers generally agree on the two major psychological contributions to anxiety disorders: *faulty cognitive processes* and *maladaptive learning.*

People with anxiety disorders tend to have habits of thinking, or cognitive processes, that make them prone to fear. These faulty cognitions tend to make them hypervigilant—meaning they constantly scan their environment for signs of danger and ignore signs of safety. They also tend to magnify ordinary threats and failures and to be hypersensitive to others' opinions of them.

In contrast to this cognitive explanation, learning theorists suggest that anxiety disorders result from maladaptive learning, such as inadvertent and improper conditioning and social learning (Chapter 6) (Gazendam et al., 2013; Grills-Taquechel & Ollendick, 2013; Lovibond, 2011). During classical conditioning, for example, a stimulus that is originally neutral (say a harmless spider) becomes paired with a frightening event (a sudden panic attack) so that it becomes a conditioned stimulus that elicits anxiety. The person then begins to avoid spiders in order to reduce anxiety (an operant conditioning process known as negative reinforcement) (Chapter 6) **(Figure 12.7)**.

Some researchers contend that because most people with phobias cannot remember a specific instance that led to their fear, and because frightening experiences do not always trigger phobias, conditioning may not be the only explanation. Social learning theorists propose that some phobias result from modeling and imitation. For example, children whose parents, especially fathers, are afraid of going to the dentist are much more likely to also have such a fear themselves (Lara-Sacido et al., 2012).

Biological Factors

Some researchers believe phobias reflect an evolutionary predisposition to fear things that were dangerous to our ancestors (Beckers et al., 2013; Glover, 2011; Mineka & Oehlberg, 2008; Noggle & Dean, 2013; Soares & Esteves, 2013). Some people with panic disorder also seem genetically predisposed toward an overreaction of the autonomic nervous system, further supporting the argument for a biological

---

FIGURE 12.7 **CONDITIONING AND PHOBIAS**

Classical conditioning combined with operant conditioning can lead to phobias. Consider the example of Little Albert's classically conditioned fear of rats, discussed in Chapter 6.

Benjamin Harris

Ⓐ Classical conditioning
By pairing the white rat with a loud noise, experimenters used classical conditioning to teach Little Albert to fear rats.

Ⓑ Operant conditioning
Later Albert might have learned to avoid rats through operant conditioning. Avoiding rats would reduce Albert's fear, giving unintended reinforcement to his fearful behavior.

Ⓒ Phobia
Over time, this cycle of fear and avoidance could produce an even more severe fear, or phobia.

component. In addition, stress and arousal seem to play a role in panic attacks, and drugs such as caffeine or nicotine and even hyperventilation can trigger an attack, all suggesting a biochemical disturbance.

Sociocultural Factors

In addition to psychological and biological components, sociocultural factors can contribute to anxiety. There has been a sharp rise in anxiety disorders in the past 50 years, particularly in Western industrialized countries. Can you see how our fast-paced lives—along with our increased mobility, decreased job security, and decreased family support—might contribute to anxiety? Unlike the dangers early humans faced in our evolutionary history, today's threats are less identifiable and less immediate. This may in turn lead some people to become hypervigilant and predisposed to anxiety disorders.

Further support for sociocultural influences on anxiety disorders is our recognition that they can have dramatically different forms in other cultures. For example, in a collectivist twist on anxiety, some Japanese experience a type of social phobia called *taijin kyofusho* (*TKS*), a morbid dread of doing something to embarrass *others*. This disorder is quite different from the Western version of social phobia, which centers on a fear of criticism.

RETRIEVAL PRACTICE: ANXIETY DISORDERS

Self-Test

Completing this self-test and comparing your answers with those in Appendix B provides immediate feedback and helpful practice for exams. Additional interactive, self-tests are available at www.wiley.com/college/huffman.

1. Label the three key anxiety disorders.

2. Anxiety disorders are _____.

  a. characterized by overwhelming tension, irrational fear, and physiological arousal

  b. the least frequent of the mental disorders

  c. twice as common in men as in women

  d. all these options

3. Persistent, uncontrollable, and free-floating, non-specified anxiety might be diagnosed as a _____.

  a. generalized anxiety disorder   b. panic disorder

  c. phobia   d. all these options

4. In the Japanese social phobia called TKS, people fear that they will _____.

  a. evaluate others negatively   b. embarrass themselves

  c. embarrass others   d. be embarrassed by others

Think Critically

1 Why do you suppose anxiety disorders are among the easiest disorders to treat?

2 How would you explain the high number of anxiety disorders in the United States?

realworldpsychology

Do people with a phobia see the object that frightens them as larger than it really is?

HINT: LOOK IN THE MARGIN FOR (Q2)

DEPRESSIVE AND BIPOLAR DISORDERS

RETRIEVAL PRACTICE While reading the upcoming sections, respond to each Learning Objective in your own words. Then compare your responses with those found at www.wiley.com/college/huffman.

LEARNING OBJECTIVES

1 **EXPLAIN** how depressive disorders and bipolar disorders differ.

2 **SUMMARIZE** research on the biological and psychological factors that contribute to depressive and bipolar disorders.

3 **DISCUSS** what to do if someone is suicidal.

Both depressive disorders and bipolar disorders are characterized by extreme disturbances in emotional states.

Describing Depressive and Bipolar Disorders

We all feel "blue" sometimes—especially following the loss of a job, end of a relationship, or death of a loved one. People suffering from **depressive disorders**, however, are so deeply sad and discouraged that they often have trouble sleeping, are likely to lose (or gain) significant weight, and may feel so fatigued that they cannot go to work or school or even comb their hair and brush their teeth. They may sleep constantly, have problems concentrating, and feel so profoundly sad and guilty that they consider suicide. Seriously depressed individuals have a hard time thinking clearly or recognizing their own problems (Hammen & Keenan-Miller, 2013; Wyrobeck et al., 2013).

Depressive disorders A group of mental disorders, including disruptive mood dys-regulation disorder and major depressive disorder, characterized by sad, empty, or irritable moods that interfere with the ability to function.

realworldpsychology   Hollywood's Depiction of Bipolar Disorder

Did you know that the Oscar nominated film *Silver Linings Playbook* was originally a gift from the director to his son, Matthew, who suffers from *bipolar disorder*? Viewers and mental health professionals, however, all agree that it's a gift for all because it casts a sensitive subject in a warmer light and helps offset the stigma so commonly associated with mental illness (Lopez, 2013).

© The Weinstein Company/ Photofest

Non Sequitur by Wiley7. Distributed by Universal Press Syndicate/ UniversalUclick. All Rights Reserved.

Bipolar disorder A mental disorder characterized by repeated episodes of mania (unreasonable elation, often with hyperactivity) alternating with depression.

When depression is *unipolar*, and the depressive episode ends, the person generally returns to a normal emotional level. People with **bipolar disorders**, however, rebound to the opposite state, known as *mania* (**Figure 12.8**).

During a manic episode, the bipolar person is overly excited, extremely active, and easily distracted. In addition, he or she exhibits unrealistically high self-esteem, an inflated sense of importance, and poor judgment—giving away valuable possessions or going on wild spending sprees. The person also is often hyperactive and may not sleep for days at a time yet does not become fatigued. Thinking is faster than normal and can change abruptly to new topics, showing "rapid flight of ideas." Speech is also rapid ("pressured speech"), making it difficult for others to get a word in edgewise. A manic episode may last a few days or a few months, and it generally ends abruptly. The ensuing depressive episode generally lasts three times as long.

The lifetime risk for bipolar disorder is low—between 0.5 and 1.6%—but it can be one of the most debilitating and lethal disorders, with a suicide rate between 10 and 20% among sufferers (Bender & Alloy, 2011; Hammen & Keenan-Miller, 2013; Thaler et al., 2013). Suicide also is a serious risk for anyone suffering from several other mental health issues, particularly depressive disorders. See *Test Yourself: Danger Signs for Suicide* to first test your own level of depression and then to learn more about common suicide myths.

Explaining Depressive and Bipolar Disorders

Biological factors appear to play a significant role in both depressive disorders and bipolar disorders. For example, both disorders are sometimes treated with antidepressants, which affect the amount or functioning of norepinephrine, dopamine, and/or serotonin in the brain. In addition, recent research suggests that structural brain changes may contribute to these mood disorders. Sadly, NFL players are at greater risk of developing depression as they age, possibly due to brain damage caused by repeated concussions. One recent study on former NFL players revealed that 41% show cognitive problems and 24% show clinical depression, which may result from neurological changes caused by concussions (Hart et al., 2013). Their brain scans also revealed changes in blood flow within the brain and

---

FIGURE 12.8 **DEPRESSIVE VERSUS BIPOLAR DISORDERS**

If depressive disorders and bipolar disorders were depicted on a graph, they might look something like this. Note that only in bipolar disorders do people experience manic episodes.

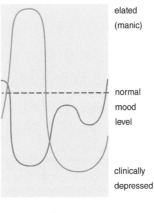

elated (manic)

normal mood level

clinically depressed

—— Bipolar Disorder

—— Major Depressive Disorder

TEST YOURSELF: DANGER SIGNS FOR SUICIDE
psychology and you

Let's begin with a measure of your own symptoms of depression. Answer the following questions, based on how you have been feeling over the past two weeks. Use a scale of 1 = at no time to 6 = all the time.

Have you felt low in spirits or sad?

Have you lost interest in your daily activities?

Have you felt lacking in energy and strength?

Have you felt less self-confident?

Have you had a bad conscience or feelings of guilt?

Have you felt that life wasn't worth living?

Have you had difficulty concentrating?

Have you felt very restless?

Have you felt subdued or slowed down?

Have you had trouble sleeping at night?

Have you suffered from reduced appetite?

Have you suffered from increased appetite?

Higher numbers on this scale indicate higher levels of depression (Bech et al., 2011; Olsen et al., 2003). If you're currently feeling suicidal, seek help immediately! If not, read on about some misconceptions and stereotypes surrounding suicide. Can you correctly identify which of the following is true or false?

1. People who talk about suicide are less likely to commit suicide.

2. Suicide usually takes place with little or no warning.

3. Suicidal people are fully intent on dying.

4. Children of parents who attempt suicide are at greater risk of committing suicide.

5. Suicidal people remain so forever.

6. Men are more likely than women to actually kill themselves by suicide.

7. When a suicidal person has been severely depressed and seems to be "snapping out of it," the danger of suicide decreases substantially.

8. Only depressed people commit suicide.

9. Thinking about suicide is rare.

10. Asking a depressed person about suicide will push him or her over the edge and cause a suicidal act that would not otherwise have occurred.

Now, compare your responses to the experts' answers and explanations (Bailey et al., 2011; Baldessarini & Tondo, 2008; Callanan & Davis, 2012; Lilienfeld et al., 2010; Schneidman, 1981; Stricker et al., 2013; Taub & Thompson, 2013; Walsh et al., 2013).

1. and 2. **False**. Up to three-quarters of those who take their own lives talk about it and give warnings about their intentions beforehand. They may say, "If something happens to me, I want you to . . . " or "Life just isn't worth living." They also provide behavioral clues, such as giving away valued possessions, withdrawing from family and friends, and losing interest in favorite activities.

3. **False**. Only about 3 to 5% of suicidal people truly intend to die. Most are just unsure about how to go on living. They cannot see their problems objectively enough to realize that they have alternative courses of action. They often gamble with death, arranging it so that fate or others will save them. Moreover, once the suicidal crisis passes, they are generally grateful to be alive.

4. **True**. Children of parents who attempt or commit suicide are at much greater risk of following in their footsteps. As Schneidman (1969) puts it, "The person who commits suicide puts his psychological skeleton in the survivor's emotional closet" (p. 225).

5. **False**. People who want to kill themselves are usually suicidal only for a limited period.

6. **True**. Although women are much more likely to attempt suicide, men are far more likely to actually commit suicide. Men are also more likely to use stronger methods, such as guns instead of pills.

7. **False**. When people are first coming out of a depression, they are in fact at greater risk because they now have the energy to actually commit suicide.

8. **False**. Suicide rates are highest among people with major depressive disorders. However, suicide is also the leading cause of premature death in people who suffer from schizophrenia, and a major cause of death in people with anxiety disorders and alcohol and other substance-related disorders. Furthermore, suicide is not limited to people with depression. Poor physical health, serious illness, substance abuse (particularly of alcohol), loneliness, unemployment, and even natural disasters may push many over the edge.

9. **False**. Estimates from various studies are that 40 to 80% of the general public have thought about committing suicide at least once in their lives.

10. **False**. Because society often considers suicide a terrible, shameful act, asking directly about it can give the person permission to talk. In fact, not asking might lead to further isolation and depression.

abnormalities in various parts of the brain. Sadly, these changes may contribute to serious depression and increased risk of suicide **(Figure 12.9)**.

Other research points to imbalances of the neurotransmitters serotonin, norepinephrine, and dopamine as possible causes of mood disorders (Barton et al., 2008; Lopez-Munoz & Alamo, 2011; Pu et al., 2011; Wiste et al., 2008). Drugs that alter the activity of these neurotransmitters also decrease the symptoms of depression (and are therefore called antidepressants) (Chuang, 1998). Interestingly, researchers in one study found that people who regularly ate fast food and commercially produced baked goods (such as croissants and doughnuts) were 51% more likely to develop depression later on. This may be the result of the chemicals in such foods leading to physiological changes in the brain and body (Sanchez-Villegas et al., 2011).

Some biological research indicates that both depressive and bipolar disorders may be inherited (Boardman et al., 2011; Gonzales et al., 2013; McGue & Christensen, 2013; Melas et al., 2013). In contrast, research that takes an evolutionary perspective suggests that moderate depression may be a normal and healthy adaptive response to a very real loss, such as the death of a loved one, which helps us to step back and reassess our goals (Baddeley, 2013; Carvalho et al., 2013; Nettle, 2011; Raison & Miller, 2013). And clinical, severe depression may just be an extreme version of this generally adaptive response.

FIGURE 12.9 BRAIN DAMAGE AND PROFESSIONAL SPORTS

Junior Seau, who played in the NFL for 20 years, committed suicide with a gunshot wound to his chest in 2012 at the age of 43. Later studies concluded that he suffered from *chronic traumatic encephalopathy* (CTE), a form of concussion-related brain damage that has also been found in other NFL players.

Kent C. Horner/Getty Images

Psychosocial theories of depression focus on environmental stressors, disturbances in the person's interpersonal relationships or self-concept, and on any history of abuse or assault (Betancourt et al., 2011; Herrenkohl et al., 2013; Jewkes, 2013; Mendelson et al., 2011; Mota et al., 2012; Neri et al., 2012). The psychoanalytic explanation sees depression as the result of experiencing a real or imagined loss, which in internalized as guilt, shame, self-hatred and ultimately self-blame. The cognitive perspective explains depression as caused, at least in part, by negative thinking patterns, including a tendency to ruminate, or obsess, about problems (Brinker et al., 2013; Demeyer et al., 2012; Gibb et al., 2012). The humanistic school says that depression results when a person demands perfection of him- or herself or when positive growth is blocked (Keen, 2011; O'Connell, 2008; Stricker et al., 2013).

According to the **learned helplessness** theory (Seligman, 1975, 2007), depression occurs when people (and other animals) become resigned to the idea that they are helpless to escape from something painful. Learned helplessness may be particularly likely to trigger depression if the person attributes failure to causes that are internal ("my own weakness"), stable ("this weakness is long-standing and unchanging"), and global ("this weakness is a problem in lots of settings") (Alloy et al., 2011; Barnum et al., 2013; Newby & Moulds, 2011; Reivich et al., 2013).

Keep in mind that suicide is a major danger associated with both depressive disorder and bipolar disorder. Given that some people who suffer with these disorders are so disturbed that they lose contact with reality, they may fail to recognize the danger signs or to seek help. *What To Do If You Think Someone Is Suicidal* offers important information for both the sufferers and their family and friends.

Learned helplessness Seligman's term for a state of helplessness or resignation, in which human or nonhuman animals learn that escape from something painful is impossible; the organism stops responding and may become depressed.

WHAT TO DO IF YOU THINK SOMEONE IS SUICIDAL
psychology and you

If you believe someone is contemplating suicide, act on your beliefs. Stay with the person if there is any immediate danger. Encourage him or her to talk to you rather than withdraw. Show the person that you care but do not give false reassurances that "everything will be okay." This type of response may make the suicidal person feel *more* alienated. Instead, openly ask whether the person is feeling hopeless and suicidal. Do not be afraid to discuss suicide with people who feel depressed or hopeless, fearing that you will put ideas into their heads. The reality is that people who are left alone or who are told they can't be serious about suicide often attempt it.

If you suspect that someone is imminently suicidal, it is vitally important that you help the person obtain counseling. Get help immediately! Consider calling the police for emergency intervention, the person's therapist, and/or the toll-free 24/7 hotline 1-800-SUICIDE (784-2433). Most cities also have walk-in centers that provide emergency counseling.

In addition, share your suspicions with parents, friends, or others who can help in a suicidal crisis. To save a life, you may have to betray a secret when someone confides in you. If you feel you can't do this alone, get another person to help you.

Mirek Towski/DMI/Time LifePictures/Getty Images

Even people who enjoy fame and success may be at risk for suicide. Famous musicians like Mindy McCready (pictured here) and Kurt Cobain; professional athletes such as Olympic medalist Jeret Peterson, or football player Junior Seau; and well known writers and artists like Hunter S. Thompson, Virginia Woolf, Ernest Hemingway, and Vincent van Gogh have all died as a result of suicide.

RETRIEVAL PRACTICE: DEPRESSIVE AND BIPOLAR DISORDERS

Self-Test

Completing this self-test and comparing your answers with those in Appendix B provides immediate feedback and helpful practice for exams. Additional interactive, self-tests are available at www.wiley.com/college/huffman.

1. A major difference between depressive disorder and bipolar disorder is that only in bipolar disorder do people have _____.

   a. hallucinations or delusions   b. depression
   c. manic episodes   d. a biochemical imbalance

2. Depressive and bipolar disorders are sometimes treated by _____ drugs, which affect the amount or functioning of norepinephrine, dopamine, and serotonin in the brain.

   a. antidepressant   b. antipsychotics
   c. mood congruence   d. none of the above

3. Which of the following is a myth about suicide?

   a. People who talk about it are less likely to actually do it   b. Suicide usually occurs with little or no warning
   c. Most people have never thought about suicide   d. all of these options

4. According to the theory known as _____, when faced with a painful situation from which there is no escape, animals and people enter a state of helplessness and resignation.

   a. autonomic resignation   b. helpless resignation
   c. resigned helplessness   d. learned helplessness

Think Critically

1 Have you ever felt seriously depressed? How would you distinguish between "normal" depression and a serious depressive disorder?

2 Can you think of a personal example of how major depression served as a possible evolutionary advantage?

realworldpsychology

Can eating fast food lead to depression later on?

HINT: LOOK IN THE MARGIN FOR

SCHIZOPHRENIA

LEARNING OBJECTIVES

RETRIEVAL PRACTICE While reading the upcoming sections, respond to each Learning Objective in your own words. Then compare your responses with those found at www.wiley.com/college/huffman.

1 **IDENTIFY** schizophrenia and its common symptoms.
2 **COMPARE** the traditional five-subtype system for classifying different types of schizophrenia with the two-group system that has recently emerged.
3 **SUMMARIZE** the biological and psychosocial factors that contribute to schizophrenia.

Imagine that your 17-year-old son's behavior has changed dramatically over the past few months, and he has gone from being actively involved in sports and clubs to suddenly quitting all activities and refusing to go to school. He now also talks to himself—mumbling and yelling out at times—and no longer regularly showers or washes his hair. Recently he announced, "The voices are telling me to jump out the window" (Kotowski, 2012).

This description is taken from the true case history of a patient who suffers from **schizophrenia**. People with schizophrenia have serious problems caring for themselves, relating to others, and holding a job. In extreme cases, the illness is considered a *psychosis*, meaning the person is out of touch with reality, and treatment often requires institutional or custodial care.

Schizophrenia is one of the most widespread and devastating mental disorders. Approximately 1 of every 100 people will develop it in his or her lifetime, and

Schizophrenia A group of severe disorders involving major disturbances in perception, language, thought, emotion, and behavior.

approximately half of all people who are admitted to mental hospitals are diagnosed with this disorder (Gottesman, 1991; Harvey & Bowie, 2013; Kessler et al., 1994; Regier et al., 1993). Schizophrenia usually emerges between the late teens and the mid-30s and only rarely prior to adolescence or after age 45. It seems to be equally prevalent in men and women, but it's generally more severe and strikes earlier in men (Chang et al., 2011; Goldstein et al., 2013; Gottesman, 1991; Harvey & Bowie, 2013; Lee et al., 2011).

Many people confuse schizophrenia with dissociative identity disorder, which is sometimes referred to as *split* or *multiple personality disorder* (see *Real World Psychology*). *Schizophrenia* means "split mind," but when Eugen Bleuler coined the term in 1911, he was referring to the fragmenting of thought processes and emotions, not of personalities (Neale et al., 1983). As we discuss later in this chapter, dissociative identity disorder is popularly referred to as having a "split personality"—the rare and controversial condition of having more than one distinct personality.

---

realworldpsychology **Do People with Schizophrenia Have Multiple Personalities?** As shown in this cartoon and in popular movies and television shows, schizophrenia is commonly confused with *multiple personality disorder* (now known as *dissociative identity disorder*, p. 357). This widespread error persists in part because of confusing terminology. Literally translated, *schizophrenia* means "split mind," referring to a split from reality that shows itself in disturbed perceptions, language, thought, emotions, and/or behavior.

In contrast, dissociative identity disorder (DID) refers to the condition in which two or more distinct personalities exist within the same person at different times. People with schizophrenia have only one personality.

Why does this matter? Confusing schizophrenia with multiple personalities is not only technically incorrect, it also trivializes the devastating effects of both disorders, which may include severe anxiety, social isolation, unemployment, homelessness, substance abuse, clinical depression, and even suicide (Lilienfeld et al., 2010; Preventing Suicide, 2009; Smith et al., 2011; Stricker et al., 2013).

Dave Parker/CartoonStock

"THANKS FOR CURING MY SCHIZOPHRENIA— WE'RE BOTH FINE NOW!"

Symptoms of Schizophrenia

Schizophrenia is a group of disorders characterized by a disturbance in one or more of the following areas: *perception, language, thought, affect* (emotions), and *behavior.*

Perception

The senses of people with schizophrenia may be either enhanced or blunted. The filtering and selection processes that allow most people to concentrate on whatever they choose are impaired, and sensory stimulation is jumbled and distorted. People with schizophrenia may also experience **hallucinations**, false, imaginary sensory perceptions that occur without external stimuli. Auditory hallucinations (hearing voices and sounds) is one of the most commonly noted and reported symptoms of schizophrenia.

On rare occasions, people with schizophrenia hurt others in response to their distorted perceptions. But a person with schizophrenia is more likely to be self-destructive and suicidal than violent toward others.

Hallucination A false, imaginary sensory perception that occurs without an external, objective source.

Language and Thought

For people with schizophrenia, words lose their usual meanings and associations, logic is impaired, and thoughts are disorganized and bizarre. When language and thought disturbances are mild, the individual jumps from topic to topic. With more severe disturbances, the person jumbles phrases and words together (into a "word salad") or creates artificial words. The most common—and frightening—thought disturbance experienced by people with schizophrenia is lack of contact with reality (psychosis).

Delusions, false beliefs or opinions despite invalidating evidence, are also common in people with schizophrenia. We all experience exaggerated thoughts from time to time, such as thinking a friend is trying to avoid us, but the delusions of schizophrenia are much more extreme. For example, if someone falsely believed that the postman who routinely delivered mail to his house every afternoon was a co-conspirator in a plot to kill him, it would likely qualify as a *delusion of persecution*. In *delusions of grandeur*, people believe that they are someone very important, perhaps Jesus Christ or the queen of England. In *delusions of reference*, unrelated events are given special significance, as when a person believes a radio program is sending him or her special messages.

A recent trend among individuals suffering from various mental disorders is to join Internet groups where they can share their experiences with others. For example, people with schizophrenia and other psychotic disorders can now share with fellow sufferers their belief that they are being stalked or that their minds are being controlled by technology. Some experts consider Internet groups that offer peer support to be helpful to mentally ill individuals, but others believe they may reinforce troubled thinking and impede treatment. Those who use the sites report feeling relieved by the sense that they are not alone in their suffering, but the groups are not moderated by professionals and pose the danger of amplifying the symptoms of mentally ill individuals (Kershaw, 2008).

Delusion A false or irrational belief maintained despite clear evidence to the contrary.

"That's the doctor who is treating me for paranoia. I don't trust him."

Emotion

Changes in emotion usually occur in people with schizophrenia. In some cases, emotions are exaggerated and fluctuate rapidly. At other times, they become blunted. Some people with schizophrenia have *flattened affect*—almost no emotional response of any kind.

Behavior

Disturbances in behavior may take the form of unusual actions that have special meaning to the sufferer. For example, one patient massaged his head repeatedly to "clear it" of unwanted thoughts. People with schizophrenia also may become *cataleptic* and assume a nearly immobile stance for an extended period.

Types of Schizophrenia

For many years, researchers divided schizophrenia into five subtypes: *paranoid, catatonic, disorganized, undifferentiated,* and *residual.* Critics suggested that this system does not differentiate in terms of prognosis, cause, or response to treatment and that the undifferentiated type was merely a catchall for cases that are difficult to diagnose (American Psychiatric Association, 2013). For these reasons, researchers have proposed an alternative classification system:

1. **Positive schizophrenia symptoms** are additions to or exaggerations of normal thought processes and behaviors, including bizarre delusions and hallucinations.

2. **Negative schizophrenia symptoms** include the loss or absence of normal thought processes and behaviors and appear as impaired attention, limited or toneless speech, flat or blunted affect, and social withdrawal.

Positive symptoms are more common when schizophrenia develops rapidly, whereas negative symptoms are more often found in slow-developing schizophrenia. Positive symptoms are associated with better adjustment before the onset and a better prognosis for recovery.

Explaining Schizophrenia

Because schizophrenia comes in many different forms, it probably has multiple biological and psychosocial bases. Let's look at biological contributions first.

Prenatal stress and viral infections, birth complications, immune responses, maternal malnutrition, and advanced paternal age all may contribute to the development of schizophrenia (Kneeland & Fatemi, 2013; Miller et al., 2013; Noggle & Dean, 2013; Weinberger & Harrison, 2011). However, most biological theories of schizophrenia focus on genetics, neurotransmitters, and brain abnormalities:

- **Genetics** Although researchers are beginning to identify specific genes related to schizophrenia, most genetic studies have focused on twins and adoptions (Drew et al., 2011; Gilman et al., 2012; Owens et al., 2011; Svrakic et al., 2013; Wiener et al., 2013). This research indicates that the risk for schizophrenia increases with genetic similarity; that is, people who share more genes with a person who has schizophrenia are more likely to develop the disorder **(Figure 12.10)**.

- **Neurotransmitters** Precisely how genetic inheritance produces schizophrenia is unclear. According to the *dopamine hypothesis*, overactivity of certain dopamine neurons in the brain causes some forms of schizophrenia (Fusar-Poli & Meyer-Lindenberg, 2013; Madras, 2013; Nord & Farde, 2011; Sokoloff et al., 2013). This hypothesis is based on two observations. First, administering amphetamines increases the amount of dopamine and can produce (or worsen) some symptoms of schizophrenia, especially in people with a genetic predisposition to the disorder. Second, drugs that reduce dopamine activity in the brain reduce or eliminate some symptoms of schizophrenia.

- **Brain abnormalities** A third major biological theory for schizophrenia looks at abnormalities in brain function and structure. Researchers have found larger cerebral ventricles (fluid-filled spaces in the brain) in some people with schizophrenia (Agartz et al., 2011; Fusar-Poli et al., 2011; Pepe et al., 2013).

Also, some people with chronic schizophrenia have a lower level of activity in their frontal and temporal lobes—areas we use in language, attention, and memory **(Figure 12.11)**. Damage in

FIGURE 12.10 **GENETICS AND SCHIZOPHRENIA**

Biological relatives of people with schizophrenia have a higher risk than the general population of developing the disorder during their lifetimes. Closer relatives (who have a more similar genetic makeup) have a greater risk than more distant relatives (Gottesman, 1991).

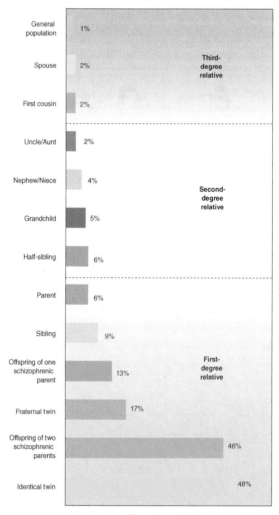

FIGURE 12.11 **BRAIN ACTIVITY IN SCHIZOPHRENIA**

Using these positron emission tomography (PET) scans, compare the normal levels of brain activity (upper left) with those of a person with schizophrenia (upper right), and then with those of a person with depression (lower left). Warmer colors (reds, yellows) indicate increased brain activity, whereas cooler colors (blues and greens) indicate decreased activity.

Science Source/Photo Researchers, Inc.

Diathesis-stress model A hypothesis about the cause of certain disorders, such as schizophrenia, which suggests that people inherit a predisposition (or "diathesis") that increases their risk for mental disorders if they are exposed to certain extremely stressful life experiences.

these regions might explain the thought and language disturbances that characterize schizophrenia. This lower level of brain activity, and schizophrenia itself, may also result from an overall loss of gray matter (neurons in the cerebral cortex) (Salgado-Pineda et al., 2011; Trost et al., 2013; Williams et al., 2013).

Clearly, biological factors play a key role in schizophrenia. But the fact that the heritability of schizophrenia is only 48% even in identical twins—who share identical genes—tells us that nongenetic factors must contribute the remaining percentage. Most psychologists believe there are at least two possible psychosocial contributors.

According to the **diathesis-stress model** of schizophrenia, stress plays an essential role in triggering schizophrenic episodes in people with an inherited predisposition (or diathesis) toward the disease (Arnsten, 2011; Beaton & Simon, 2011; Gallagher & Jones, 2013). In line with this model, children who experience severe trauma before age 16 are three times more likely than other people to develop schizophrenia (Bentall et al., 2012). People who experience stressful living environments, including poverty, unemployment, and crowding, are also at increased risk (Burns, 2013; Kirkbride et al., 2013).

Some investigators suggest that communication disorders in family members may also be a predisposing factor for schizophrenia. Such disorders include unintelligible speech, fragmented communication, and parents' frequently sending severely contradictory messages to children. Several studies have also shown greater rates of relapse and worsening of symptoms among hospitalized patients who went home to families that were critical and hostile toward them or overly involved in their lives emotionally (McFarlane, 2011; Roisko et al., 2011; Wasserman et al., 2013).

How should we evaluate the different theories about the causes of schizophrenia? Critics of the dopamine hypothesis and the brain damage theory argue that those theories fit only some cases of schizophrenia. Moreover, with both theories, it is difficult to determine cause and effect. The disturbed-communication theories are also hotly debated, and research is inconclusive. Like almost all forms of mental illness, schizophrenia is probably the result of a combination of known and unknown interacting factors **(Figure 12.12)**.

FIGURE 12.12 **THE BIOPSYCHOSOCIAL MODEL AND SCHIZOPHRENIA**

RETRIEVAL PRACTICE: SCHIZOPHRENIA

Self-Test

Completing this self-test and comparing your answers with those in Appendix B provides immediate feedback and helpful practice for exams. Additional interactive, self-tests are available at www.wiley.com/college/huffman.

1. Major disturbances in perception, language, thought, emotion, and behavior may be diagnosed as _____.

    a. schizophrenia   b. multiple dissociative disorder
    c. borderline psychosis   d. neurotic psychosis

2. _____ refers to "split mind," whereas refers to "split personality."

    a. Psychosis; neurosis   b. Insanity; multiple personalities
    c. Schizophrenia; dissociative   d. Paranoia; borderline
        identity disorder (DID)

3. In extreme cases, schizophrenia is also a form of _____, a term describing general lack of contact with reality.

    a. multiple personality   b. psychosis
       disorder
    c. borderline polar psychosis   d. all the above

4. Perceptions for which there are no appropriate external stimuli are called _____, and the most common type among people suffering from schizophrenia is _____.

    a. hallucinations; auditory   b. hallucinations; visual
    c. delusions; auditory   d. delusions; visual

Think Critically

1 Most of the disorders discussed in this chapter have some evidence for a genetic predisposition. What would you tell a friend who has a family member with one of these disorders and fears that he or she might develop the same disorder?

2 What do you think are the most important biological and psychosocial factors that contribute to schizophrenia?

realworldpsychology

Why might children who experience trauma be at increased risk of developing schizophrenia later in life?

HINT: LOOK IN THE MARGIN FOR

OTHER DISORDERS

RETRIEVAL PRACTICE While reading the upcoming sections, respond to each Learning Objective in your own words. Then compare your responses with those found at www.wiley.com/college/huffman.

1 **SUMMARIZE** the major features of obsessive-compulsive disorder.
2 **DESCRIBE** dissociative disorders.
3 **IDENTIFY** the major characteristics of personality disorders.

LEARNING OBJECTIVES

Having discussed anxiety disorders, mood disorders, and schizophrenia, we now explore three additional disorders: obsessive-compulsive, dissociative, and personality disorders.

Obsessive-Compulsive Disorder (OCD)

OCD involves persistent, unwanted, fearful thoughts (obsessions) and/or irresistible urges to perform an act or repeated rituals (compulsions) to help relieve the anxiety created by the obsession. In adults, women are affected at a slightly higher rate than men, whereas men are more commonly affected in childhood (American Psychiatric Association, 2013).

Common examples of obsessions are fear of germs, fear of being hurt or of hurting others, and troubling religious or sexual thoughts. Examples of compulsions are repeatedly checking, counting, cleaning, washing all or specific body

Obsessive-compulsive disorder (OCD) A mental disorder characterized by persistent, anxiety-provoking thoughts that will not go away (obsessions) and/or irresistible urges to perform repetitive behaviors (compulsions) performed according to certain rules or in a ritualized manner; compulsive behaviors persist because they help relieve the anxiety created by the obsessions.

parts, or putting things in a certain order. While everyone worries and sometimes double-checks, people with OCD have these thoughts and do these rituals for at least an hour or more each day, often longer (Chang et al., 2013; Roth et al., 2013).

Imagine what it would be like to worry so obsessively about germs that you compulsively wash your hands hundreds of times a day, until they are raw and bleeding. Most sufferers of **obsessive compulsive disorder (OCD)** realize that their actions are senseless. But when they try to stop the behavior, they experience mounting anxiety, which is relieved only by giving in to the compulsions. Given that numerous biological and psychological factors contribute to OCD, it is most often treated with a combination of drugs and cognitive-behavior therapy (CBT) **(Figure 12.13)** (Amin & Noggle, 2013; Roth et al., 2013) (Chapter 13).

Voices from the Classroom

OCD and Counting Stairs When we discuss *obsessive-compulsive disorder* in my class, I explain that everyone has some obsessive-compulsive behaviors, but it's not considered a disorder unless it becomes disruptive to your life. Some people count stairs as they go up or down (you know who you are)—not out loud but just silently.

After making this same statement in class one day, a student replied: "But you HAVE to count them. And if you get to the top or bottom and they're an odd number, you have to go back and start over. This time you have to continue counting with the number you stopped with so that they come out even." Counting the stairs to yourself is just a little obsessive-compulsive behavior, but having to go back and do it again so that they come out even is disruptive.

Professor Mike Majors
Delgado Community College
New Orleans, Louisiana

FIGURE 12.13 **MANAGING OCD**

Many celebrities suffer from OCD, including soccer star David Beckham, actors Megan Fox (pictured here) and Leonardo DiCaprio, and singer/actor Justin Timberlake. Fortunately, people can learn to manage the symptoms of OCD, through therapy and/or medication, and lead highly productive and fulfilling lives.

Kevin Winter/Getty Images

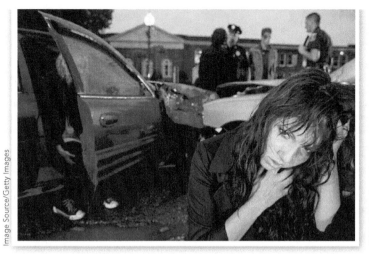

Image Source/Getty Images

FIGURE 12.14 **DISSOCIATION AS AN ESCAPE**

The major force behind all dissociative disorders is the need to escape from anxiety. Imagine witnessing a loved one's death in a horrible car accident. Can you see how your mind might cope by blocking out all memory of the event?

Dissociative Disorders

The most dramatic psychological disorders are **dissociative disorders**, psychological dysfunctions characterized by a major loss of memory without a clear physical cause. There are several types, but all are characterized by a splitting apart (a *dis-association*) of significant aspects of experience from memory or consciousness **(Figure 12.14)**. Unlike most other psychological disorders, dissociative disorders appear to be primarily caused by environmental variables, with little or no genetic influence (Hulette et al., 2011; Sinason, 2011; Waller & Ross, 1997).

The most severe dissociative disorder is **dissociative identity disorder (DID)**—previously known as multiple personality disorder (MPD)—in which at least two separate and distinct personalities exist within a person at the same time **(Figure 12.15)**. Each personality has unique memories, behaviors, and social relationships. Transition from one personality to another occurs suddenly and is often triggered by psychological stress. Usually, the original personality has no knowledge or awareness of the alternate personalities, but all the personalities may be aware of lost periods of time. The disorder is diagnosed about equally among men and women (American Psychiatric Association, 2013).

Dissociative disorder A psychological disorder marked by a disturbance in the integration of consciousness, identity, memory, and other features.

Dissociative identity disorder (DID) A mental disorder characterized by the presence of two or more distinct personality systems in the same individual at different times; previously known as multiple personality disorder (MPD).

DID is a controversial diagnosis. Some experts suggest that many cases are faked or result from false memories and an unconscious need to please the therapist (Boysen & VanBergen, 2013; Kihlstrom, 2005; Ost et al., 2013; Stafford & Lynn, 2002). On the other side of the debate are psychologists who accept the validity of DID and provide treatment guidelines (Brown, 2011; Chu, 2011; Dalenberg et al., 2007; Lipsanen et al., 2004; Moline, 2013).

Stephen Dunn / Allsport / GettyImages.

FIGURE 12.15 **A PERSONAL ACCOUNT OF DID**

Herschel Walker, professional football player, pro bowler, Olympic bobsledder, and business and family man, now suggests that none of the people who played these roles were really he. They were his "alters," or alternate personalities. He has been diagnosed with the controversial diagnosis of *dissociative identity disorder* (*DID*). Although some have suggested that the disorder helped him succeed as a professional athlete, it played havoc with his personal life. He's now in treatment and has written a book, *Breaking Free*, hoping to change the public's image of DID.

Personality disorder A mental disorder characterized by chronic, inflexible, maladaptive personality traits, which cause significant impairment of social and occupational functioning.

Antisocial personality disorder The pervasive pattern of disregard for, and violation of, the rights of others beginning in childhood or early adolescence and continuing into adulthood; includes traits like unlawful behaviors, deceitful and manipulative behaviors, impulsivity, irritability and aggressiveness, consistent irresponsibility, reckless disregard for self and others, and lack of remorse.

Personality Disorders

What would happen if the characteristics of a personality were so inflexible and maladaptive that they significantly impaired someone's ability to function? This is what occurs with **personality disorders**. Several types of personality disorders are included in this category in the fifth edition of the *DSM*, but here we will focus on antisocial personality disorder and borderline personality disorder (American Psychiatric Association, 2013).

Antisocial Personality Disorder

People with **antisocial personality disorder**—also sometimes referred to as *psychopathy, sociopathy*, or *dissocial personality disorder*—show a pattern of disregard for, and violation of, the rights of others. These labels describe behavior so far outside the ethical and legal standards of society that many consider it the most serious of all mental disorders. Unlike people with anxiety, mood disorders, and schizophrenia, those with this diagnosis feel little personal distress (and may not be motivated to change). Yet their maladaptive traits generally bring considerable harm and suffering to others (Hervé et al., 2004; Noggle et al., 2013; Trull et al., 2013). Although serial killers are often seen as classic examples of people with antisocial personality disorder, most people who have this disorder generally harm others in less dramatic ways—for example, as ruthless businesspeople and crooked politicians.

RJ Sangostri_Sangostri /AFP /NewsCom

realworldpsychology **The Media and Mental Illness** The world was shocked and deeply saddened on July 20, 2012, when 25-year-old James Holmes went on a horrific shooting spree, killing 12 people and wounding or injuring 58 in a movie theater in Aurora, Colorado. The shootings prompted intense debate over gun control and violence in the media. Perhaps because he had been seeing a psychiatrist prior to the shooting, it also heightened attention to the detection and treatment of mental illness. But few questions were asked about the intensive media coverage. Given what you've learned in this chapter, how might news and social media discussions of tragic shooting events like these increase myths and misconceptions about people with a mental illness?

Unlike most other adults, individuals with antisocial personality disorder act impulsively, without giving thought to the consequences. They are usually poised when confronted with their destructive behavior and feel contempt for anyone they are able to manipulate. They also change jobs and relationships suddenly, and they often have a history of truancy from school and of being expelled for destructive behavior. People with antisocial personalities can be charming and persuasive, and they have remarkably good insight into the needs and weaknesses of other people.

Twin and adoption studies suggest a possible genetic predisposition to antisocial personality disorder (Beaver et al., 2011; Kendler & Prescott, 2006). Biological contributions are also suggested by studies that have found abnormally low autonomic activity during stress, right hemisphere abnormalities, and reduced gray matter in the frontal lobes and biochemical disturbances (Anderson et al., 2011; Bertsch et al., 2013; Portnoy et al., 2013; Schiffer et al., 2011; Sundram et al., 2011). For example, MRI brain scans of criminals currently in prison for violent crimes, such as rape, murder, or attempted murder, and showing little empathy and remorse for their crimes, revealed reduced gray matter volume in the prefrontal cortex (Gregory et al., 2012). (Recall from Chapter 2 that this is the area of the brain responsible for emotions, such as fear, empathy, and/or guilt.)

Evidence also exists for environmental or psychological causes. People with antisocial personality disorder often come from homes characterized by abusive parenting styles, emotional deprivation, harsh and inconsistent disciplinary practices, and antisocial parental behavior (Calkins & Keane, 2009; Noggle et al., 2013; Torry & Billick, 2011; Wachlarowicz et al., 2012). Still other studies show a strong

Q5

interaction between both heredity and environment (Douglas et al., 2011; Hudziak, 2008; Philibert et al., 2011; Trull et al., 2013).

Borderline Personality Disorder

Borderline personality disorder (BPD) is among the most commonly diagnosed and most functionally disabling of all mental disorders (Ansell & Grilo, 2007; Chanen & McCutcheon, 2013; Gunderson, 2011; Rizvi & Salters-Pedneault, 2013).

The core features of this disorder are impulsivity and instability in mood, relationships, and self-image. Originally, the term implied that the person was on the borderline between neurosis and schizophrenia (Schroeder et al., 2013). The modern conceptualization no longer has this connotation, but BPD remains one of the most complex and debilitating of all the personality disorders.

People with BPD experience extreme difficulties in relationships. Subject to chronic feelings of depression, emptiness, and intense fear of abandonment, they also engage in destructive, impulsive behaviors, such as sexual promiscuity, drinking, gambling, and eating sprees. In addition, they may attempt suicide and sometimes engage in self-mutilating behavior (Chapman et al., 2008; Lynam et al., 2011; Muehlenkamp et al., 2011; Turnbull et al., 2013).

Those with BPD also tend to see themselves and everyone else in absolute terms—as either perfect or worthless (Mak & Lam, 2013; Rizvi & Salters-Pedneault, 2013; Scott et al., 2011). Constantly seeking reassurance from others, they may quickly erupt in anger at the slightest sign of disapproval. The disorder is also typically marked by a long history of broken friendships, divorces, and lost jobs.

In short, people with this disorder appear to have a deep well of intense loneliness and a chronic fear of abandonment and they often seek therapy. Unfortunately, given their troublesome personality traits, friends, lovers, and even family members and therapists often do "abandon" them—thus creating a tragic self-fulfilling prophecy. The good news is that BPD can be reliably diagnosed and it does respond to professional intervention—particularly in young people (Chanen & McCutcheon, 2013; Fleischhaker et al., 2011; Leichsenring et al., 2011; Rizvi & Salters-Pedneault, 2013).

What causes BPD? Some research points to environmental factors, such as a childhood history of neglect, emotional deprivation, and physical, sexual, or emotional abuse (Chanen & McCutcheon, 2013; Distel et al., 2011). From a biological perspective, BPD also tends to run in families, and some data suggest that it is a result of impaired functioning of the brain's frontal lobes and limbic system, areas that control impulsive behaviors (Leichsenring et al., 2011; Mak & Lam, 2013; Schulze et al., 2011). For example, research using neuroimaging reveals that people with BPD show more activity in parts of the brain associated with the experience of negative emotions, coupled with less activity in parts of the brain that help suppress negative emotion (Ruocco et al., 2013). As in many cases, most researchers agree that BPD results from an interaction between the environment and biology (Carpenter et al., 2013; Ripoll et al., 2013).

Borderline personality disorder (BPD) A mental disorder characterized by severe instability in emotion and self-concept, along with impulsive and self-destructive behaviors.

RETRIEVAL PRACTICE: OTHER DISORDERS

Self-Test

Completing this self-test and comparing your answers with those in Appendix B provides immediate feedback and helpful practice for exams. Additional interactive, self-tests are available at www.wiley.com/college/huffman.

1. Repetitive, ritualistic behaviors, such as hand washing, counting, or putting things in order, are called a(n) _____.

a. obsessions
b. compulsions
c. ruminations
d. phobias

2. A disorder characterized by disturbances in consciousness, identity, memory, and other features is known as a(n) _____.

a. dissociative disorder
b. disoriented disorder
c. displacement disorder
d. identity disorder

3. A serial killer would likely be diagnosed as a(n) _____ personality in the *Diagnostic and Statistical Manual (DSM)*.

a. dissociative disorder

b. antisocial personality disorder

c. multiple personality disorder

d. borderline psychosis

4. One possible biological contributor to BPD is a(n) _____.

a. childhood history of neglect

b. emotional deprivation

c. impaired functioning of the frontal lobes

d. all these options

Think Critically

1 How would you explain to others that schizophrenia is not the same as dissociative identity disorder (DID) (formerly called multiple personality disorder [MPD])?

2 Does the fact that research shows a genetic component to antisocial personality disorder change your opinion regarding the degree of guilt and responsibility someone like Adam Lanza has for the Sandy Hook shooting spree?

realworldpsychology

How do changes in the brain help explain severe antisocial personality disorder?

HINT: LOOK IN THE MARGIN FOR

GENDER AND CULTURAL EFFECTS

LEARNING OBJECTIVES

RETRIEVAL PRACTICE While reading the upcoming sections, respond to each Learning Objective in your own words. Then compare your responses with those found at www.wiley.com/college/huffman.

1 DISCUSS the possible gender differences in psychological disorders.

2 EXPLAIN why it is difficult to directly compare mental disorders across cultures.

3 OUTLINE strategies for avoiding ethnocentrism in psychological disorders.

Among the Chippewa, Cree, and Montagnais-Naskapi Indians in Canada, there is a disorder called *windigo*—or *wiitiko*—*psychosis*, characterized by delusions and cannibalistic impulses. Believing they have been possessed by the spirit of a windigo, a cannibal giant with a heart and entrails of ice, victims become severely depressed (Faddiman, 1997). As the malady begins, the individual typically experiences loss of appetite, diarrhea, vomiting, and insomnia, and he or she may see people turning into beavers and other edible animals. In later stages, the victim becomes obsessed with cannibalistic thoughts and may even attack and kill loved ones in order to devour their flesh (Berreman, 1971).

If you were a therapist, how would you treat this disorder? Does it fit neatly into any of the categories of psychological disorders that you have learned about? We began this chapter by discussing the complexities and problems with defining, identifying, and classifying abnormal behavior. Before we close, we need to add two additional confounding factors: gender and culture. In this section, we explore a few of the many ways in which men and women differ in their experience of abnormal behavior. We also look at cultural variations in abnormal behavior.

Gender Differences

When you picture someone suffering from depression, anxiety, alcoholism, or antisocial personality disorder, what is the gender of each person? Most people tend to visualize a woman for the first two and a man for the last two. There is some truth to these stereotypes.

Research has found many gender differences in the prevalence rates of various mental disorders. Let's start with the well-established fact that around the world, the rate of severe depression for women is about double that for men (Dillard et al., 2012; Luppa et al., 2012; Sonnenberg et al., 2013; World Health Organization, 2011). Why is there such a striking gender difference?

Certain risk factors for depression (such as genetic predisposition, marital problems, pain, and medical illness) are common to both men and women. However, poverty is a well-known contributor to many psychological disorders, and women are far more likely than men to fall into the lowest socioeconomic groups. Women also experience more sexual trauma, partner abuse, and chronic stress in their daily lives, and these are all well-known contributing factors in depression (Doornbos et al., 2013; Harkness et al., 2010; Mapayi et al., 2013; Mota et al., 2012; Neri et al., 2012; Oram et al., 2013).

Recent research also suggests that some gender differences in depression may relate to the way women and men tend to internalize or externalize their emotions. Using structured interview techniques, researchers found that women ruminate more frequently than men, which means they are more likely to focus repetitively on their *internal* negative emotions and problems rather than engage in more external problem-solving strategies. In contrast, men tend to be more disinhibited and more likely to *externalize* their emotions and problems (Dawson et al., 2010; Schirmer, 2013; Tarter et al., 2003; Tompkins et al., 2011; Xu et al., 2012).

On the other hand, gender differences may result from misapplied gender role stereotypes. For example, the most common symptoms of depression, such as crying, low energy, dejected facial expressions, and withdrawal from social activities, are more socially acceptable for women than for men. And the fact that gender differences in depression are more pronounced in cultures with traditional gender roles (e.g., Seedat et al., 2009) suggests that male depression may be underdiagnosed because men are raised to be better at hiding and redirecting their emotions (Fields & Cochran, 2011). In U.S. society, men are typically socialized to suppress their emotions and to show their distress by acting out (showing aggression), acting impulsively (driving recklessly and committing petty crimes), or engaging in substance abuse.

To examine different expectations about depression as a function of gender, researchers in one study asked participants to read a story about a fictitious person (Kate in one version, Jack in the other). The story was exactly the same in both conditions and included the following information: "For the past two weeks, Kate/Jack has been feeling really down. S/he wakes up in the morning with a flat, heavy feeling that stick with her/him all day. S/he isn't enjoying things the way s/he normally would. S/he finds it hard to concentrate on anything." Although all participants read the same story, those who read about Kate rated her symptoms as more distressing, deserving of sympathy, and difficult to treat (Swami et al., 2012).

psychology and you   **Strategies for Managing Depression** Do you, or does someone you know, suffer from depression? Fortunately, many strategies can help both men and women cope with depression. For example, in order to prevent or reduce depression, women may benefit from learning better coping and cognitive skills to reduce the likelihood of rumination and just wallowing in sad feelings. On the other hand, if it's true that men more often express their depression through impulsive, acting-out behaviors, then rewarding deliberate, planned behaviors over unintentional, spur-of-the moment ones may be helpful for treating some forms of male depression (Eaton et al., 2012).

© Piotr Marcinski / Shutterstock

Understanding the importance of genetic predispositions, external environmental factors (like poverty), and cognitive factors (like internalizing versus externalizing emotions and problems) may help mental health professionals better understand individual and gender-related differences in depression.

Culture and Schizophrenia

Peoples of different cultures experience mental disorders in a variety of ways. For example, the reported incidence of schizophrenia varies in different cultures around the world. It is unclear whether these differences result from actual differences in prevalence of the disorder or from differences in definition, diagnosis, or reporting (Berry et al., 2011; Butler et al., 2011; Zandi, 2013). The symptoms of schizophrenia also vary across cultures (Barnow & Balkir, 2013; Burns, 2013), as do the particular stressors that may trigger its onset **(Figure 12.16)**.

Finally, despite the advanced treatment facilities and methods in industrialized nations, the prognosis for people with schizophrenia is actually better in nonindustrialized societies. The reason may be that the core symptoms of schizophrenia (poor rapport with others, incoherent speech, and so on) make it more difficult to survive in highly industrialized countries. In addition, in most industrialized nations, families and other support groups are less likely to feel responsible for relatives and friends who have schizophrenia (Barnow & Balkir, 2013; Eaton et al., 2011).

Avoiding Ethnocentrism

Most research on psychological disorders originates and is conducted primarily in Western cultures. Such a restricted sampling can limit our understanding of disorders in general and can lead to an ethnocentric view of mental disorders.

Fortunately, cross-cultural researchers have devised ways to overcome these difficulties (Matsumoto & Juang, 2013; Triandis, 2007). For example, Robert Nishimoto (1988) has found several *culture-general symptoms* that are useful in diagnosing disorders across cultures **(Table 12.3)**.

In addition, Nishimoto found several *culture-bound symptoms*. For example, Vietnamese Chinese respondents reported "fullness in head," Mexican respondents had "problems with [their] memory," and Anglo-American respondents reported "shortness of breath" and "headaches." Apparently, people learn to express their problems in ways that are acceptable to others in the same culture (Brislin, 1997, 2000; Butler et al., 2011; Dhikav et al., 2008; Iwata et al., 2011; Kanayama & Pope, 2011; Marques et al., 2011).

FIGURE 12.16 **WHAT IS STRESSFUL?**

Ⓐ Some stressors are culturally specific, such as feeling possessed by evil forces or being the victim of witchcraft.

Ⓑ Other stressors are shared by many cultures, such as the unexpected death of a loved one or loss of a job (Al-Issa, 2000; Cechnicki et al., 2011; Neria et al., 2002; Ramsay et al., 2012).

TABLE 12.3	CULTURE-GENERAL SYMPTOMS OF MENTAL HEALTH DIFFICULTIES	
Nervous	Trouble sleeping	Low spirits
Weak all over	Personal worries	Restless
Feel apart, alone	Can't get along	Hot all over
Worry all the time	Can't do anything worthwhile	Nothing turns out right

Source: Brislin, 2000.

This division between culture-general and culture-bound symptoms also helps us better understand depression. Certain symptoms of depression (such as intense sadness, poor concentration, and low energy) seem to exist across all cultures (Walsh & Cross, 2013; World Health Organization, 2011). But there is also evidence of some culture-bound symptoms. For example, feelings of guilt are found more often in North America and Europe than in other parts of the world. And in China, *somatization* (the conversion of depression into bodily complaints) occurs more frequently than it does in other parts of the world (Helms & Cook, 1999; Lawrence et al., 2011; Lim et al., 2011).

Just as there are culture-bound and culture-general symptoms, researchers have found that mental disorders are themselves sometimes culturally bound and generally only appear in one population group **(Figure 12.17)**. The earlier example of windigo psychosis, a disorder limited to a small group of Canadian Indians, illustrates just such a case.

As you can see, culture has a strong effect on mental disorders. Studying the similarities and differences across cultures can lead to better diagnosis and understanding. It also helps mental health professionals who work with culturally diverse populations understand both culturally general and culturally bound symptoms.

FIGURE 12.17 CULTURE-BOUND DISORDERS

Some disorders are fading as remote areas become more Westernized, whereas other disorders (such as anorexia nervosa) are spreading as other countries adopt Western values.

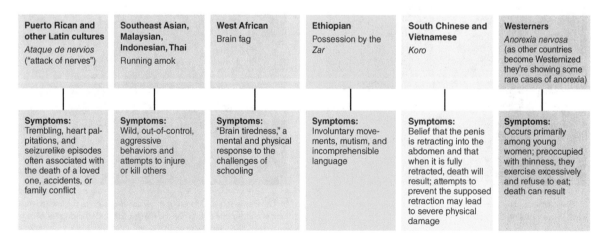

RETRIEVAL PRACTICE: GENDER AND CULTURAL EFFECTS

Self-Test

Completing this self-test and comparing your answers with those in Appendix B provides immediate feedback and helpful practice for exams. Additional interactive, self-tests are available at www.wiley.com/college/huffman.

1. When studying gender differences in mental health, researchers found that _____.

   a. women ruminate more frequently than men
   b. men tend to be more disinhibited and more likely to externalize their emotions and problems
   c. men are typically socialized to suppress their emotions
   d. all these options

2. Which of the following are examples of culture-general symptoms of mental health difficulties that are useful in diagnosing disorders across cultures?

   a. trouble sleeping
   b. worry all the time
   c. can't get along
   d. all the above

3. Symptoms of mental illness that generally only appear in one population group are known as _____.

   a. culture-bound symptoms
   b. group specific disorders
   c. group-think syndrome
   d. none of these

4. What disorder has the following symptoms: wild, out-of-control, aggressive behaviors and attempts to injure or kill others?

   a. *Ataque de nervios* ("attack of nerves")
   b. Running amok
   c. Possession by the Zar
   d. Koro

Think Critically

1 Culture clearly has strong effects on mental disorders. How does this influence what you think about what is normal or abnormal?

2 Some research suggests that depression in men is often overlooked because men are socialized to suppress their emotions and encouraged to express their distress by acting out, being impulsive, or engaging in substance abuse. Does this ring true with your own experiences and/or observations of others? If so, how might we change this situation?

realworldpsychology

Are symptoms of depression in women more distressing, deserving of sympathy, and difficult to treat than the same signs in men?

HINT: LOOK IN THE MARGIN FOR Q6

Summary

1 STUDYING PSYCHOLOGICAL DISORDERS   334

- Criteria for **psychological disorders** include *deviance, dysfunction, distress*, and *danger*. None of these criteria alone is adequate for classifying abnormal behavior.
- Superstitious explanations for abnormal behavior were replaced by the **medical model**, which eventually gave rise to the modern specialty of **psychiatry**. In contrast to the medical model, psychology offers a multifaceted approach to explaining abnormal behavior.

2 ANXIETY DISORDERS   340

- **Anxiety disorders** include **generalized anxiety disorder (GAD)**, **panic disorder**, and **phobias** (including agoraphobia, specific phobias, and social phobias).
- Psychological (faulty cognitions and maladaptive learning), biological (evolutionary and genetic predispositions, biochemical disturbances), and sociocultural (cultural pressures toward hypervigilance) factors likely all contribute to anxiety. Classical and operant conditioning also can contribute to phobias.

3 DEPRESSIVE AND BIPOLAR DISORDERS   345

- Both depressive and bipolar disorders are characterized by extreme disturbances in emotional states. People suffering from **depressive disorders** may experience a lasting depressed mood without a clear trigger. In contrast, people with **bipolar disorder** alternate between periods of depression and mania (characterized by hyperactivity and poor judgment).
- Biological factors play a significant role in mood disorders. Psychosocial theories of depression focus on environmental stressors and disturbances in interpersonal relationships, thought processes, self-concept, and learning history, including **learned helplessness**.

4 SCHIZOPHRENIA   350

- **Schizophrenia** is a group of disorders, each characterized by a disturbance in perception (including **hallucinations**), language, thought (including **delusions**), emotions, and/or behavior.
- In the past, researchers divided schizophrenia into multiple subtypes. More recently, researchers have proposed focusing

instead on **positive schizophrenia symptoms** versus **negative schizophrenia symptoms**.

- Most biological theories of schizophrenia focus on genetics, neurotransmitters, and brain abnormalities. Psychologists believe that there are also at least two possible psychosocial contributors: stress and communication disorders in families.

5 OTHER DISORDERS 355

- **Obsessive-compulsive disorder (OCD)** involves persistent, unwanted, fearful thoughts (obsessions) and/or irresistible urges to perform an act or repeated rituals (compulsions), which help relieve the anxiety created by the obsession. Given that numerous biological and psychological factors contribute to OCD, its most often treated with a combination of drugs and cognitive-behavior therapy (CBT).
- **Dissociative disorders** are characterized by a major loss of memory without a clear physical cause, and a subtype of these disorders, **dissociative identity disorder (DID)**, involves the presence of two or more distinct personality systems in the same individual at different times. Environmental variables appear to be the primary cause of dissociative disorders. Dissociation can be a form of escape from a past trauma.

- **Personality disorders** occur when inflexible, maladaptive personality traits cause significant impairment of social and occupational functioning. **Antisocial personality disorder** is a pattern of disregard for, and violation of, the rights of others. The most common personality disorder is **borderline personality disorder (BPD)**. Its core features are impulsivity and instability in mood, relationships, and self-image. Although some therapists have success with drug therapy and behavior therapy, the prognosis is not favorable.

6 GENDER AND CULTURAL EFFECTS 360

- Men and women differ in their rates and experiences of abnormal behavior. For instance, in the case of depression, modern research suggests that the gender-ratio differences may reflect an underlying predisposition toward internalizing or externalizing emotions and problems.
- Peoples of different cultures experience mental disorders in a variety of ways. For example, the reported incidence of schizophrenia varies in different cultures around the world, as do the disorder's symptoms, triggers, and prognosis.
- Some symptoms of psychological disorders, as well as some disorders themselves, are *culture general*, whereas others are *culture bound*.

◎ applyingrealworldpsychology

We began this chapter with five intriguing Real World Psychology questions, and you were asked to revisit these questions at the end of each section. Questions like these have an important and lasting impact on all of our lives. See if you can answer these additional critical thinking questions related to real world examples.

Jodi Cobb/NG Image Collection

1 Is this man's behavior abnormal? Which criteria for psychological disorders do his piercings and tattoos meet? Which do they not?

2 Can you think of any behavior *you* exhibit that might be considered abnormal if your own cultural norms were not taken into account?

3 We've all experienced anxiety. Which of the explanations described in this section do you feel best describes your personal experiences with it? Why?

4 Recall an experience you've had with depression. How was it similar to or different from what was discussed in the section on major depressive disorders?

5 In the section on schizophrenia, we pointed out that if one identical twin develops schizophrenia, there is a 48% chance that the other twin will do so as well. How does this high correlation support the diathesis-stress model?

6 Think about someone you know—a friend, a family member, or yourself—who suffers from one of the disorders described in this chapter. How does the information we've provided differ from or match what you've discovered from your own or others' experiences?

Key Terms

RETRIEVAL PRACTICE Write a definition for each term before turning back to the referenced page to check your answer.

- abnormal behavior 334
- antisocial personality disorder 358
- anxiety disorder 340
- bipolar disorder 346
- borderline personality disorder (BPD) 359
- comorbidity 337
- delusion 352
- depressive disorders 345
- *Diagnostic and Statistical Manual of Mental Disorders* (DSM) 337

- diathesis-stress model 354
- dissociative disorder 357
- dissociative identity disorder (DID) 357
- generalized anxiety disorder (GAD) 341
- hallucination 351
- insanity 337
- learned helplessness 349
- medical model 336
- neurosis 337
- obsessive-compulsive disorder (OCD) 356

- panic disorder 341
- personality disorder 358
- phobia 342
- psychiatry 336
- psychosis 337
- schizophrenia 350

chapterthirteen

Therapy

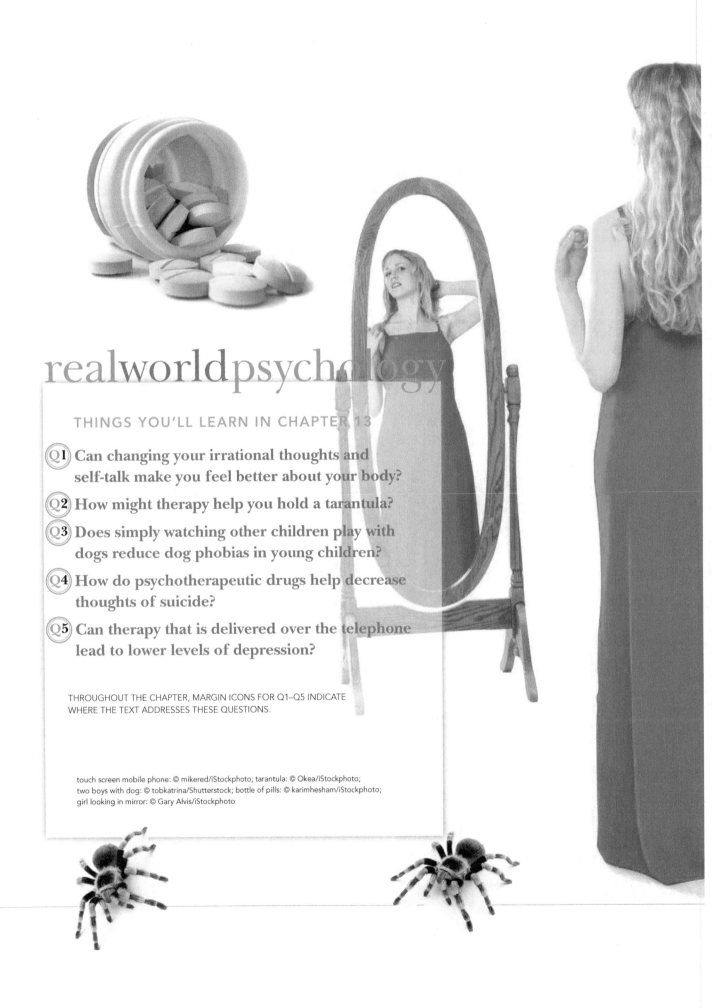

realworldpsychology

THINGS YOU'LL LEARN IN CHAPTER 13

Q1 Can changing your irrational thoughts and self-talk make you feel better about your body?

Q2 How might therapy help you hold a tarantula?

Q3 Does simply watching other children play with dogs reduce dog phobias in young children?

Q4 How do psychotherapeutic drugs help decrease thoughts of suicide?

Q5 Can therapy that is delivered over the telephone lead to lower levels of depression?

THROUGHOUT THE CHAPTER, MARGIN ICONS FOR Q1–Q5 INDICATE WHERE THE TEXT ADDRESSES THESE QUESTIONS.

chapteroverview

Throughout this text, we have emphasized the *science* of psychology, and this chapter is no exception. However, psychology is also a *practice*, in which psychologists conduct research and apply psychological principles to help people suffering from psychological disorders (Chapter 12). In this chapter, we'll discuss the three major approaches to psychotherapy **(Figure 13.1)**, its general goals and effectiveness, and other important issues and topics in the field. Along the way, we'll work to demystify and destigmatize its practice and dispel some common myths **(Table 13.1)**.

FIGURE 13.1 AN OVERVIEW OF THE THREE MAJOR APPROACHES TO THERAPY

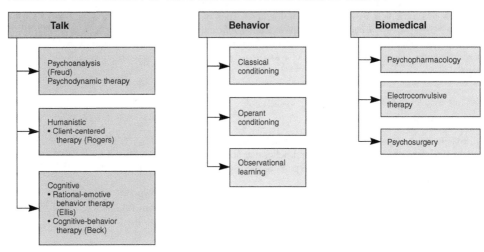

TABLE 13.1   **MYTHS ABOUT THERAPY** | realworldpsychology

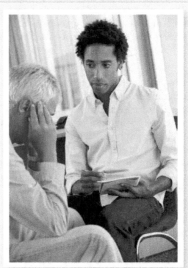

- **Myth: There is one best therapy.**
  Fact: Many problems can be treated equally well with many different forms of therapy.

- **Myth: Therapists can read your mind.**
  Fact: Good therapists often seem to have an uncanny ability to understand how their clients are feeling and to know when someone is trying to avoid certain topics. This is not due to any special mind-reading ability; it simply reflects their specialized training and daily experience working with troubled people.

- **Myth: People who go to therapists are crazy or weak.**
  Fact: Most people seek counseling because of stress in their lives or because they realize that therapy can improve their level of functioning. It is difficult to be objective about our own problems. Seeking therapy is a sign of wisdom and personal strength.

- **Myth: Only the rich can afford therapy.**
  Fact: Therapy can be expensive. But many clinics and therapists charge on a sliding scale, based on the client's income. Some insurance plans also cover psychological services.

- **Myth: If I am taking meds, I don't need therapy.**
  Fact: Medications, such as antidepressants, are only one form of therapy. They can change brain chemistry, but they can't teach us to think, feel, or behave differently. Research suggests that a combination of drugs and psychotherapy may be best for some situations, whereas in other cases, psychotherapy or drug therapy alone may be most effective.

© Mark Bowden/iStockphoto

TALK THERAPIES

RETRIEVAL PRACTICE While reading the upcoming sections, respond to each Learning Objective in your own words. Then compare your responses with those found at www.wiley.com/college/huffman.

LEARNING OBJECTIVES

1 DESCRIBE the core treatment techniques in psychoanalysis and modern psychodynamic therapies.

2 SUMMARIZE the key characteristics of humanistic therapies.

3 EXPLAIN the principles underlying cognitive therapies.

We begin our discussion of professional **psychotherapy** with traditional psychoanalysis and its modern counterpart, psychodynamic therapies. Then we explore humanistic and cognitive therapies. Although these therapies differ significantly, they're often grouped together as "talk therapies" because they emphasize communication between the therapist and client, as opposed to the behavioral and biomedical therapies we discuss later.

Psychotherapy Any of a group of therapies used to treat psychological disorders and to improve psychological functioning and adjustment to life.

Psychoanalysis/Psychodynamic Therapies

In **psychoanalysis**, a person's *psyche* (or mind) is *analyzed*. Traditional psychoanalysis is based on Sigmund Freud's central belief that abnormal behavior is caused by unconscious conflicts among the three parts of the psyche—the id, the ego, and the superego (Chapter 11).

During psychoanalysis, these conflicts are brought to consciousness. The patient comes to understand the reasons for his or her dysfunction and realizes that the childhood conditions under which the conflicts developed no longer exist. Once this realization or insight occurs, the conflicts can be resolved, and the patient can develop more adaptive behavior patterns (Altman, 2013; Cordón, 2012; Johnson, 2011).

Unfortunately, according to Freud, the ego has strong *defense mechanisms* that block unconscious thoughts from coming to light. Thus, to gain insight into the unconscious, the ego must be "tricked" into relaxing its guard. To meet that goal, psychoanalysts employ five major methods: *free association, dream analysis, analyzing resistance, analyzing transference,* and *interpretation.*

Psychoanalysis A type of psychodynamic therapy developed by Freud; an intensive and prolonged technique for bringing unconscious conflicts into conscious awareness.

Free association In psychoanalysis, reporting whatever comes to mind without monitoring its contents.

Free Association

According to Freud, when you let your mind wander and remove conscious censorship over thoughts—a process called **free association**—interesting and even bizarre connections seem to spring into awareness. Freud believed that the first thing to come to a patient's mind is often an important clue to what the person's unconscious wants to conceal. Having the patient recline on a couch, with only the ceiling to look at, is believed to encourage free association **(Figure 13.2)**.

Dream Analysis

Recall from Chapter 5 that, according to Freud, our psychological defenses are lowered during sleep. Therefore, our forbidden desires and unconscious conflicts are supposedly more freely expressed during dreams. Even while dreaming, however, we recognize these feelings and conflicts as unacceptable and must disguise them as

Sigmund Freud (1856–1939)
Freud believed that during psychoanalysis, the therapist's (or psychoanalyst's) major goal was to bring unconscious conflicts into consciousness.

© Hulton-Deutsch Collection/©Corbis

FIGURE 13.2 FREUD'S FREE ASSOCIATION

Psychoanalysis is often portrayed as a patient lying on a couch engaging in free association. Freud believed that this arrangement—with the patient relaxed and the therapist out of his or her view—helps the patient let down his or her defenses, making the unconscious more accessible.

"The way this works is that you say the first thing that comes to your mind..."

© Joseph Farris/CartoonStock

Dream analysis In psychoanalysis, interpretation of the underlying true meaning of dreams to reveal unconscious processes.

images that have deeper symbolic meaning. Thus, using Freudian **dream analysis**, a therapist might interpret a dream of riding a horse or driving a car—the surface description, or *manifest content*—as a desire for, or concern about, sexual intercourse—the hidden, underlying meaning, or *latent content*.

Analysis of Resistance

Resistance In psychoanalysis, the inability or unwillingness of a patient to discuss or reveal certain memories, thoughts, motives, or experiences.

During free association or dream analysis, Freud found that patients often show an inability or unwillingness to discuss or reveal certain memories, thoughts, motives, or experiences. For example, if the patient suddenly "forgets" what he or she was saying or completely changes the subject, it is the therapist's job to identify these possible cases of **resistance** and then help the patient face his or her problems and learn to deal with them more realistically.

Analysis of Transference

Transference In psychoanalysis, the process by which a client attaches (transfers) to a therapist feelings formerly held toward some significant person who figured in a past emotional conflict.

Freud believed that during psychoanalysis, patients disclose intimate feelings and memories, and the relationship between the therapist and patient may become complex and emotionally charged. As a result, patients often apply, or *transfer*, some of their unresolved emotions and attitudes from past relationships onto the therapist. The therapist uses this process of **transference** to help the patient "relive" painful past relationships in a safe, therapeutic setting so that he or she can move on to healthier relationships.

Interpretation

Interpretation A psychoanalyst's explanation of a patient's free associations, dreams, resistance, and transference; more generally, any statement by a therapist that presents a patient's problem in a new way.

The core of all psychoanalytic therapy is **interpretation**. During free association, dream analysis, resistance, and transference, the analyst listens closely and tries to find patterns and hidden conflicts. At the right time, the therapist explains or interprets the underlying meanings to the client.

Evaluating Psychoanalysis

As you can see, psychoanalysis is largely rooted in the assumption that repressed memories and unconscious conflicts actually exist. But, as we noted in Chapters 7 and 11, this assumption is the subject of heated, ongoing debate. Critics also point to two other problems with psychoanalysis (Messer & Gurman, 2011; Miltenberger, 2011; Siegel, 2010):

- **Limited applicability** Psychoanalysis is time-consuming (often lasting several years with four to five sessions a week) and expensive. In addition, critics suggest that it applies only to a select group of highly motivated, articulate patients with less severe disorders and not to more complex disorders, such as schizophrenia.

- **Lack of scientific credibility** According to critics, it is difficult, if not impossible, to scientifically document the major tenets of psychoanalysis. How do we prove or disprove the importance or meaning of unconscious conflicts or symbolic dream images?

Despite these criticisms, research shows that traditional psychoanalysis can be effective for those who have the time and money (Altman, 2013; Barratt, 2013; Lambert, 2013; Spurling, 2011).

Stockbyte/SUPERSTOCK

FIGURE 13.3 INTERPERSONAL THERAPY (IPT)

IPT, a variation of psychodynamic therapy, focuses on current relationships, with the goal of relieving immediate symptoms and teaching better ways to solve interpersonal problems. Research shows that it's effective for a variety of disorders, including depression, marital conflict, eating disorders, and drug addiction (Aldenhoff, 2011; Cuijpers et al., 2011; Hardy, 2011; Stricker et al., 2013).

Psychodynamic Therapy

A modern derivative of Freudian psychoanalysis, **psychodynamic therapy**, includes both Freud's theories and those of his major followers—Jung, Adler, and Erikson. In contrast to psychoanalysis, psychodynamic therapy is shorter and less intensive (one or twice a week vs. several times a week and only a few weeks or months vs. years). In addition, the patient is treated face-to-face rather than reclining on a couch, and the therapist takes a more directive approach rather than waiting for unconscious memories and desires to slowly be uncovered.

Also, contemporary psychodynamic therapists focus less on unconscious, early-childhood roots of problems and more on conscious processes and current problems (Frew & Spiegler, 2013; Hunsley & Lee, 2010; Zuckerman, 2011). Such refinements have helped make treatments shorter, more available, and more effective for an increasing number of people. See **Figure 13.3** for one of the most popular modern forms of psychodynamic therapy.

Psychodynamic therapy A type of therapy that focuses on conscious processes and current problems; a briefer, more directive, and more modern form of psychoanalysis.

Humanistic therapy A type of therapy that emphasizes maximizing a client's inherent capacity for self-actualization by providing a non-judgmental, accepting atmosphere.

Humanistic Therapies

In contrast to the rather aloof doctor-to-patient approach of the psychoanalytic and psychodynamic therapies, the humanistic approach emphasizes the *human* characteristics of a person's potential, free will, and self-awareness.

Humanistic therapy assumes that people with problems are suffering from a disruption of their normal growth potential and, hence, their self-concept. When obstacles are removed, the individual is free to become the self-accepting, genuine person everyone is capable of being.

One of the best-known humanistic therapists is Carl Rogers (Rogers, 1961, 1980), who developed an approach that encouraged people to actualize their potential and to relate to others in genuine ways. His approach is referred to as

Michael Rougier/Time & Life Pictures/Getty Images

Carl Rogers (1902–1987)

Comstock/SUPERSTOCK

FIGURE 13.4 NURTURING GROWTH

Recall how you've felt when you've been with someone who believes that you are a good person with unlimited potential, a person who believes that your "real self" is unique and valuable. These are the feelings that are nurtured in humanistic therapy.

Client-centered therapy Rogers's humanistic approach to therapy, which emphasizes the client's natural tendency to become healthy and productive; techniques include empathy, unconditional positive regard, genuineness, and active listening.

Empathy In Rogerian terms, an insightful awareness and ability to share another's inner experience.

Unconditional positive regard Rogers's term for complete love and acceptance of another, such as a parent for a child, with no conditions attached.

Genuineness In Rogerian terms, authenticity or congruence; the awareness of one's true inner thoughts and feelings and being able to share them honestly with others.

Active listening Listening with total attention to what another is saying; it includes reflecting, paraphrasing, and clarifying what the person says and means.

client-centered therapy (Figure 13.4). (Rogers used the term *client* because he believed the label *patient* implied that someone was sick or mentally ill rather than responsible and competent.)

Client-centered therapy, like psychoanalysis and psychodynamic therapies, explores thoughts and feelings as a way to obtain insight into the causes for behaviors. For Rogerian therapists, however, the focus is on providing an accepting atmosphere and encouraging healthy emotional experiences. Clients are responsible for discovering their own maladaptive patterns.

Rogerian therapists create a therapeutic relationship by focusing on four important qualities of communication: *empathy, unconditional positive regard, genuineness*, and *active listening*.

Empathy

Using the technique of **empathy**, a sensitive understanding and sharing of another person's inner experience, therapists pay attention to body language and listen for subtle cues to help them understand the emotional experiences of clients. To further help clients explore their feelings, the therapist uses open-ended statements such as "You found that upsetting" or "You haven't been able to decide what to do about this" rather than asking questions or offering explanations.

Unconditional Positive Regard

Regardless of the clients' problems or behaviors, humanistic therapists offer them **unconditional positive regard**, a genuine caring and nonjudgmental attitude toward people based on their innate value as individuals. They avoid evaluative statements such as "That's good" and "You did the right thing" because such comments imply that the therapist is judging the client. Rogers believed that most of us receive conditional acceptance from our parents, teachers, and others, which leads to poor self-concepts and psychological disorders **(Figure 13.5)**.

Genuineness

Humanists believe that when therapists use **genuineness** and honestly share their thoughts and feelings with their clients, the clients will in turn develop self-trust and honest self-expression.

Active Listening

Using **active listening**, which includes reflecting, paraphrasing, and clarifying what the client is saying, the clinician communicates that he or she is genuinely interested and paying close attention (see *Psychology and You*).

FIGURE 13.5 UNCONDITIONAL VERSUS CONDITIONAL POSITIVE REGARD

According to Rogers, clients need to feel unconditionally accepted by their therapists in order to recognize and value their own emotions, thoughts, and behaviors. As this cartoon implies, some parents withhold their love and acceptance unless the child lives up to their expectations.

Pat Byrnes/The Cartoon Bank, Inc.

P. BYRNES.

"Just remember, son, it doesn't matter whether you win or lose—unless you want Daddy's love."

psychology and you Using Active Listening Personally and Professionally If you want to try active listening in your personal life, note that to *reflect* is to hold a mirror in front of the person, enabling that person to see him- or herself. To *paraphrase* is to summarize in different words what the other person is saying. To *clarify* is to check that both the speaker and listener are on the same wavelength.

When a professional uses active listening, he or she might notice a client's furrowed brow and downcast eyes while he is discussing his military experiences and then might respond, "It sounds like you're angry with your situation and feeling pretty miserable right now." Can you see how this statement reflects the client's anger, paraphrases his complaint, and gives feedback to clarify the communication? This type of attentive, active listening is a relatively simple and well-documented technique that you can use to improve your communication with virtually anyone—professors, employers, friends, family, and especially your love partner.

© Mark Bowden/iStockphoto

Evaluating Humanistic Theories

Supporters say that there is empirical evidence for the efficacy of client-centered therapy (Benjamin, 2011; Cain, 2013; Hazler, 2011; Messer & Gurman, 2011). However, critics argue that outcomes such as self-actualization and self-awareness are difficult to test scientifically, and research on specific humanistic techniques has had mixed results (Decker et al., 2013; Hodges & Biswas-Diener, 2007; Norcross & Wampold, 2011; Stiles, 2013).

Cognitive Therapies

Cognitive therapy assumes that faulty thought processes—beliefs that are irrational or overly demanding or that fail to match reality—create problem behaviors and emotions (Friedberg & Belsford, 2011; Palmer & Williams, 2013; Pomerantz, 2013).

Like psychoanalysts, cognitive therapists believe that exploring unexamined beliefs can produce insight into the reasons for disturbed thoughts, feelings, and behaviors. However, instead of believing that a change occurs because of insight, cognitive therapists suggest that negative *self-talk*, the unrealistic things a person tells himself or herself, is most important. For example, research with women suffering from eating disorders found that changing a patient's irrational thoughts and self-talk, such as "If I eat that cake, I will become fat instantly" or "I'll never have a dating relationship if I don't lose 20 pounds," resulted in their having fewer negative thoughts about their bodies (Bhatnagar et al., 2013).

Through a process called **cognitive restructuring**, clients are taught to identify and then challenge this type of negative self-talk, as well as change the way they interpret events and modify their maladaptive behaviors **(Figure 13.6)**.

Cognitive therapy A type of therapy that treats problem behaviors and mental processes by focusing on faulty thought processes and beliefs.

Cognitive restructuring A process in cognitive therapy that is designed to change destructive thoughts or inappropriate interpretations.

FIGURE 13.6 **USING COGNITIVE RESTRUCTURING TO IMPROVE SALES** | realworldpsychology

Internal Self-Talk and Beliefs

Lost important sales account

- "I hate sales."
- "I'm a shy person, and I'll never be any good at this."
- "I have to find another job before they fire me."

- "Selling can be difficult, but hard work pays off."
- "I'm shy but people respect my honesty and low-key approach."
- "I had the account before, and I'll get it back."

Possible Outcomes

Decreased efforts
Low energy
Depression

Increased efforts
Increased energy
No depression

A Note how the negative interpretation and destructive self-talk leads to destructive and self-defeating outcomes.

B Cognitive therapy teaches clients to challenge and change their negative beliefs and negative self-talk into positive ones, which, in turn, leads to more positive outcomes. Can you think of other situations in which such reinterpretation could be helpful?

Albert Ellis (1913–2007)

© Bettman/Corbis

Rational-emotive behavior therapy (REBT) Ellis's cognitive therapy that focuses on eliminating emotional reactions through logic, confrontation, and examination of irrational beliefs.

Ellis's REBT

One of the best-known cognitive therapists, Albert Ellis, suggested that irrational beliefs are the primary culprit in problem emotions and behaviors. He proposed that most people mistakenly believe they are unhappy or upset because of external, outside events, such as receiving a bad grade on an exam. Ellis suggested that, in reality, these negative emotions result from faulty interpretations and irrational beliefs (such as interpreting the bad grade as a sign of your incompetence and an indication that you'll never qualify for graduate school or a good job).

To deal with these irrational beliefs, Ellis developed **rational-emotive behavior therapy (REBT)** (Ellis, 2008; Ellis & Ellis, 2011; Vernon, 2011). (See below.)

ELLIS'S RATIONAL-EMOTIVE BEHAVIOR THERAPY (REBT)
psychology and you

If you receive a poor performance evaluation at work, you might directly attribute your bad mood to the negative feedback. Psychologist Albert Ellis would argue that your self-talk ("I always mess up") between the event and the feeling is what actually upsets you. Furthermore, ruminating on all the other bad things in your life maintains your negative emotional state and may even lead to anxiety disorders, depression, and other psychological disorders.

To treat these problems, Ellis developed an A–B–C–D approach: **A** stands for *activating event*, **B** the person's *belief system*, **C** the emotional and behavioral *consequences*, and **D** the act of *disputing* erroneous beliefs. During therapy, Ellis helped his clients identify the A, B, C's underlying their irrational beliefs by actively arguing with, cajoling, and teasing them—sometimes in very blunt, confrontational language. Once clients recognized their self-defeating thoughts, he worked with them on how to *dispute* those beliefs and create and test out new, rational ones. These new beliefs then changed the maladaptive emotions—thus breaking the vicious cycle.

oices from the Classroom

REBT and Your Grades Students put lots of pressure on themselves by thinking "I *must* do well on this test" or "I *have to* get a good test grade." We discuss this in terms of Ellis's REBT. First, this kind of pressure may hinder their performance. Second, I ask students, "Do you really *have to* get a good grade? What is the worst thing that would happen if you didn't?" They might fail the class, which might lower their GPA and/or cause them to retake the class, but plenty of people retake classes. Plus, a low grade probably won't cause them to fail the class. They are more likely to just get a lower class grade than desired. I encourage students to think more positively ("I hope to do well") or to come up with a success plan ("I will study nightly for at least one hour to get a good test score").

Professor David Baskind
Delta College
University Center, Michigan

Beck's Cognitive-Behavior Therapy (CBT)

Another well-known cognitive therapist, Aaron Beck, also believes psychological problems result from illogical thinking and destructive self-talk (Beck, 1976, 2000; Beck & Grant, 2008). But Beck seeks to directly confront and change the behaviors associated with destructive cognitions. Beck's **cognitive-behavior therapy (CBT)** is designed to reduce *both* self-destructive thoughts *and* self-destructive behaviors.

Using cognitive-behavior therapy, clients are first taught to recognize and keep track of their thoughts. Next, the therapist trains the client to develop ways to test these automatic thoughts against reality. This approach helps depressed people discover that negative attitudes are largely a product of faulty thought processes.

At this point, Beck introduces the second phase of therapy—persuading the client to actively pursue pleasurable activities. Depressed individuals often lose motivation, even for experiences they used to find enjoyable. Simultaneously taking an active rather than a passive role and reconnecting with enjoyable experiences can help in recovering from depression (see *A Cognitive Approach to Lifting Depression*).

Cognitive-behavior therapy (CBT) A type of therapy that combines cognitive therapy (changing faulty thinking) with behavior therapy (changing maladaptive behaviors).

A COGNITIVE APPROACH TO LIFTING DEPRESSION
realworldpsychology

As we've just seen, one of the most successful applications of Beck's CBT is in the treatment of depression (Beck, 1976, 2000; Beck et al., 2012; Hollon, 2011; Roelofs et al., 2013). Beck identified several thinking patterns believed to be common among depression-prone people. Recognizing these patterns in our own thought processes may help prevent or improve the occasional bad moods we all experience. To fully benefit from this approach, use what therapists call the "three C's"—*c*atch the faulty thought, *c*hallenge it, and then *c*hange it. Here we provide an example of the three C's for the first thought pattern, and then you should try to do the same for the other three:

- **Selective perception** Focusing selectively on negative events while ignoring positive events. (*Catch the thought* ="Why am I the only person alone at this party?"; *Challenge it* = "I notice four other single people at this party"; *Change it* = "Being single has several advantages. I'll bet some of the couples are actually envying my freedom.")
- **Overgeneralization** Overgeneralizing and drawing negative conclusions about our own self-worth. ("I'm worthless because I failed that exam.")
- **Magnification** Exaggerating the importance of undesirable events or personal shortcomings and seeing them as catastrophic and unchangeable. ("She left me, and I'll never find anyone like her again!")
- **All-or-nothing thinking** Seeing things as black-or-white categories—where everything is either totally good or bad, right or wrong, a success or a failure. ("If I don't get straight A's, I'll never get a good job.")

Aaron Beck

Clem Murray/MCT/NewsCom

Evaluating Cognitive Therapies

Cognitive therapies are highly effective treatments for depression, as well as anxiety disorders, bulimia nervosa, anger management, addiction, and even some symptoms of schizophrenia and insomnia (Craighead et al., 2013; Grave, 2013; Thomas et al., 2011; Turner & Barker, 2013; Young et al., 2011). However, both Beck and Ellis have been criticized for ignoring or denying the client's unconscious dynamics, overemphasizing rationality, and minimizing the importance of the client's past (Granillo et al., 2013; Hammack, 2003).

Other critics suggest that cognitive therapies are successful because they employ behavior techniques, not because they change the underlying cognitive structure (Bandura, 1969, 1997, 2006, 2008; Corey, 2013; Frew & Spiegler, 2013; Pomerantz, 2013). Imagine that you sought treatment for depression and learned to construe events more positively and to curb your all-or-nothing thinking. Further imagine that your therapist also helped you identify activities and behaviors that lessened your depression. Obviously, it's difficult to identify whether changing your cognitions or changing your behavior was the most significant therapeutic factor. But for our everyday use, it doesn't matter. CBT combines both, and it has a proven track record for lifting depression!

RETRIEVAL PRACTICE: TALK THERAPIES

Self-Test

Completing this self-test and comparing your answers with those in Appendix B provides immediate feedback and helpful practice for exams. Additional interactive, self-tests are available at www.wiley.com/college/huffman.

1. Psychoanalysis/psychodynamic, humanistic, and cognitive therapies are often grouped together as _____.

   a. talk therapies   b. behavior therapies
   c. analytic therapies   d. cognitive restructuring

2. The system of psychotherapy developed by Freud that seeks to bring unconscious conflicts into conscious awareness is known as _____.

   a. transference   b. cognitive restructuring
   c. psychoanalysis   d. the "hot seat" technique

3. _____ therapy emphasizes conscious processes and current problems.

   a. Self-talk   b. Belief-behavior
   c. Psychodynamic   d. Thought analysis

4. Aaron Beck practices _____ therapy, which attempts to change not only destructive thoughts and beliefs but the associated behaviors as well.

   a. psycho-behavior   b. cognitive-behavior
   c. thinking-acting   d. belief-behavior

Think Critically

1 Would you rather go to a therapist who uses modern psychodynamic therapy or one who practices traditional psychoanalysis? Why?

2 What is the significance of the term *client-centered therapy*?

realworldpsychology

Can changing your irrational thoughts and self-talk make you feel better about your body?

HINT: LOOK IN THE MARGIN FOR (Q1)

BEHAVIOR THERAPIES

RETRIEVAL PRACTICE While reading the upcoming sections, respond to each Learning Objective in your own words. Then compare your responses with those found at www.wiley.com/college/huffman.

LEARNING OBJECTIVES

1 **DESCRIBE** how classical conditioning is used in therapy.
2 **EXPLORE** how operant conditioning can be used in therapy.
3 **SUMMARIZE** how observational learning is used in therapy.
4 **DESCRIBE** two major criticisms of behavior therapies.

Sometimes having insight into a problem does not automatically solve it. In **behavior therapy**, the focus is on the problem behavior itself rather than on any underlying causes. Although the person's feelings and interpretations are not disregarded, they are also not emphasized. The therapist diagnoses the problem by listing maladaptive behaviors that occur and adaptive behaviors that are absent. The therapist then attempts to shift the balance of the two, drawing on the learning principles of classical conditioning, operant conditioning, and observational learning (Chapter 6).

Classical Conditioning

Behavior therapists use the principles of classical conditioning to decrease maladaptive behaviors by creating new associations to replace the faulty ones. We will explore two techniques based on these principles: *systematic desensitization* and *aversion therapy*.

Recall from Chapter 6 that classical conditioning occurs when a neutral stimulus (NS) becomes associated with an unconditioned stimulus (US) to elicit a conditioned response (CR). Sometimes a classically conditioned fear response becomes so extreme that we call it a "phobia." To treat phobias, behavior therapists often use **systematic desensitization**, which begins with relaxation training, followed by imagining or directly experiencing various versions of a feared object or situation while remaining deeply relaxed (Wolpe & Plaud, 1997). See **Figure 13.7** for a description of systematic desensitization useful for overcoming a driving phobia.

SidneyHarris/Science CartoonsPlus.com

Behavior therapy A group of techniques based on learning principles to change maladaptive behaviors.

Systematic desensitization A behavioral therapy technique in which a client learns to prevent the arousal of anxiety by gradually confronting the feared stimulus while relaxed.

FIGURE 13.7 SYSTEMATIC DESENSITIZATION

In systematic desensitization, the therapist and client together construct a *fear hierarchy*, a ranked listing of 10 or so related anxiety-arousing images. While in a state of relaxation, the client mentally visualizes or physically experiences mildly anxiety-producing items at the lowest level of the hierarchy and then works his or her way up to the most anxiety-producing items at the top. Each progressive step on the fear hierarchy is repeatedly paired with relaxation, until the fear response or phobia is extinguished.

Sitting behind the wheel of a nonmoving car in the driveway.

Driving along an empty, quiet street on a sunny day.

Driving along a busy street on a sunny day.

Driving on a busy expressway on a rainy night.

Least — 1 — Amount of anxiety — 2 — 3 — 4 — Most

©Syracuse Newspapers/D. Lassman/The Image Works

FIGURE 13.8 **VIRTUAL REALITY THERAPY**

Rather than use mental imaging or actual physical experiences of a fearful situation, virtual-reality headsets and data gloves allow a client with a fear of heights, for example, to have experiences ranging from climbing a stepladder all the way to standing on the edge of a tall building.

Aversion therapy A type of behavioral therapy characterized by the pairing of an aversive (unpleasant) stimulus with a maladaptive behavior in order to elicit a negative reaction to the target stimulus.

Similarly, if you or a friend suffers from a spider phobia, you may be amazed to know that after just two or three hours of therapy, starting with simply looking at photos of spiders and then moving next to a tarantula in a glass aquarium, patients are able to eventually pet and hold the spider with their bare hands (Hauner et al., 2012)!

How does relaxation training desensitize someone? Recall from Chapter 2 that the parasympathetic nerves control autonomic functions when we are relaxed. Because the opposing sympathetic nerves are dominant when we are anxious, it is physiologically impossible to be both relaxed and anxious at the same time. The key to success is teaching the client how to replace his or her fear response with relaxation when *exposed* to the fearful stimulus, which explains why these and related approaches are often referred to as *exposure therapies*. Modern virtual reality technology also uses systematic desensitization to expose clients to feared situations right in a therapist's office **(Figure 13.8)**.

In contrast to systematic desensitization, **aversion therapy** uses classical conditioning techniques to create anxiety rather than extinguish it. People who engage in excessive drinking, for example, build up a number of pleasurable associations with alcohol. These pleasurable associations cannot always be prevented. However, aversion therapy provides *negative associations* to compete with the pleasurable ones **(Figure 13.9)**.

FIGURE 13.9 **AVERSION THERAPY**

The goal of aversion therapy is to create an undesirable, or *aversive*, response to a stimulus a person would like to avoid, such as alcohol.

❶ During conditioning
Someone who wants to stop drinking, for example, could take a drug called Antabuse that causes vomiting whenever alcohol enters the system.

❷ After conditioning
When the new connection between alcohol and nausea has been classically conditioned, engaging in the once desirable habit will cause an immediate aversive response.

US (drug)
+
Neutral stimulus
(alcoholic drink) → UR (nausea)

CS
(alcoholic drink without drug) → CR (nausea)

Operant Conditioning

Shaping is a common operant conditioning technique used for bringing about a desired or target behavior. Recall from Chapter 6 that shaping provides immediate rewards for successive approximations of the target behavior. Therapists have found this technique particularly successful in developing language skills in children with autism. First, the child is rewarded for connecting pictures or other devices with words; later, rewards are given only for using the pictures to communicate with others.

© DRB Images, LLC/iStockphoto

psychology and you **Overcoming Shyness** Shaping can help people acquire social skills and greater assertiveness. If you are painfully shy, for example, a clinician might first ask you to role-play simply saying hello to someone you find attractive. Then you might practice behaviors that gradually lead you to suggest a get-together or date. During such role-playing, or behavior rehearsal, the clinician gives you feedback and reinforcement for each successive step you take toward the end goal.

FIGURE 13.10 OBSERVATIONAL LEARNING

During modeling therapy, a client might learn how to interview for a job by first watching the therapist role-play the part of the interviewee. The client then imitates the therapist's behavior and plays the same role. Over the course of several sessions, the client becomes gradually desensitized to the anxiety of interviews.

Adaptive behaviors can also be taught or increased with techniques that provide immediate reinforcement in the form of tokens (Craighead et al., 2013; Reed & Martens, 2011; Spiegler, 2013). For example, patients in an inpatient treatment facility might at first be given tokens (to be exchanged for primary rewards, such as food, treats, TV time, a private room, or outings) for merely attending group therapy sessions. Later they will be rewarded only for actually participating in the sessions. Eventually, the tokens can be discontinued when the patient receives the reinforcement of being helped by participation in the therapy sessions.

Observational Learning

We all learn many things by observing others. Therapists use this principle in **modeling therapy**, in which clients are asked to observe and imitate appropriate models as they perform desired behaviors. For example, researchers successfully treated 4- and 5-year-old children with severe dog phobias by asking them first to watch other children play with dogs and then to gradually approach and get physically closer to the dogs themselves (May et al., 2012). When this type of therapy combines live modeling with direct and gradual practice, it is called *participant modeling*. This type of modeling is also effective in social skills training and assertiveness training **(Figure 13.10)**.

Modeling therapy A type of therapy characterized by watching and imitating models that demonstrate desirable behaviors.

Evaluating Behavior Therapies

Criticisms of behavior therapy fall into two major categories:

- **Generalizability** Critics argue that in the real world, patients are not consistently reinforced, and their newly acquired behaviors may disappear. To deal with this possibility, behavior therapists work to encourage clients to better recognize existing external real world rewards and to generate their own internal reinforcements, which they can then apply at their own discretion.

- **Ethics** Critics contend that it is unethical for one person to control another's behavior. Behaviorists, however, argue that rewards and punishments already control our behaviors. Behavior therapy actually increases our freedom by making these controls overt and by teaching people how to change their own behavior.

Despite these criticisms, behavior therapy is generally recognized as one of the most effective treatments for numerous problems, including phobias, obsessive-compulsive disorder, eating disorders, sexual dysfunctions, autism, intellectual disabilities, and delinquency (Ahearn & Tiger, 2013; Bergman, 2013; Haynes et al., 2011; Spiegler, 2013). For an immediate practical application of behavior therapy to your college life, see *Do You Have Test Anxiety?*

TEST YOURSELF: DO YOU HAVE TEST ANXIETY?

psychology and you

Nearly everyone is somewhat anxious before an important exam. If you find this anxiety helpful and invigorating, skip ahead to the next section. However, if the days and evenings before a major exam are ruined by your anxiety and you sometimes "freeze up" while taking a test, try these tips, based on the three major forms of behavior therapy.

Stockbyte/Getty Images

1. Classical Conditioning

This informal type of systematic desensitization will help decrease your feelings of anxiety:

Step 1: Review and practice the relaxation technique taught in Chapter 3 (p. 87).

Step 2: Create a 10-step "test-taking" hierarchy—starting with the least anxiety-arousing image (perhaps the day your instructor first mentions an upcoming exam) and ending with actually taking the exam.

Step 3: Beginning with the least-arousing image—say, hearing about the exam—picture yourself at each stage. While maintaining a calm, relaxed state, mentally work your way through all 10 steps. If you become anxious at any stage, stay there, repeating your relaxation technique until the anxiety diminishes.

Step 4: If you start to feel anxious the night before the exam, or even during the exam itself, remind yourself to relax. Take a few moments to shut your eyes and review how you worked through your hierarchy.

2. Operant Conditioning

One of the best ways to avoid "freezing up" or "blanking out" on a test is to be fully prepared. To maximize your preparation, "shape" your behavior! Start small by answering the multiple-choice questions at the end of each major section of each chapter and comparing your answers with those in Appendix B. Then move on to the longer self-grading quizzes that are available on our website, www.wiley.com/college/huffman. Following each of these "successive approximations," be sure to reward yourself in some way—call a friend, play with your children or pets, watch a video, or maybe check your Facebook page.

3. Observational Learning

Talk with your classmates who are getting good grades. Ask them for tips on how they prepare for exams and how they handle their own test anxieties. This type of modeling and observational learning can be very helpful—and it's a nice way to make friends.

RETRIEVAL PRACTICE: BEHAVIOR THERAPIES

Self-Test

Completing this self-test and comparing your answers with those in Appendix B provides immediate feedback and helpful practice for exams. Additional interactive, self-tests are available at www.wiley.com/college/huffman.

1. The main focus in behavior therapy is to increase _____ and decrease _____.

a. positive thoughts and feelings; negative thoughts and feelings

b. adaptive behaviors; maladaptive behaviors

c. coping resources; coping deficits

d. all these options

2. The three steps in systematic desensitization include all *except* _____.

a. learning to become deeply relaxed

b. arranging anxiety-arousing stimuli into a hierarchy from least to most arousing

c. practicing relaxation in response to anxiety-arousing stimuli, starting with the most arousing

d. all these options

3. In behavior therapy, _____ techniques use shaping and reinforcement to increase adaptive behaviors.

a. classical conditioning

b. modeling

c. operant conditioning

d. social learning

4. In contrast to systematic desensitization, _____ uses classical conditioning techniques to create anxiety rather than prevent its arousal.

a. anxiety-modeling therapy

b. aversion therapy

c. anxiety therapy

d. subversion therapy

HINT: LOOK IN THE MARGIN FOR (Q2) AND (Q3)

Think Critically

1 Imagine that you were going to use the principles of cognitive-behavioral therapy to change some aspect of your own thinking and behavior. If you'd like to quit smoking, or be more organized, how would you identify the faulty thinking perpetuating these behaviors and fears?

2 Once you've identified your faulty thinking patterns, what could you do to change your behavior?

3 Under what circumstances might behavior therapy be unethical?

realworldpsychology

How might therapy help you hold a tarantula?

Does simply watching other children play with dogs reduce dog phobias in young children?

BIOMEDICAL THERAPIES

RETRIEVAL PRACTICE While reading the upcoming sections, respond to each Learning Objective in your own words. Then compare your responses with those found at www.wiley.com/college/huffman.

1 **DESCRIBE** biomedical therapies.
2 **IDENTIFY** the major types of drugs used to treat psychological disorders.
3 **EXPLAIN** what happens in electroconvulsive therapy and psychosurgery.
4 **DESCRIBE** the risks and benefits associated with biomedical therapies.

LEARNING OBJECTIVES

Some problem behaviors seem to be caused, at least in part, by chemical imbalances or disturbed nervous system functioning, and, as such, they can treated with **biomedical therapies**. Psychiatrists or other medical personnel are generally the only ones who use biomedical therapies. However, in some states, licensed psychologists can prescribe certain medications, and they often work with patients receiving biomedical therapies. In this section, we will discuss three aspects of biomedical therapies: *psychopharmacology, electroconvulsive therapy (ECT)*, and *psychosurgery*.

Biomedical therapy A treatment for psychological disorders that alters brain functioning with biological or physical interventions (for example, drugs, electroconvulsive therapy, psychosurgery).

Psychopharmacology

Since the 1950s, drug companies and **psychopharmacology** have helped correct chemical imbalances that underly some abnormal behaviors. In these instances, using a psychotherapeutic drug is similar to administering insulin to people with diabetes, whose own bodies fail to manufacture enough. In other cases, drugs have been used to relieve or suppress the symptoms of psychological disturbances even when the underlying cause was not thought to be biological. As shown in **Table 13.2**, psychotherapeutic drugs are classified into four major categories: *anti-anxiety, antipsychotic, mood stabilizer*, and *antidepressant*.

How do drug treatments such as antidepressants actually work? Although we don't fully understand all the mechanisms at play, some studies suggest that antidepressants increase *neurogenesis*, the production of new neurons, or *synaptogenesis*, the production of new synapses, and/or stimulate activity in various areas of the brain (Anacker et al., 2011; Castrén & Hen, 2013; Ferreira et al., 2012; Li et al., 2012; Surget et al., 2011). The best-understood action of the drugs is to correct an imbalance in the levels of neurotransmitters in the brain

Psychopharmacology The study of the effect of drugs on behavior and mental processes.

TABLE 13.2	PSYCHOTHERAPEUTIC DRUG TREATMENTS FOR PSYCHOLOGICAL DISORDERS	
	Description	**Examples (trade names)**
Antianxiety drugs Medications used to reduce anxiety and decrease overarousal in the brain.	**Antianxiety drugs**, also known as *anxiolytics* and "minor tranquilizers," lower the sympathetic activity of the brain—the crisis mode of operation—so that anxiety is diminished and the person is calmer and less tense. However, they are potentially dangerous because they can reduce alertness, coordination, and reaction time. They also can have a synergistic (intensifying) effect with other drugs, which may lead to severe drug reactions and even death.	Ativan Halcion Librium Restoril Valium Xanax
Antipsychotic drugs Medications used to diminish or eliminate hallucinations, delusions, withdrawal, and other symptoms of psychosis; also known as neuroleptics or major tranquilizers.	**Antipsychotic drugs**, or *neuroleptics*, reduce the agitated behaviors, hallucinations, delusions, and other symptoms associated with psychotic disorders, such as schizophrenia. Traditional antipsychotics work by decreasing activity at the dopamine receptors in the brain. A large majority of patients markedly improve when treated with antipsychotic drugs.	Clozaril Haldol Mellaril Navane Prolixin Risperdal Seroquel Thorazine
Mood-stabilizer drugs Medications used to treat the combination of manic episodes and depression characteristic of bipolar disorders.	**Mood-stabilizer drugs** help steady mood swings, particularly for those suffering from bipolar disorder, a condition marked by extremes of both mania and depression. Because lithium acts relatively slowly—requiring up to three or four weeks to take effect—its primary use is in preventing future episodes and helping to break the manic-depressive cycle.	Eskalith CR Lithium Tegretol
Antidepressant drugs Medications used to treat depression, some anxiety disorders, and certain eating disorders (such as bulimia).	**Antidepressant drugs** are used primarily to treat people with depression, but they are also effective for some anxiety disorders and eating disorders. There are five types of antidepressant drugs: *tricyclics, monoamine oxidase inhibitors (MAOIs), selective serotonin reuptake inhibitors (SSRIs), serotonin and norepinephrine reuptake inhibitors (SNRIs)*, and *atypical antidepressants*. Each class of drugs affects neurochemical pathways in the brain in a slightly different way, increasing or decreasing the availability of certain chemicals. SSRIs (such as *Paxil* and *Prozac*) are by far the most commonly prescribed antidepressants. The atypical antidepressants are prescribed for patients who fail to respond to or experience undesirable side effects from other antidepressants.	Anafranil Celexa Cymbalta Effexor Elavil Nardil Norpramin Parnate Paxil Prozac Tofranil Wellbutrin Zoloft

"Before Prozac, she loathed company."

(Figure 13.11). For example, researchers know that the drug ketamine works for bipolar disorders because it changes the levels of brain neurotransmitters, but another study found that 79% of those who received even a single dose of ketamine also showed lower rates of depression, including thoughts of suicide (Zarate et al., 2012). The next time you hear someone say that mental illness isn't real or that "it's all in your head," you can describe to them how changing the levels of brain chemicals has been successful for both bipolar disorder and major depression.

FIGURE 13.11 HOW ANTIDEPRESSANTS AFFECT THE BRAIN

Antidepressants work at the neural transmission level by increasing the availability of serotonin or norepinephrine, neurotransmitters that normally elevate mood and arousal. Shown here is the action of some of the most popular antidepressants—Prozac, Paxil, and other selective serotonin reuptake inhibitors (SSRIs).

Ⓐ Serotonin's effect on the brain

People with depression are known to have lower levels of serotonin. Serotonin works in the prefrontal cortex, the hippocampus, and other parts of the brain to regulate mood, sleep, and appetite, among other things.

MedioImages/Photodisc/Getty Images, Inc.

Ⓑ Normal neural transmission

The sending neuron releases an excess of neurotransmitters, including serotonin. Some of the serotonin locks into receptors on the receiving neuron, but excess serotonin is pumped back into the sending neuron (called *reuptake*) for storage and reuse. If serotonin is reabsorbed too quickly, there is less available to the brain, which may result in depression.

Ⓒ Partial blockage of reuptake by SSRIs

SSRIs, like Prozac, partially block the normal reuptake of excess serotonin, which leaves more serotonin molecules free to stimulate receptors on the receiving neuron. This increased neural transmission restores the normal balance of serotonin in the brain.

Electroconvulsive Therapy and Psychosurgery

There is a long history of using electrical stimulation to treat psychological disorders. In **electroconvulsive therapy (ECT)**, also known as electroshock therapy (EST), a moderate electrical current is passed through the brain between two electrodes placed on the outside of the head. The current triggers a widespread firing of neurons, or brief seizures. ECT can quickly reverse symptoms of certain mental illnesses and often works when other treatments have been unsuccessful. The electric current produces many changes in the central and peripheral nervous systems, including activation of the autonomic nervous system, increased secretion of various hormones and neurotransmitters, and changes in the blood–brain barrier **(Figure 13.12)**.

Despite not knowing exactly how ECT works, or that it may cause some short-term memory loss immediately after treatment, and possible long-term memory

Electroconvulsive therapy (ECT) A biomedical therapy based on passing electrical current through the brain; it is used almost exclusively to treat serious depression when drug therapy fails.

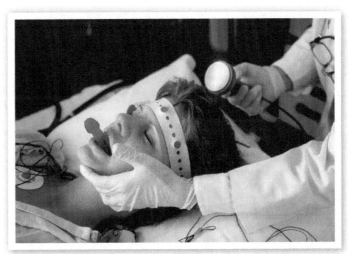

FIGURE 13.12 ELECTROCONVULSIVE THERAPY (ECT)

Modern ECT treatments are conducted with considerable safety precautions, including muscle-relaxant drugs that dramatically reduce muscle contractions and medication to help patients sleep through the procedure. ECT is used less often today and generally only when other treatments have failed, despite a 70% improvement rate for depression (Case et al., 2013; Perugi et al., 2012).

Psychosurgery A neurosurgical alteration of the brain to bring about desirable behavioral, cognitive, or emotional changes, which is generally used when patients have not responded to other forms of treatment; also called neurosurgery for mental disorder (NMD).

Lobotomy An outmoded neurosurgical procedure for mental disorders, which involved cutting nerve pathways between the frontal lobes and the thalamus and hypothalamus.

problems, the risks of untreated, severe depression are generally considered greater than the risks of ECT. It is used primarily on patients who have not responded to drugs and psychotherapy, and on suicidal patients, because it works faster than antidepressant drugs (Kobeissi et al., 2011; Loo et al., 2011; Pfeiffer et al., 2011).

The most extreme, and least used, biomedical therapy is **psychosurgery**—brain surgery performed to reduce serious debilitating psychological problems. Attempts to change disturbed thoughts, feelings, and behavior by altering the brain have a long history. In Roman times, for example, it was believed that a sword wound to the head could relieve insanity. In 1936, Portuguese neurologist Egaz Moniz first treated uncontrollable psychoses with a form of *psychosurgery* called a **lobotomy**, in which he cut the nerve fibers between the frontal lobes (where association areas for monitoring and planning behavior are found) and the thalamus and hypothalamus. Although these surgeries did reduce emotional outbursts and aggressiveness, patients were left with permanent brain damage.

realworldpsychology **A Modern Alternative to Lobotomies** Two of the most notable examples of the damage from early lobotomies are Rosemary Kennedy, the sister of President John F. Kennedy, and Rose Williams, sister of American playwright Tennessee Williams. Both women were permanently incapacitated from lobotomies performed in the early 1940s. Thankfully, in the mid-1950s, when antipsychotic drugs came into use, psychosurgery virtually stopped.

Recently, however, psychiatrists have been experimenting with a much more limited and precise neurosurgical procedure called *deep brain stimulation* (*DBS*). The surgeon drills two tiny holes into the patient's skull and implants electrodes in the area of the brain believed to be associated with a specific disorder. These electrodes are then connected to a "pacemaker" implanted in the chest or stomach that sends low-voltage electricity to the problem areas in the brain.

Over time, this repeated stimulation can bring about significant improvement in Parkinson's disease, epilepsy, major depression and other disorders (Campbell et al., 2012; Chopra et al., 2012; Kennedy et al., 2011; Lageman et al., 2013; Spindler et al., 2013). In addition, research has shown that patients who receive this type of DBS along with antidepressants show lower rates of depression than those who receive either treatment alone (Brunoni et al., 2013).

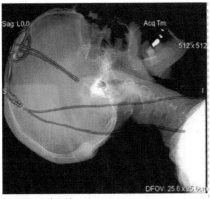

Photo Researchers/Getty Images

Evaluating Biomedical Therapies

Like all other forms of therapy, biomedical therapies have both proponents and critics.

Pitfalls of Psychopharmacology

Drug therapy poses several potential problems. First, although drugs may relieve symptoms for some people, they seldom provide cures. In addition, some patients become physically dependent on the drugs. Also, researchers are still learning about the drugs' long-term effects and potential interactions. Furthermore, psychiatric medications can cause a variety of side effects, ranging from mild fatigue to severe impairments in memory and movement. A final potential problem with drug treatment is that its relatively low cost and generally fast results have led to its overuse in some cases. Despite the problems associated with them, psychotherapeutic drugs have led to revolutionary changes in mental health. Before the use of drugs, some patients were destined to spend a lifetime in psychiatric institutions. Today, most improve enough to return to their homes and live successful lives if they continue to take their medications to prevent relapse.

Challenges to ECT and Psychosurgery

ECT currently serves as a valuable last-resort treatment for severe depression. However, similar benefits may be available through the latest advances in **repetitive transcranial magnetic stimulation (rTMS)**, which uses an electromagnet placed on the scalp that generates magnetic field pulses roughly the strength of an MRI scan **(Figure 13.13)**. To treat depression, the coil is usually placed over the prefrontal cortex, a region linked to deeper parts of the brain that regulate mood. Currently, rTMS's advantages over ECT are still unclear, but studies have shown marked improvement in depression, and patients experience fewer side effects (Berlim et al., 2013; Guse et al., 2013; Husain & Lisanby, 2011; Polley et al., 2011).

Because all forms of psychosurgery are potentially dangerous and have serious or even fatal side effects, some critics say that it should be banned altogether. Furthermore, the consequences are generally irreversible. For these reasons, psychosurgery is considered experimental and remains a highly controversial treatment.

Repetitive transcranial magnetic stimulation (rTMS) A biomedical treatment that uses repeated magnetic field pulses targeted at specific areas of the brain.

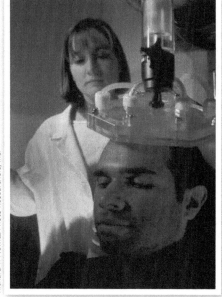

Richard T. Nowitz/Photo Researchers, Inc.

FIGURE 13.13 REPETITIVE TRANSCRANIAL MAGNETIC STIMULATION (rTMS)

Powerful electromagnets generate pulsed magnetic fields that are targeted at specific areas of the brain to treat depression.

RETRIEVAL PRACTICE: BIOMEDICAL THERAPIES

Self-Test

Completing this self-test and comparing your answers with those in Appendix B provides immediate feedback and helpful practice for exams. Additional interactive, self-tests are available at www.wiley.com/college/huffman.

1. The study of the effects of drugs on behavior and mental processes is known as _____.

   a. psychiatry
   b. psychoanalysis
   c. psychosurgery
   d. psychopharmacology

2. The effectiveness of antipsychotic drugs is thought to result primarily from decreasing activity at the _____ receptors.

   a. serotonin
   b. dopamine
   c. epinephrine
   d. all these options

3. In electroconvulsive therapy (ECT), _____.

   a. current is never applied to the left hemisphere
   b. seizures activate the central and peripheral nervous systems, stimulate hormone and neurotransmitter release, and change the blood–brain barrier
   c. convulsions are extremely painful and long lasting
   d. most patients receive hundreds of treatments because it is safer than in the past

4. ECT is used primarily to treat _____.

   a. phobias
   b. conduct disorders
   c. severe depression
   d. schizophrenia

Think Critically

1 Are the potential benefits of psychopharmacology worth the risks? Is it ever ethical to force someone to take drugs to treat his or her mental illness?

2 If you, or someone you loved, were seriously depressed would you be in favor of ECT? Why or why not?

realworldpsychology

How do psychotherapeutic drugs help decrease thoughts of suicide?

HINT: LOOK IN THE MARGIN FOR Q4

PSYCHOTHERAPY IN PERSPECTIVE

LEARNING OBJECTIVES

RETRIEVAL PRACTICE While reading the upcoming sections, respond to each Learning Objective in your own words. Then compare your responses with those found at www.wiley.com/college/huffman.

1 **SUMMARIZE** the goals and overall effectiveness of psychotherapy.
2 **DESCRIBE** group, marital, family, and telehealth/electronic therapies.
3 **IDENTIFY** the key cultural and gender issues important in therapy.
4 **SUMMARIZE** the major career options for someone interested in being a therapist.

Given that it's currently estimated that there are more than 400 forms of therapy, how would you choose one for yourself or someone you know? In the first part of this section, we discuss five goals common to all psychotherapies. Then we explore specific formats for therapy as well as considerations about culture and gender. Our aim is to help you synthesize the material in this chapter and put what you have learned about each of the major forms of therapy into a broader context.

Therapy Goals and Effectiveness

All major forms of therapy are designed to help the client in five specific areas **(Figure 13.14)**.

FIGURE 13.14 THE FIVE MOST COMMON GOALS OF THERAPY

Most therapies focus on one or more of these five goals. Can you identify which would be of most interest to psychodynamic, humanistic, cognitive, and behavioristic therapists?

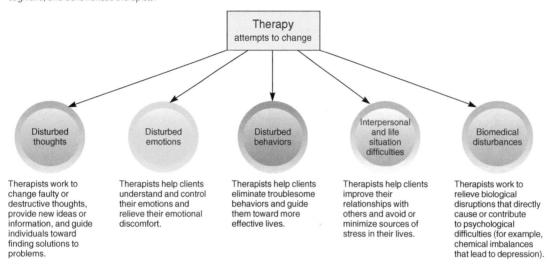

Therapists work to change faulty or destructive thoughts, provide new ideas or information, and guide individuals toward finding solutions to problems.

Therapists help clients understand and control their emotions and relieve their emotional discomfort.

Therapists help clients eliminate troublesome behaviors and guide them toward more effective lives.

Therapists help clients improve their relationships with others and avoid or minimize sources of stress in their lives.

Therapists work to relieve biological disruptions that directly cause or contribute to psychological difficulties (for example, chemical imbalances that lead to depression).

Although most therapists work with clients in several of these areas, the emphasis varies according to the therapist's training and whether it is psychodynamic, cognitive, humanistic, behaviorist, or biomedical. Clinicians who regularly borrow freely from various theories are said to take an **eclectic approach**.

Does therapy work? After years of controlled studies and *meta-analysis*—a method of statistically combining and analyzing data from many studies—researchers have fairly clear evidence that it does. For example, one early meta-analytic review combined studies of almost 25,000 people and found that the average person who received treatment was better off than 75% of the untreated control clients **(Figure 13.15)**.

Studies also show that short-term treatments can be as effective as long-term treatments and that most therapies are equally effective for various disorders (Dewan et al., 2011; Gillies et al., 2012; Messer et al., 2013; Wachtel, 2011). Even informal therapy techniques, like simple writing exercises, have led to increased marital satisfaction (see *Psych Science*).

Eclectic approach A perspective on therapy that combines techniques from various theories to find the most appropriate treatment.

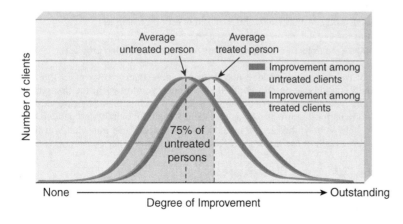

FIGURE 13.15 IS THERAPY GENERALLY EFFECTIVE?

The average person who receives therapy is better off after it than a similar person who does not get treatment (Campbell et al., 2013; Corey, 2013; Miller et al., 2013; Shedler, 2010; Smith et al., 1980). An analysis of more than 435 studies on the effectiveness of therapy for treating psychological disorders in children and adolescents revealed that therapy can lead to improvements in many different types of psychological disorders, including anxiety, autism, depression, disruptive behavior, eating problems, substance use, and traumatic stress (Chorpita et al., 2011).

PSYCHSCIENCE

CAN WRITING SAVE YOUR MARRIAGE?

© asiseeit/iStockphoto

Self-reflection and journaling are proven successful therapy techniques, so researchers in one study asked 120 volunteer married couples to describe the most significant disagreement they had experienced with their spouse during the past four months (Finkel et al., 2013). Half of the couples were then asked to complete a series of three seven-minute writing exercises. These writing exercises asked both spouses to reflect on the disagreement while taking the perspective of a neutral third party who wants the best for all involved. The researchers then contacted the couples every four months for the next two years. During these follow-up contacts, couples also were asked to provide a similar neutral summary of their most significant marital disagreement in the past four months and to report their level of relationship satisfaction, love, intimacy, trust, passion, and commitment.

Couples in both groups showed decreased marital satisfaction over the first year (a typical finding in married couples), but those that completed the writing exercises by taking the perspective of a neutral third party showed no additional decline in marital satisfaction in the second year. In contrast, couples that did not take this neutral perspective continued to show even greater declines in satisfaction.

Can you see how taking the perspective of a neutral third party might have indirectly trained the couples to use more *empathy* and *unconditional positive regard with one another*—two terms we discussed earlier in this chapter? Similarly, can you understand how this writing exercise might have helped these couples avoid Beck's negative thinking patterns of *selective perception, overgeneralization, magnification*, and *all-or-nothing thinking*? Most importantly, can you apply the results of this research, and the terms we've just identified, to improving your own relationships with love partners, family members, and friends?

RESEARCH CHALLENGE

1 Based on the information provided, did this study (Finkel et al., 2013) use descriptive, correlational, and/or experimental research?

2 If you chose:
- descriptive research, is this a naturalistic observation, survey/interview, case study, or archival research?
- correlational research, is this a positive, negative, or zero correlation?
- experimental research, label the IV, DV, experimental group(s), and control group.

>>CHECK YOUR ANSWERS IN APPENDIX B.
NOTE: The information provided in this study is admittedly limited, but the level of detail is similar to what is presented in most textbooks and public reports of research findings. Answering these questions, and then comparing your answers to those in the Appendix, will help you become a better critical thinker and consumer of scientific research.

As we've just seen, some studies find that most therapies are equally effective for various disorders. However, other studies suggest that specific therapies are more effective for certain problems than others. For example, phobias and marital problems seem to respond best to behavioral therapies, whereas depression and obsessive-compulsive disorders can be significantly relieved with cognitive-behavior therapy (CBT) accompanied by medication (Craighead et al., 2013; Spiegler, 2013; Wilson, 2011).

Finally, in recent years, the *empirically supported*, or *evidence-based practice (EBP), movement* has been gaining momentum because it seeks to identify which therapies have received the clearest research support for particular disorders (Biegel et al., 2013; Duncan & Reese, 2013; Sharf, 2012; Thyer & Myers, 2011).

Like all other movements, it has been criticized, but this type of empirically based research promises to be helpful for therapists and clients alike in their treatment decisions. For specific tips on finding therapy for yourself or a loved one, see *Choosing a Therapist*.

Therapy Formats

The therapies described earlier in this chapter are conducted primarily in a face-to-face, therapist-to-client format. In this section, we focus on several major alternatives: *group*, *family*, and *marital therapies*, which treat multiple individuals simultaneously, and *telehealth/electronic therapy*, which treats individuals via the Internet, e-mail, and/or smart phones.

Group Therapy

In **group therapy**, multiple people meet together to work toward therapeutic goals. Typically, a group of 8 to 10 people meet with a therapist on a regular basis to talk about problems in their lives.

A variation on group therapy is the **self-help group**. Unlike other group approaches, self-help groups are not guided by a professional. They are simply circles of people who share a common problem, such as alcoholism, obesity, or breast cancer, and who meet to give and receive support. Faith-based Twelve-Step programs such as Alcoholics Anonymous, Narcotics Anonymous, and Spenders

Group therapy A form of therapy in which a number of people meet together to work toward therapeutic goals.

Self-help group A leaderless or nonprofessionally guided group in which members assist each other with a specific problem, as in Alcoholics Anonymous.

Anonymous are examples of self-help groups. Although group members don't get the same level of individual attention found in one-on-one therapies, group and self-help therapies provide their own unique advantages (Corey, 2011; Jaffe & Kelly, 2011; Kivlighan et al., 2012; Messer & Gurman, 2011; Piper & Hernandez, 2013). They are far less expensive than one-on-one therapies and provide a broader base of social support. Group members also can learn from each other's experiences, share insights and coping strategies, and role-play social interactions together.

Therapists often refer their patients to group therapy and to self-help groups in order to supplement individual therapy. For example, recovering alcoholics who choose to help others in Alcoholics Anonymous group sessions actually show lower levels of alcohol use themselves as long as 10 years later (Pagano et al., 2013). In sum, research on self-help groups for alcoholism, obesity, and other disorders suggests that they can be very effective, either alone or in addition to individual psychotherapy (Donovan et al., 2013; Jaffe & Kelly, 2011; Majer et al., 2013; Pomerantz, 2013).

Marital and Family Therapies

Given that a family or marriage is a system of interdependent parts, the problem of any one individual inevitably affects everyone, and therefore all members are potential beneficiaries of therapy (Dattilio & Nichols, 2011; Friedlander et al., 2011; Hills, 2013; Lebow & Stroud, 2013). The line between family and marital or couples therapy is often blurred. Here, our discussion will focus on *family therapy*, in which the primary aim is to change maladaptive family interaction patterns **(Figure 13.16)**. All members of the family attend therapy sessions, though at times the therapist may see family members individually or in twos or threes.

Family therapy is also useful in treating a number of disorders and clinical problems. As we discussed in Chapter 12, schizophrenic patients are at increased risk of relapsing if their family members express emotions, attitudes, and behaviors that suggest criticism, hostility, or emotional overinvolvement (Lobban et al., 2013; Pharoah et al., 2010; Quinn et al., 2003). Family therapy can help family members modify their behavior toward the patient. It can also be the most favorable setting for the treatment of adolescent drug abuse (Alexander et al., 2013; Mead, 2012; Morgan et al., 2013; O'Farrell, 2011).

Telehealth/Electronic Therapy

Today millions of people are receiving advice and professional therapy in newer, electronic formats, such as the Internet, e-mail, virtual reality (VR), and interactive web-based conference systems such as Skype. This latest form of electronic therapy,

FIGURE 13.16 **FAMILY THERAPY**

Many families initially come into therapy believing that one member is the cause of all their problems. However, family therapists generally find that this "identified patient" is a scapegoat for deeper disturbances. How could changing ways of interacting within the family system promote the health of individual family members and the family as a whole?

© vgajic/iStockphoto

often referred to as *telehealth*, allows clinicians to reach more clients and provide them with greater access to information regarding their specific problems (see *Real World Psychology* feature).

realworldpsychology

Therapy—Is There an App for That? Studies have long shown that therapy outcomes improve with increased client contact, and the electronic/telehealth format may be the easiest and most cost-effective way to increase this contact (Campbell et al., 2013; DeAngelis, 2012; Myers & Turvey, 2013). For example, a recent study compared the effectiveness of cognitive behavioral therapy delivered over the telephone with the effectiveness of in-person visits for patients with major depressive disorder. The researchers found that those who received phone therapy showed improvement, but not as much as those who received face-to-face therapy. However, the phone therapy patients were more likely to continue with therapy over time (Mohr et al., 2012).

© David Ahn/iStockphoto

Using electronic options such as the Internet and smart phones does provide alternatives to traditional one-on-one therapies, but, as you might expect, these unique approaches also raise concerns (DeAngelis, 2012; Nagy, 2012; Nelson et al., 2013). Professional therapists fear, among other things, that without interstate and international licensing, or a governing body to regulate this type of therapy, there are no means to protect clients from unethical practices or incompetent therapists. What do you think? Would you be more likely to participate in therapy if it were offered via your smart phone, e-mail, or a website? Or is this too impersonal and high tech for you?

Cultural Issues in Therapy

The therapies described in this chapter are based on Western European and North American culture. Does this mean they are unique? Or do these psychotherapists accomplish some of the same things that, say, a native healer or shaman does? Are there similarities in therapies across cultures? Conversely, are there fundamental therapeutic differences among cultures?

When we look at therapies in all cultures, we find that they have certain key features in common (Barnow & Balkir, 2013; Berry et al., 2011; Buss 2011; Markus & Kitayama, 2010; Matsumoto & Juang, 2013):

- **Naming the problem** People often feel better just knowing that others experience the same problem and that the therapist has had experience with it.

- **Demonstrating the right qualities** Clients must feel that the therapist is caring, competent, approachable, and concerned with finding solutions to their problems.

- **Establishing credibility** Word-of-mouth testimonials and status symbols, such as diplomas on the wall, establish a therapist's credibility. A native healer may earn credibility by serving as an apprentice to a revered healer.

- **Placing the problem in a familiar framework** Some cultures believe evil spirits cause psychological disorders, so therapy is directed toward eliminating these spirits. Similarly, in cultures that emphasize the importance of early childhood experiences and the unconscious mind as the cause of mental disorders, therapy will be framed around these familiar issues.

- **Applying techniques to bring relief** In all cultures, therapy includes action. Either the client or the therapist must do something. Moreover, what therapists do must fit the client's expectations—whether it is performing a ceremony to expel demons or talking with the client about his or her thoughts and feelings.

- **Meeting at a special time and place** The fact that therapy occurs outside the client's everyday experiences seems to be an important feature of all therapies.

Although there are basic similarities in therapies across cultures, there are also important differences. In the traditional Western European and North American model, the emphasis is on the patient's self and on his or her having independence and control over his or her life—qualities that are highly valued in individualistic cultures. In collectivist cultures, however, the focus of therapy is on interdependence and the patient's accepting the realities of his or her life (Ross, 2013).

Sky Bonillo/PhotoEdit

realworldpsychology **Emphasizing Interdependence** In Japanese Naikan therapy, patients sit quietly from 5:30 a.m. to 9:00 p.m. for seven days and are visited by an interviewer every 90 minutes. During this time, they reflect on their relationships with others in order to discover personal guilt for having been ungrateful and troublesome and to develop gratitude toward those who have helped them (Moodley & Sutherland, 2010; Nakamura, 2006; Ozawa-de Silva, 2007; Shinfuku & Kitanishi, 2010).

Not only does culture affect the types of therapy that are developed, it also influences the perceptions of the therapist. What one culture considers abnormal behavior may be quite common—and even healthy—in others. For this reason, recognizing cultural differences is very important for building trust between therapists and clients and for effecting behavioral change (Barnow & Balkir, 2013; Frew & Spiegler, 2013; Moodley, 2012).

Gender and Therapy

In our individualistic Western culture, men and women present different needs and problems to therapists. Research has identified five unique concerns related to gender and psychotherapy (Bruns & Kaschak, 2011; Geller et al., 2013; Jordan, 2011; Remer, 2013):

1. **Rates of diagnosis and treatment of mental disorders** Women are diagnosed and treated for mental illness at a much higher rate than men. Are women "sicker" than men as a group, or are they just more willing to admit their problems? Or are the categories of illness biased against women? More research is needed to answer these questions.

2. **Stresses of poverty** Women are disproportionately likely to be poor. Poverty contributes to stress, which is directly related to many psychological disorders.

3. **Violence against women** Rape, incest, and sexual harassment—which are much more likely to happen to women than to men—may lead to depression, insomnia, posttraumatic stress disorders, eating disorders, and other problems.

4. **Stresses of multiple roles** Women today are mothers, wives, homemakers, wage earners, students, and more. The conflicting demands of their multiple roles often create special stresses.

Therapists must be sensitive to possible connections between clients' problems and their gender. Rather than prescribing drugs to relieve depression in women, for example, it may be more appropriate for therapists to explore ways to relieve the stresses of multiple roles or poverty. Can you see how helping a single mother identify parenting resources, such as play groups, parent support groups, and high-quality child care, might be just as effective at relieving depression as prescribing drugs? In the case of men, how might relieving loneliness or depression help decrease their greater problems with substance abuse and aggression?

If you've enjoyed this section on cultural and gender issues in therapy, as well as the earlier description of the various forms and formats of psychotherapy, you may be considering a possible career as a therapist. If so, see *Careers in Mental Health* below.

CAREERS IN MENTAL HEALTH | psychology and you

Most colleges have counseling or career centers with numerous resources and trained staff to help you with your career choices. However, to get you started and give you an overview of the general field of psychotherapy, we've included a brief summary of the major types of mental health professionals, their degrees, years of required education beyond the bachelor's degree, and type of training.

MAJOR TYPES OF MENTAL HEALTH PROFESSIONALS

Occupational Title	Degree	Nature of Training
Clinical psychologists	Ph.D. (doctor of philosophy), Psy.D. (doctor of psychology)	Most clinical psychologists have a doctoral degree with training in research and clinical practice and a supervised one-year internship in a psychiatric hospital or mental health facility. As clinicians, they work with patients suffering from mental disorders, but many also work in colleges and universities as teachers and researchers in addition to having their own private practice.
Counseling psychologists	Ph.D. (doctor of philosophy), Psy.D. (doctor of psychology), Ed.D. (doctor of education	Counseling psychologists have a doctoral degree with training that focuses on less severe mental disorders, such as emotional, social, vocational, educational, and health-related concerns. In addition to providing psychotherapy, other career paths are open, such as teaching, research, and vocational counseling.
Psychiatrists	M.D. (doctor of medicine)	After four years of medical school, an internship and residency in psychiatry are required, which includes supervised practice in psychotherapy techniques and biomedical therapies. In most states in the United States, psychiatrists, because they are M.D.s, are the only mental health specialists who can regularly prescribe drugs.
Psychiatric nurses	R.N. (registered nurse), M.A. (master of arts), Ph.D. (doctor of philosophy)	Psychiatric nurses usually have a bachelor's or master's degree in nursing, followed by advanced training in the care of mental patients in hospital settings and mental health facilities.
Psychiatric social workers	M.S.W. (master's in social work), D.S.W. (doctorate in social work), Ph.D. (doctor of philosophy)	Psychiatric social workers usually have a master's degree in social work, followed by advanced training and experience in hospitals or outpatient settings working with people who have psychological problems.
School psychologists	M.A. (master of arts), Ph.D. (doctor of philosophy), Psy.D. (doctor of psychology), Ed.D. (doctor of education)	School psychologists generally begin with a bachelor's degree in psychology, followed by graduate training in psychological assessment and counseling for school-related issues and problems.

Self-Test

Completing this self-test and comparing your answers with those in Appendix B provides immediate feedback and helpful practice for exams. Additional interactive, self-tests are available at www.wiley.com/college/huffman.

1. Which of the following is *not* a culturally universal feature of therapy?

   a. Naming the problem
   b. Demonstrating the right qualities
   c. Establishing rapport among family members
   d. Placing the problem in a familiar framework

2. A Japanese therapy designed to help clients discover personal guilt for having been ungrateful and troublesome to others and to develop gratitude toward those who have helped them is known as _____.

   a. Kyoto therapy
   b. Okado therapy
   c. Naikan therapy
   d. Nissan therapy

3. A(n) _____ group does not have a professional leader, and members assist each other in coping with a specific problem.

   a. self-help
   b. encounter
   c. peer
   d. behavior

4. _____ treats the family as a unit, and members work together to solve problems.

   a. Aversion therapy
   b. An encounter group
   c. A self-help group
   d. Family therapy

Think Critically

1 Which of the universal characteristics of therapists do you believe is the most important? Why?

2 If a friend were having marital problems, how would you convince him or her to go to a marriage or family therapist, using information you've gained in this chapter?

real**world**psychology

Can therapy that is delivered over the telephone lead to lower levels of depression?

HINT: LOOK IN THE MARGIN FOR (Q5)

Summary

1 TALK THERAPIES 369

- Talk therapies are forms of **psychotherapy** that seek to increase insight into clients' difficulties.
- In **psychoanalysis**, the therapist seeks to identify the patient's unconscious conflicts and to help the patient resolve them. In modern **psychodynamic therapy**, treatment is briefer, and the therapist takes a more directive approach (and puts less emphasis on unconscious childhood memories) than in traditional psychoanalysis.
- **Humanistic therapy**, such as Rogers's **client-centered therapy**, seeks to maximize personal growth, encouraging people to actualize their potential and relate to others in genuine ways.
- **Cognitive therapy** seeks to help clients challenge faulty thought processes and adjust maladaptive behaviors. Ellis's **rational-emotive behavior therapy (REBT)** and Beck's **cognitive-behavior therapy (CBT)** are important examples of cognitive therapy.

2 BEHAVIOR THERAPIES 377

- In **behavior therapy**, the focus is on the problem behavior itself rather than on any underlying causes. The therapist uses learning principles to change behavior.
- Classical conditioning techniques include **systematic desensitization** and **aversion therapy**.
- Operant conditioning techniques used to increase adaptive behaviors include *shaping* and *reinforcement*.
- In **modeling therapy**, clients observe and imitate others who are performing the desired behaviors.

3 BIOMEDICAL THERAPIES 381

- **Biomedical therapies** are based on the premise that chemical imbalances or disturbed nervous system functioning contributes to problem behaviors.
- **Psychopharmacology** is the most common form of biomedical therapy. Major classes of drugs used to treat psychological disorders are **antianxiety drugs, antipsychotic drugs, mood stabilizer drugs**, and **antidepressant drugs**.

- In **electroconvulsive therapy (ECT)**, an electrical current is passed through the brain, stimulating convulsions that produce changes in the central and peripheral nervous systems. ECT is used primarily in cases of severe depression that do not respond to other treatments.
- In **repetitive transcranial magnetic stimulation (rTMS)**, powerful electromagnets generate pulsed magnetic fields that are targeted at specific areas of the brain to treat depression.
- The most extreme biomedical therapy is **psychosurgery**. **Lobotomy**, an older form of psychosurgery, is now outmoded. Recently, psychiatrists have been experimenting with a more limited and precise surgical procedure called *deep brain stimulation* (DBS).

4 PSYCHOTHERAPY IN PERSPECTIVE 386

- All major forms of therapy are designed to address disturbed thoughts, disturbed emotions, disturbed behaviors, interpersonal and life situation difficulties, and biomedical disturbances. Research indicates that, overall, therapy does work.
- In **group therapy**, multiple people meet together to work toward therapeutic goals. A variation is the **self-help group**, which is not guided by a professional. Therapists often refer their patients to group therapy and self-help groups in order to supplement individual therapy.
- In family therapy, the aim is to change maladaptive family interaction patterns. All members of the family attend therapy sessions, though at times the therapist may see family members individually or in twos or threes.
- Therapies in all cultures have certain key features in common; however, there are also important differences among cultures. Therapists must recognize cultural differences in order to build trust with clients and effect behavioral change. Therapists must also be sensitive to possible gender issues in therapy.

◉ applyingrealworldpsychology

We began this chapter with five intriguing Real World Psychology questions, and you were asked to revisit these questions at the end of each section. Questions like these have an important and lasting impact on all of our lives. See if you can answer these additional critical thinking questions related to real world examples.

1 In the 2013 movie *Side Effects*, Rooney Mara and Channing Tatum portray a successful young couple, Emily and Martin, whose entire world falls apart when Emily's psychiatrist prescribes a new (fictional) psychoactive drug called Ablixa to treat her anxiety. The true *side effects* of the drug, as well as the underlying motivations and mental health of the main characters, are revealed only during the film's final scenes. How might this film contribute to negative stereotypes of psychotherapy and psychopharmacology?

2 Given that advertising for the fictional drug in this *Side Effects* movie closely matches the ads for actual psychoactive drugs, what special dangers and applications does widespread advertising for psychotherapeutic drugs pose for the real world?

3 Can you think of a Hollywood film that offers a positive portrayal of psychotherapy and/or psychopharmacology?

4 You undoubtedly had certain beliefs and ideas about therapy before reading this chapter. Has studying this chapter changed any of those beliefs and ideas?

5 Which form of therapy described in this chapter do you personally find most appealing? Why?

Snap Stills/Rex Features/AP Photos

Key Terms

RETRIEVAL PRACTICE   Write a definition for each term before turning back to the referenced page to check your answer.

chapterfourteen

Social Psychology

CHAPTER OUTLINE

realworldpsychology

Q1 Why do athletes often blame their losses on bad officiating?

Q2 If popular high-school students are anti-drinking, does that reduce underage drinking among their peers?

Q3 Are women less likely than men to share their opinions in a group?

Q4 Are men still more likely to get hired than equally qualified women?

Q5 How does simple nearness (proximity) influence attraction?

THROUGHOUT THE CHAPTER, MARGIN ICONS FOR Q1–Q5 INDICATE WHERE THE TEXT ADDRESSES THESE QUESTIONS.

woman peeking through paper hole: © PIKSEL/iStockphoto;
two children studying: © Gelpi JM/Shutterstock; resume: © mstahlphoto/iStockphoto;
beer: © flubydust/iStockphoto; soccer referee: © RTimages/iStockphoto

chapteroverview

For many students and psychologists, your authors included, *social psychology* is the most exciting of all fields because it's about you and me and because almost everything we do is *social*! Unlike earlier chapters that focused on individual processes, like sensation and perception, memory, or personality, this chapter studies how large social forces, such as groups, social roles, and norms, bring out the best and worst in all of us. It is organized around three central themes: *social cognition*, *social influence*, and *social relations*. Before reading on, check the misconceptions you may have about these topics in *How Much Do You Know About the Social World?*

TEST YOURSELF: HOW MUCH DO YOU KNOW ABOUT THE SOCIAL WORLD?

psychology and you

TRUE OR FALSE?

____1. Most people judge others more harshly than they judge themselves.

____2. Persuasion is the most effective way to change attitudes.

____3. Groups generally make riskier or more conservative decisions than a single individual does.

____4. People wearing masks are more likely than unmasked individuals to engage in aggressive acts.

____5. Emphasizing gender differences may create and perpetuate prejudice.

____6. Substance abuse (particularly alcohol abuse) is a major factor in aggression.

____7. When people are alone, they are more likely to help another individual than when they are in a group.

____8. Looks are the primary factor in our initial feelings of attraction, liking, and love.

____9. Opposites attract.

___10. Romantic love generally starts to fade after 6 to 30 months.

Answers: Two of these statements are false. You'll find the answers within this chapter.

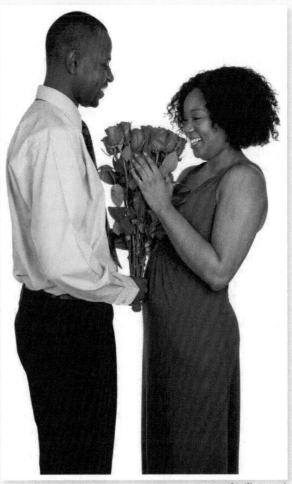

Jason Stitt/Shutterstock

SOCIAL COGNITION

RETRIEVAL PRACTICE While reading the upcoming sections, respond to each Learning Objective in your own words. Then compare your responses with those found at www.wiley.com/college/huffman.

LEARNING OBJECTIVES

1 **DESCRIBE** the field of social psychology.

2 **EXPLAIN** how attributions and their errors affect the way we perceive and judge others.

3 **IDENTIFY** attitudes and their three components.

4 **SUMMARIZE** how attitudes are formed and changed.

5 **DISCUSS** how culture affects cognitive dissonance.

Social psychology, one of the largest branches in the field of psychology, focuses on how others influence our thoughts, feelings, and actions. In turn, one of its largest and most important subfields, **social cognition**, examines the way we think about and interpret ourselves and others. In this section, we will look at two of the most important topics in social cognition—*attributions* and *attitudes*.

Social psychology The branch of psychology that studies how others influence our thoughts, feelings, and actions; it also studies group and intergroup phenomena.

Social cognition How we think about and interpret ourselves and others.

Attributions

Have you ever been in a serious verbal fight with a loved one—perhaps a parent, close friend, or romantic partner? If so, how did you react? Were you overwhelmed with feelings of anger? Did you attribute the fight to the other person's ugly, mean temper and consider ending the relationship? Or did you calm yourself with thoughts of how he or she is normally a rational person and therefore must be unusually upset by something that happened at work or college?

Can you see how these two alternative explanations for the causes of behavior or events (or **attributions**) can either destroy or maintain relationships? The study of attributions is a major topic in *social cognition and social psychology*. Everyone wants to understand and explain why people behave as they do and why events occur as they do. Humans are known to be the only reason-seeking animals! But social psychologists have discovered another explanation: Developing logical attributions for people's behavior makes us feel safer and more in control (Bodenhausen & Morales, 2013; Cushman & Greene, 2012; Ferrucci et al., 2011; Heider, 1958). In addition, they've found that the key to making correct attributions begins with the decision of whether a given action stems mainly from the person's internal disposition or from the external situation. Unfortunately, our attributions are frequently marred by two major errors: the *fundamental attribution error* (*FAE*) and the *self-serving bias*. Let's explore each of these.

Attribution The principles we follow when making judgments about the causes of events, others' behavior, and our own behavior.

Fundamental Attribution Error (FAE)

Think back to the example above. Do you recognize that attributing the fight to the bad character of the other person without considering possible situational factors, like pressures at work, may be the result of your own misguided bias in thinking? Suppose a new student joins your class and seems distant, cold, and uninterested in interaction. It's easy to conclude that she's unfriendly, and maybe even "stuck-up"—a dispositional (personality) attribution. If you later saw her in a one-to-one interaction with close friends, you might be surprised to find that she is very warm and friendly. In other words, her behavior depends on the situation. This bias toward personal, dispositional factors rather than situational factors in our explanations for others' behavior is so common that it is called the **fundamental attribution error (FAE)** (Arkes & Kajdasz, 2011; Coleman, 2013; Ross, 1977).

One reason for the FAE is that human personalities and behaviors are more salient or noticeable than situational factors. The **saliency bias** helps explain why people sometimes suggest that homeless people begging for money "should just go out and get a job"—a phenomenon also called "blaming the victim."

Keep in mind that when we focus on possible *situational* influences on behavior, we're more likely to make better and more accurate judgments of the causes of events and other people's behavior. Unfortunately, given people's enduring personality traits (Chapter 11), our shared tendency to take cognitive shortcuts (Chapter 8), and the saliency bias, we more often focus on dispositional (personality) factors—thus leading us to commit the FAE.

Fundamental attribution error (FAE) The tendency of observers to overestimate the influence of internal, dispositional factors on a person's behavior, while underestimating the impact of external, situational factors.

Saliency bias A type of attributional bias in which people tend to focus on the most noticeable (salient) factors when explaining the causes of behavior.

Self-serving bias A type of attributional bias in which people tend to take credit for their successes and externalize or deny responsibility for their failures.

Actor–observer effect The tendency to attribute one's own actions to external (situational) factors while attributing others' actions to internal (dispositional) causes.

Self-Serving Bias

Unlike the FAE, which commonly occurs when we're explaining others' behaviors, the **self-serving bias** more often happens when we explain our own behavior. In this case, we tend to favor internal (personality) attributions for our successes and external (situational) attributions for our failures. This bias is motivated by our desire to maintain positive self-esteem and a good public image (Martin & Carron, 2012; Sanjuán & Magallares, 2013; Vaillancourt, 2013). For example, students often take personal credit for doing well on an exam. If they fail a test, however, they tend to blame the instructor, the textbook, or the "tricky" questions. Similarly, elite Olympic athletes more often attribute their wins to internal (personal) causes, such as their skill and effort, while attributing their losses to external (situational) causes, such as bad equipment or poor officiating (Aldridge & Islam, 2012).

How do we explain the discrepancy between the attributions we make for ourselves and those we make for others? According to the **actor–observer effect** (Jones & Nisbett, 1971), when examining our own behaviors, we are the *actors* in the situation and know more about our own intentions and behaviors and naturally look to the environment for explanations: "I didn't tip the waiter because I got really bad service." In contrast, when explaining the behavior of others, we are *observing* the actors and therefore tend to blame the person, using a personality attribution: "She didn't tip the waiter because she's cheap" **(Figure 14.1)**.

FIGURE 14.1 THE ACTOR–OBSERVER EFFECT

We tend to explain our own behavior in terms of external factors (situational attributions) and others' behavior in terms of their internal characteristics (dispositional attributions).

Actor		Observer
Situational attribution		**Dispositional attribution**
Focuses attention on external factors		Focuses on the personality of the actor
"I don't even like drinking beer, but it's the best way to meet women."		"He seems to always have a beer in his hand; he must have a drinking problem."

Christine Schneider/© Corbis

Culture and Attributional Biases

Interestingly, both the fundamental attribution error and the self-serving bias may depend in part on cultural factors (Han et al., 2011; Imada & Ellsworth, 2011; Lien et al., 2006; Sanjuán & de Lopez, 2013; Wirtz & Chiu, 2008). In highly individualistic cultures, like the United States, people are defined and understood as individual selves, largely responsible for their own successes and failures.

In contrast, people in collectivistic cultures, like China and Japan, are primarily defined as members of their social network, responsible for doing as others expect. Accordingly, they tend to be more aware of situational constraints on behavior, making the FAE less likely (Leung et al., 2012; Matsumoto & Juang, 2013; McClure et al., 2011).

The self-serving bias is also much less common in collectivistic cultures because self-esteem is related not to doing better than others but to fitting in with the group (Berry et al., 2011; Markus & Kitayama, 2003; Smith, 2011). In Japan, for instance, the ideal person is aware of his or her shortcomings and continually works to overcome them—rather than thinking highly of himself or herself (Heine & Renshaw, 2002; Shand, 2013).

Attitudes

When we observe and respond to the world around us, we are seldom completely neutral. Rather, our responses toward subjects as diverse as pizza, AIDS, and abortion

FIGURE 14.2 **ATTITUDE FORMATION**

When social psychologists study attitudes, they measure each of the three ABC components: Affective, Behavioal, and Cognitive.

reflect our **attitudes**, which are *learned* predispositions to respond to a particular object in a particular way. Social psychologists generally agree that most attitudes have three ABC components: *affect*, or feelings; *behavior*, or actions; and *cognitions*, or thoughts and beliefs **(Figure 14.2)**.

Attitude The learned predisposition to respond cognitively, affectively, and behaviorally to a particular object, person, place, thing, or event in an evaluative way.

Attitude Formation

As mentioned, we tend to learn our attitudes—generally from direct instruction, through personal experiences, and by watching others. In some cases, these sources may differ, depending on our gender. For example, researchers have found that teenage boys are more likely to learn sexual attitudes from media representations of sexual behavior, whereas teenage girls tend to learn their sexual attitudes from their mothers, as long as they feel close to their mothers (Vanderbosch & Eggermont, 2011).

HEALTH AND SELF-IMAGE realworldpsychology

Given the high prevalence of very thin women and lean, "ripped" men displayed on magazines, TV, and movies, it's easy to see why many people in our Western culture develop a shared preference for a certain, limited body type. Thankfully, research finds that just showing 100 women photographs of plus-size models (with a minimum clothing size of 16 and a BMI between 36 and 42) caused them to change their initial attitudes, which had been to prefer the thin ideal (Boothroyd et al., 2012). Can you see how ads that offer more realistic images, as well as the devastating effects of anorexia (like the two photos on the right), might improve the overall health and self-image of both men and women? Sadly, the model in the photo on the far right, Isabel Caro, died of anorexia in 2010 at age 28.

Agencia el Universal/El Universal de Mexico/NewsCom

Attitude Change

Although attitudes begin to form in early childhood, they're obviously not permanent, a fact that advertisers and politicians know and exploit. As we've just seen in the study described above, we can sometimes change attitudes through experiments. However, a much more common method is to make direct, persuasive appeals, such as in ads that say, "Friends Don't Let Friends Drive Drunk!" Interestingly, psychologists have identified an even more efficient strategy, which is to create contradictions between our attitudes, or between our attitudes and our behaviors, that lead to

Cognitive dissonance The unpleasant tension and anxiety caused by a discrepancy between two or more conflicting attitudes or between attitudes and behaviors.

feelings of discomfort, known as **cognitive dissonance** (Baumeister & Bushman, 2014; Moghaddam, 2013; Samnani et al., 2012; Sanderson, 2010; Sharpe et al., 2013). (See *Psych Science.*)

Once we've created or experienced cognitive dissonance, how can we reduce it **(Figure 14.3)**?

Culture and Cognitive Dissonance

The experience of cognitive dissonance may depend on a distinctly Western way of thinking about and evaluating the self. As we mentioned earlier, people in Eastern cultures tend not to define themselves in terms of their individual accomplishments. For this reason, making a bad decision may not pose the same threat to self-esteem that it would in more individualistic cultures, such as the United States (Dessalles, 2011; Imada & Kitayama, 2010; Kokkoris & Kühnen, 2013; Stephens & Swartz, 2013).

In sum, psychologists have long been particularly interested in how attitudes are formed—and how they can change. This emphasis on attitudes is important because they often, but not always, predict behavior. For example, research has found that teenage drivers' attitudes about speeding are a strong predictor of whether they actually speed—and receive speeding tickets—later on (Rowe et al., 2013).

PSYCHSCIENCE

WOULD YOU LIE FOR $1.00?

In one of the best-known tests of cognitive dissonance theory, Leon Festinger and J. Merrill Carlsmith (1959) paid participants either $1 or $20 to lie to fellow research participants by telling them that a boring experimental task in which they had just participated was actually very enjoyable and fun. Surprisingly, those who were paid just $1 to lie subsequently changed their minds about the task and actually reported more positive attitudes toward it than those who were paid $20.

Why was there more attitude change among those who were paid only $1? All participants who lied to other participants presumably recognized the discrepancy between their initial attitude (the task was boring) and their behavior (telling others it was enjoyable and fun). However, as you can see in the figure above, the participants who were given insufficient monetary justification for lying (the $1 liars) apparently experienced greater

cognitive dissonance. Therefore, they expressed more liking for the dull task than those who received sufficient monetary justification (the $20 liars). This second group had little or no motivation to change their attitude—they lied for the money! (Note that in 1959, when the experiment was done, $20 would be worth about $200 today.)

RESEARCH CHALLENGE

1 Based on the information provided, did this study (Festinger & Carlsmith, 1959) use descriptive, correlational, and/or experimental research?

2 If you chose:

- descriptive research, is this a naturalistic observation, survey/interview, case study, or archival research?
- correlational research, is this a positive, negative, or zero correlation?
- experimental research, label the IV, DV, experimental group(s), and control group.

>> CHECK YOUR ANSWERS IN APPENDIX B.

NOTE: The information provided in this study is admittedly limited, but the level of detail is similar to what is presented in most textbooks and public reports of research findings. Answering these questions, and then comparing your answers to those in the Appendix, will help you become a better critical thinker and consumer of scientific research.

FIGURE 14.3 REDUCING COGNITIVE DISSONANCE

Why do some health professionals, who obviously know the dangers of smoking, continue to smoke?

1 When inconsistencies or conflicts exist between our thoughts, feelings, and actions, they can lead to strong tension and discomfort (*cognitive dissonance*).

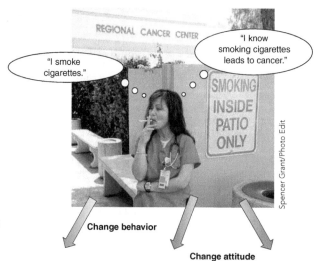

"I smoke cigarettes."

"I know smoking cigarettes leads to cancer."

REGIONAL CANCER CENTER

SMOKING INSIDE PATIO ONLY

Spencer Grant/Photo Edit

2 To reduce this cognitive dissonance, we are motivated to change our behavior or our attitude.

Change behavior

Change attitude

3a Changing behavior, such as quitting smoking, can be hard to do.

"I don't smoke cigarettes any more."

3b If unable or unwilling to change their behavior, individuals can use one or more of the four methods shown here to change their attitude.

Change perceived importance of one of the conflicting cognitions: "Experiments showing that smoking causes cancer have only been done on animals."

Modify one or both of the conflicting cognitions: "I don't smoke that much."

Add additional cognitions: "I only eat healthy foods, so I'm better protected from cancer."

Deny conflicting cognitions are related: "There's no real evidence linking cigarettes and cancer."

RETRIEVAL PRACTICE: SOCIAL COGNITION

Self-Test

Completing this self-test and comparing your answers with those in Appendix B provides immediate feedback and helpful practice for exams. Additional interactive, self-tests are available at www.wiley.com/college/huffman.

1. The study of how other people influence our thoughts, feelings, and actions is called _____.

   a. social cognition   b. social science
   c. social psychology   d. social influence

2. The principles we follow in making judgments about the causes of events, others' behavior, and our own behavior are known as _____.

   a. impression management   b. stereotaxic determination
   c. attributions   d. person perception

3. The two major attribution mistakes we make are the _____ and the _____.

   a. fundamental attribution error; self-serving bias
   b. situational attributions; dispositional attributions
   c. actor bias; observer bias
   d. stereotypes; biases

4. Label the three components of attitudes.

Attitude

a. _____   b. _____   c. _____

Measured by self-report techniques (surveys and questionnaires)

Measured by physiological techniques (heart rate, respiration)

Measured by self-reported or directly observed behavioral changes

5. According to _____ theory, we're motivated to change our attitudes because of tension created by a mismatch between two or more competing attitudes or between our attitudes and behavior.

   a. social learning   b. cognitive dissonance
   c. defense mechanisms   d. power of inconsistencies

Think Critically

1 Why do we tend to blame others for their misfortunes but deny responsibility for our own failures?

2 Have you ever changed a strongly held attitude? What caused you to do so?

3 Can you think of an example of cognitive dissonance from your own life?

realworldpsychology

Why do athletes often blame their losses on bad officiating?

HINT: LOOK IN THE MARGIN FOR Q1

SOCIAL INFLUENCE

LEARNING OBJECTIVES

RETRIEVAL PRACTICE While reading the upcoming sections, respond to each Learning Objective in your own words. Then compare your responses with those found at www.wiley.com/college/huffman.

1 IDENTIFY conformity and the factors that contribute to it.
2 DESCRIBE obedience and the factors that contribute to it.
3 EXPLAIN how groups affect behavior and decision making.

Social influence How situational factors and other people affect us.

In the previous section, we explored the way we think about and interpret ourselves and others through *social cognition*. We now focus on **social influence**: how situational factors and other people affect us. In this section, we explore three key topics—*conformity*, *obedience*, and *group processes*.

Conformity

Imagine that you have volunteered for a psychology experiment on visual perception. All participants are shown two cards. The first card has only a single vertical line on it, while the second card has three vertical lines of varying lengths. Your task is to determine which of the three lines on the second card (marked A, B, or C) is the same length as the single line on the first card (marked X).

You are seated around a table with six other people, and everyone is called on in order. Because you are seated to the left of the seventh participant, you are always next to last to provide your answers. On the first two trials, everyone agrees on the correct line. However, on the third trial, your group is shown two cards like those in **Figure 14.4**. The first participant chooses line A as the closest in length to line

FIGURE 14.4 **SOLOMON ASCH'S STUDY OF CONFORMITY**
Which line (A, B, or C) is most like line X? Could anyone convince you otherwise?

X, an obvious wrong answer! When the second, third, fourth, and fifth participants also say line A, you really start to wonder: "What's going on here? Are they wrong, or am I?"

What do you think you would do at this point in the experiment? Would you stick with your convictions and say line B, regardless of what the others have answered? Or would you go along with the group? In the original version of this experiment, conducted by Solomon Asch (1951), six of the seven participants were actually *confederates* of the experimenter (that is, they were working with the experimenter and purposely gave wrong answers). Their incorrect responses were designed to test the participant's degree of **conformity**.

More than one-third of Asch's participants conformed—they agreed with the group's obviously incorrect choice. (Participants in a control group experienced no group pressure and almost always chose correctly.) Asch's study has been conducted dozens of times, in at least 17 countries, and always with similar results (Mori & Arai, 2010; Tennen et al., 2013).

Why would so many people conform? To the onlooker, conformity is often difficult to understand. Even the conformer sometimes has a hard time explaining his or her behavior. Let's look at three factors that drive conformity:

- **Normative social influence** One of the first reasons we conform is that we want to go along with group *norms*, which are expected behaviors generally adhered to by members of a group. Most often norms are quite subtle and only implied (see *Psychology and You* and *Cultural Norms for Personal Space*).

Conformity Changes in behavior, attitudes, or values because of real or imagined group pressure.

Normative social influence Conformance to group pressure out of a need to be liked, accepted, and approved of by others.

psychology and you   **Norms in Everyday Life** Have you ever asked what others are wearing to a party or copied your neighbor at a dinner party to make sure you picked up the right fork? We generally submit to normative social influence out of our need for approval and acceptance by the group and because conforming to group norms makes us feel good (Irwin & Simpson, 2013).

© cstar55/iStockphoto

CULTURAL NORMS FOR PERSONAL SPACE
realworldpsychology

Culture and socialization have a lot to do with shaping norms for personal space. If someone invades the invisible "personal bubble" around our bodies, we generally feel very uncomfortable. This may help explain why some people from the United States feel awkward when traveling to Mediterranean and Latin American countries where people generally maintain smaller interpersonal distances (Axtell, 2007; Steinhart, 1986). As you can see in this photo, these Middle Eastern men are apparently comfortable with a small personal space and with showing male-to-male affection.

Interestingly, children in our own Western culture also tend to stand very close to others until they are socialized to recognize and maintain greater personal distance. Furthermore, friends stand closer than strangers, women tend to stand closer than men, and violent prisoners prefer approximately three times as much personal space as nonviolent prisoners (Axtell, 2007; Gilmour & Walkey, 1981; Lawrence & Andrews, 2004).

AFP/Getty Images, Inc.

Think Critically

1 How might cultural differences in personal space help explain why U.S. travelers abroad are sometimes seen as being "too loud and brassy"?

2 Given that men and women have different norms for personal space, what effect might this have on their relationships?

Informational social influence
Conformance to a group out of a need for information and direction.

• **Informational social influence** Have you ever bought a specific product simply because of a friend's recommendation? In this case, you probably conformed not to gain your friend's approval, a case of normative social influence, but because you assumed that he or she had more information than you did, a case of informational social influence. Given that participants in Asch's experiment observed all the other participants giving unanimous decisions on the length of the lines, can you see how they may have conformed because they believed the others had more information than they did?

Voices from the Classroom

Santa and Informational Social Influence Conformity is a fun and pertinent topic because there is always a good, recent example to which students can relate. For example, when discussing *informational social influence*, I talk about kids lining up to meet Santa. It's a relatively novel experience for them, and they are often unsure of how to act, so they look to others for information. When one child becomes frightened by Santa or an elf and screams or cries, there's a ripple effect throughout the line. Soon all the other kids also are scared and crying.

Professor Rebekah Wanic
University of California, San Diego
La Jolla, California

Reference groups The people we conform to, or go along with, because we like, admire, and want to be like them.

Obedience Following direct commands, usually from an authority figure.

• **Reference groups** The third major factor in conformity is the power of *reference groups*—people we most admire, like, and want to resemble. Attractive actors and popular sports stars are paid millions of dollars to endorse products because advertisers know that we want to be as cool as LeBron James or as beautiful as Natalie Portman. Of course, we also have more important reference groups in our lives—parents, friends, family members, teachers, religious leaders, and classmates—all of whom affect our willingness to conform. For example, popular high school students' attitudes about alcohol use have been shown to have a substantial influence on alcohol consumption by other students in their high school (Teunissen et al., 2012). Surprisingly, popular peers who had *negative* attitudes toward alcohol use were even more influential in determining rates of teenage drinking than those with positive attitudes! This finding suggests that capitalizing on popular peers who have negative drinking attitudes might be a very effective strategy for reducing underage drinking.

FIGURE 14.5 GOOD REASONS FOR CONFORMING AND OBEYING

These people willingly obey the firefighters who order them to evacuate a building, and many lives are saved. What would happen to our everyday functioning if most people did not go along with the crowd or generally did not obey orders?

David McNew/Getty Images

Obedience

As we've seen, conformity means going along with the group. A second form of social influence, **obedience**, involves going along with direct commands, usually from someone in a position of authority. From very early childhood, we're socialized to respect and obey our parents, teachers, and other authority figures.

Conformity and obedience aren't always bad **(Figure 14.5)**. In fact, we generally conform and obey most of the time because it's in our own best interests (and everyone else's) to do so. Like most other North Americans, we stand in line at a movie theatre instead of pushing ahead of others. This allows an orderly purchasing of tickets. Conformity and obedience allow social life to proceed with safety, order, and predictability.

However, on some occasions, it is important not to conform or obey. We don't want teenagers (or adults) engaging in risky sex or drug use just to be part of the crowd. And we don't want soldiers (or anyone else) mindlessly following orders just because they were told to do so by an authority figure. Recognizing and resisting destructive forms of obedience are particularly important to our society—and to social psychology. Let's start with an examination of a classic series of studies on obedience by Stanley Milgram (1963, 1974).

Imagine that you have responded to a newspaper ad seeking volunteers for a study on memory. At the Yale University laboratory, an experimenter explains to you and another participant that he is studying the effects of punishment on learning and memory. You are selected to play the role of the "teacher." The experimenter leads you into a room where he straps the other participant—the "learner"—into a chair. He applies electrode paste to the learner's wrist "to avoid blisters and burns" and attaches an electrode that is connected to a shock generator.

Next, you're led into an adjacent room and told to sit in front of this same shock generator, which is wired through the wall to the chair of the learner. (The setup for the experiment is illustrated in **Figure 14.6**.*) The shock machine consists of 30 switches representing successively higher levels of shock, from 15 volts to 450 volts. Written labels appear below each group of switches, ranging from "Slight Shock" to "Danger: Severe Shock," all the way to "XXX." The experimenter explains that it is your job to teach the learner a list of word pairs and to punish any errors by administering a shock. With each wrong answer, you are to increase the shock by one level.*

You begin teaching the word pairs, but the learner's responses are often wrong. Before long, you are inflicting shocks that you can only assume must be extremely painful. After you administer 150 volts, the learner begins to protest: "Get me out of here . . . I refuse to go on."

You hesitate, and the experimenter tells you to continue. He insists that even if the learner refuses to answer, you must keep increasing the shock levels. But the other person is obviously in pain. What will you do?

It's important to note that the "learners" were confederates, who helped with the experiment and never received actual shocks. They only pretended to be in pain. However, the real subjects, the "teachers," believed they were delivering shocks to a person in obvious pain. Although the "teachers" sweated, trembled, stuttered, laughed nervously, and repeatedly protested that they did not want to hurt the learner, they still obeyed!

The psychologist who designed this study, Stanley Milgram, was actually investigating not punishment and learning but obedience to authority: Would participants obey the experimenter's prompts and commands to shock another human being? In Milgram's public survey, fewer than 25% thought they would go beyond 150 volts. And no respondents predicted that they would go past the 300-volt level. Yet 65% of the teacher-participants in this series of studies obeyed completely—going all the way to the end of the scale (450 volts), even beyond the point when the "learner" (Milgram's confederate) stopped responding altogether.

Even Milgram was surprised by his results. Before the study began, he polled a group of psychiatrists, and they predicted that most people would refuse to go

FIGURE 14.6 **MILGRAM'S STUDY ON OBEDIENCE**

Under orders from an experimenter, would you, as "teacher," use this shock generator to shock a man (the "learner") who is screaming and begging to be released? Few people believe they would, but research shows otherwise.

Milgram's Shock Generator

Experimental Set Up

beyond 150 volts and that fewer than 1% of those tested would "go all the way." But, as Milgram discovered, 65% of his participants—men and women of all ages and from all walks of life—administered the highest voltage. The study was replicated many times and in many other countries, with similarly high levels of obedience.

Although there have been some recent partial replications of Milgram's study (e.g., Burger, 2009), his full, original setup could never be undertaken today due to ethical and moral considerations. Deception is a necessary part of some research, but the degree of it in Milgram's research and the discomfort of the participants would never be allowed under today's research standards. Keep in mind, however, that immediately following the study, Milgram carefully debriefed each subject and then followed up with the participants for several months. Most of his "teachers" reported finding the experience personally informative and valuable.

One final, important reminder: The *"learner" was an accomplice of the experimenter and only pretended to be shocked.* Milgram provided specific scripts that they followed at every stage of the experiment. In contrast, the "teachers" were true volunteers who believed they were administering real shocks. Although they suffered and protested, in the final analysis, they still obeyed.

Why did the teachers in Milgram's study obey the orders to shock a fellow subject, despite their moral objections? Are there specific circumstances that increase or decrease obedience? In a series of follow-up studies, Milgram found several important factors that influenced obedience: *legitimacy and closeness of the authority figure, remoteness of the victim, assignment of responsibility,* and *modeling or imitation of others* (Blass, 1991, 2000; De Vos, 2010; Forsyth, 2013; Moghaddam, 2013; Pina e Cunha et al., 2010) **(Figure 14.7)**.

In addition to the four factors that Milgram identified, other social psychologists have emphasized several additional influences, including the following:

- **Socialization** Can you see how socialization might help explain many instances of mindless and sometimes destructive obedience? From an early age, we're all taught to listen to and respect people in positions of authority. In this case, participants in Milgram's study came into the research lab with a lifetime of

FIGURE 14.7 FOUR FACTORS THAT AFFECT WHY WE OBEY

As you can see in the first bar on the graph, 65% of the participants in Milgram's early studies gave the learner the full 450-volt level of shocks. Note also how the color coding on the other bars on the graph (dark pink, yellow, green, and blue) corresponds to the four major conditions that either increased or decreased obedience to authority.

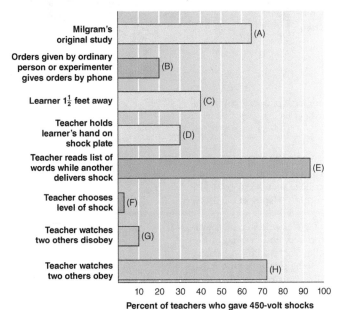

Percent of teachers who gave 450-volt shocks

1. Legitimacy and closeness of the authority figure
When orders came from an ordinary person, and when the experimenter left the room and gave orders by phone, 20% of the teachers gave the full 450-volt shocks. (Bar B on graph.)

2. Remoteness of the victim
When the learner was only 1½ feet away from the teacher, 40% of the teachers gave the highest level of shocks. However, when the teacher had to actually hold the learner's hand on the shock plate, obedience was only 30%. (Bars C and D on graph.)

3. Assignment of responsibility
When the teacher simply read the list of words, while another delivered the shock, obedience jumped to almost 94%. However, when the teacher was responsible for choosing the level of shock, only 3% obeyed. (Bars E and F on graph.)

4. Modeling or imitating others
When teachers watched two other teachers refuse to shock the learner, only 10% gave the full 450-volt shocks. However, when they watched two other teachers obey, their obedience jumped to over 70% (Milgram, 1963, 1974). (Bars G and Hon graph.)

socialization toward the value of scientific research and respect for the experimenter's authority. They couldn't suddenly step outside themselves and question the morality of this particular experimenter and his orders.

- **The foot-in-the-door technique** The step-wise actions in many obedience situations may also help explain why so many people were willing to give the maximum shocks in Milgram's study. The initial mild level of shocks may have worked as a **foot-in-the-door technique**, in which a first, small request is used as a setup for later, larger requests. Once Milgram's participants complied with the initial request, they might have felt obligated to continue.

- **Relaxed moral guard** One common intellectual illusion that hinders critical thinking about obedience is the belief that only evil people do evil things, or that evil announces itself. The experimenter in Milgram's study looked and acted like a reasonable person who was simply carrying out a research project. Because he was not seen as personally corrupt and evil, the participants' normal moral guard was down, which can maximize obedience. As philosopher Hannah Arendt has suggested, the horrifying thing about the Nazis was not that they were so deviant but that they were so "terrifyingly normal."

Foot-in-the-door technique An initial, small request is used as a setup for a later, larger request.

realworldpsychology   **A Model of Civil Disobedience**

Although the forces underlying obedience can be loud and powerful, even one quiet, courageous, dissenting voice can make a difference. Perhaps the most beautiful and historically important example of just this type of bravery occurred in Alabama in 1955. Rosa Parks boarded a bus and, as expected in those times, obediently sat in the back section marked "Negroes." When the bus became crowded, the driver told her to give up her seat to a white man. Surprisingly for those days, Parks quietly but firmly refused and was eventually forced off the bus by police and arrested. This single act of disobedience was the catalyst for the civil rights movement and the later repeal of Jim Crow laws in the South. Today, Rosa Parks's courageous stand also inspires the rest of us to carefully consider when it is appropriate and good to obey authorities and when we must resist unethical or dangerous demands.

© Bettmann/Corbis

Group Processes

Although we seldom recognize the power of group membership, social psychologists have identified several important ways that groups affect us.

Group Membership

How do the roles that we play within groups affect our behavior? This question fascinated social psychologist Philip Zimbardo. In his famous study at Stanford University, 24 carefully screened, well-adjusted young college men were paid $15 a day for participating in a two-week simulation of prison life (Haney et al., 1978; Zimbardo, 1993).

The students were randomly assigned to the role of either prisoner or guard. Prisoners were "arrested," frisked, photographed, fingerprinted, and booked at the police station. They were then blindfolded and driven to the "Stanford Prison." There, they were given ID numbers, deloused, issued prison clothing (tight nylon caps, shapeless gowns, and no underwear), and locked in cells. Participants assigned to be guards were outfitted with official-looking uniforms, official police nightsticks ("billy clubs"), and whistles, and they were given complete control.

FIGURE 14.8 POWER CORRUPTS
Zimbardo's prison study showed how the demands of roles and situations could produce dramatic changes in behavior in just a few days. Can you imagine what happens to prisoners during life imprisonment, six-year sentences, or even a few nights in jail?

Not even Zimbardo foresaw how the study would turn out. Although some guards were nicer to the prisoners than others, they all engaged in some abuse of power. The slightest disobedience was punished with degrading tasks or the loss of "privileges" (such as eating, sleeping, and washing). As demands increased and abuses began, the prisoners became passive and depressed. Only one prisoner fought back with a hunger strike, which ended with a forced feeding by the guards.

Four prisoners had to be released within the first four days because of severe psychological reactions. The study was stopped after only six days because of the alarming psychological changes in the participants.

Note that this was not a true experiment in that it lacked control groups and clear measurements of the dependent variable (Chapter 1). However, it did provide valuable insights into the potential effects of roles on individual behavior **(Figure 14.8)**. According to interviews conducted after the study, the students became so absorbed in their roles that they forgot they were participants in a university study (Zimbardo et al., 1977).

Zimbardo's study also demonstrates **deindividuation**. To be deindividuated means that we feel less self-conscious, less inhibited, and less personally responsible as a member of a group than when we're alone **(Figure 14.9)**. Groups sometimes actively promote deindividuation by requiring members to wear uniforms, for example, as a way to increase allegiance and conformity.

Deindividuation The reduced self-consciousness, inhibition, and personal responsibility that sometimes occurs in a group, particularly when the members feel anonymous.

Group Decision Making

We've just seen how group membership affects the way we think about ourselves, but how do groups affect our decisions? Are two heads truly better than one?

Most people assume that group decisions are more conservative, cautious, and middle-of-the-road than individual decisions. But is this true? Initial investigations indicated that after discussing an issue, groups actually supported riskier decisions than decisions they made as individuals before the discussion (Stoner, 1961).

Subsequent research on this *risky-shift phenomenon*, however, shows that some groups support riskier decisions while others support conservative decisions (Liu & Latané, 1998; Tindale et al., 2013). How can we tell whether a given group's decision will be risky or conservative? A group's final decision depends primarily on its dominant *preexisting* tendencies. If the dominant initial position is risky, the final decision will be even riskier, and the reverse is true if the initial position is conservative—a process called **group polarization** (Baumeister & Bushman, 2014; Sanderson, 2010; Tindale & Posavac, 2011; Zhu, 2013).

Group polarization The tendency for groups to make decisions that are more extreme (either riskier or more conservative), depending on the members' initial dominant tendency.

Why? It appears that as individuals interact and share their opinions, they pick up new and more persuasive information that supports their original opinions, which may help explain why American politics has become so polarized in recent years (Miller, 2013). Can you see how if we only interact and work with like-minded people, or only talk politics with those who agree with us, we're likely to become even more polarized? An interesting study in Washington, DC found that interns

Don Emmert/AFP/Getty Images

FIGURE 14.9 **LOST IN THE CROWD**

One of the most compelling explanations for deindividuation is the fact that the presence of others tends to increase arousal and feelings of anonymity, which is a powerful disinhibitor. As you can see in this photo, deindividuation can be healthy and positive when we're part of a happy, celebratory crowd. However, it also helps explain why vandalism seems to increase on Halloween (when people commonly wear masks) and why most crimes and riots occur at night—under the cover of darkness (Haines & Mann, 2011; Lammers & Stapel, 2011; Rodrigues et al., 2005; Spears, 2011; Zimbardo, 2007). Can you imagine your own behavior changing under such conditions?

who worked in a partisan workplace became more polarized in their opinions than those who worked in less partisan environments (Jones, 2013).

Group polarization is also important within the legal system. Imagine yourself as a member of a jury **(Figure 14.10)**. In an ideal world, attorneys from both sides would present the essential facts of the case. Then, after careful deliberation, each individual juror would move from his or her initially neutral position toward the defendant to a more extreme position—either conviction or acquittal. In a not-so-ideal world, the quality of legal arguments from opposing sides may not be equal, you and the other members of the jury may not be neutral at the start, and group polarization may cause most jurors to make riskier or more conservative judgments than they would have on their own.

A related phenomenon is **groupthink (Figure 14.11)**. When a group is highly cohesive (a couple, a family, a panel of military advisers, an athletic team), the members' desire for agreement may lead them to ignore important information or points of view held by outsiders or critics (Hergovich & Olbrich, 2003; Hogg, 2013; Vaughn, 1996). To make matters worse, women are especially likely to refrain from speaking up in a group setting, so their opinions are less likely to be heard than men's (Karpowitz et al., 2012).

Many highly-publicized tragedies—from Franklin Roosevelt's failure to anticipate the attack on Pearl Harbor in 1941 to the Jerry Sandusky Penn State sex scandal in 2012—have been blamed on groupthink. In addition, groupthink may have contributed to the losses of the space shuttles *Challenger* and *Columbia*, the terrorist attack of September 11, 2001, the war in Iraq, and other important decisions (Barlow, 2008; Burnette et al., 2011; Ehrenreich, 2004; Janis, 1972, 1989; Post, 2011; Redd & Mintz, 2013; Strozier, 2011).

Groupthink The faulty decision making that occurs when a highly cohesive group strives for agreement, especially if it is in line with the leader's viewpoint, and avoids inconsistent information.

 Q3

Exactostock/SuperStock

FIGURE 14.10 **JURIES AND GROUP POLARIZATION**

When might group polarization be both a desirable and an undesirable part of jury deliberation?

FIGURE 14.11 HOW GROUPTHINK OCCURS | realworldpsychology

A The process of groupthink begins when group members feel a strong sense of cohesiveness and isolation from the judgments of qualified outsiders. Add a directive leader and little chance for debate, and we have the recipe for a potentially dangerous decision.

Vstock LLC/Getty Images

B Few people realize that the decision to marry can be a form of groupthink. (Remember that a "group" can have as few as two members.) When planning a marriage, a couple may show symptoms of groupthink such as an illusion of invulnerability ("We're different—we won't ever get divorced"), collective rationalizations ("Two can live more cheaply than one"), shared stereotypes of the outgroup ("Couples with problems just don't know how to communicate"), and pressure on dissenters ("If you don't support our decision to marry, we don't want you at the wedding").

Groupthink

Antecedent Conditions

1. A highly cohesive group of decision makers
2. Insulation of the group from outside influences
3. A directive leader
4. Lack of procedures to ensure careful consideration of the pros and cons of alternative actions
5. High stress from external threats with little hope of finding a better solution than that favored by the leader

↓

Strong desire for group consensus—the groupthink tendency

↓

Symptoms of Groupthink

1. Illusion of invulnerability
2. Belief in the morality of the group
3. Collective rationalizations
4. Stereotypes of outgroups
5. Self-censorship of doubts and dissenting opinions
6. Illusion of unanimity
7. Direct pressure on dissenters

↓

Symptoms of Poor Decision Making

1. An incomplete survey of alternative courses of action
2. An incomplete survey of group objectives
3. Failure to examine risks of the preferred choice
4. Failure to reappraise rejected alternatives
5. Poor search for relevant information
6. Selective bias in processing information
7. Failure to develop contingency plans

↓

Low probability of successful outcome

RETRIEVAL PRACTICE: SOCIAL INFLUENCE

Self-Test

Completing this self-test and comparing your answers with those in Appendix B provides immediate feedback and helpful practice for exams. Additional interactive, self-tests are available at www.wiley.com/college/huffman.

1. The act of changing behavior as a result of real or imagined group pressure is called _____.

   a. norm compliance   b. obedience
   c. conformity   d. mob rule

2. What percentage of people in Milgram's original study were willing to give the highest level of shock (450 volts)?

   a. 45 percent   b. 90 percent
   c. 65 percent   d. 10 percent

3. Which of the following factors may contribute to destructive obedience?

   a. remoteness of the victim   b. foot-in-the-door
   c. socialization   d. All these options.

4. One of the most critical factors in deindividuation is _____.

   a. loss of self-esteem   b. anonymity
   c. identity diffusion   d. group cohesiveness

5. Faulty decision making resulting from a highly cohesive group striving for agreement to the point of avoiding inconsistent information is known as _____.

   a. the risky-shift   b. group polarization
   c. groupthink   d. destructive conformity

Think Critically

1 Explain how group membership has affected your own behavior and decision making.

2 How might Milgram's results relate to some aspects of modern warfare?

3 Have you ever done something wrong in a group that you would not have done if you were alone? What have you learned from this chapter that might help you avoid this behavior in the future?

realworldpsychology

If popular high-school students are anti-drinking, does that reduce underage drinking among their peers?

Are women less likely than men to share their opinions in a group?

HINT: LOOK IN THE MARGIN FOR AND

SOCIAL RELATIONS

RETRIEVAL PRACTICE While reading the upcoming sections, respond to each Learning Objective in your own words. Then compare your responses with those found at www.wiley.com/college/huffman.

1 **EXPLAIN** the difference between prejudice and discrimination.
2 **IDENTIFY** the factors that contribute to, and those that combat, prejudice and discrimination.
3 **DISCUSS** aggression and the factors that increase and decrease it.
4 **DESCRIBE** altruism and the factors that increase and decrease it.
5 **SUMMARIZE** the factors that influence interpersonal attraction and love.

LEARNING OBJECTIVES

Kurt Lewin (1890–1947), often considered the "father of social psychology," was among the first person to suggest that all behavior results from interactions between the individual and the environment. In this final section, on **social relations**, we explore how we develop and are affected by interpersonal relations, including prejudice, aggression, altruism, and interpersonal attraction.

Social relations How we develop and are affected by interpersonal relationships.

Prejudice and Discrimination

Prejudice, which literally means prejudgment, creates enormous problems for its victims and also limits a perpetrator's ability to accurately judge others and to process information.

    Like all other attitudes, prejudice is composed of three ABC elements: *affective* (emotions about the group), *behavioral* (predispositions and negative actions toward members of the group), and *cognitive* (**stereotypes** about group members). Although the terms *prejudice* and *discrimination* are often used interchangeably, they are not the same. Prejudice refers to an attitude, whereas **discrimination** refers to action (Fiske, 1998). The two often coincide, but not always **(Figure 14.12)**.

Prejudice A learned, generally negative, attitude toward members of a group; it includes thoughts (stereotypes), feelings, and behavioral tendencies (possible discrimination).

Stereotypes Generalizations about a group of people in which the same characteristics are assigned to all members of the group; also, the cognitive component of prejudice.

Discrimination Negative behaviors directed at others because of their membership in a particular group.

		Prejudice	
		Yes	**No**
Discrimination	**Yes**	A minority person is *denied* a job because the owner of a business is prejudiced.	A minority person is *denied* a job because the owner of a business fears white customers won't buy from a minority salesperson.
	No	A minority person is *given* a job because the owner of a business hopes to attract minority customers.	A minority person is *given* a job because he or she is the best suited for it.

FIGURE 14.12 PREJUDICE AND DISCRIMINATION

Prejudice and discrimination are closely related, but either condition can exist without the other. The only situation without prejudice or discrimination in this example occurs when someone is given a job simply because he or she is the best candidate.

How do prejudice and discrimination originate? Why do they persist? Five commonly cited sources of prejudice are *learning*, *personal experience*, *limited resources*, *displaced aggression*, and *mental shortcuts*.

Learning

People learn prejudice the same way they learn other attitudes—primarily through *classical* and *operant conditioning* and *social learning* (Chapter 6). For example, repeated exposure to stereotypical portrayals of minorities and women in movies, online, magazines, and TV teach children that such images are correct. Similarly, hearing parents, friends, and teachers express their prejudices also reinforces prejudice (Amodio & Hamilton, 2013; Biernat & Danaher, 2013; Conger et al., 2013; Ferguson & Porter, 2013). *Ethnocentrism*, believing our own culture represents the norm or is superior to others, is also a form of a learned prejudice.

 Voices from the Classroom

Learning and Gender Role Stereotypes My friends were working outside with their 2 ½-year-old son nearby, when a heavy hammer fell on one parent's foot, followed by a very "colorful" exclamation of intense pain. Both parents quickly distracted their child, hoping to prevent him from learning and repeating the word. Disaster seemed to have been averted until the next day at church, when the boy dropped a Bible on his own foot and loudly repeated the same "colorful" word! Knowing that the parents were very embarrassed, the minister reassured the couple after the service by joking to the dad about thinking twice before using "colorful" language again. To his surprise, the father responded that he was not the one who used the word. It was his wife!

Like the minister, students in my class are equally surprised by this story. I use it as an example of gender-role stereotypes and how societal expectations and assumptions may not always be accurate.

Professor Ronnie Naramore

Angelina College

Lufkin, Texas

Personal Experience

We also develop prejudice through direct experience. For example, when people make prejudicial remarks or "jokes," they often gain attention and even approval from others. Sadly, denigrating others also seems to boost some people's self-esteem (Fein & Spencer, 1997; Hodson et al., 2010; Nelson, 2013). Also, once someone has one or more negative interactions or experiences with members of a specific group, he or she may generalize the resulting bad feelings and prejudice to all members of that group.

Limited Resources

Most of us understand that prejudice and discrimination exact a high price on their victims, but few appreciate the significant economic and political advantages they offer to the dominant group (Costello & Hodson, 2011; Danso & Lum, 2013; Kteily et al., 2011; Schaefer, 2008). For example, the stereotype that African Americans and Mexicans are inferior to European Americans helps justify and perpetuate a social order in the United States in which European Americans hold disproportionate power and resources.

Displaced Aggression

As we discuss in the next section, frustration sometimes leads people to attack the perceived cause of that frustration. But, as history has shown, when the source is ambiguous, or too powerful and capable of retaliation, people often redirect their aggression toward an alternative, innocent target, known as a *scapegoat*. There is strong historical evidence of the dangers of scapegoating. Jewish people were blamed for economic troubles in Germany before World War II. In the United States beginning in the 1980s, gay men were blamed for the AIDS epidemic, and Hispanic immigrant groups are now being blamed for the nation's recent economic troubles **(Figure 14.13)**.

Mental Shortcuts

Prejudice is also believed to develop from everyday *mental shortcuts* that we create to simplify our complex social world (Ambady & Adams, 2011; Dotsch et al., 2011; Ferguson & Porter, 2013; Sternberg, 2007, 2009). Stereotypes allow quick judgments about others, thereby freeing up mental resources for other activities. Note, however, that these mental shortcuts too often lead to negative outcomes. For example, when science faculty were sent identical résumés from a male and a female student applying for a job as a laboratory manager, both male and female faculty members rated the male applicant as more competent and hirable than the female (Moss-Racusin et al., 2012). Can you see how such stereotypes might have serious real-world consequences for women in the work force—especially for those trying to enter careers in stereotypically male fields?

People use stereotypes as mental shortcuts when they classify others in terms of their membership in a group. Given that people generally classify themselves as part of the preferred group, they also create ingroups and outgroups. An *ingroup* is any category to which people see themselves as belonging; an *outgroup* is any other category.

Compared with the way they judge members of the outgroup, people tend to judge ingroup members as being more attractive, having better personalities, and so on—a phenomenon known as **ingroup favoritism** (DiDonato et al., 2011; Jackson & Rose, 2013; Reyes-Jaquez & Echols, 2013). People also tend to recognize greater diversity among members of their ingroup than they do among members of outgroups (Bendle, 2011; Kang & Lau, 2013; Ratner & Amodio, 2013). A danger of this **outgroup homogeneity effect** is that when members of minority groups are not recognized as varied and complex individuals, it is easier to treat them in discriminatory ways.

A good example is war. Viewing people on the other side as simply faceless enemies makes it easier to kill large numbers of soldiers and civilians. This dehumanization and facelessness also help perpetuate our current high levels of fear and anxiety associated with terrorism (Buckels & Trapnell, 2013; Dunham, 2011; Hutchison & Rosenthal, 2011; Savage, 2013).

Ingroup favoritism Viewing members of the ingroup more positively than members of an outgroup.

Outgroup homogeneity effect Judging members of an outgroup as more alike and less diverse than members of the ingroup.

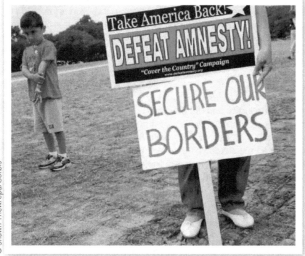

FIGURE 14.13 PREJUDICE AND IMMIGRATION

Can you identify which of the five sources of prejudice best explains this behavior?

© Shawn Thew/epa/Corbis

Implicit bias A hidden, automatic attitude that may guide behaviors independent of a person's awareness or control.

Unfortunately, stereotypes and prejudice can operate even without a person's conscious awareness or control. This process is known as automatic bias, or **implicit bias** (Cattaneo et al., 2011; Chapman et al., 2013; Columb & Plant, 2011; Soderberg & Sherman, 2013). The most prominent method for measuring implicit bias, the *Implicit Association Test* (*IAT*), measures how quickly people sort stimuli into particular categories.

Overcoming Prejudice and Discrimination

What can we do to reduce and combat prejudice and discrimination? Four major approaches have been suggested: *cooperation and common goals, intergroup contact, cognitive retraining,* and *cognitive dissonance* **(Figure 14.14)**.

Cooperation and common goals Research shows that one of the best ways to combat prejudice and discrimination is to encourage *cooperation* rather than *competition* (Kuchenbrandt et al., 2013; Price et al., 2013). Muzafer Sherif and his colleagues (1966, 1998) conducted an ingenious study to show the role of competition in promoting prejudice. The researchers artificially created strong feelings of ingroup and outgroup identification in a group of 11- and 12-year-old boys at a summer camp. They did this by physically separating the boys into different cabins and assigning different projects to each group, such as building a diving board or cooking out in the woods.

Once each group developed strong feelings of group identity and allegiance, the researchers set up a series of competitive games, including tug-of-war and touch football. They awarded desirable prizes to the winning teams. Because of this treatment, the groups began to pick fights, call each other names, and raid each other's camps. Researchers pointed to these behaviors as evidence of the experimentally produced prejudice.

The good news is that after using competition to create prejudice between the two groups, the researchers created "mini-crises" and tasks that required expertise, labor, and cooperation from both groups. Prizes were awarded to all and prejudice between the groups slowly began to dissipate. By the end of the camp, the earlier hostilities and *ingroup favoritism* had vanished. Sherif's study showed not only the importance of cooperation as opposed to competition but also the importance of *superordinate goals* (the "mini-crises") in reducing prejudice.

Intergroup Contact A second approach to reducing prejudice is to increase contact and positive experiences between groups (Butz & Plant, 2011; Cameron et al., 2007;

FIGURE 14.14 HOW CAN WE REDUCE PREJUDICE?

realworldpsychology

Can you see how the four approaches to combatting prejudice are at work in this simple game of tug-of-war? Similarly, how might large changes in social policy, such as school busing, integrated housing, and increased civil rights legislation gradually change attitudes and eventually lead to decreased prejudice and discrimination?

Dovidio et al., 2011; Hodson & Hewstone, 2013; Orta, 2013). However, as you just discovered with Sherif's study of the boys at the summer camp, contact can sometimes increase prejudice. Increasing contact works only under certain conditions that provide for *close interaction, interdependence* (superordinate goals that require cooperation), and *equal status.*

Cognitive Retraining One of the most recent strategies in prejudice reduction requires taking another's perspective or undoing associations of negative stereotypical traits (Biernat & Danaher, 2013; Müller et al., 2011; Todd et al., 2011). For example, televised specials and recent movies, like *42* and *The Butler*, help the viewing public understand and empathize with the pressures and heroic struggles of Blacks to gain equal rights. People can also learn to be less prejudiced if they are taught to selectively pay attention to *similarities* rather than *differences* (Motyl et al., 2011; Phillips & Ziller, 1997). Can you see how emphasizing gender differences (as in the book title *Men Are from Mars, Women Are from Venus*) may increase and perpetuate gender stereotypes?

Cognitive Dissonance One of the most efficient methods to change an attitude uses the earlier discussed principle of *cognitive dissonance*. Each time we meet someone who does not conform to our prejudiced views, we experience dissonance—"I thought all gay men were effeminate. This guy is a deep-voiced professional athlete. I'm confused." To resolve the dissonance, we can maintain our stereotypes by saying, "This gay man is an exception to the rule." However, if we continue our contact with a large variety of gay men, or when the media shows more instances of non-stereotypical gay individuals, this "exception to the rule" defense eventually breaks down and attitude change occurs. As you may recall from Chapter 10, on May 6, 2013, Jason Collins became the first openly male gay athlete playing in a major American team sport. Why did he decide to publicly announce his sexual orientation? One of his many reasons was: "I want to march for tolerance, acceptance, and understanding" (Collins & Lidz, 2013).

Aggression

Why do people act aggressively? In this section, we explore both biological and psychosocial explanations for **aggression** and how aggression can be controlled or reduced.

Aggression Any behavior intended to cause psychological or physical harm to another individual.

Biological Explanations
Because aggression has such a long history and is found in all cultures, some scientists believe that humans are instinctively aggressive (Buss, 2008, 2011; DeWall et al., 2013; Glenn et al., 2011; Mehta et al., 2013). Most social psychologists, however, reject this "instinct" argument, but do accept the fact that biology plays a role. For example, twin studies suggest that some individuals are genetically predisposed to have hostile, irritable temperaments and to engage in aggressive acts (Åslund, 2013; Rhee & Waldman, 2011; Weyandt et al., 2011). Research with brain injuries and other disorders also has identified possible aggression circuits in the brain (Denson, 2011; Hammond & Hall, 2011; Pardini et al., 2011; Wood & Thomas, 2013). In addition, studies have linked the male hormone testosterone and lowered levels of some neurotransmitters with aggressive behavior (Ducci et al., 2013; Geniole et al., 2011; Mazur, 2013; Popma et al., 2007; Takahashi et al., 2011).

Psychosocial Explanations
Substance abuse (particularly alcohol abuse) is a major factor in many forms of aggression (Levinthal, 2011; Quinn et al., 2013; White et al., 2013). Similarly, aversive stimuli, such as loud noise, heat, pain, bullying, insults, and foul odors, also may increase aggression (Anderson, 2001; Anderson et al., 2008; Barash & Lipton, 2011; DeWall et al., 2013). According to the **frustration–aggression hypothesis**,

Frustration–aggression hypothesis A hypothesis which states that the blocking of a desired goal (frustration) creates anger that may lead to aggression.

developed by John Dollard and colleagues (1939), another aversive stimulus—frustration—creates anger, which for some leads to aggression (see *Real World Psychology*).

Rich Schultz/Getty Images

realworldpsychology   **Aggression in Major League Baseball**
Researchers who examined 57,293 Major League Baseball games from 1952 through 2009 found that on hot days baseball pitchers were more likely to deliberately throw and hit a batter in retaliation after a batter on their own team has been hit by the opposing pitcher (Larrick et al., 2011)! Can you see how this finding supports both aversive stimuli and frustration as psychosocial explanations for aggression?

In addition, social-learning theory suggests that people raised in a culture with aggressive models will develop more aggressive responses (Cohen & Leung, 2011; Matsumoto & Juang, 2013; Rhee & Waldman, 2011). For example, the United States has a high rate of violent crime, and there are widespread portrayals of violence on TV, the Internet, movies, and video games which may contribute to aggression in both children and adults (Anderson et al., 2010; Bastian et al., 2012; Donnerstein, 2011; Hasan et al., 2013; Huesmann et al., 2013). However, the research is controversial (Ferguson, 2010, 2012, 2013; Valadez & Ferguson, 2012), and the link between violent media and aggression appears to be at least a two-way street. Laboratory studies, correlational research, and cross-cultural studies have found both that exposure to violence increases aggressiveness and that aggressive children tend to seek out violent programs (Bartlett et al., 2008; Carnagey et al., 2007; Kalnin et al., 2011; Krahé, 2013; Qian et al., 2013).

How can we control or eliminate aggression? Some therapists advise their clients to release their aggressive impulses by engaging in harmless forms of aggression, such as exercising vigorously, punching a pillow, or watching competitive sports. But studies suggest that this type of *catharsis* doesn't really help and may only intensify the feeling (Bushman, 2002; Kuperstok, 2008).

A more effective approach is to introduce *incompatible responses*. Because certain emotional responses, such as empathy and humor, are incompatible with aggression, purposely making a joke or showing some sympathy for an opposing person's point of view can reduce anger and frustration (Baumeister & Bushman, 2014; DeWall et al., 2013; Kaukiainen et al., 1999; Weiner, 2006).

Altruism

After reading about prejudice, discrimination, and aggression, you will no doubt be relieved to discover that human beings also behave in positive ways. People help and support one another by donating blood, giving time and money to charities, helping stranded motorists, and so on. There are also times when people do not help. Let's consider both responses.

Altruism, or *prosocial behavior*, consists of actions designed to help others, with no obvious benefit to the helper. There are three key approaches to explaining why we help others, and a five-step decision process explains when and why we don't help **(Figure 14.15)**.

The **evolutionary theory of helping** suggests that altruism is an instinctual behavior that has evolved because it favors survival of the altruist's genes (Boyd et al., 2011; Curry et al., 2013; McNamara et al., 2008; Preston, 2013). By helping our own child or other relative, for example, we increase the odds of our genes' survival.

Other research suggests that altruism may actually be self-interest in disguise. According to this **egoistic model of helping**, we help others only because we

Altruism Prosocial behaviors designed to help others, with no obvious benefit to the helper.

Evolutionary theory of helping A theory which states that altruism is an instinctual behavior that has evolved because it favors survival of one's genes.

Egoistic model of helping A theory which states that altruism is motivated by anticipated gain—later reciprocation, increased self-esteem, or avoidance of distress and guilt.

FIGURE 14.15 THREE MODELS FOR HELPING

Note how each of these three helping model focuses on a different motivation. Which of the three models for helping shown in this figure do you think provides the best explanation for why someone might give food or money to the man in this photo?

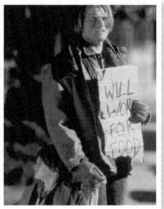

Bruce Ayers/Getty Images

hope for later reciprocation, because it makes us feel virtuous, or because it helps us avoid feeling guilty (Cialdini, 2009; Williams et al., 1998).

Opposing the evolutionary and egoistic models is the **empathy–altruism hypothesis** (Batson, 1991, 1998, 2006, 2011; Cao, 2013; Edele et al., 2013; Park et al., 2011). This perspective holds that simply seeing or hearing of another person's suffering can create *empathy*—a subjective grasp of that person's feelings or experiences. And when we feel empathic toward another, we are motivated to help that person for his or her own sake. The ability to empathize may even be innate. Research with infants in the first few hours of life shows that they become distressed and cry at the sound of another infant's cries (Hay, 1994; Hoffman, 1993).

Social psychologists have a long history of researching the impact of others on helping behavior (e.g., Fischer et al., 2011). But one of the most compelling and comprehensive explanations for helping or not helping comes from the research of John Darley and Bibb Latané (1970). They found that whether or not someone helps depends on a series of interconnected events and decisions: The potential helper must notice what is happening, interpret the event as an emergency, accept personal responsibility for helping, decide how to help, and then actually initiate the helping behavior **(Figure 14.16)**.

Empathy–altruism hypothesis A theory which states that we help because of empathy for someone in need.

FIGURE 14.16 WHEN AND WHY DON'T WE HELP?

According to Latané and Darley's five step decision process (1968), if our answer at each step is "yes," we will help others. If our answer is "no" at any point, the helping process ends.

Sam Sarkis/Photodisc/Getty

Bystander effect A phenomenon in which the greater the number of bystanders, the less likely it is that any one individual will feel responsible for seeking help or giving aid to someone who is in need of help.

How does this sequence explain television news reports and "caught on tape" situations in which people are robbed or attacked, and no one comes to their aid? The breakdown generally comes at the third stage—*taking personal responsibility for helping*. In follow-up interviews, most onlookers report that they failed to intervene because they were certain that someone must already have called the police. This so-called **bystander effect** is a well-known problem that affects our helping behaviors (see *Psychology and You*).

© Andrew.Johnson/iStockphoto

> **psychology and you** **Saving Your Own Life!** In one of the earliest studies of the power of the bystander effect, participants were asked to complete a questionnaire, either alone or with others. While they were working, a large amount of smoke was pumped into the room through a wall vent to simulate an emergency. As you might expect, most of the participants working alone, about 75%, quickly reported the smoke. In contrast, fewer than 40% reported smelling smoke when three other participants were in the room, and only 10% reported the smoke when they were with passive participants who ignored the smoke (Latane & Darley, 1968). Keep this study in mind when you're in a true emergency situation. Do not simply rely on others for information. Make your own quick decisions to act. It may save your life!

Why are we less likely to help when others are around? Researchers have suggested that when others are present we assume the responsibility for acting is shared, or diffused, among all onlookers. In contrast, when we're the lone observer, we recognize that we have the sole responsibility for acting. How can we promote helping? Considering what we've just learned about the bystander effect and the *diffusion of responsibility*, it's important to clarify when help is needed and then assign responsibility. For example, most parents teach their children to scream as loud as they can if they're being abducted by a stranger. Given that children often scream, can you see why this might not work? Instead, they should be taught to make eye contact with anyone who may be watching and then to shout something like: "This isn't my parent. Help me!" On the other hand, if you notice a situation in which it seems unclear whether someone needs help, simply ask: "Do you need help?" Highly publicized television programs, like ABC's "What Would You Do?" and "CNN Heroes," which honor and reward altruism, also increase helping. Finally, enacting laws that protect helpers from legal liability, so-called "good Samaritan" laws, also encourages helping behavior.

Interpersonal Attraction

Interpersonal attraction Positive feelings toward another.

What causes us to feel admiration, liking, friendship, intimacy, lust, or love? All these social experiences are reflections of **interpersonal attraction**, our positive feelings toward another. Psychologists have found three compelling factors in interpersonal attraction: *physical attractiveness*, *proximity*, and *similarity*. Each influences our attraction in different ways.

Physical Attractiveness

The way we look—including facial characteristics, body size and shape, and manner of dress—is one of the most important factors in our initial attraction, liking, or loving of others (Back et al., 2011; Buss, 2003, 2008, 2011; Cunningham et al., 2008; Regan, 2011, Sanderson, 2010). In addition, attractive individuals are seen as more poised, interesting, cooperative, achieving, sociable, independent, intelligent, healthy, and sexually warm than unattractive people (Jaeger, 2011; McColl & Truong, 2013; Moore et al., 2011; Tsukiura & Cabeza, 2011).

Interestingly, standards for attractiveness appear consistent across cultures, with most people showing a preference for faces that are average as opposed to "distinct" (Cunningham et al., 1995, 2002; Langlois et al., 2000; McArthur & Berry, 1987; Swami

& Harris, 2012). Cultures also show consistency in what they want in a mate. Women are valued more for looks and youth, whereas men are valued more for maturity, ambitiousness, and financial resources (Bryan et al., 2011; Buss, 1989, 2008, 2011; Chang et al., 2011; Li et al., 2011; Swami, 2011).

Why? Evolutionary psychologists would suggest that men prefer attractive women because youth and good looks generally indicate better health, sound genes, and high fertility. Similarly, women prefer men with maturity and resources because the responsibility of rearing and nurturing children has historically fallen primarily on women's shoulders.

So how do those of us who are not "superstar beautiful" manage to find mates? The good news is that people usually do not hold out for partners who are ideally attractive. Instead, both men and women tend to select partners whose physical attractiveness approximately matches their own (Regan, 1998, 2011; Sprecher & Regan, 2002; Taylor et al., 2011). Also, people use nonverbal flirting behavior to increase their attractiveness and signal interest to a potential romantic partner. Note that in heterosexual couples, the generally accepted norms are for the woman to first signal her interest and for the man to make the first approach (Lott, 2000, Moore, 1998).

Proximity

Attraction also depends on the two persons' being in the same place at the same time. Thus, *proximity*, or geographic nearness, is another major factor in attraction. One examination of over 300,000 Facebook users found that even though people can have relationships with people throughout the world, the likelihood of a friendship decreases as distance between people increases (Nguyen & Szymanski, 2012). If you're wondering if this is a case of correlation being confused with causation, that's great! You're becoming an educated consumer of research and a good critical thinker.

In fact, there is experimental evidence supporting a causative link between proximity and attraction. For example, oxytocin, a naturally occurring bodily chemical, is known to be a key facilitator of interpersonal attraction and parental attachment (Goodson, 2013; Weisman et al., 2012). In one very interesting experiment, the intranasal administration of oxytocin stimulated men in monogamous relationships, but not single ones, to keep a much greater distance between themselves and an attractive woman during a first encounter (Scheele et al., 2012). The researchers concluded that oxytocin may help maintain monogamous relationships by making men avoid close personal proximity to other women.

Why is proximity so important? It's largely due to the **mere-exposure effect**. Just as familiar people become more physically attractive over time, repeated exposure also increases overall liking (Monin, 2003; Rhodes et al., 2001). This makes sense from an evolutionary point of view. Things we have seen before are less likely to pose a threat than novel stimuli. It also explains why modern advertisers tend to run highly redundant ad campaigns with familiar faces and jingles. In short, repeated exposure increases liking! (See **Figure 14.17**.)

Mere-exposure effect A developed preference for people or things simply because they are familiar.

FIGURE 14.17 **THE FACE IN THE MIRROR**

As a result of the mere-exposure effect, we generally prefer a reversed image of ourselves (the one on the left, in this case) because it is the familiar face we're accustomed to seeing in the mirror. However, when presented with reversed and nonreversed photos, close friends prefer the nonreversed images (Mita et al., 1977).

Bernhard Kuhmsted/Retna

Similarity

The major cementing factor for long-term relationships, whether liking or loving, is *similarity*. We tend to prefer, and stay with, people who are most like us—those who share our ethnic background, social class, interests, and attitudes (Böhm et al., 2010; Caprara et al., 2007; Morry et al., 2011; Sanbonmatsu et al., 2011). In other words, "Birds of a feather flock together."

What about the old saying "opposites attract"? The term *opposites* here probably refers to personality traits rather than to social background or values. An attraction to a seemingly opposite person is more often based on the recognition that in one or two important personality traits, that person offers something we lack. In sum, lovers can enjoy some differences, but the more alike people are, the more both their loving and their liking endure.

The following *Psychology and You* feature offers a fun test of your understanding of the three factors in interpersonal attraction. Try it!

TEST YOURSELF: UNDERSTANDING INTERPERSONAL ATTRACTION

psychology and you

Based on your reading of this section, can you explain Kvack's love for the wooden dummy?

Answers: Research shows that similarity is the best predictor of long-term relationships. As shown here, however, many people ignore dissimilarities and hope that their chosen partner will change over time.

Loving Others

It's easy to see why interpersonal attraction is a fundamental building block of our feelings about others. But how do we make sense of love? Why do we love some people and not others? Many people find the subject to be alternately mysterious, exhilarating, comforting—and even maddening. In this section, we explore four perspectives on love—*Sternberg's triarchic theory, consummate love, romantic love,* and *companionate love.*

Robert Sternberg, a well-known researcher on creativity and intelligence (Chapter 8), produced a **triarchic** (triangular) **theory of love** (Sternberg, 1986, 1988, 2006) **(Figure 14.18)**, which suggests that different types and stages of love result from three basic components:

- **Intimacy**—emotional closeness and connectedness, mutual trust, friendship, warmth, private sharing of self-disclosure, and forming of "love maps."
- **Passion**—sexual attraction and desirability, physical excitement, a state of intense longing to be with the other.
- **Commitment**—permanence and stability, the decision to stay in the relationship for the long haul, and the feelings of security that go with this intention.

Triarchic theory of love Sternberg's theory that different stages and types of love result from three basic components—*intimacy, passion,* and *commitment.*

FIGURE 14.18 STERNBERG'S TRIARCHIC THEORY OF LOVE

According to Sternberg, we all experience various forms and stages of love, six of which are seen as being on the outside of the triangle. Only true *consummate love* is inside the triangle because it includes a healthy balance of intimacy, passion, and commitment. The balance among these three components naturally shifts and changes over the course of a relationship, but relationships based on only one or two of these elements are generally less fulfilling and less likely to survive.

For Sternberg, a healthy degree of all three components in both partners characterizes the fullest form of love, **consummate love**. Trouble occurs when one of the partners has a higher or lower need for one or more of the components. For example, if one partner has a much higher need for intimacy and the other partner has a stronger interest in passion, this lack of compatibility can be fatal to the relationship—unless the partners are willing to compromise and strike a mutually satisfying balance (Sternberg, 1988).

Consummate love Sternberg's strongest and most enduring type of love, based on a balanced combination of intimacy, passion, and commitment.

Romantic Love

When you think of romantic love, do you imagine falling in love, a magical experience that puts you on cloud nine? **Romantic love** has intrigued people throughout history. Its intense joys and sorrows also have inspired countless poems, novels, movies, and songs around the world. A cross-cultural study by anthropologists William Jankowiak and Edward Fischer found romantic love in 147 of the 166 societies they studied. They concluded that "romantic love constitutes a human universal or, at the least, a near universal" (1992, p. 154).

Romantic love may be almost universal, but even in the most devoted couples, the intense attraction and excitement of romantic love generally begin to fade 6 to 30 months after the relationship begins, whereas companionate love grows and evolves **(Figure 14.19)** (Hatfield & Rapson, 1996; Livingston, 1999). Why? Further research explains that **companionate love** is based on deep and lasting trust, caring, tolerance, and friendship, which slowly develops as couples grow and spend more time together. In contrast, romantic love is largely based on mystery and fantasy. People often fall in love with what they want another person to be—and these illusions usually fade with the realities of everyday living (Fletcher & Simpson, 2000; Levine, 2001).

Romantic love An intense feeling of attraction to another in an erotic context.

Companionate love Strong and lasting attraction characterized by deep and lasting trust, caring, tolerance, and friendship.

424

NetPhotos/Alamy

realworldpsychology **Can You Find Lasting Love Via On-Line Dating?** To test this question, researchers conducted an on-line survey of over 19,000 Americans (Cacioppo et al., 2013). Participants were asked if they were currently married, if they had ever been divorced, and/or if they met their current or former spouse on-line. Those who were married also completed a measure of relationship satisfaction.

Researchers then compared divorce rates and marital satisfaction for those who met their spouse on-line versus not on-line. Interestingly, they found a higher level of marital satisfaction and a significantly lower divorce rate for those whose marriages started on-line versus those that started off-line. Can you think of topics from this or any other chapter in this text, or from your own life experiences, that might explain why relationships which start on-line may in fact be longer lasting and more satisfying than those that start in more traditional ways?

FIGURE 14.19 **LOVE OVER THE LIFESPAN**

How can we keep romantic love alive? One of the most constructive ways is to recognize its fragile nature and nurture it with carefully planned surprises, flirting, flattery, and special dinners and celebrations. In the long run, however, romantic love's most important function might be to keep us attached long enough to move on to the deeper and more enduring companionate love.

As you can see in the figure, romantic love is high in the beginning of a relationship, but it tends to diminish over time, with periodic resurgences, or "spikes." In contrast, companionate love usually steadily increases over time. One reason may be that satisfaction grows as we come to recognize the lasting value of companionship and

— Romantic love
— Companionate love

Years of relationship

intimacy (Gottman, 2012; Jacobs Bao & Lyubomirsky, 2013; Regan, 2011). One tip for maximizing companionate love is to overlook each other's faults. People are more satisfied with relationships when they have a somewhat idealized perception of their partner (Barelds & Dijkstra, 2011; Campbell et al., 2001; Fletcher & Simpson, 2000; Regan, 2011). This makes sense in light of research on cognitive dissonance (discussed earlier). Idealizing our mates allows us to believe we have a good deal—and thereby avoid any cognitive dissonance that might arise when we see an attractive alternative. As Benjamin Franklin wisely said, "Keep your eyes wide open before marriage, and half shut afterwards."

Sisse Brimberg & Cotton Coulson/NG Image Collection

Annie Griffiths Belt/NG Image Collection

Alaska Stock Images/NG Image Collection

RETRIEVAL PRACTICE: SOCIAL RELATIONS

Self-Test

Completing this self-test and comparing your answers with those in Appendix B provides immediate feedback and helpful practice for exams. Additional interactive, self-tests are available at www.wiley.com/college/huffman.

1. _____ is a learned, generally negative, attitude toward specific people solely because of their membership in an identified group.

   a. Discrimination   b. Stereotyping
   c. Cognitive biasing   d. Prejudice

2. Research suggests that one of the best ways to decrease prejudice is to encourage _____.

   a. cooperation   b. friendly competition
   c. reciprocity of liking   d. conformity

3. Onlookers to crimes sometimes fail to respond to cries for help because of the _____ phenomenon.

   a. empathy–altruism   b. egoistic model
   c. inhumanity of large cities   d. diffusion of responsibility

4. The positive feelings we have toward others is called _____.

   a. affective relations   b. interpersonal attraction
   c. interpersonal attitudes   d. affective connections

5. A strong and lasting attraction characterized by deep and lasting trust, caring, tolerance, and friendship called _____.

   a. companionate love   b. intimate love
   c. passionate love   d. all these options

Think Critically

1 Do you believe you are free of prejudice? After reading this chapter, which of the many factors that cause prejudice do you think is most important to change?

2 Which of the three major theories of helping do you find best explains why you tend to help others?

realworldpsychology

Are men still more likely to get hired than equally qualified women?

How does simple nearness (proximity) influence attraction?

HINT: LOOK IN THE MARGIN FOR (Q4) AND (Q5)

Summary

1 SOCIAL COGNITION   399

- **Social psychology** is the study of the way other people influence our thoughts, feelings, and actions. **Social cognition**, the way we think about and interpret ourselves and others, relies on **attributions**, which help us explain behaviors and events. However, these attributions are frequently marred by the **fundamental attribution error (FAE)** and the **self-serving bias**. Both biases may depend in part on cultural factors.
- **Attitudes** have three ABC components: *affective, behavioral,* and *cognitive*. An efficient strategy for changing attitudes is to create **cognitive dissonance**. Like the tendency toward attributional biases, our experience of cognitive dissonance may depend on culture.

2 SOCIAL INFLUENCE   404

- Three factors drive conformity: *normative social influence, informational social influence,* and the role of *reference groups.* **Conformity** means going along with a group, while **obedience** means going along with a direct command, usually from someone in a position of authority. Milgram's research demonstrated the startling power of social situations to create obedience. The degree of deception and discomfort to which Milgram's participants were subjected raises serious ethical questions, and the same study would never be done today.
- The roles we play within groups strongly affect our behavior, as Zimbardo's Stanford Prison experiment showed. Zimbardo's study also demonstrated **deindividuation**. In addition, as we interact with others and discuss our opinions, **group**

polarization—a group's movement toward more extreme decisions—and **groupthink**—a group's tendency to strive for agreement and to avoid inconsistent information—tend to occur. Both processes may hinder effective decision making.

3 SOCIAL RELATIONS   413

- Like all other attitudes, **prejudice** includes three ABC components: *affective, behavioral,* and *cognitive.* Although the terms prejudice and **discrimination** are often used interchangeably, they are not the same. Five commonly cited sources of prejudice are *learning, personal experience, limited resources, displaced aggression,* and *mental shortcuts.*
- Several biological factors may help explain **aggression**, including genetic predisposition, aggression circuits in the brain, hormones, and neurotransmitters. Psychosocial explanations for aggression include substance abuse, aversive stimuli, media violence, and social learning.

- Evolutionary theory suggests that **altruism** is an evolved, instinctual behavior. Other research suggests that helping may actually be self-interest in disguise—the **egoistic model**. The **empathy–altruism hypothesis** proposes that although altruism is occasionally based on selfish motivations, it is sometimes truly selfless and motivated by empathy or concern for others. Latané and Darley found that in order for helping to occur, the potential helper must notice what is happening, interpret the event as an emergency, take personal responsibility for helping, decide how to help, and then actually initiate the helping behavior.
- Psychologists have found three compelling factors in **interpersonal attraction:** physical attractiveness, proximity, and similarity. Sternberg suggests that **consummate love** depends on a healthy degree of intimacy, passion, and commitment. **Romantic love** is an intense but generally short-lived attraction based on mystery and fantasy, whereas **companionate love** is a strong, lasting attraction based on trust, caring, tolerance, and friendship.

William Philpott/Reuters/© Corbis

⊚ applyingrealworldpsychology

We began this chapter with five intriguing Real World Psychology questions, and you were asked to revisit these questions at the end of each section. Questions like these have an important and lasting impact on all of our lives. See if you can answer these additional critical thinking questions related to real world examples.

1 What were the major social factors that contributed to Rosa Parks, pictured here, being willing to stand up against the bus driver who ordered her to give her seat to a white man? Does her model of disobedience encourage you to follow her example? Why or why not?

2 Can you think of an example from your own life, or from the life of one of your friends, in which attitudes did not match behavior? How might strong attitudes be a better predictor of actual behavior than weak ones?

3 In both Asch's conformity experiment and Milgram's study of obedience, the presence of another person greatly affected the behaviors of the research participants. How would you explain this?

4 Thinking about the most important romantic relationship in your life, explain how each of the major factors in interpersonal attraction—physical attractiveness, proximity, and similarity—affect this relationship.

5 Imagine yourself with a career as a social psychologist. Which of the key factors discussed in this chapter would you be most and least interested in studying? Why?

Key Terms

RETRIEVAL PRACTICE Write a definition for each term before turning back
to the referenced page to check your answer.

- actor–observer effect 400
- aggression 417
- altruism 418
- attitude 401
- attribution 399
- bystander effect 420
- cognitive dissonance 402
- companionate love 423
- conformity 405
- consummate love 423
- deindividuation 410
- discrimination 413
- egoistic model of helping 418

- empathy–altruism hypothesis 419
- evolutionary theory of helping 418
- foot-in-the-door technique 409
- frustration–aggression hypothesis 417
- fundamental attribution error (FAE) 399
- group polarization 410
- groupthink 411
- implicit bias 416
- Informational social influence 406
- ingroup favoritism 415
- interpersonal attraction 420
- mere-exposure effect 421
- normative social influence 405

- obedience 406
- outgroup homogeneity effect 415
- prejudice 413
- reference groups 406
- romantic love 423
- saliency bias 399
- self-serving bias 400
- social cognition 399
- social influence 404
- social psychology 399
- social relations 413
- stereotype 413
- triarchic theory of love 422

Appendix A

STATISTICS AND PSYCHOLOGY

We are constantly bombarded by numbers: "On sale for 30 percent off," "70 percent chance of rain," "9 out of 10 doctors recommend," "Your scores on the SAT were in the 75th percentile." Business and advertisers use numbers to convince us to buy their products. College admission officers use SAT percentile scores to help them decide who to admit to their programs. And, as you've seen throughout this text, psychologists use numbers to support or refute psychological theories and demonstrate that certain behaviors are indeed results of specific causal factors.

When we use numbers in these ways, we're all using statistics. **Statistics** is a branch of applied mathematics that uses numbers to describe and analyze information on a subject.

Statistics The branch of applied mathematics that deals with the collection, calculation, analysis, interpretation, and presentation of numerical facts or data.

If you're considering a major in psychology, you may be surprised to learn that a full course in statistics is generally required for this major. Why? Statistics make it possible for psychologists to quantify the information we obtain in our studies. We can then critically analyze and evaluate this information. Statistical analysis is imperative for researchers to describe, predict, or explain behavior. For instance, Albert Bandura (1973) proposed that watching violence on television causes aggressive behavior in children. In carefully controlled experiments, he gathered numerical information and analyzed it according to specific statistical methods. The statistical analysis helped him substantiate that the aggression of his participants and the aggressive acts they had seen on television were related, and that the relationship was not mere coincidence.

Although statistics is a branch of applied mathematics, you don't have to be a math whiz. Simple arithmetic is all we need for most of the calculations. For more complex statistics involving more complicated mathematics, computer programs are readily available. What is more important than learning the mathematical computations, however, is developing an understanding of when and why each type of statistic is used. The purpose of this appendix is to help you develop this understanding and to become a better consumer of the statistics that bombard us each day. In addition, we hope to increase your appreciation for the important role this form of math plays in the science of psychology.

GATHERING AND ORGANIZING DATA

Psychologists design their studies to facilitate gathering information about the factors they want to study. The information they obtain is known as *data* (data is plural; its singular is datum). When the data are gathered, they are generally in the form of numbers; if they aren't, they are converted to numbers. After they are gathered, the data must be organized in such a way that statistical analysis is possible. In the following section, we will examine the methods used to gather and organize information.

Variables

When studying a behavior, psychologists normally focus on one particular factor to determine whether it has an effect on the behavior. This factor is known as a *variable*, which is in effect anything that can assume more than one value (see Chapter 1). Height, weight, sex, eye color, and scores on an IQ test or a video game are all factors that can assume more than one value and are therefore variables. Some will vary between people, such as sex (you are either male *or* female but not both at the same time). Some may even vary within one person, such as scores on a video game (the same person might get 10,000 points on one try and only 800 on another). Opposed to a variable, anything that remains the same and does not vary is called a *constant*. If researchers use only women in their research, then sex is a constant, not a variable.

In nonexperimental studies, variables can be factors that are merely observed through naturalistic observation or case studies, or they can be factors about which people are questioned in a test or survey. In experimental studies, the two major types of variables are independent and dependent variables.

Independent variables are those that are manipulated by the experimenter. For example, suppose we were to conduct a study to determine whether the sex of the debater influences the outcome of a debate. In this study, one group of participants watches a videotape of a debate between a man arguing the "pro" side and a woman arguing the "con"; another group watches the same debate, but with the pro and con roles reversed. In such a study, the form of the presentation viewed by each group (whether "pro" is argued by a man or a woman) is the independent variable because the experimenter manipulates the form of presentation seen by each group. Another example might be a study to determine whether a particular drug has any effect on a manual dexterity task. To study this question, we would administer the drug to one group and no drug to another. The independent variable would be the amount of drug given (some or none). The independent variable is particularly important when using *inferential statistics*, which we will discuss later.

The *dependent variable* is a factor that results from, or depends on, the independent variable. It is a measure of some outcome or, most commonly, a measure of the participants' behavior. In the debate example, each subject's choice of the winner of the debate would be the dependent variable. In the drug experiment, the dependent variable would be each subject's score on the manual dexterity task.

Frequency Distributions

After conducting a study and obtaining measures of the variable(s) being studied, psychologists need to organize the data in a meaningful way. **Table A.1** presents test scores from a Math Aptitude Test collected from 50 college students. This information is called *raw data* because there is no order to the numbers. They are presented as they were collected and are therefore "raw."

The lack of order in raw data makes them difficult to study. Thus, the first step in understanding the results of an experiment is to impose some order on the raw data. There are several ways to do this. One of the simplest is to create a *frequency distribution*, which shows the number of times a score or event occurs. Although frequency distributions are helpful in several ways, the major advantages are that

TABLE A.1	MATH APTITUDE TEST SCORES FOR 50 COLLEGE STUDENTS			
73	57	63	59	50
72	66	50	67	51
63	59	65	62	65
62	72	64	73	66
61	68	62	68	63
59	61	72	63	52
59	58	57	68	57
64	56	65	59	60
50	62	68	54	63
52	62	70	60	68

they allow us to see the data in an organized manner and they make it easier to represent the data on a graph.

The simplest way to make a frequency distribution is to list all the possible test scores, then tally the number of people *(N)* who received those scores. **Table A.2** presents a frequency distribution using the raw data from Table A.1. As you can see, the data are now easier to read. Note how most of the test scores lie in the middle with only a few at the very high or very low end. This was not at all evident from looking at the raw data.

TABLE A.2	FREQUENCY DISTRIBUTION OF 50 STUDENTS ON MATH APTITUDE TEST		
Score	Frequency	Score	Frequency
73	2	61	2
72	3	60	2
71	0	59	5
70	1	58	1
69	0	57	3
68	5	56	1
67	1	55	0
66	2	54	1
65	3	53	0
64	2	52	2
63	5	51	1
62	5	50	3
Total			50

This type of frequency distribution is practical when the number of possible scores is 20 or fewer. However, when there are more than 20 possible scores it can be even harder to make sense out of the frequency distribution than the raw data. This can be seen in **Table A.3**, which presents the hypothetical Psychology Aptitude Test scores for 50 students. Even though there are only 50 actual scores in this table, the number of possible scores ranges from a high of 1390 to a low of 400. If we included zero frequencies there would be 100 entries in a frequency distribution of

TABLE A.3	PSYCHOLOGY APTITUDE TEST SCORES FOR 50 COLLEGE STUDENTS			
1350	750	530	540	750
1120	410	780	1020	430
720	1080	1110	770	610
1130	620	510	1160	630
640	1220	920	650	870
930	660	480	940	670
1070	950	680	450	990
690	1010	800	660	500
860	520	540	880	1090
580	730	570	560	740

this data, making the frequency distribution much more difficult to understand than the raw data. If there are more than 20 possible scores, therefore, a *group frequency distribution* is normally used.

In a *group frequency distribution*, individual scores are represented as members of a group of scores or as a range of scores (see **Table A.4**). These groups are called *class intervals*. Grouping these scores makes it much easier to make sense out of the distribution, as you can see from the relative ease in understanding Table A.4 as compared to Table A.3. Group frequency distributions are easier to represent on a graph.

TABLE A.4	GROUP FREQUENCY DISTRIBUTION OF PSYCHOLOGY APTITUDE TEST SCORES FOR 50 COLLEGE STUDENTS

Class Interval	Frequency
1300–1390	1
1200–1290	1
1100–1190	4
1000–1090	5
900–990	5
800–890	4
700–790	7
600–690	10
500–590	9
400–490	4
Total	50

When graphing data from frequency distributions, the class intervals are represented along the *abscissa* (the horizontal or *x* axis). The frequency is represented along the *ordinate* (the vertical or *y* axis). Information can be graphed in the form of a bar graph, called a *histogram*, or in the form of a point or line graph, called a *polygon*. **Figure A.1** shows a histogram presenting the data from Table A.4. Note that the class intervals are represented along the bottom line of the graph (the *x* axis) and the height of the bars indicates the frequency in each class interval. Now look at **Figure A.2**. The information presented here is exactly the same as that in Figure A.1 but is represented in the form of a polygon rather than a histogram. Can you see how both graphs illustrate the same information? Even though graphs like these are quite common today, we have found that many students have never been formally taught how to read graphs, which is the topic of our next section.

FIGURE A.1 **A HISTOGRAM ILLUSTRATING THE INFORMATION FOUND IN TABLE A4**

FIGURE A.2 **A POLYGON ILLUSTRATING THE INFORMATION FOUND IN TABLE A4**

How to Read a Graph

Every graph has several major parts. The most important are the labels, the axes (the vertical and horizontal lines), and the points, lines, or bars. Find these parts in Figure A.1.

The first thing we should all notice when reading a graph are the labels because they tell what data are portrayed. Usually the data consist of the descriptive statistics, or the numbers used to measure the dependent variables. For example, in Figure A.1 the horizontal axis is labeled "Psychology Aptitude Test Scores," which is the dependent variable measure; the vertical axis is labeled "Frequency," which means the number of occurrences. If a graph is not labeled, as we sometimes see in TV commercials or magazine ads, it is useless and should be ignored. Even when a graph *is* labeled, the labels can be misleading. For example, if graph designers want to distort the information, they can elongate one of the axes. Thus, it is important to pay careful attention to the numbers as well as the words in graph labels.

Next, we need to focus on the bars, points, or lines on the graph. In the case of histograms like the one in Figure A.1, each bar represents the class interval. The width of the bar stands for the width of the class interval, whereas the height of the bar stands for the frequency in that interval. Look at the third bar from the left in Figure A.1. This bar represents the interval "600 to 690 Psychology Aptitude Scores," which has a frequency of 10. Can you see how this directly corresponds to the same class interval in Table A.4? Graphs and tables are both merely alternate ways of illustrating information.

Reading point or line graphs is the same as reading a histogram. In a point graph, each point represents two numbers, one found along the horizontal axis and the other found along the vertical axis. A polygon is identical to a point graph except that it has lines connecting the points. Figure A.2 is an example of a polygon, where each point represents a class interval and is placed at the center of the interval and at the height corresponding to the frequency of that interval. To make the graph easier to read, the points are connected by straight lines.

Displaying the data in a frequency distribution or in a graph is much more useful than merely presenting raw data and can be especially helpful when researchers are trying to find relations between certain factors. However, as we explained earlier, if psychologists want to make precise predictions or explanations, we need to perform specific mathematical computations on the data. How we use these computations, or statistics, is the topic of our next section.

USES OF THE VARIOUS STATISTICS

The statistics psychologists use in a study depend on whether they are trying to describe and predict behavior or explain it. When they use statistics to describe behavior, as in reporting the average score on the hypothetical Psychology Aptitude Test, they are using **descriptive statistics**. When they use them to explain behavior, as Bandura did in his study of children modeling aggressive behavior seen on TV, they are using **inferential statistics**.

Descriptive statistics Mathematical methods used to describe and summarize sets of data in a meaningful way.

Inferential statistics Mathematical procedures that provide a measure of confidence about how likely it is that a certain result appeared by chance.

Descriptive Statistics

Descriptive statistics are the numbers used to describe the dependent variable. They can be used to describe characteristics of a *population* (an entire group, such as all people living in the United States) or a *sample* (a part of a group, such as a randomly selected group of 25 students from Cornell University). The major descriptive statistics include measures of central tendency (mean, median, and mode), measures of variation (variance and standard deviation), and correlation.

Mean The arithmetic average of a distribution, which is obtained by adding the values of all the scores and dividing by the number of scores (N).

Median The halfway point in a set of data; half the scores fall above the median, and half fall below it.

Mode The score that occurs most frequently in a data set.

Measures of Central Tendency

Statistics indicating the center of the distribution are called *measures of central tendency* and include the mean, median, and mode. They are all scores that are typical of the center of the distribution. The **mean** is the arithmetic average, and it is what most of us think of when we hear the word "average." The **median** is the middle score in a distribution—half the scores fall above it and half fall below it. The **mode** is the score that occurs most often.

Mean What is your average exam score in your psychology class? What is the average yearly rainfall in your part of the country? What is the average reading test score in your city? When these questions ask for the average, they are really asking for the "mean." The arithmetic *mean* is the weighted average of all the raw scores, which is computed by totaling all the raw scores and then dividing that total by the number of scores added together. In statistical computation, the mean is represented by an *"X"* with a bar above it ($\overline{X}$, pronounced *"X* bar"), each individual raw score by an "X," and the total number of scores by an *"N."* For example, if we wanted to compute the $\overline{X}$ of the raw statistics test scores in Table A.1, we would sum all the X's (Σ, with Σ meaning sum) and divide by N (number of scores). In Table A.1, the sum of all the scores is equal to 3100 and there are 50 scores. Therefore, the mean of these scores is

$$\overline{X} = \frac{3100}{50} = 62$$

Table A.5 illustrates how to calculate the mean for 10 IQ scores.

TABLE A.5	COMPUTATION OF THE MEAN FOR 10 IQ SCORES
IQ Scores X	
143	
127	
116	
98	
85	
107	
106	
98	
104	
116	
$\Sigma X = 1100$	
Mean $= \overline{X} = \dfrac{\Sigma X}{N} = \dfrac{1{,}100}{10} = 110$	

Median The *median* is the middle score in the distribution once all the scores have been arranged in rank order. If N (the number of scores) is odd, then there actually is a middle score and that middle score is the median. When N is even, there are two middle scores and the median is the mean of those two scores. **Table A.6** shows the computation of the median for two different sets of scores, one set with 15 scores and one with 10.

TABLE A.6	COMPUTATION OF MEDIAN FOR ODD AND EVEN NUMBERS OF IQ SCORES
IQ	IQ
139	137
130	135
121	121
116	116
107	108 ← middle score
101	106 ← middle score
98	105
96 ← middle score	101
84	98
83	97
82	N = 10
75	N is even
75	
68	
65	Median = $\dfrac{106 + 108}{2}$ = 107
N = 15	
N is odd	

TABLE A.7	FINDING THE MODE FOR TWO DIFFERENT DISTRIBUTIONS
IQ	IQ
139	139
138	138
125	125
116 ←	116 ←
116 ←	116 ←
116 ←	116 ←
107	107
100	98 ←
98	98 ←
98	98 ←
Mode = most frequent score	Mode = 116 and 98
Mode = 116	

Mode Of all the measures of central tendency, the easiest to compute is the *mode*, which is merely the most frequent score. It is computed by finding the score that occurs most often. Whereas there is always only one mean and only one median for each distribution, there can be more than one mode. **Table A.7** shows how to find the mode in a distribution with one mode (unimodal) and in a distribution with two modes (bimodal).

There are several advantages to each of these measures of central tendency, but in psychological research the mean is used most often. A book solely covering psychological statistics will provide a more thorough discussion of the relative values of these measures.

Measures of Variation

When describing a distribution, it is not sufficient merely to give the central tendency; it is also necessary to give a *measure of variation*, which is a measure of the spread of the scores. By examining this **range**, or spread of scores, we can determine whether the scores are bunched around the middle or tend to extend away from the middle. **Figure A.3** shows three different distributions, all with the same mean but with different spreads of scores. You can see from this figure that, in order to describe these different distributions accurately, there must be some measures of the variation in their spread. The most widely used measure of variation is the **standard deviation**, which is represented by a lowercase s. The standard deviation is a standard measurement of how much the scores in a distribution deviate from the mean. The formula for the standard deviation is

$$s = \sqrt{\frac{\Sigma(X - \bar{X})^2}{N}}$$

Table A.8 illustrates how to compute the standard deviation.

Most distributions of psychological data are bell-shaped. That is, most of the scores are grouped around the mean, and the farther the scores are from the mean in either direction, the fewer the scores. Notice the bell shape of the distribution

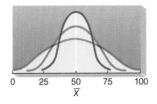

0   25   50   75   100
$\bar{X}$

FIGURE A.3 THREE DISTRIBUTIONS HAVING THE SAME MEAN BUT A DIFFERENT VARIABILITY

Range A measure of the dispersion of scores between the highest and lowest scores.

Standard deviation A computed measure of how much scores in a sample differ from the mean of the sample.

415

TABLE A.8	COMPUTATION OF THE STANDARD DEVIATION FOR 10 IQ SCORES	
IQ Scores X	$X - \overline{X}$	$(X - \overline{X})^2$
143	33	1089
127	17	289
116	6	36
98	−12	144
85	−25	625
107	−3	9
106	−4	16
98	−12	144
104	−6	36
116	6	36
$\Sigma X = 1100$		$\Sigma(X - \overline{X})^2 = 2424$

Standard Deviation = s

$$= \sqrt{\frac{\Sigma(X - \overline{X})^2}{N}} - \sqrt{\frac{2424}{10}}$$

$$= \sqrt{242.4} = 15.569$$

Percent of cases under portions of the normal curve

0.13% 2.15% 13.59% 34.13% 34.13% 13.59% 2.15% 0.13%

−4 −3 −2 −1 0 +1 +2 +3 +4

Standard deviations

FIGURE A.4 THE NORMAL DISTRIBUTION FORMS A BELL-SHAPED CURVE

In a normal distribution, two-thirds of the scores lie between one standard deviation above and one standard deviation below the mean.

Normal distribution A symmetrical, bell-shaped curve that represents a set of data in which most scores occur in the middle of the possible range, with fewer and fewer scores near the extremes.

in **Figure A.4**. Distributions such as this are called **normal distributions**. In normal distributions, as shown in Figure A.4, approximately two-thirds of the scores fall within a range that is one standard deviation below the mean to one standard deviation above the mean. For example, the Wechsler IQ tests (see Chapter 7) have a mean of 100 and a standard deviation of 15. This means that approximately two-thirds of the people taking these tests will have scores between 85 and 115.

Correlation

Suppose for a moment that you are sitting in the student union with a friend. To pass the time, you and your friend decide to play a game in which you try to guess the height of the next man who enters the union. The winner, the one whose guess is closest to the person's actual height, gets a piece of pie paid for by the loser. When it is your turn, what do you guess? If you're like most people, you'll probably try to estimate the mean of all the men in the union and use that as your guess. The mean is almost always our best guess when we have no other information.

Now let's change the game a little and add a friend who stands outside the union and weighs the next man who enters the union. If your friend texts you with the information that this man weighs 125 pounds, without seeing him would you still predict that he's of average height? Probably not. You'd most likely guess that he's below the mean. Why? Because you intuitively understand that there is a *correlation* (Chapter 1), a relationship, between height and weight, with tall people usually weighing more than short people. Given that 125 pounds is less than the average weight for men, you'll probably guess a less-than-average height. The statistic used to measure this type of relationship between two variables is called a correlation coefficient.

Correlation Coefficient A *correlation coefficient* (Chapter 1), measures the relationship between two variables, such as height and weight or IQ and annual income. Given any two variables, there are three possible relationships between them: *positive, negative*, and *zero* (no relationship). A *positive relationship* exists when the two variables vary in the same direction (e.g., as height increases, weight normally also increases). A *negative relationship* occurs when the two variables vary in opposite directions (e.g., as temperatures go up, hot chocolate sales go down). There is a *zero*

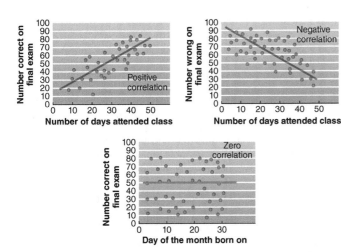

Positive correlation (top left): as the number of days of class attendance increases, so does the number of correct exam items. Negative correlation (top right): as the number of days of class attendance increases, the number of incorrect exam items decreases. Zero correlation (bottom): the day of the month on which one is born has no relationship to the number of exam items correct.

(no) *relationship* when the two variables vary totally independently of one another (e.g., there is no relationship between your height and the color of your toothbrush). **Figure A.5** illustrates these three types of correlations.

The computation and the formula for a correlation coefficient (correlation coefficient is delineated by the letter *"r")* are shown in **Table A.9**. The correlation coefficient *(r)* always has a value between +1 and −1 (it is never greater than +1 and it is never smaller than −1). When *r* is close to +1, it signifies a high positive relationship between the two variables (as one variable goes up, the other variable also goes up). When *r* is close to −1, it signifies a high negative relationship between the two variables (as one variable goes up, the other variable goes down). When *r* is 0, there is no linear relationship between the two variables being measured.

TABLE A.9	COMPUTATION OF CORRELATION COEFFICIENT BETWEEN HEIGHT AND WEIGHT FOR 10 MEN			
Height (inches) X	X^2	Weight (pounds) Y	Y^2	XY
73	5,329	210	44,100	15,330
64	4,096	133	17,689	8,512
65	4,225	128	16,384	8,320
70	4,900	156	24,336	10,920
74	5,476	189	35,721	13,986
68	4,624	145	21,025	9,860
67	4,489	145	21,025	9,715
72	5,184	166	27,556	11,952
76	5,776	199	37,601	15,124
71	5,041	159	25,281	11,289
700	49,140	1,630	272,718	115,008

$$r = \frac{N \cdot \Sigma XY - \Sigma X \cdot \Sigma Y}{\sqrt{[N \cdot \Sigma X^2 - (\Sigma X)^2]} \sqrt{[N \cdot \Sigma Y^2 - (\Sigma Y)^2]}}$$

$$r = \frac{10 \cdot 115,008 - 700 \cdot 1,630}{\sqrt{[10 \cdot 49,140 - 700^2]} \sqrt{[10 \cdot 272,718 - 1,630^2]}}$$

$$r = 0.92$$

Correlation coefficients can be quite helpful in making predictions. Bear in mind, however, that predictions are just that: *predictions*. They will have some error as long as the correlation coefficients on which they are based are not perfect (+1 or −1). Also, correlations cannot reveal any information regarding causation. Merely because two factors are correlated, it does not mean that one factor causes the other. Consider, for example, ice cream consumption and swimming pool use. These two variables are positively correlated with one another, in that as ice cream consumption increases, so does swimming pool use. But nobody would suggest that eating ice cream *causes* swimming, or vice versa. Similarly, just because LeBron James eats Wheaties and can do a slam dunk it does not mean that you will be able to do one if you eat the same breakfast. The only way to determine the *cause* of behavior is to conduct an experiment and analyze the results by using inferential statistics.

Inferential Statistics

Knowing the descriptive statistics associated with different distributions, such as the mean and standard deviation, can enable us to make comparisons between various distributions. By making these comparisons, we may be able to observe whether one variable is related to another or whether one variable has a causal effect on another. When we design an experiment specifically to measure causal effects between two or more variables, we use *inferential statistics* to analyze the data collected. Although there are many inferential statistics, the one we will discuss is the t-test, since it is the simplest.

t-Test Suppose we believe that drinking alcohol causes a person's reaction time to slow down. To test this hypothesis, we recruit 20 participants and separate them into two groups. We ask the participants in one group to drink a large glass of orange juice with one ounce of alcohol for every 100 pounds of body weight (e.g., a person weighing 150 pounds would get 1.5 ounces of alcohol). We ask the control group to drink an equivalent amount of orange juice with no alcohol added. Fifteen minutes after the drinks, we have each participant perform a reaction time test that consists of pushing a button as soon as a light is flashed. (The reaction time is the time between the onset of the light and the pressing of the button.) **Table A.10** shows the data from this hypothetical experiment. It is clear from the data that there is definitely a difference in the reaction times of the two groups: There is an obvious difference between the means. However, it is possible that this difference is due merely to chance. To determine whether the difference is real or due to chance, we can conduct a *t*-test. We have run a sample *t*-test in Table A.10.

The logic behind a *t*-test is relatively simple. In our experiment we have two samples. If each of these samples is from the *same* population (e.g., the population of all people, whether drunk or sober), then any difference between the samples will be due to chance. On the other hand, if the two samples are from *different* populations (e.g., the population of drunk individuals *and* the population of sober individuals), then the difference is a significant difference and not due to chance.

If there is a significant difference between the two samples, then the independent variable must have caused that difference. In our example, there is a significant difference between the alcohol and the no alcohol groups. We can tell this because *p* (the probability that this *t* value will occur by chance) is less than .05. To obtain the *p*, we need only look up the *t* value in a statistical table, which is found in any statistics book. In our example, because there is a significant difference between the groups, we can reasonably conclude that the alcohol did cause a slower reaction time.

TABLE A.10	REACTION TIMES IN MILLISECONDS (MSEC) FOR PARTICIPANTS IN ALCOHOL AND NO ALCOHOL CONDITIONS AND COMPUTATION OF *t*

RT (msec) Alcohol X_1	RT (msec) No Alcohol X_2
200	143
210	137
140	179
160	184
180	156
187	132
196	176
198	148
140	125
159	120
$SX_1 = 1{,}770$	$SX_2 = 1{,}500$
$N_1 = 10$	$N_2 = 10$
$\bar{X}_1 = 177$	$\bar{X}_2 = 150$
$s_1 = 24.25$	$s_2 = 21.86$

$$\Sigma_{\bar{X}1} = \frac{s}{\sqrt{N_1 - 1}} = 8.08 \qquad \Sigma_{\bar{X}2} = \frac{s}{\sqrt{N_2 - 1}} = 7.29$$

$$S_{\bar{X}_1 - \bar{X}_2} = \sqrt{S_{\bar{X}_1}^2 + S_{\bar{X}_2}^2} = \sqrt{8.08^2 + 7.29^2} = 10.88$$

$$t = \frac{\bar{X}_1 - \bar{X}_2}{S_{\bar{X}1 - \bar{X}2}} \quad \frac{177 - 150}{10.88} = 2.48$$

$$t = 2.48, p < .05$$

Appendix B

ANSWERS TO SELF-TEST RETRIEVAL PRACTICE QUESTIONS AND RESEARCH CHALLENGES

Chapter 1   Introduction and Research Methods

Self-Test—*Introducing Psychology* (p. 13) 1. d. 2. a. 3. c. 4. a. **Self-Test—*The Science of Psychology* (p. 17)** 1. c. 2. d. 3. b. 4. Step 1 = Observation and literature review, Step 2 = Testable hypothesis, Step 3 = Research design, Step 4 = Data collection and analysis, Step 5 = Publication, Step 6 = Theory development. **Self-Test—*Research Methods* (p. 27)** 1. b. 2. b. 3. c. 4. d. 5. b. **Self-Test—*Strategies for Student Success* (p. 30)** 1. Survey, Question, Read, Recite, Review, and wRite. 2. a. 3. d. 4. a. ***Research Challenge* (p. 25)**. Question 1: Study 1 = experimental; Study 2 = descriptive and correlational. As you'll discover in later psychology classes, descriptive and correlational studies often overlap. Question 2: Study 1: IV = political similarity; DV = interest in dating, ratings of physical attractiveness. Study 2: If you chose descriptive, the answer is archival research. If you chose correlational, this is a positive correlation.

Chapter 2   Neuroscience and Biological Foundations

Self-Test—*Our Genetic Inheritance* (pp. 36–37) 1. b. 2. d. 3. a. 4. a. **Self-Test—*Neural Bases of Behavior* (p. 42)** 1. c. 2. b. 3. c. 4. b. **Self-Test—*Nervous System Organization* (p. 48)** 1. d. 2. d. 3. d. 4. a. **Self-Test—*A Tour Through the Brain* (pp. 57–58)** 1. Compare your answers to Figure 2.19 (p. 49). 2. Compare your answers to Figure 2.24 (p. 53). 3. b. 4. b. ***Research Challenge* (p. 54)**. Question 1: Descriptive. Question 2: Case study.

Chapter 3   Stress and Health Psychology

Self-Test—*Understanding Stress* (pp. 68–69) 1. d. 2. c. 3. c. 4. b. **Self-Test—*Stress and Illness* (p. 74)** 1. d. 2. d. 3. c. 4. b. **Self-Test—*Health Psychology and Stress Management* (p. 79)** 1. d. 2. a. 3. b. 4. d. ***Research Challenge* (p. 70)**. Question 1: Descriptive and correlational. As you'll discover in later psychology classes, descriptive and correlational studies often overlap. Question 2: If you chose descriptive, the answer is survey/interview. If you chose correlational, this is a positive correlation.

Chapter 4   Sensation and Perception

Self-Test—*Understanding Sensation* (p. 89) 1. a. 2. c. 3. a. 4. b. **Self-Test—*How We See and Hear* (pp. 94–95)** 1. Compare your answers to Figure 4.8 (p. 91). 2. c. 3. Compare your answers to Figure 4.9 (p. 93). 4. c. **Self-Test—*Our Other Important Senses* (p. 99)** 1. c. 2. c. 3. d. 4. d. **Self-Test—*Understanding Perception* (p. 108–109)** 1. c. 2. b. 3. a. 4. b. 5. b. ***Research Challenge* (p. 97)**. Question 1: Experimental. Question 2: IV = whether and when drank carrot juice. DV = liking of carrot-flavored cereal, amount of cereal eaten. Note that experiments, like this one, often contain more than one level (or treatment) for the independent variable (IV), as well as multiple measures for the dependent variable (DV).

Chapter 5   States of Consciousness

Self-Test—*Consciousness, Sleep, and Dreaming* (pp. 125–126) 1. b. 2. d. 3. c. 4. a. **Self-Test—*Psychoactive Drugs* (pp. 132–133)** 1. a. 2. c. 3. a. 4. d. **Self-Test—*Meditation and Hypnosis* (p. 136)** 1. d. 2. d. 3. c. 4. c. ***Research Challenge* (p. 116)**. Question 1: Study 1 = Descriptive. Study 2 = Experimental. Question 2: Study 1 = Naturalistic observation. Study 2: IV = condition (no cell phone, cell phone, intoxicated). DV = number of accidents, brake reaction time, speed. Note that experiments, like this one, often contain more than one level (or treatment) for the independent variable (IV), as well as multiple measures for the dependent variable (DV).

Chapter 6   Learning

Self-Test—*Classical Conditioning* (p. 159) 1. c. 2. c. 3. d. 4. d. **Self-Test—*Operant Conditioning* (pp. 167–168)** 1. b. 2. a. 3. c. 4. c. **Self-Test—*Cognitive-Social Learning* (p. 172)** 1. c. 2. c. 3. a. 4. b. **Self-Test—*Biology of Learning* (p. 175)** 1. d. 2. b. 3. d. 4. c. ***Research Challenge* (p. 171)**. Question 1: Descriptive. Question 2: Survey/interview.

Chapter 7   Memory

Self-Test—*The Nature of Memory* (p. 188) 1. d. 2. a. 3. b. 4. c. **Self-Test—*Forgetting* (p. 193)** 1. a. 2. b. 3. c. 4. b. **Self-Test—*Biological Bases of Memory* (p. 199)** 1. c. 2. d. 3. d. 4. c. **Self-Test—*Memory Distortions* (p. 204)** 1. c. 2. a. 3. c. 4. d. ***Research Challenge* (p. 202)**. Question 1: Descriptive. Question 2: Survey/interview.

Chapter 8   Thinking, Language, and Intelligence

Self-Test—*Thinking* (p. 215) 1. c. 2. b. 3. a. 4. d. **Self-Test—*Language* (p. 221)** 1. d. 2. a. 3. b. 4. d. **Self-Test—*Intelligence* (p. 233)** 1. d. 2. b. 3. c. 4. d. ***Research Challenge* (p. 231)**. Question 1: Descriptive. Question 2: Archival research.

Chapter 9   Lifespan Development

Self-Test—*Studying Development* (p. 242) 1. d. 2. d. 3. a. 4. c. **Self-Test—*Physical Development* (pp. 250–251)** 1. b. 2. d. 3. a. 4. a. 5. d. **Self-Test—*Cognitive Development* (p. 259)** 1. c. 2. d. 3. d. 4. c. **Self-Test—*Social-Emotional Development* (pp. 269–270)** 1. a. 2. d. 3. c. 4. b. ***Research Challenge* (p. 239)**. Question 1: Descriptive. Question 2: Case study.

Chapter 10   Motivation and Emotion

Self-Test—*Theories of Motivation* (p. 279) 1. a 2. d. 3. b. 4. d. **Self-Test— *Motivation and Behavior* (p. 290)** 1. a. 2. c. 3. c. 4. c. **Self-Test—*Components and Theories of Emotion* (p. 298)** 1. a. 2. a. 3. d. 4. a. *Research Challenge* **(p. 286)**. Question 1: Descriptive. Question 2: Survey/interview.

Chapter 11   Personality

Self-Test—*Psychoanalytic/Psychodynamic Theories* (pp. 308–309) 1. d. 2. b. 3. d. 4. c. 5. c. **Self-Test—*Trait Theories* (p. 313)** 1. c. 2. a. 3. d. 4. e. **Self-Test— *Humanistic Theories* (p. 317)** 1. a. 2. c. 3. c. 4. c. **Self-Test—*Social-Cognitive Theories* (p. 320)** 1. c. 2. d. 3. b. 4. a. **Self-Test—*Biological Theories* (p. 323)** 1. b. 2. d. 3. a. 4. b. **Self-Test—*Personality Assessment* (p. 329)** 1. d. 2. a. 3. d. 4. b. *Research Challenge* **(p. 311)**. Question 1: Descriptive and correlational. As you'll discover in later psychology classes, descriptive and correlational studies often overlap. Question 2: If you chose descriptive, the answer is naturalistic observation. If you chose correlational, this is a positive correlation.

Chapter 12   Psychological Disorders

Self-Test—*Studying Psychological Disorders* (p. 340) 1. c. 2. b. 3. a. 4. Compare your answers with Figure 12.2 (p. 334). **Self-Test—*Anxiety Disorders* (p. 344)** 1. Compare your answers with Figure 12.4 (p. 341). 2. a. 3. a. 4. c. **Self-Test— *Depressive and Bipolar Disorders* (p. 350)** 1. c. 2. a. 3. d. 4. d. **Self-Test— *Schizophrenia* (p. 355)** 1. a. 2. c. 3. b. 4. a. **Self-Test—*Other Disorders* (pp. 359–360)** 1. b. 2. a. 3. b. 4. d. **Self-Test— *Gender and Cultural Effects* (p. 364)** 1. d. 2. d. 3. a. 4. b. *Research Challenge* (p. 337). Question 1: Descriptive. Question 2: Survey/interview.

Chapter 13   Therapy

Self-Test—*Talk Therapies* (p. 376) 1. a. 2. c. 3. c. 4. b. **Self-Test—*Behavior Therapies* (pp. 380–381)** 1. b. 2. c. 3. c. 4. b. **Self-Test—*Biomedical Therapies* (p. 386)** 1. d. 2. b. 3. b. 4. c. **Self-Test— *Psychotherapy in Perspective* (p. 394)** 1. c. 2. c. 3. a. 4. d. *Research Challenge* **(p. 388)**. Question 1: Experimental. Question 2: IV = condition (whether completed writing exercises or not). DV = change in marital satisfaction.

Chapter 14   Social Psychology

Self-Test—*Social Cognition* (pp. 403–404) 1. c. 2. c. 3. a. 4. a. cognitive, b. affective, c. behavioral. 5. b. **Self-Test— *Social Influence* (pp. 412–413)** 1. c. 2. c. 3. d. 4. b. 5. c. **Self-Test—*Social Relations* (p. 425)** 1. d. 2. a. 3. d. 4. b. 5. a. *Research Challenge* **(p. 402)**. Question 1: Experimental. Question 2: IV = amount paid ($1, $20). DV = attitudes towards the task.

Glossary

Abnormal behavior Patterns of behaviors, thoughts, or emotions considered pathological (diseased or disordered) for one or more of these four reasons: deviance, dysfunction, distress, or danger.

Absolute threshold The minimum amount of stimulation necessary to consciously detect a stimulus 50% of the time.

Accommodation According to Piaget, the process of adjusting (accommodating) existing mental patterns (schemas) or developing new ones to better fit with new information; works in tandem with assimilation (Chapter 9).

Accommodation The process by which the eye's ciliary muscles change the shape (thickness) of the lens so that light is focused on the retina; adjustment of the eye's lens permitting focusing on near and distant objects (Chapter 4).

Achievement motivation The desire to excel, especially in competition with others.

Acquisition The final step in a classical conditioning experiment during which the conditioned stimulus (CS) elicits the conditioned response (CR).

Action potential A neural impulse, or brief electrical charge, that carries information along the axon of a neuron; movement is generated when positively charged ions move in and out through channels in the axon's membrane.

Activation–synthesis hypothesis of dreams The perspective that dreams are by-products of random stimulation of brain cells, which the brain attempts to combine (or synthesize) into coherent patterns, known as dreams.

Active listening Listening with total attention to what another is saying; it includes reflecting, paraphrasing, and clarifying what the person says and means.

Actor–observer effect The tendency to attribute one's own actions to external (situational) factors while attributing others' actions to internal (dispositional) causes.

Adaptation/protection theory of sleep The theory that sleep evolved to conserve energy and provide protection from predators.

Addiction A broad term that describes a condition in which the body requires a drug (or specific activity) in order to function without physical and psychological reactions to its absence; it is often the outcome of tolerance and dependence.

Ageism Prejudice or discrimination based on physical age; similar to racism and sexism in its negative stereotypes.

Aggression Any behavior intended to cause psychological or physical harm to another individual.

Agonist drug A drug that binds to a receptor and triggers a response in the cell; a substance that mimics or enhances a neurotransmitter's effect.

AIDS (Acquired Immunodeficiency Syndrome) A disease in which human immunodeficiency virus (HIV) destroys the immune system's ability to fight other diseases, thus leaving the body vulnerable to a variety of opportunistic infections and cancers.

Algorithm A logical, step-by-step procedure that, if followed correctly, will always eventually solve the problem.

Alternate state of consciousness (ASC) A mental state, other than ordinary waking consciousness, that occurs during sleep, dreaming, psychoactive drug use, and hypnosis.

Altruism Prosocial behaviors designed to help others, with no obvious benefit to the helper.

Alzheimer's disease (AD) A chronic organic brain syndrome characterized by gradual loss of memory, decline in intellectual ability, and deterioration of personality.

Amygdala A part of the limbic system structure linked to the production and regulation of emotions; also responsible for the formation of emotional memory.

Androgyny [an-DRAH-juh-nee] Exhibiting both masculine and feminine traits; from the Greek *andro* for "male" and *gyn* for "female."

Anorexia nervosa An eating disorder characterized by severe loss of weight resulting from self-imposed starvation and an obsessive fear of obesity.

Antagonist drug A drug that binds to a receptor and triggers a response in the cell, which blocks a neurotransmitter's effect.

Anterograde amnesia The inability to form new memories after a brain injury; forward-acting amnesia.

Antianxiety drugs Medications used to reduce anxiety and decrease overarousal in the brain.

Antidepressant drugs Medications used to treat depression, some anxiety disorders, and certain eating disorders (such as bulimia).

Antipsychotic drugs Medications used to diminish or eliminate hallucinations, delusions, withdrawal, and other symptoms of psychosis; also known as neuroleptics or major tranquilizers.

Antisocial personality disorder The pervasive pattern of disregard for, and violation of, the rights of others beginning in childhood or early adolescence and continuing into adulthood; includes traits like unlawful behaviors, deceitful and manipulative behaviors, impulsivity, irritability and aggressiveness, consistent irresponsibility, reckless disregard for self and others, and lack of remorse.

Anxiety disorder A mental disorder characterized by overwhelming tension and irrational fear accompanied by physiological arousal.

Applied research Research that is generally conducted outside the laboratory; its data are typically used for real world application.

Approach–approach conflict The forced choice between two options, both of which have equally desirable characteristics.

Approach–avoidance conflict The forced choice within one option, which has equally desirable and undesirable characteristics.

Archetypes According to Jung, the universal, inherited, primitive, and symbolic representations of a particular experience or object, which reside in the collective unconscious.

Archival research A descriptive research approach that studies existing data to find answers to research questions.

Artificial concept A clearly defined concept based on a set of logical rules; also known as a formal concept.

Assertiveness The act of confidently and directly standing up for your rights, or putting forward your views, without infringing on the rights or views of others; striking a balance between passivity and aggression.

Assimilation In Piaget's theory, applying existing mental patterns (schemas) to new information; new information is incorporated (assimilated) into existing schemas; works in tandem with accommodation.

Association areas The "quiet" areas in the cerebral cortex involved in interpreting, integrating, and acting on information processed by other parts of the brain.

Attachment A strong emotional bond with special others that endures over time.

Attitude The learned predisposition to respond cognitively, affectively, and behaviorally to a particular object, person, place, thing, or event in an evaluative way.

Attribution The principles we follow when making judgments about the causes of events, others' behavior, and our own behavior.

Audition The sense or act of hearing.

Autocratic (authoritarian) leader A leader whose leadership style generally emerges during times of crisis; such a leader makes all major decisions, assigns tasks to members of the group, and demands full obedience.

Autonomic nervous system (ANS) The subdivision of the peripheral nervous system (PNS) that controls the body's involuntary motor responses by connecting the sensory receptors to the central nervous system (CNS) and the CNS to the smooth muscle, cardiac muscle, and glands.

Availability heuristic A cognitive strategy (or shortcut) that involves making judgments based on information that is readily available in memory.

Aversion therapy A type of behavioral therapy characterized by the pairing of an aversive (unpleasant) stimulus with a maladaptive behavior in order to elicit a negative reaction to the target stimulus.

Avoidance–avoidance conflict The forced choice between two options, both of which have equally undesirable characteristics.

Axon A long, tube-like structure that conveys impulses away from a neuron's cell body toward other neurons or to muscles or glands.

Babbling The vowel/consonant combinations that infants begin to produce at about 4 to 6 months of age.

Basic anxiety According to Horney, feelings of helplessness and insecurity that adults experience because as children they felt alone and isolated in a hostile environment.

Basic research Research that typically focuses on fundamental principles and theories; most often conducted in universities and research laboratories.

Behavior therapy A group of techniques based on learning principles to change maladaptive behaviors.

Behavioral genetics The study of the relative effects of heredity and the environment on behavior and mental processes.

Behavioral perspective An approach to understanding behavior and mental processes that emphasizes objective, observable environmental influences on overt behavior.

Binge-eating disorder An eating disorder characterized by recurrent episodes of consuming large amounts of food in a discrete period of time, while feeling a lack of control, but not followed by purge behaviors.

Binocular cues Visual input from two eyes that allows perception of depth or distance.

Biological perspective An approach to understanding behavior and mental processes that focuses on genetics and biological processes in the brain and other parts of the nervous system.

Biological preparedness The built-in (innate) readiness to form associations between certain stimuli and responses.

Biomedical therapy A treatment for psychological disorders that alters brain functioning with biological or physical interventions (for example, drugs, electroconvulsive therapy, psychosurgery).

Biopsychosocial model An integrative, unifying theme of modern psychology that sees biological, psychological, and social processes as interacting influences.

Bipolar disorder A mental disorder characterized by repeated episodes of mania (unreasonable elation, often with hyperactivity) alternating with depression.

Blind spot The point at which the optic nerve leaves the eye, which contains no receptor cells for vision—thus creating a "blind spot."

Borderline personality disorder (BPD) A mental disorder characterized by severe instability in emotion and self-concept, along with impulsive and self-destructive behaviors.

Bottom-up processing Perceptual analysis that begins "at the bottom," with raw sensory data being sent "up" to the brain for higher-level analysis; it is data-driven processing that moves from the parts to the whole.

Bulimia nervosa An eating disorder characterized by recurrent episodes of consuming large quantities of food (bingeing), followed by self-induced vomiting (purging), extreme exercise, laxative use, and other medications.

Burnout A state of psychological and physical exhaustion that results from chronic exposure to high levels of stress, with little personal control.

Bystander effect A phenomenon in which the greater the number of bystanders, the less likely it is that any one individual will feel responsible for seeking help or giving aid to someone who is in need of help.

Cannon-Bard theory A theory which states that emotions and physiological changes occur simultaneously ("I'm crying and feeling sad at the same time"); in this view, all emotions are physiologically similar.

Case study An in-depth study of a single research participant or a small group of individuals.

Cataclysmic event A stressful occurrence that occurs suddenly and generally affects many people simultaneously.

Cell body The part of a neuron that contains the cell nucleus and other structures that help the neuron carry out its functions; also known as the soma.

Central nervous system (CNS) The part of the nervous system consisting of the brain and spinal cord.

Cerebellum The hindbrain structure responsible for coordinating fine muscle movement, balance, and some perception and cognition.

Cerebral cortex The thin surface layer on the cerebral hemispheres that regulates most complex behavior, including sensations, motor control, and higher mental processes.

Child sexual abuse The unlawful sexual act involving a child that is intended to provide sexual gratification to a parent, caregiver, or other individual, including physical contact and non-contact exploitation.

Chronic stress A continuous state of arousal in which demands are perceived as greater than the inner and outer resources available for dealing with them.

Chunking The process of grouping separate pieces of information into a single unit (or chunk) on the basis of similarity or some other organizing principle.

Circadian rhythm A consistent pattern of cyclical bodily activities, governed by an internal biological clock, that generally occurs on a 24- to 25-hour cycle. (*Circa* means "about," and *dies* means "day.")

Classical conditioning A type of learning that develops through involuntarily paired associations; a previously neutral stimulus (NS) is paired (associated) with an unconditioned stimulus (US) to elicit a conditioned response (CR).

Client-centered therapy Rogers's humanistic approach to therapy, which emphasizes the client's natural tendency to become healthy and productive; techniques include empathy, unconditional positive regard, genuineness, and active listening.

Cochlea [KOK-lee-uh] The fluid-filled, coiled tube in the inner ear that contains the receptors for hearing.

Coding The process in which neural impulses travel by different routes to different parts of the brain; it allows us to detect various physical stimuli as distinct sensations.

Coercive power Authority based on the ability to use or threaten punishment.

Cognition The mental activities involved in acquiring, storing, retrieving, and using knowledge.

Cognitive dissonance The unpleasant tension and anxiety caused by a discrepancy between two or more conflicting attitudes or between attitudes and behaviors.

Cognitive map A mental image of a three-dimensional space that an organism has navigated.

Cognitive perspective An approach to understanding behavior and mental processes that focuses on thinking, perceiving, and information processing.

Cognitive restructuring A process in cognitive therapy that is designed to change destructive thoughts or inappropriate interpretations.

Cognitive therapy A type of therapy that treats problem behaviors and mental processes by focusing on faulty thought processes and beliefs.

Cognitive view of dreams The perspective that dreams are a type of information processing that help interpret daily experiences and organize them into memories.

Cognitive-behavior therapy (CBT) A type of therapy that combines cognitive therapy (changing faulty thinking) with behavior therapy (changing maladaptive behaviors).

Cognitive-social learning theory A theory that emphasizes the roles of thinking and social learning.

Collective unconscious Jung's concept of the part of an individual's unconscious that is inherited, evolutionarily developed, and common to all members of the species.

Communication The interdependent process of sending, receiving, and understanding messages.

Comorbidity The co-occurrence of two or more disorders in the same person at the same time, as when a person suffers from both depression and alcoholism.

Companionate love Strong and lasting attraction characterized by deep and lasting trust, caring, tolerance, and friendship.

Concept The mental representation of a group or category.

Concrete operational stage Piaget's third stage of cognitive development (roughly age 7 to 11), in which the child can perform mental operations on concrete objects and understand reversibility and conservation, but thinking is tied to concrete, tangible objects and events.

Conditioned emotional response (CER) Through classical conditioning, an emotion, such as fear, becomes a conditioned response to a previously neutral stimulus (NS).

Conditioned response (CR) In classical conditioning, a learned reaction to a conditioned stimulus (CS) that occurs because of previous repeated pairings with an unconditioned stimulus (US).

Conditioned stimulus (CS) In classical conditioning, a previously neutral stimulus (NS) becomes conditioned through repeated pairings with an unconditioned stimulus (US), and it now elicits a conditioned response (CR).

Conditioning The process of learning associations between stimuli and behavioral responses.

Conduction hearing loss A type of hearing loss that results from damage to the mechanical system that conducts sound waves to the cochlea; also called conduction deafness.

Cones Visual receptor cells that are concentrated near the center of the retina and are responsible for color vision and fine detail; they are most sensitive in brightly lit conditions.

Confirmation bias The bias of preferring information that confirms preexisting positions or beliefs, while ignoring or discounting contradictory evidence.

Conflict A forced choice between two or more incompatible goals or impulses.

Conformity Changes in behavior, attitudes, or values because of real or imagined group pressure.

Confounding variable A stimulus, other than the variable an experimenter inadvertently introduces into a research setting, that may affect the outcome of the study and lead to erroneous conclusions.

Conscious In Freudian terms, thoughts or motives that a person is currently aware of or is remembering.

Consciousness An organism's awareness of internal events and of the external environment.

Conservation According to Piaget, the understanding that certain physical characteristics (such as volume) remain unchanged, even though appearances may change.

Consolidation The process by which neural changes associated with recent learning become durable and stable.

Constructive process The process of organizing and shaping information during processing, storage, and retrieval of memories.

Consummate love Sternberg's strongest and most enduring type of love, based on a balanced combination of intimacy, passion, and commitment.

Continuous reinforcement A reinforcement pattern in which every correct response is reinforced.

Control group The group that is not manipulated (i.e., receives no treatment) during an experiment.

Conventional level The second level of Kohlberg's theory of moral development, where moral judgments are based on compliance with the rules and values of society.

Convergence A binocular depth cue in which the eyes turn inward (or converge) to fixate on an object.

Cooing The vowel-like sounds infants produce beginning around 2 to 3 months of age.

Corpus callosum A bundle of neural fibers that connects the brain's two hemispheres.

Correlation coefficient A number from −1.00 to +1.00 that indicates the direction and strength of the relationship between two variables.

Correlational research Research that measures the degree of relationship (if any) between two or more variables in order to determine how well one variable predicts another.

Creativity The ability to produce original, appropriate, and valued outcomes in a novel way; consists of three characteristics—originality, fluency, and flexibility.

Critical period A time of special sensitivity to specific types of learning, which shapes the capacity for future development.

Critical thinking The process of objectively evaluating, comparing, analyzing, and synthesizing information.

Cross-dressing The practice of wearing clothing and adopting gender role behaviors commonly associated with the other sex.

Cross-sectional design A research technique that measures individuals of various ages at one point in time and provides information about age differences.

Crystallized intelligence (*gc*) Knowledge and skills gained through experience and education and the ability to access that knowledge; intelligence that tends to increase over the life span.

Debriefing A discussion procedure conducted at the end of an experiment or study; participants are informed of the study's design and purpose, possible misconceptions are clarified, questions answered, and explanations are provided for any possible deception.

Defense mechanisms Freud's description of the strategies the ego supposedly uses to protect itself from anxiety, which distorts reality and may increase self-deception.

Deindividuation The reduced self- consciousness, inhibition, and personal responsibility that sometimes occurs in a group, particularly when the members feel anonymous.

Delusion A false or irrational belief maintained despite clear evidence to the contrary.

Democratic (participative) leader A leader whose leadership style is to encourage group discussion and decision making through consensus.

Dendrites The branching fibers of neurons that receive neural impulses from other neurons and convey impulses toward the cell body.

Dependent variable (DV) The variable that is observed and measured for change; the factor that is affected by (or dependent on) the independent variable.

Depressant A drug that decreases bodily processes and overall responsiveness.

Depressive disorders A group of mental disorders, including disruptive mood dysregulation disorder and major depressive disorder, characterized by sad, empty, or irritable moods that interfere with the ability to function.

Depth perception The ability to perceive three-dimensional space and to accurately judge distance.

Descriptive research A research method in which the researcher observes and records behavior and mental processes without manipulating variables.

Descriptive statistics Mathematical methods used to describe and summarize sets of data in a meaningful way.

Developmental psychology The study of age-related changes in behavior, mental processes, and stages of growth, from conception to death.

Diagnostic and Statistical Manual of Mental Disorders (DSM) A classification system developed by the American Psychiatric Association that is used to describe abnormal behaviors.

Diathesis-stress model A hypothesis about the cause of certain disorders, such as schizophrenia, which suggests that people inherit a predisposition (or "diathesis") that increases their risk for mental disorders if they are exposed to certain extremely stressful life experiences.

Difference threshold The smallest physical difference between two stimuli that is consciously detectable 50% of the time; also called the *just noticeable difference (JND)*.

Discrimination Negative behaviors directed at others because of their membership in a particular group.

Dissociative disorder A psychological disorder marked by a disturbance in the integration of consciousness, identity, memory, and other features.

Dissociative identity disorder (DID) A mental disorder characterized by the presence of two or more distinct personality systems in the same individual at different times; previously known as multiple personality disorder (MPD).

Distributed practice A study technique in which practice (or study) sessions are interspersed with rest periods.

Divergent thinking An aspect of creativity characterized by an ability to produce unusual but appropriate alternatives from a single starting point.

Double-blind study An experimental technique in which both the researcher and the participants are unaware of (blind to) who is in the experimental or control groups.

Dream analysis In psychoanalysis, interpretation of the underlying true meaning of dreams to reveal unconscious processes.

Drive-reduction theory The theory that motivation begins with a physiological need (a lack or deficiency) that elicits a drive toward behavior that will satisfy the original need; once the need is met, a state of balance (homeostasis) is restored, and motivation decreases.

Drug abuse Drug taking that causes emotional or physical harm to the drug user or others.

Eclectic approach A perspective on therapy that combines techniques from various theories to find the most appropriate treatment.

Ego In Freud's theory, the rational, decision-making component of personality that operates according to the reality principle; from the Latin term *ego*, meaning "I."

Egocentrism In cognitive development, the inability to take the perspective of another person; a hallmark of Piaget's preoperational stage.

Egoistic model of helping A theory which states that altruism is motivated by anticipated gain—later reciprocation, increased self-esteem, or avoidance of distress and guilt.

Elaborative rehearsal A technique for improving memory by linking new information to previously stored material; also known as deeper levels of processing.

Electroconvulsive therapy (ECT) A biomedical therapy based on passing electrical current through the brain; it is used almost exclusively to treat serious depression when drug therapy fails.

Embryonic period The second stage of prenatal development, which begins after uterine implantation and lasts through the eighth week.

Emotion A complex pattern of feelings that includes arousal (heart pounding), cognitions (thoughts, values, and expectations), and expressive behaviors (smiles, frowns, and gestures).

Emotion-focused coping The strategies we use to relieve or regulate the emotional impact of a stressful situation.

Emotional intelligence (EI) The ability to perceive, appraise, express, and regulate emotions accurately and appropriately.

Empathy In Rogerian terms, an insightful awareness and ability to share another's inner experience.

Empathy–altruism hypothesis A theory which states that we help because of empathy for someone in need.

Encoding The process by which a mental representation is formed in memory.

Encoding, storage, and retrieval (ESR) model A memory model which suggests that memory is formed through three processes: *encoding* (getting information in), *storage* (retaining information for future use), and *retrieval* (recovering information).

Encoding-specificity principle The principle that retrieval of information is improved if cues received at the time of recall are consistent with those present at the time of encoding.

Endocrine system A network of glands located throughout the body that manufacture and secrete hormones into the bloodstream.

Endorphin A chemical substance in the nervous system similar in structure and action to opiates; involved in pain control, pleasure, and memory.

Episodic memory A subsystem of long-term memory (LTM) that stores autobiographical events and the contexts in which they occurred; a mental diary of a person's life.

Equity theory A cognitive theory of work motivation which proposes that workers are motivated by a need for a sense of balance between output and input.

Ethnocentrism The belief that one's culture is typical of all cultures; also, viewing one's own ethnic group (or culture) as central and "correct" and judging others according to this standard.

Evolutionary perspective An approach to understanding behavior and mental processes that stresses natural selection, adaptation, and evolution; it assumes that mental capabilities evolved over millions of years to serve particular adaptive purposes.

Evolutionary psychology The branch of psychology that studies the application of the principles of evolution to explain behavior and mental processes.

Evolutionary theory of helping A theory which states that altruism is an instinctual behavior that has evolved because it favors survival of one's genes.

Expectancy theory A cognitive theory of work motivation which proposes that workers are motivated by the expectancy of outcomes, their desirability, and the effort needed to achieve them.

Experimental group The group that is manipulated (i.e., receives treatment) in an experiment.

Experimental research A carefully controlled scientific procedure that involves the manipulation of variables to determine cause and effect.

Experimenter bias Bias that occurs when a researcher influences research results in the expected direction.

Expert power Authority based on experience and expertise (physician, lawyer).

Explicit/declarative memory A subsystem within long-term memory (LTM) that consciously stores facts, information, and personal life experiences.

External locus of control The belief that chance or outside forces beyond our control determine our fate.

Extinction The gradual disappearance of a conditioned response (CR); it occurs when an unconditioned stimulus (US) is withheld whenever the conditioned stimulus (CS) is presented.

Extrasensory perception (ESP) The perceptual, so-called "psychic," abilities that supposedly go beyond the known senses (for example, telepathy, clairvoyance, precognition, and psychokinesis).

Extrinsic motivation Motivation based on external rewards or threats of punishment.

Facial-feedback hypothesis The hypothesis that movements of the facial muscles produce and/or intensify our subjective experience of emotion.

Feature detectors Specialized neurons that respond only to certain sensory information.

Fetal alcohol syndrome (FAS) A combination of birth defects, including organ deformities and mental, motor, and/or growth retardation, that result from maternal alcohol abuse.

Fetal period The third, and final, stage of prenatal development (eight weeks to birth); characterized by rapid weight gain in the fetus and the fine detailing of bodily organs and systems.

Five-factor model (FFM) A comprehensive descriptive personality system that includes openness, conscientiousness, extroversion, agreeableness, and neuroticism; informally called the Big Five.

Fixed interval (FI) schedule A schedule of reinforcement in which a reinforcer is delivered for the first response made after a fixed period of time.

Fixed ratio (FR) schedule A schedule of reinforcement in which a reinforcer is delivered for the first response made after a fixed number of responses.

Flashbulb memory (FBM) A recall of vivid, detailed, and near-permanent images associated with surprising or strongly emotional events; it may or may not be accurate.

Fluid intelligence (gf) Aspects of innate intelligence, including reasoning abilities, memory, and speed of information processing; relatively independent of education and tends to decline as people age.

Foot-in-the-door technique An initial, small request is used as a setup for a later, larger request.

Forebrain The collection of upper-level brain structures including the thalamus, hypothalamus, limbic system, and cerebral cortex.

Formal operational stage Piaget's fourth stage of cognitive development (around age 11 and beyond), characterized by abstract and hypothetical thinking.

Fovea A tiny pit in the center of the retina that is densely filled with cones; it is responsible for sharp vision.

Free association In psychoanalysis, reporting whatever comes to mind without monitoring its contents.

Frequency theory for hearing The theory that pitch perception occurs when a tone produces a rate of vibration in the basilar membrane equal to its frequency, with the result that pitch can be coded by the frequency of the neural response.

Frontal lobes The two lobes at the front of the brain that govern motor control, speech production, and higher functions, such as thinking, personality, emotion, and memory.

Frustration Unpleasant tension, anxiety, and heightened sympathetic activity that results from a blocked goal.

Frustration–aggression hypothesis A hypothesis which states that the blocking of a desired goal (frustration) creates anger that may lead to aggression.

Functional fixedness The inability to think of an object functioning other than in its usual or customary way; adversely affects problem solving and creativity.

Fundamental attribution error (FAE) The tendency of observers to overestimate the influence of internal, dispositional factors on a person's behavior, while underestimating the impact of external, situational factors.

Gate-control theory of pain The theory that pain sensations are processed and altered by certain cells in the spinal cord, which act as gates to interrupt and block some pain signals while sending others on to the brain.

Gender A psychological and sociocultural phenomenon referring to learned sex-related behaviors and attitudes of males and females.

Gender identity Our self-identification as being a man or a woman or some transgendered position between the two; usually includes awareness and acceptance of our biological sex.

Gender role A set of learned societal expectations for behaviors and attitudes considered "appropriate" for men and women and expressed publicly by an individual.

Gene A segment of DNA (deoxyribonucleic acid) that occupies a specific place on a particular chromosome and carries the code for hereditary transmission.

General adaptation syndrome (GAS) Selye's three-stage (alarm, resistance, exhaustion) reaction to chronic stress; a pattern of non-specific, adaptational response to a continuing stressor.

General intelligence (g) Spearman's term for overall, general intellectual ability.

Generalized anxiety disorder (GAD) An anxiety disorder characterized by persistent, uncontrollable, and free-floating, nonspecified anxiety.

Genuineness In Rogerian terms, authenticity or congruence; the awareness of one's true inner thoughts and feelings and being able to share them honestly with others.

Germinal period The first stage of prenatal development, beginning with ovulation and followed by conception and implantation in the uterus; the first two weeks of pregnancy.

Glial cells The cells that provide structural, nutritional, and other support for neurons, as well as communication within the nervous system; also called glia or neuroglia.

Goal-setting theory The theory that setting specific and difficult, but attainable, goals leads to higher performance.

Grammar The system of rules (syntax and semantics) used to create language and communication.

Great-person theory A theory that leadership results from specific, inherited personality traits.

Group polarization The tendency for groups to make decisions that are more extreme (either riskier or more conservative), depending on the members' initial dominant tendency.

Group therapy A form of therapy in which a number of people meet together to work toward therapeutic goals.

Groupthink The faulty decision making that occurs when a highly cohesive group strives for agreement, especially if it is in line with the leader's viewpoint, and avoids inconsistent information.

Growth/development theory of sleep The theory that deep sleep (Stage 4) is correlated with physical development, including changes in the structure and organization of the brain; infants spend far more time in Stage 4 sleep than adults.

Gustation The sense or act of taste.

Habituation The brain's reduced responsiveness due to repeated stimulation of the same receptors.

Hallucination A false, imaginary sensory perception that occurs without an external, objective source.

Hallucinogen A drug that produces sensory or perceptual distortions.

Halo error The tendency to rate individuals either too high or too low based on one outstanding trait.

Hassle Any small problem of daily living that accumulates and sometimes become a major source of stress.

Hawthorne effect A change in behavior resulting from the novelty of the research situation or from simply being observed.

Health psychology A subfield of psychology that studies how people stay healthy, why they become ill, and how they respond when they become ill.

Heritability A statistical formula that provides a percentage of variation in a population attributable to genetic factors rather than to differences in the environment.

Heuristic A cognitive strategy, or "rule of thumb," often used as a shortcut for problem solving; does not guarantee a solution to a problem but does narrow the alternatives.

Hierarchy of needs Maslow's view that basic human motives form a hierarchy; the lower motives (such as physiological and safety needs) must be met before advancing to higher needs (such as belonging and self-actualization).

Higher-order conditioning A process in which a neutral stimulus (NS) becomes a conditioned stimulus (CS) through repeated pairings with a previously conditioned stimulus (CS).

Hindbrain The lower or hind region of the brain; collection of structures including the medulla, pons, and cerebellum.

Hippocampus The sea-horse shaped part of the limbic system involved in forming and retrieving memories.

HIV positive The state of being infected by the human immuno-deficiency virus (HIV).

Homeostasis Our body's tendency to maintain a relatively balanced and stable internal state, such as a constant internal temperature.

Hormone Chemical messengers manufactured and secreted by the endocrine glands, which circulate in the bloodstream to produce bodily changes or maintain normal bodily functions.

HPA axis Our body's delayed stress response, involving the hypothalamus, pituitary, and adrenal cortex; also called the hypothalamic–pituitary–adrenocortical (HPA) axis.

Humanistic perspective An approach to understanding behavior and mental processes that perceives human nature as naturally positive and growth seeking; it emphasizes free will and self-actualization.

Humanistic therapy A type of therapy that emphasizes maximizing a client's inherent capacity for self-actualization by providing a non-judgmental, accepting atmosphere.

Hypnosis An alternate state of consciousness characterized by deep relaxation and a trancelike state of heightened suggestibility and intense focus.

Hypothalamus The small brain structure beneath the thalamus that helps govern drives (hunger, thirst, sex, and aggression) and hormones.

Hypothesis A tentative and testable explanation about the relationship between two or more variables; a testable prediction or question.

Id According to Freud, the primitive, unconscious component of personality that operates irrationally and acts on the pleasure principle.

Illusion A false or misleading perception shared by others in the same perceptual environment.

Implicit bias A hidden, automatic attitude that may guide behaviors independent of a person's awareness or control.

Implicit/nondeclarative memory A subsystem within long-term memory (LTM) that unconsciously stores procedural skills and simple classically conditioned responses.

Imprinting An inherited, primitive form of rapid learning (within a critical period) in which some infant animals physically follow and form an attachment to the first moving object they see and/or hear.

Incentive theory The theory that motivation results from external stimuli that "pull" an organism in certain directions.

Independent variable (IV) The variable that is manipulated to determine its causal effect on the dependent variable; also called the treatment variable.

Industrial/organizational (I/O) psychology The field of psychology concerned with the development and application of scientific principles to the workplace.

Inferiority complex Adler's idea that feelings of inferiority develop from early childhood experiences of helplessness and incompetence.

Inferential statistics Mathematical procedures that provide a measure of confidence about how likely it is that a certain result appeared by chance.

Informational social influence Conformance to a group out of a need for information and direction.

Informed consent A participant's agreement to take part in a study after being told what to expect.

Ingroup favoritism Viewing members of the ingroup more positively than members of an outgroup.

Inner ear The semicircular canals, vestibular sacs, and cochlea, which generate neural signals that are sent to the brain.

Insanity The legal (not clinical) designation for the state of an individual judged to be legally irresponsible or incompetent to manage his or her own affairs because of mental illness.

Insight A sudden understanding or realization of how a problem can be solved.

Insomnia A sleep disorder characterized by persistent problems falling asleep, staying asleep, or awakening too early.

Instinct Fixed, unlearned response patterns found in almost all members of a species.

Instinctive drift The tendency for conditioned responses to revert (drift back) to innate response patterns.

Intelligence The global capacity to think rationally, act purposefully, profit from experience, and deal effectively with the environment.

Intelligence quotient (IQ) An index of intelligence initially derived from standardized tests and by dividing mental age by chronological age and then multiplying by 100; now derived by comparing individual scores with the scores of others of the same age.

Internal locus of control The belief that we control our own fate.

Interpersonal attraction Positive feelings toward another.

Interpretation A psychoanalyst's explanation of a patient's free associations, dreams, resistance, and transference; more generally, any statement by a therapist that presents a patient's problem in a new way.

Intrinsic motivation Motivation resulting from internal, personal satisfaction from a task or activity.

James-Lange theory A theory of emotion which suggests that the subjective experience of emotion results from physiological changes rather than being their cause ("I feel sad because I'm crying"); in this view, each emotion is physiologically distinct.

Job analysis A detailed description of the tasks involved in a job, as well as the knowledge, skills, abilities, and other personal characteristics (KSAOs) a successful employee must possess.

Kinesics A form of nonverbal communication using the body language and gestures of a particular culture.

Kinesthesis The sense, located in muscles, joints, and tendons, that detects bodily posture, orientation, and movement of body parts relative to each other.

Laissez-faire leader A leader whose leadership style features minimal involvement in the decision-making process; such a leader encourages worker to self-manage.

Language A form of communication using sounds and symbols combined according to specified rules.

Language acquisition device (LAD) According to Chomsky, an innate mechanism that enables a child to analyze language and extract the basic rules of grammar.

Latent content of dreams According to Freud, a dream's unconscious, hidden meaning transformed into symbols within the dream's manifest content (story line).

Latent learning Hidden learning that exists without behavioral signs.

Law of effect Thorndike's rule that responses that produce a satisfying effect are more likely to occur again, whereas those that produce a discomforting effect become less likely to occur again.

Leadership The process of using interpersonal influence to inspire or persuade others to support the goals and perform the tasks desired by the leader.

Learned helplessness Seligman's term for a state of helplessness or resignation, in which human or nonhuman animals learn that escape from something painful is impossible; the organism stops responding and may become depressed.

Learning A relatively permanent change in behavior or mental processes caused by experience.

Learning/memory theory of sleep The theory that sleep is important for learning and for the consolidation, storage, and maintenance of memories.

Legitimate power Authority based on a job title or position (president, police officer).

Limbic system The interconnected group of forebrain structures involved with emotions, drives, and memory, as well as major physiological functions.

Lobotomy An outmoded neurosurgical procedure for mental disorders, which involved cutting nerve pathways between the frontal lobes and the thalamus and hypothalamus.

Long-term memory (LTM) The third stage of memory, which stores information for long periods of time; the capacity is virtually limitless, and the duration is relatively permanent.

Long-term potentiation (LTP) A long-lasting increase in neural excitability, which may be a biological mechanism for learning and memory.

Longitudinal design A research design that measures a single individual or group of individuals over an extended period and gives information about age changes.

Maintenance rehearsal The memory-improvement technique of repeating information over and over to maintain it in short-term memory (STM).

Manifest content of dreams In Freudian dream analysis, the "surface," or remembered, story line, which contains symbols that mask the dream's latent content (the true meaning).

Massed practice A study technique in which time spent learning is grouped (or massed) into long, unbroken intervals; also known as cramming.

Maturation The continuing influence of heredity throughout development; age-related physical and behavioral changes characteristic of a species.

Mean The arithmetic average of a distribution, which is obtained by adding the values of all the scores and dividing by the number of scores (N).

Median The halfway point in a set of data; half the scores fall above the median, and half fall below it.

Medical model The diagnostic perspective which assumes that diseases (including mental illness) have physical causes that can be diagnosed, treated, and possibly cured.

Meditation A group of techniques designed to alter consciousness; it's believed to enhance self-knowledge and well-being through reduced self-awareness.

Medulla The hindbrain structure responsible for vital, automatic functions, such as respiration and heartbeat.

Memory The internal record or representation of some prior event or experience; the mental capacity to encode, store, and retrieve information.

Mental image The mental representation of a previously stored sensory experience, including visual, auditory, olfactory, tactile, motor, or gustatory imagery (for example, visualizing a train and hearing its horn).

Mental set A problem-solving strategy that has worked in the past, which we continue to use rather than try new strategies.

Mere-exposure effect A developed preference for people or things simply because they are familiar.

Meta-analysis A statistical technique for combining and analyzing data from many studies in order to determine overall trends.

Midbrain The collection of structures in the middle of the brain responsible for coordinating movement patterns, sleep, and arousal.

Middle ear The hammer, anvil, and stirrup structures of the ear, which concentrate eardrum vibrations onto the cochlea's oval window.

Mindfulness-based stress reduction (MBSR) A stress reduction strategy based on developing a state of consciousness that attends to ongoing events in a receptive and non-judgmental way.

Minnesota Multiphasic Personality Inventory (MMPI) The most widely researched and clinically used self-report personality test. (MMPI-2 is the revised version.)

Mirror neuron A type of neuron that fires (or activates) when an action is performed, as well as when observing the actions or emotions of another; believed to be responsible for empathy, imitation, language, and the deficits of some mental disorders.

Misinformation effect A memory distortion that results from misleading post-event information.

Mnemonic A strategy or device that uses familiar information during the encoding of new information to enhance subsequent access to the information in memory.

Mode The score that occurs most frequently in a data set.

Modeling therapy A type of therapy characterized by watching and imitating models that demonstrate desirable behaviors.

Monocular cues Visual input from a single eye alone that contributes to perception of depth or distance.

Mood-stabilizer drugs Medications used to treat the combination of manic episodes and depression characteristic of bipolar disorders.

Morality principle In Freudian terms, the principle on which the superego operates; feelings of guilt result if its rules are violated.

Morpheme The smallest meaningful unit of language; formed from a combination of phonemes.

Motivation A set of factors that activate, direct, and maintain behavior, usually toward some goal.

Myelin sheath The layer of fatty insulation wrapped around the axon of some neurons that increases the rate at which neural impulses travel along the axon.

Narcolepsy The sudden and irresistible compulsion to sleep during the daytime. (*Narco* means "numbness," and *lepsy* means "seizure.")

Natural selection The process by which heritable traits that increase an organism's chances of survival or reproduction are favored over less beneficial traits.

Naturalistic observation The process of observing and recording a research participant's behavior and mental processes in his or her natural setting, without interfering.

Nature–nurture controversy An ongoing dispute about the relative contributions of nature (heredity) and nurture (environment) in determining the development of behavior and mental processes.

Negative punishment The taking away (or removing) of a stimulus, thereby weakening a response and making it less likely to recur.

Negative reinforcement The taking away (or removing) of a stimulus, thereby strengthening a response and making it more likely to recur.

Neurogenesis The process by which new neurons are generated.

Neuron The basic building block (nerve cell) of the nervous system, responsible for receiving, processing, and transmitting electrochemical information.

Neuroplasticity The brain's ability to reorganize and change its structure and function throughout the life span.

Neurosis An outmoded term and category dropped from *DSM-111*, in which a person does not have signs of brain abnormalities and does not display grossly irrational thinking or violate basic norms but does experience subjective distress.

Neurotransmitter A chemical messenger released by neurons that travels across the synapse and allows neurons to communicate with one another.

Neutral stimulus (NS) A stimulus that, before conditioning, does not naturally bring about the response of interest.

Nightmares Anxiety-arousing dreams that generally occur near the end of the sleep cycle, during REM sleep.

Non-rapid-eye-movement (NREM) sleep Stages 1 through 4 of sleep during which a sleeper does not show rapid eye movements.

Nonverbal communication The process of sending and receiving messages through means other than words.

Normal distribution A symmetrical, bell-shaped curve that represents a set of data in which most scores occur in the middle of the possible range, with fewer and fewer scores near the extremes.

Normative social influence Conformance to group pressure out of a need to be liked, accepted, and approved of by others.

Obedience Following direct commands, usually from an authority figure.

Obesity Having a body mass index of 30 or above, based on height and weight.

Object permanence The Piagetian term for an infant's recognition that objects (or people) continue to exist even when they cannot be seen, heard, or touched directly.

Observational learning The learning of new behaviors or information by watching and imitating others (also known as social learning or modeling).

Obsessive-compulsive disorder (OCD) A mental disorder characterized by persistent, anxiety-provoking thoughts that will not go away (obsessions) and/or irresistible urges to perform repetitive behaviors (compulsions) performed according to certain rules or in a ritualized manner; compulsive behaviors persist because they help relieve the anxiety created by the obsessions.

Occipital lobes The two lobes at the back of the brain that are primarily responsible for vision and visual perception.

Olfaction The sense or act of smelling.

Operant conditioning Learning through voluntary behavior and its subsequent consequences; reinforcement increases behavioral tendencies, whereas punishment decreases them.

Operational definition A precise description of how the variables in a study will be observed, manipulated, and measured.

Opiate A drug derived from opium that numbs the senses and relieves pain.

Opponent-process theory of color The theory that all color perception is based on three systems, each of which contains two color opposites (red versus green, blue versus yellow, and black versus white).

Optimal-arousal theory The theory that organisms are motivated to achieve and maintain an optimal level of arousal.

Organizational citizenship behavior (OCB) Actions that go beyond formal job requirements and are beneficial to an organization.

Organizational culture A group's shared pattern of thought and action; common perception held by the organization's members.

Organizational psychology A branch of the I/O field of psychology that focuses on the employee within the social context of the workplace.

Outer ear The pinna, auditory canal, and eardrum structures which funnel sound waves to the middle ear.

Outgroup homogeneity effect Judging members of an outgroup as more alike and less diverse than members of the ingroup.

Overextension The overly broad use of a word to include objects that do not fit the word's meaning (or example, calling all men "Daddy").

Overgeneralization The grammatical error of applying the basic rules of grammar even to cases that are exceptions to the rule (for example, saying "mans" instead of "men"); also known as overregularization.

Panic disorder An anxiety disorder in which sufferers experience sudden and inexplicable panic attacks; symptoms include difficulty breathing, heart palpitations, dizziness, trembling, terror, and feelings of impending doom.

Paralanguage A form of nonverbal communication that includes pace, pitch, volume, tone of voice and inflection.

Paraphilic disorder Any of a group of psychosexual disorders characterized by distress about one's sexual interests, including disturbing and repetitive sexual fantasies, urges, or behaviors.

Parasympathetic nervous system The subdivision of the autonomic nervous system (ANS) that is responsible for calming the body and conserving energy.

Parietal lobes The two lobes located at the top of the brain, in which bodily sensations are received and interpreted.

Partial (intermittent) reinforcement A reinforcement pattern in which some, but not all, correct responses are reinforced.

Participant bias Bias that can occur when experimental conditions influence the participant's behavior or mental processes.

Perception The processes of selecting, organizing, and interpreting sensory information into meaningful patterns; interpreting sensory images as having been produced by stimuli from the external, three-dimensional world.

Perceptual constancy The ability to retain an unchanging perception of an object despite changes in the sensory input.

Perceptual set The readiness to perceive in a particular manner, based on expectations.

Performance anxiety The fear of being judged in connection with sexual activities.

Performance evaluation The formal procedure used to assess employee job performance.

Peripheral nervous system (PNS) The part of the nervous system composed of the nerves and neurons connecting the central nervous system (CNS) to the rest of the body.

Personality A unique and relatively stable pattern of thoughts, feelings, and actions.

Personality disorder A mental disorder characterized by chronic, inflexible, maladaptive personality traits, which cause significant impairment of social and occupational functioning.

Personality–job fit theory The theory that job satisfaction is determined by a "good fit" between personality type and occupation.

Pheromones [FARE-oh-mones] Chemical signals released by organisms to communicate with other; they may affect behavior, including recognition of family members, aggression, territorial marking, and sexual mating.

Phobia A persistent and intense, irrational fear and avoidance of a specific object or situation.

Phoneme The smallest basic unit of speech or sound in any given language that makes a meaningful difference in speech production and reception.

Physical dependence The changes in bodily processes that make a drug necessary for minimal functioning.

Place theory for hearing The theory that pitch perception is linked to the particular spot on the cochlea's basilar membrane that is most stimulated; pitch is coded by the place at which activation occurs.

Placebo An inactive substance or fake treatment used as a control technique, usually in drug research, or given by a medical practitioner to a patient.

Pleasure principle In Freud's theory, the principle on which the id operates—seeking immediate gratification.

Polygraph An instrument that measures sympathetic arousal (heart rate, respiration rate, blood pressure, and skin conductivity) to detect emotional arousal, which in turn supposedly reflects lying versus truthfulness.

Pons The hindbrain structure involved in respiration, movement, waking, sleep, and dreaming.

Positive affect Demonstrating a sense of pleasure in the environment, including feelings of happiness, joy, enthusiasm, and contentment.

Positive psychology The study of optimal human functioning; it emphasizes positive emotions, traits, and institutions.

Positive punishment The addition (or presenting) of a stimulus, thereby weakening a response and making it less likely to recur.

Positive reinforcement The adding (or presenting) of a stimulus, thereby strengthening a response and making it more likely to recur.

Postconventional level The highest level of Kohlberg's theory of moral development, where individuals develop personal standards for right and wrong and define morality in terms of abstract principles and values that apply to all situations and societies.

Posttraumatic stress disorder (PTSD) A trauma- and stressor-related disorder that develops from directly or indirectly experiencing actual or threatened death, serious injury, or violence.

Preconscious Freud's term for thoughts, motives, or memories that exist just beneath the surface of awareness and can be called to consciousness when necessary.

Preconventional level The first level of Kohlberg's theory of moral development, where morality is based on rewards, punishment, and exchange of favors.

Prejudice A learned, generally negative, attitude toward members of a group; it includes thoughts (stereotypes), feelings, and behavioral tendencies (possible discrimination).

Premack principle The use of a naturally occurring high-frequency response to reinforce and increase low-frequency responses.

Preoperational stage Piaget's second stage of cognitive development (roughly age 2 to 7), characterized by the ability to employ significant language and to think symbolically, but the child lacks operations (reversible mental processes), and thinking is egocentric and animistic.

Primary punishers Any stimuli that decrease the probability of a response because of their innate, biological value, such as hunger and thirst.

Primary reinforcers Any stimuli that increase the probability of a response because of their innate, biological value, such as food and water.

Priming A process in which a prior exposure to a stimulus (or prime) facilitates or inhibits the processing of new information, even when one has no conscious memory of the initial learning and storage.

Proactive interference A memory error in which old information interferes with remembering new information; it is forward-acting interference.

Problem-focused coping The strategies we use to deal directly with a stressor to eventually decrease or eliminate it.

Projective test A method of personality assessment in which an individual is presented with a standardized set of ambiguous stimuli, such as inkblots or abstract drawings, which allow the test taker to project his or her unconscious onto the test material; the individual's responses are assumed to reveal inner feelings, motives, and conflicts.

Prototype The example that embodies the "best" or most typical features of a concept or category.

Proxemics The form of nonverbal communication involving physical and personal space.

Psychiatry The branch of medicine that deals with the diagnosis, treatment, and prevention of mental disorders.

Psychoactive drug A chemical that changes mental processes and conscious awareness, mood, and/or perception.

Psychoanalysis A type of psychodynamic therapy developed by Freud; an intensive and prolonged technique for bringing unconscious conflicts into conscious awareness.

Psychoanalytic perspective An approach to understanding behavior and mental processes developed by Freud, which focuses on unconscious processes and unresolved conflicts.

Psychodynamic perspective An approach to understanding behavior and mental processes that emphasizes unconscious dynamics, internal motives, conflicts, and past experiences; actions are viewed as stemming from inherited instincts, biological drives, and attempts to resolve conflicts between personal needs and social requirements.

Psychodynamic therapy A type of therapy that focuses on conscious processes and current problems; a briefer, more directive, and more modern form of psychoanalysis.

Psychological dependence The psychological desire or craving to achieve a drug's effect.

Psychology The scientific study of behavior and mental processes.

Psychoneuroimmunology The interdisciplinary field that studies the effects of psychological and other factors on the immune system.

Psychopharmacology The study of the effect of drugs on behavior and mental processes.

Psychophysics The study of the link between the physical characteristics of stimuli and the psychological experience of them.

Psychosexual stages In Freudian theory, five developmental periods (oral, anal, phallic, latency, and genital) during which particular kinds of pleasures must be gratified if personality development is to proceed normally.

Psychosis A serious mental disorder characterized by extreme mental disruption and defective or lost contact with reality.

Psychosocial stages Erikson's theory that individuals pass through eight developmental stages, each involving a specific crisis that must be successfully resolved; each stage incorporates both the sexual and social aspects of an individual's development.

Psychosurgery A neurosurgical alteration of the brain to bring about desirable behavioral, cognitive, or emotional changes, which is generally used when patients have not responded to other forms of treatment; also called neurosurgery for mental disorder (NMD).

Psychotherapy Any of a group of therapies used to treat psychological disorders and to improve psychological functioning and adjustment to life.

Puberty The biological changes during adolescence that lead to an adult-sized body and sexual maturity.

Punishment The adding or taking away of a stimulus following a response, which decreases the likelihood of that response being repeated.

Random assignment A research technique that involves using chance to assign participants to experimental or control conditions, thus minimizing the possibility of biases or preexisting differences in the group.

Range A measure of the dispersion of scores between the highest and lowest scores.

Rape The unlawful act of coercing oral, anal, or vaginal penetration upon a person without consent, or upon someone incapable of giving consent (due to age or physical or mental incapacity).

Rapid-eye-movement (REM) sleep The fifth stage of sleep marked by rapid eye movements, high-frequency brain waves, paralysis of large muscles, and often dreaming.

Rational-emotive behavior therapy (REBT) Ellis's cognitive therapy that focuses on eliminating emotional reactions through logic, confrontation, and examination of irrational beliefs.

Reality principle According to Freud, the principle on which the conscious ego operates as it seeks to delay gratification of the id's impulses until appropriate outlets and situations can be found.

Reciprocal determinism Bandura's belief that a complex reciprocal interaction exists among the individual, his or her behavior, and environmental stimuli.

Reference groups The people we conform to, or go along with, because we like, admire, and want to be like them.

Referent power Authority derived from identification with another (movie stars, athletes, friends).

Reflex An innate, automatic response to a stimulus that has a biological relevance for an organism (for example, knee-jerk reflex).

Reinforcement The adding or taking away of a stimulus following a response, which increases the likelihood of that response being repeated.

Relationship-oriented leader A leader whose leadership style is to seek to maintain group morale, satisfaction, and motivation.

Reliability The degree to which a test produces similar scores each time it is used; stability or consistency of the scores produced by an instrument.

Repair/restoration theory of sleep The theory that sleep allows organisms to repair or recuperate from depleting daily waking activities.

Repetitive transcranial magnetic stimulation (rTMS) A biomedical treatment that uses repeated magnetic field pulses targeted at specific areas of the brain.

Representativeness heuristic A cognitive strategy (or shortcut) that involves making judgments based on how well an object or event matches (represents) an existing prototype in our minds.

Resistance In psychoanalysis, the inability or unwillingness of a patient to discuss or reveal certain memories, thoughts, motives, or experiences.

Reticular formation (RF) The diffuse set of neurons that helps screen incoming information and controls arousal.

Retina The light-sensitive inner surface of the back of the eye, which contains the receptor cells for vision (rods and cones).

Retinal disparity The binocular cue of distance in which the separation of the eyes causes different images to fall on each retina.

Retrieval The recovery of information from memory storage.

Retrieval cue A prompt or stimulus that aids recall or retrieval of a stored piece of information from long-term memory (LTM).

Retroactive interference A memory error in which new information interferes with remembering old information; it is backward-acting interference.

Retrograde amnesia The loss of memory for events before a brain injury; backward-acting amnesia.

Reward power Authority based on the ability to give or promise rewards.

Rods Photoreceptors concentrated in the periphery of the retina that are most active in dim illumination; rods do not produce sensation of color.

Romantic love An intense feeling of attraction to another in an erotic context.

Rorschach Inkblot Test A projective test based on 10 cards with symmetrical abstract patterns, known as inkblots, which asks respondents to describe what they "see" in the image; the participant's response is thought to be a projection of unconscious processes.

Saliency bias A type of attributional bias in which people tend to focus on the most noticeable (salient) factors when explaining the causes of behavior.

SAM system Our body's initial, rapid-acting stress response, involving the sympathetic nervous system and the adrenal medulla; called the sympatho–adreno–medullary (SAM) system.

Sample bias A bias that may occur when research participants are unrepresentative of the larger population.

Savant syndrome A condition in which a person with generally limited mental abilities exhibits exceptional skill or brilliance in some limited field.

Schedules of reinforcement Specific patterns of reinforcement (either fixed or variable) that determine when a behavior will be reinforced.

Schema The cognitive structures, framework, or "blueprints" of knowledge, regarding objects, people, and situations, which grow and differentiate with experience.

Schizophrenia A group of severe disorders involving major disturbances in perception, language, thought, emotion, and behavior.

Scientific method The cyclical and cumulative research process used for gathering and interpreting objective information in a way that minimizes error and yields dependable results.

Secondary punishers Any stimuli that decrease the probability of a response because of their learned value, such as poor grades or a parking ticket.

Secondary reinforcers Any stimuli that increase the probability of a response because of their learned value, such as money and material possessions.

Selective attention The process of filtering out and attending only to important sensory messages.

Self-actualization The humanistic term for the inborn drive to realize one's full potential and to develop all one's inherent talents and capabilities.

Self-concept A person's relatively stable self-perception, or mental model, based on life experiences, particularly the feedback and perception of others.

Self-efficacy Bandura's term for a person's learned expectation of success in a given situation; also, another term for self-confidence.

Self-help group A leaderless or nonprofessionally guided group in which members assist each other with a specific problem, as in Alcoholics Anonymous.

Self-serving bias A type of attributional bias in which people tend to take credit for their successes and externalize or deny responsibility for their failures.

Semantic memory A subsystem of long-term memory (LTM) that stores general knowledge; a mental encyclopedia or dictionary.

Sensation The process of detecting, converting, and transmitting raw sensory information from the external and internal environments to the brain.

Sensorimotor stage Piaget's first stage of cognitive development (birth to approximately age 2), in which schemas are developed through sensory and motor activities.

Sensorineural hearing loss A type of hearing loss resulting from damage to cochlea's receptor (hair) hearing cells or to the auditory nerve; also called nerve deafness.

Sensory adaptation The process by which receptor cells become less sensitive due to constant stimulation.

Sensory memory The initial memory stage, which holds sensory information; it has relatively large capacity but the duration is only a few seconds.

Serial-position effect A characteristic of memory retrieval in which information at the beginning and end of a series is remembered better than material in the middle.

Sex The biological differences between men and women, such as having a penis or vagina; also, physical activities, such as masturbation and intercourse.

Sexual dysfunction A problem that interferes with initiation of, consummation of, or satisfaction with sexual activities.

Sexual orientation Our emotional and erotic attraction, which can be primarily toward members of the same sex (homosexual, gay, lesbian), both sexes (bisexual), or the other sex (heterosexual).

Sexual prejudice A negative attitude toward an individual because of her or his sexual orientation.

Sexual response cycle Masters and Johnson's description of the four-stage bodily response to sexual arousal, which consists of excitement, plateau, orgasm, and resolution.

Sexual scripts The learned and socially constructed blueprint and guidelines for our sexual interactions.

Shaping A training method where reinforcement is delivered for successive approximations of the desired response.

Short-term memory (STM) The second memory stage, which temporarily stores sensory information and decides whether to send it on to long-term memory (LTM); its capacity is limited to five to nine items and it has a duration of about 30 seconds.

Single-blind study An experiment where only the researcher, and not the participants, knows who is in either the experimental or control group.

Sleep apnea A sleep disorder of the upper respiratory system that causes a repeated interruption of breathing during sleep; it also leads to loud snoring or poor-quality sleep and excessive daytime sleepiness.

Sleep terrors Abrupt awakenings from NREM (non-rapid-eye-movement) sleep accompanied by intense physiological arousal and feelings of panic.

Sleeper effect A memory error in which information from an unreliable source that was initially discounted later gains credibility because the source is forgotten.

Social cognition How we think about and interpret ourselves and others.

Social influence How situational factors and other people affect us.

Social psychology The branch of psychology that studies how others influence our thoughts, feelings, and actions; it also studies group and intergroup phenomena.

Social relations How we develop and are affected by interpersonal relationships.

Sociocultural perspective An approach to understanding behavior and mental processes that emphasizes the social interaction and cultural determinants of behavior and mental processes.

Somatic nervous system (SNS) A subdivision of the peripheral nervous system (PNS) that connects the central nervous system (CNS) to sensory receptors and controls skeletal muscles.

Source amnesia A memory error caused by forgetting the true source of a memory (also called source confusion or source misattribution).

Split-brain surgery The cutting of the corpus callosum to separate the brain's two hemispheres; used medically to treat severe epilepsy; also provides information on the functions of the two hemispheres.

Spontaneous recovery The sudden, reappearance of a previously extinguished conditioned response (CR) after a rest period.

SQ4R method A study technique based on six steps: Survey, Question, Read, Recite, Review, and wRite.

Standardization A set of uniform procedures for treating each participant in a test, interview, or experiment or for recording data.

Standard deviation A computed measure of how much scores in a sample differ from the mean of the sample.

Statistics The branch of applied mathematics that deals with the collection, calculation, analysis, interpretation, and presentation of numerical facts or data.

Statistical significance A statistical statement of how likely it is that a study's result occurred merely by chance.

Stem cells Immature (uncommitted) cells that have the potential to develop into almost any type of cell, depending on the chemical signals they receive.

Stereotype threat Awareness of a negative stereotype that affects oneself and may lead to impairment in performance.

Stereotypes Generalizations about a group of people in which the same characteristics are assigned to all members of the group; also, the cognitive component of prejudice.

Stimulant A drug that increases overall activity and general responsiveness.

Stimulus discrimination A conditioning process in which an organism learns to respond differently to stimuli that differ from the conditioned stimulus on some dimension.

Stimulus generalization The conditioned response (CR) is elicited not only by the conditioned stimulus (CS) but also by stimuli similar to the conditioned stimulus (CS).

Storage The retention of encoded information over time.

Stress The interpretation of specific events, called *stressors*, as threatening or challenging; the physical and psychological reactions to stress, known as the *stress response*.

Stressor A trigger or stimulus that induces stress.

Subliminal perception The perception of stimuli presented below conscious awareness.

Superego In Freud's theory, the aspect of personality that operates on the morality principle; the "conscience" that internalizes society's values, standards, and morals.

Survey/interview A research technique that questions a large sample of people to assess their behaviors and mental processes.

Sympathetic nervous system The subdivision of the autonomic nervous system (ANS) that is responsible for arousing the body and mobilizing its energy during times of stress; also called the "fight-or-flight" system.

Synapse The gap between the axon tip of the sending neuron and the dendrite and/or cell body of the receiving neuron; during an action potential, neurotransmitters are released and flow across the synapse.

Systematic desensitization A behavioral therapy technique in which a client learns to prevent the arousal of anxiety by gradually confronting the feared stimulus while relaxed.

Task-oriented leader A leader whose leadership style is characterized by direct assistance with group tasks to help reach a particular goal.

Taste-aversion A classically conditioned dislike for, and avoidance of, a specific food whose ingestion is followed by illness.

Telegraphic speech The two- or three-word sentences of young children that contain only the most necessary words.

Temporal lobes The two lobes on each side of the brain above the ears that are involved in audition (hearing), language comprehension, memory, and some emotional control.

Teratogen An environmental agent that causes damage during prenatal development; comes from the Greek word *teras*, meaning "malformation."

Thalamus The forebrain structure at the top of the brainstem that serves as the brain's switchboard, relaying sensory messages to the cerebral cortex.

Thematic Apperception Test (TAT) A projective test in which pictures of ambiguous scenes are presented to an individual, who is encouraged to generate stories about them; the responses supposedly reflect a projection of the respondent's unconscious processes.

Theory An organized, interrelated set of concepts that explain a phenomenon or body of data.

Three-stage memory model A memory model which suggests that memory storage requires passage of information through three stages (sensory, short-term, and long-term memory).

Tip-of-the-tongue (TOT) phenomenon Feeling that specific information is stored in your long-term memory but being temporarily unable to retrieve it.

Tolerance The bodily adjustment to continued use of a drug in which the drug user requires greater dosages to achieve the same effect.

Top-down processing Perceptual analysis that starts "at the top," with higher-level cognitive processes (such as expectations and knowledge), and then works down; it is conceptually driven processing that moves from the whole to the parts.

Trait A relatively stable personality characteristic that can be used to describe someone.

Transduction The process whereby sensory receptors convert stimuli into neural impulses to be sent to the brain (for example, transforming light waves into neural impulses).

Transference In psychoanalysis, the process by which a client attaches (transfers) to a therapist feelings formerly held toward some significant person who figured in a past emotional conflict.

Transgendered Being gender diverse and nonconforming to social expectations of masculinity and femininity; being between, beyond, or some combination of genders.

Transsexualism The state of being born with the biological characteristics of one sex but feeling psychologically as if belonging to the other gender; having a gender identity that does not match the biological sex.

Triarchic theory of love Sternberg's theory that different stages and types of love result from three basic components—*intimacy*, *passion*, and *commitment*.

Trichromatic theory of color The theory that color perception results from three types of cones in the retina, each most sensitive to either red, green, or blue; other colors result from a mixture of these three.

Two-factor theory Schachter and Singer's theory that emotion depends upon two factors—physiological arousal and cognitive labeling of that arousal.

Type A A pattern of behaviors and emotions that includes intense ambition, competition, exaggerated time urgency, and a cynical, hostile outlook; hostility increases the risk of coronary heart disease.

Type B A pattern of behaviors and emotions that is less competitive, less aggressive, more relaxed, and less hostile than a Type A.

Unconditional positive regard Rogers's term for complete love and acceptance of another, such as a parent for a child, with no conditions attached.

Unconditioned response (UR) In classical conditioning, a learned reaction to an unconditioned stimulus (US) that occurs without previous conditioning.

Unconditioned stimulus (US) In classical conditioning, a stimulus that elicits an unconditioned response (UR) without previous conditioning.

Unconscious Freud's term for a part of the psyche that stores repressed urges and primitive impulses.

Validity The degree to which a test measures what it is intended to measure.

Variable interval (VI) schedule A schedule of reinforcement in which a reinforcer is delivered for the first response made after a variable period of time whose average is predetermined.

Variable ratio (VR) schedule A schedule of reinforcement in which a reinforcer is delivered for the first response made after a variable number of responses whose average is predetermined.

Vestibular sense The sense, located in the inner ear, that detects body movement and position with respect to gravity; also called the sense of balance.

Wish-fulfillment view of dreams The Freudian belief that dreams provide an outlet for unacceptable desires.

Withdrawal The discomfort and distress, including physical pain and intense cravings, experienced after stopping the use of an addictive drug.

Working memory An alternate term for short-term memory (STM), which emphasizes the active processing of information.

Zone of proximal development (ZPD) In Vygotsky's theory of cognitive development, the area between what children can accomplish on their own and what they can accomplish with the help of others who are more competent.

References

Abadinsky, H. (2011). *Drug use and abuse: A comprehensive introduction* (7th ed.). Belmont, CA: Cengage.

Abadinsky, H. (2014). *Drug use and abuse: A comprehensive introduction* (8th ed.). Independence, KY: Cengage.

Abedi, J. (2013). Testing of English language learner students. In K. F. Geisinger, B. A. Bracken, J. F. Carlson, J.-I. C. Hansen, N. R. Kuncel, S. P. Reise, & M. C. Rodriguez (Eds.), *APA handbooks in psychology. APA handbook of testing and assessment in psychology, Vol. 3. Testing and assessment in school psychology and education* (pp. 355–368). Washington, DC: American Psychological Association.

Aboa-Éboulé, C. (2008). Job strain and recurrent coronary heart disease events—Reply. *Journal of the American Medical Association, 299*, 520–521.

Abrams, J. (2011). Napping is prevalent among N.B.A. players. *New York Times*, March 6. Retrieved from http://www.nytimes.com/2011/03/07/sports/basketball/07naps.html?pagewanted=all&_r=0&gwh=F4B759C38E8986D45D92E0A629B0EED2

Acerbi, A., & Nunn, C. L. (2011). Predation and the phasing of sleep: An evolutionary individual-based model. *Animal Behaviour, 81*, 801–811.

Acheson, K., Blondel-Lubrano, A., Oguey-Araymon, S., Beaumont, M., Emady-Azar, S., Ammon-Zufferey, C., . . . Bovetto, L. (2011). Protein choices targeting thermogenesis and metabolism. *The American Journal of Clinical Nutrition, 93*, 525–534.

Ackermann, K., Revell, V. L., Lao, O., Rombouts, E. J., Skene, D. J., & Kayser, M. (2012). Diurnal rhythms in blood cell populations and the effect of acute sleep deprivation in healthy young men. *Sleep, 35*, 933–940.

Adams, M. (2011). Evolutionary genetics of personality in nonhuman primates. In M. Inoue-Murayama, S. Kawamura, & A. Weiss (Eds.), *From genes to animal behavior* (pp. 137–164). Tokyo, Japan: Springer.

Adelmann, P. K., & Zajonc, R. B. (1989). Facial efference and the experience of emotion. *Annual Review of Psychology, 40*, 249–280.

Adler, A. (1964). The individual psychology of Alfred Adler. In H. L. Ansbacher & R. R. Ansbacher (Eds.), *The individual psychology of Alfred Adler*. New York: Harper & Row.

Adler, A. (1998). *Understanding human nature*. Center City, MN: Hazelden Information Education.

Adolph, K. E., & Berger, S. E. (2012). Physical and motor development. In M. H. Bornstein & M. E. Lamb (Eds.), *Cognitive development: An advanced textbook* (pp. 257–318). New York: Psychology Press.

Adolph, K. E., & Kretch, K. S. (2012). Infants on the edge. Developmental psychology: Revisiting the classic studies. Retrieved from http://www.psych.nyu.edu/adolph/publications/Adolph%20KE%20Kretch%20KS-Infants%20on%20the%20Edge%20Beyond%20the%20Visual%20Cliff.pdf

Adolph, K. E., Cole, W. G., Komati, M., Garciaguirre, J. S., Badaly, D., Lingeman, J. M., . . . Sotsky, R. B. (2012). How do you learn to walk? Thousands of steps and dozens of falls per day. *Psychological Science, 23*, 1387–1394.

Agartz, I., Brown, A., Rimol, L., Hartberg, C., Dale, A., Melle, I., . . . Andreassen, O. (2011). Common sequence variants in the major histocompatibility complex region associate with cerebral ventricular size in schizophrenia. *Biological Psychiatry, 10*, 696–698.

Agarwal, P. K., Bain, P. M., & Chamberlain, R. W. (2012). The value of applied research: Retrieval practice improves classroom learning and recommendations from a teacher, a principal, and a scientist. *Educational Psychology Review, 24*, 437–448.

Aggleton, J. P., O'Mara, S. M., Vann, S. D., Wright, N. F., Tsanov, M., & Erichsen, J. T. (2010). Hippocampal anterior thalamic pathways for memory: Uncovering a network of direct and indirect actions. *European Journal of Neuroscience, 31*, 2292–2307.

Agopian, A. J., Lupo, P. J., Herdt-Losavio, M. L., Langlois, P. H., Rocheleau, C. M., Mitchell, L. E., & National Birth Defects Prevention Study. (2012). Differences in folic acid use, prenatal care, smoking, and drinking in early pregnancy by occupation. *Preventive Medicine: An International Journal Devoted to Practice and Theory, 55*, 341–345.

Ahearn, W. H., & Tiger, J. H. (2013). Behavioral approaches to the treatment of autism. In G. J. Madden, W. V. Dube, T. D. Hackenberg, G. P. Hanley, & K. A. Lattal (Eds.), *APA handbook of behavior analysis, Vol. 2. Translating principles into practice* (pp. 301–327). Washington, DC: American Psychological Association.

Ahmetoglu, G., & Chamorro-Premuzic, T. (2013). *Psych 101. Personality 101*. New York: Springer.

Ahola, K., Sirén, I., Kivimäki, M., Ripatti, S., Aromaa, A., Lönnqvist, J., & Hovatta, I. (2012). Work-related exhaustion and telomere length: A population-based study. *PLoS ONE 7*: e40186.

Ainsworth, M. D. S. (1967). *Infancy in Uganda: Infant care and the growth of love*. Baltimore, MD: Johns Hopkins University Press.

Ainsworth, M. D. S. (2010). Security and attachment. In R. Volpe (Ed.), *The secure child: Timeless lessons in parenting and childhood education* (pp. 43–53). Charlotte, NC: IAP Information Age Publishing.

Ainsworth, M. D. S., Blehar, M., Waters, E., & Wall, S. (1978). *Patterns of attachment: Observations in the strange situation and at home*. Hillsdale, NJ: Erlbaum.

Akers, R. M., & Denbow, D. (2008). *Anatomy and physiology of domestic animals*. Hoboken, NJ: Wiley.

Akey, J. E., Rintamaki, L. S., & Kane, T. L. (2013). Health belief model deterrents of social support seeking among people coping with eating disorders. *Journal of Affective Disorders, 145*, 246–252.

Akins, C. K., & Panicker, S. (2012). Ethics and regulation of research with nonhuman animals. In H. Cooper, P. M. Camic, D. L. Long, A. T. Panter, D. Rindskopf, & K. J. Sher (Eds.), *APA handbook of research methods in psychology, Vol. 1. Foundations, planning, measures, and psychometrics* (pp. 75–82). Washington, DC: American Psychological Association.

Aknin, L. B., Hamlin, J. K., & Dunn, E. W. (2012). Giving leads to happiness in young children. *PLoS ONE 7*: e39211.

Alberts, A., Elkind, D., & Ginsberg, S. (2007). The personal fable and risk-taking in early adolescence. *Journal of Youth and Adolescence, 36*, 71–76.

Alcock, J. (2011). Back from the future: Parapsychology and the Bem affair. The

Committee for Skeptical Inquiry (CSI). Retrieved from http://www.csicop.org/specialarticles/show/back_from_the_future

Aldenhoff, J. (2011). Interpersonal therapy. *European Psychiatry, 26,* 1782.

Aldridge, L. J., & Islam, M. R. (2012). Cultural differences in athlete attributions for success and failure: The sports pages revisited. *International Journal of Psychology, 47,* 67–75.

Alexander, J. F., Waldron, H. B., Robbins, M. S., & Neeb, A. A. (2013). *Functional family therapy for adolescent behavior problems* (pp. 113–128). Washington, DC: American Psychological Association.

Al-Issa, I. (2000). Culture and mental illness in Algeria. In I. Al-Issa (Ed.), *Al-Junun: Mental illness in the Islamic world* (pp. 101–119). Madison, CT: International Universities Press.

Allan, R. F. J. (2011). Type A behavior pattern. In R. F. J. Allan (Ed.), *Heart and mind: The practice of cardiac psychology* (2nd ed., pp. 287–290). Washington, DC: American Psychological Association.

Allemand, M., Steiger, A. E., & Hill, P. L. (2013). Stability of personality traits in adulthood: Mechanisms and implications. *GeroPsych: The Journal of Gerontopsychology and Geriatric Psychiatry, 26,* 5–13.

Alloy, L. B., Wagner, C. A., Black, S. K., Gerstein, R. K., & Abramson, L. Y. (2011). The breakdown of self-enhancing and self-protecting cognitive biases in depression. In M. D. Alicke & C. Sedikides (Eds.), *Handbook of self-enhancement and self-protection* (pp. 358–379). New York: Guilford Press.

Allport, G. W., & Odbert, H. S. (1936). Trait-names: A psycho-lexical study. *Psychological Monographs: General and Applied, 47,* 1–21.

Almas, A. N., Degnan, K. A., Radulescu, A., Nelson, C. A., Zeanah, C. H., & Fox, N. A. (2012). Effects of early intervention and the moderating effects of brain activity on institutionalized children's social skills at age 8. *Proceedings of the National Academy of Sciences, 109,* 17228–17231.

Almela, M., Hidalgo, V., Villada, C., Espín, L., Gómez-Amor, J., & Salvador, A. (2011). The impact of cortisol reactivity to acute stress on memory: Sex differences in middle-aged people. *Stress: The International Journal on the Biology of Stress, 14,* 117–127.

Altman, N. (2013). Psychoanalytic therapy. In J. Frew & M. D. Spiegler (Eds.), *Contemporary psychotherapies for a diverse world* (1st rev. ed., pp. 39–86). New York: Routledge/Taylor & Francis Group.

Ambady, N., & Adams, R. B., Jr. (2011). Us versus them: The social neuroscience of perceiving out-groups. In A. Todorov, S. T. Fiske, & D. A. Prentice (Eds.), *Oxford series in social cognition and social neuroscience. Social neuroscience: Toward understanding the underpinnings of the social mind* (pp. 135–143). New York: Oxford University Press.

American Heart Association (2013). *Statistical fact sheet: 2013 update.* Retrieved from: http://www.heart.org/idc/groups/heart-public/@wcm/@sop/@smd/documents/downloadable/ucm_319588.pdf

American Psychiatric Association (2013). *Diagnostic and statistical manual of mental disorders* (5th ed.). Washington, DC: American Psychiatric Association.

Amin, A. R., & Noggle, C. A. (2013). The neuropsychology of psychopathology: Historical shifts. In C. A. Noggle & R. S. Dean (Eds.), *Contemporary neuropsychology. The neuropsychology of psychopathology* (pp. 3–9). New York: Springer.

Amodio, D. M., & Hamilton, H. K. (2012). Intergroup anxiety effects on implicit racial evaluation and stereotyping. *Emotion, 12,* 1273–1280.

Amundson, J. K., & Nuttgens, S. A. (2008). Strategic eclecticism in hypnotherapy: Effectiveness research considerations. *American Journal of Clinical Hypnosis, 50,* 233–245.

Anacker, C., Zunszain, P. A., Cattaneo, A., Carvalho, L. A., Garabedian, M. J., Thuret, S., . . . Pariante, C. M. (2011). Antidepressants increase human hippocampal neurogenesis by activating the glucocorticoid receptor. *Molecular Psychiatry, 16,* 738–750.

Anderman, E., & Dawson, H. (2011). Learning with motivation. In R. Mayer & P. Alexander (Eds.), *Handbook of research on learning and instruction* (pp. 219–242). New York: Routledge.

Andersen, B. L., Thornton, L. M., Shapiro, C. L., Farrar, W. B., Mundy, B. L., Yang, H. C., & Carson, W. E. 3rd. (2010). Biobehavioral, immune, and health benefits following recurrence for psychological intervention participants. *Clinical Cancer Research, 16,* 3270–3278.

Anderson, C. A. (2001). Heat and violence. *Current Directions in Psychological Science, 10,* 33–38.

Anderson, C. A., Buckley, K. E., & Carnegey, N. L. (2008). Creating your own hostile environment: A laboratory examination of trait aggressiveness and the violence escalation cycle. *Personality and Social Psychology Bulletin, 34,* 462–473.

Anderson, J. R., Betts, S., Ferris, J. L., & Fincham, J. M. (2011). Cognitive and metacognitive activity in mathematical problem solving: Prefrontal and parietal patterns. *Cognitive, Affective and Behavioral Neuroscience, 11,* 52–67.

Anderson, M. C., Ochsner, K. N., Kuhl, B., Cooper, J., Robertson, E., Gabrieli, S. W., . . . Gabrieli, J. D. E. (2004). Neural systems underlying the suppression of unwanted memories. *Science, 303,* 232–235.

Andersson, J., & Walley, A. (2011). The contribution of heredity to clinical obesity. In R.H. Lustig (Ed.), *Obesity before birth* (pp. 25–52). New York: Springer.

Ando, J., Fujisawa, K. K., Shikishima, C., Hiraishi, K., Nozaki, M., Yamagata, S., . . . Ooki, S. (2013). Two cohort and three independent anonymous twin projects at the Keio Twin Research Center (KoTReC). *Twin Research & Human Genetics, 16,* 202–216.

Andrade, T. G., & Graeff, F. G. (2001). Effect of electrolytic and neurotoxic lesions of the median raphe nucleus on anxiety and stress. *Pharmacology, Biochemistry and Behavior, 70,* 1–14.

Andreassen, C. S., Torsheim, T., Brunborg, G. S., & Pallesen, S. (2012). Development of a Facebook addiction scale. *Psychological Reports, 110,* 501–517.

Anik, L., Aknin, L. B., Norton, M. L., & Dunn, E. W. (2011). Feeling good about giving: The benefits (and costs) of self-interested charitable behavior. In D. M. Oppenheimer & C. Y. Olivola (Eds.), *The science of giving: Experimental approaches to the study of charity. Society for Judgment and Decision Making series* (pp. 3–23). New York: Psychology Press.

Ansell, E. B., & Grilo, C. M. (2007). Personality disorders. In M. Hersen, S. M. Turner, & D. C. Beidel (Eds.), *Adult psychopathology and diagnosis* (5th ed., pp. 633–678). Hoboken, NJ: Wiley.

Antúnez, E., Palomino, A. J., Marfil, R., & Bandera, J. P. (2013). Perceptual organization and artificial attention for visual landmarks detection. *Cognitive Processing, 14,* 13–18.

Aoyama, S., Toshima, T., Saito, Y., Konishi, N., Motoshige, K., Ishikawa, N., . . . Kobayashi, M. (2010). Maternal breast milk odour induces frontal lobe activation in neonates: A NIRS study. *Early Human Development, 86,* 541–545.

Appel, M., & Richter, T. (2007). Persuasive effects of fictional narratives increase over time. *Media Psychology, 10,* 113–134.

Arango, C., Rapado-Castro, M., Reig, S., Castro-Fornieles, J., Gonzalez-Pinto, A., Otero, S., . . . Desco, M. (2012). Progressive brain changes in children and adolescents with first-episode psychosis. *Archives of General Psychiatry, 69,* 16–26.

Archer, T. (2011). Physical exercise alleviates debilities of normal aging and Alzheimer's disease. *Acta Neurologica Scandinavica, 123,* 221–238.

Arkes, H., & Kajdasz, J. (2011). Intuitive theories of behavior. In National Research Council (Ed.), *Intelligence analysis: Behavioral and social scientific foundations* (pp. 143–168). Washington, DC: The National Academies Press.

Armony, J. L. (2013). Current emotion research in behavioral neuroscience: The role(s) of the amygdala. *Emotion Review, 5,* 104–115.

Armstrong, K., Hangauer, J., & Agazzi, H. (2013). Intellectual and developmental disabilities and other low-incidence disorders. In L. A. Reddy, A. S. Weissman, & J. B. Hale (Eds.), *Neuropsychological assessment and intervention for youth: An evidence-based approach to emotional and behavioral disorders* (pp. 227–246). Washington, DC: American Psychological Association.

Arnsten, A. F. T. (2011). Prefrontal cortical network connections: Key site of vulnerability in stress and schizophrenia. *International Journal of Developmental Neuroscience, 29,* 215–223.

Aronson, J., Jannone, S., McGlone, M., & Johnson-Campbell, T. (2009). The Obama effect: An experimental test. *Journal of Experimental Social Psychology, 45,* 957–960.

Arumugam, V., Lee, J-S., Nowak, J. K., Pohle, R. J., Nyrop, J. E., Leddy, J. J., & Pelkman, C. L. (2008). A high-glycemic meal pattern elicited increased subjective appetite sensations in overweight and obese women. *Appetite, 50,* 215–222.

Asaoka, S., Aritake, S., Komada, Y., Ozaki, A., Odagiri, Y., Inoue, S., . . . Inoue, Y. (2013). Factors associated with shift work disorder in nurses working with rapid-rotation schedules in Japan: The Nurses Sleep Health Project. *Chronobiology International, 30,* 628–636.

Asch, S. E. (1951). Effects of group pressure upon the modification and distortion of judgment. In H. Guetzkow (Ed.), *Groups, leadership, and men.* Pittsburgh, PA: Carnegie Press.

Ashley, K. B. (2013). The science on sexual orientation: A review of the recent literature. *Journal of Gay & Lesbian Mental Health, 17,* 175–182.

Åslund, C., Comasco, E., Nordquist, N., Leppert, J., Oreland, L., & Nilsson, K. W. (2013). Self-reported family socioeconomic status, the 5-HTTLPR genotype, and delinquent behavior in a community-based adolescent population. *Aggressive Behavior, 39,* 52–63.

Atkinson, R. C., & Shiffrin, R. M. (1968). Human memory: A proposed system and its control processes. In K. W. Spence & J. T. Spence (Eds.), *The psychology of learning and motivation* (Vol. 2, pp. 90–91). New York: Academic Press.

Atun-Einy, O., Berger, S. E., & Scher, A. (2012). Pulling to stand: Common trajectories and individual differences in development. *Developmental Psychobiology, 54,* 187–198.

Aunola, K., Viljaranta, J., Lehtinen, E., & Nurmi, J. E. (2013). The role of maternal support of competence, autonomy and relatedness in children's interests and mastery orientation. *Learning and Individual Differences, 25,* 171–177.

Austin, J. E., & Rini, C. (2013). Bone marrow and stem cell transplant. In A. R. Block & D. B. Sarwer (Eds.), *Presurgical psychological screening: Understanding patients, improving outcomes* (pp. 103–125). Washington, DC: American Psychological Association.

Avidan, G., Tanzer, M., Hadj-Bouziane, F., Liu, N., Ungerleider, L. G., & Behrmann, M. (2013). Selective dissociation between core and extended regions of the face processing network in congenital prosopagnosia. *Cerebral Cortex.* Retrieved from http://cercor.oxfordjournals.org/content/early/2013/01/31/cercor.bht007.full

Axtell, R. E. (2007). *Essential do's and taboos: The complete guide to international business and leisure travel.* Hoboken, NJ: Wiley.

Babula, M. W. (2013). The unlikely Samaritans. *Journal of Applied Social Psychology, 43,* 899–908.

Baddeley, A. D. (1992). Working memory. *Science, 255,* 556–559.

Baddeley, A. D. (2007). Working memory, thought, and action. *Oxford psychology series.* New York: Oxford University Press.

Baddeley, A. D. (2013). Working memory and emotion: Ruminations on a theory of depression. *Review of General Psychology, 17,* 20–27

Baer, J. (2013). Teaching for creativity: Domains and divergent thinking, intrinsic motivation, and evaluation. In M. Banks Gregerson, H. T. Snyder, & J. C. Kaufman (Eds.), *Teaching creatively and teaching creativity* (pp. 175–181). New York: Springer.

Bagermihl, B. (1999). *Biological exuberance: Animal homosexuality and natural diversity.* New York: St Martins Press.

Bagley, S. L., Weaver, T. L., & Buchanan, T. W. (2011). Sex differences in physiological and affective responses to stress in remitted depression. *Physiology and Behavior, 104,* 180–186.

Bailey, J. M., Dunne, M. P., & Martin, N. G. (2000). Genetic and environmental influences on sexual orientation and its correlates in an Australian twin sample. *Journal of Personality and Social Psychology, 78,* 524–536.

Baird, A. A. (2010). The terrible twelves. In P. D. Zelazo, M. Chandler, & E. Crone (Eds.), *Developmental social cognitive neuroscience. The Jean Piaget symposium series* (pp. 191–207). New York: Psychology Press.

Baker, D. G., Nievergelt, C. M., & O'Connor, D. T. (2011). Biomarkers of PTSD: Neuropeptides and immune signaling. *Neuropharmacology, 62,* 663–673.

Baker, D., & Nieuwenhuijsen, M. J. (Eds.) (2008). *Environmental epidemiology: Study methods and application.* New York: Oxford University Press.

Baker, S. C., & Serdikoff, S. L. (2013). Addressing the role of animal research in psychology. In D. S. Dunn, R. A. R. Gurung, K. Z. Naufel, & J. H. Wilson (Eds.), *Controversy in the psychology classroom: Using hot topics to foster critical thinking* (pp. 105–112). Washington, DC: American Psychological Association.

Baldessarini, R. J., & Tondo, L. (2008). Lithium and suicidal risk. *Bipolar Disorders, 10,* 114–115.

Bandura, A. (1969). *Principles of behavior modification.* New York: Holt, Rinehart & Winston.

Bandura, A. (1986). *Social foundations of thought and action: A social cognitive theory.* Englewood Cliffs, NJ: Prentice Hall.

Bandura, A. (1991). Human agency: The rhetoric and the reality. *American Psychologist, 46,* 157–162.

Bandura, A. (1997). *Self-efficacy: The exercise of control.* New York: Freeman.

Bandura, A. (2006). Going global with social cognitive theory: From prospect to paydirt. In D. E. Berger & K. Pezdek (Eds.), *The rise of applied psychology: New frontiers and rewarding careers* (pp. 53–79). Mahwah, NJ: Erlbaum.

Bandura, A. (2008). Reconstrual of "free will" from the agentic perspective of social cognitive theory. In J. Baer, J. C. Kaufman, & R. F. Baumeister (Eds.), *Are we free? Psychology and free will* (pp. 86–127). New York: Oxford University Press.

Bandura, A. (2012). On the functional properties of perceived self-efficacy revisited. *Journal of Management, 38,* 9–44.

Bandura, A. (2012). Social cognitive theory. In P. A. M. Van Lange, A. W. Kruglanski, &

E. T. Higgins (Eds.), *Handbook of theories of social psychology* (Vol. 1, pp. 349–373). Thousand Oaks, CA: Sage Publications.

Bankó, É. M., & Vidnyánszky, Z. (2010). Retention interval affects visual short-term memory encoding. *Journal of Neurophysiology, 103*, 1425–1430.

Banks, M. S., & Salapatek, P. (1983). Infant visual perception. In M. M. Haith & J. J. Campos (Eds.), *Handbook of child psychology*. Hoboken, NJ: Wiley.

Bao, A., & Swaab, D. (2011). Sexual differentiation of the human brain: Relation to gender identity, sexual orientation and neuropsychiatric disorders. *Frontiers in Neuroendocrinology, 32*, 214–226.

Barash, D. P., & Lipton, J. E. (2011). *Payback: Why we retaliate, redirect aggression, and take revenge*. New York: Oxford University Press.

Barbeau, E.-J., Puel, M., & Pariente, J. (2010). La mémoire déclarative antérograde et ses modèles [Anterograde declarative memory and its models]. *Revue Neurologique, 166*, 661–672.

Barbui, C., Cipriani, A., Patel, V., Ayuso-Mateos, J. L., & Ommeren, M. V. (2011). Efficacy of antidepressants and benzodiazepines in minor depression: Systematic review and meta-analysis. *The British Journal of Psychiatry, 198*, 11–16.

Barelds, D. P. H., & Dijkstra, P. (2011). Positive illusions about a partner's personality and relationship quality. *Journal of Research in Personality, 45*, 37–43.

Barenbaum, N. B., & Winter, D. G. (2013). Personality. In D. K. Freedheim & I. B. Weiner (Eds.), *Handbook of psychology, Vol. 1. History of psychology* (2nd ed., pp. 198–223). Hoboken, NJ: Wiley.

Barlow, D. H. (Ed.). (2008). *Clinical handbook of psychological disorders: A step-by-step treatment manual (4th ed.)*. New York: Guilford Press.

Barnes, J. (2013). *Essential biological psychology*. London, UK: Sage.

Barnow, S., & Balkir, N. (Eds.). (2013). *Cultural variations in psychopathology: From research to practice*. Cambridge, MA: Hogrefe Publishing.

Barnum, S. E., Woody, M. L., & Gibb, B. E. (2013). Predicting changes in depressive symptoms from pregnancy to postpartum: The role of brooding rumination and negative inferential styles. *Cognitive Therapy and Research, 37*, 71–77.

Barratt, B. B. (2013). *What is psychoanalysis? 100 years after Freud's 'secret committee.'* New York: Routledge/Taylor & Francis Group.

Barrouillet, P., & Camos, V. (2012). As time goes by: Temporal constraints in working memory. *Current Directions in Psychological Science, 21*, 413–419.

Bartlett, C. P., Harris, R. J., & Bruey, C. (2008). The effect of the amount of blood in a violent video game on aggression, hostility, and arousal. *Journal of Experimental Social Psychology, 44*, 539–546.

Barton, J. J. S. (2008). Prosopagnosia associated with a left occipitotemporal lesion. *Neuropsychologia, 46*, 2214–2224.

Bastien, C. H. (2011). Insomnia: Neurophysiological and neuropsychological approaches. *Neuropsychology Review, 21*, 22–40.

Bateman, C. R., & Valentine, S. R. (2010). Investigating the effects of gender on consumers' moral philosophies and ethical intentions. *Journal of Business Ethics, 95*, 393–414.

Batson, C. D. (1991). *The altruism question: Toward a social-psychological answer*. Hillsdale, NJ: Erlbaum.

Batson, C. D. (1998). Altruism and prosocial behavior. In D.T. Gilbert, S.T. Fiske, & G. Lindzey (Eds.), *The handbook of social psychology, Vol. 2* (4th ed., pp. 282–316). Boston, MA: McGraw-Hill.

Batson, C. D. (2006). "Not all self-interest after all": Economics of empathy-induced altruism. In D. De Cremer, M. Zeelenberg, & J. K. Murnighan (Eds.), *Social psychology and economics* (pp. 281–299). Mahwah, NJ: Erlbaum.

Batson, C. D. (2011). *Altruism in humans*. New York: Oxford University Press.

Baucom, B. R., Weusthoff, S., Atkins, D. C., & Hahlweg, K. (2012). Greater emotional arousal predicts poorer long-term memory of communication skills in couples. *Behaviour Research and Therapy, 50*, 442–447.

Bauer, P. J., & Lukowski, A. F. (2010). The memory is in the details: Relations between memory for the specific features of events and long-term recall during infancy. *Journal of Experimental Child Psychology, 107*, 1–14.

Baumann, M. H., Partilla, J. S., Lehner, K. R., Thorndike, E. B., Hoffman, A. F., Holy, M., . . . Schindler, C. W. (2013). Powerful cocaine-like actions of 3,4-methylenedioxypyrovalerone (MPDV), a principal constituent of psychoactive "bath salts" products. *Neuropsychopharmacology, 38*, 552–562.

Baumeister, R. F., & Bushman, B. J. (2014). *Social psychology and human nature* (3rd ed.). Belmont, CA: Thomson Wadsworth.

Baumrind, D. (2013). Authoritative parenting revisited: History and current status. In R. E. Larzelere, A. S. Morris, & A. W. Harrist (Eds.), *Authoritative parenting: Synthesizing nurturance and discipline for optimal child development* (pp. 11–34). Washington, DC: American Psychological Association.

Beacham, A., Stetson, B., Braekkan, K., Rothschild, C., Herbst, A., & Linfield, K. (2011). Causal attributions regarding personal exercise goal attainment in exerciser schematics and aschematics. *International Journal of Sport and Exercise Psychology, 9*, 48–63.

Beaton, E. A., & Simon, T. J. (2011). How might stress contribute to increased risk for schizophrenia in children with Chromosome 22q11.2 deletion syndrome? *Journal of Neurodevelopmental Disorders, 3*, 68–75.

Beauchamp, M. R., Rhodes, R. E., Kreutzer, C., & Rupert, J. L. (2011). Experiential versus genetic accounts of inactivity: Implications for inactive individuals' self-efficacy beliefs and intentions to exercise. *Behavioral Medicine, 37*, 8–14.

Beaver, K. M., Barnes, J. C., May, J. S., & Schwartz, J. A. (2011). Psychopathic personality traits, genetic risk, and gene-environment correlations. *Criminal Justice and Behavior, 38*, 896–912.

Bech, P., Fava, M., Trivedi, M. H., Wisniewski, S. R., & Rush, A. J. (2011). Factor structure and dimensionality of the two depression scales in STAR*D using level 1 datasets. *Journal of Affective Disorders, 132*, 396–400.

Beck, A. T., & Grant, P. M. (2008). Negative self-defeating attitudes: Factors that influence everyday impairment in individuals with schizophrenia. *American Journal of Psychiatry, 165*, 772.

Beck, A. T., Haigh, E. A. P., & Baber, K. F. (2012). Biological underpinnings of the cognitive model of depression: A prototype for psychoanalytic research. *Psychoanalytic Review, 99*, 515–537.

Beckers, T., Krypotos, A.-M., Boddez, Y., Effting, M., & Kindt, M. (2013). What's wrong with fear conditioning? *Biological Psychology, 92*, 90–96.

Beilin, H. (1992). Piaget's enduring contribution to developmental psychology. *Developmental Psychology, 28*, 191–204.

Belar, C. D., McIntyre, T. M., & Matarazzo, J. D. (2013). Health psychology. In D. K. Freedheim & I. B. Weiner (Eds.), *Handbook of psychology, Vol. 1. History of psychology* (2nd ed., pp. 488–506). Hoboken, NJ: Wiley.

Bellebaum, C., & Daum, I. (2011). Mechanisms of cerebellar involvement in associative learning. *Cortex: A Journal Devoted to* *the Study of the Nervous System and Behavior, 47,* 128–136.

Bem, D. J. (2011). Feeling the future: Experimental evidence for anomalous retroactive influences on cognition and affect. Journal of *Personality & Social Psychology, 100,* 407–425.

Bem, S. L. (1981). Gender schema theory: A cognitive account of sex typing. *Psychological Review, 88,* 354–364.

Bem, S. L. (1993). *The lenses of gender: Transforming the debate on sexual inequality.* New Haven, CT: Yale University Press.

Bender, R. E., & Alloy, L. B. (2011). Life stress and kindling in bipolar disorder: Review of the evidence and integration with emerging biopsychosocial theories. *Clinical Psychology Review, 31,* 383–398.

Bendle, N. T. (2011). Out-group homogeneity bias and strategic market entry. *Dissertation Abstracts International Section A: Humanities and Social Sciences, 71,* 3341.

Benjamin Neelon, S. E., Oken, E., Taveras, E. M., Rifas-Shiman, S. L., & Gillman, M. W. (2012). Age of achievement of gross motor milestones in infancy and adiposity at age 3 years. *Maternal and Child Health Journal, 16,* 1015–1020.

Benjamin, E. (2011). Humanistic psychology and the mental health worker. *Journal of Humanistic Psychology, 51,* 82–111.

Bennett, E., English, M. W., Rennoldson, M., & Starza-Smith, A. (2013). Predicting parenting stress in caregivers of children with brain tumours. *Psycho-Oncology, 22,* 629–636.

Ben-Porath, Y. S. (2013). Self-report inventories: Assessing personality and psychopathology. In J. R. Graham, J. A. Naglieri, & I. B. Weiner (Eds.), *Handbook of psychology, Vol. 10. Assessment psychology* (2nd ed., pp. 622–644). Hoboken, NJ: Wiley.

Bentall, R. P., Wickham, S., Shevlin, M., & Varese, F. (2012). Do specific early-life adversities lead to specific symptoms of psychosis? A study from the 2007 The Adult Psychiatric Morbidity Survey. *Schizophrenia Bulletin, 38,* 734–740.

Berger, M., Speckmann, E.-J., Pape, H. C., & Gorji, A. (2008). Spreading depression enhances human neocortical excitability in vitro. *Cephalalgia, 28,* 558–562.

Bergman, R. L. (2013). *Programs that work. Treatment for children with selective mutism: An integrative behavioral approach.* New York: Oxford University Press.

Bergstrom-Lynch, C. A. (2008). Becoming parents, remaining childfree: How same-sex couples are creating families and confronting social inequalities. *Dissertation Abstracts International Section A: Humanities and Social Sciences, 68,* 3608.

Berlim, M. T., Van den Eynde, F., & Daskalakis, Z. J. (2013). Clinically meaningful efficacy and acceptability of low-frequency repetitive transcranial magnetic stimulation (rTMS) for treating primary major depression: A meta-analysis of randomized, double-blind and sham-controlled trials. *Neuropsychopharmacology, 38,* 543–551.

Berman, S. M., Paz-Filho, G., Wong, M.-L., Kohno, M., Licinio, J., & London, E. D. (2013). Effects of leptin deficiency and replacement on cerebellar response to food-related cues. *The Cerebellum, 12,* 59–67.

Bermeitinger, C., Goelz, R., Johr, N., Neumann, M., Ecker, U. K. H., & Doerr, R. (2009). The hidden persuaders break into the tired brain. *Journal of Experimental Social Psychology, 45,* 320–326.

Bernabé, D. G., Tamae, A. C., Biasoli, É. R., & Oliveira, S. H.P. (2011). Stress hormones increase cell proliferation and regulates interleukin-6 secretion in human oral squamous cell carcinoma cells. *Brain, Behavior, and Immunity, 25,* 574–583.

Bernard, L. L. (1924). *Instinct.* New York: Holt.

Bernhard, F., Landgraf, K., Klöting, N., Berthold, A., Büttner, P., Friebe, D., . . . Körner, A. (2013). Functional relevance of genes implicated by obesity genome-wide association study signals for human adipocyte biology. *Diabetologia, 56,* 311–322.

Berreman, G. (1971). *Anthropology today.* Del Mar, CA: CRM Books.

Berry, J., Poortinga, Y., Breugelmans, S., Chasiotis, A., & Sam, D. (2011). *Cross-cultural psychology: Research and applications* (3rd ed.). Cambridge, UK: Cambridge University Press.

Bertsch, K., Grothe, M., Prehn, K., Vohs, K., Berger, C., Haunstein, K., . . . Herpetz, S. C. (2013). Brain volumes differ between diagnostic groups of violent criminal offenders. *European Archives of Psychiatry and Clinical Neuroscience, 263,* 593–606.

Betancourt, T. S., Borisova, I. I., de la Soudière, M., & Williamson, J. (2011). Sierra Leone's child soldiers: War exposures and mental health problems by gender. *Journal of Adolescent Health, 49,* 21–28.

Bettens, K., Sleegers, K., & Van Broeckhoven, C. (2013). Genetic insights in Alzheimer's disease. *The Lancet Neurology, 12,* 92–104.

Beutler, L. E. (2009). Making science matter in clinical practice: Redefining psychotherapy. *Clinical Psychology: Science and Practice, 16,* 301–317.

Beyers, W., & Seiffge-Krenke, I. (2010). Does identity precede intimacy? Testing Erikson's theory on romantic development in emerging adults of the 21st century. *Journal of Adolescent Research, 25,* 387–415.

Bhatnagar, K. A. C., Wisniewski, L., Solomon, M., & Heinberg, L. (2013). Effectiveness and feasibility of a cognitive-behavioral group intervention for body image disturbance in women with eating disorders. *Journal of Clinical Psychology, 69,* 1–13.

Bhattacharya, S. K., & Muruganandam, A. V. (2003). Adaptogenic activity of Withania somnifera: An experimental study using a rat model of chronic stress. *Pharmacology, Biochemistry and Behavior, 75,* 547–555.

Bianchi, M., Franchi, S., Ferrario, P., Sotgiu, M. L., & Sacerdote, P. (2008). Effects of the bisphosphonate ibandronate on hyperalgesia, substance P, and cytokine levels in a rat model of persistent inflammatory pain. *European Journal of Pain, 12,* 284–292.

Biegel, D. E., Kola, L. A., Ronis, R. J., & Kruszynski, R. (2013). Evidence-based treatment for adults with co-occurring mental and substance use disorders: Current practice and future directions. In J. Rosenberg & S. J. Rosenberg (Eds.), *Community mental health: Challenges for the 21st century* (2nd ed., pp. 215–237). New York: Routledge/Taylor & Francis Group.

Biernat, M., & Danaher, K. (2013). Prejudice. In H. Tennen, J. Suls, & I. B. Weiner (Eds.), *Handbook of psychology, Vol. 5. Personality and social psychology* (2nd ed., pp. 341–367). Hoboken, NJ: Wiley.

Bjork, J. M., Smith, A. R., Chen, G., & Hommer, D. W. (2012). Mesolimbic recruitment by nondrug rewards in detoxified alcoholics: Effort anticipation, reward anticipation, and reward delivery. *Human Brain Mapping, 33,* 2174–2188.

Blacha, C., Schmid, M. M., Gahr, M., Freudenmann, R. W., Plener, P. L., Finter, F., . . . Schönfeldt-Lecuona, C. (2013). Self-inflicted testicular amputation in first lysergic acid diethylamide use. *Journal of Addiction Medicine, 7,* 83–84.

Blair, R. J. R., & Lee, T. M. (2013). The social cognitive neuroscience of aggression, violence, and psychopathy. *Social Neuroscience, 8,* 108–111.

Blampied, N. M., & Bootzin, R. R. (2013). Sleep: A behavioral account. In G. J. Madden, W. V. Dube, T. D. Hackenberg, G. P. Hanley, & K. A. Lattal (Eds.), *APA handbook of behavior analysis, Vol. 2. Translating principles into practice* (pp. 425–453). Washington, DC: American Psychological Association.

Blass, T. (1991). Understanding behavior in the Milgram obedience experiment: The role of personality, situations, and their interactions. *Journal of Personality and Social Psychology, 60,* 398–413.

Blass, T. (2000). Stanley Milgram. In A. E. Kazdin (Ed.), *Encyclopedia of psychology* (Vol. 5, pp. 248–250). Washington, DC: American Psychological Association.

Blecha, P. (2004). *Taboo tunes: A history of banned bands and censored songs.* San Francisco, CA: Backbeat Books.

Blum, H. P. (2011). To what extent do you privilege dream interpretation in relation to other forms of mental representations? *The International Journal of Psychoanalysis, 92,* 275–277.

Blum, K., Oscar-Berman, M., Barh, D., Giordano, J., & Gold, M. S. (2013). Dopamine genetics and function in food and substance abuse. *Journal of Genetic Syndromes & Gene Therapy, 4:* 1000121.

Blume-Marcovici, A. (2010). Gender differences in dreams: Applications to dream work with male clients. *Dreaming, 20,* 199–210.

Boag, S. (2012). *Freudian repression, the unconscious, and the dynamics of inhibition.* London, England: Karnac Books.

Boardman, J., Alexander, K., & Stallings, M. (2011). Stressful life events and depression among adolescent twin pairs. *Biodemography and Social Biology, 57,* 53–66.

Bodenhausen, G. V., & Morales, J. R. (2013). Social cognition and perception. In H. Tennen, J. Suls, & I. B. Weiner (Eds.), *Handbook of psychology (Vol. 5). Personality and social psychology* (2nd ed., pp. 225–246). Hoboken, NJ: Wiley.

Boer, D., & Fischer, R. (2013). How and when do personal values guide our attitudes and sociality? Explaining cross-cultural variability in attitude–value linkages. *Psychological Bulletin, 139,* 1113–1147.

Boland, E. M., & Alloy, L. B. (2013). Sleep disturbance and cognitive deficits in bipolar disorder: Toward an integrated examination of disorder maintenance and functional impairment. *Clinical Psychology Review, 33,* 33–44.

Bones, A. K. (2012). We knew the future all along: Scientific hypothesizing is much more accurate than other forms of precognition—A satire in one part. *Perspectives on Psychological Science, 7,* 307–309.

Bonk, W. J., & Healy, A. F. (2010). Learning and memory for sequences of pictures, words, and spatial locations: An exploration of serial position effects. *The American Journal of Psychology, 123,* 137–168.

Boothroyd, L. G., Tovee, M. T., & Pollett, T. (2012). Mechanisms of change in body size preferences. *PLOS One, 7:* e48691.

Bor, J., Brunelin, J., Sappey-Marinier, D., Ibarrola, D., d'Amato, T., Suaud-Chagny, M.-F., & Saoud, M. (2011). Thalamus abnormalities during working memory in schizophrenia. An fMRI study. *Schizophrenia Research, 125,* 49–53.

Borgelt, L. M., Franson, K. L., Nussbaum, A. M., & Wang, G. S. (2013). The pharmacologic and clinical effects of medical cannabis. *Pharmacotherapy: The Journal of Human Pharmacology and Drug Therapy, 33,* 195–209.

Bornstein, R. F., Denckla, C. A., & Chung, W.-J. (2013). Psychodynamic models of personality. In H. Tennen, J. Suls, & I. B. Weiner (Eds.), *Handbook of psychology, Vol. 5. Personality and social psychology* (2nd ed., pp. 43–64). Hoboken, NJ: Wiley.

Borst, G., Kievit, R. A., Thompson, W. L., & Kosslyn, S. M. (2011). Mental rotation is not easily cognitively penetrable. *Journal of Cognitive Psychology, 23,* 60–75.

Bouchard, T. J., Jr. (1997). The genetics of personality. In K. Blum & E. P. Noble (Eds.), *Handbook of psychiatric genetics* (pp. 273–296). Boca Raton, FL: CRC Press.

Bouchard, T. J., Jr. (2004). Genetic influence on human psychological traits: A survey. *Current Directions in Psychological Science, 13,* 148–151.

Bouchard, T. J., Jr. & McGue, M. (1981). Familial studies of intelligence: A review. *Science, 212,* 1055–1059.

Bouchard, T. J., Jr., McGue, M., Hur, Y., & Horn, J. M. (1998). A genetic and environmental analysis of the California Psychological Inventory using adult twins reared apart and together. *European Journal of Personality, 12,* 307–320.

Bourne, L. E., Dominowski, R. L., & Loftus, E. F. (1979). *Cognitive processes.* Englewood Cliffs, NJ: Prentice Hall.

Bouton, M. E., Winterbauer, N. E., & Todd, T. P. (2012). Relapse processes after the extinction of instrumental learning: Renewal, resurgence, and reacquisition. *Behavioural Processes, 90,* 130–141.

Bowden, M. G., Woodbury, M. L., & Duncan, P. W. (2013). Promoting neuroplasticity and recovery after stroke: Future directions for rehabilitation clinical trials. *Current Opinion in Neurology, 26,* 37–42.

Bowlby, J. (1969). *Attachment and loss: Vol. 1. Attachment.* New York: Basic Books.

Bowlby, J. (1989). *Secure attachment.* New York: Basic Books.

Bowlby, J. (2000). *Attachment.* New York: Basic Books.

Bowling, A. C., & Mackenzie, B. D. (1996). The relationship between speed of information processing and cognitive ability. *Personality and Individual Differences, 20,* 775–800.

Boxer, P., Huesmann, L. R., Dubow, E. F., Landau, S. F., Gvirsman, S. D., Shikaki, K., & Ginges, J. (2013). Exposure to violence across the social ecosystem and the development of aggression: A test of ecological theory in the Israeli–Palestinian conflict. *Child Development, 84,* 163–177.

Boyce, C. J., Wood, A. M., & Powdthavee, N. (2013). Is personality fixed? Personality changes as much as "variable" economic factors and more strongly predicts changes to life satisfaction. *Social Indicators Research, 111,* 287–305.

Boyd, R., Richerson, P. J., & Henrich, J. (2011). Rapid cultural adaptation can facilitate the evolution of large-scale cooperation. *Behavioral Ecology and Sociobiology, 65,* 431–444.

Boyle, S. H., Williams, R. B., Mark, D. B., Brummett, B. H., Siegler, I. C., Helms, M. J., & Barefoot, J. C. (2004). Hostility as a predictor of survival in patients with coronary artery disease. *Psychosomatic Medicine, 66,* 629–632.

Boysen, G. A., & VanBergen, A. (2013). A review of published research on adult dissociative identity disorder: 2000–2010. *The Journal of Nervous and Mental Disease, 201,* 5–11.

Bradshaw, D. H., Chapman, C. R., Jacobson, R. C., & Donaldson, G. W. (2012). Effects of music engagement on responses to painful stimulation. *Clinical Journal of Pain, 28,* 418–427.

Brady, M. L., Diaz, M. R., Iuso, A., Everett, J. C., Valenzuela, C. F., & Caldwell, K. K. (2013). Moderate prenatal alcohol exposure reduces plasticity and alters NMDA receptor subunit composition in the dentate gyrus. *The Journal of Neuroscience, 33,* 1062–1067.

Brady, T. F., & Tenenbaum, J. B. (2013). A probabilistic model of visual working memory: Incorporating higher order regularities into working memory capacity estimates. *Psychological Review, 120,* 85–109.

Bratter, J., & Gorman, B. K. (2011). Does multiracial matter? A study of racial disparities in self-rated health. *Demography, 48,* 127–152.

Braunlich, K., & Seger, C. (2013). The basal ganglia. *Wiley Interdisciplinary Reviews: Cognitive Science, 4,* 135–148.

Brewer, J. B., Zhao, N., Desmond, J. E., Glover, G. H., & Gabriel, J. D. E. (1998). Making memories: Brain activity that predicts how well visual experience will be remembered. *Science, 281,* 1185–1187.

Brewer, N., Weber, N., Wootton, D., & Lindsay, D. (2012). Identifying the bad guy in a lineup using confidence judgments under deadline pressure. *Psychological Science, 23,* 1208–1214.

Brim, B. L., Haskell, R., Awedikian, R., Ellinwood, N. M., Jin, L., Kumar, A., . . . Magnusson, K. R. (2013). Memory in aged mice is rescued by enhanced expression of the GluN2B subunit of the NMDA receptor. *Behavioural Brain Research, 238,* 211–226.

Brink, M., & van Bronswijk, J. E. M. H. (2013). Addressing Maslow's deficiency needs in smart homes. *Gerontechnology, 11,* 445–451.

Brinker, J. K., Campisi, M., Gibbs, L., & Izzard, R. (2013). Rumination, mood and cognitive performance. *Psychology, 4,* 224–231.

Brislin, R. W. (1997). *Understanding culture's influence on behavior* (2nd ed.). San Diego, CA: Harcourt Brace.

Brislin, R. W. (2000). *Understanding culture's influence on behavior* (3rd ed.). Ft. Worth, TX: Harcourt.

Brodin, T., Lind, M., & Johansson, F. (2013). Personality trait differences between mainland and island populations in the common frog (*Rana temporaria*). *Behavioral Ecology and Sociobiology, 67,* 135–143.

Brooks, S. J., O'Daly, O. G., Uher, R., Schiöth, H. B., Treasure, J., & Campbell, I. C. (2012). Subliminal food images compromise superior working memory performance in women with restricting anorexia nervosa. *Consciousness & Cognition: An International Journal, 21,* 751–763.

Brown, L. M., Frahm, K. A., & Bongar, B. (2013). Crisis intervention. In G. Stricker, T. A. Widiger, & I. B. Weiner (Eds.), *Handbook of psychology, Vol. 8. Clinical psychology* (2nd ed., pp. 408–430). Hoboken, NJ: Wiley.

Brown, L. S. (2011). Guidelines for treating dissociative identity disorder in adults, third revision: A tour de force for the dissociation field. *Journal of Trauma and Dissociation, 12,* 113–114.

Brown, R., & Kulik, J. (1977). Flashbulb memories. *Cognition, 5,* 73–99.

Brown, W. A. (2013). *The placebo effect in clinical practice.* New York: Oxford University Press.

Brumbaugh, C. C., & Wood, D. (2013). Mate preferences across life and across the world. *Social Psychological and Personality Science, 4,* 100–107.

Brunoni, A. R., Valiengo, L., Baccaro, A., Zanão, T. A., de Oliveira, J. F., Goulart, A., . . . Fregni, F. (2013). The sertraline vs electrical current therapy for treating depression clinical study: Results from a factorial, randomized, controlled trial. *JAMA Psychiatry, 70,* 383–391.

Bruns, C. M., & Kaschak, E. (2011). Feminisms: Feminist therapies in the 21st century. *Women and Therapy, 34,* 1–5.

Bryan, A. D., Webster, G. D., & Mahaffey, A. L. (2011). The big, the rich, and the powerful: Physical, financial, and social dimensions of dominance in mating and attraction. *Personality and Social Psychology Bulletin, 37,* 365–382.

Brzezinski, A., Vangel, M. G., Wurtman, R. J., Norrie, G., Zhdanova, I., Ben-Shushan, A., & Ford, I. (2005). Effects of exogenous melatonin on sleep: A meta-analysis. *Sleep Medicine Reviews, 9,* 41–50.

Buckels, E. E., & Trapnell, P. D. (2013). Disgust facilitates outgroup dehumanization. *Group Processes & Intergroup Relations, 16,* 771–780.

Bull, R., Cleland, A. A., & Mitchell, T. (2013). Sex differences in the spatial representation of number. *Journal of Experimental Psychology: General, 142,* 181–192.

Bunde, J., & Suls, J. (2006). A quantitative analysis of the relationship between the Cook-Medley hostility scale and traditional coronary artery disease risk factors. *Health Psychology, 25,* 493–500.

Buneviciute, J., Staniute, M., Brozaitiene, J., Girdler, S. S., & Bunevicius, R. (2013). Mood symptoms and personality dimensions as determinants of health related quality of life in patients with coronary artery disease. *Journal of Health Psychology, 18,* 1493–1504.

Bunge, S. A., & Toga, A. W. (2013). Introduction to frontal lobe development. In D. Stuss & R. Knight (Eds.), *Oxford handbook of frontal lobe functions.* New York: Oxford University Press.

Burnette, J., Pollack, J., & Forsyth, D. (2011). Leadership in extreme contexts: A groupthink analysis of the May 1996 Mount Everest disaster. *Journal of Leadership Studies, 4,* 29–40.

Burns, J. K. (2013). The social determinants of schizophrenia: An African journey in social epidemiology. *Public Health Reviews, 34.* Retrieved from http://www.publiche althreviews.eu/upload/pdf_files/12/00_ Burns.pdf

Burnstock, G. (2013). Introduction to purinergic signalling in the brain. *Glioma Signaling, 986,* 1–12.

Buss, D. M. (1989). Sex differences in human mate preferences: Evolutionary hypotheses tested in 37 cultures. *Behavioral and Brain Sciences, 12,* 1–49.

Buss, D. M. (1994). Mate preferences in 37 countries. In W. J. Lonner & R. Malpass (Eds.), *Psychology and culture.* Boston, MA: Allyn & Bacon.

Buss, D. M. (2003). *The evolution of desire: Strategies of human mating.* New York: Basic Books.

Buss, D. M. (2008). *Evolutionary psychology: The new science of the mind* (3rd ed.). Boston: Allyn & Bacon.

Buss, D. M. (2011). *Evolutionary psychology: The new science of the mind* (4th ed.). Upper Saddle River, NJ: Prentice-Hall.

Buss, D. M., Abbott, M., Angleitner, A., Asherian, A., Biaggio, A., Blanco-Villasenor, A., . . . Yang, K. -S. (1990). International preferences in selecting mates: A study of 37 cultures. *Journal of Cross-Cultural Psychology, 21,* 5–47.

Buszewski, B., Rudnicka, J., Ligor, T., Walczak, M., Jezierski, T., & Amann, A. (2012). Analytical and unconventional methods of cancer detection using odor. *Trends in Analytical Chemistry, 38,* 1–12.

Butcher, J. N. (2000). Revising psychological tests: Lessons learned from the revision of the MMPI. *Psychological Assessment, 12,* 263–271.

Butcher, J. N. (2011). *A beginner's guide to the MMPI-2* (3rd ed.). Washington, DC: American Psychological Association.

Butcher, J. N., & Perry, J. N. (2008). *Personality assessment in treatment planning: Use of the MMPI-2 and BTPI.* New York: Oxford University Press.

Butz, D. A., & Plant, E. A. (2011). Approaching versus avoiding intergroup contact: The role of expectancies and motivation. In L. R. Tropp & R. K. Mallett (Eds.), *Moving beyond prejudice reduction: Pathways to positive intergroup relations* (pp. 81–98). Washington, DC: American Psychological Association.

Buxton, O. M., Cain, S. W., O'Connor, S. P., Porter, J. H., Duffy, J. F., Wang, W. . . . Shea, S. A. (2012). Adverse metabolic consequences in humans of prolonged sleep restriction combined with circadian disruption. *Science Translational Medicine, 4,* 129ra43.

Cacioppo, J. T., Cacioppo, S., Gonzaga, G. C., Ogburn, E. L., & VanderWeele, T. J. (2013). Marial satisfaction and break-ups differ across on-line and off-line meeting venues. *Proceedings of the National Academy of Sciences, 110,* 10135–10140.

Cain, D. J. (2013). Person-centered therapy. In J. Frew & M. D. Spiegler (Eds.), *Contemporary psychotherapies for a diverse world* (1st rev. ed., pp. 165–213). New York: Routledge/Taylor & Francis Group.

Calkins, S. D., & Keane, S. P. (2009). Developmental origins of early antisocial behavior. *Development and Psychopathology, 21,* 1095–1109.

Call, D., Miron, L., & Orcutt, H. (2013). Effectiveness of brief mindfulness techniques in reducing symptoms of anxiety and stress. *Mindfulness.* Advance online publication. doi: 10.1007/s12671-013-0218-6.

Call, J. (2011). How artificial communication affects the communication and cognition of the great apes. *Mind and Language, 26,* 1–20.

Camarena, B., Santiago, H., Aguilar, A., Ruvinskis, E., González-Barranco, J., & Nicolini, H. (2004). Family-based association study between the monoamine oxidase A gene and obesity: Implications for psychopharmacogenetic studies. *Neuropsychobiology, 49,* 126–129.

Cameron, L., Rutland, A. & Brown, R. (2007). Promoting children's positive intergroup attitudes towards stigmatized groups: Extended contact and multiple classification skills training. *International Journal of Behavioral Development, 31,* 454–466.

Campbell, J. L., Britten, N., Green, C., Holt, T. A., Lattimer, V., Richards, S.H., . . . Fletcher, E. (2013). The effectiveness and cost-effectiveness of telephone triage of patients requesting same day consultations in general practice: study protocol for a cluster randomised controlled trial comparing nurse-led and GP-led management systems (ESTEEM). *Trials, 14,* 4.

Campbell, J. R., & Feng, A. X. (2011). Comparing adult productivity of American mathematics, physics, and chemistry Olympians with Terman's longitudinal study. *Roeper Review: A Journal on Gifted Education, 33,* 18–25.

Campbell, L. F., Norcross, J. C., Vasquez, M. J. T., & Kaslow, N. J. (2013). Recognition of psychotherapy effectiveness: The APA resolution. *Psychotherapy, 50,* 98–101.

Campbell, L., Simpson, J. A., Kashy, D. A., & Fletcher, G. J. O. (2001). Ideal standards, the self, and flexibility of ideals in close relationships. *Personality and Social Psychology Bulletin, 27,* 447–462.

Campbell, M. C., Black, K. J., Weaver, P. M., Lugar, H. M., Videen, T. O., Tabbal, S. D., . . . Hershey, T. (2012). Mood response to deep brain stimulation of the subthalamic nucleus in Parkinson's Disease. *Journal of Neuropsychiatry and Clinical Neurosciences, 24,* 28–36.

Camperio Ciani, A. S., Edelman, S., & Ebstein, R. P. (2013). The dopamine D4 receptor (DRD4) Exon 3 VNTR contributes to adaptive personality differences in an Italian small island population. *European Journal of Personality.* doi: 10.1002/per.1917

Cao, X. (2013). The effects of facial close-ups and viewers' sex on empathy and intentions to help people in need. *Mass Communication and Society, 16,* 161–178.

Caprara, G. V., Vecchione, M., Barbaranelli, C., & Fraley, R. C. (2007). When likeness goes with liking: The case of political preference. *Political Psychology, 28,* 609–632.

Caqueo-Urízar, A., Ferrer-García, M., Toro, J., Gutiérrez-Maldonado, J., Peñaloza, C., Cuadros-Sosa, Y., & Gálvez-Madrid, M. J. (2011). Associations between sociocultural pressures to be thin, body distress, and eating disorder symptomatology among Chilean adolescent girls. *Body Image, 8,* 78–81.

Cardeña, E., Butler, L. D., Reijman, S., & Spiegel, D. (2013). Disorders of extreme stress. In G. Stricker, T. A. Widiger, & I. B. Weiner (Eds.), *Handbook of psychology, Vol. 8. Clinical psychology (2nd ed.,* pp. 193–216). Hoboken, NJ: Wiley.

Carey, B. (2008, December 4). H. M., an unforgettable amnesiac, dies at 82. *The New York Times.* Retrieved from http://www .nytimes.com/2008/12/05/us/05hm.html

Carlesimo, G. A., Costa, A., Serra, L., Bozzali, M., Fadda, L., & Caltagirone, C. (2011). Prospective memory in thalamic amnesia. *Neuropsychologia, 49,* 2199–2208.

Carlo, G., Mestre, M. V., McGinley, M., Tur-Porcar, A., Samper, P., & Streit, C. (2013). The structure and correlates of a measure of prosocial moral reasoning in adolescents from Spain. *European Journal of Developmental Psychology, 10,* 174–189.

Carlson, J. D., & Englar-Carlson, M. (2013). Adlerian therapy. In J. Frew & M. D. Spiegler (Eds.), *Contemporary psychotherapies for a diverse world* (1st rev. ed., pp. 87–129). New York: Routledge/Taylor & Francis Group.

Carnagey, N. L., Anderson, C. A., & Bartholow, B. D. (2007). Media violence and social neuroscience: New questions and new opportunities. *Current Directions in Psychological Science, 16,* 178–182.

Carpenter, R. W., Tomko, R. L., Trull, T. J., & Boomsma, D. I. (2013). Gene-environment studies and borderline personality disorder: A review. *Current Psychiatry Reports, 15,* 1–7.

Carpenter, S. K. (2012). Testing enhances the transfer of learning. *Current Directions in Psychological Science, 21,* 279–283.

Carroll, J. E., Low, C. A., Prather, A. A., Cohen, S., Fury, J. M., Ross, D. C., & Marsland, A. L. (2011). Negative affective responses to a speech task predict changes in interleukin (IL)-6. *Brain, Behavior, and Immunity, 25,* 232–238.

Carskadon, M. A., Wolfson, A. R., Acebo, C., Tzischinsky, O., & Seifer, R. (1998). Adolescent sleep patterns, circadian timing, and sleepiness at a transition to early school days. *Sleep, 21,* 871–881.

Carvalho, S., Pinto-Gouveia, J., Pimentel, P., Maia, D., Gilbert, P., & Mota-Pereira, J. (2013). Entrapment and defeat perceptions in expressive symptomatology: Through an evolutionary approach. *Psychiatry: Interpersonal & Biological Processes, 76,* 53–67.

Case, B. G., Bertollo, D. N., Laska, E. M., Price, L. H., Siegel, C. E., Olfson, M., & Marcus, S. C. (2013). Declining use of electroconvulsive therapy in United States general hospitals. *Biological Psychiatry, 73,* 119–126.

Casey, B. M. (2013). Individual and group differences in spatial ability. In D. Waller & L. Nadel (Eds.), *Handbook of spatial cognition* (pp. 117–134). Washington, DC: American Psychological Association.

Castrén, E., & Hen, R. (2013). Neuronal plasticity and antidepressant actions. *Trends in Neurosciences, 36,* 259–267.

Cathers-Schiffman, T. A., & Thompson, M. S. (2007). Assessment of English-and Spanish-speaking students with the WISC-III and Leiter-R. *Journal of Psychoeducational Assessment, 25,* 41–52.

Cattaneo, Z., Mattavelli, G., Platania, E., & Papagno, C. (2011). The role of the prefrontal cortex in controlling gender-stereotypical associations: A TMS investigation. *NeuroImage, 56,* 1839–1846.

Cattell, R. B. (1950). *Personality: A systematic, theoretical, and factual study.* New York: McGraw-Hill.

Cattell, R. B. (1965). *The scientific analysis of personality.* Baltimore, MD: Penguin.

Cattell, R. B. (1990). Advances in Cattellian personality theory. In L. A. Pervin (Ed.), *Handbook of personality: Theory and research.* New York: Guilford Press.

Cautin, R. L. (2011). A century of psycho-therapy, 1860–1960. In J. C. Norcross, G. R. VandenBos, & D. K. Freedheim (Eds.), *History of psychotherapy: Continuity and change* (2nd ed., pp. 3–38). Washington, DC: American Psychological Association.

Cavazos-Rehg, P. A., Krauss, M. J., Spitznagel, E. L., Chaloupka, F. J., Schootman, M., Grucza, R. A., & Bierut, L. J. (2012). Associations between selected state laws and teenagers' drinking and driving behaviors. *Alcoholism: Clinical and Experimental Research, 36*, 1647–1652.

Cechnicki, A., Helms, J. E., & Cook, D. A. (1999). *Using race and culture in counseling and psychotherapy: Theory and process.* Boston, MA: Allyn & Bacon.

Celes, L. A. M. (2010). Clinica psicanalitica: Aproximações histórico-conceituais e contemporâneas e perspectivas futuras [Psychoanalytic practice: Historical, conceptual and contemporary approaches and future perspectives]. *Psicologia: Teoria e Pesquisa, 26*, 65–80.

Centers for Disease Control and Prevention (2011). *Healthy weight—it's not a diet, it's a lifestyle!* Retrieved from: http://www .cdc.gov/healthyweight/assessing/bmi/ adult_bmi/english_bmi_calculator/bmi_ calcula tor.html

Cervone, D., & Pervin, L. A. (2010). *Personality theory and research* (11th ed.). Hoboken, NJ: Wiley.

Ceschi, G., & Scherer, K. R. (2001). Contrôler l'expression faciale et changer l'émotion: Une approche développementale. The role of facial expression in emotion: A developmental perspective. *Enfance, 53*, 257–269.

Chadwick, R. (2011). Personal genomes: No bad news? *Bioethics, 25*, 62–65.

Challem, J., Berkson, B., Smith, M. D., & Berkson, B. (2000). *Syndrome X: The complete program to prevent and reverse insulin resistance.* Hoboken, NJ: Wiley.

Chamberlin, N. L., & Saper, C. B. (2009). The agony of the ecstasy: Serotonin and obstructive sleep apnea. *Neurology, 73*, 1947–1948.

Chamorro-Premuzic, T. (2011). *Personality and individual differences.* Malden, MA: Blackwell.

Chanen, A. M., & McCutcheon, L. (2013). Prevention and early intervention for borderline personality disorder: current status and recent evidence. *The British Journal of Psychiatry, 202*, s24–s29.

Chang, C.-Y. (2012). The survey research of kindergarten children's dreams. *Chinese Journal of Guidance and Counseling, 33*, 1–23.

Chang, L., Wang, Y., Shackelford, T. K., & Buss, D. M. (2011). Chinese mate preferences: Cultural evolution and continuity across a quarter of a century. *Personality and Individual Differences, 50*, 678–683.

Chang, S. W., O'Neill, J., & Rosenberg, D. (2013). Obsessive-compulsive disorder. In L. A. Reddy, A. S. Weissman, & J. B. Hale (Eds.), *Neuropsychological assessment and intervention for youth: An evidence-based approach to emotional and behavioral disorders* (pp. 41–71). Washington, DC: American Psychological Association.

Chao, O. Y. H., Pum, M. E., & Huston, J. P. (2013). The interaction between the dopaminergic forebrain projections and the medial prefrontal cortex is critical for memory of objects: Implications for Parkinson's disease. *Experimental Neurology, 247*, 373–382.

Chapman, A. L., Leung, D. W., & Lynch, T. R. (2008). Impulsivity and emotion dysregulation in borderline personality disorder. *Journal of Personality Disorders, 22*, 148–164.

Chapman, E. N., Kaatz, A., & Carnes, M. (2013). Physicians and implicit bias: How doctors may unwittingly perpetuate health care disparities. *Journal of General Internal Medicine, 28*, 1504–1510.

Charles, K. (2011). Retrieved from www .napier.ac.uk/media/Pages/NewsDetails .aspx?NewsID=187.

Chellappa, S. L., Frey, S., Knoblauch, V., & Cajochen, C. (2011). Cortical activation patterns herald successful dream recall after NREM and REM sleep. *Biological Psychology, 87*, 251–256.

Chen, C-F., & Kao, Y-L. (2013). The connection between the hassles–burnout relationship, as moderated by coping, and aberrant behaviors and health problems among bus drivers. *Accident Analysis and Prevention, 53*, 105–111.

Cheng, C., Cheung, S-F., Chio, J. H., & Chan, M. S. (2013). Cultural meaning of perceived control: A meta-analysis of locus of control and psychological symptoms across 18 cultural regions. *Psychological Bulletin, 139*, 152–188.

Cheung, F., van de Vijver, F., & Leong, F. (2011). Toward a new approach to the study of personality in culture. *American Psychologist, 66*, 596–603.

Chi, L. (2013). Intergenerational transmission of educational attainment: Three levels of parent–child communication as mediators. *PsyCh Journal, 2*, 26–38.

Chiang, Y. Y., Tsai, P. Y., Chen, P. C., Yang, M. H., Li, C. Y., Sung, F. C., & Chen, K. B. (2012). Sleep disorders and traffic accidents. *Epidemiology, 23*, 643–644.

Chica, A. B., Bartolomeo, P., & Lupiáñez, J. (2013). Two cognitive and neural systems for endogenous and exogenous spatial attention. *Behavioural Brain Research, 237*, 107–123.

Choca, J. P. (2013). Interpretative basics. In J. P. Choca (Ed.), *The Rorschach inkblot test: An interpretive guide for clinicians* (pp. 27–33). Washington, DC: American Psychological Association.

Chopra, A., Tye, S. J., Lee, K. H., Sampson, S., Matsumoto, J., Adams, A., . . . Frye, M. A. (2012). Underlying neurobiology and clinical correlates of mania status after subthalamic nucleus deep brain stimulation in Parkinson's Disease: A review of the literature. *Journal of Neuropsychiatry and Clinical Neurosciences, 24*, 102–110.

Chorpita, B. F., Daleiden, E. L., Ebesutani, C., Young, J., Becker, K. D., Nakamura, B. J., . . . Starace, N. (2011). Evidence-based treatments for children and adolescents: An updated review of indicators of efficacy and effectiveness. *Clinical Psychology: Science and Practice, 18*, 154–172.

Chou, Y.-C., Chiao, C., & Fu, L.-Y. (2011). Health status, social support, and quality of life among family carers of adults with profound intellectual and multiple disabilities (PIMD) in Taiwan. *Journal of Intellectual and Developmental Disability, 36*, 73–79.

Chrisler, J. C. (2008). The menstrual cycle in a biopsychosocial context. In F. Denmark & M. A. Paludi (Eds.), *Psychology of women: A handbook of issues and theories* (2nd ed., pp. 400–439). *Women's psychology.* Westport, CT: Praeger/Greenwood.

Christakou, A., Brammer, M., & Rubia, K. (2011). Maturation of limbic corticostriatal activation and connectivity associated with developmental changes in temporal discounting. *NeuroImage, 54*, 1344–1354.

Christandl, F., Fetchenhauer, D., & Hoelzl, E. (2011). Price perception and confirmation bias in the context of a VAT increase. *Journal of Economic Psychology, 32*, 131–141.

Christenfeld, N. J. S., & Mandler, G. (2013). Emotion. In D. K. Freedheim & I. B. Weiner (Eds.), *Handbook of psychology, Vol. 1. History of psychology* (2nd ed., pp. 177–197). Hoboken, NJ: Wiley.

Christensen, D. (2000). Is snoring a diZ-ZZease? Nighttime noises may serve as a wake-up call for future illness. *Science News, 157*, 172–173.

Christensen, H., Anstey, K. J., Leach, L. S., & Mackinnon, A. J. (2008). Intelligence, education, and the brain reserve hypothesis. In F. I. M. Craik & T. A. Salthouse (Eds.), *The handbook of aging and cognition* (3rd ed., pp. 133–188). New York: Psychology Press.

Chu, J. (2011). *Rebuilding shattered lives: Treating complex PTSD and dissociative disorders* (2nd ed.). Hoboken, NJ: Wiley.

Chu, Y. L., Farmer, A., Fung, C., Kuhle, S., Storey, K. E., & Veugelers, P. J. (2013). Involvement in home meal preparation is associated with food preference and self-efficacy among Canadian children. *Public Health Nutrition, 16,* 108–112.

Chuang, D. (1998). Cited in J. Travis, Simulating clue hints how lithium works. *Science News, 153,* 165.

Cini, F., Kruger, S., & Ellis, S. (2013). A model of intrinsic and extrinsic motivations on subjective well-being: The experience of overnight visitors to a national park. *Applied Research in Quality of Life, 8,* 45–61.

Claes, L., Bijttebier, P., Mitchell, J. E., de Zwaan, M., & Mueller, A. (2011). The relationship between compulsive buying, eating disorder symptoms, and temperament in a sample of female students. *Comprehensive Psychiatry, 52,* 50–55.

Claydon, L. (2012). Are there lessons to be learned from a more scientific approach to mental condition defences? *International Journal of Law and Psychiatry, 35,* 88–98.

Cohen, C., Janicki-Deverts, D., Doyle, W. J., Miller, G. E., Frank, E., Rabin, B. S., & Turner, R. B. (2012). Chronic stress, glucocorticoid receptor resistance, inflammation, and disease risk. *Proceedings of the National Academy of Sciences, 109,* 5995–5999.

Cohen, D., & Leung, A. K. (2011). Violence and character: A CuPS (culture 3 person 3 situation) perspective. In P. R. Shaver & M. Mikulincer (Eds.), *Herzilya series on personality and social psychology. Human aggression and violence: Causes, manifestations, and consequences* (pp. 187–200). Washington, DC: American Psychological Association.

Cohen, S., & Lemay, E. P. (2007). Why would social networks be linked to affect and health practices? *Health Psychology, 26,* 410–417.

Cohen, S., Doyle, W. J., Alper, C. M., Janicki-Deverts, D., & Turner, R. B. (2009). Sleep habits and susceptibility to the common cold. *Archives of Internal Medicine, 169,* 62–67.

Cohen, S., Doyle, W. J., Turner, R. B., Alper, C. M., & Skoner, D. P. (2003). Sociability and susceptibility to the common cold. *Psychological Science, 14,* 389–395.

Cole, M., & Gajdamaschko, N. (2007). Vygotsky and culture. In H. Daniels, J. Wertsch, & M. Cole (Eds.), *The Cambridge companion to Vygotsky* (pp. 193–211). New York: Cambridge University Press.

Coleborne, C., & MacKinnon, D. (2011). *Exhibiting madness in museums: Remembering psychiatry through collection and display.* New York: Routledge.

Coleman, M. D. (2013). Emotion and the ultimate attribution error. *Current Psychology, 32,* 71–81.

Collins, J., & Lidz, F. (2013). Why NBA center Jason Collins is coming out now. *SI: The Magazine.* Retrieved from http://sportsillustrated.cnn.com/magazine/news/20130429/jason-collins-gay-nba-player/

Collins, R. (2011). Content analysis of gender roles in media: Where are we now and where should we go? *Sex Roles, 64,* 290–298.

Collins, R. O., & Adams, J. L. (2013). *Prefrontal cortex: Developmental, executive, and cognitive functions and role in neurological disorders.* Hauppauge, NY: Nova Science.

Colom, R., Burgaleta, M., Román, F. J., Karama, S., Álvarez-Linera, J., Abad, F., . . . Haier, R. J. (2013). Neuroanatomic overlap between intelligence and cognitive factors: Morphometry methods provide support for the key role of the frontal lobes. *NeuroImage, 72,* 143–152.

Colombo, J., Brez, C. C., & Curtindale, L. M. (2013). Infant perception and cognition. In R. M: Lerner, M. A. Easterbrooks, J. Mistry, & I. B. Weiner (Eds.), *Handbook of psychology, Vol. 6. Developmental psychology (2nd ed.,* pp. 61–89). Hoboken, NJ: Wiley.

Colrain, I. M. (2011). Sleep and the brain. *Neuropsychology Review, 21,* 1–4.

Columb, C., & Plant, E. A. (2011). Revisiting the Obama Effect: Exposure to Obama reduces implicit prejudice. *Journal of Experimental Social Psychology, 47,* 499–501.

Colzato, L. S., Ozturk, A., & Hommel, B. (2012). Meditate to create: The impact of focused-attention and open-monitoring training on convergent and divergent thinking. *Frontiers in Psychology, 3,* 116.

Conger, A. J., Dygdon, J. A., & Rollock, D. (2013). Conditioned emotional responses in racial prejudice. *Ethnic and Racial Studies, 35,* 298–319.

Conger, K. (2011). Embryonic stem cell therapy for paralysis given to first patient in western United States. *Stanford School of Medicine.* Retrieved from http://med.stanford.edu/ism/2011/september/geron.html

Connelly, B. S., & Hülsheger, U. R. (2012). A narrower scope or a clearer lens of personality? Examining sources of observers' advantages over self-reports for predicting performance. *Journal of Personality, 80,* 603–631.

Connelly, B. S., & Ones, D. S. (2012). An other perspective on personality: Meta-analytic integration of observers' accuracy and predictive validity. *Psychological Bulletin, 136,* 1092–1122.

Connolly, I., Zaleon, C., & Montagnini, M. (2013). Management of severe neuropathic cancer pain: An illustrative case and review. *American Journal of Hospice & Palliative Medicine, 30,* 83–90.

Constantino, M. J., Manber, R., Ong, J., Kuo, T. F., Huang, J. S., & Arnow, B. A. (2007). Patient expectations and therapeutic alliance as predictors of outcome in group cognitive-behavioral therapy for insomnia. *Behavioral Sleep Medicine, 5,* 210–228.

Conzen, P. (2010). Erik H. Erikson: Pionier der psychoanalytischen identitätstheorie [Erik H. Erikson: A pioneer of the psychoanalytic identity theory]. *Forum der Psychoanalyse: Zeitschrift für klinische Theorie and Praxis, 26,* 389–411.

Cook, M. (2013). *Levels of personality* (3rd ed.). New York: Cambridge University Press.

Cooper, J. A., Watras, A. C., Paton, C. M., Wegner, F. H., Adams, A. K., & Schoeller, D. A. (2011). Impact of exercise and dietary fatty acid composition from a high-fat diet on markers of hunger and satiety. *Appetite, 56,* 171–178.

Cooper, W. E. Jr., Pérez-Mellado, V., Vitt, L. J., & Budzinsky, B. (2002). Behavioral responses to plant toxins in two omnivorous lizard species. *Physiology and Behavior, 76,* 297–303.

Cordón, L. (2012). *All things Freud: An encyclopedia of Freud's world* (Vols. 1–2). Santa Barbara, CA: Greenwood.

Coren, S. (2013). Sensation and perception. In D. K. Freedheim & I. B. Weiner (Eds.), *Handbook of psychology, Vol. 1. History of psychology* (2nd ed., pp. 100–128). Hoboken, NJ: Wiley.

Corey, G. (2013). *Theory and practice of counseling and psychotherapy (9th ed.).* Belmont, CA: Brooks/Cole Cengage Learning.

Corkin, S. (2002). What's new with the amnesic patient H.M.? *Nature Reviews Neuroscience, 3,* 153–160.

Corr, C. A., Nabe, C. M., & Corr, D. M. (2009). *Death and dying: Life and living* (6th ed.). Belmont, CA: Wadsworth.

Correll, J., Park, B., Judd, C. M., & Wittenbrink, B. (2002). The police officer's dilemma: Using ethnicity to disambiguate potentially threatening individuals. *Journal of Personality & Social Psychology, 83,* 1314–1329.

Corsica, J. A., & Perri, M. G. (2013). Understanding and managing obesity. In A. M. Nezu, C. M. Nezu, P. A. Geller, & I. B. Weiner (Eds.), *Handbook of psychology, Vol. 9. Health psychology* (2nd ed., pp. 128–148). Hoboken, NJ: Wiley.

Costa, P. T., Jr., & McCrae, R. R. (2011). The five-factor model, five-factor theory, and interpersonal psychology. In L. M. Horowitz & S. Strack (Eds.), *Handbook of interpersonal psychology: Theory, research, assessment, and therapeutic interventions* (pp. 91–104). Hoboken, NJ: Wiley.

Cotter, D., Hermsen, J., & Vanneman, R. (2011). The end of the gender revolution? Gender role attitudes from 1977–2008. *American Journal of Sociology, 116*, 1–31.

Cougle, J. R., Bonn-Miller, M. O., Vujanovic, A. A., Zvolensky, M. J., & Hawkins, K. A. (2011). Posttraumatic stress disorder and Cannabis use in a nationally representative sample. *Psychology of Addictive Behaviors, 25*, 554–558.

Courage, M. L., & Adams, R. J. (1990). Visual acuity assessment from birth to three years using the acuity card procedures: Cross-sectional and longitudinal samples. *Optometry and Vision Science, 67*, 713–718.

Coyne, J. C., & Tennen, H. (2010). Positive psychology in cancer care: Bad science, exaggerated claims, and unproven medicine. *Annals of Behavioral Medicine, 39*, 16–26.

Craighead, W. E., Craighead, L. W., Ritschel, L. A., & Zagoloff, A. (2013). Behavior therapy and cognitive-behavioral therapy. In G. Stricker, T. A. Widiger, & I. B. Weiner (Eds.), *Handbook of psychology, Vol. 8. Clinical psychology* (2nd ed., pp. 291–319). Hoboken, NJ: Wiley.

Creaven, A-M, Howard, S., & Hughes, B. M. (2013). Social support and trait personality are independently associated with resting cardiovascular function in women. *British Journal of Health Psychology, 18*, 556–573.

Crum, A. J., Salovey, P., & Achor, S. (2013). Rethinking stress: The role of mindsets in determining the stress response. *Journal of Personality & Social Psychology, 104*, 716–733.

Cuijpers, P., Geraedts, A., van Oppen, P., Andersson, G., Markowitz, J., & van Straten, A. (2011). Interpersonal psychotherapy for depression: A meta-analysis. *American Journal of Psychiatry, 168*, 581–592.

Culebras, A. (2012). Sleep, stroke and post-stroke. *Neurologic Clinics, 30*, 1275–1284.

Cullen, D., & Gotell, L. (2002). From orgasms to organizations: Maslow, women's sexuality and the gendered foundations of the needs hierarchy. *Gender, Work and Organization, 9*, 537–555.

Cummins, R. A. (2013). Positive psychology and subjective well-being homeostasis: A critical examination of congruence. In A.

Efklides & D. Moraitou (Eds.), *Quality of life: A positive psychology perspective* (pp. 67–86). New York: Springer.

Cunningham, M. R., Barbee, A. P., & Philhower, C. L. (2002). Dimensions of facial physical attractiveness: The intersection of biology and culture. In G. Rhodes & L. A. Zebrowitz (Eds.), *Facial attractiveness: Evolutionary, cognitive, and social perspectives. Advances in visual cognition* (Vol. 1, pp. 193–238). Westport, CT: Ablex Publishing.

Cunningham, M. R., Roberts, A. R., Barbee, A. P., Druen, P. B., & Wu, C. (1995). "Their ideas of beauty are, on the whole, the same as ours": Consistency and variability in the cross-cultural perception of female physical attractiveness. *Journal of Personality and Social Psychology, 38*, 181–192.

Curry, O., Roberts, S. G. B., & Dunbar, R. I. M. (2013). Altruism in social networks: Evidence for a 'kinship premium'. *British Journal of Psychology, 104*, 283–295.

Curt, A. (2012). Talk given at the Interdependence 2012 Global SCI Conference, Vancouver, British Columbia, May 15–17, 2012.

Curtiss, S. (1977). *Genie: A psycholinguistic study of a modern-day "wild child."* New York: Academic Press.

Cushman, F., & Greene, J. (2012). The philosopher in the theater. In M. M. P. R. Shaver (Ed.), *The social psychology of morality: Exploring the causes of good and evil* (pp. 33–50). Washington, DC: American Psychological Association.

Cusimano, M., Biziato, D., Brambilla, E., Donegà, M., Alfaro-Cervello, C., Snider, S., . . . Pluchino, S. (2012). Transplanted neural stem/precursor cells instruct phagocytes and reduce secondary tissue damage in the injured spinal cord. *Brain: A Journal of Neurology, 135*, 447–460.

Cutler, B. l., & Kovera, M. B. (2013). Evaluation for eyewitness identification. In R. Roesch & P. A. Zapf (Eds.), *Best practices in forensic mental health assessment. Forensic assessments in criminal and civil law: A handbook for lawyers* (pp. 118–132). New York: Oxford University Press.

Cvetkovic, D., & Cosic, I. (Eds.). (2011). *States of consciousness: Experimental insights into meditation, waking, sleep and dreams.* New York: Springer.

Daan, S. (2011). How and why? The lab versus the field. *Sleep and Biological Rhythms, 9*, 1–2.

Dalal, S., & Bruera, E. (2013). Access to opioid analgesics and pain relief for patients with cancer. *Nature Reviews Clinical Oncology, 10*, 108–116.

Dalenberg, C., Loewenstein, R., Spiegel, D., Brewin, C., Lanius, R., Frankel, S., . . . Paulson, K. (2007). Scientific study of the dissociative disorders. *Psychotherapy and Psychosomatics, 76*, 400–401.

Dana, R. H. (2005). *Multicultural assessment: Principles, applications, and examples.* Mahwah, NJ: Erlbaum.

Dandekar, M. P., Nakhate, K. T., Kokare, D. M., & Subhedar, N. K. (2011). Effect of nicotine on feeding and body weight in rats: Involvement of cocaine- and amphetamine-regulated transcript peptide. *Behavioural Brain Research, 219*, 31–38.

Danner, F., & Phillips, B. (2008). Adolescent sleep, school start times, and teen motor vehicle crashes. *Journal of Clinical Sleep Medicine, 4*, 533–535.

Danso, K., & Lum, T. (2013). Intergroup relations and predictors of immigrant experience. *Journal of Ethnic and Cultural Diversity in Social Work, 22*, 60–75.

Dantzer, R., O'Connor, J. C., Freund, G. C., Johnson, R. W., & Kelley, K. W. (2008). From inflammation to sickness and depression: When the immune system subjugates the brain. *Nature Reviews Neuroscience, 9*, 46–57.

Darwin, C. (1872). *The expression of emotions in man and animals.* New York: Appleton & Company.

Dattilio, F. M., & Nichols, M. P. (2011). Reuniting estranged family members: A cognitive-behavioral-systemic perspective. *American Journal of Family Therapy, 39*, 88–99.

David, S. P., McClure, J. B., & Swan, G. E. (2013). Nicotine dependence. In A. M. Nezu, C. M. Nezu, P. A. Geller, & I. B. Weiner (Eds.), *Handbook of psychology, Vol. 9. Health psychology* (2nd ed., pp. 149–181). Hoboken, NJ: Wiley.

Davies, G., Tenesa, A., Payton, A., Yang, J., Harris, S. E., Liewald, D., . . . Deary, I. J. (2011). Genome-wide association studies establish that human intelligence is highly heritable and polygenic. *Molecular Psychiatry, 16*, 996–1005.

Davies, I. (1998). A study of colour grouping in three languages: A test of the linguistic relativity hypothesis. *British Journal of Psychology, 89*, 433–452.

Dawson, D. A., Goldstein, R. B., Moss, H. B., Li, T. K., & Grant, B. F. (2010). Gender differences in the relationship of internalizing and externalizing psychopathology to alcohol dependence: Likelihood, expression and course. *Drug and Alcohol Dependence, 112*, 9–17.

Dawson, D., Noy, Y. I., Härmä, M., Åkerstedt, T., & Belenky, G. (2011). Modelling fatigue and the use of fatigue models in work settings. *Accident Analysis and Prevention, 43*, 549–564.

De Leersnyder, J., Boiger, M., & Mesquita, B. (2013). Cultural regulation of emotion: individual, relational, and structural sources. *Frontiers in Psychology, 4, 55*.

De Smet, H. J., Paquier, P., Verhoeven, J., & Mariën, P. (2013). The cerebellum: Its role in language and related cognitive and affective functions. *Brain and Language*. Advance online publication. doi: 10.1016/j.bandl.2012.11.001

De Sousa, A. (2011). Freudian theory and consciousness: A conceptual analysis. *Brain, Mind and Consciousness, 9*, 210–217.

De Vos, J. (2010). From Milgram to Zimbardo: The double birth of postwar psychology/psychologization. *History of the Human Sciences, 23*, 156–175.

Deaner, R. O. (2013). Distance running as an ideal domain for showing a sex difference in competitiveness. *Archives of Sexual Behavior, 42*, 413–428.

DeAngelis, T. (2012). Practicing distance therapy, legally and ethically. *Monitor on Psychology, 43*, 52.

Deary, I. J., Ferguson, K. J., Bastin, M. E., Barrow, G. W. S., Reid, L. M., Seckl, J. R., . . . MacLullich, A. M. J. (2007). Skull size and intelligence, and King Robert Bruce's IQ. *Intelligence, 35*, 519–528.

Deci, E. L., & Moller, A. C. (2005). The concept of competence: A starting place for understanding intrinsic motivation and self-determined extrinsic motivation. In A. J. Elliot & C. S. Dweck (Eds.), *Handbook of competence and motivation* (pp. 579–597). New York: Guilford.

Deci, E. L., & Ryan, R. M. (2012). Self-determination theory. In P. A. M. Van Lange, A. W. Kruglanski, & E. T. Higgins (Eds), *Handbook of theories of social psychology* (Vol. 1, pp. 416–436). Thousand Oaks, CA: Sage Publications.

Decker, S. E., Nich, C., Carroll, K. M., & Martino, S. (2013). Development of the therapist empathy scale. *Behavioural and Cognitive Psychotherapy, 6*, 1–16.

DeClue, G. (2003). The polygraph and lie detection. *Journal of Psychiatry and Law, 31*, 361–368.

Dekel, S., & Farber, B. A. (2012). Models of intimacy of securely and avoidantly attached young adults. *The Journal of Nervous and Mental Disease, 200*, 156–162.

Del Giudice, M., Booth, T., & Irwing, P. (2012). The distance between Mars and Venus: Measuring global sex differences in personality. *PLoS ONE, 7*, e29265.

DeMaria, S. (2012). Club drugs. In E. O. Bryson & E. A. M. Frost (Eds.), *Periopera-tive addiction: Clinical management of the addicted patient* (pp. 111–128). New York: Springer Science + Business Media.

Dement, W. C., & Wolpert, E. (1958). The relation of eye movements, bodily motility, and external stimuli to dream content. *Journal of Experimental Psychology, 53*, 543–553.

Demeyer, I., De Lissnyder, E., Koster, E., & De Raedt, R. (2012). Rumination mediates the relationship between impaired cognitive control for emotional information and depressive symptoms: A prospective study in remitted depressed adults. *Behaviour Research and Therapy, 50*, 292–297.

Dempster, M., McCorry, N. K., Brennan, E., Donnelly, M., Murray, L. J., & Johnston, B. T. (2011). Do changes in illness perceptions predict changes in psychological distress among oesophageal cancer survivors? *Journal of Health Psychology, 16*, 500–509.

Denmark, F. L., Rabinovitz, V. C., & Sechzer, J. A. (2005). *Engendering psychology: Women and gender revisited* (2nd ed.). Boston, MA: Allyn and Bacon.

Denson, T. F. (2011). A social neuroscience perspective on the neurobiological bases of aggression. In P. R. Shaver & M. Mikulincer (Eds.), *Herzilya series on personality and social psychology. Human aggression and violence: Causes, manifestations, and consequences* (pp. 105–120). Washington, DC: American Psychological Association.

Depue, B. E. (2012). A neuroanatomical model of prefrontal inhibitory modulation of memory retrieval. *Neuroscience and Biobehavioral Reviews, 36*, 1382–1399.

Derntl, B., Schöpf, V., Kollndorfer, K., & Lanzenberger, R. (2013). Menstrual cycle phase and duration of oral contraception intake affect olfactory perception. *Chemical Senses, 38*, 67–75.

DeRobertis, E. M. (2013). Humanistic psychology: Alive in the 21st century?. *Journal of Humanistic Psychology*. doi:10.1177/00221678 12473369.

Desbordes, G., Negi, L. T., Pace, T. W. W., Wallace, B. A., Raison, C. L., & Schwartz, E. L. (2012). Effects of mindful-attention and compassion meditation training on amygdala response to emotional stimuli in an ordinary, non-meditative state. *Frontiers in Human Neuroscience, 6*, 292.

Dessalles, J. (2011). Sharing cognitive dissonance as a way to reach social harmony. *Social Science Information/Sur Les Sciences Sociales, 50*, 116–127.

Deutscher, G. (2010). *Through the language glass: Why the world looks different in other languages*. New York: Metropolitan Books/Henry Holt & Company.

DeWall, C. N., Anderson, C. A., & Bushman, B. J. (2013). Aggression. In H. Tennen, J. Suls, & I. B. Weiner (Eds.), *Handbook of psychology, Vol. 5. Personality and social psychology* (2nd ed., pp. 449–466). Hoboken, NJ: Wiley

Dewan, M. J., Steenbarger, B. N., & Greenberg, R. P. (2011). Brief psychotherapies. In R. E. Hales, S. C. Yudofsky, & G. O. Gabbard (Eds.), *Essentials of psychiatry* (3rd ed., pp. 525–539). Arlington, VA: American Psychiatric Publishing.

Dewar, M., Alber, J., Butler, C., Cowan, N., & Della Sala, S. (2012). Brief wakeful resting boosts new memories over the long term. *Psychological Science, 23*, 955–960.

Dhikav, V., Aggarwal, N., Gupta, S., Jadhavi, R., & Singh, K. (2008). Depression in Dhat syndrome. *Journal of Sexual Medicine, 5*, 841–844.

Di Iorio, C. R., Watkins, T. J., Dietrich, M. S., Cao, A., Blackford, J. U., Rogers, B., . . . Cowan, R. L. (2012). Evidence for chronically altered serotonin function in the cerebral cortex of female 3,4-methylenedioxymethamphetamine polydrug users. *Archives of General Psychiatry, 69*, 399–409.

Dickens, W. T., & Flynn, J. R. (2001). Heritability estimates versus large environmental effects: The IQ paradox resolved. *Psychological Review, 108*, 346–369.

DiDonato, T. E., Ullrich, J., & Krueger, J. I. (2011). Social perception as induction and inference: An integrative model of intergroup differentiation, ingroup favoritism, and differential accuracy. *Journal of Personality and Social Psychology, 100*, 66–83.

Diego, M. A., & Jones, N. A. (2007). Neonatal antecedents for empathy. In T. Farrow & P. Woodruff (Eds.), *Empathy in mental illness* (pp. 145–167). New York: Cambridge University Press.

Diener, E., & Chan, M. Y. (2011). Happy people live longer: Subjective well-being contributes to health and longevity. *Applied Psychology: Health and Well-Being, 3*, 1–43.

Dierdorff, E. C., Bell, S. T., & Belohlav, J. A. (2011). The power of "we": Effects of psychological collectivism on team performance over time. *Journal of Applied Psychology, 96*, 247–262.

DiFeliceantonio, A. G., Mabrouk, O. S., Kennedy, R. T., & Berridge, K. C. (2012). Enkephalin surges in dorsal neostriatum as a signal to eat. *Current Biology, 22*, 1918–1924.

DiGrazia, J., McKelvey, K., Bollen, J., & Rojas, F. (2013). More tweets, more votes: Social media as a quantitative indicator of political behavior. *Social Science Research Network*. Advance online publication. doi .org/10.2139/ssrn.2235423

Dillard, D. A., Smith, J. J., Ferucci, E. D., & Lanier, A. P. (2012). Depression prevalence and associated factors among Alaska native people: The Alaska education and research toward health (EARTH) study. *Journal of Affective Disorders, 136,* 1088–1097.

Dimberg, U., & Söderkvist, S. (2011). The voluntary facial action technique: A method to test the facial feedback hypothesis. *Journal of Nonverbal Behavior, 35,* 17–33.

DiPietro, J. A. (2000). Baby and the brain: Advances in child development. *Annual Review of Public Health, 21,* 455–471.

Dirks-Linhorst, P. A. (2013). An analysis of Missouri's insanity acquittee population, 1980–2009: Differences within African American insanity acquittees. *Journal of Ethnicity in Criminal Justice, 11,* 44–70.

Distel, M. A., Middeldorp, C. M., Trul, T. J., Derom, C. A, Willemsen, G., & Boomsma, D. I. (2011). Life events and borderline personality features: The influence of gene-environment interaction and gene-environment correlation. *Psychological Medicine: A Journal of Research in Psychiatry and the Allied Sciences, 41,* 849–860.

Doane, L. D., Kremen, W. S., Eaves, L. J., Eisen, S. A., Hauger, R., Hellhammer, D., . . . Jacobson, K. C. (2010). Associations between jet lag and cortisol diurnal rhythms after domestic travel. *Health Psychology, 29,* 117–123.

Doghramji, K. (2000, December). *Sleepless in America: Diagnosing and treating insomnia.* Retrieved from http://psychiatry. medscape.com/Medscape/psychiatry/ClinicalMgmt/CM.v02/public/indexCM.v02.html.

Dolev-Cohen, M. & Barak, A. (2013). Adolescents' use of instant messaging as a means of emotional relief. *Computers in Human Behavior, 29,* 58–63.

Domhoff, G. W. (2003). *The scientific study of dreams: Neural networks, cognitive development, and content analysis.* Washington, DC: American Psychological Association.

Domhoff, G. W. (2007). Realistic simulation and bizarreness in dream content: Past findings and suggestions for future research. In D. Barrett & P. McNamara (Eds.), *The new science of dreaming: Volume 2. Content, recall, and personality correlates* (pp. 1–27). Westport, CT: Praeger.

Domhoff, G. W. (2010). Dream content is continuous with waking thought, based on preoccupations, concerns, and interests. *Sleep Medicine Clinics, 5,* 203–215.

Domjan, M. (2005). Pavlovian conditioning: A functional perspective. *Annual Review of Psychology, 56,* 179–206.

Donnerstein, E. (2011). The media and aggression: From TV to the internet. In J. P. Forgas, A. W. Kruglanski & K. D. Williams (Eds.), *The psychology of social conflict and aggression* (pp. 267–284). New York: Psychology Press.

Donovan, D. M., Daley, D. C., Brigham, G. S., Hodgkins, C. C., Perl, H. I., Garrett, S.B., . . . Zammarelli, L. (2013). Stimulant abuser groups to engage in 12-step: A multisite trial in the National Institute on Drug Abuse Clinical Trials Network. *Journal of Substance Abuse Treatment, 44,* 103–114.

Doornbos, M. M., Zandee, G. L., DeGroot, J., & Warpinski, M. (2013). Desired mental health resources for urban, ethnically diverse, impoverished women struggling with anxiety and depression. *Qualitative Health Research, 23,* 78–92.

Dotsch, R., Wigboldus, D. H. J., & van Knippenberg, A. (2011). Biased allocation of faces to social categories. *Journal of Personality and Social Psychology, 100,* 999–1014.

Dougall, A. L., Wroble Biglan, M. C., Swanson, J. N., & Baum, A. (2013). Stress, coping, and immune function. In R. J. Nelson, S. J. Y. Mizumori, & I. B. Weiner (Eds.), *Handbook of psychology, Vol. 3. Behavioral neuroscience (2nd ed.,* pp. 440–460). Hoboken, NJ: Wiley.

Douglass, A. B. & Pavletic, A. (2012). Eyewitness confidence malleability. In B. L. Cutler (Ed.), *Conviction of the innocent: Lessons from psychological research* (pp. 149–165). Washington DC: American Psychological Association.

Dovidio, J. F., Eller, A., & Hewstone, M. (2011). Improving intergroup relations through direct, extended and other forms of indirect contact. *Group Processes and Intergroup Relations, 14,* 147–160.

Drapeau, V., & Gallant, A. R. (2013). Homeostatic and circadian control of food intake: Clinical strategies to prevent overconsumption. *Current Obesity Reports, 2,* 93–103.

Drew, L. (2013). What is the point of sleep? *New Scientist, 217,* 38–39.

Drew, L. J., Crabtree, G. W., Markx, S., Stark, K. L., Chaverneff, F., Xu, B., . . . Karayiorgou, M. (2011). The 22q11.2 microdeletion: Fifteen years of insights into the genetic and neural complexity of psychiatric disorders. *International Journal of Developmental Neuroscience, 29,* 259–281.

Drucker, D. J. (2010). Male sexuality and Alfred Kinsey's 0–6 Scale: Toward "a sound understanding of the realities of sex." *Journal of Homosexuality, 57,* 1105–1123.

Ducci, F., Bevilacqua, L., Landi, P., & Goldman, D. (2013). Genetic variation within serotonin genes, hormones, and aggression. In D. W. Pfaff & Y. Christen (Eds.), *Multiple origins of sex differences in the brain* (pp. 81–102). Berlin, Germany: Springer.

Duffey, K. J., & Popkin, B. M. (2013). Causes of increased energy intake among children in the US, 1977–2010. *American Journal of Preventive Medicine, 44,* e1-e8.

Dufresne, T. (2007). *Against Freud: Critics talk back.* Palo Alto, CA: Stanford University Press.

Duncan, B. L., & Reese, R. J. (2013). Empirically supported treatments, evidence-based treatments, and evidence-based practice. In G. Stricker, T. A. Widiger, & I. B. Weiner (Eds.), *Handbook of psychology, Vol. 8. Clinical psychology (2nd ed.,* pp. 489–513). Hoboken, NJ: Wiley.

Dunlosky, J., Rawson, K. A., Marsh, E. J., Nathan, M. J., & Willingham, D. T. (2013). Improving students' learning with effective learning techniques: Promising directions from cognitive and educational psychology. *Psychological Science in the Public Interest, 14,* 4–58.

Dunn, D. S., Saville, B. K., Baker, S. C., & Marek, P. (2013). Evidence–based teaching: Tools and techniques that promote learning in the psychology classroom. *Australian Journal of Psychology, 65,* 5–13.

Dunn, D., & Goodnight, L. (2014). *Communication: Embracing difference* (4th ed.). Upper Saddle River, NJ: Pearson.

Dunn, E. W., Aknin, L. B., & Norton, M. I. (2008). Spending money on others promotes happiness. *Science, 319,* 1687–1688.

Dunning, D., & Balcetis, E. (2013). Wishful seeing how preferences shape visual perception. *Current Directions in Psychological Science, 22,* 33–37.

Durgin, F. H., Ruff, A. J., & Russell, R. C. (2012). Constant enough: On the kinds of perceptual constancy worth having. In G. Hatfield & S. Allred (Eds.), *Visual experience: Sensation, cognition, and constancy* (pp. 87–102). New York: Oxford University Press.

Durrant, R., & Ellis, B. J. (2013). Evolutionary psychology. In R. J. Nelson, S. J. Y. Mizumori, & I. B. Weiner (Eds.), *Handbook of psychology, Vol. 3. Behavioral neuroscience (2nd ed.,* pp. 26–51). Hoboken, NJ: Wiley.

Duval, D. C. (2006). The relationship between African centeredness and psychological androgyny among African American women in middle adulthood. *Dissertation Abstracts International: Section B: The Sciences and Engineering, 67,* 1146.

Eagly, A. H., Karau, S. J., & Makhijani, M. G. (1995). Gender and the effectiveness of leaders: A meta-analysis. *Psychological Bulletin, 117,* 125–145.

Eaton, N. R., Keyes, K. M., Krueger, R. F., Balsis, S., Skodol, A. E., Markon, K. E., . . . Hasin, D. S. (2012). An invariant dimensional liability model of gender differences in mental disorder prevalence: Evidence from a national sample. *Journal of Abnormal Psychology, 121,* 282–288.

Eckel-Mahan, K., & Sassone-Corsi, P. (2013). Metabolism and the circadian clock converge. *Physiological Reviews, 93,* 107–135.

Ecker, U. K. H., Lewandowsky, S., & Apai, J. (2011). Terrorists brought down the plane!—No, actually it was a technical fault: Processing corrections of emotive information. *The Quarterly Journal of Experimental Psychology, 64,* 283–310.

Edele, A., Dziobek, I., & Keller, M. (2013). Explaining altruistic sharing in the dictator game: The role of affective empathy, cognitive empathy, and justice sensitivity. *Learning and Individual Differences, 24,* 96–102.

Edelstein, B. A., Martin, R. R., & Gerolimatos, L. A. (2013). Assessment in geriatric settings. In J. R. Graham, J. A. Naglieri, & I. B. Weiner (Eds.), *Handbook of psychology, Vol. 10. Assessment psychology* (2nd ed., pp. 425–447). Hoboken, NJ: Wiley.

Ehrenreich, B. (2004, July 15). *All together now.* Retrieved from http://select.nytimes .com/gst/abstract.html?res5F00E16FA3C5E 0C768DDDAE0894DC404482.

Eichenbaum, H. (2013). Memory systems. In R. J. Nelson, S. J. Y. Mizumori, & I. B. Weiner (Eds.), *Handbook of psychology, Vol. 3. Behavioral neuroscience* (2nd ed., pp. 551–573). Hoboken, NJ: Wiley.

Eisenberger, R., & Armeli, S. (1997). Can salient reward increase creative performance without reducing intrinsic creative interest? *Journal of Personality and Social Psychology, 72,* 652–663.

Eisenberger, R., & Rhoades, L. (2002). Incremental effects of reward on creativity. *Journal of Personality and Social Psychology, 81,* 728–741.

Ekas, N. V., Haltigan, J. D., & Messinger, D. S. (2013). The dynamic still-face effect: Do infants decrease bidding over time when parents are not responsive? *Developmental Psychology, 49,* 1027–1035.

Ekman, P., & Friesen, W. V. (1971). Constants across cultures in the face and emotion. *Journal of Personality and Social Psychology, 17,* 124–129.

Ekman, P., & Keltner, D. (1997). Universal facial expressions of emotion: An old controversy and new findings. In U. C. Segerstrale & P. Molnar (Eds.), *Nonverbal communication: Where nature meets culture* (pp. 27–46). Mahwah, NJ: Erlbaum.

Elkind, D. (1967). Egocentrism in adolescence. *Child Development, 38,* 1025–1034.

Elkind, D. (2000). A quixotic approach to issues in early childhood education. *Human Development, 43,* 279–283.

Ellis, A. (2008). Rational emotive behavior therapy. In K. Jordan (Ed.), *The quick theory reference guide: A resource for expert and novice mental health professionals,* (pp. 127–139). Hauppauge, NY: Nova Science Publishers.

Ellis, A., & Ellis, D. J. (2011a). *Rational emotive behavior therapy.* Washington, DC: American Psychological Association.

Ellis, A., & Ellis, D. J. (2011b). *Theories of psychotherapy. Rational emotive behavior therapy.* Washington, DC: Amreican Psychological Association.

Elsesser, K., Wannemüller, A., Lohrmann, T., Jöhren, P., & Sartory, G. (2013). Attention focusing versus distraction during exposure in dental phobia. *Behavioural and Cognitive Psychotherapy, 41,* 173–187.

Emdin, M., Passino, C., & Giannoni, A. (2013). Breathless heart: Only when the neck is deep in water? *Journal of the American College of Cardiology, 61,* 1167–1168.

Emery, C. F., Anderson, D. R., & Goodwin, C. L. (2013). Coronary heart disease and hypertension. In A. M. Nezu, C. M. Nezu, P. A. Geller, & I. B. Weiner (Eds.), *Handbook of psychology, Vol. 9. Health psychology* (2nd ed., pp. 340–364). Hoboken, NJ: Wiley.

Emmett, J., & McGee, D. (2013). Extrinsic motivation for large-scale assessments: A case study of a student achievement program at one urban high school. *The High School Journal, 96,* 116–137.

Endendijk, J. J., Groeneveld, M. G., van Berkel, S. R., Hallers-Haalboom, E. T., Mesman, J., & Bakermans-Kranenburg, M. J. (2013). Gender stereotypes in the family context: Mothers, fathers, and siblings. *Sex Roles, 68,* 577–590.

Eng, P. M., Rimm, E. B., Fitzmaurice, G., & Kawachi, I. (2002). Social ties and change in social ties in relation to subsequent total and cause-specific mortality and coronary heart disease incidence in men. *American Journal of Epidemiology, 155,* 700–709.

Enoch, M.-A. (2011). The role of early life stress as a predictor for alcohol and drug dependence. *Psychopharmacology, 214,* 17–31.

Epley, N. (2008) Rebate psychology. *New York Times.* Retrieved from http://select.nytimes.com/mem/tnt.html?tnt get2008/01/31/opinion/31epley.html.

Epstein, L. H., Handley, E. A., Dearing, K. K., Cho, D. D., Roemmich, J. N., Paluch, R. A., . . . Spring, B. (2006). Purchases of food in youth: Influence of price and income. *Psychological Science, 17,* 82–89.

Erlacher, D., & Schredl, M. (2004). Dreams reflecting waking sport activities: A comparison of sport and psychology students. *International Journal of Sport Psychology, 35,* 301–308.

Ersche, K. D., Jones, P. S., Williams, G. B., Robbins, T. W., & Bullmore, E. T. (2012). Cocaine dependence: A fast-track for brain ageing? *Molecular Psychiatry, 18,* 134–140.

Espy, K. A., Fang, H., Johnson, C., Stopp, C., Wiebe, S. A., & Respass, J. (2011). Prenatal tobacco exposure: Developmental outcomes in the neonatal period. *Developmental Psychology, 47,* 153–169.

Esquivel, G. B., & Acevedo, M. (2013). Testing for language competence in children and adolescents. In K. F. Geisinger, B. A. Bracken, J. F. Carlson, J.-I. C. Hansen, N. R. Kuncel, S. P. Reise, & M. C. Rodriguez (Eds.), *APA handbooks in psychology. APA handbook of testing and assessment in psychology, Vol. 3. Testing and assessment in school psychology and education* (pp. 213–230). Washington, DC: American Psychological Association.

Essau, C. A., & Petermann, F. (Eds.). (2013). *Anxiety disorders in children and adolescents: Epidemiology, risk factors and treatment* (Vol. 4). New York: Routledge.

Ethical Principles of Psychologists and Code of Conduct. (2010). *American Psychologist, 65,* 493.

Eysenck, H. J. (1967). *The biological basis of personality.* Springfield, IL: Charles C Thomas.

Eysenck, H. J. (1982). *Personality, genetics, and behavior: Selected papers.* New York: Prager.

Eysenck, H. J. (1990). Biological dimensions of personality. In L. A. Pervin (Ed.), *Handbook of personality: Theory and research* (pp. 244–276). New York: Guilford Press.

Fabre, B., Grosman, H., Mazza, O., Nolazco, C., Machulsky, N. F., Mesch, V., . . . Berg, G. (2013). Relationship between cortisol, life events and metabolic syndrome in men. *Stress: The International Journal on the Biology of Stress, 161,* 16–23.

Faddiman, A. (1997). *The spirit catches you and you fall down.* New York: Straus & Giroux.

Farber, I., & Banks, W. P. (2013). Consciousness. In A. F. Healy, R. W. Proctor, & I. B. Weiner (Eds.), *Handbook of psychology,*

Vol. 4. *Experimental psychology* (2nd ed., pp. 3–31). Hoboken, NJ: Wiley.

Fazio, L. K., Barber, S. J., Rajaram, S., Ornstein, P. A., & Marsh, E. J. (2013). Creating illusions of knowledge: Learning errors that contradict prior knowledge. *Journal of Experimental Psychology: General, 142*, 1–5.

Fein, S., & Spencer, S. J. (1997). Prejudice as selfimage maintenance: Affirming the self through derogating others. *Journal of Personality and Social Psychology, 73*, 31–44.

Feinstein, J. S. (2013). Lesion studies of human emotion and feeling. *Current Opinion in Neurobiology, 23*, 304–309.

Feldman, R. (2014). Synchrony and the neurobiological basis of social affiliation. In M. Mikulincer & P. R. Shaver (Eds.), *Mechanisms of social connection: From brain to group. The Herzliya series on personality and social psychology* (pp. 145–166). Washington, DC: American Psychological Association.

Fenn, K. M., & Hambrick, D. Z. (2012). What drives sleep-dependent memory consolidation: Greater gain or less loss? *Psychonomic Bulletin & Review, 20*, 501–506.

Fennis, B. M., & Stroebe, W. (2010). *The psychology of advertising.* New York: Psychology Press.

Ferguson, C. J. (2010). Violent crime research: An introduction. In C. J. Ferguson (Ed.), *Violent crime: Clinical and social implications* (pp. 3–18). Thousand Oaks, CA: Sage.

Ferguson, C. J. (2012). Violence in video games: Advocating for the wrong cause? *Child and Family Policy and Practice Advocate, 35*, 16–18.

Ferguson, M. J., & Porter, S. C. (2013). An examination of categorization processes in organizations: The root of intergroup bias and a route to prejudice reduction. In Q. M. Roberson (Ed.), *Oxford library of psychology. The Oxford handbook of diversity and work* (pp. 98–114). New York: Oxford University Press.

Fernández-Dols, J. M. (2013). Advances in the study of facial expression: An introduction to the special section. *Emotion Review, 5*, 3–7.

Ferreira, G. K., Rezin, G. T., Cardoso, M. R., Gonçalves, C. L., Borges, L. S., Vieira, J. S., . . . Streck, E. L. (2012). Brain energy metabolism is increased by chronic administration of bupropion. *Acta Neuropsychiatrica, 24*, 115–121.

Ferrucci, L. M., Cartmel, B., Turkman, Y. E., Murphy, M. E., Smith, T., Stein, K. D., & McCorkle, R. (2011). Causal attribution among cancer survivors of the 10 most common cancers. *Journal of Psychosocial Oncology, 29*, 121–140.

Festinger, L. A., & Carlsmith, J. M. (1959). Cognitive consequences of forced compliance. *Journal of Abnormal and Social Psychology, 58*, 203–210.

Field, K. M., Woodson, R., Greenberg, R., & Cohen, D. (1982). Discrimination and imitation of facial expressions by neonates. *Science, 218*, 179–181.

Fields, A., & Cochran, S. (2011). Men and depression: Current perspectives for health care professionals. *American Journal of Lifestyle Medicine, 5*, 92–100.

Figlewicz, D. P., & Sipols, A. J. (2010). Energy regulatory signals and food reward. *Pharmacology, Biochemistry & Behavior, 97*, 15–24.

Figueredo, A., Jacobs, W., Burger, S., Gladden, P., & Olderbak, S. (2011). The biology of personality. In G. Terzis & R. Arp (Eds.), *Information and living systems: Philosophical and scientific perspectives* (pp. 371–406). Boston, MA: MIT Press.

Filipović, D., Zlatković, J., Gass, P., & Inta, D. (2013). The differential effects of acute vs. chronic stress and their combination on hippocampal parvalbumin and Hsp70i expression. *Neuroscience, 236*, 47–54.

Fink, G. (2011). Stress controversies: Post-traumatic stress disorder, hippocampal volume, gastroduodenal ulceration. *Journal of Neuroendocrinology, 23*, 107–117.

Finkel, E. J., Slotter, E. B., Luchies, L. B., Walton, G. M., & Gross, J. J. (2013). A brief intervention to promote conflict-reappraisal preserves marital quality over time. *Psychological Science, 24*, 1595–1601.

Fischer, P., Krueger, J. I., Greitemeyer, T., Vogrincic, C., Kastenmüller, A., Frey, D., . . . Kainbacher, M. (2011). The bystander-effect: A meta-analytic review on bystander intervention in dangerous and non-dangerous emergencies. *Psychological Bulletin, 137*, 517–537.

Fischer, S., Peterson, C. M., & McCarthy, D. (2013). A prospective test of the influence of negative urgency and expectancies on binge eating and purging. *Psychology of Addictive Behaviors, 27*, 294–300.

Fisher, J. O., Birch, L. L., Zhang, J., Grusak, M. A., & Hughes, S. O. (2013). External influences on children's self-served portions at meals. *International Journal of Obesity, 37*, 954–960.

Fisher, M. A. (2013). *The ethics of conditional confidentiality: A practice model for mental health professionals.* New York: Oxford University Press.

Fishman, I., & Ng, R. (2013). Error-related brain activity in extraverts: Evidence for altered response monitoring in social context. *Biological Psychology, 93*, 225–230.

Fisk, J. E., Bury, A. S., & Holden, R. (2006). Reasoning about complex probabilistic concepts in childhood. *Scandinavian Journal of Psychology, 47*, 497–504.

Fiske, S. T. (1998). Stereotyping, prejudice, and discrimination. In D. T. Gilbert, S. T. Fiske, & G. Lindzey (Eds.), *The handbook of social psychology* (4th ed., Vol. 2, pp. 357–411). New York: Oxford University Press.

Fitzgerald, C. S., & Clark, S. (2013). Work locus of control and perceptions of practice. *Journal of Public Child Welfare, 7*, 59–78.

Fitzpatrick, D., & Mooney, R. D. (2012). The somatic sensory system: Touch and proprioception. In D. Purves, G. J. Augustine, D. Fitzpatrick, W. C. Hall, A.-S. LaManita, & L. E. White (Eds.), *Neuroscience* (5th ed., pp. 189–208). Sunderland, MA: Sinauer Associates.

Fivush, R., Bohanek, J. G., Zaman, W., & Grapin, S. (2012). Gender differences in adolescents' autobiographical narratives. *Journal of Cognition and Development, 13*, 295–319.

Flaherty, S. C., & Sadler, L. S. (2011). A review of attachment theory in the context of adolescent parenting. *Journal of Pediatric Health Care, 25*, 114–121.

Flavell, J. H., Miller, P. H., & Miller, S. A. (2002). *Cognitive development* (4th ed.). Upper Saddle River, NJ: Prentice-Hall.

Fleischhaker, C., Böhme, R., Sixt, B., Brück, C., Schneider, C., & Schulz, E. (2011). Dialectical Behavioral Therapy for Adolescents (DBT-A): A clinical trial for patients with suicidal and self-injurious behavior and borderline symptoms with a one-year follow-up. *Child and Adolescent Psychiatry and Mental Health, 5*, Article ID 3.

Fletcher, B. R., & Rapp, P. R. (2013). Normal neurocognitive aging. In R. J. Nelson, S. J. Y. Mizumori, & I. B. Weiner (Eds.), *Handbook of psychology, Vol. 3. Behavioral neuroscience* (2nd ed., pp. 643–663). Hoboken, NJ: Wiley.

Fletcher, G. J. O., & Simpson, J. A. (2000). Ideal standards in close relationships: Their structure and functions. *Current Directions in Psychological Science, 9*, 102–105.

Flint, M. S., Baum, A., Episcopo, B., Knickelbein, K. Z., Liegey Dougall, A. J., Chambers, W. H., & Jenkins, F. J. (2013). Chronic exposure to stress hormones promotes transformation and tumorigenicity of 3T3 mouse fibroblasts. *Stress: The International Journal on the Biology of Stress, 16*, 114–121.

Flo, E., Pallesen, S., Åkerstedt, T., Magerøy, N., Moen, B. E., Grønli, J., . . .

Bjorvatn, B. (2013). Shift-related sleep problems vary according to work schedule. *Occupational and Environmental Medicine 70*, 238–245.

Flor, H. (2013). Cultural influences on perceptions of pain. In S. Barnow & N. Balkir (Eds.), *Cultural variations in psychopathology: From research to practice* (pp. 173–183). Cambridge, MA: Hogrefe Publishing.

Flynn, J. R. (1987). Massive IQ gains in 14 nations: What IQ tests really measure. *Psychological Bulletin, 101*, 171–191.

Flynn, J. R. (2007). *What is intelligence?: Beyond the Flynn Effect.* New York: Cambridge University Press.

Flynn, J. R. (2010). Problems with IQ gains: The huge vocabulary gap. *Journal of Psychoeducational Assessment, 28*, 412–433.

Foa, E. B., Gillihan, S. J., & Bryant, R. A. (2013). Challenges and successes in dissemination of evidence-based treatments for posttraumatic stress: Lessons learned from prolonged exposure therapy for PTSD. *Psychological Science in the Public Interest, 14*, 65–111.

Foell, J., & Flor, H. (2012). Phantom limb pain. In R. J. Moore (Ed.), *Handbook of pain and palliative care* (pp. 417–430). New York: Springer.

Foerde, K., & Shohamy, D. (2011). The role of the basal ganglia in learning and memory: Insight from Parkinson's disease. *Neurobiology of Learning and Memory, 96*, 624–636.

Fok, H. K., Hui, C. M., Bond, M. H., Matsumoto, D., & Yoo, S. H. (2008). Integrating personality, context, relationship, and emotion type into a model of display rules. *Journal of Research in Personality, 42*, 133–150.

Font, E., & Carazo, P. (2010). Animals in translation: Why there is meaning (but probably no message) in animal communication. *Animal Behaviour, 80*, e1–e6.

Forgas, J. P., & Eich, E. (2013). Affective influences on cognition: Mood congruence, mood dependence, and mood effects on processing strategies. In A. F. Healy, R. W. Proctor, & I. B. Weiner (Eds.), *Handbook of psychology, Vol. 4. Experimental psychology (2nd ed.,* pp. 61–82). Hoboken, NJ: Wiley.

Forshaw, M. (2013). *Critical thinking for psychology: A student guide.* Malden, MA: Wiley-Blackwell.

Forsyth, D. R. (2013). Social influence and group behavior. In H. Tennen, J. Suls, & I. B. Weiner (Eds.), *Handbook of psychology (Vol. 5). Personality and social psychology* (2nd ed., pp. 305–328). Hoboken, NJ: Wiley.

Fortune, E. E., & Goodie, A. S. (2012). Cognitive distortions as a component and treatment focus of pathological gambling: A review. *Psychology of Addictive Behaviors, 26*, 298–310.

Fouladi, D. B., Nassiri, P., Monazzam, E. M., Farahani, S., Hassanzadeh, G., & Hoseini, M. (2012). Industrial noise exposure and salivary cortisol in blue collar industrial workers. *Noise & Health, 14*, 184–189.

Foulkes, D. (1993). Children's dreaming. In D. Foulkes & C. Cavallero (Eds.), *Dreaming as cognition* (pp. 114–132). New York: Harvester Wheatsheaf.

Fraley, R. C., & Shaver, P. R. (1997). Adult attachment and the suppression of unwanted thoughts. *Journal of Personality and Social Psychology, 73*, 1080–1091.

Fraley, R. C., Roisman, G. I., Booth-LaForce, C., Owen, M. T., & Holland, A. S. (2013). Interpersonal and genetic origins of adult attachment styles: A longitudinal study from infancy to early adulthood. *Journal of Personality and Social Psychology, 104*, 817–338.

Francis, G. (2012). Publication bias and the failure of replication in experimental psychology. *Psychonomic Bulletin & Review, 19*, 975–991.

Franconeri, S. L., Alvarez, G. A., & Cavanagh, P. (2013). Flexible cognitive resources: competitive content maps for attention and memory. *Trends in Cognitive Sciences, 17*, 134–141.

Franklin, A., Bevis, L., Ling, Y., & Hurlbert, A. (2010). Biological components of color preference in infancy. *Developmental Science, 21*, 346–354.

Franko, D. L., Lovering, M. E., & Thompson-Brenner, H. (2013). Ethnicity, race and binge eating disorder. *A Clinician's Guide to Binge Eating Disorder, 14*, 93–112.

Freedheim, D. K., & Weiner, I. B. (Eds.). (2013). *Handbook of psychology, Vol. 1. History of psychology* (2nd ed.). Hoboken, NJ: Wiley.

Freeman, J. B., & Ambady, N. (2011). A dynamic interactive theory of person construal. *Psychological Review, 118*, 247–279.

Frenda, S. J., Knowles, E. D., Saletan, W., & Loftus, E. F. (2013). False memories of fabricated political events. *Journal of Experimental Social Psychology, 49*, 280–286.

Frew, J., & Spiegler, M. D. (Eds.). (2013). *Contemporary psychotherapies for a diverse world (1st rev. ed.).* New York: Routledge/ Taylor & Francis Group.

Fridlund, A. J., Beck, H. P., Goldie, W. D., & Irons, G. (2012). Little Albert: A neurologically impaired child. *History of Psychology, 15*, 302–327.

Friedberg, R. D., & Brelsford, G. M. (2011). Core principles in cognitive therapy with youth. *Child and Adolescent Psychiatric Clinics of North America, 20*, 369–378.

Friederich, H.-C., Wu, M., Simon, J. J., & Herzog, W. (2013). Neurocircuit function in eating disorders. *International Journal of Eating Disorders, 46*, 425–432.

Friedlander, M. L., Escudero, V., Heatherington, L., & Diamond, G. M. (2011). Alliance in couple and family therapy. *Psychotherapy, 48*, 25–33.

Friedman, D. D., Ertegun, L., Lupi, T., Beebe, B., & Deutsch, S. (2013). Securing attachment: Mother–infant research informs. In J. E. Bettmann & D. D. Friedman (Eds.), *Attachment-based clinical work with children and adolescents* (pp. 45–60). New York: Springer.

Fryer, R. G., Jr. (2010). Financial incentives and student achievement: Evidence from randomized trials. *National Bureau of Economic Research*, Working Paper No. 15898.

Fujimura, J. H., Rajagopalan, R., Ossorio, P. N., & Doksum, K. A. (2010). Race and ancestry: Operationalizing populations in human genetic variation studies. In I. Whitmarsh & D. S. Jones (Eds.), *What's the use of race? Modern governance and the biology of difference* (pp. 169–183). Cambridge, MA: MIT Press.

Fukase, Y., & Okamoto, Y. (2010). Psychosocial tasks of the elderly: A reconsideration of the eighth stage of Erikson's epigenetic scheme. *Japanese Journal of Developmental Psychology, 21*, 266–277.

Fuller-Rowell, T. E., Doan, S. N., & Eccles, J. S. (2012). Differential effects of perceived discrimination on the diurnal cortisol rhythm of African Americans and Whites. *Psychoneuroendocrinology, 37*, 107–118.

Fulton, L. V., Ivanitskaya, L. V., Bastian, N. D., Erofeev, D. A., & Mendez, F. A. (2013). Frequent deadlines: Evaluating the effect of learner control on healthcare executives' performance in online learning. *Learning and Instruction, 23*, 24–32.

Fumagalli, M., Ferrucci, R., Mameli, F., Marceglia, S., Mrakic-Sposta, S., Zago, S., . . . Priori, A. (2010). Gender-related differences in moral judgments. *Cognitive Processing, 11*, 219–226.

Funder, D. C. (2000). Personality. *Annual Review of Psychology, 52*, 197–221.

Furguson, E., Chamorro-Premuzic, T., Pickering, A., & Weiss, A. (2011). Five into one does go: A critique of the general factor of personality. In T. Chamorro-Premuzic, S. von Stumm, & A. Furnam (Eds.), *Wiley-Blackwell handbook of individual differences* (pp. 162–186). Chichester, UK: Wiley-Blackwell.

Furukawa, T., Nakano, H., Hirayama, K., Tanahashi, T., Yoshihara, K., Sudo, N., . . . Nishima, S. (2010). Relationship between snoring sound intensity and day-time blood pressure. *Sleep and Biological Rhythms, 8,* 245–253.

Fusar-Poli, P., & Meyer-Lindenberg, A. (2013). Striatal presynaptic dopamine in schizophrenia, Part I: Meta-analysis of dopamine active transporter (DAT) density. *Schizophrenia Bulletin, 39,* 22–32.

Gabry, K. E., Chrousos, G. P., Rice, K. C., Mostafa, R. M., Sternberg, E., Negrao, A. B., . . . Gold, P. W. (2002). Marked suppression of gastric ulcerogenesis and intestinal responses to stress by a novel class of drugs. *Molecular Psychiatry, 7,* 474–483.

Gacono, C. B., Evans, F. B., & Viglione, D. J. (2008). Essential issues in the forensic use of the Rorschach. In C. B. Gacono (Ed.), F. B. Evans (Ed.), N. Kaser-Boyd (Col.), & L. A. Gacono (Col.), *The handbook of forensic Rorschach assessment (pp. 3–20). The LEA series in personality and clinical psychology.* New York: Routledge/Taylor & Francis Group.

Gaetz, M., Weinberg, H., Rzempoluck, E., & Jantzen, K. J. (1998). Neural network classifications and correlational analysis of EEG and MEG activity accompanying spontaneous reversals of the Necker Cube. *Cognitive Brain Research, 6,* 335–346.

Galak, J., LeBoeuf, R. A., Nelson, L. D., & Simmons, J. P. (2012). Correcting the past: Failures to replicate psi. *Journal of Personality & Social Psychology, 103,* 933–948.

Gallagher III, B. J., & Jones, B. J. (2013). Childhood stressors and symptoms of schizophrenia. *Clinical Schizophrenia & Related Psychoses, 8,* 1–19.

Gallup Wellbeing. (2013). *Snapshot: Obesity rate ticking up.* Retrieved from http://www.gallup.com/poll/163205/snapshot-obesity-rate-ticking.aspx

Ganis, G., & Schendan, H. E. (2013). Cognitive neuroscience of mental imagery: Methods and paradigms. In S. Lacey & R. Lawson (Eds.), *Multisensory imagery* (pp. 283–298). New York: Springer.

Ganis, G., Rosenfeld J. P., Meixner, J., Kievit, R. A., & Schendan, H. E. (2011). Lying in the scanner: Covert countermeasures disrupt deception detection by functional magnetic resonance imaging. *Neuroimage, 55,* 312–319.

Gans, J. J., O'Sullivan, P., & Bircheff, V. (2013). Mindfulness based tinnitus stress reduction pilot study: A symptom perception-shift program. *Mindfulness, 12*(Suppl. 1): P76.

García, E. E., & Náñez, J. E., Sr. (2011). Education circumstances. In E. E. García & J. E. Náñez, Sr. (Eds.), *Bilingualism and cognition: Informing research, pedagogy, and policy* (pp. 103–114). Washington, DC: American Psychological Association.

Gardner, H. (1983). *Frames of mind.* New York: Basic Books.

Gardner, H. (1999, February). Who owns intelligence? *Atlantic Monthly,* pp. 67–76.

Gardner, H. (2008). Who owns intelligence? In M. H. Immordino-Yang (Ed.), *Jossey-Bass Education Team. The Jossey-Bass reader on the brain and learning* (pp. 120–132). San Francisco, CA: Jossey-Bass.

Gardner, H. (2011). *Frames of mind.* New York: Basic Books.

Garfield, A.S., Cowley, M., Smith, F.M., Moorwood, K., Stewart-Cox, J.E., Gilroy, K. . . . Ward, A. (2011). Distinct physiological and behavioural functions for parental alleles of imprinted Grb10. *Nature, 469,* 534–538.

Gasser, S., & Raulet, D. H. (2006). The DNA damage pathway regulates innate immune system ligands of the NKG2D receptor arouses the immune system. *Cancer Research, 66,* 3959–3962.

Gazendam, F. J., Kamphuis, J. H., & Kindt, M. (2013). Deficient safety learning characterizes high trait anxious individuals. *Biological Psychology, 92,* 342–352.

Gazzaniga, M. S. (2009). The fictional self. Personal identity and fractured selves: Perspectives from philosophy, ethics, and neuroscience. In D. J. H. Mathews, H. Bok, & P. V. Rabins (Eds.), *Personal identity and fractured selves: Perspectives from philosophy, ethics, and neuroscience* (pp. 174–185). Baltimore, MD: Johns Hopkins University Press.

Geangu, E., Benga, O., Stahl, D., & Striano, T. (2010). Contagious crying beyond the first days of life. *Infant Behavior and Development, 33,* 279–288.

Geisinger, K. F. (2013). Reliability. In K. F. Geisinger, B. A. Bracken, J. F. Carlson, J.-I. C. Hansen, N. R. Kuncel, S. P. Reise, & M. C. Rodriguez (Eds.), *APA handbooks in psychology. APA handbook of testing and assessment in psychology, Vol. 1. Test theory and testing and assessment in industrial and organizational psychology* (pp. 21–42). Washington, DC: American Psychological Association.

Gelder, B. D., Meeren, H. K., Righart, R. Stock, J. V., van de Riet, W. A., & Tamietto, M. (2006). Beyond the face: Exploring rapid influences of context on face processing. *Progress in Brain Research, 155,* 37–48.

Geller, P. A., Nelson, A. R., & Bonacquisti, A. (2013). Women's health psychology. In A. M. Nezu, C. M. Nezu, P. A. Geller, & I. B. Weiner (Eds.), *Handbook of psychology, Vol. 9. Health psychology* (2nd ed., pp. 477–511). Hoboken, NJ: Wiley.

Gellerman, D. M., & Lu, F. G. (2011). Religious and spiritual issues in the outline for cultural formulation. In J. R. Peteet, F. G. Lu, & W. E Narrow (Eds.), *Religious and spiritual issues in psychiatric diagnosis: A research agenda for DSM-V* (pp. 207–220). Washington, DC: American Psychiatric Association.

Geniole, S. N., Carré, J. M., & McCormick, C. M. (2011). State, not trait, neuroendocrine function predicts costly reactive aggression in men after social exclusion and inclusion. *Biological Psychology, 87,* 137–145.

Gerber, A. J., Posner, J., Gorman, D., Colibazzi, T., Yu, S., Wang, Z., . . . Peterson, B. S. (2008). An affective circumplex model of neural systems subserving valence, arousal, and cognitive overlay during the appraisal of emotional faces. *Neuropsychologia, 46,* 2129–2139.

Giacobbi, P., Jr., Foore, B., & Weinberg, R. S. (2004). Broken clubs and expletives: The sources of stress and coping responses of skilled and moderately skilled golfers. *Journal of Applied Sport Psychology, 16,* 166–182.

Gibb, B. E., Grassia, M., Stone, L. B., & Uhrlass, D. J. (2012). Brooding rumination and risk for depressive disorders in children of depressed mothers. *Journal of Abnormal Child Psychology, 40,* 317–326.

Gibbs, N. (1995, October 2). The EQ factor. *Time,* pp. 60–68.

Gibson, E. J., & Walk, R. D. (1960). The visual cliff. *Scientific American, 202,* 67–71.

Giles, L. C., Glonek, G. F. V., Luszcz, M. A., & Andrews, G. R. (2005). Effect of social networks on 10 year survival in very old Australians: The Australian longitudinal study of aging. *Journal of Epidemiology and Community Health, 59,* 574–579.

Gilles, F. H., & M. D. Nelson (2013). *The developing human brain: Growth and adversities.* Hoboken, NJ: Wiley.

Gillies, D., Taylor, F., Gray, C., O'Brien, L., & D'Abrew, N. (2012). Psychological therapies for the treatment of post-traumatic stress disorder in children and adolescents. *Cochrane Database of Systematic Reviews 2012,* Issue 12.

Gilman, S. R., Chang, J., Xu, B., Bawa, T. S., Gogos, J. A., Karayiorgou, M., & Vitkup, D. (2012). Diverse types of genetic variation converge on functional gene networks involved in schizophrenia. *Nature Neuroscience, 15,* 1723–1728.

Gilmour, D. R., & Walkey, F. H. (1981). Identifying violent offenders using a video measure of interpersonal distance. *Journal of Consulting and Clinical Psychology, 49,* 287–291.

Gimbel, S. I., & Brewer, J. B. (2011). Reaction time, memory strength, and fMRI activity during memory retrieval: Hippocampus and default network are differentially responsive during recollection and familiarity judgments. *Cognitive Neuroscience, 2,* 19–26.

Gini, M., Oppenheim, D., & Sagi-Schwartz, A. (2007). Negotiation styles in mother-child narrative co-construction in middle childhood: Associations with early attachment. *International Journal of Behavioral Development, 31,* 149–160.

Giummarra, M., & Moseley, L. (2011). Phantom limb pain and bodily awareness:current concepts and future directions. *Current Opinions in Anesthesiology, 24,* 524–531.

Glavis-Bloom, C., Alvarado, M. C., & Bachevalier, J. (2013). Neonatal hippocampal damage impairs specific food/place associations in adult macaques. *Behavioral Neuroscience, 127,* 9–22.

Glenn, A. L., Kurzban, R., & Raine, A. (2011). Evolutionary theory and psychopathy. *Aggression and Violent Behavior, 16,* 371–380.

Glicksohn, A., & Cohen, A. (2011). The role of Gestalt grouping principles in visual statistical learning. *Attention, Perception, and Psychophysics, 73,* 708–713.

Glikson, E., & Erez, M. (2013). Emotion display norms in virtual teams. *Journal of Personnel Psychology, 12,* 22–32.

Glover, V. (2011). Annual research review: Prenatal stress and the origins of psychopathology: An evolutionary perspective. *Journal of Child Psychology and Psychiatry, 52,* 356–367.

Go, A. S., Mozaffarian, D., Roger, V. L., Benjamin, E. J., Berry, J. D., Borden, W. B., . . . Turner, M. B. (2013). Heart disease and stroke statistics—2013 update: A report from the American Heart Association. *Circulation, 127,* e6-e245.

Goldfield, G. S. (2012). Making access to TV contingent on physical activity: Effects on liking and relative reinforcing value of TV and physical activity in overweight and obese children. *Journal of Behavioral Medicine, 35,* 1–7.

Goldstein, A. M., Morse, S. J., & Packer, I. K. (2013). Evaluation of criminal responsibility. In R. K. Otto & I. B. Weiner (Eds.), *Handbook of psychology, Vol. 11. Forensic psychology* (2nd ed., pp. 440–472). Hoboken, NJ: Wiley.

Goldstein, E. B. (2014). *Sensation and perception.* Belmont, CA: Wadsworth Publishing.

Goldstein, G., Brown, L. H., Haas, G. L., & Allen, D. N. (2013). Schizophrenia. In C. A. Noggle & R. S. Dean (Eds.), *Contemporary neuropsychology. The neuropsychology of psychopathology* (pp. 325–343). New York: Springer.

Goldstein, I. (2010). Looking at sexual behavior 60 years after Kinsey. *Journal of Sexual Medicine, 7,* 246–247.

Goldstone, R. L., Kersten, A., & Carvalho, P. F. (2013). Concepts and categorization. In A. F. Healy, R. W. Proctor, & I. B. Weiner (Eds.), *Handbook of psychology, Vol. 4. Experimental psychology* (2nd ed., pp. 607–630). Hoboken, NJ: Wiley.

Gómez-Restrepo, C. (2007). 'Nada más que la verdad': Muchos cuestionamientos, pocas respuestas, parcas acciones. Dónde quedan la ética, los derechos fundamentales y la salud mental? Una opinión desde la academia. / 'Nothing but the Truth': Many questions, few answers, little action. What happened to ethics, human rights and mental health? An opinion from the academy. *Revista Colombiana de Psiquiatría, 36,* 675–690.

Gonzalez, S., Xu, C., Ramirez, M., Zavala, J., Armas, R., Contreras, S. A., . . . Escamilla, M. (2013). Suggestive evidence for association between L-type voltage-gated calcium channel (CACNA1C) gene haplotypes and bipolar disorder in Latinos: A family-based association study. *Bipolar Disorders, 15,* 206–214.

Goodson, J. L. (2013). Deconstructing sociality, social evolution and relevant nonapeptide functions. *Psychoneuroendocrinology, 38,* 465–478.

Goodwin, C. J. (2011). *Research in psychology: Methods and design* (6th ed.). Hoboken, NJ: Wiley.

Goodwin, C. J. (2012). *A history of modern psychology* (4th ed.). Hoboken, NJ: Wiley.

Goodwin, C. J. (2012). United States. In D. B. Baker (Ed.), *Oxford library of psychology. The Oxford handbook of the history of psychology: Global perspectives* (pp. 571–593). New York: Oxford University Press.

Goodwin, K. A., Kukucka, J. P., & Hawks, I. M. (2013). Co-witness confidence, conformity, and eyewitness memory: An examination of normative and informational social influences. *Applied Cognitive Psychology, 27,* 91–100.

Gooneratne, N. S., Edwards, A. Y. Z., Zhou, C., Cuellar, N., Grandner, M. A., & Barrett, J. S. (2012). Melatonin pharmacokenetics following two different oral surge-sustained release does in older adults. *Journal of Pineal Research: Molecular, Biolgical, Physiological, and Clinical Aspects of Melatonin, 52,* 437–445.

Gorelick, D. A., Goodwin, R. S., Schwilke, E., Schwope, D. M., Darwin, W. D., Kelly, D. L., . . . Huestis, M. A. (2013). Tolerance to effects of high-dose oral Δ9-tetrahydro-cannabinol and plasma cannabinoid concentrations in male daily cannabis smokers. *Journal of Analytical Toxicology, 37,* 11–16.

Gosling, S. D., & John, O. P. (1999). Personality dimensions in non-human animals: A cross-species review. *Current Directions in Psychological Science, 8,* 69–75.

Gosling, S. D., Vazire, S., Srivastava, S., & John, O. P. (2004). Should we trust Web-based studies? A comparative analysis of six preconceptions about Internet questionnaires. *American Psychologist, 59,* 93–104.

Gottesman, I. I. (1991). *Schizophrenia genesis: The origins of madness.* New York: Freeman.

Gottman, J., & Silver, N. (2012). *What makes love last? How to build trust and avoid betrayal.* New York: Simon & Schuster.

Gracely, R. H., Farrell, M. J., & Grant, M. A. (2002). Temperature and pain perception. In H. Pashler & S. Yantis (Eds.), *Steven's handbook of experimental psychology: Vol. 1. Sensation and perception* (3rd ed., pp. 619–651). Hoboken, NJ: Wiley.

Graham, J. M. (2011). Measuring love in romantic relationships: A meta-analysis. *Journal of Social and Personal Relationships, 28,* 748–771.

Graham, J. R. (1991). Comments on Duckworth's review of the Minnesota Multiphasic Personality Inventory-2. *Journal of Counseling and Development, 69,* 570–571.

Grand, A. P., Kuhar, C. W., Leighty, K. A., Bettinger, T. L., & Laudenslager, M. L. (2012). Using personality ratings and cortisol to characterize individual differences in African elephants (*Loxodonta africana*). *Applied Animal Behaviour Science, 142,* 69–75.

Granillo, M. T., Perron, B. E., Jarman, C., & Gutowski, S. M. (2013). Cognitive behavioral therapy with substance use disorders: Theory, evidence, and practice. In M. G. Vaughn & B. E. Perron (Eds.), *Social work practice in the addictions* (pp. 101–118). New York: Springer.

Granrud, C. E. (2012). Judging the size of a distant object: Strategy use by children and adults. In G. Hatfield & S. Allred (Eds.), *Visual experience: Sensation, cognition, and constancy* (pp. 13–34). New York: Oxford University Press.

Grant, J. A., Courtemanche, J., & Rainville, P. (2011). A non-elaborative mental stance and decoupling of executive and pain-related cortices predicts low pain sensitivity in Zen meditators. *Pain, 152,* 150–156.

Grave, R. D. (2013). *Multistep cognitive behavioral therapy for eating disorders: Theory, practice, and clinical cases.* Lanham, MD: Jason Aronson.

Graven, L. J., & Grant, J. S. (2013). Coping and health-related quality of life in individuals with heart failure: An integrative review. *Heart & Lung, 42,* 183–194.

Green, A. J., & De-Vries, K. (2010). Cannabis use in palliative care—An examination of the evidence and the implications for nurses. *Journal of Clinical Nursing, 19,* 2454–2462.

Greenberg, D. L. (2004). President Bush's false "flashbulb" memory of 9/11/01. *Applied Cognitive Psychology, 18,* 363–370.

Greenberg, J. (2002). Who stole the money, and when? Individual and situational determinants of employee theft. *Organizational Behavior and Human Decision Processes, 89,* 985–1003.

Greenberg, L., Elliott, R., Lietaer, G., & Watson, J. (2013). The humanistic-experiential approach. In G. Stricker, T. A. Widiger, & I. B. Weiner (Eds.), *Handbook of psychology, Vol. 8. Clinical psychology* (2nd ed., pp. 320–344). Hoboken, NJ: Wiley.

Greene, C. A., & Murdock, K. K. (2013). Multidimensional control beliefs, socioeconomic status, and health. *American Journal of Health Behavior, 37,* 227–237.

Greenfield, P. M., & Quiroz, B. (2013). Context and culture in the socialization and development of personal achievement values: Comparing Latino immigrant families, European American families, and elementary school teachers. *Journal of Applied Developmental Psychology, 34,* 108–118.

Gregory, R. J. (2011). *Psychological testing: History, principles, and applications* (6th ed.). Boston, MA: Allyn & Bacon.

Gregory, S., Ffytche, D., Simmons, A., Kumari, V., Howard, M., Hodgins, S., & Blackwood, N. (2012). The antisocial brain: Psychopathy matters. *Archives of General Psychiatry, 69,* 962–972.

Gremore, T. M., Baucom, D. H., Porter, L. S., Kirby, J. S., Atkins, D. C., & Keefe, F. J. (2011). Stress buffering effects of daily spousal support on women's daily emotional and physical experiences in the context of breast cancer concerns. *Health Psychology, 30,* 20–30.

Griffin, R., & Moorhead, G. (2012). *Organizational behavior: Managing people and organizations* (10th ed.). Mason, OH: South-Western Cengage.

Griffith, R. M., Miyagi, O., & Tago, A. (1958/2009). The universality of typical dreams: Japanese vs. Americans. Retrieved from http://onlinelibrary.wiley.com/doi/10.1525/aa.1958.60.6.02a00110/pdf

Grills-Taquechel, A. E., & Ollendick, T. H. (2013). *Advances in psychotherapy. Phobic and anxiety disorders in children and adolescents.* Cambridge, MA: Hogrefe Publishing.

Groch, S., Wilhelm, I., Diekelmann, S., & Born, J. (2013). The role of REM sleep in the processing of emotional memories: Evidence from behavior and event-related potentials. *Neurobiology of Learning and Memory, 99,* 1–9.

Grossman, T. (2013). The early development of processing emotions in face and voice. In P. Belin, S. Campanella, & T. Ethofer (Eds.), *Integrating face and voice in person perception* (pp. 95–116). New York: Springer Science + Business Media.

Gruber, T. R. (2013). Nature, nurture, and knowledge acquisition. *International Journal of Human-Computer Studies, 71,* 191–194.

Grubin, D. (2010). The polygraph and forensic psychiatry. *Journal of the American Academy of Psychiatry and the Law, 38,* 446–451.

Guastello, S. J., Guastello, D. D., & Craft, L. L. (1989). Assessment of the Barnum effect in computer-based test interpretations. *Journal of Psychology: Interdisciplinary and Applied, 123,* 477–484.

Guenzel, F. M., Wolf, O. T., & Schwabe, L. (2013). Stress disrupts response memory retrieval. *Psychoneuroendocrinology, 38,* 1460–1465.

Gupta, M. A., & Gupta, A. K. (2013). Sleep-wake disorders and dermatology. *Clinics in Dermatology, 31,* 118–126.

Gurven, M., von Rueden, C., Massenkoff, M., Kaplan, H., & Lero Vie, M. (2013). How universal is the big five? Testing the five-factor model of personality variation among forager-farmers in the Bolivian Amazon. *Journal of Personality and Social Psychology, 104,* 354–370.

Guse, B., Falkai, P., Gruber, O., Whalley, H., Gibson, L., Hasan, A., . . . Wobrock, T. (2013). The effect of long-term high frequency repetitive transcranial magnetic stimulation on working memory in schizophrenia and healthy controls—A randomized placebo-controlled, double-blind fMRI study. *Behavioural Brain Research, 237,* 300–307.

Haab, L., Trenado, C., Mariam, M., & Strauss, D. J. (2011). Neurofunctional model of large-scale correlates of selective attention governed by stimulus-novelty. *Cognitive Neurodynamics, 5,* 103–111.

Hackley, C. (2007). Marketing psychology and the hidden persuaders. *The Psychologist, 20,* 488–490.

Haghighi, A., Schwartz, D. H., Abrahamowicz, M., Leonard, G. T., Perron, M., Richer, L., . . . Pausova, Z. (2013). Prenatal exposure to maternal cigarette smoking, amygdala volume and fat intake in adolescence. *Journal of the American Medical Association Psychiatry, 70,* 98–105.

Haines, R., & Mann, J. (2011). A new perspective on de-individuation via computer-mediated communication. *European Journal of Information Systems, 20,* 156–167.

Halbesleben, J. R. B., Wheeler, A. R., & Paustian-Underdahl, S. C. (2013). The impact of furloughs on emotional exhaustion, self-rated performance, and recovery experiences. *Journal of Applied Psychology, 98,* 492–503.

Hall, E. T. (2008). Adumbration as a feature of intercultural communication. In D. C. Mortensen (Ed.), *Communication theory* (2nd ed., pp. 420–432). Piscataway, NJ: Transaction Publishers.

Hall, P. A., & Schaeff, C. M. (2008). Sexual orientation and fluctuating asymmetry in men and women. *Archives of Sexual Behavior, 37,* 158–165.

Hall, W., & Degenhardt, L. (2010). "Adverse health effects of non-medical cannabis use"— Authors' reply. *The Lancet, 375,* 197.

Hallvig, D., Anund, A., Fors, C., Kecklund, G., Karlsson, J. G., Wahde, M., & Åkerstedt, T. (2013). Sleepy driving on the real road and in the simulator—A comparison. *Accident Analysis and Prevention, 50,* 44–50.

Hamby, S., & Grych, J. (2013). Implications for research: Toward a more comprehensive understanding of interpersonal violence. In S. Hamby & J. Grych (Eds.), *The web of violence* (pp. 67–79). New York: Springer.

Hamilton, G. F., Boschen, K. E., Goodlett, C. R., Greenough, W. T., & Klintsova, A. Y. (2012). Housing in environmental complexity following wheel running augments survival of newly generated hippocampal neurons in a rat model of binge alcohol exposure during the third trimester equivalent. *Alcoholism: Clinical and Experimental Research, 36,* 1196–1204.

Hamlett, J., & Hoskins, L. (2013). Comfort in small things? Clothing, control and agency in county lunatic asylums in nineteenth-and early twentieth-century England. *Journal of Victorian Culture, 6,* 1–22.

Hammack, P. L. (2003). The question of cognitive therapy in a postmodern world. *Ethical Human Sciences and Services, 5,* 209–224.

Hammen, C., & Keenan-Miller, D. (2013). Mood disorders. In G. Stricker, T. A. Widiger, & I. B. Weiner (Eds.), *Handbook of psychology, Vol. 8. Clinical psychology* (2nd ed., pp. 121–146). Hoboken, NJ: Wiley.

Hammond, J. L., & Hall, S. S. (2011). Functional analysis and treatment of aggressive behavior following resection of a craniopharyngioma. *Developmental Medicine and Child Neurology, 53*, 369–374.

Han, S., Mao, L., Qin, J., Friederici, A. D., & Ge, J. (2011). Functional roles and cultural modulations of the medial prefrontal and parietal activity associated with causal attribution. *Neuropsychologia, 49*, 83–91.

Handler, M., Honts, C. R., Krapohl, D. J., Nelson, R., & Griffin, S. (2009). Integration of pre-employment polygraph screening into the police selection process. *Journal of Police and Criminal Psychology, 24*, 69–86.

Haney, C., Banks, C., & Zimbardo, P. (1978). Interpersonal dynamics in a simulated prison. *International Journal of Criminology and Penology, 1*, 69–97.

Hardy, G., Barkham, M., Shapiro, D., Guthrie, E., & Margison, F. (Eds.). (2011). *Psychodynamic-interpersonal therapy*. Thousand Oaks, CA: Sage.

Harkness, K. L., Alavi, N., Monroe, S. M., Slavich, G. M., Gotlib, I. H., & Bagby, R. M. (2010). Gender differences in life events prior to onset of major depressive disorder: The moderating effect of age. *Journal of Abnormal Psychology, 119*, 791–803.

Harlow, J. (1868). Recovery from the passage of an iron bar through the head. *Publications of the Massachusetts Medical Society, 2*, 237–246.

Harriger, J. A., Calogero, R. M., Witherington, D. C., & Smith, J. E. (2010). Body size stereotyping and internalization of the thin ideal in preschool girls. *Sex Roles, 63*, 609–620.

Hart, C., & Ksir, C. (2013). *Drugs, society, and human behavior (15th ed.)*. New York: McGraw-Hill.

Hart, J., Kraut, M. A., Womack, K. B., Strain, J., Didehbani, N., Bartze, E., . . . Cullum, C. M. (2013). Neuroimaging of cognitive dysfunction and depression in aging retired National Football League players: A cross-sectional study. *JAMA Neurology, 70*, 326–335.

Harvey, P. D., & Bowie, C. R. (2013). Schizophrenia spectrum conditions. In G. Stricker, T. A. Widiger, & I. B. Weiner (Eds.), *Handbook of psychology, Vol. 8. Clinical psychology* (2nd ed., pp. 240–261). Hoboken, NJ: Wiley.

Hasan, Y., Bègue, L., Scharkow, M., & Bushman, B. J. (2013). The more you play, the more aggressive you become: A long-term experimental study of cumulative violent video game effects on hostile expectations and aggressive behavior. *Journal of Experimental Social Psychology, 49*, 224–227.

Hashimoto, T., Mojaverian, T., & Kim, H. S. (2012). Culture, interpersonal stress, and psychological distress. *Journal of Cross-Cultural Psychology, 43*, 527–532.

Hassan, S., Karpova, Y., Baiz, D., Yancey, D., Pullikuth, A., Flores, A., . . . Kulik, G. (2013). Behavioral stress accelerates prostate cancer development in mice. *The Journal of Clinical Investigation, 123*, 874–886.

Hasson, D., Theorell, T., Bergquist, J., & Canlon, B. (2013). Acute stress induces hyperacusis in women with high levels of emotional exhaustion. *PloS one, 8*, e52945.

Hatemi, P. K., & McDermott, R. (2012). The genetics of politics: Discovery, challenges and progress. *Trends in Genetics, 28*, 525–533.

Hatfield, E., & Rapson, R. L. (1996). *Love and sex: Cross-cultural perspectives*. Needham Heights, MA: Allyn & Bacon.

Haukkala, A., Konttinen, H., Laatikainen, T., Kawachi, I., & Uutela, A. (2010). Hostility, anger control, and anger expression as predictors of cardiovascular disease. *Psychosomatic Medicine, 72*, 556–562.

Hauner, K. K., Mineka, S., Voss, J. L., & Paller, K. A. (2012). Exposure therapy triggers lasting reorganization of neural fear processing. *Proceedings of the National Academy of Sciences, 109*, 9203–9208.

Hauser, S. L., & Johnston, S. C. (2013). DSM-V: Psychodrama on the public stage. *Annals of Neurology, 73*, A5–A6.

Hay, D. F. (1994). Prosocial development. *Journal of Child Psychology and Psychiatry, 35*, 29–71.

Haynes, S., O'Brien, W., & Kaholokula, J. (2011). *Behavioral assessment and case formulation*. Hoboken, NJ: Wiley.

Hazan, C., & Shaver, P. (1987). Romantic love conceptualized as an attachment process. *Journal of Personality and Social Psychology, 52*, 511–524.

Hazler, R. J. (2011). Person-centered theory. In D. Capuzzi & D. R. Gross (Eds.), *Counseling and psychotherapy* (5th ed., pp. 143–166). Alexandria, VA: American Counseling Association.

Hazlett, E. A., Collazo, T., Zelmanova, Y., Entis, J. J., Chu, K.-W., Goldstein, K. E., . . . Byne, W. (2012). Anterior limb of the internal capsule in schizotypal personality disorder: Fiber-tract counting, volume, and anisotropy. *Schizophrenia Research, 141*, 119–127.

Heaner, M. K., & Walsh, B. T. (2013). A history of the identification of the characteristic eating disturbances of bulimia nervosa, binge eating disorder and anorexia nervosa. *Appetite, 65*, 185–188.

Heider, F. (1958). *The psychology of interpersonal relations*. Hoboken, NJ: Wiley.

Heine, S. J., & Renshaw, K. (2002). Interjudge agreement, self-enhancement, and liking: Cross-cultural divergences. *Personality and Social Psychology Bulletin, 28*, 578–587.

Heinicke, M. R., Carr, J. E., Eastridge, D., Kupfer, J., & Mozzoni, M. P. (2013). Assessing preferences of individuals with acquired brain injury using alternative stimulus modalities. *Brain Injury, 27*, 48–59.

Hellström, P. M. (2013). Satiety signals and obesity. *Current Opinion in Gastroenterology, 29*, 222–227.

Herbert, H. S., Manjula, M., & Philip, M. (2013). Resilience and factors contributing to resilience among the offsprings of parents with schizophrenia. *Psychological Studies, 58*, 80–88.

Hergovich, A., & Olbrich, A. (2003). The impact of the Northern Ireland conflict on social identity, groupthink and integrative complexity in Great Britain. *Review of Psychology, 10*, 95–106.

Herholz, S. C., Halpern, A. R., & Zatorre, R. J. (2012). Neuronal correlates of perception, imagery, and memory for familiar tunes. *Journal of Cognitive Neuroscience, 24*, 1382–1397.

Herman, C. P., & Polivy, J. (2008). External cues in the control of food intake in humans: The sensory-normative distinction. *Physiology and Behavior, 94*, 722–728.

Herman, L. M., Richards, D. G., & Woltz, J. P. (1984). Comprehension of sentences by bottlenosed dolphins. *Cognition, 16*, 129–139.

Hernandez, I., & Preston, J. L. (2013). Disfluency disrupts the confirmation bias. *Journal of Experimental Social Psychology, 49*, 178–182.

Herrenkohl, T. I., Hong, S., Klika, J. B., Herrenkohl, R. C., & Russo, M. J. (2013). Developmental impacts of child abuse and neglect related to adult mental health, substance use, and physical health. *Journal of Family Violence, 28*, 191–199.

Hervé, H. F., Cooper, B. S., & Yuille, J. C. (2013). Biopsychosocial perspectives on memory variability in eyewitnesses. In B. S. Cooper, D. Griesel, & M. Ternes (Eds.), *Applied issues in investigative interviewing, eyewitness memory, and credibility assessment* (pp. 99–142). New York: Springer.

Hervé, H., Mitchell, D., Cooper, B. S., Spidel, A., & Hare, R. D. (2004). Psychopathy and unlawful confinement: An examination of perpetrator and event characteristics.

REFERENCES

Canadian Journal of Behavioural Science, 36, 137–145.

Hess, T. M., Popham, L. E., Emery, L., & Elliott, T. (2012). Mood, motivation, and misinformation: Aging and affective state influences on memory. *Aging, Neuropsychology and Cognition, 19*, 13–34.

Higley, E. R. (2008). Nighttime interactions and mother-infant attachment at one year. *Dissertation Abstracts International: Section B: The Sciences and Engineering, 68*, 5575.

Hilgard, E. R. (1978). Hypnosis and consciousness. *Human Nature, 1*, 42–51.

Hilgard, E. R. (1992). Divided consciousness and dissociation. *Consciousness and Cognition, 1*, 16–31.

Hill, J. S., Robbins, R. R., & Pace, T. M. (2012). Cultural validity of the Minnesota Multiphasic Personality Inventory–2 empirical correlates: Is this the best we can do? *Journal of Multicultural Counseling and Development, 40*, 104–116.

Hill, P. L., & Lapsley, D. K. (2011). Adaptive and maladaptive narcissism in adolescent development. In C. T. Barry, P. K. Kerig, K. K. Stellwagen, & T. D. Barry (Eds.), *Narcissism and Machiavellianism in youth: Implications for the development of adaptive and maladaptive behavior* (pp. 89–105). Washington, DC: American Psychological Association.

Hills, J. (2013). *Basic texts in counselling and psychotherapy. Introduction to systemic and family therapy: A user's guide.* New York: Palgrave Macmillan.

Hines, M. (2013). Gonadal hormone influences on human neurobehavioral development: Outcomes and mechanisms. In D. W. Pfaff & Y. Christen (Eds.), *Multiple origins of sex differences in brain* (pp. 59–69). New York: Springer.

Hirst, W., Phelps, E. A., Buckner, R. L., Budson, A. E., Cuc, A., Gabrieli, J. D. E., . . . Vaidya, C. J. (2009). Long-term memory for the terrorist attack of September 11: Flashbulb memories, event memories, and the factors that influence their retention. *Journal of Experimental Psychology: General, 138*, 161–176.

Hiscock, H., & Davey, M. J. (2013). Sleep disorders in infants and children. *Journal of Paediatrics & Child Health.* Advance online publication. doi: 10.1111/jpc.12033

Hoar, S. D., Evans, M. B., & Link, C. A. (2012). How do master athletes cope with pre-competitive stress at a "Senior Games?" *Journal of Sport Behavior, 35*, 181–203.

Hobson, J. A., Sangsanguan, S., Arantes, H., & Kahn, D. (2011). Dream logic—The inferential reasoning paradigm. *Dreaming, 21*, 1–15.

Hobson, J. A., & Silvestri, L. (1999). Parasomnias. *The Harvard Mental Health Letter, 15*, 3–5.

Hodges, S. D., & Biswas-Diener, R. (2007). Balancing the empathy expense account: Strategies for regulating empathic response. In T. Farrow & P. Woodruff (Eds.), *Empathy in mental illness* (pp. 389–407). New York: Cambridge University Press.

Hodson, G., & Hewstone, M. (Eds.). (2013). *Advances in intergroup contact.* New York: Psychology Press.

Hoff, E. (2013). *Language development* (5th ed.). Belmont, CA: Wadsworth Publishing.

Hoffman, M. L. (1993). Empathy, social cognition, and moral education. In A. Garrod (Ed.), *Approaches to moral development: New research and emerging themes* (pp. 157–179). New York: Teachers College Press.

Hogan, T. P. (2006). *Psychological testing: A practical Introduction (2nd ed.).* Hoboken, NJ: Wiley.

Hogg, D. (2013). Application of groupthink to Generation Y decision making processes within a professional services context in New Zealand. *International Journal of Business and Management, 8*, 69.

Hollander, J., Renfrow, D., & Howard, J. (2011). *Gendered situations, gendered selves: A gender lens on social psychology* (2nd ed.). Lanham, MD: Rowman and Littlefield.

Hollon, S. D. (2011). Cognitive and behavior therapy in the treatment and prevention of depression. *Depression and Anxiety, 28*, 263–266.

Hölzel, B. K, Carmody, J., Vangel, M., Congleton, C., Yerramsetti, S. M, Gard, T., & Lazar, S. W. (2011). Mindfulness practice leads to increases in regional brain gray matter density. *Psychiatry Research: Neuroimaging, 191*, 36–43.

Honig, A. S., & Nealis, A. L. (2012). What do young children dream about? *Early Child Development & Care, 182*, 771–795.

Honts, C. R., & Kircher, J. C. (1994). Mental and physical countermeasures reduce the accuracy of polygraph tests. *Journal of Applied Psychology, 79*, 252–259.

Hooley, J. M., Maher, W. B., & Maher, B. A. (2013). Abnormal psychology. In D. K. Freedheim & I. B. Weiner (Eds.), *Handbook of psychology, Vol. 1. History of psychology* (2nd ed., pp. 340–376). Hoboken, NJ: Wiley.

Hopfer, C. (2011). Club drug, prescription drug, and over-the-counter medication abuse: Description, diagnosis, and intervention. In Y. Kaminer & K. C. Winters (Eds.), *Clinical manual of adolescent substance abuse treatment* (pp. 187–212). Arlington, VA: American Psychiatric Publishing.

Hoppe, A. (2011). Psychosocial working conditions and well-being among immigrant and German low-wage workers. *Journal of Occupational Health Psychology, 16*, 187–201.

Hopwood, C. J., & Wright, A. G. (2012). A comparison of passive–aggressive and negativistic personality disorders. *Journal of Personality Assessment, 94*, 296–303.

Hora, M., & Klassen, R. D. (2012). Learning from others' misfortune: Factors in influencing knowledge acquisition to reduce operational risk. *Journal of Operations Management, 31*, 52–61.

Houlfort, N. (2006). The impact of performance-contingent rewards on perceived autonomy and intrinsic motivation. *Dissertation Abstracts International Section A: Humanities and Social Sciences, 67*, 460.

Howe, M. L., & Malone, C. (2011). Mood-congruent true and false memory: Effects of depression. *Memory, 19*, 192–201.

Hrobjartsson, A., Ravaud, P., Tendal, B., Thomsen, A. S. S., Boutron, I., Emanuelsson, F., . . . Brorson, S. (2013). Observer bias in randomized clinical trials with measurement scale outcomes: A systematic review of trials with both blinded and nonblinded assessors. *Canadian Medical Association Journal, 185*, E201-E211.

Hsiao, S. S., & Gomez-Ramirez, M. (2013). Neural mechanisms of tactile perception. In R. J. Nelson, S. J. Y. Mizumori, & I. B. Weiner (Eds.), *Handbook of psychology, Vol. 3. Behavioral neuroscience* (2nd ed., pp. 206–239). Hoboken, NJ: Wiley.

Huang, M., & Hauser, R. M. (1998). Trends in Black–White test-score differentials: II. The WORDSUM Vocabulary Test. In U. Neisser (Ed.), *The rising curve: Long-term gains in IQ and related measures* (pp. 303–334). Washington, DC: American Psychological Association.

Huang, X., Zhu, X., Zheng, J., Zhang, L. & Shiomi, K. (2012). Relationships among androgyny, self-esteem, and trait coping style of Chinese university students. *Social Behavior and Personality, 40*, 1005–1014.

Huber, G., & Malhotra, N. (2012). Political sorting in social relationships. Working paper. Retrieved from http://huber .research.yale.edu/materials/38_paper.pdf.

Huesmann, L. R., Dubow, E. F., & Yang, G. (2013). Why it is hard to believe that media violence causes aggression. *The Oxford handbook of media psychology, Oxford library of psychology* (pp. 159–171). New York: Oxford University Press.

Hulette, A., Freyd, J., & Fisher, P. (2011). Dissociation in middle childhood among foster children with early maltreatment experiences. *Child Abuse and Neglect, 35*, 123–126.

Hull, C. (1952). *A behavior system.* New Haven, CT: Yale University Press.

Hull, E. M. (2011). Sex, drugs and gluttony: How the brain controls motivated behaviors. *Physiology and Behavior, 104,* 173–177.

Hülsheger, U. R., Alberts, H. J., Feinholdt, A., & Lang, J. W. B. (2013). Benefits of mindfulness at work: The role of mindfulness in emotion regulation, emotional exhaustion, and job satisfaction. *Journal of Applied Psychology, 98,* 310–325.

Hunsley, J., & Lee, E. M. (2010). *Introduction to clinical psychology* (2nd ed.). Toronto, ON: Wiley.

Hunt, E. (2011). *Human intelligence.* New York: Cambridge University Press.

Hupbach, A., & Fieman, R. (2012). Moderate stress enhances immediate and delayed retrieval of educationally relevant material in healthy young men. *Behavioral Neuroscience, 126,* 819–825.

Husain, M. M., & Lisanby, S. H. (2011). Repetitive transcranial magnetic stimulation (rTMS): A noninvasive neuromodulation probe and intervention. *The Journal of ECT, 27,* 2.

Hutchison, P., & Rosenthal, H. E. S. (2011). Prejudice against Muslims: Anxiety as a mediator between intergroup contact and attitudes, perceived group variability and behavioural intentions. *Ethnic and Racial Studies, 34,* 40–61.

Hyde, J. S. (2005). The genetics of sexual orientation. In J. S. Hyde (Ed.), *Biological substrates of human sexuality* (pp. 9–20). Washington, DC: American Psychological Association.

Hyman, R. (1981). Cold reading: How to convince strangers that you know all about them. In K. Fraizer (Ed.), *Paranormal borderlands of science* (pp. 232–244). Buffalo, NY: Prometheus.

Hyman, R. (1996). The evidence for psychic functioning: Claims vs. reality. *Skeptical Inquirer, 20,* 24–26.

Iacono, W. G. (2008). Accuracy of polygraph techniques: Problems using confessions to determine ground truth. *Physiology and Behavior, 95,* 24–26.

Imada, T., & Ellsworth, P. C. (2011). Proud Americans and lucky Japanese: Cultural differences in appraisal and corresponding emotion. *Emotion, 11,* 329–345.

Inden, M., Takata, K., Nishimura, K., Kitamura, Y., Ashihara, E., Yoshimoto, K., . . . Shimohama, S. (2013). Therapeutic effects of human mesenchymal and hematopoietic stem cells on rotenone-treated Parkinsonian mice. *Journal of Neuroscience Research, 91,* 62–72.

Inostroza, M., Binder, S., & Born, J. (2013). Sleep-dependency of episodic-like memory consolidation in rats. *Behavioural Brain Research, 237,* 15–22.

Insel, T. (2012). Director's blog: Spotlight on eating disorders. *National Institute for Mental Health (NIMH).* Retrieved from http://www.nimh.nih.gov/about/director/2012/spotlight-on-eating-disorders.shtml

Inui, K., Urakawa, T., Yamashiro, K., Otsuru, N., Takeshima, Y., Nishihara, M., . . . Kakigi, R. (2010). Echoic memory of a single pure tone indexed by change-related brain activity. *BMC Neuroscience, 11,* Article ID 135.

Inzlicht, M., & Al-Khindi, T. (2012). ERN and the placebo: A misattribution approach to studying the arousal properties of the error-related negativity. *Journal of Experimental Psychology: General, 141,* 799–807.

Irish, M., Lawlor, B. A., O'Mara, S. M., & Coen, R. F. (2011). Impaired capacity for autonoetic reliving during autobiographical event recall in mild Alzheimer's disease. *Cortex: A Journal Devoted to the Study of the Nervous System and Behavior, 47,* 236–249.

Irvine, E. (2013). The scientific study of consciousness: Consciousness as a scientific concept. *Studies in Brain and Mind, 5,* 1–14.

Irwin, K., & Simpson, B. (2013). Do descriptive norms solve social dilemmas? Conformity and contributions in collective action groups. *Social Forces, 91,* 1057–1084.

Irwin, M. (2008). There's no good proof the real *Medium,* Allison DuBois, has ever cracked a case, but her fans don't care. *Phoenix New Times.* Retrieved from http://www.phoenixnewtimes.com/2008-06-12/news/there-s-no-good-proof-the-real-medium-allison-dubois-has-ever-cracked-a-case-but-her-fans-don-t-care/

Iwata, Y., Suzuki, K., Takei, N., Toulopoulou, T., Tsuchiya, K. J., Matsumato, K., . . . Mori, N. (2011). Jiko-shisen-kyofu (fear of one's own glance), but not taijin-kyofusho (fear of interpersonal relations), is an east Asian culture-related specific syndrome. *Australian and New Zealand Journal of Psychiatry, 45,* 148–152.

Izard, C. E. (1971). *The face of emotion.* New York: Appleton-Century-Crofts.

Jackendoff, R. (2003). Foundations of language, brain, meaning, grammar, evolution. *Applied Cognitive Psychology, 17,* 121–122.

Jackson, J. W., & Rose, J. (2013). The stereotype consistency effect is moderated by group membership and trait valence. *The Journal of Social Psychology, 153,* 51–61.

Jackson, M. L., Croft, R. J., Kennedy, G. A., Owens, K., & Howard, M. E. (2013). Cognitive components of simulated driving performance: Sleep loss effects and predictors. *Accident Analysis & Prevention, 50,* 438–444.

Jacobs Bao, K., & Lyubomirsky, S. (2013). Making it last: Combating hedonic adaptation in romantic relationships. *The Journal of Positive Psychology, 8,* 196–206.

Jaeger, A., Cox, J. C., & Dobbins, I. G. (2012). Recognition confidence under violated and confirmed memory expectations. *Journal of Experimental Psychology: General, 141,* 282–301.

Jaeger, M. (2011). "A thing of beauty is a joy forever"? Returns to physical attractiveness over the life course. *Social Forces, 89,* 983–1003.

Jaehne, E. J., Majumder, I., Salem, A., & Irvine, R. J. (2011). Increased effects of 3, 4-methylenedioxymethamphetamine (ecstasy) in a rat model of depression. *Addiction Biology, 16,* 7–19.

Jaffe, S. L., & Kelly, J. F. (2011). Twelve-step mutual-help programs for adolescents. In Y. Kaminer & K. C. Winters (Eds.), *Clinical manual of adolescent substance abuse treatment* (pp. 269–282). Arlington, VA: American Psychiatric Publishing.

James, W. (1890). *The principles of psychology* (Vol. 2). New York: Holt.

Jamieson, G. A., & Hasegawa, H. (2007). New paradigms of hypnosis research. In G. A. Jamieson (Ed.), *Hypnosis and conscious states: The cognitive neuroscience perspective* (pp. 133–144). New York: Oxford University Press

Jang, K. L., Taylor, S., & Livesley, W. J. (2006). The University of British Columbia Twin Project: Personality is something and personality does something. *Twin Research and Human Genetics, 9,* 739–742.

Janis, I. L. (1972). *Victims of groupthink: A psychological study of foreign-policy decisions and fiascoes.* Boston, MA: Houghton Mifflin.

Janis, I. L. (1989). *Crucial decisions: Leadership in policymaking and crisis management.* New York: Free Press.

Jaremka, L. M., Glaser, R., Loving, T. J., Malarkey, W. B., Stowell, J. R., & Kiecolt-Glaser, J. K. (2013). Attachment anxiety is linked to alterations in cortisol production and cellular immunity. *Psychological Science, 24,* 272–279.

Jarvis, S. (2011). Conceptual transfer: Crosslinguistic effects in categorization and construal. *Bilingualism: Language and Cognition, 14,* 1–8.

Jenkins, P. E., Meyer, C., & Blissett, J. M. (2013). Childhood abuse and eating psychopathology: The mediating role of core beliefs. *Journal of Aggression, Maltreatment & Trauma, 22,* 248–261.

Jensen, K. B., Kaptchuk, T. J., Kirsch, I., Raicek, J., Lindstrom, K. M., Berna, C., ... Kong, J. (2012). Nonconscious activation of placebo and nocebo pain responses. *Proceedings of the National Academy of Sciences, 109*, 15959–15964.

Jensen, L. A. (2011). The cultural-developmental theory of moral psychology: A new synthesis. In L. A. Jensen (Ed.), *Bridging cultural and developmental approaches to psychology: New syntheses in theory, research, and policy* (pp. 3–25). New York: Oxford University Press.

Jensen, M. P., Hakimian, S., Sherlin, L. H., & Fregni, F. (2008). New insights into neuromodulatory approaches for the treatment of pain. *The Journal of Pain, 9*, 193–199.

Jern, A., & Kemp, C. (2013). A probabilistic account of exemplar and category generation. *Cognitive Psychology, 66*, 85–125.

Jeste, D. V., Savla, G. N., Thompson, W. K., Vahia, I. V., Glorioso, D. K., Martin, A. S., . . . Depp, C. A. (2012). Association between older age and more successful aging: Critical role of resilience and depression. *American Journal of Psychiatry, 170*, 188–196.

Jewkes, R. (2013). Intimate partner violence as a risk factor for mental health problems in South Africa. In C. Garcia-Moreno & A. Riecher-Rössler (Eds.), *Violence against women and mental health. Key issues mental health* (pp. 65–74). Switzerland: Basel, Karger.

Ji, G., Yan, L., Liu, W., Qu, J., & Gu, A. (2013). OGG1 Ser326Cys polymorphism interacts with cigarette smoking to increase oxidative DNA damage in human sperm and the risk of male infertility. *Toxicology Letters, 218*, 144–149.

Jinap, S., & Hajeb, P. (2010). Glutamate: Its applications in food and contribution to health. *Appetite, 55*, 1–10.

Joanisse, M., Gagnon, S., & Voloaca, M. (2013). The impact of stereotype threat on the simulated driving performance of older drivers. *Accident Analysis and Prevention, 50*, 530–538.

Joeng, J. R., Turner, S. L., & Lee, K. H. (2013). South Korean college students' Holland Types and career compromise processes. *The Career Development Quarterly, 61*, 64–73.

Johns, M. M., Zimmerman, M., & Bauermeister, J. A. (2013). Sexual attraction, sexual identity, and psychosocial wellbeing in a national sample of young women during emerging adulthood. *Journal of Youth and Adolescence, 42*, 82–95.

Johnson, D. M., Delahanty, D. L., & Pinna, K. (2008). The cortisol awakening response as a function of PTSD severity and abuse chronicity in sheltered battered women. *Journal of Anxiety Disorders, 22*, 793–800.

Johnson, S. C., Dweck, C. S., & Chen, F. S. (2007). Evidence for infants' internal working method of attachment. *Psychological Science, 18*, 501–502.

Johnson, W., & Bouchard Jr., T. J. (2007). Sex differences in mental ability: A proposed means to link them to brain structure and function. *Intelligence, 35*, 197–209.

Johnston, C. C., Campbell-Yeo, M., & Filion, F. (2011). Paternal vs. maternal kangaroo care for procedural pain in preterm neonates: A randomized crossover trial. *Archives of Pediatrics & Adolescent Medicine, 165*, 792–796.

Johnston, L., Titov, N., Andrews, G., Dear, B. F., & Spence, J. (2013). Comorbidity and internet-delivered transdiagnostic cognitive behavioural therapy for anxiety disorders. *Cognitive Behaviour Therapy, 42*, 180–192.

Johnston, M. E., Sherman, A., & Grusec, J. E. (2013). Predicting moral outrage and religiosity with an implicit measure of moral identity. *Journal of Research in Personality, 47*, 209–217.

Jolliffe, C. D., & Nicholas, M. K. (2004). Verbally reinforcing pain reports: An experimental test of the operant conditioning of chronic pain. *Pain, 107*, 167–175.

Jones, D. A. (2013). The polarizing effect of a partisan workplace. *PS: Political Science & Politics, 46*, 67–73.

Jones, D. E., Hammond, P., & Platoni, K. (2013). Traumatic event management in Afghanistan: A field report on combat applications in regional command-south. *Military Medicine, 178*, 4–10.

Jones, E. E., & Nisbett, R. E. (1971). *The actor and the observer: Divergent perceptions of the causes of behavior.* Morristown, NJ: General Learning Press.

Jones, S. G., & Benca, R. M. (2013). Sleep and biological rhythms. In R. J. Nelson, S. J. Y. Mizumori, & I. B. Weiner (Eds.), *Handbook of psychology, Vol. 3. behavioral neuroscience (2nd ed.,* pp. 365–394). Hoboken, NJ: Wiley.

Jopp, D. S., & Schmitt, M. (2010). Dealing with negative life events: Differential effects of personal resources, coping strategies, and control beliefs. *European Journal of Ageing, 7*, 167–180.

Jost, K., Bryck, R. L., Vogel, E. K., & Mayr, U. (2011) Are old adults just like low working memory young adults? Filtering effi-

ciency and age differences in visual working memory. *Cerebral Cortex, 21*, 1147–1154.

Jung, C. G. (1946). *Psychological types.* New York: Harcourt Brace.

Jung, C. G. (1959). The archetypes and the collective unconscious. In H. Read, M. Fordham, & G. Adler (Eds.), *The collected works of C. G. Jung, Vol. 9.* New York: Pantheon.

Jung, C. G. (1969). The concept of collective unconscious. In *Collected Works* (Vol. 9, Part 1). Princeton, NJ: Princeton University Press (Original work published 1936).

Jung, J., & Kim, Y. (2012). Causes of newspaper firm employee burnout in Korea and its impact on organizational commitment and turnover intention. *The International Journal of Human Resource Management, 23*, 3636–3651.

Jung, R. E., & Haier, R. J. (2007). The Parieto-Frontal Integration Theory (P-FIT) of intelligence: Converging neuroimaging evidence. *Behavioral and Brain Sciences, 30*, 135–154.

Jurado-Berbel, P., Costa-Miserachs, D., Torras-Garcia, M., Coll-Andreu, M., & Portell-Cortés, I. (2010). Standard object recognition memory and "what" and "where" components: Improvement by post-training epinephrine in highly habituated rats. *Behavioural Brain Research, 207*, 44–50.

Kahneman, D., & Tversky, A. (1973). On the psychology of prediction. *Psychological Review, 80*, 237–251.

Kaida, K., Akerstedt, T., Takahashi, M., Vestergren, P., Gillberg, M., Lowden, A., . . . Portin, C. (2008). Performance prediction by sleepiness- related subjective symptoms during 26-hour sleep deprivation. *Sleep & Biological Rhythms, 6*, 234–241.

Kalat, J. W. (2013). *Biological psychology* (11th ed.). Belmont, CA: Wadsworth, Cengage Learning.

Kalnin, A. J., Edwards, C. R., Wang, Y., Kronenberger, W. G., Hummer, T. A., Mosier, K. M., . . . Mathews, V. P. (2011). The interacting role of media violence exposure and aggressive–disruptive behavior in adolescent brain activation during an emotional Stroop task. *Psychiatry Research: Neuroimaging, 192*, 12–19.

Kan, K.-J., Dolan, C. V., Nivard, M. G., Middeldorp, C. M., van Beijsterveldt, C. E., Willemsen, G., & Boomsa, D. I. (2013). Genetic and environmental stability in attention problems across the lifespan: Evidence from the Netherlands Twin Register. *Journal of the American Academy of Child & Adolescent Psychiatry, 52*, 12–25.

Kanayama, G., & Pope, H. G., Jr. (2011). Gods, men, and muscle dysmorphia. *Harvard Review of Psychiatry, 19*, 95–98.

Kandler, C., Bleidorn, W., Riemann, R., Angleitner, A., & Spinath, F. (2012). Life events as environmental states and genetic traits and the role of personality: A longitudinal twin study. *Behavior Genetics, 42,* 57–72.

Kang, H. J., Voleti, B., Hajszan, T., Rajkowska, G., Stockmeier, C. A., Licznerski, P., . . . Duman, R. S. (2012). Decreased expression of synapse-related genes and loss of synapses in major depressive disorder. *Nature Medicine,* 18, 1413–1417.

Kang, S.-M., & Lau, A. S. (2013). Revisiting the out-group advantage in emotion recognition in a multicultural society: Further evidence for the in-group advantage. *Emotion, 13,* 203–215.

Kar, B. R. (Ed.). (2013). Development of selection and control. In B. R. Kar, N.K. Srinivasan, & R. Bhoomika (Eds.), *APA human brain development series. Cognition and brain development: Converging evidence from various methodologies* (pp. 11–32). Washington, DC: American Psychological Association.

Karatsoreos, I. N., Bhagat, S., Bloss, E. B., Morrison, J. H., & McEwen, B. S. (2011). Disruption of circadian clocks has ramifications for metabolism, brain, and behavior. *Proceedings of the National Academy of Sciences, 108,* 1657–1662.

Karavolos, S., Stewart, J., Evbuomwan, I., McEleny, K., & Aird, I. (2013). Assessment of the infertile male. *The Obstetrician & Gynaecologist, 15,* 1–9.

Kariuki, C. M., & Stein, D. J. (2013). Social anxiety disorder. In S. M. Stahl & B. A. Moore (Eds.), *Anxiety disorders: A guide for integrating psychopharmacology and psychotherapy* (pp. 221–258). New York: Routledge.

Kark, R., Waismel-Manor, R., & Shamir, B. (2012). Does valuing androgyny and femininity lead to a female advantage? The relationship between gender-role, transformational leadership and identification. *The Leadership Quarterly, 23,* 620–640.

Karpicke, J. D., & Bauernschmidt, A. (2011). Spaced retrieval: Absolute spacing enhances learning regardless of relative spacing. *Journal of Experimental Psychology: Learning, Memory, and Cognition,* 37, 1250–1257.

Karpicke, J. D., & Smith, M. A. (2012). Separate mnemonic effects of retrieval practice and elaborative encoding. *Journal of Memory & Language, 67,* 17–29.

Karpowitz, C. F., Mendelberg, T., & Shaker, L. (2011). Gender inequality in deliberative participation. *American Political Science Review, 106,* 533–547.

Karra, E., O'Daly, O. G., Choudhury, A. I., Yousseif, A., Millership, S., Neary, M. T., . . . Batterham, R. L. (2013). A link between FTO, ghrelin, and impaired brain food-cue responsivity. *Journal of Clinical Investigations, 123,* 3539–3551.

Kato, K., Zweig, R., Barzilai, N., & Atzmon, G. (2012). Positive attitude towards life and emotional expression as personality phenotypes for centenarians. *Aging, 4,* 359–367.

Katz, I., Kaplan, A., & Buzukashvily, T. (2011). The role of parents' motivation in students' autonomous motivation for doing homework. *Learning and Individual Differences, 21,* 376–386.

Kaukiainen, A., Björkqvist, K., Lagerspetz, K., Österman, K., Salmivalli, C., Rothberg, S., & Ahlbom, A. (1999). The relationships between social intelligence, empathy, and three types of aggression. *Aggressive Behavior, 25,* 81–89.

Kaye, W. H., Wierenga, C. E., Bailer, U. F., Simmons, A. N., & Bischoff-Grethe, A. (2013). Nothing tastes as good as skinny feels: The neurobiology of anorexia nervosa. *Trends in Neurosciences, 36,* 110–120.

Keats, D. M. (1982). Cultural bases of concepts of intelligence: A Chinese versus Australian comparison. In P. Sukontasarp, N. Yongsiri, P. Intasuwan, N. Jotiban, & C. Suvannathat (Eds.), *Proceedings of the second Asian workshop on child and adolescent development* (pp. 67–75). Bangkok, India: Burapasilpa Press.

Keen, E. (2011). Emotional narratives: Depression as sadness—Anxiety as fear. *The Humanistic Psychologist, 39,* 66–70.

Keller, J., & Bless, H. (2008). The interplay of stereotype threat and regulatory focus. In Y. Kashima, K. Fiedler, & P. Freytag (Eds.), *Stereotype dynamics: Language-based approaches to the formation, maintenance, and transformation of stereotypes* (pp. 367–389). Mahwah, NJ: Erlbaum.

Kellogg, R. (2011). *Fundamentals of cognitive psychology* (2nd ed.). Thousand Oaks, CA: Sage.

Keltner, D., Kring, A. M., & Bonanno, G. A. (1999). Fleeting signs of the course of life: Facial expression and personal adjustment. *Current Directions in Psychological Science, 8,* 18–22.

Kendler, K. S., & Prescott, C. A. (2006). *Genes, environment, and psychopathology: Understanding the causes of psychiatric and substance use disorders.* New York: Guilford Press.

Kennedy, S. H., Giacobbe, P., Rizvi, S. J., Placenza, F. M., Nishikawa, Y., Mayberg, H. S., & Lozano, A. M. (2011). Deep brain stimulation for treatment-resistant depression: Follow-up after 3 to 6 years. *American Journal of Psychiatry, 168,* 502–510.

Kerr, N. L., Feltz, D. L., & Irwin, B. C. (2013). To pay or not to pay? Do extrinsic incentives alter the Köhler group motivation gain? *Group Processes & Intergroup Relations, 16,* 257–268.

Kershaw, S. (2008). Sharing their demons on the Web. *New York Times.* Retrieved from http://www.nytimes.com/2008/11/13/fashion/13psych.html

Kessler, R. C., McGonagle, K. A., Zhao, S., Nelson, C. B., Hughes, M., Eshleman, S., . . . Kendler, K. S. (1994). Lifetime and 12-month prevalence of DSM-IIIR psychiatric disorders in the United States. *Archives of General Psychiatry, 51,* 8–19.

Khaleque, A., & Rohner, R. P. (2011). Transnational relations between perceived parental acceptance and personality dispositions of children and adults: A meta-analytic review. *Personality and Social Psychology Review, 16,* 103–115.

Kiefer, F., & Dinter, C. (2013). New approaches to addiction treatment based on learning and memory. In W. H. Sommer & R. Spanagel (Eds.), *Current topics in behavioral neurosciences: Vol. 13. Behavioral neurobiology of alcohol addiction* (pp. 671–684). New York: Springer Science + Business Media

Kihlstrom, J. F. (2005). Dissociative disorders. *Annual Review of Clinical Psychology, 1,* 227–253.

Kilmann, P. R., Finch, H., Parnell, M. M., & Downer, J. T. (2013). Partner attachment and interpersonal characteristics. *Journal of Sex & Marital Therapy, 39,* 144–159.

Kilpatrick, L. A., Suyenobu, B. Y., Smith, S. R., Bueller, J. A., Goodman, T., Creswell, J. D., . . . Naliboff, B. D. (2011). Impact of mindfulness-based stress reduction training on intrinsic brain connectivity. *NeuroImage, 56,* 290–298.

Kim, J-H., & Park, E-Y. (2012). The factor structure of the Center for Epidemiologic Studies Depression Scale in stroke patients. *Topics in Stroke Rehabilitation, 19,* 54–62.

Kim, K-S., Kim, H. S., Park, J-M., Kim, H. W., Park, M-K., Lee, H-S., . . . Moon, J. (2013). Long-term immunomodulatory effect of amniotic stem cells in an Alzheimer's disease model. *Neurobiology of Aging, 34,* 2408–2420.

King, B. M. (2012). *Human sexuality today* (7th ed.). Boston, MA: Allyn & Bacon.

Kircher, T., Arolt, V., Jansen, A., Pyka, M., Reinhardt, I., Kellermann, T., . . . Straube, B. (2013). Effect of cognitive-behavioral therapy on neural correlates of fear conditioning in panic disorder. *Biological Psychiatry, 73,* 93–101.

Kirisci, L., Tarter, R., Ridenour, T., Zhai, Z. W., Fishbein, D., Reynolds, M., & Vanyukov, M. (2013). Age of alcohol and cannabis use onset mediates the association of transmissible risk in childhood and development of alcohol and cannabis disorders: Evidence for common liability. *Experimental and Clinical Psychopharmacology, 21,* 38.

Kirkbride, J. B., Jones, P. B., Ullrich, S., & Coid, J. W. (2012). Social deprivation, inequality, and the neighborhood-level incidence of psychotic syndromes in East London. *Schizophrenia Bulletin.* doi: 10.1093/schbul/sbs151

Kite, M. E. (2013). Teaching about race and ethnicity. In D. S. Dunn, R. A. R. Gurung, K. Z. Naufel, & J. H. Wilson (Eds.), *Controversy in the psychology classroom: Using hot topics to foster critical thinking* (pp. 169–184). Washington, DC: American Psychological Association.

Kivimäki, M., Nyberg, S. J., Batty, G. D., Fransson, E. I., Heikkila, K., Alfredsson, L., . . . Theorell, T. (2012). Job strain as a risk factor for coronary heart disease: A collaborative meta-analysis of individual participant data. *Lancet, 380,* 1491–1497.

Kivlighan Jr, D. M., London, K., & Miles, J. R. (2012). Are two heads better than one? The relationship between number of group leaders and group members, and group climate and group member benefit from therapy. *Group Dynamics: Theory, Research, and Practice, 16,* 1–13.

Kleider, H. M., Pezdek, K., Goldinger, S. D., & Kirk, A. (2008). Schema-driven source misattribution errors: Remembering the expected from a witnessed event. *Applied Cognitive Psychology, 22,* 1–20.

Klein, S. B. (2012). *Learning: Principles and applications* (6th ed.). Thousand Oaks, CA: SAGE.

Kluger, J., & Masters, C. (2006, August 28). How to spot a liar. *Time,* 46–48.

Kneeland, R. E., & Fatemi, S. H. (2013). Viral infection, inflammation and schizophrenia. *Progress in Neuro-Psychopharmacology & Biological Psychiatry, 42,* 35–48.

Knutson, K. L. (2012). Does inadequate sleep play a role in vulnerability to obesity? *American Journal of Human Biology, 24,* 361–371.

Kobeissi, J., Aloysi, A., Tobias, K., Popeo, D., & Kellner, C. H. (2011). Resolution of severe suicidality with a single electroconvulsive therapy. *The Journal of ECT, 27,* 86–88.

Kohl, J. V. (2012). Human pheromones and food odors: Epigenetic influences on the socioaffective nature of evolved behaviors.

Socioaffective Neuroscience & Psychology, 2: 17338.

Kohlberg, L. (1964). Development of moral character and moral behavior. In L. W. Hoffman & M. L. Hoffman (Eds.), *Review of child development research* (Vol. 1, pp. 383–431). New York: Sage.

Kokkoris, M. D., & Kühnen, U. (2013). Choice and dissonance in a European cultural context: The case of Western and Eastern Europeans. *International Journal of Psychology.* Advance online publication. doi: 10.1080/00207594.2013.766746

Kolb, B. (2013). *Introduction to brain and behavior.* New York: Worth.

Kolen, M. J., & Hendrickson, A. B. (2013). Scaling, norming, and equating. In K. F. Geisinger, B. A. Bracken, J. F. Carlson, J.-I. C. Hansen, N. R. Kuncel, S. P. Reise, & M. C. Rodriguez (Eds.), *APA handbooks in psychology. APA handbook of testing and assessment in psychology, Vol. 1. Test theory and testing and assessment in industrial and organizational psychology* (pp. 201–222). Washington DC: American Psychological Association.

Kontak, A. C., Victor, R. G., & Vongpatanasin, W. (2013). Dexmedetomidine as a novel countermeasure for cocaine-induced central sympathoexcitation in cocaine-addicted humans: Novelty and significance. *Hypertension, 61,* 388–394.

Koopmann-Holm, B., & Matsumoto, D. (2011). Values and display rules for specific emotions. *Journal of Cross-Cultural Psychology, 42,* 355–371.

Koran, L. M. (2007). Obsessive-compulsive disorder: An update for the clinician. *Focus, 5,* 299–313.

Kotagal, S., & Kumar, S. (2013). Childhood onset narcolepsy cataplexy-more than just a sleep disorder. *Sleep, 36,* 161.

Kotowski, A. (2012). Case study: A young male with auditory hallucinations in paranoid schizophrenia. *International Journal of Nursing Knowledge, 23,* 41–44.

Kracher, B., & Marble, R. P. (2008). The significance of gender in predicting the cognitive moral development of business practitioners using the Socioemotional Reflection Objective Measure. *Journal of Business Ethics, 78,* 503–526.

Kraft, T. L., & Pressman, S. D. (2012). Grin and bear it: The influence of manipulated positive facial expression on the stress response. *Psychological Science, 23,* 1372–1378.

Krahé, B. (2013). *The social psychology of aggression (2nd ed.).* New York: Psychology Press.

Krebs, D. L. (2007). Deciphering the structure of the moral sense: A review of moral minds: How nature designed our universal

sense of right and wrong. *Evolution and Human Behavior, 28,* 294–296.

Kreger Silverman, L. (2013). *Psych 101: Giftedness 101.* New York: Springer.

Kreipe, R. E., Starr, T. B., & Simeone, R. E. (2012). Eating disorders. In O. J. Z. Sahler, J. E. Carr, J. B. Frank, & J. V. Nunes (Eds.), *The behavioral sciences and health care* (3rd ed., pp. 199–205). Cambridge, MA: Hogrefe.

Kress, T., Aviles, C., Taylor, C., & Winchell, M. (2011). Individual/collective human needs: (Re) theorizing Maslow using critical, sociocultural, feminist, and indigenous lenses. In C. Malott & B. Porfilio (Eds.), *Critical pedagogy in the twenty-first century: A new generation of scholars (*pp. 135–157). Charlotte, NC: Information Age Publishing.

Kress, V. E., Hoffman, R. M., Adamson, N., & Eriksen, K. (2013). Informed consent, confidentiality, and diagnosing: Ethical guidelines for counselor practice. *Journal of Mental Health Counseling, 35,* 15–28.

Krettenauer, T., Campbell, S., & Hertz, S. (2013). Moral emotions and the development of the moral self in childhood. *European Journal of Developmental Psychology, 10,* 159–173.

Kring, A. M., Johnson, S. L. , Davison, G. C., & Neale, J. M. (2012). *Abnormal psychology* (12th ed.). Hoboken, NJ: Wiley.

Krohne, H. W., & Slangen, K. E. (2005). Influence of social support on adaptation to surgery. *Health Psychology, 24,* 101–105.

Krug, S. E. (2013). Objective personality testing. In K. F. Geisinger, B. A. Bracken, J. F. Carlson, J.-I. C. Hansen, N. R. Kuncel, S. P. Reise, & M. C. Rodriguez (Eds.), *APA handbooks in psychology. APA handbook of testing and assessment in psychology, Vol. 1. Test theory and testing and assessment in industrial and organizational psychology* (pp. 315–328). Washington, DC: American Psychological Association.

Krugman, H. E. (2013). *Consumer behavior and advertising involvement: Selected works of Herbert E. Krugman.* New York: Routledge Academic.

Krukowski, K., Eddy, J., Kosik, K. L., Konley, T., Janusek, L. W., & Mathews, H. L. (2011). Glucocorticoid dysregulation of natural killer cell function through epigenetic modification. *Brain, Behavior, and Immunity, 25,* 239–249.

Krusemark, E. A., Campbell, W. K., & Clementz, B. A. (2008). Attributions, deception, and event related potentials: An investigation of the self-serving bias. *Psychophysiology, 45,* 511–515.

Krypel, M. N., & Henderson-King, D. (2010). Stress, coping styles, and optimism: Are they related to meaning of education in students' lives? *Social Psychology of Education, 13,* 409–424.

Kteily, N. S., Sidanius, J., & Levin, S. (2011). Social dominance orientation: Cause or 'mere effect'?: Evidence for SDO as a causal predictor of prejudice and discrimination against ethnic and racial outgroups. *Journal of Experimental Social Psychology, 47,* 208–214.

Kubiak, T., Vögele, C., Siering, M., Schiel, R., & Weber, H. (2008). Daily hassles and emotional eating in obese adolescents under restricted dietary conditions—The role of ruminative thinking. *Appetite, 51,* 206–209.

Kubota, M., Miyata, J., Sasamoto, A., Sugihara, G., Yoshida, H., Kawada, R., . . . Murai, T. (2013). Thalamocortical disconnection in the orbitofrontal region associated with cortical thinning in schizophrenia thalamocortical disconnection. *Journal of the American Medical Association Psychiatry, 70,* 12–21.

Kuchenbrandt, D., Eyssel, F., & Seidel, S. K. (2013). Cooperation makes it happen: Imagined intergroup cooperation enhances the positive effects of imagined contact. *Group Processes & Intergroup Relations, 16,* 636–648.

Kukucka, J., & Kassin, S. M. (2012). *Do confessions taint juror perceptions of handwriting evidence?* Paper presented at the annual meeting of the American Psychology-Law Society, San Juan, Puerto Rico.

Kullmann, D. M., & Lamsa, K. P. (2011). LTP and LTD in cortical GABAergic interneurons: Emerging rules and roles. *Neuropharmacology, 60,* 712–719.

Kumar, S., & Mellsop, G. (2013). Burnout: Gender aspects. In S. Bährer-Kohler (Ed.), *Burnout for experts: Prevention in the context of living and working* (pp. 99–117). New York: Springer Science + Business Media.

Kvavilashvili, L., Mirani, J., Schlagman, S., Erskine, J. A. K., & Kornbrot, D. E. (2010). Effects of age on phenomenology and consistency of flashbulb memories of September 11 and a staged control event. *Psychology and Aging, 25,* 391–404.

Kyaga, S., Landén, M., Boman, M., Hultman, C. M., Långström, N., & Lichtenstein, P. (2012). Mental illness, suicide and creativity: 40-year prospective total population study. *Journal of Psychiatric Research, 47,* 83–90.

Kyriacou, C. P., & Hastings, M. H. (2010). Circadian clocks: Genes, sleep, and cognition. *Trends in Cognitive Sciences, 14,* 259–267.

Lageman, S. K., Mickens, M., Verkerke, T., & Holloway, K. (2013). Deep brain stimulation for Parkinson's disease. In A.

R. Block & D. B. Sarwer (Eds.), *Presurgical psychological screening: Understanding patients, improving outcomes* (pp. 127–149). Washington, DC: American Psychological Association.

Laier, C., Schulte, F. P., & Brand, M. (2013). Pornographic picture processing interferes with working memory performance. *Journal of Sex Research, 50,* 642–652.

Lakein, A. (1998). *Give me a moment and I'll change your life: Tools for moment management.* New York: Andrews McMeel Publishing.

Lambert, A. J., Good, K. S., & Kirk, I. J. (2010). Testing the repression hypothesis: Effects of emotional valence on memory suppression in the think—no think task. *Consciousness and Cognition, 19,* 281–293.

Lambert, M. J. (2013). Outcome in psychotherapy: The past and important advances. *Psychotherapy, 50,* 42–51.

Lammers, J., & Stapel, D. (2011). Power increases dehumanization. *Group Processes and Intergroup Relations, 14,* 113–126.

Lamy, D., Leber, A. B., & Egeth, H. E. (2013). Selective attention. In A. F. Healy, R. W. Proctor, & I. B. Weiner (Eds.), *Handbook of psychology, Vol. 4. Experimental psychology* (2nd ed., pp. 267–294). Hoboken, NJ: Wiley.

Lancaster, R. S. (2007). *Stop Sylvia Browne: Sylvia Browne's best evidence.* Retrieved from http://www.stopsylvia.com/articles/ac360_brownesbestevidence.shtml.

Landsbergis, P. A., Schnall, P. L., Belkic, K. L., Baker, D., Schwartz, J. E., & Pickering, T. G. (2011). Workplace and cardiovascular disease: Relevance and potential role for occupational health psychology. In J. C. Quick & L. E. Tetrick (Eds.), *Handbook of occupational health psychology* (2nd ed., pp. 243–264). Washington, DC: American Psychological Association.

Lanfer, A., Bammann, K., Knof, K., Buchecker, K., Russo, P., Veidebaum, T., . . . Ahrens, W. (2013). Predictors and correlates of taste preferences in European children: The IDEFICS study. *Food Quality and Preference, 27,* 128–136.

Langenecker, S. A., Bieliauskas, L. A., Rapport, L. J., Zubieta, J-K., Wilde, E. A., & Berent, S. (2005). Face emotion perception and executive functioning deficits in depression. *Journal of Clinical and Experimental Neuropsychology, 27,* 320–333.

Langlois, J. H., Kalakanis, L., Rubenstein, A., Larson, A., Hallam, M., & Smoot, M. (2000). Maxims or myths of beauty? A meta-analytic and theoretical review. *Psychological Bulletin, 126,* 390–423.

Langmeyer, A., Guglhör-Rudan, A., & Tarnai, C. (2012). What do music preferences reveal about personality: A cross-cultural replication using self-ratings and ratings of music samples. *Journal of Individual Differences, 33,* 119–130.

Långström, N., Rahman, Q., Carlström, E., & Lichtenstein, P. (2010). Genetic and environmental effects on same-sex sexual behavior: A population study of twins in Sweden. *Archives of Sexual Behavior, 39,* 75–80.

LaPointe, L. L. (Ed.) (2005). Feral children. *Journal of Medical Speech-Language Pathology, 13,* vii–ix.

Lapsley, D. K. (2006). Moral stage theory. In M. Killen & J. Smetana (Eds.), *Handbook of moral development* (pp. 37–66). Mahwah, NJ: Erlbaum.

Lara-Sacido, A., Crego, A., & Romero-Maroto, M. (2012). Emotional contagion of dental fear to children: The fathers' mediating role in parental transfer of fear. *International Journal of Paediatric Dentistry, 22,* 324–330.

Lariscy, R. A. W., & Tinkham, S. F. (1999). The sleeper effect and negative political advertising. *Journal of Advertising, 28,* 13–30.

Larkby, C. A., Goldschmidt, L., Hanusa, B. H., & Day, N. L. (2011). Prenatal alcohol exposure is associated with conduct disorder in adolescence: Findings from a birth cohort. *Journal of the American Academy of Child and Adolescent Psychiatry, 50,* 262–271.

Larrick, R. P., Timmerman, T. A., Carton, A. M., & Abrevaya, J. (2011). Temper, temperature, and temptation: Heat-related retaliation in baseball. *Psychological Science, 22,* 423–428.

Lasnier, G. (2013). Popping the question is his job. *Newscenter.* Retrieved from http://news.ucsc.edu/2013/01/marriage-traditions.html

Latane, B., & Darley, J. M. (1968). Group inhibition of bystander intervention in emergencies. *Journal of Personality and Social Psychology, 10,* 215–221.

Lavner, J. A., & Bradbury, T. N. (2012). Why do even satisfied newlyweds eventually go on to divorce? *Journal of Family Psychology, 26,* 1–10.

Lawrence, C., & Andrews, K. (2004). The influence of perceived prison crowding on male inmates' perception of aggressive events. *Aggressive Behavior, 30,* 273–283.

Lawrence, V., Murray, J., Klugman, A., & Banerjee, S. (2011). Cross-cultural variation in the experience of depression in older people in the UK. In M. Abou-Saleh, C. Katona, & A. Kumar (Eds.), *Principle and*

practice of geriatric psychiatry (3rd ed., pp. 711–716). Hoboken, NJ: Wiley.

Lazar, S. W., Kerr, C. E., Wasserman, R. H., Gray, J. R., Greve, D. N., Treadway, M. T., . . . Fischl, B. (2005). Meditation experience is associated with increased cortical thickness. *Neuroreport, 16*, 1893–1897.

Lazarus, R. S. (1991). *Emotion and adaptation.* New York: Oxford University Press.

Lazarus, R. S. (1998). *The life and work of an eminent psychologist.* New York: Oxford University Press.

Leaper, C. (2013). Gender development during childhood. In P. D. Zelazo (Ed.), *Oxford handbook of developmental psychology* (pp. 327–377). New York: Oxford University Press.

Lebow, J., & Stroud, C. B. (2013). Family therapy. In G. Stricker, T. A. Widiger, & I. B. Weiner (Eds.), *Handbook of psychology, Vol. 8. Clinical psychology* (2nd ed., pp. 384–407). Hoboken, NJ: Wiley.

LeDoux, J. E. (1998). *The emotional brain.* New York: Simon & Schuster.

LeDoux, J. E. (2002). *Synaptic self: How our brains become who we are.* New York: Viking.

LeDoux, J. E. (2003). The emotional brain, fear, and the amygdala. *Cellular and Molecular Neurobiology, 23*, 727–738.

LeDoux, J. E. (2007). Emotional memory. *Scholarpedia, 2*, 180.

Lee, A. M., & Messing, R. O. (2011). Protein kinase C epsilon modulates nicotine consumption and dopamine reward signals in the nucleus accumbens. *Proceedings of the National Academy of Sciences, 108*, 16080–16085.

Lee, J., Jiang, J., Sim, K., Tay, J., Subramaniam, M., & Chong, S. (2011). Gender differences in Singaporean Chinese patients with schizophrenia. *Asian Journal of Psychiatry, 4*, 60–64.

Lee, J-H., Chung, W-H., Kang, E-H., Chung, D-J., Choi, C-B., Chang, H-S., . . . Kim, H-Y. (2011). Schwann cell-like remyelination following transplantation of human umbilical cord blood (hUCB)-derived mesenchymal stem cells in dogs with acute spinal cord injury. *Journal of the Neurological Sciences, 300*, 86–96.

Leichsenring, F., Leibing, E., Kruse, J., New, A., & Leweke, F. (2011). Borderline personality disorder. *The Lancet, 377*, 74–84.

Leichtman, M. D. (2006). Cultural and maturational influences on long-term event memory. In L. Balter & C. S. Tamis-LeMonda (Eds.), *Child psychology: A handbook of contemporary issues* (2nd ed., pp. 565–589). New York: Psychology Press.

LePage, P., Akar, H., Temli, Y., Sen, D., Hasser, N., & Ivins, I. (2011). Comparing teachers' views on morality and moral education, a comparative study in Turkey and the United States. *Teaching and Teacher Education, 27*, 366–375.

Leslie, M. (2000, July/August). The Vexing Legacy of Lewis Terman. *Stanford Magazine.* Retrieved from http://www.stanfordalumni.org/news/magazine/2000/julaug/articles/terman.html.

Lessov-Schlaggar, C. N., Agrawal, A., & Swan, G. E. (2013). Behavior genetics. In J. A. Schinka, W. F. Velicer, & I. B. Weiner (Eds.), *Handbook of psychology, Vol. 2. Research methods in psychology* (2nd ed., pp. 342–365). Hoboken, NJ: Wiley.

Leung, A. K. Y., Kim, Y. H., Zhang, Z. X., Tam, K. P., & Chiu, C. Y. (2012). Cultural construction of success and epistemic motives moderate American-Chinese differences in reward allocation biases. *Journal of Cross-Cultural Psychology, 43*, 46–52.

LeVay, S. (2003). Queer science: The use and abuse of research into homosexuality. *Archives of Sexual Behavior, 32*, 187–189.

Levine, J. R. (2001). *Why do fools fall in love: Experiencing the magic, mystery, and meaning of successful relationships.* New York: Jossey-Bass.

Levinson, D. B., Smallwood, J., & Davidson, R. J. (2012). The persistence of thought: Evidence for a role of working memory in the maintenance of task-unrelated thinking. *Psychological Science, 23*, 375–380.

Levinthal, C. (2011). *Drugs, behavior, and modern society (7th ed.).* Boston, MA: Prentice Hall.

Leyfer, O., Gallo, K., Cooper-Vince, C., & Pincus, D. (2013). Patterns and predictors of comorbidity of DSM-IV anxiety disorders in a clinical sample of children and adolescents. *Journal of Anxiety Disorders, 27*, 306–311.

Li, Y., Li, Y., McKay, R., Riethmacher, D., & Parada, L. F. (2012). Neurofibromin modulates adult hippocampal neurogenesis and behavioral effects of antidepressants. *The Journal of Neuroscience, 32*, 3529–3539.

Li, Y., Liu, J., Wang, W., Yong, Q., Zhou, G., Wang, M., . . . Zhao, D. (2012). Association of self-reported snoring with carotid artery intima-media thickness and plaque. *Journal of Sleep Research, 21*, 87–93.

Libby, D. J., Worhunsky, P. D., Pilver, C. E., & Brewer, J. A. (2012). Meditation-induced changes in high-frequency heart rate variability predict smoking outcomes. *Frontiers in Human Neuroscience, 6*, Article ID 54.

Libon, D. J., Xie, S. X., Moore, P., Farmer, J., Antani, S., McCawley, . . . Grossman, M. (2007). Patterns of neuropsychological impairment in frontotemporal dementia. *Neurology, 68*, 369–375.

Liem, D. G., Toraman Aydin, N., & Zandstra, E. H. (2012). Effects of health labels on expected and actual taste perception of soup. *Food Quality & Preference, 29*, 192–197.

Lien, Y-W., Chu, R-L., Jen, C-H., & Wu, C-H. (2006). Do Chinese commit neither fundamental attribution error nor ultimate attribution error? *Chinese Journal of Psychology, 48*, 163–181.

Lilienfeld, S. O., Lynn, S. J., Ruscio, J., & Beyerstein, B. L. (2010). *50 great myths of popular psychology: Shattering widespread misconceptions about human behavior.* Malden, MA: Wiley-Blackwell.

Lilienfeld, S. O., Waldman, I. D., Landfield, K., Watts, A. L., Rubenzer, S., & Faschingbauer, T. R. (2012). Fearless dominance and the U.S. presidency: Implications of psychopathic personality traits for successful and unsuccessful political leadership. *Journal of Personality and Social Psychology, 103*, 489–505.

Lim, L., Chang, W., Yu, X., Chiu, H., Chong, M., & Kua, E. (2011). Depression in Chinese elderly populations. *Asia-Pacific Psychiatry, 3*, 46–53.

Lim, S. S., Vos, T., Flaxman, A. D., Danaei, G., Shibuya, K., Adair-Rohani, H., . . . Degenhardt, L. (2013). A comparative risk assessment of burden of disease and injury attributable to 67 risk factors and risk factor clusters in 21 regions, 1990–2010: A systematic analysis for the Global Burden of Disease Study 2010. *The Lancet, 380*, 2224–2260.

Lin, C. S., Niddam, D. M., Hsu, M. L., & Hsieh, J. C. (2013). Pain catastrophizing is associated with dental pain in a stressful context. *Journal of Dental Research, 92*, 130–135.

Lin, C.-C. J., Chen, W.-N., Chen, C.-J., Lin, Y.-W., Zimmer, A., & Chen, C.-C. (2012). An antinociceptive role for substance P in acid-induced chronic muscle pain. *Proceeding of the National Academy of Sciences, 109*, E76–E83.

Lin, T.-C. E., Dumigan, N. M., Dwyer, D. M., Good, M. A., & Honey, R. C. (2013). Assessing the encoding specificity of associations with sensory preconditioning procedures. *Journal of Experimental Psychology: Animal Behavior Processes, 39*, 67–75.

Lindner, I., Echterhoff, G., Davidson, P. S. R., & Brand, M. (2010). Observation inflation: Your actions become mine. *Psychological Science, 21*, 1291–1299.

Liu, H. (2009). Till death do us part: Marital status and US mortality trends, 1986–2000.

Journal of Marriage and Family, 71, 1158–1173.

Liu, J. H., & Latané, B. (1998). Extremitization of attitudes: Does thought- and discussion-induced polarization cumulate? *Basic and Applied Social Psychology, 20,* 103–110.

Livingston, J. A. (1999). Something old and something new: Love, creativity, and the enduring relationship. *Bulletin of the Menninger Clinic, 63,* 40–52.

Lo, P. C., & Chang, C. H. (2013). Effects of long-term Dharma-Chan meditation on cardiorespiratory synchronization and HRV behavior. *Rejuvenation Research, 16,* 115–123.

Lobban, F., Postlethwaite, A., Glentworth, D., Pinfold, V., Wainwright, L., Dunn, G., . . . Haddock, G. (2013). A systematic review of randomised controlled trials of interventions reporting outcomes for relatives of people with psychosis. *Clinical Psychology Review, 33,* 372–382.

LoBue, V., & DeLoache, J. S. (2008). Detecting the snake in the grass: Attention to fear-relevant stimuli by adults and young children. *Psychological Science, 19,* 284–289.

Loftus, E. F. (2000). Remembering what never happened. In E. Tulving (Ed.), *Memory, consciousness, and the brain: The Tallinn Conference* (pp. 106–118). New York: Psychology Press.

Loftus, E. F. (2001). Imagining the past. *Psychologist, 14,* 584–587.

Loftus, E. F. (2007). Memory distortions: Problems solved and unsolved. In M. Garry, & H. Hayne (Eds.), *Do justice and let the skies fall* (pp. 1–14). Mahwah, NJ: Erlbaum.

Loftus, E. F. (2011). How I got started: From semantic memory to expert testimony. *Applied Cognitive Psychology, 25,* 347–348.

Loftus, E. F., & Cahill, L. (2007). Memory distortion from misattribution to rich false memory. In J. S. Nairne (Ed.), *The foundations of remembering: Essays in honor of Henry L. Roediger, III* (pp. 413–425). New York: Psychology Press.

Longino, H. (2013). *Studying human behavior: How scientists investigate aggression and sexuality.* Chicago: University of Chicago Press.

Loo, C. K., Mahon, M., Katalinic, N., Lyndon, B., & Hadzi-Pavlovic, D. (2011). Predictors of response to ultrabrief right unilateral electroconvulsive therapy. *Journal of Affective Disorders, 130,* 192–197.

Lopez, K. (2013). *"Silver Linings" hits close to home for director Russell.* Retrieved from http://www.usatoday.com/story/news/nation/2013/02/08/silver-lining-playbook-mental-illness/1891065/

Lopez-Munoz, F., & Alamo, C. (2011). *Neurobiology of depression.* Boca Raton, FL: CRC Press.

Lotem, A., & Halpern, J. Y. (2012). Coevolution of learning and data-acquisition mechanisms: A model for cognitive evolution. *Philosophical Transactions of the Royal Society B: Biological Sciences, 367,* 2686–2694.

Lovibond, P. (2011). Learning and anxiety: A cognitive perspective. In T. Schachtman & S. Reilly (Eds.), *Associative learning and conditioning theory: Human and non-human applications* (pp. 104–120). Oxford, UK: Oxford University Press.

Luby, J. L., Barch, D. M., Belden, A., Gaffrey, M.S., Tillman, R., Babb, C., . . . Botteron, K. N. (2012). Maternal support in early childhood predicts larger hippocampal volumes at school age. *Proceedings of the National Academy of Sciences, 109,* 2854–2859.

Luchies, L.B., Wieselquist, J., Rusbult, C. E., Kumashiro, M., Eastwick, P.W., Coolsen, M. K., & Finkel, E.J. (2013). Trust and biased memory of transgressions in romantic relationships. *Journal of Personality and Social Psychology, 104,* 673–694.

Luo, S., Romero, A., Hu, H. H., Monterosso, J, & Page, K. A. (2013). Abdominal fat is associated with a greater brain reward response to high-calorie food cues in Hispanic women. *Obesity, 21,* 2029–2036.

Luppa, M., Sikorski, C., Luck, T., Ehreke, L., Konnopka, A., Wiese, B., . . . Riedel-Heller, S. G. (2012). Age- and gender-specific prevalence of depression in latest-life – Systematic review and meta-analysis. *Journal of Affective Disorders, 136,* 212–221.

Lyn, H., Greenfield, P. M., Savage-Rumbaugh, S., Gillespie-Lynch, K., & Hopkins, W. D. (2011). Nonhuman primates do declare! A comparison of declarative symbol and gesture use in two children, two bonobos, and a chimpanzee. *Language and Communication, 31,* 63–74.

Lynam, D. R., Miller, J. D., Miller, D. J., Bornovalova, M. A., & Lejuez, C. W. (2011). Testing the relations between impulsivity-related traits, suicidality, and nonsuicidal self-injury: A test of the incremental validity of the UPPS model. *Personality Disorders: Theory, Research, and Treatment, 2,* 151–160.

Lynn, S. J., Condon, L., & Colletti, G. (2013). The treatment of dissociative identity disorder: Questions and considerations. In W. O'Donohue & S. O. Lilienfeld (Eds.), *Case studies in clinical science* (pp. 329–351). New York: Oxford University Press.

Lynn, S. J., Rhue, J. W., & Kirsch, I. (Eds.). (2010). *Handbook of clinical hypnosis* (2nd ed.). Washington, DC: American Psychological Association.

Lyubimov, N. N. (1992). Electrophysiological characteristics of sensory processing and mobilization of hidden brain reserves. *2nd Russian-Swedish Symposium New Research in Neurobiology.* Moscow: Russian Academy of Science Institute of Human Brain.

Maas, J., B., Wherry, M. L., Axelrod, D. J., Hogan, B. R., & Bloomin, J. (1999). *Power sleep: The revolutionary program that prepares your mind for peak performance.* New York: HarperPerennial.

Macmillan, M. (2000). *An odd kind of fame: Stories of Phineas Gage.* Cambridge, MA: MIT Press.

Macmillan, M. (2008). Phineas Gage — Unravelling the myth. *Psychologist, 21,* 828–831.

Macmillan, M., & Lena, M.L. (2010). Rehabilitating Phineas Gage. *Neuropsychological Rehabilitation, 20,* 641–658.

Madden, K., Middleton, P., Cyna, A. M., Matthewson, M., & Jones, L. (2012). Hypnosis for pain management during labour and childbirth. *Cochrane Database of Systematic Reviews,* 11:CD009356.

Madras, B. K. (2013). History of the discovery of the antipsychotic dopamine D2 receptor: A basis for the dopamine hypothesis of schizophrenia. *Journal of the History of the Neurosciences, 22,* 62–78.

Mahn, H., & John-Steiner, V. (2013). Vygotsky and sociocultural approaches to teaching and learning. In W. M. Reynolds, G. E. Miller, & I. B. Weiner (Eds.), *Handbook of psychology, Vol. 7. Educational psychology* (2nd ed., pp. 117–145). Hoboken, NJ: Wiley.

Maier, S. F. (1970). Failure to escape traumatic electric shock: Incompatible skeletal-motor responses or learned helplessness? *Learning and Motivation, 1,* 157–169.

Main, M., & Solomon, J. (1986). Discovery of an insecure-disorganized attachment pattern. In T. Brazelton & M. W. Yogman (Eds.), *Affective development in infancy* (pp. 95–124). Westport, CT: Ablex Publishing.

Maisto, S. A., Galizio, M., & Connors, G., J. (2014). *Drug use and abuse* (7th ed.). Belmont, CA: Cengage.

Majer, J. M., Jason, L. A., Aase, D. M., Droege, J. R., & Ferrari, J. R. (2013). Categorical 12-step involvement and continuous abstinence at 2 years. *Journal of Substance Abuse Treatment, 44,* 46–51.

Mak, A. S. P., & Lam, L. C. W. (2013). Neurocognitive profiles of people with borderline personality disorder. *Current Opinion in Psychiatry, 26*, 90–96.

Makinodan, M., Rosen, K. M., Ito, S., & Corfas, G. (2012). A critical period for social experience–dependent oligodendrocyte maturation and myelination. *Science, 337*, 1357–1360.

Malhi, G. S. (2013). DSM-5: Ordering disorder? *Australian and New Zealand Journal of Psychiatry, 47*, 7–9.

Malinowski, P. (2013). Neural mechanisms of attentional control in mindfulness meditation. *Frontiers in Neuroscience, 7*, 8.

Malti, T. (Ed.). (2013). *New directions for youth development: Theory practice research. Adolescent emotions: Development, morality, and adaptation.* San Francisco, CA: Jossey-Bass.

Mancia, M., & Baggott, J. (2008). The early unrepressed unconscious in relation to Matte-Blanco's thought. *International Forum of Psychoanalysis, 17*, 201–212.

Maner, J. K., & Menzel, A. J. (2013). Evolutionary social psychology. In H. Tennen, J. Suls, & I. B. Weiner (Eds.), *Handbook of psychology, Vol. 5. Personality and social psychology* (2nd ed., pp. 487–506). Hoboken, NJ: Wiley.

Manganelli, F., Dubbioso, R., Pisciotta, C., Antenora, A., Nolano, M., De Michele, G., . . . Santoro, L. (2013). Somatosensory temporal discrimination threshold is increased in patients with cerebellar atrophy. *Cerebellum, 12*, 456–459.

Manna, G., Faraci, P., & Como, M. R. (2013). Factorial structure and psychometric properties of the Sensation Seeking Scale-Form V (SSS-V) in a sample of Italian adolescents. *Europe's Journal of Psychology, 9*, 276–288.

Mansukhani, M. P., Kolla, B. P., Surani, S., Varon, J., & Ramar, K. (2012). Sleep deprivation in resident physicians, work hour limitations, and related outcomes: A systematic review of the literature. *Postgraduate Medicine, 124*, 241–249.

Mapayi, B., Makanjuola, R. O. A., Mosaku, S. K., Adewuya, O. A., Afolabi, O., Aloba, O. O., & Akinsulore, A. (2013). Impact of intimate partner violence on anxiety and depression amongst women in Ile-Ife, Nigeria. *Archives of Women's Mental Health, 16*, 11–18.

Marazziti, D., Masala, I., Baroni, S., Polini, M., Massimetti, G., Giannaccini, G., . . . Mauri, M. (2010). Male axillary extracts modify the affinity of the platelet serotonin transporter and impulsiveness in women. *Physiology and Behavior, 100*, 364–368.

Marcia, J., & Josselson, R. (2013). Eriksonian personality research and its implications for psychotherapy. *Journal of Personality.* Advance online publication. doi: 10.1111/jopy.12014

Marcotte, K., Perlbarg, V., Marrelec, G., Benali, H., & Ansaldo, A. I. (2013). Default-mode network functional connectivity in aphasia: Therapy-induced neuroplasticity. *Brain & Language, 124*, 45–55.

Mares, M. L., & Woodard, E. (2005). Positive effects of television on children's social interactions: A meta-analysis. *Media Psychology, 7*, 301–322.

Marks, D. F., Murray, M. D., Evans, B., & Estacio, E. V. (2011). *Health psychology: Theory, research and practice* (3rd ed.). London, UK: Sage.

Markus, H. R., & Kitayama, S. (2003). Culture, self, and the reality of the social. *Psychological Inquiry, 14*, 277–283.

Marques, L., Robinaugh, D., LeBlanc, N., & Hinton, D. (2011). Cross-cultural variations in the prevalence and presentation of anxiety disorders. *Expert Review of Neurotherapeutics, 11*, 313–322.

Martella, D., Casagrande, M., & Lupiáñez, J. (2011). Alerting, orienting and executive control: The effects of sleep deprivation on attentional networks. *Experimental Brain Research, 210*, 81–89.

Marti, F., Arib, O., Morel, C., Dufresne, V., Maskos, U., Corringer, P-J., . . . Faure, P. (2012). Smoke extracts and nicotine, but not tobacco extracts, potentiate firing and burst activity of ventral tegmental area dopaminergic neurons in mice. *Neuropsychopharmacology, 36*, 2244–2257.

Martin, C. L., & Fabes, R. (2009). *Discovering child development* (2nd ed.). Belmont, CA: Cengage.

Martin, L. J., & Carron, A. V. (2012). Team attributions in sport: A meta-analysis. *Journal of Applied Sport Psychology, 24*, 157–174.

Martinko, M. J., Harvey, P., & Dasborough, M. T. (2011). Attribution theory in the organizational sciences: A case of unrealized potential. *Journal of Organizational Behavior, 32*, 144–149.

Martin-Storey, A., Serbin, L. A., Stack, D. M., Ledingham, J. E., & Schwartzman, A. E. (2012). Self and peer perceptions of childhood aggression, social withdrawal and likeability predict adult personality factors: A prospective longitudinal study. *Personality and Individual Differences, 53*, 843–848.

Marusich, J. A., Darna, M., Charnigo, R. J., Dwoskin, L. P., & Bardo, M. T. (2011). A multivariate assessment of individual differences in sensation seeking and impulsivity as predictors of amphetamine self-administration and prefrontal dopamine function in rats. *Experimental and Clinical Psychopharmacology, 19*, 275–284.

Marx, D. M., Ko, S. J., & Friedman, R. A. (2009). The "Obama effect": How a salient role model reduces race-based performance differences. *Journal of Experimental Social Psychology, 45*, 953–956.

Maslow, A. H. (1954). *Motivation and personality.* New York: Harper & Row.

Maslow, A. H. (1970). *Motivation and personality* (2nd ed.). New York: Harper & Row.

Maslow, A. H. (1999). *Toward a psychology of being* (3rd ed.). Hoboken, NJ: Wiley.

Master, S. L., Eisenberger, N. I., Taylor, S. E., Naliboff, B. D., Shirinyan, D., & Lieberman, M. D. (2009). A picture's worth: Partner photographs reduce experimentally induced pain. *Psychological Science, 20*, 1316–1318.

Masters, W. H., & Johnson, V. E. (1961). Orgasm, anatomy of the female. In A. Ellis & A. Abarbonel (Eds.), *Encyclopedia of sexual behavior*, Vol. 2. New York: Hawthorn.

Masters, W. H., & Johnson, V. E. (1966). *Human sexual response.* Boston, MA: Little, Brown.

Masters, W. H., & Johnson, V. E. (1970). *Human sexual inadequacy.* Boston, MA: Little, Brown.

Mathis, J., & Hess, C. (2009). Sleepiness and vigilance tests. *Swiss Medical Weekly, 139*, 214–219.

Matlin, M. W. (2012). *The psychology of women* (7th ed.). Belmont, CA: Cengage.

Matlin, M. W. (2013). *Cognition* (8th ed.). Hoboken, NJ: Wiley.

Matsumoto, D. (2000). *Culture and psychology: People around the world.* Belmont, CA: Wadsworth.

Matsumoto, D. (2010). *APA handbook of interpersonal communication.* Washington, DC: American Psychological Association.

Matsumoto, D., & Hwang, H. S. (2011). Cooperation and competition in intercultural interactions. *International Journal of Intercultural Relations, 35*, 677–685.

Matsumoto, D., & Hwang, H. S. (2012). Culture and emotion: The integration of biological and cultural contributions. *Journal of Cross-Cultural Psychology, 43*, 91–118.

Matsumoto, D., & Juang, L. (2008). *Culture and psychology* (4th ed.). Belmont, CA: Cengage.

Matsumoto, D., & Juang, L. (2013). *Culture and psychology (5th ed.).* Belmont, CA: Wadsworth Publishing.

Maxson, S. C. (2013). Behavioral genetics. In R. J. Nelson, S. J. Y. Mizumori, & I. B.

Weiner (Eds.), *Handbook of psychology, Vol. 3. Behavioral neuroscience* (2nd ed., pp. 1–25). Hoboken, NJ: Wiley.

May, A. C., Rudy, B. M., Davis, T. E. III, & Matson, J. L. (2013). Evidence-based behavioral treatment of dog phobia with young children: Two case examples. *Behavior Modification, 37,* 143–160.

May-Collado, L. J. (2010). Changes in whistle structure of two dolphin species during interspecific associations. *Ethology, 116,* 1065–1074.

Mazur, A. (2013). Dominance, violence, and the neurohormonal nexus. In D. D. Franks & J. H. Turner (Eds.), *Handbooks of sociology and social research* (pp. 359–368). New York: Springer Science + Business Media.

McAllister, K. A., Saksida, L. M., & Bussey, T. J. (2013). Dissociation between memory retention across a delay and pattern separation following medial prefrontal cortex lesions in the touchscreen TUNL task. *Neurobiology of Learning and Memory, 101,* 120–126.

McArthur, L. Z., & Berry, D. S. (1987). Cross-cultural agreement in perceptions of babyfaced adults. *Journal of Cross-Cultural Psychology, 18,* 165–192.

McCauley, J. L., Killeen, T., Gros, D. F., Brady, K. T., & Back, S. E. (2012). Posttraumatic stress disorder and co-occurring substance use disorders: Advances in assessment and treatment. *Clinical Psychology: Science and Practice, 19,* 283–304.

McClelland, D. C. (1958). Risk-taking in children with high and low need for achievement. In J. W. Atkinson (Ed.), *Motives in fantasy, action, and society* (pp. 306–321). Princeton, NJ: Van Nostrand.

McClelland, D. C. (1987). Characteristics of successful entrepreneurs. *Journal of Creative Behavior, 3,* 219–233.

McClelland, D. C. (1993). Intelligence is not the best predictor of job performance. *Current Directions in Psychological Science, 2,* 5–6.

McClure, J., Meyer, L. H., Garisch, J., Fischer, R., Weir, K. F., & Walkey, F. H. (2011). Students' attributions for their best and worst marks: Do they relate to achievement? *Contemporary Educational Psychology, 36,* 71–81.

McColl, R., & Truong, Y. (2013). The effects of facial attractiveness and gender on customer evaluations during a web-video sales encounter. *Journal of Personal Selling and Sales Management, 33,* 117–128.

McCrae, R. R. (2004). Human nature and culture: A trait perspective. *Journal of Research in Personality, 38,* 3–14.

McCrae, R. R., & Costa, P. T., Jr. (2013). Introduction to the empirical and theoretical status of the five-factor model of personality traits. In T. A. Widiger & P. T. Costa, Jr. (Eds.), *Personality disorders and the five-factor model of personality* (3rd ed., pp. 15–27). Washington, DC: American Psychological Association.

McCulloch, M., Turner, K., & Broffman, M. (2012). Lung cancer detection by canine scent: Will there be a lab in the lab? *European Respiratory Journal, 39,* 511–512.

McDougall, D. (2013). Applying single-case design innovations to research in sport and exercise psychology. *Journal of Applied Sport Psychology, 25,* 33–45.

McFarlane, W. R. (2011). Integrating the family in the treatment of psychotic disorders. In R. Hagen, D. Turkington, T. Berge, & R. W. Gråwe (Eds.), *International Society for the Psychological Treatments of the Schizophrenias and Other Psychoses. CBT for psychosis: A symptom-based approach* (pp. 193–209). New York: Routledge/Taylor & Francis Group.

McGeehan, P. (2012). Driver fatigue and speed caused fatal bus crash, investigators say. *The New York Times,* June 5. Retrieved from http://www.nytimes.com/2012/06/06/nyregion/fatal-bronx-bus-crash-caused-by-driver-fatigue-board-says.html?gwh=3D1913CEAAD0A9F19130A6E6C337ED84

McGue, M., & Christensen, K. (2013). Growing old but not growing apart: Twin similarity in the latter half of the lifespan. *Behavior Genetics, 43,* 1–12.

McIntyre, C. K., McGaugh, J. L., & Williams, C. L. (2012). Interacting brain systems modulate memory consolidation. *Neuroscience and Biobehavioral Reviews, 36,* 1750–1762.

McKee, A. C., Stein, T. D., Nowinski, C. J., Stern, R. A., Daneshvar, D. H., Alvarez, V. E., . . . Cantu, R. C. (2013). The spectrum of disease in chronic traumatic encephalopathy. *Brain, 136,* 43–64.

McKellar, P. (1972). Imagery from the standpoint of introspection. In P. W. Sheehan (Ed.), *The function and nature of imagery.* New York: Academic Press.

McKinney, C., Donnelly, R., & Renk, K. (2008). Perceived parenting, positive and negative perceptions of parents, and late adolescent emotional adjustment. *Child and Adolescent Mental Health, 13,* 66–73.

McKoon, G., & Ratcliff, R. (2012). Aging and IQ effects on associative recognition and priming in item recognition. *Journal of Memory and Language, 66,* 416–437.

McLoyd, V. C. (2011). How money matters for children's socioemotional adjustment: Family processes and parental investment.

In G. Carlo, L. J. Crockett, & M. A. Carranza (Eds.), *Nebraska symposium on motivation. Health disparities in youth and families: Research and applications* (pp. 33–72). New York: Springer.

McNally, R. J. (2012). Searching for repressed memory. *Nebraska Symposium on Motivation, 58,* 121–147.

McNamara, J. M., Barta, Z., Fromhage, L., & Houston, A. I. (2008). The coevolution of choosiness and cooperation. *Nature, 451,* 189–201.

Mead, E. (2012). *Family therapy education and supervision.* Hoboken, NJ: Wiley.

Mead, M. (1928). *Coming of age in Samoa: A psychological study of primitive youth for western civilisation.* New York: Morrow.

Mednick, S. C., Makovski, T., Cai, D. J., & Jiang, Y. V. (2009). Sleep and rest facilitate implicit memory in a visual search task. *Vision Research, 49,* 2557–2565.

Mehrabian, A. (1968). A relationship of attitude to seated posture orientation and distance. *Journal of Personality and Social Psychology, 10,* 26–30.

Mehrabian, A. (1971). *Silent messages.* Belmont, CA: Wadsworth.

Mehrabian, A. (2007). *Nonverbal communication.* New Brunswick, NJ: Aldine Transaction.

Mehta, P. H., Goetz, S. M., & Carré, J. M. (2013). Genetic, hormonal, and neural underpinnings of human aggressive behavior. In D. D. Franks & J. H. Turner (Eds.), *Handbooks of sociology and social research. Handbook of neurosociology* (pp. 47–65). Dordrecht, Netherlands: Springer Science + Business Media B.V.

Mehta, P. H., & Gosling, S. D. (2006). How can animal studies contribute to research on the biological bases of personality? In T. Canli (Ed.), *Biology of personality and individual differences* (pp. 427–448). New York: Guilford.

Mehta, R., Zhu, R. J., & Cheema, A. (2012). Is noise always bad? Exploring the effects of ambient noise on creative cognition. *Journal of Consumer Research, 39,* 784–799.

Meier, M. H., Caspi, A., Ambler, A., Harrington, H., Houts, R., Keefe, R. S. E., . . . Moffitt, T. E. (2012). Persistent cannabis users show neuropsychological decline from childhood to midlife. *Proceedings of the National Academy of Sciences, 109,* E2657–E2664.

Melas, P. A., Wei, Y., Wong, C. C., Sjöholm, L. K., Åberg, E., Mill, J., . . . Lavebratt, C. (2013). Genetic and epigenetic associations of MAOA and NR3C1 with depression and childhood adversities. *The International Journal of Neuropsychopharmacology/Official Scientific*

Journal of the Collegium Internationale Neuropsychopharmacologicum (CINP), 1, 1–16.

Melton, J. (2011). Organizational training in Japan: A case study of the spaces localization. *Technical Communication, 58*, 19–33.

Meltzoff, A. N., & Moore, M. K. (1985). Cognitive foundations and social functions of imitation and intermodal representation in infancy. In J. Mehler & R. Fox (Eds.), *Neonate cognition: Beyond the blooming buzzing confusion* (pp. 139–156). Hillsdale, NJ: Erlbaum.

Melzack, R. (1999). Pain and stress: A new perspective. In R. J. Gatchel & D. C. Turk (Eds.), *Psychosocial factors in pain: Critical perspectives* (pp. 89–106). New York: Guilford Press.

Mendelson, T., Turner, A. K., & Tandon, S. D. (2010). Violence exposure and depressive symptoms among adolescents and young adults disconnected from school and work. *Journal of Community Psychology, 38*, 607–621.

Menegaux, F. Truong, T., Anger, A., Cordina-Suverger, E., Lamkarkach, F., Arveux, P., . . . Guenel, P. (2013). Night work and breast cancer: A population-based case-control study in France (the CECILE study). *International Journal of Cancer, 132*, 924–931.

Mennella, J. A., Jagnow, C. P., & Beauchamp, G. K. (2001). Prenatal and postnatal flavor learning by human infants. *Pediatrics, 107*, E88.

Mercadillo, R. E., Díaz, J. L., Pasaye, E. H., & Barrios, F. A. (2011). Perception of suffering and compassion experience: Brain gender disparities. *Brain and Cognition, 76*, 5–14.

Messer, S. B., & Gurman, A. (2011). *Essential psychotherapies: Theory and practice* (3rd ed.). New York: Guilford Press.

Messer, S. B., Sanderson, W. C., & Gurman, A. S. (2013). Brief psychotherapies. In G. Stricker, T. A. Widiger, & I. B. Weiner (Eds.), *Handbook of psychology, Vol. 8. Clinical psychology* (2nd ed., pp. 431–453). Hoboken, NJ: Wiley.

Meyer, L. H. (2011). Making sense of differently able minds. *PsyCRITIQUES*. Retrieved from http://psycnet.apa.org/critiques/56/9/6.html.

Mieg, H. A. (2011). Focused cognition: Information integration and complex problem solving by top inventors. In K. L. Mosier & U. M. Fischer (Eds.), *Expertise: Research and applications. Informed by knowledge: Expert performance in complex situations* (pp. 41–54). New York: Psychology Press.

Milgram, S. (1963). Behavioral study of obedience. *Journal of Abnormal and Social Psychology, 67*, 371–378.

Milgram, S. (1974). *Obedience to authority: An experimental view*. New York: Harper & Row.

Miller, B. J., Culpepper, N., Rapaport, M. H., & Buckley, P. (2013). Prenatal inflammation and neurodevelopment in schizophrenia: A review of human studies. *Progress in Neuro-Psychopharmacology & Biological Psychiatry, 42*, 92–100.

Miller, F. M., & Allen, C. T. (2012). Corrigendum to "How does celebrity meaning transfer? Investigating the process of meaning transfer with celebrity affiliates and mature brands." *Journal of Consumer Psychology, 22*, 606.

Miller, J. G., & Bersoff, D. M. (1998). The role of liking in perceptions of the moral responsibility to help: A cultural perspective. *Journal of Experimental Social Psychology, 34*, 443–469.

Miller, K. B., Lund, E., & Weatherly, J. (2012). Applying operant learning to the stay-leave decision in domestic violence. *Behavior and Social Issues, 21*, 135–151.

Miller, P. K., Rowe, L., Cronin, C., & Bampouras, T. M. (2012). Heuristic reasoning and the observer's view: The influence of example-availability on ad-hoc frequency judgments in sport. *Journal of Applied Sport Psychology, 24*, 290–302.

Miller, S. D., Hubble, M. A., Chow, D. L., & Seidel, J. A. (2013). The outcome of psychotherapy: Yesterday, today, and tomorrow. *Psychotherapy, 50*, 88–97.

Miller, W. J. (2013). The polarized America: Coverage, characters, and issues in the new decade. *American Behavioral Scientist, 57*, 3–7.

Millings, A., Walsh, J., Hepper, E., & O'Brien, M. (2013). Good partner, good parent: Responsiveness mediates the link between romantic attachment and parenting style. *Personality and Social Psychology Bulletin, 39*, 170–180.

Millon, T. (2004). *Masters of the mind: Exploring the story of mental illness from ancient times to the new millennium*. Hoboken, NJ: Wiley.

Miltenberger, R. G. (2011). *Behavior modification: Principles and procedures*. (5th ed.). Beverly, MA: Wadsworth.

Mineka, S., & Oehlberg, K. (2008). The relevance of recent developments in classical conditioning to understanding the etiology and maintenance of anxiety disorders. *Acta Psychologica, 127*, 567–580.

Minnameier, G., & Schmidt, S. *(2013).* Situational moral adjustment and the happy victimizer. *European Journal of Developmental Psychology, 10*, 253–268.

Miranda-Contreras, L., Gómez-Pérez, R., Rojas, G., Cruz, I., Berrueta, L., Salmen, S., . . . Osuna, J. A. (2013). Occupational exposure to organophosphate and carbamate pesticides affects sperm chromatin integrity and reproductive hormone levels among Venezuelan farm workers. *Journal of Occupational Health, 55*, 195–203.

Mischel, W., Shoda, Y., & Ayduk, O. (2008). *Introduction to personality: Toward an integrative science of the person* (8th ed.). Hoboken, NJ: Wiley.

Mischel, W. (1968). *Personality and assessment*. Hoboken, NJ: Wiley.

Mischel, W. (1984). Convergences and challenges in the search for consistency. *American Psychologist, 39*, 351–364.

Mischel, W. (2004). Toward an integrative science of the person. *Annual Review of Psychology, 55*, 1–22.

Mischel, W., & Shoda, Y. (2008). Toward a unified theory of personality: Integrating dispositions and processing dynamics within the cognitive-affective processing system. In O. P. John, R. W. Robins & L. A. Pervin (Eds.), *Handbook of personality: Theory and research* (3rd ed., pp. 208–241). New York: Guilford Press.

Mita, T. H., Dermer, M., & Knight, J. (1977). Reversed facial images and the mere-exposure hypothesis. *Journal of Personality and Social Psychology, 35*, 597–601.

Mitchell, J. M., O'Neil, J. P., Janabi, M., Marks, S. M., Jagust, W. J., & Fields, H. L. (2012). Alcohol consumption induces endogenous opioid release in the human orbitofrontal cortex and nucleus accumbens. *Science Translational Medicine, 4*: 116ra6.

Mitchell, P., & Ziegler, F. (2013). *Fundamentals of developmental psychology* (2nd ed.). New York: Psychology Press.

Miyamoto, Y, & Ryff, C. D. (2011). Cultural differences in the dialectical and non-dialectical emotional styles and their implications for health. *Cognition & Emotion, 25*, 22–39.

Moayedi, M., & Davis, K. D. (2013). Theories of pain: From specificity to gate control. *Journal of Neurophysiology, 109*, 5–12.

Moghaddam, F. M. (2013). Conformity, obedience, and behavior regulation. In F. M. Moghaddam (Ed.), *The psychology of dictatorship* (pp. 123–139). Washington, DC: American Psychological Association.

Moghaddam, F. M. (2013). From torture to cognitive dissonance: Varieties of coercion in dictatorship. In F. M. Moghaddam (Ed.), *The psychology of dictatorship* (pp. 141–158). Washington, DC: American Psychological Association.

Mohamad, O., Song, M., Wei, L., & Yu, S. P. (2013). Regulatory roles of the NMDA receptor Glun3A subunit in locomotion, pain perception and cognitive functions in adult mice. *The Journal of Physiology, 591,* 149–168.

Mohr, D. C., Ho, J., Duffecy, J., Reifler, D., Sokol, L., Burns, M. N., . . . Siddique, J. (2012). Effect of telephone-administered vs face-to-face cognitive behavioral therapy on adherence to therapy and depression outcomes among primary care patients: A randomized trial. *Journal of the American Medical Association, 307,* 2278–2285.

Moilanen, J., Aalto, A.-M., Hemminki, E., Aro, A. R., Raitanen, J., & Luoto, R. (2010). Prevalence of menopause symptoms and their association with lifestyle among Finnish middle-aged women. *Maturitas, 67,* 368–374.

Moitra, E., Beard, C., Weisberg, R. B., & Keller, M. B. (2011). Occupational impairment and social anxiety disorder in a sample of primary care patients. *Journal of Affective Disorders, 130,* 209–212.

Mokrova, I. L., O'Brien, M., Calkins, S. D., Leerkes, E. M., & Marcovitch, S. (2013). The role of persistence at preschool age in academic skills at kindergarten. *European Journal of Psychology of Education.* Advance online publication. doi:10.1007/s10212-013-0177-2

Molenaar, D., Sluis, S., Boomsma, D. I., Haworth, C. M. A., Hewitt, J. K., Martin, N. G., . . . Dolan, C. V. (2013). Genotype by environment interactions in cognitive ability: A survey of 14 studies from four countries covering four age groups. *Behavior Genetics, 43,* 208–219.

Moline, R. A. (2013). *The diagnosis and treatment of dissociative identity disorder: A case study and contemporary perspective.* Lanham, MD: Jason Aronson.

Moll, J., Bado, P., de Oliveira-Souza, R., Bramati, I. E., Lima, D. O., Paiva, F. F., . . . Zahn, R. (2012). A neural signature of affiliative emotion in the human septohypothalamic area. *The Journal of Neuroscience, 32,* 12499–12505.

Mommersteeg, P. M. C., & Pouwer, F. (2012). Personality as a risk factor for the metabolic syndrome: A systematic review. *Journal of Psychosomatic Research, 73,* 326–333.

Monin, B. (2003). The warm glow heuristic: When liking leads to familiarity. *Journal of Personality and Social Psychology, 85,* 1035–1048.

Montangero, J. (2012). Dreams are narrative simulations of autobiographical episodes, not stories or scripts: A review. *Dreaming, 22,* 157–172.

Montgomery, G. H., Schnur, J. B., & Kravits, K. (2013). Hypnosis for cancer care: Over 200 years young. *CA: A Cancer Journal for Clinicians, 63,* 31–44.

Montoro-García, S., Shantsila, E., & Lip, G. Y. H. (2011). Platelet reactivity in prolonged stress disorders—A link with cardiovascular disease? *Psychoneuroendocrinology, 36,* 159–160.

Moodley, R., & Sutherland, P. (2010). Psychic retreats in other places: Clients who seek healing with traditional healers and psychotherapists. *Counselling Psychology Quarterly, 23,* 267–282.

Moon, C., Lagercrantz, H., & Kuhl, P. K. (2013). Language experienced in utero affects vowel perception after birth: A two-country study. *Acta Paediatrica, 102,* 156–160.

Moore, D. L. (2013). USA's Manteo Mitchell runs 4x400 relay on broken leg. USA Today Sports. Retrieved from http://usatoday30.usa today.com/sports/olympics/london/track/story/2012-08-09/usa-man teo-mitchell-runs-4x400-relay-on-broken-leg/56915070/1

Moore, F., Filippou, D., & Perrett, D. (2011). Intelligence and attractiveness in the face: Beyond the attractiveness halo effect. *Journal of Evolutionary Psychology, 9,* 205–217.

Moore, T. S., Lapan, S. D., & Quartaroli, M. T. (2012). Case study research. In S. D. Lapan, M. T. Quartaroli, & F. J. Riemer (Eds.), *Qualitative research: An introduction to methods and designs* (pp. 243–270). San Francisco, CA: Jossey-Bass.

Moran, T., & Dailey, M. (2011). Intestinal feedback signaling and satiety. *Physiology and Behavior, 105,* 77–81.

Moreno, J. P., & Johnston, C. A. (2013). The role of confirmation bias in the treatment of diverse patients. *American Journal of Lifestyle Medicine, 7,* 20–22.

Morey, L. C. (2013). Measuring personality and psychopathology. In J. A. Schinka, W. F. Velicer, & I. B. Weiner (Eds.), *Handbook of psychology, Vol. 2. Research methods in psychology* (2nd ed., pp. 395–427). Hoboken, NJ: Wiley.

Morgan, C. A., Southwick, S., Steffian, G., Hazlett, G. A., & Loftus, E. F. (2013). Misinformation can influence memory for recently experienced, highly stressful events. *International Journal of Law and Psychiatry, 36,* 11–17.

Morgan, C. D., & Murphy, C. (2010). Differential effects of active attention and age on event-related potentials to visual and olfactory stimuli. *International Journal of Psychophysiology, 78,* 190–199.

Morgan, T. B., Crane, D. R., Moore, A. M., & Eggett, D. L. (2013). The cost of treating substance use disorders: Individual versus family therapy. *Journal of Family Therapy, 35,* 2–23.

Mori, K., & Arai, M. (2010). No need to fake it: Reproduction of the Asch experiment without confederates. *International Journal of Psychology, 45,* 390–397.

Morin, C. M., Savard, J., & Ouellet, M.-C. (2013). Nature and treatment of insomnia. In A. M. Nezu, C. M. Nezu, P. A. Geller, & I. B. Weiner (Eds.), *Handbook of psychology, Vol. 9. Health psychology* (2nd ed., pp. 318–339). Hoboken, NJ: Wiley.

Morton, P. M., Schafer, M. H., & Ferraro, K. F. (2012). Does childhood misfortune increase cancer risk in adulthood? *Journal of Aging and Health, 24,* 948–984.

Moshman, D. (2011). *Adolescent rationality and development: Cognition, morality, and identity* (3rd ed.). New York: Psychology Press.

Moskowitz, J. T., Epel, E. S., & Acree, M. (2008). Positive affect uniquely predicts lower risk of mortality in people with diabetes. *Health Psychology, 27,* S73–S82.

Moss-Racusin, C. A., Dovidio, J. F., Brescoll, V. L., Graham, M. J., & Handelsman, J. (2012). Science faculty's subtle gender biases favor male students. *Proceedings of the National Academy of Sciences, 109,* 16474–16479.

Mota, N. P., Medved, M., Wang, J., Asmundson, G. J. G., Whitney, D., & Sareen, J. (2012). Stress and mental disorders in female military personnel: Comparisons between the sexes in a male dominated profession. *Journal of Psychiatric Research, 46,* 159–167.

Motyl, M., Hart, J., Pyszczynski, T., Weise, D., Maxfield, M., & Siedel, A. (2011). Subtle priming of shared human experiences eliminates threat-induced negativity toward arabs, immigrants, and peace-making. *Journal of Experimental Social Psychology, 47,* 1179–1184.

Moulin, C. (Ed.). (2011). *Human memory* (Vols. 1–4). Thousand Oaks, CA: Sage.

Moutinho, A., Pereira, A., & Jorge, G. (2011). Biology of homosexuality. *European Psychiatry, 26,* 1741–1753.

Muehlenkamp, J. J., Ertelt, T. W., Miller, A. L., & Claes, L. (2011). Borderline personality symptoms differentiate non-suicidal and suicidal self-injury in ethnically diverse adolescent outpatients. *Journal of Child Psychology and Psychiatry, 52,* 148–155.

Muenssinger, J., Matuz, T., Schleger, F., Kiefer-Schmidt, I., Goelz, R., Wacher-Gussmann, A., . . . Preissl, H. (2013). Auditory habituation in the fetus and neonate: An fMEG study. *Developmental Science, 16,* 287–295.

Müller, B., Kühn, S., van Baaren, R., Dotsch, R., Brass, M., & Dijksterhuis, A. (2011). Perspective taking eliminates differences in co-representation of out-group members' actions. *Experimental Brain Research, 211,* 423–428.

Mundia, L. (2011). Social desirability, non-response bias and reliability in a long self-report measure: Illustrations from the MMPI-2 administered to Brunei student teachers. *Educational Psychology, 31,* 207–224.

Murayama, K., Perkrun, R., Lichtenfeld, S., & vom Hofe, R. (2012). Predicting long-term growth in students' mathematics achievement: The unique contributions of motivation and cognitive strategies. *Child Development, 84,* 1475–1490.

Murray, A. D., Staff, R. T., McNeil, C. J., Salarirad, S., Starr, J. M., Deary, I. J., & Whalley, L. J. (2011). Brain lesions, hypertension and cognitive ageing in the 1921 and 1936 Aberdeen birth cohorts. *Age, 34,* 451–459.

Murty, V. P., Ritchey, M., Adcock, R. A., & LaBar, K. S. (2011). Reprint of: fMRI studies of successful emotional memory encoding: A quantitative meta-analysis. *Neuropsychologia, 49,* 695–705.

Mussweiler, T., Rüter, K., & Epstude, K. (2004). The ups and downs of social comparison: Mechanisms of assimilation and contrast. *Journal of Personality & Social Psychology, 87,* 832–844.

Myers, K., & Turvey, C. L. (Eds.). (2013). *Elsevier insights. Telemental health: Clinical, technical, and administrative foundations for evidence-based practice.* Amsterdam: Elsevier.

Nabi, R. L., & Moyer-Gusé, E. (2013). The psychology underlying media-based persuasion. In K. E. Dill (Ed.), The *Oxford handbook of media psychology, Oxford library of psychology* (pp. 285–301). New York: Oxford University Press.

Nadal, K. L. (2013). Sexual orientation, microaggressions: Experiences of lesbian, gay, and bisexual people. In K. L. Nadal (Ed.), *That's so gay! Microaggressions and the lesbian, gay, bisexual, and transgender community. Contemporary perspectives on lesbian, gay, and bisexual psychology* (pp. 51–79). Washington, DC: American Psychological Association.

Nadel, L. (2013). Cognitive maps. In D. Waller & L. Nadel (Eds.), *Handbook of spatial cognition* (pp. 155–171). Washington, DC: American Psychological Association.

Nagy, T. F. (2012). Competence. In S. J. Knapp, M. C. Gottlieb, M. M. Handelsman & L. D. VandeCreek (Eds.), *APA handbook of ethics in psychology, Vol 1: Moral foundations and common themes* (pp. 147–174).

Washington, DC: American Psychological Association.

Nairne, J. S., & Neath, I. (2013). Sensory and working memory. In A. F. Healy, R. W. Proctor, & I. B. Weiner (Eds.), *Handbook of psychology, Vol. 4. Experimental psychology* (2nd ed., pp. 419–445). Hoboken, NJ: Wiley.

Nakamura, K. (2006). The history of psychotherapy in Japan. *International Medical Journal, 13,* 13–18.

Narasimamurthy, R., Hatori, M., Nayak, S. K., Liu, F., Panda, S., & Verma, I. M. (2012). Circadian clock protein cryptochrome regulates the expression of proinflammatory cytokines. *Proceedings of the National Academy of Sciences, 109,* 12662–12667.

Nasehi, M., Piri, M., Jamali-Raeufy, N., & Zarrindast, M. R. (2010). Influence of intracerebral administration of NO agents in dorsal hippocampus (CA1) on cannabinoid state-dependent memory in the step-down passive avoidance test. *Physiology and Behavior, 100,* 297–304.

National Organization on Fetal Alcohol Syndrome (2012). *FASD: What everyone should know.* Retrieved from http://www.nofas.org/wp-content/uploads/2012/10/NOFAS-FASD-What-Everyone-Should-Know-2012.pdf

National Sleep Foundation. (2012). Sleepy pilots, train operators, and drivers. Retrieved from www.sleepfoundation.org/article/press-release/sleepy-pilots-train-operators-and-drivers

Neal, D., & Chartrand, T. (2011). Embodied emotion perception: Amplifying and dampening facial feedback modulates emotion perception accuracy. *Social Psychological and Personality Science, 2,* 673–678.

Neale, J. M., Oltmanns, T. F., & Winters, K. C. (1983). Recent developments in the assessment and conceptualization of schizophrenia. *Behavioral Assessment, 5,* 33–54.

Negri, R., Di Feola, M., Di Domenico, S., Scala, M. G., Artesi, G., Valente, S., . . . Greco, L. (2012). Taste perception and food choices. *Journal of Pediatric Gastroenterology & Nutrition, 54,* 624–629.

Neher, A. (1991). Maslow's theory of motivation: A critique. *Journal of Humanistic Psychology, 31,* 89–112.

Neisser, U. (1967). *Cognitive psychology.* New York: Appleton-Century-Crofts.

Nelson, E.-L., Davis, K., & Velasquez, S. E. (2013). Ethical considerations in providing mental health services over videoteleconferencing. In K. Myers & C. L. Turvey (Eds.), *Elsevier insights. Telemental health: Clinical, technical, and administrative foundations*

for evidence-based practice (pp. 47–62). Amsterdam: Elsevier.

Nelson, N. L., & Russell, J. A. (2013). Universality revisited. *Emotion Review, 5,* 8–15.

Nelson, T. D. (2013). The neurobiology of stereotyping and prejudice. In D. D. Franks & J. H. Turner (Eds.), *Handbooks of sociology and social research* (pp. 349–358). New York: Springer Science + Business Media.

Nemoda, Z., Szekely, A., & Sasvari-Szekely, M. (2011). Psychopathological aspects of dopaminergic gene polymorphisms in adolescence and young adulthood. *Neuroscience and Biobehavioral Reviews, 35,* 1665–1686.

Neri, A. L., Yassuda, M. S., Fortes-Burgos, A. C., Mantovani, E. P., Arbex, F. S., de Souza Torres, S. V., . . . Guariento, M. E. (2012). Relationships between gender, age, family conditions, physical and mental health, and social isolation of elderly caregivers. *International Psychogeriatrics, 24,* 472–483.

Neria, Y., Bromet, E. J., Sievers, S., Lavelle, J., & Fochtmann, L. J. (2002). Trauma exposure and posttraumatic stress disorder in psychosis: Findings from a first-admission cohort. *Journal of Consulting and Clinical Psychology, 70,* 246–251.

Nestor, P. G., & Schutt, R. K. (2012). *Research methods in psychology: Investigating human behavior.* Thousand Oaks, CA: Sage.

Nettle, D. (2011). Normality, disorder, and evolved function: The case of depression. In P. Adriaens & A. de Block (Eds.), *Maladapting minds: Philosophy, psychiatry, and evolutionary theory* (pp. 198–215). New York: Oxford University Press.

Neubauer, A. C., Grabner, R. H., Freudenthaler, H. H., Beckmann, J. F., & Guthke, J. (2004). Intelligence and individual differences in becoming neurally efficient. *Acta Psychologica, 116,* 55–74.

Newby, J. M., & Moulds, M. L. (2011). Intrusive memories of negative events in depression: Is the centrality of the event important? *Journal of Behavior Therapy and Experimental Psychiatry, 42,* 277–283.

Newman, M. L., & Roberts, N. A. (Eds.). (2013). *Health and social relationships: The good, the bad, and the complicated.* Washington, DC: American Psychological Association.

Nguyen, T., & Szymanski, B. (2012). Using location-based social networks to validate human mobility and relationships models. *Proceedings of the 2012 IEEE/ACM International Conference on Advances in Social Networks Analysis and Mining,* pp. 1247–1253.

Nickerson, R. (1998). Confirmation bias: A ubiquitous phenomenon in many guises. *Review of General Psychology, 2*, 175–220.

Nicolaidis, S. (2011). Metabolic and humoral mechanisms of feeding and genesis of the ATP/ADP/AMP concept. *Physiology and Behavior, 104*, 8–14.

Nielsen, T. A., Zadra, A. L., Simard, V., Saucier, S., Saucier, S., Stenstrom, P., . . . Kuiken, D. (2003). The typical dreams of Canadian university students. *Dreaming, 13*, 211–235.

Nieto, F. J., Peppard, P. E., Young, T., Finn, L., Hla, K. M., & Farre, R. (2012). Sleep disordered breathing and cancer mortality: Results from the Wisconsin Sleep Cohort Study. *American Journal of Respiratory and Critical Care Medicine, 186*, 190–194.

Nikolaou, A., Schiza, S. E., Chatzi, L., Koudas, V., Fokos, S., Solidaki, E., & Bitsios, P. (2011). Evidence of dysregulated affect indicated by high alexithymia in obstructive sleep apnea. *Journal of Sleep Research, 20*, 92–100.

Nishitani, S., Miyamura, T., Tagawa, M., Sumi, M., Takase, R., Doi, H., . . . Shinohara, K. (2009). The calming effect of a maternal breast milk odor on the human newborn infant. *Neuroscience Research, 63*, 66–71.

Noggle, C. A., & Dean, R. S. (Eds.). (2013). *Contemporary neuropsychology: The neuropsychology of psychopathology*. New York: Springer.

Noggle, C. A., Rylander, M., & Soltys, S. (2013). Personality disorders. In C. A. Noggle & R. S. Dean (Eds.), *Contemporary neuropsychology. The neuropsychology of psychopathology* (pp. 343–388). New York: Springer.

Nolan-Poupart, S., Veldhuizen, M. G., Geha, P., & Small, D. M. (2013). Midbrain response to milkshake correlates with ad libitum milkshake intake in the absence of hunger. *Appetite, 60*, 168–174.

Norcross, J. C., & Wampold, B. E. (2011). Evidence-based therapy relationships: Research conclusions and clinical practices. *Psychotherapy, 48*, 98–102.

Northcote, J., & Livingston, M. (2011). Accuracy of self-reported drinking: Observational verification of "last occasion" drink estimates of young adults. *Alcohol and Alcoholism, 46*, 709–713.

Northup, T., & Mulligan, N. (2013). Conceptual implicit memory in advertising research. *Applied Cognitive Psychology, 27*, 127–136.

Nusbaum, F., Redouté, J., Le Bars, D., Volckmann, P., Simon, F., Hannoun, S., . . . Sappey-Marinier, D. (2011). Chronic low-back pain modulation is enhanced by hypnotic analgesic suggestion by recruiting an emotional network: A PET imaging study. *International Journal of Clinical and Experimental Hypnosis, 59*, 27–44.

O'Boyle, E.H., Forsyth, D.R., Banks, G.C., & McDaniel, M.A. (2012). A meta-analysis of the Dark Triad and work behavior: A social exchange perspective. *Journal of Applied Psychology, 97*, 557–579.

O'Brien, C. W., & Moorey, S. (2010). Outlook and adaptation in advanced cancer: A systematic review. *Psycho-Oncology, 19*, 1239–1249.

O'Connell, K. L. (2008). What can we learn? Adult outcomes in children of seriously mentally ill mothers. *Journal of Child and Adolescent Psychiatric Nursing, 21*, 89–104.

O'Farrell, T. J. (2011). Family therapy. In M. Galanter & H. D. Kleber (Eds.), *Psychotherapy for the treatment of substance abuse* (pp. 329–350). Arlington, VA: American Psychiatric Publishing.

O'Neil, D. P. (2007). Predicting leader effectiveness: Personality traits and character strengths. *Dissertation Abstracts International: Section B: The Sciences and Engineering, 68*, 4178.

O'Neill, J. W., & Davis, K. (2011). Work stress and well-being in the hotel industry. *International Journal of Hospitality Management, 30*, 385–390.

Oberauer, K., Souza, A. S., Druey, M. D., & Gade, M. (2013). Analogous mechanisms of selection and updating in declarative and procedural working memory: Experiments and a computational model. *Cognitive Psychology, 66*, 157–211.

Obschonka, M., Schmitt-Rodermund, E., Silbereisen, R. K., Gosling, S. D., & Potter, J. (2013). The regional distribution and correlates of an entrepreneurship-prone personality profile in the United States, Germany, and the United Kingdom: A socioecological perspective. *Journal of Personality and Social Psychology, 105*, 104–122.

Ogedegbe, G. O., Boutin-Foster, C., Wells, M. T., Allegrante, J. P., Isen, A. M., Jobe, J. B., & Charlson, M. E. (2012). A randomized controlled trial of positive-affect intervention and medication adherence in hypertensive African Americans. *Archives of Internal Medicine, 172*, 322–326.

Ogilvie, R. D., Wilkinson, R. T., & Allison, S. (1989). The detection of sleep onset: Behavioral, physiological, and subjective convergence. *Sleep, 12*, 458–474.

Ohayon, M. M., Mahowald, M. W., Dauvilliers, Y., Krystal, A. D., & Leger, D. (2012). Prevalence and comorbidity of nocturnal wandering in the US adult general population. *Neurology, 78*, 1583–1589.

Olds, J., & Milner, P. M. (1954). Positive reinforcement produced by electrical stimulation of septal area and other regions of rat brains. *Journal of Comparative and Physiological Psychology, 47*, 419–427.

Ollendick, T. H., Thomas, M., Sherman, P. M., & King, N. (2012). Beyond Watson and Rayner's Little Albert. In A. M. Slater & P. C. Quinn (Eds.), *Developmental psychology: Revisiting the classic studies* (pp. 38–97). Thousand Oaks, CA: Sage.

Oller, J. W., Jr., Oller, S. D., & Oller, S. N. (2014). *Milestones: Normal speech and language development across the life span* (2nd ed.). San Diego, CA: Plural Publishing.

Olsen, L. R., Jensen, D. V., Noerholm, V., Martiny, K., & Bech, P. (2003). The internal and external validity of the Major Depression Inventory in measuring severity of depressive states. *Psychological Medicine, 33*, 351–356.

Olson, I. R., Berryhill, M. E., Drowos, D. B., Brown, L., & Chatterjee, A. (2010). A calendar savant with episodic memory impairments. *Neurocase, 16*, 208–218.

Olsson, C. A., McGee, R., Nada-Raja, S., & Williams, S. M. (2012). A 32-year longitudinal study of child and adolescent pathways to well-being in adulthood. *Journal of Happiness Studies, 14*, 1069–1083.

Oram, S., Trevillion, K., Feder, G., & Howard, L. M. (2013). Prevalence of experiences of domestic violence among psychiatric patients: Systematic review. *The British Journal of Psychiatry, 202*, 94–99.

Orne, M. T. (2006). The nature of hypnosis. artifact and essence: An experimental study. *Dissertation Abstracts International: Section B: The Sciences and Engineering, 67*, 1207.

Orta, I. M. (2013). The impact of cross-group romantic relationships on intergroup prejudice. *Social Behavior and Personality, 41*, 1–6.

Ortony, A., & Turner, T. J. (1990). What's basic about basic emotions? *Psychological Review, 97*, 315–331.

Orzel-Gryglewska, J. (2010). Consequences of sleep deprivation. *International Journal of Occupational Medicine and Environmental Health, 23*, 95–114.

Ost, J., Wright, D. B., Easton, S., Hope, L., & French, C. C. (2013). Recovered memories, satanic abuse, dissociative identity disorder and false memories in the UK: A survey of clinical psychologists and hypnotherapists. *Psychology, Crime & Law, 19*, 1–19.

Ostir, G. V., Markides, K., S., Peek, M. K., & Goodwin, J. S. (2001). The association between emotional well-being and the incidence of stroke in older adults. *Psychosomatic Medicine, 63*, 210–215.

Ottenheimer, H. J. (2013). *The anthropology of language* (3rd ed.). Belmont, CA: Wadsworth Cengage Learning.

Oudiette, D., Dealberto, M.-J., Uguccioni, G., Golmard, J.-L., Merino-Andreu, M., Tafti, M., . . . Arnulf, I. (2012). Dreaming without REM sleep. *Consciousness and Cognition: An International Journal, 21*, 1129–1140.

Overstreet, M. F., & Healy, A. F. (2011). Item and order information in semantic memory: Students' retention of the "CU fight song" lyrics. *Memory and Cognition, 39*, 251–259.

Owens, J. A., Belon, K., & Moss, P. (2010). Impact of delaying school start time on adolescent sleep, mood, and behavior. *Archives of Pediatric & Adolescent Medicine, 164*, 608–614.

Owens, J., & Massey, D. S. (2011). Stereotype threat and college academic performance: A latent variables approach. *Social Science Research, 40*, 150–166.

Owens, S., Rijsdijk, F., Picchioni, M., Stahl, D., Nenadic, I., Murray, R., & Toulopoulou, T. (2011). Genetic overlap between schizophrenia and selective components of executive function. *Schizophrenia Research, 127*, 181–187.

Oz, M. (2011). Bath salts: "Evil" lurking at your corner store. *Time.* Retrieved from http://www.time.com/time/magazine/article/0,9171,2065249,00.html

Ozawa-de Silva, C. (2007). Demystifying Japanese therapy: An analysis of Naikan and the Ajase complex through Buddhist thought. *Ethos, 35*, 411–446.

Ozturk, O., Shayan, S., Liszkowski, U., & Majid, A. (2013). Language is not necessary for color categories. *Developmental Science, 16*, 111–115.

Pace, T. W. W., & Heim, C. M. (2011). A short review on the psychoneuroimmunology of posttraumatic stress disorder: From risk factors to medical comorbidities. *Brain, Behavior, and Immunity, 25*, 6–13.

Pachur, T., Hertwig, R., & Rieskamp, J. (2013). The mind as an intuitive pollster: Frugal search in social spaces. In R. Hertwig & U. Hoffrage (Eds.), *ABC research group, evolution and cognition series. Simple heuristics in a social world* (pp. 261–291). New York: Oxford University Press.

Paciello, M., Fida, R., Tramontano, C., Cole, E., & Cerniglia, L. (2013). Moral dilemma in adolescence: The role of values, prosocial moral reasoning and moral disengagement in helping decision making.

European Journal of Developmental Psychology, 10, 190–205.

Pagano, M. E., White, W. L., Kelly, J. F., Stout, R. L., & Tonigan, J. S. (2013). The 10-year course of AA participation and long-term outcomes: A follow-up study of outpatient subjects in Project MATCH. *Substance Abuse, Special Issue, 31*, 51–59.

Palmer, S., & Williams, H. (2013). Cognitive behavioral approaches. In J. Passmore, D. B. Peterson, & T. Freire (Eds.), *Wiley-Blackwell handbooks in organizational psychology. The Wiley-Blackwell handbook of the psychology of coaching and mentoring* (pp. 319–338). Hoboken, NJ: Wiley-Blackwell.

Panagopoulos, C. (2013). Extrinsic rewards, intrinsic motivation and voting. *The Journal of Politics, 75*, 266–280.

Panlilio, L. V., Zanettini, C., Barnes, C., Solinas, M., & Goldberg, S. R. (2013). Prior exposure to THC increases the addictive effects of nicotine in rats. *Neuropsychopharmacology, 38*, 1198–1208.

Papathanassoglou, E. D., Giannakopoulou, M., Mpouzika, M., Bozas, E., & Karabinis, A. (2010). Potential effects of stress in critical illness through the role of stress neuropeptides. *Nursing in Critical Care, 15*, 204–216.

Pardini, M., Krueger, F., Hodgkinson, C., Raymont, V., Ferrier, C., Goldman, D., . . . Grafman, J. (2011). Prefrontal cortex lesions and MAO-A modulate aggression in penetrating traumatic brain injury. *Neurology, 76*, 1038–1045.

Park, L., Troisi, J., & Maner, J. (2011). Egoistic versus altruistic concerns in communal relationships. *Journal of Social and Personal Relationships, 28*, 315–335.

Parker, R. & McCaffree, K. (Eds.). (2013). *Alcohol and violence: The nature of the relationship and the promise of prevention.* Lanham, MD: Lexington Books.

Partanen, E., Kujala, T., Näätänen, R., Liitola, A., Sambeth, A., & Huotilainen, M. (2013). Learning-induced neural plasticity of speech processing before birth. *Proceedings of the National Academy of Sciences, 110*, 15145–15150.

Paterson, H. M., Kemp, R. I., & Ng, J. R. (2011). Combating co-witness contamination: Attempting to decrease the negative effects of discussion on eyewitness memory. *Applied Cognitive Psychology, 25*, 43–52.

Pathman, T., & Bauer, P. J. (2013). Beyond initial encoding: Measures of the post-encoding status of memory traces predict long-term recall during infancy. *Journal of Experimental Child Psychology, 114*, 321–338.

Patra, B. N., & Balhara, Y. P. (2012). Creativity and mental disorder. *British Journal of Psychiatry, 200*, 346.

Patterson, F., & Linden, E. (1981). *The education of Koko.* New York: Holt, Rinehart and Winston.

Paul, M. A., Gray, G. W., Lieberman, H. R., Love, R. J., Miller, J. C., Trouborst, M., & Arendt, J. (2011). Phase advance with separate and combined melatonin and light treatment. *Psychopharmacology, 214*, 515–523.

Pause, B. M. (2012). Processing of body odor signals by the human brain. *Chemosensory Perception, 5*, 55–63.

Payne, J. D., Chambers, A. M., & Kensinger, E. A. (2012). Sleep promotes lasting changes in selective memory for emotional scenes. *Frontiers in Integrative Neuroscience, 6*, Article 108. doi: 10.3389/fnint.2012.00108

Payne, J. D., Tucker, M. A., Ellenbogen, J. M., Wamsley, E. J., Walker, M. P., Schacter, D. L., & Stickgold, R. (2012). Memory for semantically related and unrelated declarative information: The benefit of sleep, the cost of wake. *PLoS ONE, 7*, e33079

Paz, R., & Pare, D. (2013). Physiological basis for emotional modulation of memory circuits by the amygdala. *Current Opinion in Neurobiology, 23*, 381–386.

Pearson, J. L., Abrams, D. B., Niaura, R. S., Richardson, A., & Vallone, D. M. (2013). Public support for mandated nicotine reduction in cigarettes. *American Journal of Public Health, 103*, 562–567.

Pechtel, P., & Pizzagalli, D. A. (2011). Effects of early life stress on cognitive and affective function: An integrated review of human literature. *Psychopharmacology, 214*, 55–70.

Pedrazzoli, M., Pontes, J. C., Peirano, P., & Tufik, S. (2007). HLA-DQB1 genotyping in a family with narcolepsy-cataplexy. *Brain Research, 1165*, 1–4.

Peer, E., & Rosenbloom, T. (2013). When two motivations race: The effects of time-saving bias and sensation-seeking on driving speed choices. *Accident Analysis & Prevention, 50*, 1135–1139.

Peleg, G., Katzir, G., Peleg, O., Kamara, M., Brodsky, L., Hel-Or, H., . . . Nevo, E. (2006). Hereditary family signature of facial expression. *Proceedings of the National Academy of Sciences, 103*, 15921–15926.

Peng, A. C., Riolli, L. T., Schaubroeck, J., & Spain, E. S. P. (2012). A moderated mediation test of personality, coping, and health among deployed soldiers. *Journal of Organizational Behavior, 33*, 512–530.

Pepe, A., Zhao, L., Koikkalainen, J., Hietala, J., Ruotsalainen, U., & Tohka, J.

(2013). Automatic statistical shape analysis of cerebral asymmetry in 3D T1-weighted magnetic resonance images at vertex-level: Application to neuroleptic-naïve schizophrenia. *Magnetic Resonance Imaging, 31,* 676–687.

Pergola, G., Bellebaum, C., Gehlhaar, B., Koch, B., Schwarz, M., Daum, I., & Suchan, B. (2013). The involvement of the thalamus in semantic retrieval: A clinical group study. *Journal of Cognitive Neuroscience, 7,* 1–15.

Pergola, G., Güntürkün, O., Koch, B., Schwarz, M., Daum, I., & Suchan, B. (2012). Recall deficits in stroke patients with thalamic lesions covary with damage to the parvocellular mediodorsal nucleus of the thalamus. *Neuropsychologia, 50,* 2477–2491.

Perkmen, S., & Sahin, S. (2013). Who should study instructional technology? Vocational personality approach. *British Journal of Educational Technology, 44,* 54–65.

Perry, B. D. (2002). Childhood experience and the expression of genetic potential: What childhood neglect tells us about nature and nurture. *Brain and Mind, 3,* 79–100.

Perugi, G., Medda, P., Zanello, S., Toni, C., & Cassano, G. B. (2012). Episode length and mixed features as predictors of ect nonresponse in patients with medication-resistant major depression. *Brain Stimulation, 5,* 18–24.

Petrosini, L., Cutuli, D., & De Bartolo, P. (2013). Environmental influences on development of the nervous system. In R. J. Nelson, S. J. Y. Mizumori, & I. B. Weiner (Eds.), *Handbook of psychology, Vol. 3. Behavioral neuroscience (2nd ed.,* pp. 461–479). Hoboken, NJ: Wiley.

Petry, Y. (2011). 'Many things surpass our knowledge': An early modern surgeon on magic, witchcraft and demonic possession. *Social History of Medicine, 25,* 47–64.

Pezdek, K. (2012). Fallible eyewitness memory and identification. In B. Cutler (Ed.), *Conviction of the innocent: Lessons from psychological research* (pp. 105–124). Washington, DC: American Psychological Association.

Pfeiffer, P. N., Valenstein, M., Hoggatt, K. J., Ganoczy, D., Maixner, D., Miller, E. M., & Zivin, K. (2011). Electroconvulsive therapy for major depression within the Veterans Health Administration. *Journal of Affective Disorders, 130,* 21–25.

Pharoah, F., Mari, J. J., Rathbone, J., & Wong, W. (2011). Family intervention for schizophrenia. *Cochrane Database of Systematic Reviews 2010,* Issue 12.

Phillips, S. T., & Ziller, R. C. (1997). Toward a theory and measure of the nature of non-prejudice. *Journal of Personality and Social Psychology, 72,* 420–434.

Pietschnig, J., Voracek, M., & Formann, A. K. (2011). Female Flynn effects: No sex differences in generational IQ gains. *Personality and Individual Differences, 50,* 759–762.

Pilati, N., Ison, M. J., Barker, M., Mulheran, M., Large, C. H., Forsythe, I. D., . . . Hamann, M. (2012). Mechanisms contributing to central excitability changes during hearing loss. *Proceedings of the National Academy of Sciences, 109,* 8292–8297.

Pilcher, J. J., Burnett, M. L., & McCubbin, J. A. (2013). Measurement of sleep and sleepiness. In R. R. Sinclair, M. Wang, & L. E. Tetrick (Eds.), *Research methods in occupational health psychology: Measurement, design, and data analysis* (pp. 49–60). New York: Routledge/Taylor & Francis Group.

Pilecki, M. W., Józefik, B. & Sałapa, K. (2012). Kontekst kulturowy zaburzeodywiania si—Badania własne. / The cultural context of eating disorders—Own research. *Psychiatria Polska, 46,* 189–200.

Pina e Cunha, M., Rego, A., & Clegg, S. R. (2010). Obedience and evil: From Milgram and Kampuchea to normal organizations. *Journal of Business Ethics, 97,* 291–309.

Ping-Delfos, W., & Soares, M. (2011). Diet induced thermogenesis, fat oxidation and food intake following sequential meals: Influence of calcium and vitamin D. *Clinical Nutrition, 30,* 376–383.

Pinho, N., Moreira, K. M., Hipolide, D. C., Sinigaglia-Coimbra, R., Ferreira, T. L., Nobrega, J. N., . . . Oliveira, M. G. M. (2013). Sleep deprivation alters phosphorylated CREB levels in the amygdala: Relationship with performance in a fear conditioning task. *Behavioural Brain Research, 236,* 221–224.

Piper, W. E., & Hernandez, C. A. S. (2013). Group psychotherapies. In G. Stricker, T. A. Widiger, & I. B. Weiner (Eds.), *Handbook of psychology, Vol. 8. Clinical psychology* (2nd ed., pp. 367–383). Hoboken, NJ: Wiley.

Plassmann, H., O'Doherty, J., Shiv, B., & Rangel, A. (2008). Marketing actions can modulate neural representations of experienced pleasantness. *Proceedings of the National Academy of Sciences, 105,* 1050–1054.

Platt, T., Hofmann, J., Ruch, W., & Proyer, R. T. (2013). Duchenne display responses towards sixteen enjoyable emotions: Individual differences between no and fear of being laughed at. *Motivation and Emotion.* Advance online publication. doi: 10.1007/s11031-013-9342-9

Plöderl, M., Wagenmakers, E.-J., Tremblay, P., Ramsay, R., Kralovec, K.,

Fartacek, C., & Fartacek, R. (2013). Suicide risk and sexual orientation: A critical review. *Archives of Sexual Behavior, 42,* 715–727.

Plomin, R. (1990). The role of inheritance in behavior. *Science, 248,* 183–188.

Plomin, R., & Spinath, F. M. (2004). Intelligence: Genetics, genes, and genomics. *Journal of Personality & Social Psychology, 86,* 112–129.

Plucker, J., & Esping, A. (2013). *Intelligence 101.* New York: Springer.

Plumbe, L., Peters, S., Bennett, S., Vicenzino, B., & Coppieters, M. W. (2013). Mirror therapy, graded motor imagery and virtual illusion for the management of chronic pain. *Cochrane Database of Systematic Reviews.* doi: 10.1002/14651858.CD010329.

Plutchik, R. (1980). A general psychoevolutionary theory of emotion. In R. Plutchik & H. Kellerman (Eds.), *Emotion: Theory, research, and experience: Vol. 1. Theories of emotion* (pp. 3–31). New York: Academic Press.

Pohl, R. F., Erdfelder, E., Hilbig, B. E., Liebke, L., & Stahlberg, D. (2013). Effort reduction after self-control depletion: The role of cognitive resources in use of simple heuristics. *Journal of Cognitive Psychology, 25,* 267–276.

Pokhrel, P., Herzog, T. A., Black, D. S., Zaman, A., Riggs, N. R., & Sussman, S. (2013). Adolescent neurocognitive development, self-regulation, and school-based drug use prevention. *Prevention Science, 14,* 218–228.

Polley, K. H., Navarro, R., Avery, D. H., George, M. S., & Holtzheimer, P. E. (2011). 2010 updated Avery-George-Holtzheimer Database of rTMS depression studies. *Brain Stimulation, 4,* 115–116.

Pomerantz, A. (2013). *Clinical psychology: Science, practice, and culture (3rd ed.).* Thousand Oaks, CA: Sage.

Pomerantz, E. M., & Kempner, S. G. (2013). Mothers' daily person and process praise: Implications for children's theory of intelligence and motivation. *Developmental Psychology.* Advance online publication. doi: 10.1037/a0031840

Pomponio, A. T. (2002). *Psychological consequences of terror.* Hoboken, NJ: Wiley.

Pope, K. S., & Vasquez, M. J. T. (2011). *Ethics in psychotherapy and counseling: A practical guide* (4th ed.). Hoboken, NJ: Wiley.

Popma, A., Vermeiren, R., Geluk, C. A. M. L., Rinne, T., van den Brink, W., Knol, D. L., . . . Doreleijers, T. A. H. (2007). Cortisol moderates the relationship between testosterone and aggression in delinquent male adolescents. *Biological Psychiatry, 61,* 405–411.

Portnoy, J., Gao, Y., Glenn, A. L., Niv, S., Peskin, M., Rudo-Hutt, A., . . . Raine, A. (2013). The biology of childhood crime and antisocial behavior. In C. L. Gibson & M. D. Krohn (Eds.), *Handbook of life-course criminology: Emerging trends and directions for future research* (pp. 21–42). New York: Springer Science + Business Media.

Post, J. M. (2011). Crimes of obedience: "Groupthink" at Abu Ghraib. *International Journal of Group Psychotherapy, 61,* 49–66

Posthuma, D., de Geus, E. J. C., & Boomsma, D. I. (2001). Perceptual speed and IQ are associated through common genetic factors. *Behavior Genetics, 31,* 593–602.

Potenza, M. N. (2013). Biological contributions to addictions in adolescents and adults: Prevention, treatment, and policy implications. *Journal of Adolescent Health, 52,* S22-S32.

Poulin, M. J., Holman, E. A., & Buffone, A. (2012). The neurogenetics of nice: Receptor genes for oxytocin and vasopressin interact with threat to predict prosocial behavior. *Psychological Science, 23,* 446–452.

Pournaghash-Tehrani, S. (2011). Domestic violence in Iran: A literature review. *Aggression and Violent Behavior, 16,* 1–5.

Prasada, S., Hennefield, L., & Otap, D. (2012). Conceptual and linguistic representations of kinds and classes. *Cognitive Science, 36,* 1224–1250.

Pressman, S. D., & Cohen, S. (2005). Does positive affect influence health? *Psychological Bulletin, 131,* 925–971.

Preston, S. D. (2013). The origins of altruism in offspring care. *Psychological Bulletin.* Advance online publication. doi:10.1037/a0031755

Price, J., Lefgren, L., & Tappen, H. (2013). Interracial workplace cooperation: Evidence from the NBA. *Economic Inquiry, 51,* 1026–1034.

Prkachin, K. M., & Silverman, B. E. (2002). Hostility and facial expression in young men and women: Is social regulation more important than negative affect? *Health Psychology, 21,* 33–39.

Protzko, J., Aronson, J., & Blair, C. (2013). How to make a young child smarter: Evidence from the database of raising intelligence. *Perspectives on Psychological Science, 8,* 25–40.

Pruett, D., Waterman, E. H., & Caughey, A. B. (2013). Fetal alcohol exposure: Consequences, diagnosis, and treatment. *Obstetrical & Gynecological Survey, 68,* 62–69.

Pu, S., Yamada, T., Yokoyama, K., Matsumura, H., Kobayashi, H., Sasaki, N., . . . Nakagome, K. (2011). A multichannel near-infrared spectroscopy study of prefrontal cortex activation during working memory task in major depressive disorder. *Neuroscience Research, 70,* 91–97.

Pullum, G. K. (1991). *The great Eskimo vocabulary hoax and other irreverent essays on the study of language.* Chicago, IL: University of Chicago Press.

Purves, D., & Piatt, M. L. (2012). Sleep and wakefulness. In D. Purves, G. J. Augustine, D. Fitzpatrick, W. C. Hall, A.-S. LaManita, & L. E. White (Eds.), *Neuroscience* (5th ed., pp. 625–646). Sunderland, MA: Sinauer Associates.

Qian, Z., Zhang, D., & Wang, L. (2013). Is aggressive trait responsible for violence? Priming effects of aggressive words and violent movies. *Psychology, 4,* 96–100.

Quick, J. C., Wright, T. A., Adkins, J. A., Nelson, D. L., & Quick, J. D. (2013). Primary prevention for individuals: Managing and coping with stressors. In J. C. Quick, T. A., Wright, J. A. Adkins, D. L. Nelson, & J. D. Quick (Eds.), *Preventive stress management in organizations (2nd ed.,* pp. 147–163). Washington, DC: American Psychological Association.

Quinn, J., Barrowclough, C., & Tarrier, N. (2003). The Family Questionnaire (FQ): A scale for measuring symptom appraisal in relatives of schizophrenic patients. *Acta Psychiatrica Scandinavica, 108,* 290–296.

Quinn, P. D., Stappenbeck, C. A., & Fromme, K. (2013). An event-level examination of sex differences and subjective intoxication in alcohol-related aggression. *Experimental and Clinical Psychopharmacology, 21,* 93–102.

Raaska, H., Elovainio, M., Sinkkonen, J., Stolt, S., Jalonen, I., Matomaki, J., . . . Lapinleimu, H. (2013). Adopted children's language difficulties and their relation to symptoms of reactive attachment disorder: FinAdo study. *Journal of Applied Developmental Psychology, 34,* 152–160.

Raggi, A., Plazzi, G., Pennisi, G., Tasca, D., & Ferri, R. (2011). Cognitive evoked potentials in narcolepsy: A review of the literature. *Neuroscience and Biobehavioral Reviews, 35,* 1144–1153.

Rai, T. S., & Fiske, A. P. (2011). Moral psychology is relationship regulation: Moral motives for unity, hierarchy, equality, and proportionality. *Psychological Review, 118,* 57.

Raison, C. L., & Miller, A. H. (2013). The evolutionary significance of depression in Pathogen Host Defense (PATHOS-D). *Molecular Psychiatry, 18,* 15–37.

Ramsay, C. E., Stewart, T., & Compton, M. T. (2012). Unemployment among patients with newly diagnosed first-episode psychosis: Prevalence and clinical correlates in a US sample. *Social Psychiatry and Psychiatric Epidemiology, 47,* 797–803.

Ratner, K. G., & Amodio, D. M. (2013). Seeing "us vs. Them": Minimal group effects on the neural encoding of faces. *Journal of Experimental Social Psychology, 49,* 298–301.

Rattaz, C., Goubet, N., & Bullinger, A. (2005). The calming effect of a familiar odor on full-term newborns. *Journal of Developmental and Behavioral Pediatrics, 26,* 86–92.

Read, D., & Grushka-Cockayne, Y. (2011). The similarity heuristic. *Journal of Behavioral Decision Making, 24,* 23–46.

Redd, S. B., & Mintz, A. (2013). Policy perspectives on national security and foreign policy decision making. *Policy Studies Journal, 41,* S11–S37.

Redish, A. D., & Ekstrom, A. (2013). Hippocampus and related areas: What the place cell literature tells us about cognitive maps in rats and humans. In D. Waller & L. Nadel (Eds.), *Handbook of spatial cognition* (pp. 15–34). Washington, DC: American Psychological Association.

Reel, J. J. (2013). Mortality rates. In J. J. Reel (Ed.), *Eating disorders: An encyclopedia of causes, treatments, and prevention* (pp. 283–284). Goleta, CA: ABC-CLIO.

Regan, P. (1998). What if you can't get what you want? Willingness to compromise ideal mate selection standards as a function of sex, mate value, and relationship context. *Personality and Social Psychology Bulletin, 24,* 1294–1303.

Reinhard, M.-A., & Dickhäuser, O. (2011). How affective states, task difficulty, and self-concepts influence the formation and consequences of performance expectancies. *Cognition and Emotion, 25,* 220–228.

Reivich, K., Gillham, J. E., Chaplin, T. M., & Seligman, M. E. (2013). From helplessness to optimism: The role of resilience in treating and preventing depression in youth. In S. Goldstein & R. B. Brooks (Eds.), *Handbook of resilience in children* (pp. 201–214). New York: Springer Science + Business Media.

Remer, P. (2013). Feminist therapy. In J. Frew & M. D. Spiegler (Eds.), *Contemporary psychotherapies for a diverse world* (1st rev. ed., pp. 317–414). New York: Routledge/Taylor & Francis Group.

Rentfrow, P. J., Gosling, S. D., & Potter, J. (2008). A theory of the emergence, persistence, and expression of geographic variation in . psychological characteristics. *Perspectives on Psychological Science, 3,* 339–369.

Rest, J., Narvaez, D., Bebeau, M., & Thoma, S. (1999). A neo-Kohlbergian approach: The DIT and schema theory. *Educational Psychology Review, 11*, 291–324.

Reyes-Jaquez, B., & Echols, C. H. (2013). Developmental differences in the relative weighing of informants' social attributes. *Developmental Psychology, 49*, 602–613.

Rhee, S. H., & Waldman, I. D. (2011). Genetic and environmental influences on aggression. In P. R. Shaver & M. Mikulincer (Eds.), *Herzilya series on personality and social psychology. Human aggression and violence: Causes, manifestations, and consequences* (pp. 143–163). Washington, DC: American Psychological Association.

Rimmele, U., Davachi, L., & Phelps, E. A. (2012). Memory for time and place contributes to enhanced confidence in memories for emotional events. *Emotion, 12*, 834–846.

Ripoll, L. H., Snyder, R., Steele, H., & Siever, L. J. (2013). The neurobiology of empathy in borderline personality disorder. *Current Psychiatry Reports, 15*, 1–11.

Risman, B. J., & Davis, G. (2013). From sex roles to gender structure. *Current Sociology, 61*, 733–755.

Riva, M. A., Tremolizzo, L., Spicci, M., Ferrarese, C., De Vito, G., Cesana, G. C., & Sironi, V. A. (2011). The disease of the moon: The linguistic and pathological evolution of the English term "lunatic." *Journal of the History of the Neurosciences, 20*, 65–73.

Rivers, S. E., Brackett, M. A., Reyes, M. R., Elbertson, N. A., & Salovey, P. (2013). Improving the social and emotional climate of classrooms: A clustered randomized controlled trial testing the RULER approach. *Prevention Science, 14*, 77–87.

Rizvi, S. L., & Salters-Pedneault, K. (2013). Borderline personality disorder. In W. O'Donohue & S. O. Lilienfeld (Eds.), *Case studies in clinical psychological science: Bridging the gap from science to practice* (pp. 301–322). New York: Oxford University Press.

Rizzolatti, G. (2012). The mirror mechanism: A mechanism for understanding others. *International Journal of Psychophysiology, 85*, 282.

Robbins, L. (2013). Neuralstem's stem cells give spinal injury patients hope. Retrieved from http://www.gazette.net/article/20130114/NEWS/130119667/neuralstem-x2019-s-stem-cells-give-spinal-injury-patients-hope&template=gazette

Robertson, D. (2013). *The practice of cognitive-behavioural hypnotherapy: A manual for evidence-based cinical hypnosis.* London: Karnac Books.

Robichaud, M. (2013). Generalized anxiety disorder: Targeting intolerance of uncertainty. In G. Simos & S. G. Hofmann (Eds.), *CBT for anxiety disorders: A practitioner book* (pp. 57–85). Oxford, UK: Wiley.

Robnett, R. D., & Leaper, C. (2013). "Girls don't propose! Ew.": A mixed-methods examination of marriage tradition preferences and benevolent sexism in emerging adults. *Journal of Adolescent Research, 28*, 96–121.

Rodkey, E. N., & Riddell, R. P. (2013). The infancy of infant pain research: The experimental origins of infant pain denial. *The Journal of Pain, 14*, 338–350.

Rodrigues, A., Assmar, E. M., & Jablonski, B. (2005). Social-psychology and the invasion of Iraq. *Revista de Psicología Social, 20*, 387–398.

Roehrs, T., & Roth, T. (2012). Sleep and sleep disorders. In J. C. Verster, K. Brady, M. Galanter, & P. Conrod (Eds.), *Drug abuse and addiction in medical illness: Causes, consequences and treatment* (pp. 375–384). New York: Springer Science + Business Media.

Roelofs, J., van Breukelen, G., de Graaf, L. E., Beck, A. T., Arntz, A., & Huibers, M. J. H. (2013). Norms for the Beck Depression Inventory (BDI-II) in a large Dutch community sample. *Journal of Psychopathology and Behavioral Assessment, 35*, 93–98.

Roeser, R. W., Schonert-Reichl, K. A., Jha, A., Cullen, M., Wallace, L., Wilensky, R., . . . Harrison, J. (2013). Mindfulness training and reductions in teacher stress and burnout: Results from two randomized, waitlist-control field trials. *Journal of Educational Psychology, 105*, 787–804.

Roisko, R., Wahlberg, K.-E., Hakko, H., Wynne, L., & Tienari, P. (2011). Communication deviance in parents of families with adoptees at a high or low risk of schizophrenia-spectrum disorders and its associations with attributes of the adoptee and the adoptive parents. *Psychiatry Research, 185*, 66–71.

Rood, L., Roelofs, J., Bogels, S. M., & Arntz, A. (2012). The effects of experimentally induced rumination, positive reappraisal, acceptance, and distancing when thinking about a stressful event on affect states in adolescents. *Journal of Abnormal Child Psychology, 40*, 73–84.

Rooke, S. E., Norberg, M. M., Copeland, J., & Swift, W. (2013). Health outcomes associated with long-term regular cannabis and tobacco smoking. *Addictive Behaviors, 38*, 2207–2213.

Rosch, E. (1978). Principles of organization. In E. Rosch & H. L. Lloyd (Eds.), *Cognition and categorization*. Hillsdale, NJ: Erlbaum.

Rose, S. A., Feldman, J. F., Jankowski, J. J., & Van Rossem, R. (2011). The structure of memory in infants and toddlers: An SEM study with full-terms and preterms. *Developmental Science, 14*, 83–91.

Roselli, C., Reddy, R., & Kaufman, K. (2011). The development of male-oriented behavior in rams. *Frontiers in Neuroendocrinology, 32*, 164–169.

Rosenström, T., Hintsanen, M., Kivimäki, M., Jokela, M., Juonala, M., Viikari, J. S., . . . Keltikangas-Järvinen, L. (2011). "Change in job strain and progression of atherosclerosis: The cardiovascular risk in young Finns study": Correction to Rosenström et al. (2011). *Journal of Occupational Health Psychology, 16*, 201.

Rosenzweig, M. R., Bennett, E. L., & Diamond, M. C. (1972). Brain changes in response to experience. *Scientific American, 226*, 22–29.

Roskies, A. L., Schweitzer, N. J., & Saks, M. J. (2013). Neuroimages in court: Less biasing than feared. *Trends in Cognitive Sciences, 17*, 99–101.

Ross, A. (2013). Handbook of counseling and psychotherapy in an international context. *European Journal of Psychotherapy & Counselling, 5*, 1–4.

Ross, D., Kincaid, H., Spurrett, D., & Collins, P. (Eds.). (2010). *What is addiction?* Cambridge, MA: MIT Press.

Ross, L. (1977). The intuitive psychologist and his shortcomings. Distortions in the attribution process. In L. Berkowitz (Ed.), *Advances in experimental social psychology* (Vol. 10, pp. 173–220). New York: Academic Press.

Rossi, S. L. (2011). The characterization and transplantation of human embryonic stem cell-derived motor neuron progenitors following bilateral cervical spinal cord injury. *Dissertation Abstracts International: Section B. The Sciences and Engineering, 71*, 59–63.

Roth, R. M., Lavoie, M. E., Mason, E. A., & O'Connor, K. P. (2013). Obsessive-compulsive disorder. In C. A. Noggle & R. S. Dean (Eds.), *Contemporary neuropsychology. The neuropsychology of psychopathology* (pp. 261–286). New York: Springer.

Roth, T. (2012). Appropriate therapeutic selection for patients with shift work disorder. *Sleep Medicine, 13*, 335–341.

Rotter, J. B. (1954). *Social learning and clinical psychology.* Englewood Cliffs, NJ: Prentice Hall.

Rotter, J. B. (1990). Internal versus external control of reinforcement: A case history of a variable. *American Psychologist, 45*, 489–493.

Rotter, J. B. (1996). Generalized expectancies for internal versus external control of reinforcement. *Psychological Monographs: General & Applied, 80*, 1–28.

Rouder, J. N., Morey, R. D., & Province, J. M. (2013). A Bayes factor meta-analysis of recent extrasensory perception experiments: Comment on Storm, Tressoldi, and Di Risio (2010). *Psychological Bulletin, 139,* 241–247.

Rowe, B., & Levine, D. (2011). *Concise introduction to linguistics* (3rd ed.). Upper Saddle River, NJ: Prentice Hall.

Rowe, R., Maughan, B., Gregory, A. M., & Eley, T. C. (2013). The development of risky attitudes from pre-driving to fully-qualified driving. *Injury Prevention, 19,* 244–249.

Rozencwajg, P., Cherfi, M., Ferrandez, A. M., Lautrey, J., Lemoine, C., & Loarer, E. (2005). Age related differences in the strategies used by middle aged adults to solve a block design task. *International Journal of Aging and Human Development, 60,* 159–182.

Rumbaugh, D. M., von Glasersfeld, E. C., Warner, H., Pisani, P., & Gill, T. V. (1974). Lana (chimpanzee) learning language: A progress report. *Brain and Language, 1,* 205–212.

Ruocco, A. C., Amirthavasagam, S., Choi-Kain, L. W., & McMain, S. F. (2013). Neural correlates of negative emotionality in borderline personality disorder: An activation-likelihood-estimation meta-analysis. *Biological Psychiatry, 73,* 153–160.

Ruscheweyh, R., Albers, C., Kreusch, A., Sommer, J., & Marziniak, M. (2013). The effect of catastrophizing self-statements on pain perception and the nociceptive flexor reflex (RIII Reflex). *The Clinical Journal of Pain, 27,* 578–586.

Rushton, P., & Irwing, P. (2011). The general factor of personality: Normal and abnormal. In T. Chamorro-Premuzic, S., von Stumm, & A. Furnam (Eds.), *Wiley-Blackwell handbook of individual differences* (pp. 132–161). Chichester, UK: Wiley-Blackwell.

Russ, T. C., Stamatakis, E., Hamer, M., Starr, J. M., Kivimäki, M., & Batty, G. D. (2012). Association between psychological distress and mortality: Individual participant pooled analysis of 10 prospective cohort studies. *British Medical Journal, 345,* e4933.

Ruzek, J. I., Schnurr, P. P., Vasterling, J. J., & Friedman, M. J. (2011). *Caring for veterans with deployment-related stress disorders: Iraq, Afghanistan, and beyond.* Washington, DC: American Psychological Association.

Ryan, A. M., & Sackett, P. R. (2013). Stereotype threat in workplace assessments. In K. F. Geisinger, B. A. Bracken, J. F. Carlson, J.-I. C. Hansen, N. R. Kuncel, S. P. Reise, & M. C. Rodriguez (Eds.), *APA handbooks in psychology. APA handbook of testing and assessment in psychology, Vol. 1. Test theory and testing and assessment in industrial and organizational psychology* (pp. 661–673). Washington, DC: American Psychological Association.

Rymer, R. (1993). *Genie: An abused child's first flight from silence.* New York: Harper-Collins.

Sachdev, P. S. (2013). Is DSM-5 defensible? *Australian and New Zealand Journal of Psychiatry, 47,* 10–11.

Sack, R. L. (2010). Jet lag. *The New England Journal of Medicine, 362,* 440–447.

Sacks, O. (1995). *An anthropologist on Mars.* New York: Vintage books.

Salgado-Pineda, P., Fakra, E., Delaveau, P., McKenna, P. J., Pomarol-Clotet, E., & Blin, O. (2011). Correlated structural and functional brain abnormalities in the default mode network in schizophrenia patients. *Schizophrenia Research, 125,* 101–109.

Salpeter, L. R., & Swirsky, J. I. (2012). Historical and legal implications of subliminal messaging in the multimedia: Unconscious subjects. *Nova Law Review, 36,* 497–555.

Samnani, A. K., Boekhorst, J. A., & Harrison, J. A. (2012). Acculturation strategy and individual outcomes: Cultural diversity implications for human resource management. *Human Resource Management Review, 22,* 323–335.

Sanbonmatsu, D. M., Uchino, B. N., & Birmingham, W. (2011). On the importance of knowing your partner's views: Attitude familiarity is associated with better interpersonal functioning and lower ambulatory blood pressure in daily life. *Annals of Behavioral Medicine, 41,* 131–137.

Sánchez-Villegas, A., Toledo, E., de Irala, J., Ruiz-Canela, M., Pla-Vidal, J., & Martínez-González, M. A. (2011). Fast-food and commercial baked goods consumption and the risk of depression. *Public Health Nutrition, 15,* 424–432.

Sanday, L., Zanin, K. A., Patti, C. L., Fernandes-Santos, L., Oliveira, L. C., Longo, B. M., . . . Frussa-Filho, R. (2013). Role of state-dependent learning in the cognitive effects of caffeine in mice. *The International Journal of Neuropsychopharmacology, 16,* 1547–1557.

Sander, D. (2013). Models of emotion: The affective neuroscience approach. In J. Armony, & P. Vuilleumier (Eds.), *The Cambridge handbook of human affective neuroscience* (pp. 5–53). New York: Cambridge University Press.

Sanderson, C. A. (2010). *Social psychology.* Hoboken, NJ: Wiley.

Sanderson, C. A. (2013). *Health psychology* (2nd ed.). Hoboken, NJ: Wiley.

Sangwan, S. (2001). Ecological factors as related to I.Q. of children. *Psycho-Lingua, 31,* 89–92.

Sanjuán, P., & de Lopez, K. J. (2013). Relationships between self-serving attributional bias and subjective well-being among Danish and Spanish women. In H. H. Knoop & A. Delle Fave (Eds.), *Cross-cultural advancements in positive psychology* (Vol. 3, pp. 183–194). New York: Springer Science + Business Media.

Sanjuán, P., & Magallares, A. (2013). Coping strategies as mediating variables between self-serving attributional bias and subjective well-being. *Journal of Happiness Studies.* Advance online publication. doi:10.1007/s10902-013-9430-2

Sara, S. J. (2010). Reactivation, retrieval, replay and reconsolidation in and out of sleep: Connecting the dots. *Frontiers in Behavioral Neuroscience, 4,* Article ID 185.

Sarafino, E. P. (2012). *Applied behavior analysis: Principles and procedures for modifying behavior.* Hoboken, NJ: Wiley.

Sargent, J. D., Tanski, S., & Stoolmiller, M. (2012). Influence of motion picture rating on adolescent response to movie smoking. *Pediatrics, 130,* 228–236.

Sarkhosh, K., Switzer, N. J., El-Hadi, M., Birch, D. W., Shi, X., & Karmali, S. (2013). The impact of bariatric surgery on obstructive aleep apnea: A systematic review. *Obesity Surgery, 2393,* 414–423.

Satler, C., Garrido, L. M., Sarmiento, E. P., Leme, S., Conde, C., & Tomaz, C. (2007). Emotional arousal enhances declarative memory in patients with Alzheimer's disease. *Acta Neurologica Scandinavica, 116,* 355–360.

Savage, R. (2013). Modern genocidal dehumanization: a new model. *Patterns of Prejudice, 47,* 139–161.

Savage-Rumbaugh, E. S. (1990). Language acquisition in a nonhuman species: Implications for the innateness debate. *Developmental Psychobiology, 23,* 599–620.

Saxton, M. (2010). *Child language: Acquisition and development.* Thousand Oaks, CA: Sage.

Sbarra, D. A., & Nietert, P. J. (2009). Divorce and death: Forty years of the Charleston Heart Study. *Psychological Science, 20,* 107–113.

Scarborough, P., Nnoaham, K. E., Clarke, D., Capewell, S., & Rayner, M. (2012). Modelling the impact of a healthy diet on cardiovascular disease and cancer mortality. *Journal of Epidemiology and Community Health, 66,* 420–426.

Schachter, S., & Singer, J. E. (1962). Cognitive, social, and physiological determinants of emotional state. *Psychological Review, 69,* 379–399.

Schaefer, R. T. (2008). Power and power elite. In V. Parillo (Ed.), *Encyclopedia of* *social problems.* Thousand Oaks, CA: Sage.

Scheele, D., Striepens, N., Güntürkün, O., Deutschländer, S., Maier, W., Kendrick, K. M., & Hurlemann, R. (2012). Oxytocin modulates social distance between males and females. *The Journal of Neuroscience, 32*, 16074–16079.

Scheiermann, C., Kunisaki, Y., & Frenette, P. S. (2013). Circadian control of the immune system. *Nature Reviews Immunology, 13*, 190–198.

Schiffer, B., Muller, B., Scherbaum, N., Hodgins, S., Forsting, M., Wiltfand, J., . . . Leygraf, N. (2011). Disentangling structural brain alterations associated with violent behavior from those associated with substance use disorders. *Archives of General Psychiatry, 68*, 1039–1049.

Schilling, C., Kühn, S., Romanowski, A., Banaschewski, T., Barbot, A., Barker, G. J., . . . IMAGEN Consortium. (2013). Common structural correlates of trait impulsiveness and perceptual reasoning in adolescence. *Human Brain Mapping, 34*, 374–383.

Schilling, T. M., Kölsch, M., Larra, M. F., Zech, C. M., Blumenthal, T. D., Frings, C., & Schächinger, H. (2013). For whom the bell (curve) tolls: Cortisol rapidly affects memory retrieval by an inverted U-shaped dose–response relationship. *Psychoneuroendocrinology, 38*, 1565–1567.

Schirmer, A. (2013). Sex differences in emotion. In J. Armony & P. Vuilleumier (Eds.), *The Cambridge handbook of human affective neuroscience* (pp. 591–610). New York: Cambridge University Press.

Schmid, P. F. (2013). Whence the evil? A personalistic and dialogic perspective. In A. C. Bohart, B. S. Held, E. Mendelowitz, & K. J. Schneider (Eds.), *Humanity's dark side: Evil, destructive experience, and psychotherapy* (pp. 35–55). Washington, DC: American Psychological Association.

Schmidt, A. M., Beck, J. W., & Gillespie, J. Z. (2013). Motivation. In N. W. Schmitt, S. Highhouse, & I. B. Weiner (Eds.), *Handbook of psychology, Vol. 12. Industrial and organizational psychology* (2nd ed., pp. 311–340). Hoboken, NJ: Wiley.

Schmidt, S. R. (2012). *Essays in cognitive psychology. Extraordinary memories for exceptional events.* New York: Psychology Press.

Schmitz, M., & Wentura, D. (2012). Evaluative priming of naming and semantic categorization responses revisited: A mutual facilitation explanation. *Journal of Experimental Psychology: Learning, Memory, and Cognition, 38*, 984–1000.

Schneider, C., Charpak, N., Ruiz-Peláez, J. G., & Tessier, R. (2012). Cerebral motor function in very premature-at-birth adolescents: A brain stimulation exploration of kangaroo mother care effects. *Acta Paediatrica, 101*, 1045–1053.

Schneidman, E. S. (1981). Suicide. *Suicide and Life-Threatening Behavior, 11*, 198–220.

Schott, B. H., Wüstenberg, T., Wimber, M., Fenker, D. B., Zierhut, K. C., Seidenbecher, C. I., . . . Richardson-Klavehn, A. (2013). The relationship between level of processing and hippocampal–cortical functional connectivity during episodic memory formation in humans. *Human Brain Mapping, 34*, 407–424.

Schredl, M. (2010). Nightmare frequency and nightmare topics in a representative German sample. *European Archives of Psychiatry and Clinical Neuroscience, 260*, 565–570.

Schroeder, K., Fisher, H. L., & Schäfer, I. (2013). Psychotic symptoms in patients with borderline personality disorder: Prevalence and clinical management. *Current Opinion in Psychiatry, 26*, 113–119.

Schulze, L., Domes, G., Krüger, A., Berger, C., Fleischer, M., Prehn, K., . . . Herpertz, S. C. (2011). Neuronal correlates of cognitive reappraisal in borderline patients with affective instability. *Biological Psychiatry, 69*, 564–573.

Schunk, D. H., & Zimmerman, B. J. (2013). Self-regulation and learning. In W. M. Reynolds, G. E. Miller, & I. B. Weiner (Eds.), *Handbook of psychology, Vol. 7. Educational psychology* (2nd ed., pp. 45–68). Hoboken, NJ: Wiley.

Schwabe, L., & Wolf, O. T. (2013). Stress and multiple memory systems: from 'thinking' to 'doing'. *Trends in Cognitive Sciences, 17*, 60–68.

Schwartz, S. D., Hubschman, J. P., Heilwell, G., Franco-Cardenas, V., Pan, C. K., Ostrick, R. M., . . . Lanza, R. (2012). Embryonic stem cell trials for macular degeneration: A preliminary report. *Lancet, 379*, 713–720.

Schweitzer, N. J., & Saks, M. J. (2011). Neuroimage evidence and the insanity defense. *Behavioral Sciences & the Law, 29*, 592–607.

Scott, L. N., Levy, K. N., Adams, R. B., Jr., & Stevenson, M. T. (2011). Mental state decoding abilities in young adults with borderline personality disorder traits. *Personality Disorders: Theory, Research, and Treatment, 2*, 98–112.

Segal, N. L. (2013). *Born together—reared apart: The landmark Minnesota Twin Study.* Cambridge, MA: Harvard University Press.

Segerstrom, S., C., & Miller, G. E. (2004). Psychological stress and the human immune system: A meta-analytic study of 30 years of inquiry. *Psychological Bulletin, 130*, 601–630.

Seligman, M. E. P. (1975) *Helplessness: On depression, development, and death.* San Francisco, CA: Freeman.

Seligman, M. E. P. (2003). The past and future of positive psychology. In C. L. M. Keyes & J. Daidt (Eds.), *Flourishing: Positive psychology and the life well-lived* (pp. xi–xx). Washington, DC: American Psychological Association.

Seligman, M. E. P. (2007). Coaching and positive psychology. *Australian Psychologist, 42*, 266–267.

Seligman, M. E. P. (2011). *Flourish: A visionary new understanding of happiness and well-being.* New York: Free Press.

Seligman, M. E. P., & Csikszentmihalyi, M. (2000). Positive psychology: An introduction. *American Psychologist, 55*, 5–14.

Seligman, M. E., & Maier, S. F. (1967). Failure to escape traumatic shock. *Journal of Experimental Psychology, 74*, 1–9.

Senko, C., & Hulleman, C. S. (2013). The role of goal attainment expectancies in achievement goal pursuit. *Journal of Educational Psychology, 105*, 504–521.

Serlin, I. (2011). The history and future of humanistic psychology. *Journal of Humanistic Psychology, 51*, 428–431.

Shaffer, D., & Kipp, K. (2013). *Developmental psychology: Childhood and adolescence* (9th ed.). Belmont Park, CA: Wadsworth Publishing.

Shaffer, R., & Jadwiszczok, A. (2010). Psychic defective: Sylvia Browne's history of failure. *Skeptical Inquirer, 34*. 2.

Shand, G. (2013). Culture and the self: a comparison of attitudes to study among English and Japanese students in state secondary education. *Compare: A Journal of Comparative and International Education.* Advance online publication. doi: 10.1080/03057925.2012.752623

Sharf, R. S. (2012). *Theories of psychotherapy and counseling: Concepts and cases* (5th ed.). Pacific Grove, CA: Brooks/Cole.

Sharkey, P. (2010). The acute effect of local homicides on children's cognitive performance. *Proceedings of the National Academy of Sciences, 107*, 11733–11738.

Sharpe, D. I., Walters, A. S., & Goren, M. J. (2013). Effect of cheating experience on attitudes toward infidelity. *Sexuality & Culture, 7*, 1–16.

Shaw, N. D., Butler, J. P., McKinney, S. M., Nelson, S. A., Ellenbogen, J. M., & Hall, J. E. (2012). Insights into puberty: The relationship between sleep stages and pulsatile LH secretion. *Journal of Clinical Endocrinology & Metabolism, 97*, E2055–E2062.

Sheard, M. (2013). *Mental toughness: The mindset behind sporting achievement* (2nd ed.). New York: Routledge/Taylor & Francis Group.

Shedler, J. (2010). The efficacy of psychodynamic psychotherapy. *American Psychologist, 65,* 98–109.

Shepperd, J. A., Malone, W., & Sweeny, K. (2008). Exploring causes of the self-serving bias. *Social and Personality Psychology Compass, 2,* 895–908.

Sheridan, M. A., Fox, N. A., Zeanah, C. H., McLaughlin, K. A., & Nelson, C. A. III. (2012). Variation in neural development as a result of exposure to institutionalization early in childhood. *Proceedings of the National Academy of Sciences, 109,* 12927–12932.

Sherman, G. D., Lee, J. J., Cuddy, A. J. C., Renshon, J., Oveis, C., Gross, J. J., & Lerner, J. S. (2012). Leadership is associated with lower levels of stress. *Proceedings of the National Academy of Sciences, 109,* 17903–17907.

Shimane, T., Hidaka, Y., Wada, K., & Funada, M. (2013). Ecstasy (3, 4-methylenedioxymethamphetamine) use among Japanese rave population. *Psychiatry & Clinical Neurosciences, 67,* 12–19.

Shin, R.-M., Tully, K., Li, Y., Cho, J.-H., Higuchi, M., Suhara, T., & Bolshakov, V. Y. (2010). Hierarchical order of coexisting pre- and postsynaptic forms of long-term potentiation at synapses in amygdala. *Proceedings of the National Academy of Sciences, 107,* 19073–19078.

Shinfuku, N., & Kitanishi, K. (2010). Buddhism and psychotherapy in Japan. Religion and psychiatry: Beyond boundaries. In P. J. Verhagen, H. M. van Praag, J. J., J. Jr. López-Ibor, J. L. Cox, & D. Moussaoui (Eds.), *Religion and psychiatry: Beyond boundaries* (pp. 181–191). Malden, MA: Wiley-Blackwell.

Shweder, R. A. (2011). Commentary: Ontogenetic cultural psychology. In L. A. Jensen (Ed.), *Bridging cultural and developmental approaches to psychology: New syntheses in theory, research, and policy* (pp. 303–310). New York: Oxford University Press.

Sias, P. M., Heath, R. G., Perry, T., Silva, D., & Fix, B. (2004). Narratives of workplace friendship deterioration. *Journal of Social and Personal Relationships, 21,* 321–340.

Sidhu, M., Malhi, P., & Jerath, J. (2010). Intelligence of children from economically disadvantaged families: Role of parental education. *Psychological Studies, 55,* 358–364.

Sieber-Blum, M. (2010). Epidermal neural crest stem cells and their use in mouse models of spinal cord injury. *Brain Research Bulletin, 83,* 189–193.

Siegala, M., & Varley, R. (2008). If we could talk to the animals. *Behavioral and Brain Sciences, 31,* 146–147.

Siegel, A. B. (2010). Dream interpretation in clinical practice: A century after Freud. *Sleep Medicine Clinics, 5,* 299–313.

Siegel, J. M. (2000, January). Narcolepsy. *Scientific American,* pp. 76–81.

Siegel, J. M. (2008). Do all animals sleep? *Trends in Neurosciences, 31,* 208–213.

Siegler, I. C., Elias, M. F., Brummett, B. H., & Bosworth, H. B. (2013). Adult development and aging. In A. M. Nezu, C. M. Nezu, P. A. Geller, & I. B. Weiner (Eds.), *Handbook of psychology, Vol. 9. Health psychology (2nd ed.,* pp. 459–476). Hoboken, NJ: Wiley.

Signorielli, N. (2013). Gender-role socialization in the twenty-first century. *The international encyclopedia of media studies.* Advance online publication. doi: 10.1002/9781444361506.wbiems116

Sillén, A., Lilius, L., Forsell, C., Kimura, T., Winblad, B., & Graff, C. (2011). Linkage to the 8p21.1 region including the CLU gene in age at onset stratified Alzheimer's disease families. *Journal of Alzheimer's Disease, 23,* 13–20.

Silverstein, M. L. (2013). *Personality and clinical psychology. Personality assessment in depth: A casebook.* New York: Routledge/Taylor & Francis Group.

Simmons, A. L. (2012). Distributed practice and procedural memory consolidation in musicians' skill learning. *Journal of Research in Music Education, 59,* 357–368.

Simpson, T. L., Stappenbeck, C. A., Varra, A. A., Moore, S. A., & Kaysen, D. (2012). Symptoms of posttraumatic stress predict craving among alcohol treatment seekers: Results of a daily monitoring study. *Psychology of Addictive Behaviors, 26,* 724–733.

Sinason, V. (Ed.). (2011). *Attachment, trauma, and multiplicity: Working with dissociative identity disorder* (2nd ed.). New York: Routledge.

Sinclair, L. (2011). Designer drug's rapid spread causes alarm on several fronts. *Psychiatric News, 46,* 8.

Skinner, R., Conlon, L., Gibbons, D., & McDonald, C. (2011). Cannabis use and non-clinical dimensions of psychosis in university students presenting to primary care. *Acta Psychiatrica Scandinavica, 123,* 21–27.

Slater, L. Z., Moneyham, L., Vance, D. E., Raper, J. L., Mugavero, M. J., & Childs, G. (2013). Support, stigma, health, coping, and quality of life in older gay men with HIV. *Journal of the Association of Nurses in AIDS Care, 24,* 38–49.

Slutske, W. S., Cho, S. B., Piasecki, T. M., & Martin, N. G. (2013). Genetic overlap between personality and risk for disordered gambling: Evidence from a national community-based Australian twin study. *Journal of Abnormal Psychology, 122,* 250–255.

Smink, F. R. E., van Hoeken, D., & Hoek, H. W. (2012). Epidemiology of eating disorders: Incidence, prevalence, and mortality rates. *Current Psychiatry Reports, 14,* 406–414.

Smith, B. (2011). Hypnosis today. *Monitor on Psychology, 42,* 6.

Smith, C. V., & Shaffer, M. J. (2013). Gone but not forgotten: Virginity loss and current sexual satisfaction. *Journal of Sex & Marital Therapy, 39,* 96–111.

Smith, K. C. (2012). The Obama effect on African-American students' academic performance. *Dissertation Abstracts International: Section B: The Sciences and Engineering, 72,* 7114.

Smith, K. D. (2007). Spinning straw into gold: Dynamics of Rumpelstiltskin style of leadership. *Dissertation Abstracts International Section A: Humanities and Social Sciences, 68,* 1760.

Smith, M. L. (2012). Rapid processing of emotional expressions without conscious awareness. *Cerebral Cortex, 22,* 1748–1760.

Smith, M. L., & Glass, G. V. (1977). Meta-analysis of psychotherapy outcome studies. *American Psychologist, 32,* 752–760.

Smith, M. L., Glass, G. V., & Miller, T. I. (1980). *The benefits of psychotherapy.* Baltimore: Johns Hopkins University Press.

Smith, M. T., Huang, M. I., & Manber, R. (2005). Cognitive behavior therapy for chronic insomnia occurring within the context of medical and psychiatric disorders. *Clinical Psychology Review, 25,* 559–592.

Smith, M., Robinson, L., & Segal, R. (2012). How much sleep do you need? Sleep cycles and stages, lack of sleep, and getting the hours you need. Retrieved from http://helpguide.org/life/sleeping.htm

Smith, M., Wang, L., Cronenwett, W., Goldman, M., Mamah, D., Barch, D., & Csernansky, J. (2011). Alcohol use disorders contribute to hippocampal and subcortical shape differences in schizophrenia. *Schizophrenia Research, 131,* 174–183.

Snijders, T. J., Ramsey, N. F., Koerselman, F., & van Gijn, J. (2010). Attentional modulation fails to attenuate the subjective pain experience in chronic, unexplained pain. *European Journal of Pain, 14,* e1–e10.

Soares, S. C., & Esteves, F. (2013). A glimpse of fear: Fast detection of threatening targets in visual search with brief stimulus durations. *PsyCh Journal, 2,* 11–16.

Soderberg, C. K., & Sherman, J. W. (2013). No face is an island: How implicit bias operates in social scenes. *Journal of Experimental Social Psychology, 49,* 307–313.

Sokoloff, P., Leriche, L., Diaz, J., Louvel, J., & Pumain, R. (2013). Direct and indirect interactions of the dopamine D3 receptor with glutamate pathways: implications for the treatment of schizophrenia. *Naunyn-Schmiedeberg's Archives of Pharmacology, 386,* 107–124.

Solms, M. (1997). *The neuropsychology of dreams.* Mahwah, NJ: Lawrence Erlbaum.

Somerville, L. H., Wagner, D. D., Wig, G. S., Moran, J. M., Whalen, P. J., & Kelley, W. M. (2013). Interactions between transient and sustained neural signals support the generation and regulation of anxious emotion. *Cerebral Cortex, 23,* 49–60.

Son, H., Banasr, M., Choi, M., Chae, S. Y., Licznerski, P., Lee, B., . . . Duman, R. S. (2012). Neuritin produces antidepressant actions and blocks the neuronal and behavioral deficits caused by chronic stress. *Proceedings of the National Academy of Sciences, 109,* 11378–11383.

Sonnenberg, C. M., Deeg, D. J. H., van Tilburg, T. G., Vink, D., Stek, M. L., & Beekman, A. T. F. (2013). Gender differences in the relation between depression and social support in later life. *International Psychogeriatrics, 25,* 61–70.

Sowell, E. R., Mattson, S. N., Kan, E., Thompson, P. M., Riley, E. P., Edward, P., & Toga, A. W. (2008). Abnormal cortical thickness and brain-behavior correlation patterns in individuals with heavy prenatal alcohol exposure. *Cerebral Cortex, 18,* 136–144.

Spano, R., Koenig, T. L., Hudson, J. W., & Leiste, M. R. (2010). East meets west: A nonlinear model for understanding human growth and development. *Smith College Studies in Social Work, 80,* 198–214.

Spearman, C. (1923). *The nature of "intelligence" and the principles of cognition.* London, England: Macmillan.

Spears, R. (2011). Group identities: The social identity perspective. In S. Schwartz, K. Luyckx, & V. Vignoles (Eds.), *Handbook of identity theory and research* (Vols. 1–2) (pp. 201–224). New York: Springer.

Speisman, R. B., Kumar, A., Rani, A., Pastoriza, J. M., Severance, J. E., Foster, T. C., & Ormerod, B. K. (2013). Environmental enrichment restores neurogenesis and rapid acquisition in aged rats. *Neurobiology of Aging, 34,* 263–274.

Spiegler, M. D. (Ed.). (2013). Behavior therapy II: Cognitive-behavioral therapy. In J. Frew & M. D. Spiegler (Eds.), *Contemporary psychotherapies for a diverse world (1st rev. ed.,* pp. 301–337). New York: Routledge/Taylor & Francis Group.

Spindler, M. A., Galifianakis, N. B., Wilkinson, J. R., & Duda, J. E. (2013). Globus pallidus interna deep brain stimulation for tardive dyskinesia: Case report and review of the literature. *Parkinsonism & Related Disorders, 19,* 141–147.

Sprecher, S., & Fehr, B. (2011). Dispositional attachment and relationship-specific attachment as predictors of compassionate love for a partner. *Journal of Social and Personal Relationships, 28,* 558–574.

Spurling, L. (2011). Review of Off the Couch: Contemporary psychoanalytic approaches. *Psychodynamic Practice: Individuals, Groups and Organisations, 17,* 99–100.

Stadlbauer, U., Arnold, M., Weber, E., & Langhans, W. (2013). Possible mechanisms of circulating PYY-induced satiation in male rats. *Endocrinology, 154,* 193–204.

Stafford, J., & Lynn, S. J. (2002). Cultural scripts, memories of childhood abuse, and multiple identities: A study of role-played enactments. *International Journal of Clinical and Experimental Hypnosis, 50,* 67–85.

Stalder, T., Kirschbaum, C., Heinze, K., Steudte, S., Foley, P., Tietze, A., & Dettenborn, L. (2010). Use of hair cortisol analysis to detect hypercortisolism during active drinking phases in alcohol-dependent individuals. *Biological Psychology, 85,* 357–360.

Stefanek, E., Strohmeier, D., Fandrem, H., & Spiel, C. (2012). Depressive symptoms in native and immigrant adolescents: The role of critical life events and daily hassles. *Anxiety, Stress and Coping: An International Journal, 25,* 201–217.

Stegmann, U. E. (2013). *Animal communication theory: Information and influence.* New York: Cambridge University Press.

Steiger, H., Bruce, K. R., & Israël, M. (2013). Eating disorders: Anorexia nervosa, bulimia nervosa, and binge eating disorder. In G. Stricker, T. A. Widiger, & I. B. Weiner (Eds.), *Handbook of psychology, Vol. 8. Clinical psychology* (2nd ed., pp. 73–93). Hoboken, NJ: Wiley.

Stein, D. J., Denys, D., Gloster, A. T., Hollander, E., Leckman, J. F., Rauch, S. L., & Phillips, K. A. (2009). Obsessive-compulsive disorder: Diagnostic and treatment issues. *Psychiatric Clinics of North America, 32,* 665–685.

Stein, J. L., Medland, S. E., Vasquez, A. A., Hibar, D. P., Senstad, R. E., Winkler, A. M., . . . Thompson, P. M. (2012). Identification of common variants associated with human hippocampal and intracranial volumes. *Nature Genetics, 44,* 552–561.

Steinhart, P. (1986, March). Personal boundaries. *Audubon,* pp. 8–11.

Stephens, N. J., & Swartz, T. A. (2013). Beliefs of Chinese buyers of pirated goods. *Journal of Consumer Behaviour, 12,* 42–48.

Steptoe, A., & Kivimäki, M. (2013). Stress and cardiovascular disease: An update on current knowledge. *Annual Review of Public Health, 34,* 337–354.

Sternberg, R. J. (1986). A triangular theory of love. *Psychological Review, 93,* 119–135.

Sternberg, R. J. (1988). *The triangle of love.* New York: Basic Books.

Sternberg, R. J. (2006). A duplex theory of love. In R. J. Sternberg & K. Weis (Eds.), *The new psychology of love* (pp. 184–199). New Haven, CT: Yale University Press.

Sternberg, R. J. (2012). *Cognitive psychology* (6th ed.). Belmont, CA: Cengage.

Sternberg, R. J. (2013). Contemporary theories of intelligence. In W. M. Reynolds, G. E. Miller, & I. B. Weiner (Eds.), *Handbook of psychology, Vol. 7. Educational psychology* (2nd ed., pp. 23–44). Hoboken, NJ: Wiley.

Sternberg, R. J. (2013). Intelligence. In D. K. Freedheim & I. B. Weiner (Eds.), *Handbook of psychology, Vol. 1. History of psychology (2nd ed.,* pp. 155–176). Hoboken, NJ: Wiley.

Sternberg, R. J., & Grigorenko, E. L. (2008). Ability testing across cultures. In L. Suzuki (Ed.), *Handbook of multicultural assessment* (3rd ed., pp. 449–470). New York: Jossey-Bass.

Sternberg, R. J., & Lubart, T. I. (1992). Buy low and sell high: An investment approach to creativity. *Current Directions in Psychological Science, 1,* 1–5.

Stets, J. E., & Carter, M. J. (2012). A theory of the self for the sociology of morality. *American Sociological Review, 77,* 120–140.

Stickgold, R., & Walker, M. P. (2013). Sleep-dependent memory triage: Evolving generalization through selective processing. *Nature Neuroscience, 16,* 139–145.

Stiles, W. B. (2013). The variables problem and progress in psychotherapy research. *Psychotherapy, 50,* 33–41.

Stock, M. L., Gibbons, F. X., Peterson, L. M., & Gerrard, M. (2013). The effects of racial discrimination on the HIV-risk cognitions and behaviors of Black adolescents and young adults. *Health Psychology, 32,* 543–550.

Stoll, E. E., & Ha-Brookshire, J. E. (2012). Motivations for success: Case of U.S. textile and apparel small- and medium-sized enterprises. *Clothing & Textiles Research Journal, 30,* 149–163.

Stollhoff, R., Jost, J., Elze, T., & Kennerknecht, I. (2011). Deficits in long-term recognition memory reveal dissociated subtypes in congenital prosopagnosia. *PLoS ONE, 6,* Article ID e15702.

Stoltzfus, G., Nibbelink, B., Vredenburg, D., & Hyrum, E. (2011). Gender, gender role, and creativity. *Social Behavior and Personality: An International Journal, 39,* 425–432.

Stoner, J. A. (1961). *A comparison of individual and group decisions involving risk.* Unpublished master's thesis, School of Industrial Management, MIT, Cambridge, MA.

Stoodley, C. J. (2012). The cerebellum and cognition: Evidence from functional imaging studies. *The Cerebellum, 11,* 352–365.

Stopa, L., Denton, R., Wingfield, M., & Taylor, K. N. (2013). The fear of others: A qualitative analysis of interpersonal threat in social phobia and paranoia. *Behavioural and Cognitive Psychotherapy, 41,* 188–209.

Storsve, A. B., McNally, G. P., & Richardson, R. (2012). Renewal and reinstatement of the conditioned but not the unconditioned response following habituation of the unconditioned stimulus. *Behavioural Processes, 90,* 58–65.

Stowell, J. R., Robles, T. F., & Kane, H. S. (2013). Psychoneuroimmunology: Mechanisms, individual differences, and interventions. In A. M. Nezu, C. M. Nezu, P. A. Geller, & I. B. Weiner (Eds.), *Handbook of psychology, Vol. 9. Health psychology (2nd ed.,* pp. 79–101). Hoboken, NJ: Wiley.

Strack, F., Martin, L. L., & Stepper, S. (1988). Inhibiting and facilitating conditions of the human smile: A nonobstrusive test of the facial feedback hypothesis. *Journal of Personality and Social Psychology, 54,* 768–777.

Strange, D., Garry, M., Bernstein, D. M., & Lindsay, D. S. (2011). Photographs cause false memories for the news. *Acta Psychologica, 136,* 90–94.

Straub, R. O. (2011). *Health psychology: A biopsychosocial approach* (3rd ed.). New York: Worth.

Strauss, J. R. (2010). The baby boomers meet menopause: Attitudes and roles. *Dissertation Abstracts International Section A: Humanities and Social Sciences, 70,* 3196.

Strayer, D. L., Wartson, J. M., & Drews, F. A. (2011). Cognitive distraction while multitasking in the automobile. In B. H. Ross (Ed.), *The psychology of learning and motivation: Advances in research and theory* (Vol. 54, pp. 29–58). San Diego, CA: Elsevier Academic Press.

Stricker, G., Widiger, T. A., & Weiner, I. B. (Eds.). (2013). *Handbook of psychology, Vol 8: Clinical Psychology (2nd ed.).* Hoboken, NJ: Wiley.

Stroebe, W., & Stroebe, M. S. (1996). The social psychology of social support. In E. T. Higgins & A. W. Kruglanski (Eds.), *Social psychology: Handbook of basic principles* (pp. 597–621). New York: Guilford Press.

Strozier, C. B. (2011). Torture, war, and the culture of fear after 9/11. *International Journal of Group Psychotherapy, 61,* 67–72.

Sugarman, H., Impey, C., Buxner, S., & Antonellis, J. (2011). Astrology beliefs among undergraduate students. *Astronomy Education Review, 10.* Retrieved from http://aer.aas.org/resource/1/aerscz/v10/i1/p010101_s1?view=fulltext

Sullivan, M. J. L., Tripp, D. A., & Santor, D. (1998). *Gender differences in pain and pain behavior: The role of catastrophizing.* Paper presented at the annual meeting of the American Psychological Association, San Francisco, CA.

Suls, J., Davidson, K., & Kaplan, R. (Eds.). (2010). *Handbook of health psychology and behavioral medicine.* New York: Guilford Press.

Sundram, F., Deeley, Q., Sarkar, S., Daly, E., Latham, R., Barker, G., & Murphy, D. (2011). White matter microstructural abnormalities in antisocial personality disorder: A pilot diffusion tensor imaging study. *European Psychiatry, 26,* 957.

Surtees, P. G., Wainwright, N. W. J., Luben, R. N., Khaw, K-T, & Bingham, S. A. (2009). No evidence that social stress is associated with breast cancer incidence. *Breast Cancer Research and Treatment, 120,* 169–174.

Susilo, T., & Duchaine, B. (2013). Advances in developmental prosopagnosia research. *Current Opinion in Neurobiology, 23,* 423–429.

Suthana, N., Haneef, Z., Stern, J., Mukamel, R., Behnke, E., Knowlton, B., & Fried, I. (2012). Memory enhancement and deepbrain stimulation of the entorhinal area. *New England Journal of Medicine, 366,* 502–510.

Sutin, R., Terracciano, A., Milaneschi, Y., An, Y., Ferrucci, L., & Zonderman, A. B. (2013). The effect of birth cohort on well-being: The legacy of economic hard times. *Psychological Science, 24,* 379–385.

Suzuki, L. A., Onoue, M. A., & Hill, J. S. (2013). Clinical assessment: A multicultural perspective. In K. F. Geisinger, B. A. Bracken, J. F. Carlson, J.-I. C. Hansen, N. R. Kuncel, S. P. Reise, & M. C. Rodriguez (Eds.), *APA handbooks in psychology. APA handbook of testing and assessment in psychology, Vol. 2. Testing and assessment in clinical and counseling psychology* (pp. 193–212). Washington, DC: American Psychological Association.

Svrakic, D. M., Zorumski, C. F., Svrakic, N. M., Zwir, I., & Cloninger, C. R. (2013). Risk architecture of schizophrenia: the role of epigenetics. *Current Opinion in Psychiatry, 26,* 188–195.

Swami, V. (2012). Mental health literacy of depression: Gender differences and attitudinal antecedents in a representative British sample. *PLoS ONE, 7:* e49779.

Swami, V., & Harris, A. S. (2012). Evolutionary perspectives on physical appearance. In T. F. Cash (Ed.), *Encyclopedia of body image and human appearance* (Vol. 1, pp. 404–411). San Diego, CA: Elsevier Academic Press.

Swanson, S. A., Saito, N., Borges, G., Benjet, C., Aguilar-Gaxiola, S., Medina-Mora, M. E., . . . Breslau, J. (2012). Change in binge eating and binge eating disorder associated with migration from Mexico to the US. *Journal of Psychiatric Research, 46,* 31–37.

Sylvestre, A., & Mérette, C. (2010). Language delay in severely neglected children: A cumulative or specific effect of risk factors? *Child Abuse & Neglect, 34,* 414–428.

Szanton, S. L., Rifkind, J. M., Mohanty, J. G., Miller, E. R., Thorpe, R. J., Nagababu, E., . . . Evans, M. K. (2011). Racial discrimination is associated with a measure of red blood cell oxidative stress: A potential pathway for racial disparities. *International Journal of Behavioral Medicine, 19,* 489–495.

Szasz, T. (2012). Varieties of psychiatric criticism. *History of Psychiatry, 23,* 349–355.

Takahashi, A., Quadros, I. M., de Almeida, R. M. M., & Miczek, K. A. (2011). Brain serotonin receptors and transporters: Initiation vs. termination of escalated aggression. *Psychopharmacology, 213,* 183–212.

Takahashi, E., Ohki, K., & Kim, D.-S. (2013). Dissociation and convergence of the dorsal and ventral visual working memory streams in the human prefrontal cortex. *NeuroImage, 65,* 488–498.

Tang, Y. Y., & Posner, M. I. (2013). Tools of the trade: Theory and method in mindfulness neuroscience. *Social Cognitive and Affective Neuroscience, 8,* 118–120.

Tang, Y.-P., Wang, H., Feng, R., Kyin, M., & Tsien, J. Z. (2001). Differential effects of enrichment on learning and memory function in NR2B transgenic mice. *Neuropharmacology, 41*, 779–790.

Tarter, R. E., Kirisci, L., Mezzich, A., Cornelius, J. R., Pajer, K., Vanyukov, M., . . . Clark, D. (2003). Neurobehavioral disinhibition in childhood predicts early age at onset of substance use disorder. *American Journal of Psychiatry, 160*, 1078.

Tatkin, S. (2011). *Wired for love: How understanding your partner's brain and attachment style can help you defuse conflict and build a secure relationship.* Oakland, CA: New Harbinger Publications.

Taub, D. J., & Thompson, J. (2013). College student suicide. *New Directions for Student Services, 141*, 5–14.

Taub, E. (2004). Harnessing brain plasticity through behavioral techniques to produce new treatments in neurorehabilitation. *American Psychologist, 59*, 692–704.

Taub, E. (2012). The behavior-analytic origins of constraint-induced movement therapy: An example of behavioral neurorehabilitation. *The Behavior Analyst, 35*, 155–178.

Taylor, J. Y., Caldwell, C. H., Baser, R. E., Matusko, N., Faison, N., & Jackson, J. S. (2013). Classification and correlates of eating disorders among Blacks: Findings from the National Survey of American Life. *Journal of Health Care for the Poor and Underserved, 24*, 289.

Taylor, L., Fiore, A., Mendelsohn, G., & Cheshire, C. (2011). "Out of my league": A real-world test of the matching hypothesis. *Personality and Social Psychology Bulletin, 37*, 942–954.

Taylor, S. E. (2006). Tend and befriend: Biobehavioral bases of affiliation under stress. *Current Directions in Psychological Science, 15*, 273–277.

Taylor, S. E., & Sherman, D. K. (2008). Self-enhancement and self-affirmation: The consequences of positive self-thoughts for motivation and health. In J. Y. Shah & W. L. Gardner (Eds.), *Handbook of motivation science* (pp. 57–70). New York: Guilford Press.

Tellegen, A. (1985). Structures of mood and personality and their relevance to assessing anxiety with an emphasis on self-report. In A. H. Tuma & J. D. Maser (Eds.), *Anxiety and the anxiety disorders* (pp. 681–706). Hillsdale, NJ: Erlbaum.

Tennen, H., Suls, J., & Weiner, I. B. (Eds.). (2013). *Handbook of psychology, Vol. 5. Personality and social psychology* (2nd ed.). Hoboken, NJ: Wiley.

Terhune, D. B., Cardeña, E., & Lindgren, M. (2011). Dissociative tendencies and individual differences in high hypnotic suggestibility. *Cognitive Neuropsychiatry, 16*, 113–135.

Terman, L. M. (1906). Genius and stupidity: A study of some of the intellectual processes of seven "bright" and seven "stupid" boys. *Pedagogical Seminary, 13*, 307–373.

Terracciano, A., Löckenhoff, C. E., Zonderman, A. B., Ferrucci, L., & Costa, P. T. Jr. (2008). Personality predictors of longevity: Activity, emotional stability, and conscientiousness. *Psychosomatic Medicine, 70*, 621–627.

Terrace, H. S. (1979, November). How Nim Chimpsky changed my mind. *Psychology Today*, pp. 65–76.

Tesarz, J., Schuster, A. K., Hartmann, M., Gerhardt, A., & Eich, W. (2012). Pain perception in athletes compared to normally active controls: A systematic review with meta-analysis. *Pain, 153*, 1253–1262.

Teunissen, H. A., Spijkerman, R., Prinstein, M. G., Cohen, G. L., Engles, R. C., & Scholte, R. H. (2012). Adolescents' conformity to their peers' pro-alcohol and anti-alcohol norms: The power of popularity. *Alcoholism: Clinical and Experimental Research, 36*, 1257–1267.

Thaler, J. P., Yi, C. X., Schur, E. A., Guyenet, S. J., Hwang, B. H., Dietrich, M. O., . . . Schwartz, M. W. (2012). Obesity is associated with hypothalamic injury in rodent models and humans. *Journal of Clinical Investigations, 122*, 153–162.

Thaler, N. S., Allen, D. N., & Goldstein, G. (2013). Bipolar disorders. In C. A. Noggle & R. S. Dean (Eds.), *Contemporary neuropsychology. The neuropsychology of psychopathology* (pp. 221–242). New York: Springer.

Thoits, P. A. (2010). Stress and health: Major findings and policy implications. *Journal of Health and Social Behavior, 51*, S41–S53.

Thomas, B. (2012). What's so special about mirror neurons? Retrieved from http://scientificamerican.com/2012/11/06/whats-so-special-about-mirror-neurons/

Thompson, D. (2013, July 15). Could a gene help make you obese? US News. Retrieved from http://health.usnews.com/health-news/news/articles/2013/07/15/could-a-gene-help-make-you-obese

Thompson, R. F. (2005). In search of memory traces. *Annual Review of Clinical Psychology, 56*, 1–23.

Thomson, C. J., Hanna, C. W., Carlson, S. R., & Rupert, J. L. (2013). The− 521 C/T variant in the dopamine 4 receptor gene (DRD4) is associated with skiing and snowboarding behavior. *Scandinavian Journal of Medicine & Science in Sports, 23*, 108–113.

Thornton, B., & Tizard, H. J. (2010). "Not in my back yard": Evidence for arousal moderating vested interest and oppositional behavior to proposed change. *Social Psychology, 41*, 255–262.

Thornton, M. A., & Conway, A. R. (2013). Working memory for social information: Chunking or domain-specific buffer?. *NeuroImage, 70*, 233–239.

Thurstone, L. L. (1938). *Primary mental abilities.* Chicago: University of Chicago Press.

Thyer, B. A., & Myers, L. L. (2011). The quest for evidence-based practice: A view from the United States. *Journal of Social Work, 11*, 8–25.

Thyssen, A., Stavermann, M., Buddrus, K., Doengi, M., Ekberg, J., A., St John, J. A., . . . Lohr, C. (2013). Spatial and developmental heterogeneity of calcium signaling in olfactory ensheathing cells. *Glia, 61*, 327–337.

Tindale, R. S., Talbot, M., & Martinez, R. (2013). Decision making. In J. M. Levine (Ed.), *Frontiers of social psychology. Group processes* (pp. 165–192). New York: Psychology Press.

Tindale, S., & Posavac, E. (2011). The social psychology of stakeholder processes: Group processes and interpersonal relations. In M. Mark, S. Donaldson, & B. Campbell (Eds.) *Social psychology and evaluation* (pp. 189–209). New York: Guilford Press.

Todd, A. R., Bodenhausen, G. V., Richeson, J. A., & Galinsky, A. D. (2011). Perspective taking combats automatic expressions of racial bias. *Journal of Personality and Social Psychology, 100*, 1027–1042.

Todd, P. M., & Gigerenzer, G. (2000). Precis of simple heuristics that make us smart. *Behavioral and Brain Sciences, 23*, 727.

Tomasetto, C., & Appoloni, S. (2013). A lesson not to be learned? Understanding stereotype threat does not protect women from stereotype threat. *Social Psychology of Education, 16*, 199–213.

Tomash, J. J., & Reed, P. (2013). The generalization of a conditioned response to deception across the public/private barrier. *Learning and Motivation, 44*, 196–203.

Tomkins, S. S. (1962). *Affect, imagery, consciousness: Vol. 1. The positive effects.* New York: Springer.

Tompkins, T. L., Hockett, A. R., Abraibesh, N., & Witt, J. L. (2011). A closer look at co-rumination: Gender, coping, peer functioning and internalizing/externalizing problems. *Journal of Adolescence, 34*, 801–811.

Topham, G. L., Hubbs-Tait, L., Rutledge, J. M., Page, M. C., Kennedy, T. S., Shriver, L. H., & Harrist, A. W. (2011). Parenting styles, parental response to child emotion, and family emotional responsiveness are related to child emotional eating. *Appetite, 56*, 261–264.

Torry, Z. D., & Billick, S. B. (2011). Implications of antisocial parents. *Psychiatric Quarterly, 82*, 275–285.

Trawick-Smith, J., & Dziurgot, T. (2011). 'Good-fit' teacher–child play interactions and the subsequent autonomous play of preschool children. *Early Childhood Research Quarterly, 26*, 110–123.

Tronci, V., & Balfour, D. J. K. (2011). The effects of the mGluR5 receptor antagonist 6-methyl-2-(phenylethynyl)-pyridine (MPEP) on the stimulation of dopamine release evoked by nicotine in the rat brain. *Behavioural Brain Research, 219*, 354–357.

Trost, S., Platz, B., Usher, J., Scherk, H., Wobrock, T., Ekawardhani, S., . . . Gruber, O. (2013). The DTNBP1 (dysbindin-1) gene variant rs2619522 is associated with variation of hippocampal and prefrontal grey matter Vols. in humans. *European Archives of Psychiatry and Clinical Neuroscience, 263*, 53–63.

Trull, T. J., Carpenter, R. W., & Widiger, T. A. (2013). Personality disorders. In G. Stricker, T. A. Widiger, & I. B. Weiner (Eds.), *Handbook of psychology, Vol. 8. Clinical psychology* (2nd ed., pp. 94–120). Hoboken, NJ: Wiley.

Trzaskowski, M., Davis, O. S. P., DeFries, J. C., Yang, J., Visscher, P. M., & Plomin, R. (2013). Dna evidence for strong genome-wide pleiotropy of cognitive and learning abilities. *Behavior Genetics, 43*, 267–273.

Trzaskowski, M., Yang, J., Visscher, P. M., & Plomin, R. (2013). DNA evidence for strong genetic stability and increasing heritability of intelligence from age 7 to 12. *Molecular Psychiatry*. Advance online publication. doi: 10.1038/mp.2012.191

Tsien, J. Z. (2000, April). Building a brainier mouse. *Scientific American*, pp. 62–68.

Tsoukalas, I. (2012). The origin of REM sleep: A hypothesis. *Dreaming, 22*, 253–283.

Tulving, E., & Thompson, D. M. (1973). Encoding specificity and retrieval processes in episodic memory. *Psychological Review, 80*, 352–373.

Turnbull, D. L., Cox, B. J., Oleski, J., & Katz, L. Y. (2013). The effects of borderline personality disorder and panic disorder on suicide attempts and the associated influence of affective dysregulation in the general population. *The Journal of Nervous and Mental Disease, 201*, 130–135.

Turner, M., & Barker, J. B. (2013). Examining the efficacy of rational-emotive behavior therapy (REBT) on irrational beliefs and anxiety in elite youth cricketers. *Journal of Applied Sport Psychology, 25*, 131–147.

Tversky, A., & Kahneman, D. (1974). Judgment under uncertainty: Heuristics and biases. *Science, 185*, 1124–1131.

Tversky, A., & Kahneman, D. (1993). Probabilistic reasoning. In A. I. Goldman (Ed.), *Readings in philosophy and cognitive science* (pp. 43–68). Cambridge, MA: MIT Press.

Tyson, P. J., Jones, D., & Elcock, J. (2011). *Psychology in social context: Issues and debates*. Malden, MA: Wiley-Blackwell.

Ueno, M., Uchiyama, I., Campos, J. J., Dahl, A., & Anderson, D. I. (2012). The organization of wariness of heights in experienced crawlers. *Infancy, 11*, 376–392.

Ulrich, R. E., Stachnik, T. J., & Stainton, N. R. (1963). Student acceptance of generalized personality interpretations. *Psychological Reports, 13*, 831–834.

Unsworth, N., Spillers, G. J., & Brewer, G. A. (2012). Dynamics of context-dependent recall: An examination of internal and external context change. *Journal of Memory and Language, 66*, 1–16.

Urry, H. L., Roeser, R. W., Lazar, S. W., & Poey, A. P. (2012). Prefrontal cortical activation during emotion regulation: Linking religious/spiritual practices with well-being. In A. E. A. Warren, R. M. Lerner, & E. Phelps (Eds.), *Thriving and spirituality among youth: Research perspectives and future possibilities* (pp. 19–29). Hoboken, NJ: Wiley.

Vaillancourt, T. (2013). Students aggress against professors in reaction to receiving poor grades: An effect moderated by student narcissism and self-esteem. *Aggressive Behavior, 39*, 71–84.

Van de Carr, F. R., & Lehrer, M. (1997). *While you are expecting: Your own prenatal classroom*. New York: Humanics Publishing.

Van Der Kloet, D., Giesbrecht, T., Franck, E., Van Gastel, A., De Volder, I., Van Den Eede, F., . . . Merckelbach, H. (2013). Dissociative symptoms and sleep parameters—an all-night polysomnography study in patients with insomnia. *Comprehensive Psychiatry, 54*, 658–664.

van der Laan, L. N., de Ridder, D. T. D., Viergever, M. A., & Smeets, P. A. M. (2011). The first taste is always with the eyes: A meta-analysis on the neural correlates of processing visual food cues. *NeuroImage, 55*, 296–303.

Van Gordon, W., Shonin, E., Sumich, A., Sundin, E. C., & Griffiths, M. D. (2013). Meditation awareness training (mat) for psychological well-being in a sub-clinical sample of university students: A controlled pilot study. *Mindfulness*. Advance online publication. 10.1007/s12671-012-0191-5.

Van Horn, J. D., Irimia, A., Torgerson, C. M., Chambers, M. C., Kikinis, R., & Toga, A. W. (2012). Mapping connectivity damage in the case of Phineas Gage. *PLoS ONE, 7*. Article ID e37454.

Van Iddekinge, C. H., Roth, P. L., Raymark, P. H., & Odle-Dusseau, H. N. (2012). The critical role of the research question, inclusion criteria, and transparency in meta-analyses of integrity test research: A reply to Harris et al. (2012) and Ones, Viswesvaran, and Schmidt (2012). *Journal of Applied Psychology, 97*, 543–549.

van Ijzendoorn, M. H., Bakermans-Kranenburg, M. J., Pannebakker, F., & Out, D. (2013). In defence of situational morality: Genetic, dispositional, and situational determinants of children's donation to charity. *Journal of Moral Education, 39*, 1–20.

van Laar, M. (2012). Epidemiology of alcohol and drug use. In J. C. Verster, K. Brady, M. Galanter, & P. Conrod (Eds.), *Drug abuse and addiction in medical illness: Causes, consequences and treatment* (pp. 3–23). New York: Springer Science + Business Media.

Vandenbosch, L., & Eggermont, S. (2011). *Temptation Island, The Bachelor, Joe Millionaire*: A prospective cohort study on the role of romantically themed reality television in adolescents' sexual development. *Journal of Broadcasting & Electronic Media, 56*, 563–580.

Vasey, M. W., Vilensky, M. R., Heath, J. H., Harbaugh, C. N., Buffington, A. G., & Fazio, R. H. (2012). It was as big as my head, I swear! *Journal of Anxiety Disorders, 26*, 20–24.

Vaughn, D. (1996). *The Challenger launch decision: Risky technology, culture, and deviance at NASA*. Chicago, IL: University of Chicago Press.

Vaz-Leal, F., Rodríguez-Santos, L, García-Herráiz, A., & Ramos-Fuentes, I. (2011). Neurobiological and psychopathological variables related to emotional instability: A study of their capability to discriminate patients with bulimia nervosa from healthy controls. *Neuropsychobiology, 63*, 242–251.

Verleger, R., Ludwig, J., Kolev, V., Yordanova, J., & Wagner, U. (2011). Sleep effects on slow-brain-potential reflections of associative learning. *Biological Psychology, 86,* 219–229.

Vernon, A. (2011). Rational emotive behavior therapy. In D. Capuzzi & D. R. Gross (Eds.), *Counseling and psychotherapy* (5th ed., pp. 237–261). Alexandria, VA: American Counseling Association.

Veselka, L., Schermer, J. A., & Vernon, P. (2011). Beyond the big five: The dark triad and the Supernumerary Personality Inventory. *Twin Research and Human Genetics, 14,* 158–168.

Vidal, S. G. M., Hornik, A., & Morgan, C. (2012). Cocaine induced hippocampi infarction. *BMJ Case Reports,* Retrieved from http://casereports.bmj.com/content/2012/bcr.03.2012.5998.full

Viena, T. D., Banks, J. B., Barbu, I. M., Schulman, A. H., & Tartar, J. L. (2012). Differential effects of mild chronic stress on cortisol and S-IgA responses to an acute stressor. *Biological Psychology, 91,* 307–311.

Vitulano, N., Di Marco, B. A., Re, A., Riccioni, G., Perna, F., Mormile, F., . . . Bellocci, F. (2013). Obstructive sleep apnea and heart disease: the biomarkers point of view. *Frontiers in Bioscience (Scholar edition), 5,* 588.

Vokey, J. R., & Read, J. D. (1985). Subliminal messages: Between the devil and the media. *American Psychologist, 40,* 1231–1239.

Völker, S. (2007). Infants' vocal engagement oriented towards mother versus stranger at 3 months and avoidant attachment behavior at 12 months. *International Journal of Behavioral Development, 31,* 88–95.

Völlink, T., Bolman, C. A., Dehue, F., & Jacobs, N. C. (2013). Coping with cyberbullying: Differences between victims, bully-victims and children not involved in bullying. *Journal of Community & Applied Social Psychology, 23,* 7–24.

von Dawans, B., Fischbacher, U., Kirschbaum, C., Fehr, E., & Heinrichs, M. (2012). The social dimension of stress reactivity: Acute stress increases prosocial behavior in humans. *Psychological Science, 23,* 651–660.

von Hofsten, C. (2013). Action in infancy: A foundation for cognitive development. In W. Prinz, M. Beisert, & A. Herwig (Eds.), *Action science foundation of an emerging discipline* (pp. 255–280). New York: Oxford University Press.

Voss, C., & Sandercock, G. R. H. (2013). Associations between perceived parental physical activity and aerobic fitness in schoolchildren. *Journal of Physical Activity and Health, 10,* 397–405.

Vrticka, P., Simioni, S., Fornari, E., Schluep, M., Vuilleumier, P., & Sander, D. (2013). Neural substrates of social emotion regulation: A fMRI study on imitation and expressive suppression to dynamic facial signals. *Frontiers in Psychology, 4,* Article 95. doi: 10.3389/fpsyg.2013.00095

Wachholtz, A. B., & Austin, E. T. (2013). Contemporary spiritual meditation: Practices and outcomes. In K. I. Pargament, J. J. Exline, & J. W. Jones (Eds.), *APA handbooks in psychology. APA handbook of psychology, religion, and spirituality (Vol. 1): Context, theory, and research* (pp. 311–327). Washington, DC: American Psychological Association.

Wachlarowicz, M., Snyder, J., Low, S., Forgatch, M., & DeGarmo, D. (2012). The moderating effects of parent antisocial characteristics on the effects of Parent Management Training-Oregon (PMTOTM). *Prevention Science, 13,* 229–240.

Wachtel, P. L. (2011). *Inside the session: What really happens in psychotherapy.* Washington, DC: American Psychological Association.

Waller, N. G., & Ross, C. A. (1997). The prevalence and biometric structure of pathological dissociation in the general population: Taxometric and behavior genetics findings. *Journal of Abnormal Psychology, 106,* 499–510.

Walsh, E., Hooven, C., & Kronick, B. (2013). School-wide staff and faculty training in suicide risk awareness: Successes and challenges. *Journal of Child and Adolescent Psychiatric Nursing, 26,* 53–61.

Walsh, K., & Cross, W. (2013). Depression: Classification, culture and the westernisation of mental illness. In N. Kocabasoglu (Ed.), *Mood disorders.* Retrieved from http://cdn.intechopen.com/pdfs/42233/InTech-Depression_classification_culture_and_the_westernisation_of_mental_illness.pdf

Walton, G. M. & Cohen, G. L. (2011). A brief social-belonging intervention improves academic and health outcomes of minority students. *Science, 331,* 1447–1451.

Wamsley, E. J., Hirota, Y., Tucker, M. A., Smith, M. R., Doan, T., & Antrobus, J. S. (2007). Circadian and ultradian influences on dreaming: A dual rhythm model. *Brain Research Bulletin, 71,* 347–354.

Wamsley, E. J., & Stickgold, R. (2010). Dreaming and offline memory processing. *Current Biology, 20,* 1010–1913.

Wang, H., Fang, H., Dai, J., Liu, G., & Xu, Z. J. (2013). Induced pluripotent stem cells for spinal cord injury: Current status and perspective. *Neurological Sciences, 34,* 11–17.

Wang, J., Yuan, W., & Li, M. D. (2011). Genes and pathways co-associated with the exposure to multiple drugs of abuse, including alcohol, amphetamine/methamphetamine, cocaine, marijuana, morphine, and/or nicotine: A review of proteomics analyses. *Molecular Neurobiology, 44,* 269–286.

Wansink, B., & van Ittersum, K. (2012). Fast food restaurant lighting and music can reduce calorie intake and increase satisfaction. *Psychological Reports, 111,* 228–232.

Warneken, F., & Tomasello, M. (2008). Extrinsic rewards undermine altruistic tendencies in 20-month-olds. *Developmental Psychology, 44,* 1785–1788.

Warren, K. R., & Murray, M. M. (2013). Alcohol and pregnancy: Fetal alcohol spectrum disorders and the fetal alcohol syndrome. In P. Boyle, P. Boffetta, A. B. Lowenfels, H. B. Burns, O. Brawley, W. Zatonski, & J. Rehm. (Eds.), *Alcohol: Science, Policy and Public Health* (pp. 307–347). New York: Oxford University Press.

Warren, P. (2013). *Introducing psycholinguistics.* Cambridge, UK: Cambridge University Press.

Warrington, N. M., Wu, Y. Y., Pennell, C. E., Marsh, J. A., Beilin, L. J., Palmer, L. J., . . . Briollais, L. (2013). Modelling BMI trajectories in children for genetic association studies. *PLoS ONE, 8,* e53897.

Wasserman, S., Weisman, A., & Suro, G. (2013). Nonreligious coping and religious coping as predictors of expressed emotion in relatives of patients with schizophrenia. *Mental Health, Religion & Culture, 16,* 16–30.

Watkins, M. W., & Smith, L. G. (2013). Long-term stability of the Wechsler Intelligence Scale for Children—Fourth Edition. *Psychological Assessment, 25,* 477–483.

Weaver, J. (2012). A new look at "filler cells" in the brain reveals their role in learning. *PLoS Biology, 10,* Article e1001263.

Weber, M. T., Rubin, L. H., & Maki, P. M. (2013). Cognition in perimenopause: The effect of transition stage. *Menopause, 20,* 511–517.

Wechsler, D. (1944). *The measurement of adult intelligence* (3rd ed.). Baltimore, MD: Williams & Wilkins.

Wechsler, D. (1977). *Manual for the Wechsler Intelligence Scale for Children* (Rev.). New York: Psychological Corporation.

Weems, C. F., Scott, B. G., Banks, D. M., & Graham, R. A. (2012). Is T.V. traumatic for all youths? The role of preexisting posttraumatic-stress symptoms in the link between disaster coverage and stress. *Psychological Science, 23,* 1293–1297.

Weinberger, D., & Harrison, P. (Eds.). (2011). *Schizophrenia* (3rd ed.). Hoboken, NJ: Wiley.

Weiner, B. (1972). *Theories of motivation.* Chicago, IL: Rand-McNally.

Weiner, B. (1982). The emotional consequences of causal attributions. In M. S. Clark & S. T. Fiske (Eds.), *Affect and cognition.* Hillsdale, NJ: Erlbaum.

Weiner, B. (2006). *Social motivation, justice, and the moral emotions: An attributional approach.* Mahwah, NJ: Erlbaum.

Weinstein, N., Ryan, W. S., DeHaan, C. R., Przybylski, A. K., Legate, N., & Ryan, R. M. (2012). Parental autonomy support and discrepancies between implicit and explicit sexual identities: Dynamics of self-acceptance and defense. *Journal of Personality and Social Psychology, 102,* 815–832.

Weisberg, R. & Reeves, L. (2013). *Cognition: From memory to creativity.* Hoboken, NJ: Wiley.

Weisman, O., Zagoory-Sharon, O., & Feldman, R. (2012). Oxytocin administration to parent enhances infant physiological and behavioral readiness for social engagement. *Biological Psychiatry, 72,* 982–989.

Weiss, A., Gartner, M. C., Gold, K. C., & Stoinski, T. S. (2013). Extraversion predicts longer survival in gorillas: An 18-year longitudinal study. *Proceedings of the Royal Society B.* doi: 10.1098/rspb.2012.2231

Weitlauf, J. C., Cervone, D., Smith, R. E., & Wright, P. M. (2001). Assessing-generalization in perceived self-efficacy: Multidomain and global assessments of the effects of self-defense training for women. *Personality and Social Psychology Bulletin, 27,* 1683–1691.

West, R., Meserve, R., & Stanovich, K. (2012). Cognitive sophistication does not attenuate the bias blind spot. *Journal of Personality and Social Psychology, 103,* 506–519.

Westen, D. (1998). Unconscious thought, feeling, and motivation: The end of a centurylong debate. In R. F. Bornstein & J. M. Masling (Eds.), *Empirical perspectives on the psychoanalytic unconscious* (pp. 1–43). Washington, DC: American Psychological Association.

Weyandt, L. L., Verdi, G., & Swentosky, A. (2011). Oppositional, conduct, and aggressive disorders. In S. Goldstein & C. R. Reynolds (Eds.), *Handbook of neurodevelopmental and genetic disorders in children* (2nd ed., pp. 151–170). New York: Guilford Press.

Whalen, P. J., Kim, M. J., Neta, M., & Davis, F. C. (2013). Emotion. In R. J. Nelson, S. J. Y. Mizumori, & I. B. Weiner (Eds.), *Handbook of psychology, Vol. 3. Behavioral neuroscience (2nd ed.,* pp. 422–439). Hoboken, NJ: Wiley.

Whalen, P. J., Raila, H., Bennett, R., Mattek, A., Brown, A., Taylor, J., . . .

Palmer, A. (2013). Neuroscience and facial expressions of emotion: The role of amygdala–prefrontal interactions. *Emotion Review, 5,* 78–83.

Whaley, A., Smith, M., & Hancock, A. (2011). Ethnic/racial differences in the self-reported physical and mental health correlates of adolescent obesity. *Journal of Health Psychology, 16,* 1048–1057.

Whalley, L. J. (2011). Brain lesions, hypertension and cognitive ageing in the 1921 and 1936 Aberdeen birth cohorts. *Age, 34,* 451–459.

Wheaton, A. G., Perry, G. S., Chapman, D. P., & Croft, J. B. (2012). Sleep disordered breathing and depression among U.S. adults: National Health and Nutrition Examination Survey, 2005–2008. *Sleep, 35,* 461–467.

Whitbourne, S. K. (2011). *Adult development and aging: Biopsychosocial perspectives* (4th ed.). Hoboken, NJ: Wiley.

White, H. R., Fite, P., Pardini, D., Mun, E.-Y., & Loeber, R. (2013). Moderators of the dynamic link between alcohol use and aggressive behavior among adolescent males. *Journal of Abnormal Child Psychology, 41,* 211–222.

White, T., Andreasen, N. C., & Nopoulos, P. (2002). Brain volumes and surface morphology in monozygotic twins. *Cerebral Cortex, 12,* 486–493.

Wickramasekera, I., II. (2008b). Review of hypnotizability, absorption and negative cognitions as predictors of dental anxiety: Two pilot studies. *American Journal of Clinical Hypnosis, 50,* 285–286.

Widiger, T. A. (Ed.). (2013). Diagnosis and classification. In G. Stricker, T. A. Widiger, & I. B. Weiner (Eds.), *Handbook of psychology, Vol. 8. Clinical psychology* (2nd ed., pp. 3–18). Hoboken, NJ: Wiley.

Wiener, H., Klei, L., Calkins, M., Wood, J., Nimgaonkar, V., Gur, R., . . . Go, R. (2013). Principal components of heritability from neurocognitive domains differ between families with schizophrenia and control subjects. *Schizophrenia Bulletin, 39,* 464–471.

Wikgren, M., Maripuu, M., Karlsson, T., Nordfjäll, K., Bergdahl, J., Hultdin, J., . . . Norrback, K-F. (2011). Short telomeres in depression and the general population are associated with a hypocortisolemic state. *Biological Psychiatry, 71,* 294–300.

Wille, B., De Fruyt, F., & De Clercq, B. (2013). Expanding and reconceptualizing aberrant personality at work: Validity of Five-Factor Model aberrant personality tendencies to predict career outcomes. *Personnel Psychology, 66,* 173–223.

Williams, J. E. (2010). Anger/hostility and cardiovascular disease. In M. Potegal, G.

Stemmler, & C. Spielberger (Eds.), *International handbook of anger: Constituent and concomitant biological, psychological, and social processes* (pp. 435–447). New York: Springer Science 1 Business Media.

Williams, M. R., Chaudhry, R., Perera, S., Pearce, R. K. B., Hirsch, S. R., Ansorge, O., . . . Maier, M. (2013). Changes in cortical thickness in the frontal lobes in schizophrenia are a result of thinning of pyramidal cell layers. *European Archives of Psychiatry and Clinical Neuroscience, 263,* 25–39.

Williams, S. C. P. (2013, July 15). Obesity gene linked to hunger hormone. *Science NOW.* Retrieved from http://news.sciencemag.org/sciencenow/2013/07/obesity-gene-linked-to-hunger-ho.html?ref=em#.UeTHLsf3tP0.email

Williams, S. S. (2001). Sexual lying among college students in close and casual relationships. *Journal of Applied Social Psychology, 31,* 2322–2338.

Williamson, A., Lombardi, D. A., Folkard, S., Stutts, J., Courtney, T. K., & Connor, J. L. (2011). The link between fatigue and safety. *Accident Analysis and Prevention, 43,* 498–515.

Williamson, J. M., Lounsbury, J. W., & Han, L. D. (2013). Key personality traits of engineers for innovation and technology development. *Journal of Engineering and Technology Management, 30,* 157–168.

Williamson, M. (1997). Circumcision anesthesia: A study of nursing implication for dorsal penile nerve block. *Pediatric Nursing, 23,* 59–63.

Willingham, D.B. (2001). *Cognition: The thinking animal.* Upper Saddle River, NJ: Prentice Hall.

Willyard, C. (2011). Men: A growing minority. *gradPSYCH, 9,* 40–44.

Wilner, B. (February 5, 2011). Vick wins Comeback Player award. *Associated Press.* Retrieved from http://news.yahoo.com/s/ap/20110206/ap_on_sp_fo_ne/fbn_comeback_player.

Wilson, G. T. (2011). Behavior therapy. In R. J. Corsini & D. Wedding (Eds,), *Current psychotherapy* (9th ed., pp. 235–275). Florence, KY: Cengage Learning.

Wilson, S., & Nutt, D. (2008). *Sleep disorders.* London, England: Oxford University Press.

Winder, G. S., Stern, N., & Hosanagar, A. (2013). Are "bath salts" the next generation of stimulant abuse? *Journal of Substance Abuse Treatment, 44,* 42–45.

Winerman, L. (2004). Sleep deprivation threatens public health, says research award winner. *Monitor on Psychology, 35,* 61.

Wirtz, D., & Chiu, C-Y. (2008). Perspectives on the self in the East and the West: Searching for the quiet ego. In A. H. Wayment & J. J. Bauer (Eds.), *Transcending self-interest: Psychological explorations of the quiet ego. Decade of behavior* (pp. 149–158). Washington, DC: American Psychological Association.

Wiste, A. K., Arango, V., Ellis, S. P., Mann, J. J., & Underwood, M. D. (2008). Norepinephrine and serotonin imbalance in the locus coeruleus in bipolar disorder. *Bipolar Disorders, 10,* 349–359.

Witelson, S. F., Kigar, D. L., & Harvey, T. (1999). The exceptional brain of Albert Einstein. *The Lancet, 353,* 2149–2153.

Wolpe, J., & Plaud, J. J. (1997). Pavlov's contributions to behavior therapy. *American Psychologist, 52,* 966–972.

Wood, B., Rea, M. S., Plitnick, B., & Figueiro, M. G. (2012). Light level and duration of exposure determine the impact of self-luminous tablets on melatonin suppression. *Applied Ergonomics, 44,* 237–240.

Wood, J. M., Nezworski, T., Lilienfeld, S. O., & Garb, H. N. (2011). *What's wrong with the Rorschach: Science confronts the controversial inkblot test.* Hoboken, NJ: Wiley/ JosseyBass.

Wood, J. T. (2013). *Gendered lives.* Belmont, CA: Wadsworth.

Wood, R. L., & Thomas, R. H. (2013). Impulsive and episodic disorders of aggressive behaviour following traumatic brain injury. *Brain Injury, 27,* 253–261.

Woods, R. J., & Wilcox, T. (2013). Posture support improves object individuation in infants. *Developmental Psychology, 49,* 1413–1424.

Wright, A. J. (2011). *Conducting psychological assessment: A guide for practitioners.* Hoboken, NJ: Wiley.

Wright, D. S., Wade, K. A., & Watson, D. G. (2013). Delay and déjà vu: Timing and repetition increase the power of false evidence. *Psychonomic Bulletin & Review, 20,* 812–818.

Wryobeck, J. M., Haines, M. E., Wynkoop, T. F., & Swanson, M. M. (2013). Depressive disorders. In C. A. Noggle & R. S. Dean (Eds.), *Contemporary neuropsychology. The neuropsychology of psychopathology* (pp. 201–220). New York: Springer.

Wu, T., Liu, J., Hallett, M., Zheng, Z., & Chan, P. (2013). Cerebellum and integration of neural networks in dual-task processing. *NeuroImage, 65,* 466–475.

Wulandari, L. P. L., Craig, P., & Whelan, A. K. (2013). Foetal health locus of control and iron supplementation adherence among pregnant women in Bali. *Journal of Reproductive & Infant Psychology, 31,* 94–101.

Wyman, A. J., & Vyse, S. (2008). Science versus the stars: A double-blind test of the validity of the NEO five-factor inventory and computer-generated astrological natal charts. *Journal of General Psychology, 135,* 287–300.

Wyse, C. A. (2012). Does human evolution in different latitudes influence susceptibility to obesity via the circadian pacemaker? *BioEssays, 34,* 921–924.

Xia, Q., & Grant, S. F. (2013). The genetics of human obesity. *Annals of the New York Academy of Sciences, 1281,* 178–190.

Xu, L., & Barnes, L. (2011). Measurement invariance of scores from the inventory of school motivation across Chinese and U.S. college students. *International Journal of Testing, 11,* 178–210.

Xu, Y., Schneier, F., Heimberg, R. G., Princisvalle, K., Liebowitz, M. R., Wang, S., & Blanco, C. (2012). Gender differences in social anxiety disorder: Results from the national epidemiologic sample on alcohol and related conditions. *Journal of Anxiety Disorders, 26,* 12–19.

Yamada, H. (1997). *Different games, different rules: Why Americans and Japanese misunderstand each other.* London, England: Oxford University Press.

Yantis, S. (2013). *Sensation and perception.* New York: Worth.

Yin, F., Tian, Z-M., Liu, S., Zhao, Q-J., Wang, R-M., Shen, L., . . . Yan, Y. (2012). Transplantation of human retinal pigment epithelium cells in the treatment for Parkinson disease. *CNS Neuroscience and Therapeutics, 18,* 1012–1020.

You, S., Hong, S., & Ho, H. Z. (2011). Longitudinal effects of perceived control on academic achievement. *Journal of Educational Research, 104,* 253–266.

Young, R. M., Connor, J. P., & Feeney, G. F. X. (2011). Alcohol expectancy changes over a 12-week cognitive–behavioral therapy program are predictive of treatment success. *Journal of Substance Abuse Treatment, 40,* 18–25.

Young, S. G., Brown, C. M., & Ambady, N. (2012). Priming a natural or human-made environment directs attention to context-congruent threatening stimuli. *Cognition & Emotion, 26,* 927–933.

Young, T. (1802). On the theory of light and colours. *Philosophical Transactions of the Royal Society, 92,* 12–48.

Yu, C. K.-C. (2012). Dream motif scale. *Dreaming, 22,* 18–52.

Yu, J.-T., Ma, X.-Y., Wang, Y.-L., Sun, L., Tan, L., Hu, N., & Tan, L. (2013). Genetic variation in clusterin gene and alzheimer's disease risk in han chinese. *Neurobiology of Aging, 34,* e17-e23.

Yuen, E. Y., Wei, J., Liu, W., Zhong, P., Li, X., & Yan, Z. (2012). Repeated stress causes cognitive impairment by suppressing glutamate receptor expression and function in prefrontal cortex. *Neuron, 73,* 962–977.

Zampieri, M., & Pedrosa de Souza, E. A. (2011). Locus of control, depression, and quality of life in Parkinson's Disease. *Journal of Health Psychology, 16,* 980–987.

Zandi, T. (2013). Possible misclassification of psychotic symptoms among Moroccan immigrants in the Netherlands. In S. Barnow & N. Balkir (Eds.), *Cultural variations in psychopathology: From research to practice* (pp. 219–229). Cambridge, MA: Hogrefe Publishing.

Zarate, C. A. Jr., Brutsche, N. E., Ibrahim, L., Franco-Chaves, J., Diazgranados, N., Cravchik, A., . . . Luckenbaugh, D. A. (2012). Replication of ketamine's antidepressant efficacy in bipolar depression: A randomized controlled add-on trial. *Biological Psychiatry, 71,* 939–946.

Zelazo, P. D., Chandler, M., & Crone, E. (Eds.). (2010). *The Jean Piaget symposium series. Developmental social cognitive neuroscience.* New York: Psychology Press.

Zentner, M., & Mitura, K. (2012). Stepping out of the caveman's shadow: Nations' gender gap predicts degree of sex differentiation in mate preferences. *Psychological Science, 23,* 1176–1185.

Zerr, A. A., Holly, L. E., & Pina, A. A. (2011). Cultural influences on social anxiety in African American, Asian American, Hispanic and Latino, and Native American adolescents and young adults. In C. A. Alfano & D. C. Beidel (Eds.), *Social anxiety in adolescents and young adults: Translating developmental science into practice* (pp. 203–222). Washington, DC: American Psychological Association.

Zhang, L. F., & He, Y. F. (2011). Thinking styles and the Eriksonian stages. *Journal of Adult Development, 18,* 8–17.

Zhaoping, L., & Guyader, N. (2007). Interference with bottom-up feature detection by higher-level object recognition. *Current Biology, 17,* 26–31.

Zhou, J., & Urhahne, D. (2013). Teacher judgment, student motivation, and the mediating effect of attributions. *European Journal of Psychology of Education, 28,* 275–295.

Zhu, B., Chen, C., Loftus, E. F., He, Q., Chen, C., Lei, D., . . . Dong, Q. (2012). Brief exposure to misinformation can lead to long-term false memories. *Applied Cognitive Psychology, 26,* 301–307.

Zhu, D. H. (2013). Group polarization on corporate boards: Theory and evidence on board decisions about acquisition premiums. *Strategic Management Journal, 34,* 800–822.

Zhu, L., & Zee, P. C. (2012). Circadian rhythm sleep disorders. *Neurologic Clinics, 30,* 1167–1191.

Zimbardo, P. G. (1993). Stanford prison experiment: A 20-year retrospective. *Invited presentation at the meeting of the Western Psychological Association,* Phoenix, AZ.

Zink, D. N., Ojeda, C., Hernandez, M., & Puente, A. E. (2013). Generalized anxiety disorder and panic disorder. In C. A. Noggle & R. S. Dean (Eds.), *Contemporary neuropsychology. The neuropsychology of psychopathology* (pp. 243–260). New York: Springer.

Zuckerman, M. (2011). Psychodynamic approaches. In M. Zuckerman (Ed.), *Personality science: Three approaches and their applications to the causes and treatment of depression* (pp. 11–45). Washington, DC: American Psychological Association.

Zuckerman, M. (2013). Biological bases of personality. In H. Tennen, J.Suls, & I. B Weiner (Eds.), *Handbook of psychology, Vol. 5: Personality and social psychology* (2nd ed., pp. 27–42). Hoboken, NJ: Wiley.

Zvyagintsev, M., Clemens, B., Chechko, N., Mathiak, K. A., Sack, A. T., & Mathiak, K. (2013). Brain networks underlying mental imagery of auditory and visual information. *European Journal of Neuroscience, 37,* 1421–1434.

Zweig, J. (2007). *Your money and your brain: How the new science of neuroeconomics can help make you rich.* New York: Simon & Schuster.

Subject Index

Note: Page numbers followed by a "t" indicate the entry may be found within a table. Page numbers followed by an "f" indicate the entry may be found within a figure.